SYSTEMS DEVELOPMENT

A Project Management Approach

RAYMOND McLEOD, JR.
University of Texas at Austin
Department of Management Science and Information Systems

ELEANOR JORDAN
University of Texas at Austin
Department of Management Science and Information Systems

John Wiley & Sons, Inc.

New York Chichester Weinheim Brisbane Singapore Toronto

http://www.wiley.com/college

Dedication

To our parents,
Margaret McLeod and
Will and Kitty Worley

Credits

Acquisitions editor: Beth Lang Golub
Marketing manager: Gitti Lindner
Production editor: Lari Bishop
Text design: Nicole Hazard
Illustration editor: Nicole Hazard
Cover image: Kris Pauls

This book was set in 10.5/12 Times and printed and bound by R. R. Donnelly & Sons Company.

ISBN 0-471-22089-2

Printed in the United States of America
10 9 8 7 6 5 4 3 2 1

TABLE OF CONTENTS

TECHNICAL MODULE B

Process Modeling 94

TECHNICAL MODULE C

Object Modeling 110

CHAPTER 2

Systems Concepts 140

CHAPTER 3

Systems Development Methodologies 168

TECHNICAL MODULE D

Project Planning and Control 196

TECHNICAL MODULE E

Computer-Aided Software Engineering 216

Part II SYSTEMS DEVELOPMENT 229

CHAPTER 4

Preliminary Investigation 230

TECHNICAL MODULE H

Web and Graphical User Interface Design 394

CASE STUDY INSTALLMENT 5

Preliminary and Final Construction of the ASTA System 412

CHAPTER 7

Preliminary Construction 422

CHAPTER 8

Final Construction 450

CHAPTER 9

PREFACE

This book is designed specifically to support a course in which student teams complete the software development process while working with client organizations; it also works well with the case approach. We have been offering a course in which students work with client organizations—Business Systems Development, required for all MIS majors—at the University of Texas at Austin since 1983 with excellent results. Each semester, the students develop systems for clients that include profit-seeking firms, not-for-profits, state government agencies, and university offices.

The students like the course because it gives them a chance to apply the material that they have learned prior to their senior year, and the recruiters like it because it gives the students real-word experience in system development. The clients like it because most have overworked or nonexistent IT groups and the student teams offer the only hope of getting certain systems implemented.

Since both authors have previous textbook-writing experience, it was only natural that we saw a need to write a text that supports the course in the best possible way. We developed a manuscript and first used it in class during the Summer 2000 semester, and have since used it in thirteen more sections, making improvements based on student feedback each semester. So the book is well tested, having been used by over 400 students.

A Project Management Emphasis

As the students develop the client systems, they apply the methodologies and tools of systems development. The chapters in this text support this effort by describing methodologies for approaching systems development, such as prototyping, rapid application development (RAD), and phased development. The technical modules describe the tools the students will need, such as object modeling, computer-aided software engineering (CASE), and Web and graphical user interface design.

The students gain experience in project management by applying the information in the text to their individual projects. The text supports the project management effort in a number of ways. Technical Module D is devoted to project management planning tools. Each chapter includes a Project Management Toolbox that relates the chapter material to project management. And the case study presented throughout the book describes a student team developing a system for a client, with specific discussion of their project management efforts.

Feedback from our graduates who have applied the course material in their careers confirms the value of emphasizing project management fundamentals.

Organization of the Book

There are nine chapters, eight technical modules, and five installments of a case study presented in two separate parts. The first part of the book, Systems Fundamentals, contains the first three chapters, which provide a foundation of systems concepts and systems methodologies. The remaining six chapters reside in Part II, Systems

Development, and describe the system development life cycle (SDLC), with a chapter devoted to each of the SDLC phases. The book is unique in that it gives equal treatment to each SDLC phase, rather than emphasizing the initial phases of analysis and design, and treating the later phases of construction and installation in a summary fashion.

Whereas the chapters describe the SDLC, the technical modules describe the tools that the developers use. The modular organization makes it easy for the instructor to pick and choose the tools to include in the course. For example, if the instructor wants to emphasize a data and process orientation, Technical Module A on data modeling and Module B on process modeling can be used. On the other hand, if the instructor wants to emphasize an object orientation, Technical Module C can be used.

The technical modules also enable the instructor to select the sequence in which they appear. A review of the Table of Contents will reveal that the technical modules are integrated with the chapters in a certain order, but they can be used in any sequence. The sequence that has been selected seemed the most logical to the authors.

A "Painless" Application of Systems Concepts

Both authors have extensive experience working in industry and see the value of systems concepts as the foundation for systems work. Students do not always share this respect for "theory," and have difficulty appreciating its value. The text provides a thorough coverage of the concepts, but it also includes a set of templates, or blank forms, that students use for organizing their project data.

For example, one systems concept is that a system has objectives or goals. As a way to apply this concept, there is a Goal Analysis Form that requires the students to address such considerations as system quality goals (functionality, maintainability, and portability/scalability) for their client system. In using the forms, the students apply the concepts without relating their work to "theory."

The Chapters

The organization of the chapters is one that we have used successfully in previous texts. Each chapter begins with Learning Objectives and an Introduction. The Introduction is a type of "executive summary" of the chapter, touching on the major points. Each chapter concludes with a Project Management Toolbox, discussing project management as it relates to the chapter material. The Summary again covers the important chapter topics. The students therefore receive three presentations of the material—the Introduction, the chapter content, and the Summary—a technique that serves to reinforce learning. Following the Summary are Key Terms, Key Concepts, Questions, Topics for Discussion, Problems, and one or two Case Problems. A Selected Bibliography concludes each chapter and technical module. The references tie the material to IS literature—the classics as well as current descriptions of evolving topics.

Part I: Systems Fundamentals

- *Chapter 1: Introduction to Systems Development*—Systems concepts and viewing the firm as a system; an IS infrastructure; top-down strategic planning for the firm and its IS efforts; an overview of systems development stages; composition of the project team; the functions/components matrix

- *Chapter 2: Systems Concepts*—The resources available to the firm; the environment of the firm; resource flows between the firm and its environment;

the concept of a problem chain; the systems approach to problem solving; system objectives, performance criteria constraints

- *Chapter 3: Systems Development Methodologies*—The traditional system life cycle; prototyping; rapid application development (RAD); phased development methodology

Part II: Systems Development

- *Chapter 4: Preliminary Investigation*—Project triggers; strategic planning for the firm and its IT operations; enterprise analysis; business process redesign; system constraints; goal analysis; risk evaluation and reduction strategies; the feasibility study; joint application development (JAD)

- *Chapter 5: Systems Analysis*—Analysis steps; determining functional requirements; sources of information (existing documentation, interviews, surveys, collaborative sessions, observation, and existing records); the use case as an analysis tool

- *Chapter 6: Systems Design*—Design tasks; logical and physical design; computer architectures; the systems approach to design; design of user interfaces, data, procedures, software, system interfaces, and controls; risk and control matrices; alternate solution evaluation

- *Chapter 7: Preliminary Construction*—Software and test data construction; construction of physical facilities; hardware installation, software installation and coding; software test files; decision logic tables as a software testing tool; training materials and documentation; conducting user demonstrations

- *Chapter 8: Final Construction*—Final construction tasks; constructing and testing production-ready programs and the database; hardware acquisition; facility preparation; hardware components tests; completion of documentation; training production system participants and users

- *Chapter 9: System Test and Installation*—Installation goals; the system test; an installation plan checklist; user acceptance; cutover; the post-implementation evaluation; systems maintenance

The Technical Modules

Each technical module is written in a stand-alone manner. This approach permits their use at any point in the course. Although the technical module on project management planning tools is most closely related to the overall emphasis of the text, the three modules on data, process, and object modeling appear first, assuming that instructors will want students to get started on using those tools early in the course. Each technical module includes problems that enable students to apply the material.

- *Technical Module A: Data Modeling*—Entity-relationship diagrams; the data dictionary

- *Technical Module B: Process Modeling*—Data flow diagrams; structured English

- *Technical Module C: Object Modeling*—The Unified Modeling Language (UML); use case diagrams; class diagrams; sequence diagrams; statechart diagrams; object diagrams; collaboration diagrams; activity diagrams; component diagrams; and deployment diagrams

- *Technical Module D: Project Management Planning Tools*—The project management mechanism; Gantt charts; network diagrams (PERT, CPM); project cost management
- *Technical Module E: Computer-Aided Software Engineering (CASE)*—CASE tool categories; CASE as a project management tool; CASE impact on the SDLC; current CASE tool trends
- *Technical Module F: Economic System and Project Justification*—Break-even analysis; payback analysis; net present value; a cost-benefit analysis model
- *Technical Module G: Evaluation of System Alternatives*—Evaluation tables and matrices; evaluation of software tools
- *Technical Module H: Web and Graphical User Interface Design*—Users and their main events; types of interfaces; graphical user interface (GUI) design principles; use of color in GUI design; the user interface design process; Web interface design for e-business users; Web page design guidelines; Web page color guidelines

A Running Case

As with most systems analysis and design textbooks, we include a running case-the description of a development process that provides examples of the chapter and technical module material as the work progresses.

The name of our case company is Advanced System Technology Associates (ASTA), and it is based on an actual student project involving a high-tech manufacturing services firm. By using a student project as the example, the case not only provides students with good examples of documentation that is prepared during a system development project, but it provides students with a preview of how their team will proceed from phase to phase as they work with their client during the semester. The ASTA case provides a rich resource of examples of how development tools are applied in a real organization.

Project Flexibility

During the fall and spring semesters, we provide the student teams with lists of organizations that have expressed a willingness to host a system development project. We have followed this approach during the summer semester, successfully compacting the project into a five-week term, and we have taught the course during the summer semester without using real clients. We have instead used a detailed written case study that required the teams to perform the same activities they would perform in a client project. The teams used the same project management planning tools, such as Gantt charts and network diagrams, and prepared the same three user deliveries. Rather than developing production systems, the teams developed prototypes that were demonstrated to the class.

Therefore, the text supports courses that involve student teams with real organizations, and also those where written cases are used. The Web site that supports the text provides a selection of written project cases, updated on a recurring schedule.

A Complete Support Package for Students, Instructors, and Clients

As teachers, we have provided our students with a complete support package in the form of a course Web site. The contents of this Web site have been reformatted and are provided on the John Wiley & Sons Web site for this text, www.wiley.com/college/mcleod. As teachers, we have also developed materials that we need to teach the class, and these materials are made available to instructors who adopt the text. The Web site also includes materials to help the clients understand their responsibilities concerning the project.

Web Site Materials to Help the Student

- *Class notes*—Copies of transparency masters and Microsoft PowerPoint slides for each chapter and technical module are provided so that students can review the notes when preparing for class and exams.
- *Forms*—Blank copies of the various forms that serve as tools during the system development process are provided. For some forms, completed examples in addition to those in the text are also provided.

  —Functions/components matrix

  —Goal analysis

  —Risk evaluation

  —Risk reduction strategies

  —Table of existing and proposed system components

  —Gantt chart

  —Test specifications
- *Exams*—Lists of review topics and also sample essay exams will help students prepare for exams. The sample exams include the answers.
- *Client project*—Information relating to the client project will include:

  —Team assignment instructions

  —Teammate evaluation form

  —Client project delivery 1 specifications

  —Client project delivery 1 examples

  —Client project delivery 2 specifications

  —Client project delivery 2 examples

  —Final delivery specifications

  —Final delivery examples

  —Sample project examples

Web Site Materials to Help the Client

- *Information for clients*—This feature provides an explanation of the expectations of the client in terms of the project type and interactions with the team.

Web Site Materials to Help the Instructor

- *Microsoft PowerPoint presentations*—Graphical visual aids in Microsoft PowerPoint are provided for each chapter and technical module.
- *Transparency masters*—Key topics for each chapter and technical module are provided in transparency form for use in class discussions.
- *Classroom software*—This feature provides mathematical models in Microsoft Excel spreadsheets that can be used in the classroom and by students to estimate costs, break-even points, and payback periods for system projects.
- *Instructor's Manual*—Written by the authors, the IM contains suggestions for teaching the course, sample syllabi and schedules, and answers to the end-of-chapter questions, problems, discussion topics, and cases.
- *Test item file*—Written by the authors, the TIF contains sample true/false and multiple choice questions for each chapter and technical module. The answers are also provided. An electronic version of the test bank can be fully customized for the instructors needs. Contact your Wiley representative for details.
- *Written case problems*—Instructors who wish to use written case problems rather than real clients as the basis for the development project can select from several robust, written case problems. The supply of cases is frequently updated to provide a supply of new challenges for student teams.

CASE Tool

Visible Systems Corporation's Visible Analyst Student Edition is available for those instructors who want to use a CASE (computer-aided software engineering) tool with the text. Contact your Wiley representative for more information.

ACKNOWLEDGEMENTS

We may be wrong, but we believe that the chances are good that no textbook has ever received the support of more people than this one. Without the help of many, many people, the Systems Development course at UT Austin could never have achieved its level of success, and this textbook could never have come close to containing its valuable content.

We have received help from our publishers at Leyh Publishing and John Wiley & Sons, the MSIS office staff at the University of Texas at Austin, our Teaching Assistants, and IS professionals in industry who have "bought in" to the course and willingly shared their experiences with the authors and the students.

- *Leyh Publishing*—Rick Leyh, president, Lari Bishop, managing editor, and Nicole Hazard, associate editor
- *John Wiley & Sons*—Beth Lang Golub, information systems editor, Susan Elbe, publisher, and Randy Allen, sales representative
- *Industry IS professionals*—Donna Thomas of Dell Computer; Christopher Walk of TriActive; Colby Thames and Jim Steele of EnForm Technology; Lee Aber
- *The MSIS office staff*—Barbara Zuckerman, Amanda No, Jennifer Lara, and Natalia Villon
- *Teaching assistants*—Jennifer Kern, Abhay Nash Mishra, Alana Schuman, David Nachtigall, Daniel Needham, Carrie Fields, Jahanara Taufique, Sean Burns, and Haider Virani
- *Students who worked on client projects fictionalized for examples in this text*—Kate Davenport, Laura Michalik, Elizabeth Nutt, Bryan Uzzell, Brad Wells, Bryan Henry, Jubi Joseph, Darren Rose, Kristine Santos, Kathy Tran, Doug Polega, Mike Smith, Mason Schoolfield, Frank Cortez, Stanley Eng, Matt Waldbusser, Serena Laughren, Toby Patkey, Philip Meyer, and Tracey O'Dowd

Reviewers and Other Support

The following people provided their time and interest and have helped us improve the quality of this text:

Syed Imtiaz Ahmad	*Eastern Michigan University*
Penny Brunner	*University of North Carolina, Asheville*
Allen Corbett	*University of South Carolina*
Barbara Denison	*Wright State University*
Robert Keim	*Arizona State University*
Jennifer Kreie	*New Mexico State University*
Kevin Marler	
John Melrose	*University of Wisconsin*
Russ Pearlman	*Tactica*
Ulrike Schultze	*Southern Methodist University*
Diane Walz	*University of Texas, San Antonio*
Vincent Yen	*Wright State University*

We hope that you enjoy the course and the textbook as much as we have. We look forward to hearing your comments, suggestions, and feedback.

Ray McLeod and Eleanor Jordan
Austin, Texas

ABOUT THE AUTHORS

Raymond McLeod, Jr.

Prior to accepting an appointment as assistant professor at Metropolitan State College in Denver, Ray worked in industry with IBM, Recognition Equipment Inc., and Lifson, Wilson, Ferguson, and Winick, a management consulting firm. In 1973 he accepted a faculty position at Texas Christian University and in 1980 joined the faculty at Texas A & M University. In 1998 he joined the management science and information systems faculty at the University of Texas at Austin, where he now serves as adjunct professor, teaching the undergraduate course in systems development.

Findings of Professor McLeod's research have appeared in such journals as *California Management Review, MIS Quarterly, Journal of Management Information Systems, Decision Sciences, IEEE Transactions on Engineering Management,* and *Communications of the ACM.* He is co-author with George Schell of *Management Information Systems,* Eighth Edition (Prentice-Hall, 2001) and *Management Information Systems Case Book,* Sixth Edition (Prentice-Hall, 1995). He is author of *Information Systems Concepts* (Macmillan, 1994), and *Introduction to Systems Analysis and Design: An Organizational Approach* (Dryden, 1994).

Dr. McLeod has served on the editorial boards of the *Journal of Management Information Systems, Data Base, Information Resources Management Journal,* and *Journal of Information Technology Management.* He is past chair of the ACM Special Interest Group for Computer Personnel Research (SIGCPR), and holds a Certificate in Data Processing, awarded by the Data Processing Management Association (DPMA).

Eleanor Jordan

Professor Eleanor Jordan is a member of the faculty of the management science and information systems (MSIS) department at the University of Texas at Austin, where she has taught for more than two decades. Her BA, MA, and PhD are all from UT Austin.

Before beginning her academic career, Dr. Jordan developed defense system software for Rockwell International and business application systems for the Texas Department of Transportation and Highways. Since then she has focused much of her attention on improving education in information systems. As a member of the ACM Education Board she participated in one of the major revisions of the ACM model curriculum and contributed to the initial DPMA model curriculum. In addition to teaching graduate and undergraduate classes, Professor Jordan is an active program developer and teacher in executive education programs, including workshops for IBM, Sybase, National Instruments, and 3M.

Professor Jordan's research has been published in the *Journal of System Management, The International Journal of Man-Machine Studies, Human Factors in Information Systems,* as well as a variety of journals and proceedings in both statistics and MIS education. She is an invited contributor to both *The Encyclopedia of Computers* and the *Encyclopedia of Statistical Sciences.* She is the co-author of a statistics text as well as the text, *Systems Development: Requirements, Evaluation, Design, and Implementation.*

PART I

SYSTEMS FUNDAMENTALS

Case Study Installment I

Advanced System Technology Associates

FORMING THE CLIENT PROJECT TEAM

"Hey Gary! Wanna team up again this semester?" It was three weeks into the MIS Systems Development class, and Rachel wanted to get a head start in assembling her "winner group" for the client project. After talking with other students who had completed both the infamous Advanced Programming course and Systems Development, she came to the conclusion that the Systems Development project might be even more demanding than the one in Advanced Programming. Who should she ask to be on her team? She had worked with Gary last semester on the Advanced Programming project, and he was experienced with coding. Since she assumed that those skills would be useful in Systems Development, she thought that he would be a good complement to her abilities and that the two would make a good fit in terms of work style.

Gary knew that Rachel wanted to do a good job, but he wasn't too impressed with her technical ability. However, there were two women in Dr. Konana's e-Business class with him who seemed to know much more than he did when it came to ASP, HTML, and Oracle. He had been sitting next to them in Ray McLeod's Systems Development section and thought there was a good chance they would team up with him. With this possibility in mind, Gary told Rachel that he would team up with her if they would invite the two girls from Konana's class to work with them. Rachel agreed. After the Systems Development class was dismissed, they approached Tracy and Kim with the proposal. The two techies were game, so the four new teammates decided to meet to discuss the project.

Prior to the meeting, Gary filled Kim and Tracy in on his opinion of Rachel's skill set. "Sounds to me like she'll make a good documenter" was Tracy's reply. Kim was a little hesitant to agree with Tracy. "We can't just expect Rachel to document all the work we've done if she's not the one doing it. Let's figure this out when we're all together."

THE FIRST TEAM MEETING

At the first team meeting, Gary introduced the idea of documenter to Rachel. Rachel knew this wasn't a good way to separate the workload since it creates specialists and imposes big communication responsibilities on everyone to bridge the gaps. But, at the same time, she wanted to be a team player. "If that's the best idea we can come up with for breaking down the roles, then I will be more than happy to fulfill the documenter role."

Tracy butted in, "Gary told us that you're a hard worker, Rachel. But, my main concern is that we three don't end up doing all the coding and you do nothing early in the project. If you take the main responsibility for documenting, that would take some of the pressure off the three of us."

Rachel, a little taken aback, replied, "I want to put in just as much effort as you, Tracy. I just think that there is plenty of work to be done that doesn't involve coding. I could take the role as systems analyst and project leader. I have experience with both, especially with planning tools like Gantt charts and network diagrams."

Kim, feeling a little uncomfortable at Tracy's attack, stuck up for Rachel, "I think that's a good idea. Plus, in Systems Development, the client teams have five members. Let's add a strong programmer. That would give us two systems analysts and three programmers."

"That might work out, actually," Gary said. "I agree that we could always use more programming talent and there is that guy that Ray told us about at the end of class today—Sean, I think his name is. He doesn't have a team. Anybody know him?" They all looked at each other and shook their heads "No." "I'm always against taking in someone I don't know," Gary continued. "It's too much of a risk. But, we need the help and Ray's going to assign him to somebody. If we offer to accept him, it will be clear that we will do our part to make the client project a good experience. I think we ought to tell Ray that we will take him." Everybody agreed, and Gary said he would send Ray an e-mail.

Tracy looked over at Kim and asked, "Well, I'm still uncertain about who's going to do all the documenting." Gary, realizing that the two-three arrangement might be the best said, "I guess we would all document the stuff that we work on. I think that makes the most sense. I know that you two, Tracy and Kim, have the most programming skills. Would you all like to take those roles on? I would be willing to be systems analyst when needed, and programmer when needed."

Kim and Tracy looked at each other and nodded, and Kim said, "I think that's a good idea. I know Tracy, and I can get a lot done working with her."

Rachel, relieved at the change of conversation, assured Tracy and Kim that she would be willing to help them if they felt like they were overloaded. "I think we'll be okay with the work as long as we don't let the project requirements get out of hand—you know, scope creep." To this, Tracy, Kim, and Gary all agreed.

With the main team responsibilities determined, Gary asked, "What are we going to call ourselves? We need a catchy name." Tracy suggested that they use a name that reflected the team's capabilities. That idea sounded good, so, after some discussion, they decided to call themselves The Gantt Chart Queen and Cowboy Programmers.

As they broke up, Gary told the group that he would e-mail them as soon as he got a reply from Ray about adding Sean. Later that day, Gary sent his e-mail, saying that Ray had assigned Sean to The Gantt Chart Queen and Cowboy Programmers. Up to full head-count, they were ready to go to work.

FIGURE CS 1.1

ASTA Web Posting

Skills Inventory System for
ADVANCED SYSTEM TECHNOLOGY ASSOCIATES (ASTA)

ORGANIZATIONAL BACKGROUND:
The Advanced System Technology Associates (ASTA) mission is to make our customers more competitive in their market place by providing them with creative solutions to their Process Control, Factory Automation, and Machine Design & Build challenges. We view ourselves as an extension of our customer's Engineering Department and commit to providing leading edge, technical expertise, on a long-term basis.

ASTA was recently honored as the eighth fastest growing private company in the Austin area.

Address: 8900 Burnet Road, Building 4, Austin, 78757
Office Fax: 803-3123

PROJECT:
Skills Inventory System
A. Goal:
   To design, develop and implement an easy-to-use database that allows us to match resumes of potential employees with specific Skill Sets we are searching for. This database would allow the user to query a skill set and obtain either the names or resumes of potential employees matching that query.
B. Hardware requirements:
   Database should be capable of running on 586 machines or higher.
C. Software requirements:
   The completed product should be compatible with Microsoft Office 95 or better and be developed using Microsoft Access 97.
D. Deliverables:
   We would like to have a fully running system capable of being easily updated from the Web by all employees.
E. Point of contact (POC): Yolanda Garza, 803-3150, ygarza@ASTA.com

SELECTING A PROJECT

Each semester, Eleanor Jordan, the other Systems Development instructor who makes the arrangements for the client projects, posts the client list to the course Web site and the students read the brief descriptions and decide which one or ones to request. Gary, Rachel, Tracy, Kim, and Sean sat at a workstation in one of the student labs, checking out the list and focusing on the posting for a company named ASTA, shown in Figure CS 1.1.

"It's a database application, and that is something we should be able to handle, after the Database course experience," said Gary. "I like the fact that ASTA is a high-tech start-up company. I think they would be exciting to work with, and the experience would look good on my resume." Kim joined in, "I like the idea that it is a people-oriented application. I think that would be much more interesting than one involving inventory or accounts receivable or something like that."

After checking out several other clients on the list, the team decided to make the ASTA bid and e-mailed Eleanor, asking for approval. Within a few hours, Eleanor e-mailed back the good news to go ahead. The team quickly met and figured out times that all of the members could meet, and decided to try to set up the first client meeting a week ahead of schedule. Rachel, the Gantt chart queen, sent an e-mail to Yolanda Garza, the primary client contact at ASTA, asking for an appointment. Yolanda is the director of the human resources department.

The First Client Meeting

When the day of the first meeting rolled around, the team arrived at the ASTA offices a few minutes early. Gary told the receptionist that they were from the university and had an appointment with Ms. Garza. The receptionist asked them to wait in the conference room, because that was where the presentation would be held. As soon as they heard the word "presentation," the team members looked at each other with puzzled faces. They thought it was just going to be an informal meeting in Yolanda's office.

The team members followed the receptionist into the conference room and took seats around the large table. A large screen was at one end, next to a podium with a notebook computer. The screen was displaying the ASTA logo. It looked like the beginning of a PowerPoint presentation.

Within a few minutes, Yolanda and a man came into the room. Yolanda introduced herself and the man—Mel Knowler, the ASTA CEO. The team was impressed that the CEO would take the time to meet the team. As it turned out, Mel was to help Yolanda give the presentation. Before the introduction ended, another ASTA employee joined them. He was Rick Gomez, a new engineer who had worked on the project definition and who would be responsible for the system after the team installed it and turned it over to ASTA.

Background on ASTA

Mel wasted no time. "Advanced System Technology Associates, ASTA for short, is a new high-tech firm that has grown from a dozen employees in 1995 to almost 100 today. Most of the employees work out of the headquarters and plant but ten or so are assigned to the Dallas sales office. Our workforce is unique in that practically everyone has technical expertise of some sort that relates to the broad spectrum of factory automation systems that we manufacture and market around the world. It is a very knowledgeable and capable workforce, and it is one of ASTA's real strengths in the competitive world of technical system sales."

The Skill Set Matrix

Mel asked the team if they had any questions about the company and there were none. So he brought up the screen that displayed the words "Skill Set Matrix." He continued, "When ASTA sales began to explode, I recognized that there was a real need to be able to quickly identify the employees who possess the required knowledge and skills demanded by the business opportunities as they emerge. Like most industrial marketing organizations, we respond to requests for proposals (RFPs) that are submitted by companies that have a need for our products and services. We then conduct an analysis of the company's needs and, when we feel we can compete and the business would do us good, we submit a proposal. The company evaluates all the proposals and selects the vendor that should get the sales order—hopefully us."

Each team member took notes as Mel talked, with Gary cranking out the most paper.

"In order to respond to the RFPs," Mel continued, "it became clear that what was needed was some kind of file containing lists of the various types of technical skills possessed by the employees. The employees with the needed skills could be rounded up to work on evaluating the RFP and preparing the proposal. Then, if we are awarded the contract, the same skills file could be used to identify persons to meet specific needs as design and fabrication work progresses."

Mel asked if there were any questions and Gary asked, "Could you give an example?"

"Sure," Mel replied. "An R&D engineer might be working on the design of a new conveyor system and need expert advice on the human/machine interface. And so, the question is 'Does anyone in ASTA have such expertise?' Another question is 'Are they likely to be available if we win this project and start work next month?'"

With Gary satisfied with the example, Mel went on to explain that availability of the skills information would enable ASTA to respond quickly to market opportunities and to make optimum use of its employees' capabilities. In addition to R&D, he reasoned that persons in sales and manufacturing could also use the information, although for different reasons. At this point, Mel turned the presentation over to Yolanda, who then explained the slides that described the matrix and how it is used.

"Mel devised a printed form that he named the skill set matrix, listing some 150 skills in 15 categories. The matrix form was implemented, and now when someone applies for a job, he or she completes the form, identifying which skills are possessed, and coding each with a number that specifies the skill strength (0, for no experience, through 10, for expert). If we hire them, they are supposed to update their matrix forms every time they learn a new skill. They photocopy the forms and give them to me since I maintain them in a secure file cabinet in my office. When managers need access to the matrices, they ask me to retrieve them. I make copies and hand deliver them."

Yolanda asked for questions, and Kim raised her hand. "It sounds like the system is working well. What exactly do you have in mind for us to do?"

Yolanda responded. "Initially, the matrix forms worked fine. But, as more employees were added and the pace of business picked up, it became clear that the inventory would be more valuable if it were computer-based. As with any paper-based system, the matrix forms are difficult to maintain, and access to their contents is slow and prone to human error. Some employees are really good about keeping their forms updated and others never bother."

At this point, Mel, who had taken a seat at the table, interrupted, "As soon as it became obvious that a change was in order, I asked Elizabeth James, our office manager, to assign someone the responsibility of converting the hardcopy document to a computer-based system, and to investigate the possibility that it could be Web based. Elizabeth picked Sue Kim, an office assistant, to explore the possibilities. Sue is a whiz with the small business software that we purchased for our financial record keeping and the spreadsheets that are the basis for some of the company-specific applications. Sue has just been waiting for an opportunity to create systems. She is a graduate of the local community college with an emphasis in information systems, and she believes that we can take much greater advantage of technology. As soon as we get through here, I would like you to meet both Elizabeth and Sue."

ASTA's Strategic Plans, Information Infrastructure, and Organizational Culture

Mel then returned to the podium and began to talk about ASTA's strategic direction. "ASTA has a strategic business plan, which is updated each year and looks three years into the future. One of the five strategic objectives that has guided us since our inception is quick response to market opportunities. This is the objective that is supported by the skill set matrix system. We have not had a strategic plan for information resources, a SPIR I think you call it, but are in the process of developing one. I have asked our management consulting firm to draw one up. They have a lot of experience in that area and have been gathering data for over a month. I expect to have something that we can share with you before you get too far into the project. So, we have a computer capability but it is not one that has grown as a result of a plan. It just happened. We have a LAN, which consists of a Dell server and workstations, running under Microsoft Windows NT. We use the LAN for communication, and the engineers use their workstations for design. We also use it in the manufacturing process—exploding the bills of material, keeping track of inventory, and so on. Also, as I have already said, we use the computer for our accounting work. The new skills inventory system will utilize the LAN."

Mel turned the presentation back to Yolanda to give more explanation of the organizational setting in which the student team will work. "In implementing any system, attention must be given to the organizational culture. In ASTA, the culture is just evolving and is influenced by the organizational structure. There are three major divisions—research and development (R&D), sales, and manufacturing. We also have a finance department, which houses accounting and capital budgeting. Although the divisions understand that they must work together, and the value of their stock options depends on their ability to do that, there is a natural tendency to view their own unique requirements as major concerns. This means that there is not always uniform support for projects and activities. For example, when Mel's interest in a computer-based skills system became known, the R&D people could easily see the need. However, the sales people seemed more interested in external information—about their customers and prospects. So far, the manufacturing people have exhibited an indifferent attitude but that will probably change when we get into the project."

With this introduction to ASTA and the skill set project, the team asked some questions to clear up confusing points. Sean asked for a copy of the ASTA organization chart. Mel and Yolanda exchanged glances and admitted that no one had created one so far. Sean told Yolanda that if he could get some more details, he would create a chart and bring it to their next meeting. "We have to have one for our first major report delivery for class," Rachel said. Yolanda said that it would be no problem to give Sean everything that he needed.

When it was clear that the team could think of nothing else to ask, Mel excused himself and Yolanda led the team to her office. Rick followed along to provide details that he had already worked on for the proposed system.

Getting the Project Started

Yolanda asked Elizabeth and Sue to join the team in her office, where Sue explained their ideas on the new system. "Yolanda and I decided that all ASTA employees will enter name, phone number, e-mail address, and skill levels from workstations to create their matrices, and they will be required to update the data on a quarterly basis. Each quarter, the system will send a notice to each employee, reminding him or her that it is time for an update. As data is entered into a matrix, the input screen will contain necessary instructions. Any employee can access any other employee's matrix but an employee can update only his or her form. A special skills matrix password will be required to enter the system, and statistics will be maintained by the system for the number of requests for each matrix. Output will be displayed on the workstation screens, and printed on the LAN printer when requested. It seems to us, and Mel agrees, that the ideal arrangement is to create the skill set matrix as a Web-based application, enabling the employees to enter their data through the Web, and managers to retrieve the skill set information the same way. The system would be designed to protect the managers from information overload by providing only the information of employees who possess the specified skills."

"With the overall design roughed out, we turned our attention to who could do the work. I checked with a couple of the engineers, but the experienced ones said they were too busy. They suggested Rick, but then he was pulled onto a big new project. It didn't take long for us to realize that nobody within ASTA has the time and experience necessary to put the new system on the air. We don't have any development staff, just a single network support technician who helps with office installations and trouble shooting when he isn't too busy working with engineering teams at client sites."

Elizabeth broke in, "They were just about ready to report back to Mel, telling him that the project could not be implemented. Then, I recalled that my brother worked with clients in actually implementing software systems as an MIS major at the university a couple years ago. He told me the professor who developed the course was Eleanor Jordan. I told all this to Sue and Yolanda and they agreed that a phone call should be made to Eleanor to see if ASTA could qualify for such a project. Yolanda met with Mel and received his agreement to proceed. So, here you are."

Obtaining Sample Forms

Rachel decided that it was time for someone on the team to take a proactive role in the first meeting as a way of exerting ownership of the project, and she reasoned that, if she had any expectations of being a team leader, she was the logical person to do it. So, she asked if there was any documentation on either the current system or the proposed new one.

Rick said that he'd created an entity-relationship diagram ERD before he was pulled off the project. He thought this might give them a good start. "I wasn't able to get any farther than that design step," he said as he passed around copies to all of the team members. He explained the use of the infinity symbols to show the "many" relationships since that notation is not always used. Figure CS 1.2 shows the ERD.

Kim thanked Rick for the team. She then asked whether ASTA could provide completed matrices, not just the blank forms. "If you would copy about a dozen matrices, we could use those to create a test database. That will make our first drafts of reports and updates more meaningful. Plus, that will give us a better idea of what your data looks like."

Sue said that she would copy several for them now. She'd pick some experienced employees and newer employees from different areas of the company so that the team could see a representative variety of skills. She excused herself to do the copying.

At this point, the team felt a little overwhelmed. Rick left with a quick "good luck" and made sure they had his e-mail address. He didn't plan to come to the regular weekly meetings with Yolanda—he'd just be available if they needed him.

When Sue returned with the copies of the completed matrices, the team thanked Yolanda, Elizabeth, and Sue and reminded them that they would be back next week—same time and place. They might have a few questions before then. "Sure," said Yolanda, "just call or e-mail."

Planning the Second Team Meeting

In the parking lot, the team decided that they would meet the next day to go over the next steps. Rachel offered to rough out a functions/components matrix, a comparison of existing and proposed system components, and an information dimensions table for the rest of the team to review. Of course, nobody objected to Rachel doing all of this work. Feeling that she had taken a first step toward being team leader, she suggested that they all bring a task list for the team for the next couple of weeks. She'd carefully go over the client project specification for the first delivery before the meeting, but if everyone would read it and come up with their own lists, they would have a better chance of making good use of their team meeting time.

Kim countered by volunteering to go over the ERD instead and said, "Maybe Tracy could create a first draft of a menu hierarchy like we created in our

FIGURE CS 1.2

Rick's Entity Relationship Diagram for the Proposed Skill Set System

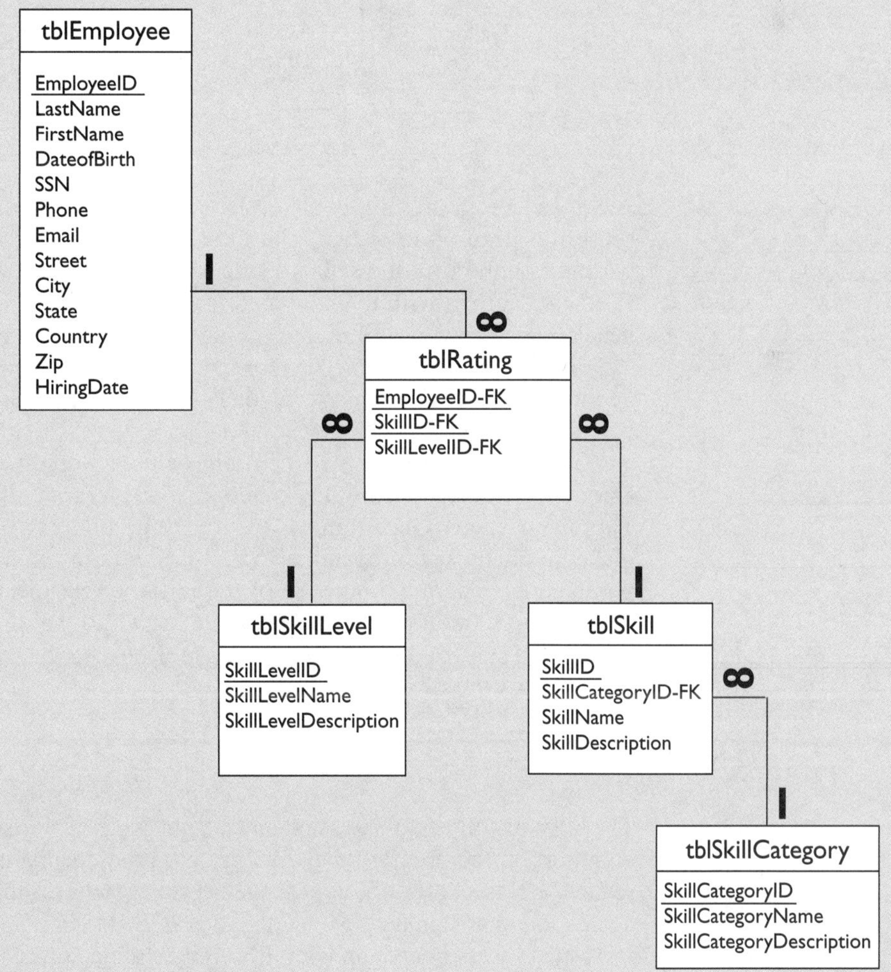

FIGURE CS 1.3

ASTA Organization Chart

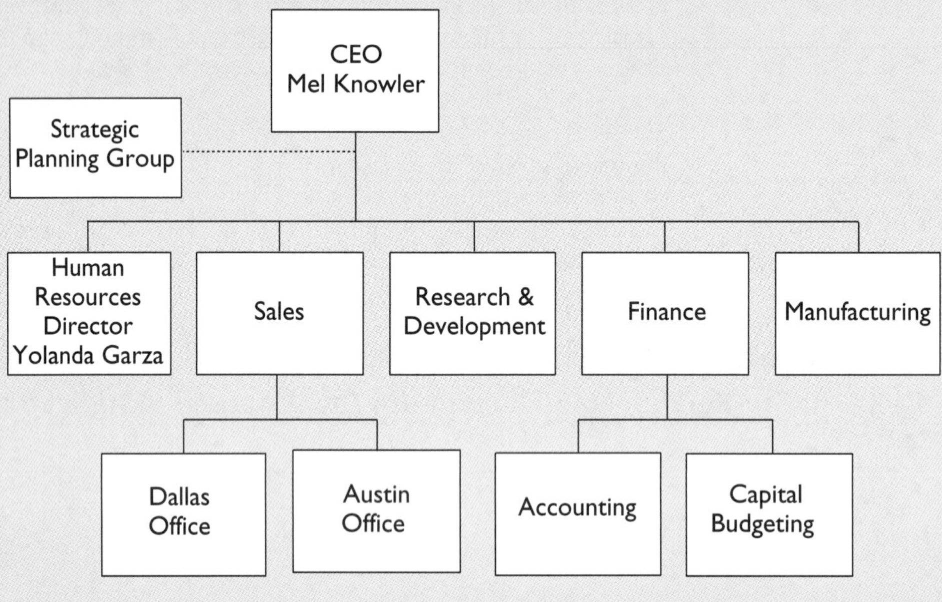

Advanced Programming course. Gary could create some DFDs. I think it makes sense for all of us to at least skim the Client Project Specification, but one of us working on the task list seems like enough to me, Rachel."

Rachel agreed with the new plan for the team meeting and deliveries. "We also need to decide who will create the agendas and minutes for client meetings. We can do that tomorrow too. The more we get started on early, the more sleep we can get at the end of the semester. None of us want another Advanced Programming course marathon."

"Getting started early will be a big help as we come to grips with our tasks," Gary added before asking the others if there was anything else that they needed. The Gantt Chart Queen and Cowboy Programmers were pleased that they had picked a client who prepared a formal presentation in advance and even the CEO participated. The main purpose of the initial client meeting is to establish a bond of trust and mutual respect between the team and the client, and they thought they had a good start on this as well as ideas for how to impress the client at their meeting at ASTA the next week.

THE SECOND TEAM MEETING

The team met the next day as planned. Sean got things rolling by suggesting that they all report on the progress they had made on the documents each had volunteered to review, and then they could put together an agenda for the client meeting. Everyone agreed that that sounded like a good idea so Sean led off with the organization chart.

"Here is what I came up with. It's pretty simple and certainly doesn't show a lot of detail. But, it does include all of the key players, or at least their positions." He passed around copies of the chart shown in Figure CS 1.3.

"This looks pretty good," Kim said. "It looks like it has all of the positions and departments and offices on it that Mel described. But, wouldn't it be better to have names for each of the slots, along with their phone extensions and e-mail addresses?" Everybody thought that added detail would help, and Sean said that he would ask Yolanda for the additional information at the next meeting.

With the organization chart put in place as a solid foundation for the study, Rachel offered to show the team her diagrams. The first one is the F/C matrix, illustrated in Figure CS 1.4.

"The second one is the comparison of the existing and the proposed systems in terms of the system components. You can just glance at it and see that the new system

FIGURE CS 1.4

ASTA's Functions/Components Matrix for the Proposed Skill Set System

	Input	Processing	Output	Storage	Control
People	Applicants and employees enter skills	Managers make RFP decisions using skill set information	Managers access skill set data		Employees can only update their skill set matrices Password required to enter system
Data	Employee ID, name, phone number, e-mail address, skill codes, skill levels, SSN, full address, birth date, hiring date	Match employee ID with skill codes		Skill set database: tblEmployee, tblProject, tblEmployee_Project_XREF, tblSkillCategory, tblRating, tblSkillLevel, tblProject_Skill_XREF, tblSkill, tblProjectType	Employees can only update their skill set matrices
Information		Collect availability information and materials requirements for RFP decision	Quarterly update notice Responses to skill set queries Employee availability report Project assignment report		
Software Tools	Java/HTML Browser software (Microsoft Internet Explorer and Netscape Navigator)	Microsoft Access	Java/HTML Browser software (Microsoft Internet Explorer and Netscape Navigator)	Microsoft Access	Microsoft Windows NT Java/HTML
Software Functions	Skills data gathered from browser	Produce skill set matrix Print quarterly update notice Respond to skill set queries	Display database content on system screens in browser	Maintain skill set database Record number of requests for each matrix	Microsoft Windows NT authentication Special skills matrix password to enter Web skill set system
Hardware	Workstations, monitors, modems	Dell server, workstations	Workstation, printers, monitors, modems	Dell server	

is going to be more robust in terms of information, hardware, and, especially software." See Figure CS 1.5.

"And, finally, I came up with this table that looks at the new system in terms of how it will contribute to the four basic dimensions of information. Since the main purpose of the new system is to provide information, it should contribute to all four dimensions." Refer to Figure CS 1.6 on page 14. The other team members agreed that Rachel had done a good job on the documents and suggested that she show them to Yolanda at the client meeting.

"What else do we have?" Sean asked. "I need to report on the ERD," Gary said. "And I need to tell you about the menu hierarchy," Tracy said. "You go first, Tracy," Sean said.

"Here is what I came up with," Tracy said as she passed around photocopies of a hand-drawn diagram. We'll have a couple of login screens—one for first time users, and the other for repetitive use. The main menu will identify the four main options—creating a new matrix, updating an existing matrix, doing a retrieval using search criteria, and preparing management reports. When the user selects the reports option, they can then specify the type of report. When they select either the create or update option, they are forced to go through all six skill categories, to make sure they don't miss one." The team discussed the diagram for a few minutes and decided that it accurately portrayed the hierarchy and that Tracy should prepare a copy using graphics software to present at the client meeting. Sean was especially excited about the menus and asked if it would be alright for him to work up some sample screens to give the client an idea of the "look and feel." Not being ones to turn down offered work, the teammates gave the green light.

Kim followed the same approach as Tracy in passing around a marked-up copy of Rick's ERD. She had added four tables that would be necessary in order to match up the employees with the projects. Since all of the team members were data modeling experts, it didn't take long for them to agree that the changes were in order. Kim promised to make a final copy to present to the client.

With nobody else stepping forward, Sean said "We want to put together an agenda for the client meeting but, first, Gary, I thought you were going to do something on the context diagram and DFDs."

Gary looked a little sheepish and said, "I thought I had some really good notes but when I started to do the drawing I realized that there is a whole lot of information that I need. I need to get with someone at ASTA who knows the process and ask some questions. I can do that at the client meeting." With that, the team discussed what they wanted to accomplish at the client meeting. The team meeting broke up and Sean went to the lab to prepare the agenda.

The Second Client Meeting

When the team arrived at ASTA, Yolanda and Sue were waiting in the conference room. Sean passed around the agenda shown in Figure CS 1.7 on page 15 and brought Yolanda and Sue up to date on the work that the team had done since the first meeting.

Sean gave Yolanda a copy of the organization chart that had been prepared and asked for names, phone numbers, and e-mail addresses. She promised to get them. Kim then explained her additions to the ERD (shown in Figure CS 1.8 on page 16) and Sue agreed that they were necessary.

Tracy then gave copies of the menu hierarchy diagram in Figure CS 1.9 on page 17 to the clients, who liked it very much.

FIGURE CS 1.5

ASTA's Existing and Proposed System Components

	Existing System	Proposed System
People	■ Employees create skill set matrix and send it to Yolanda ■ Managers ask Yolanda for copies of the skill set matrices ■ Managers make RFP decisions based on the skill set matrices	■ Employees create skill set matrix on Web ■ Managers look up employee skills on Web ■ Managers make RFP decisions using database ■ User password requirement ■ Users can only edit their own skill set
Data	■ Name ■ Company area ■ Skill codes and skill levels	■ Employee ID, name, phone number, e-mail address, SSN, full address, birth date, hire date ■ Skill codes and skill levels (improved skill set matrix) ■ Skill set database stores data in the following tables: tblEmployee, tblProject, tblEmployee_Project_XREF, tblSkillCategory, tblRating, tblSkillLevel, tblProject_Skill_XREF, tblSkill, tblProjectType
Information	■ Skill Set Matrix	■ Skill Set Matrix (improved) ■ Employees available report ■ Project assignment report ■ Quarterly update notice ■ Responses to skill set queries ■ Availability information and materials requirements are displayed for RFP decisions
Software Tools	■ None	■ Java and HTML ■ Microsoft Access ■ Browser software (Microsoft Internet Explorer and Netscape Navigator)
Software Functions	■ None	■ Data gathered from and sent to the browser ■ Access prints quarterly update notice and responds to skill set queries ■ Password verification ■ The number of requests for a matrix is captured
Hardware	■ Workstations ■ Printers ■ Monitors	■ Workstations ■ Printers ■ Monitors ■ Modems

FIGURE CS 1.6

Information Dimensions of the New ASTA Skill Set System

Dimension	Sample System Objective
Accuracy	■ The skill set database will contain current (quarterly), accurate information that will not be altered unless with a password. ■ The RFP software will make a decision based on current, accurate data about the production schedule, the bill of materials, materials requirements, and the skill set database.
Timeliness	■ Managers who retrieve the information will be able to get the results immediately. ■ The RFP decision software will make a decision without delay.
Completeness	■ The skill set retrieval software will provide managers with every employee that fits the retrieval criteria. ■ The RFP software will consider all factors (the production schedule, the bill of materials, materials requirements, and the skill set database) before making a decision.
Relevance	■ The skill set retrieval software will provide managers with only the employees who fit the specific criteria entered. No extra information will be provided. ■ The RFP decision software will base its decision on only the production schedule, the bill of materials, materials requirements, and the skill set database.

With the team clearly accomplishing its objective of impressing the client, Sean passed around copies of his screen shots, shown in Figure CS 1.10 on page 18.

Yolanda was impressed. “Hey, that’s our logo on the screens. And you’ve provided two styles in your samples.”

“I cut and pasted the logo from the ASTA Web site,” said Sean. “Which of the designs do you prefer? And do you like the use of color? You need to let us know if you like the color before we create more screens. The sooner we decide on the general look, the less changing we’ll have to do later. I’ve based the samples on the four main functions you see at the top of Tracy’s menu hierarchy diagram. Does that look right to you?”

Sue and Yolanda couldn’t believe that the team had done so much work in just a short time. They began to see how a Systems Development team could implement a working system within a semester. The team spent the remainder of the meeting asking questions, with most of the time spent by Gary asking about the processes that he would need to understand for the DFDs.

When the meeting was over, the team assembled again in the parking lot and talked over what they would do in the next team meeting. Gary promised to have some DFDs. Kim and Tracy had already decided that the team should get on the problem chain analysis, and volunteered to lead that discussion. With that, everyone went back to campus.

The Third Team Meeting

As promised, Gary showed up with his DFDs. He had three—a context diagram (Figure CS 1.11 on page 21), a figure 0 data flow diagram (Figure CS 1.12 on page 22), and a figure 3 data flow diagram (Figure CS 1.13 on page 23).

Since Gary had worked on the DFDs with Tracy and Kim, they had caught all of the careless errors such as data flow names that were not unique, or not the same from one level to the next. So the other team members gave the diagrams a seal of approval.

The team then engaged in an exhaustive discussion of the problem chain with Tracy and Kim leading the way. The team members agreed that there were a lot of symptoms and a lot of problems, some of which were systems problems and some of which were not. They ended up with three main problems—the skills inventory system, a market intelligence system, and human resources in general. For each problem, they identified objectives and performance criteria. Tracy and Kim volunteered to type up a copy to present to the client, and Sean offered to prepare another agenda.

The Third Client Meeting

Mel paid an unexpected visit to the client meeting, bringing along copies of the new SPIR for the team. He explained that it was a fairly simple plan, which he felt was

Figure CS 1.7

Agenda for the Second Client Meeting

Client Meeting Agenda

Date: January 10, 2001
Time: 2 PM
Place: ASTA Headquarters

Purpose: Review documents that team has prepared and obtain additional information as required

Team Members in Attendance: Sean Patterson, Tracy Johnson, Kim Wu, Gary Patel, Rachel Sanders

Facilitator: Rachel Sanders

Note Taker: Gary Patel

Meeting Tasks:

1. Summary of progress to date
2. Discuss the organization chart (Sean)
3. Discuss the revised ERD (Kim)
4. Present the proposed menu hierarchy (Tracy)
5. Get feedback on sample screen shots (Sean)
6. Ask questions about the new skill set system processes (Gary)
7. General question and answer session (ASTA and team members)
8. Identification of the next steps to take
9. Arrange for the next meeting

FIGURE CS 1.8

Kim's ERD with More Tables

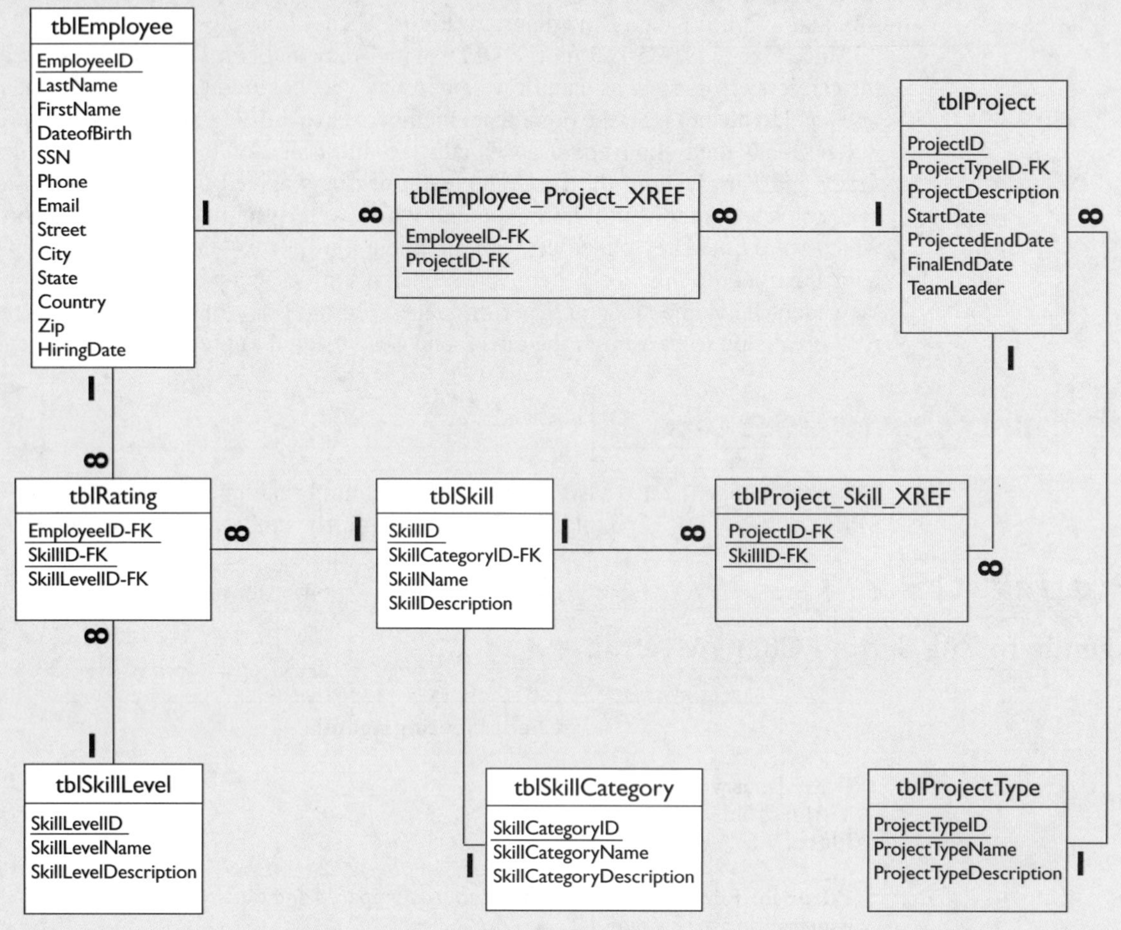

appropriate since it was their first effort. See the plan in Figure CS 1.14 on page 24. He pointed out that the plan specifies use of Gantt charts and network diagrams for project management and asked that the team conform to that guideline. He also pointed out that the Web-based skills system (planned project 6) would be accomplished by the team.

After asking the team if there were any questions about the SPIR and finding none, Mel left the meeting. From that point on the meeting was devoted almost exclusively to a discussion of the problem chain. This presentation was perhaps the most difficult for the team since the client was not familiar with the concept of a chain and its purpose. After going through the chain, illustrated in Figure CS 1.15 on page 26, the team and the client decided that the team would only address the problem with the skills inventory system, and leave the other problems to other teams at a later date. Yolanda was especially impressed with the systematic way the team had traveled down the chain to establish measurable criteria for the new system. "That's exactly what we need—something concrete to use in evaluating the system. You've done a really good job. I'm looking forward to seeing the new system."

FIGURE CS 1.9

Tracy's Initial Menu Hierarchy

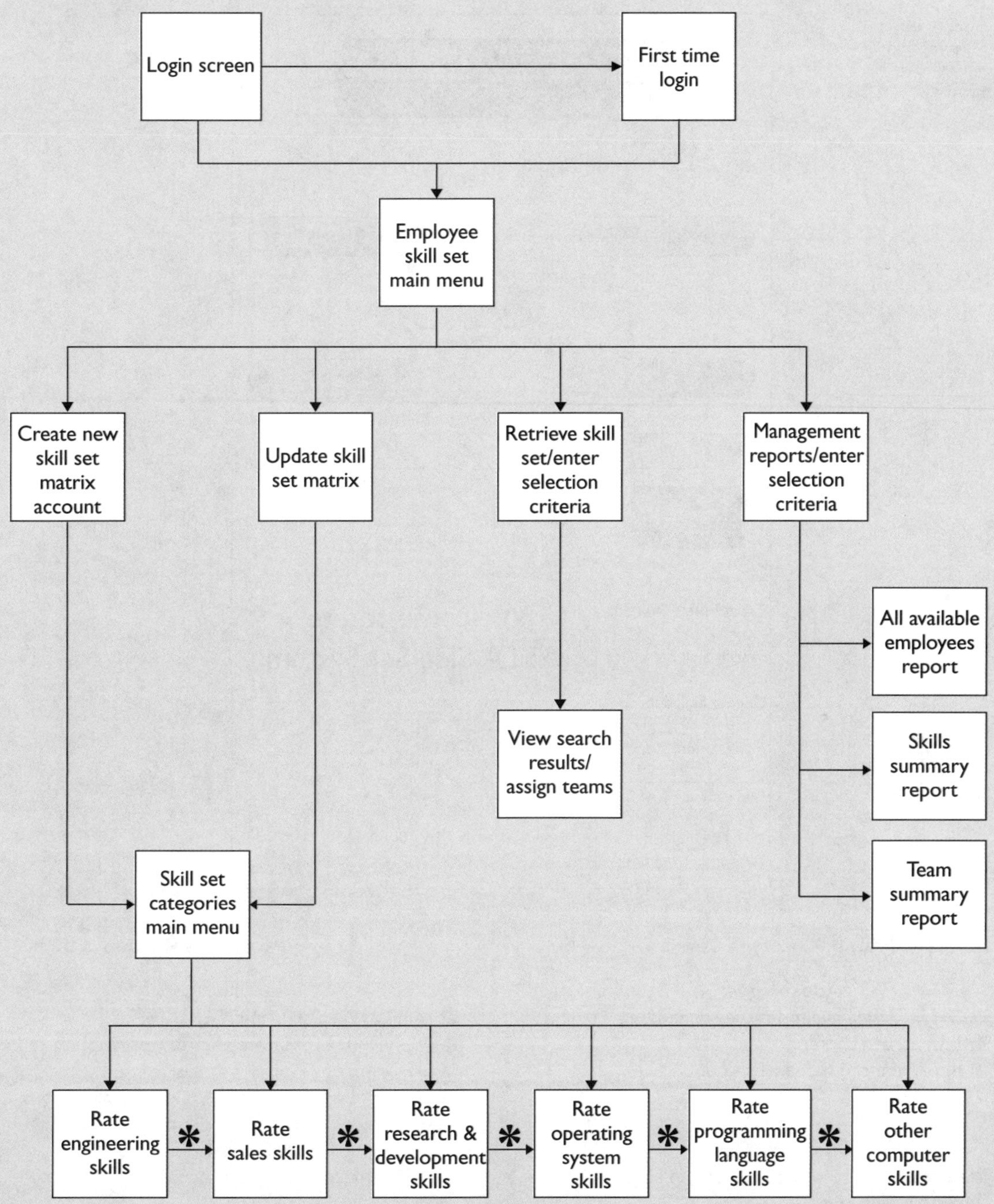

* This navigation from screen to screen will be forced to ensure that the employee will enter/review every single category of skills. Only the secretary or system administrator will be able to view/edit pages out of order.

FIGURE CS 1.10

Prototype Screen Comparison—No-Frame and Frame Versions

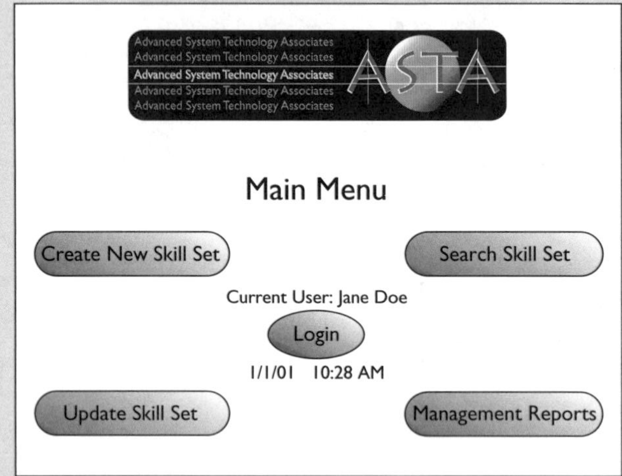

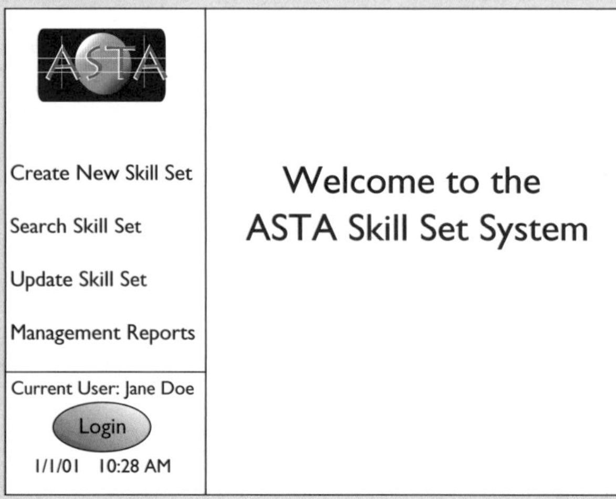

No-Frame Prototype Version

Advantages:

- Simple design minimizes user confusion
- Low screen clutter
- Intuitive menu-based navigation

Disadvantages:

- Forces users to return to menu to access system functions
- Old-style design
- Potentially more difficult to update

Frame Prototype Version

Advantages:

- Familiar Web-style interface
- Frame index is fast and easy to navigate
- Uniform design for all screens
- System functions are accessible from all screens

Disadvantages:

- Left frame adds potentially confusing clutter to all screens
- Frame occupies valuable screen space
- No familiarity advantage for non-Web users

FIGURE CS 1.10 (CONTINUED)

First Level Prototype Screens for No-Frame Version

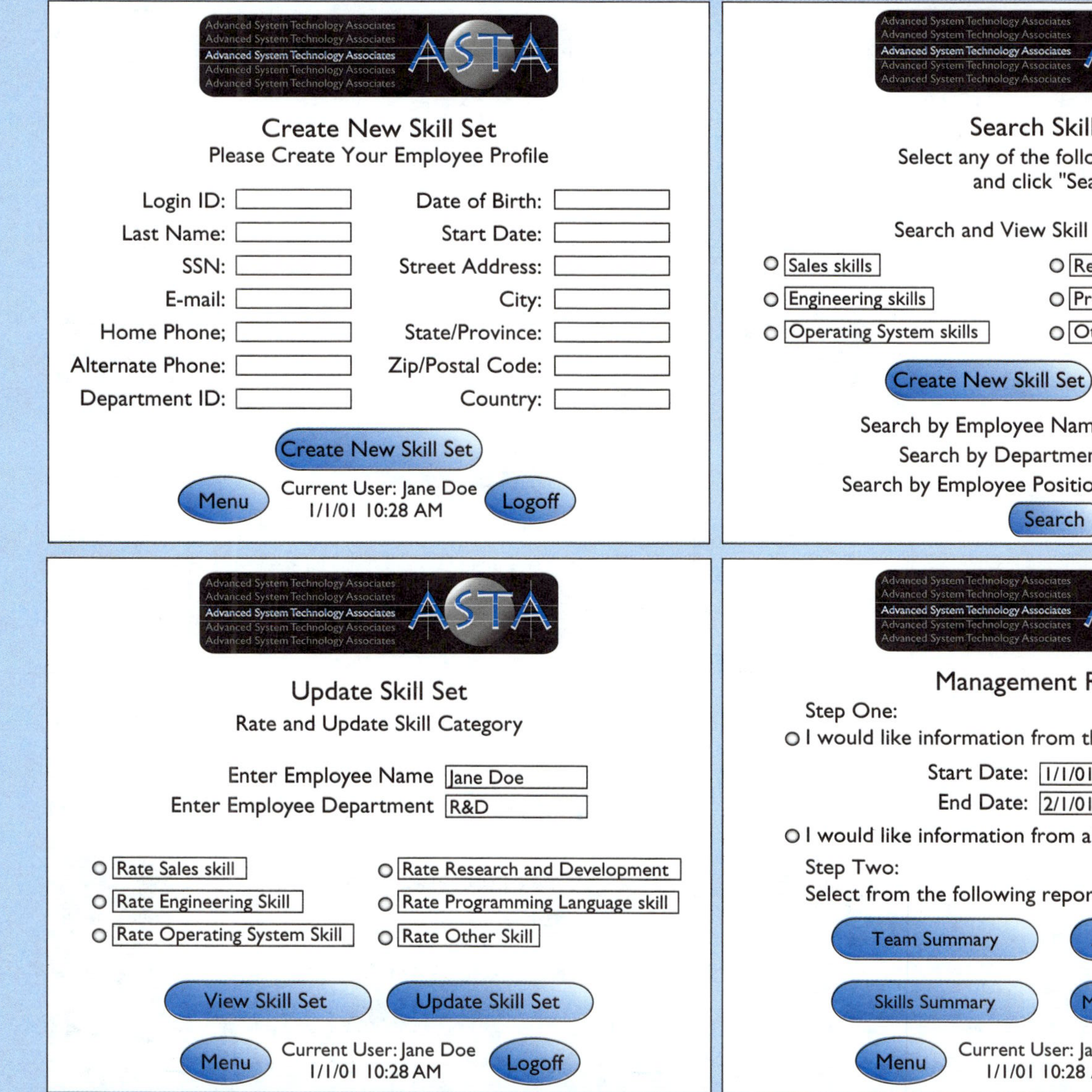
Advanced System Technology Associates
ASTA
Create New Skill Set
Please Create Your Employee Profile
Login ID:
Last Name:
SSN:
E-mail:
Home Phone;
Alternate Phone:
Department ID:
Date of Birth:
Start Date:
Street Address:
City:
State/Province:
Zip/Postal Code:
Country:
Create New Skill Set
Menu
Current User: Jane Doe
1/1/01 10:28 AM
Logoff
Search Skill Set
Select any of the following criteria
and click "Search"
Search and View Skill Set Category
Sales skills
Engineering skills
Operating System skills
Research and Development skills
Programming Language skills
Other skills
Create New Skill Set
Search
Search by Employee Name:
Search by Department: None specified
Search by Employee Position: None specified
Search
Update Skill Set
Rate and Update Skill Category
Enter Employee Name Jane Doe
Enter Employee Department R&D
Rate Sales skill
Rate Engineering Skill
Rate Operating System Skill
Rate Research and Development
Rate Programming Language skill
Rate Other Skill
View Skill Set
Update Skill Set
Menu
Current User: Jane Doe
1/1/01 10:28 AM
Logoff
Management Reports
Step One:
I would like information from the following range of dates:
Start Date: 1/1/01
End Date: 2/1/01
I would like information from all available dates:
Step Two:
Select from the following report types:
Team Summary
Available Employees
Skills Summary
Management Summary
Menu
Current User: Jane Doe
1/1/01 10:28 AM
Logoff

FIGURE CS 1.10 (CONTINUED)

First Level Prototype Screens for Frames Version

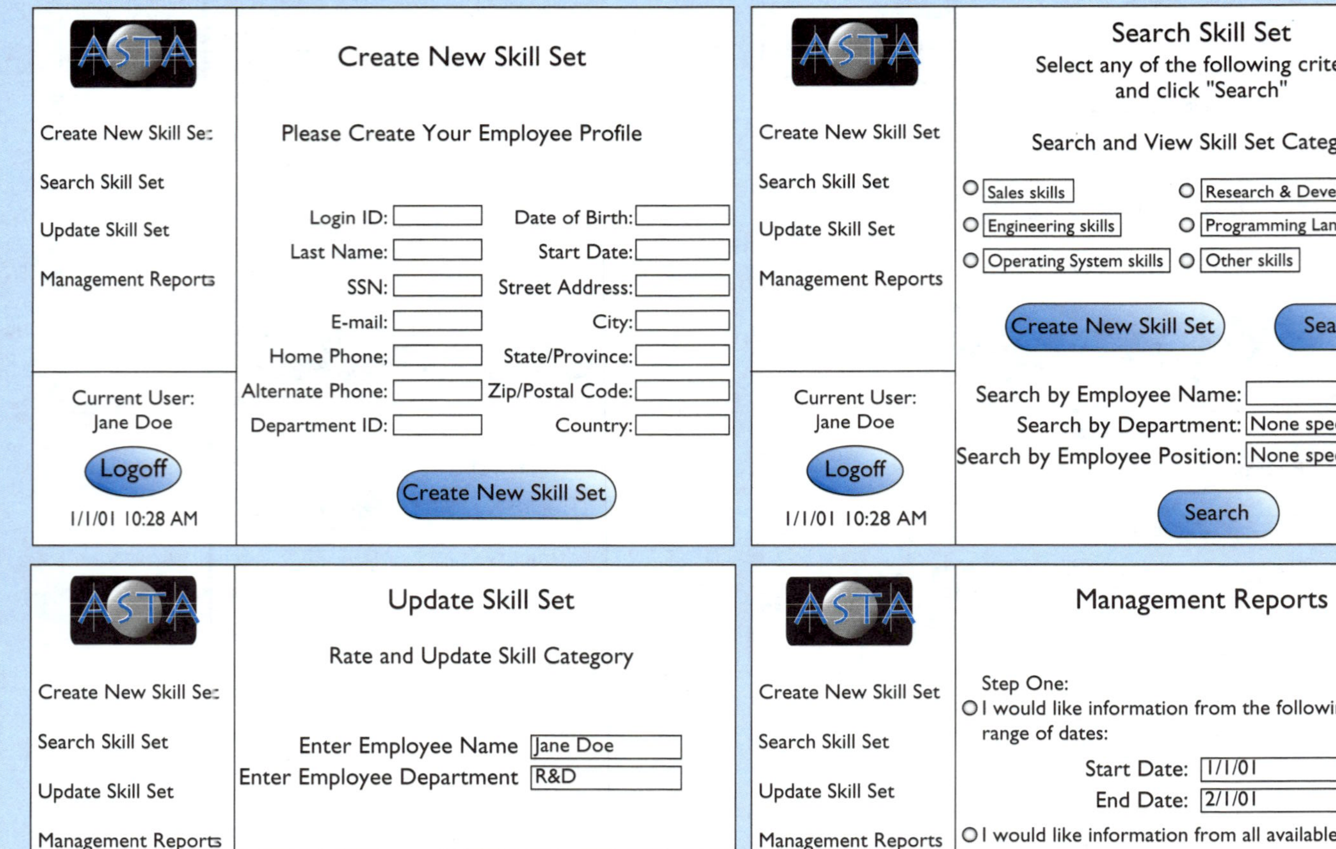
ASTA
Create New Skill Set
Search Skill Set
Update Skill Set
Management Reports
Current User:
Jane Doe
Logoff
1/1/01 10:28 AM
Create New Skill Set
Please Create Your Employee Profile
Login ID:
Last Name:
SSN:
E-mail:
Home Phone;
Alternate Phone:
Department ID:
Date of Birth:
Start Date:
Street Address:
City:
State/Province:
Zip/Postal Code:
Country:
Create New Skill Set
Search Skill Set
Select any of the following criteria and click "Search"
Search and View Skill Set Category
Sales skills
Engineering skills
Operating System skills
Research & Development skills
Programming Language skills
Other skills
Create New Skill Set
Search
Search by Employee Name:
Search by Department: None specified
Search by Employee Position: None specified
Search
Update Skill Set
Rate and Update Skill Category
Enter Employee Name Jane Doe
Enter Employee Department R&D
Rate Sales skill
Rate Engineering Skill
Rate Operating System Skill
Rate Research &Development skill
Rate Programming Language skill
Rate Other Skill
View Skill Set
Update Skill Set
Management Reports
Step One:
I would like information from the following range of dates:
Start Date: 1/1/01
End Date: 2/1/01
I would like information from all available dates
Step Two:
Select from the following report types
Team Summary
Available Employees
Skills Summary
Management Summary

FIGURE CS 1.11

Gary's Context Diagram for the Proposed Skill Set System

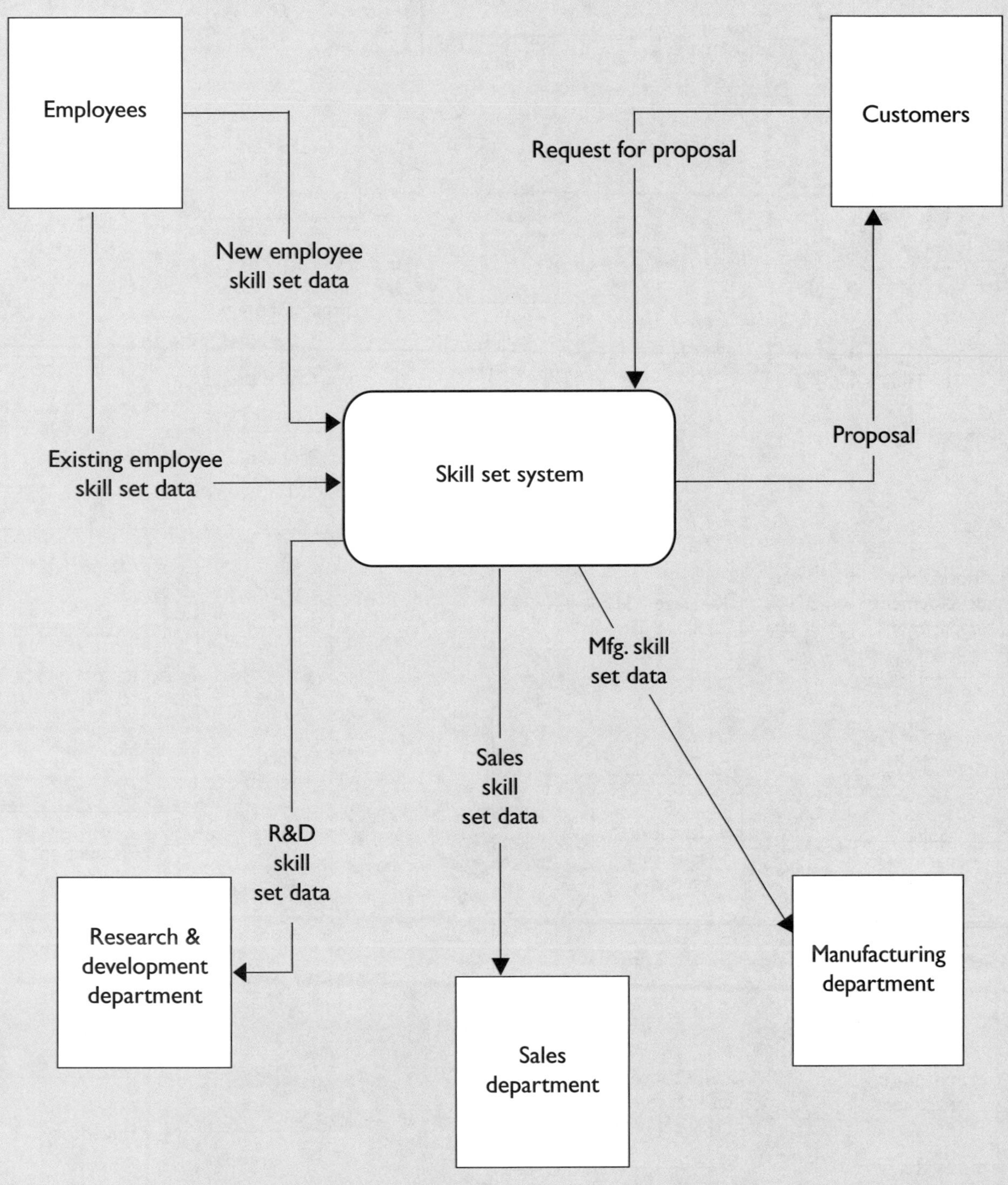

FIGURE CS 1.12

Gary's Figure 0 Data Flow Diagram for the Proposed Skill Set System

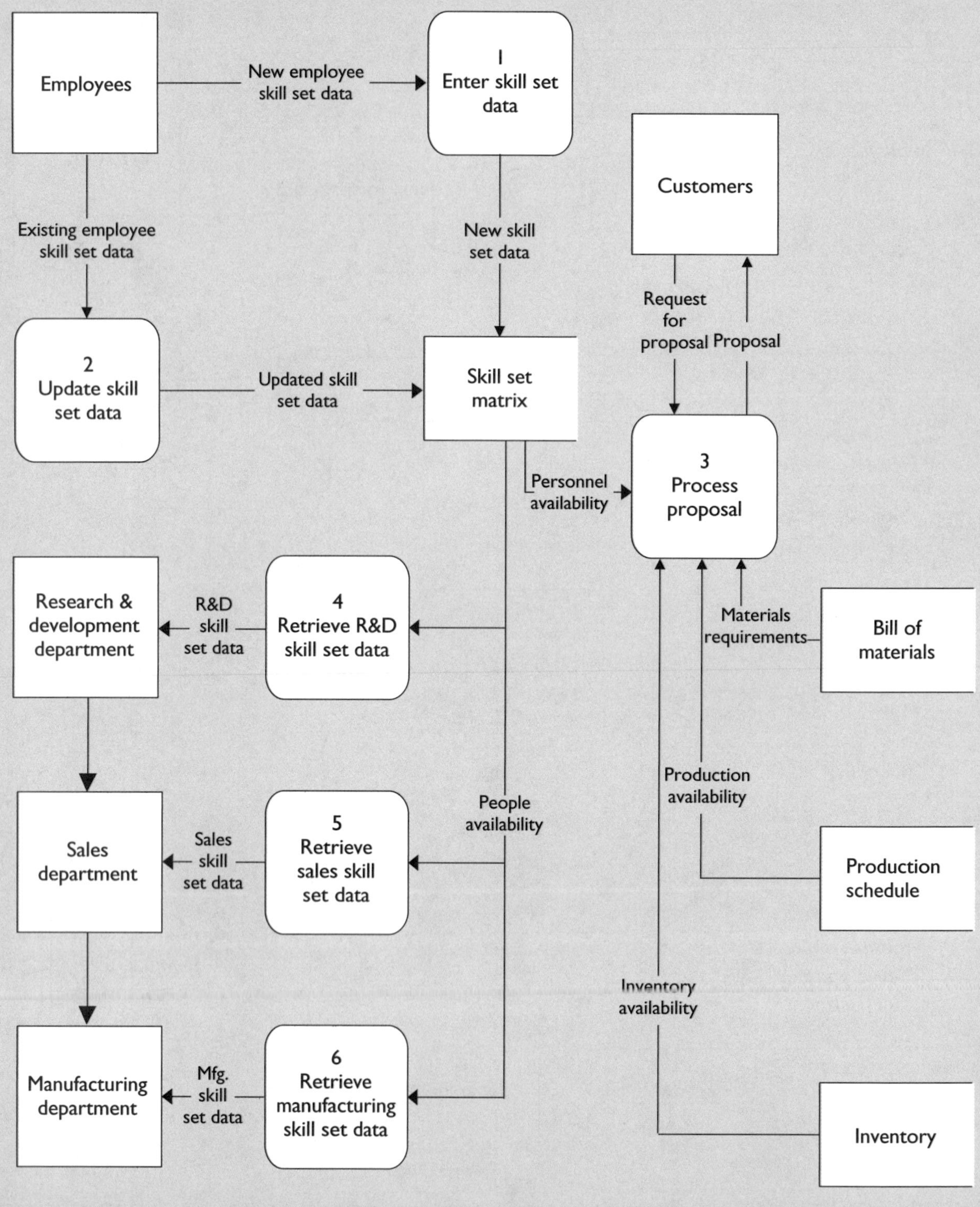

FIGURE CS 1.13

Gary's Figure 3 Data Flow Diagram for Process Proposal

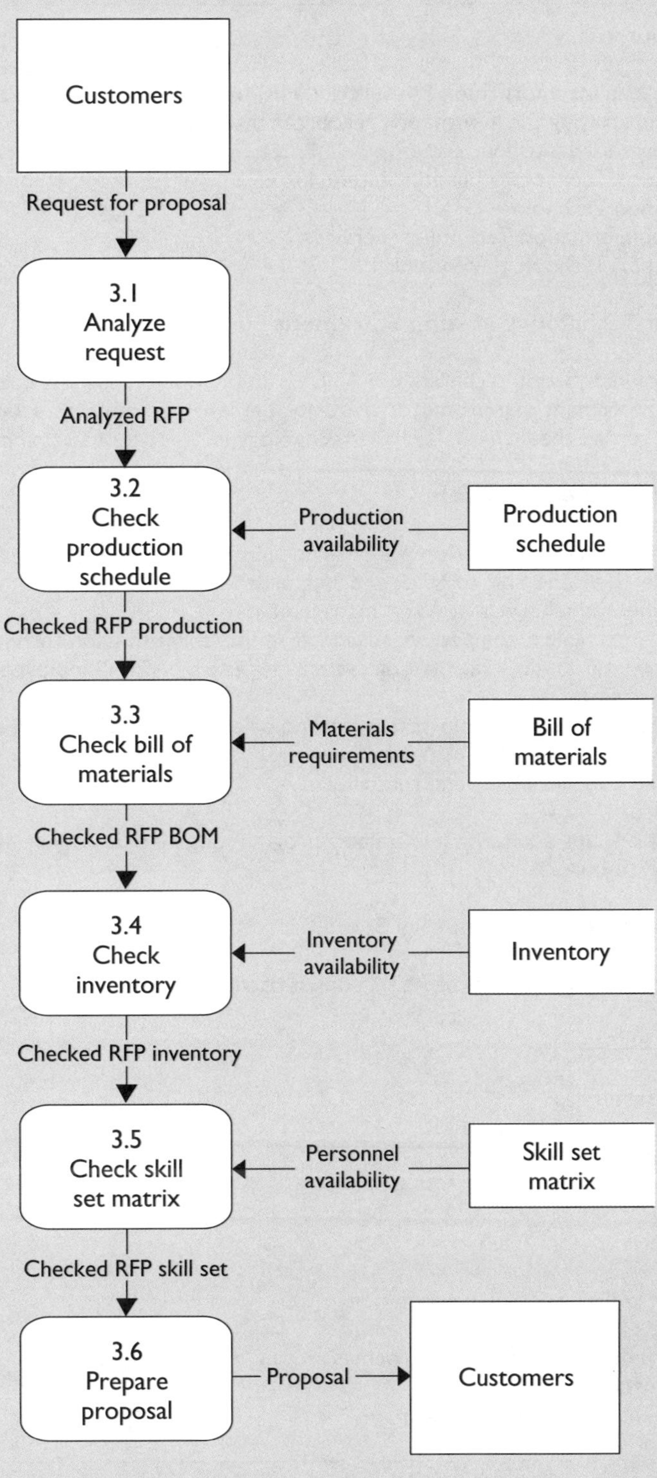

FIGURE CS 1.14

ASTA Strategic Plan for Information Resources

Executive Summary

The Strategic Plan for Information Resources (SPIR) has been developed to support the Strategic Business Plan by assembling and applying the information resources that are necessary to achieve the ASTA strategic objectives. The SPIR is organized into four sections:

- Information Technology Mission Statement
- Information Technology Goals
- Scope of Information Technology Services
- Information Technology Work Plan

Information Technology Mission Statement

The mission of information technology in ASTA is to provide the highest quality of information services in a supportive environment that promotes creativity, personal growth, interaction, diversity, and professional development so that the firm can leverage technology in support of attainment of corporate objectives.

Information Technology Goals

The information technology mission will be accomplished by pursuing the following goals:

1. Provide effective leadership to guide and support the firm through transitions in information technology, working in partnership with all levels of ASTA management.
2. Guide efforts to build a competitive advantage in use of information technology.
3. Develop the best possible information systems for use by ASTA employees and its environmental constituents in performing their tasks.
4. Stay up-to-date on evolving information technologies so that ASTA can meet the needs of its customers in a professional and businesslike manner.
5. Maintain operational stability and reliability in ASTA's information resources-people, data, facilities, hardware, and software.
6. Maintain an ongoing education and training program designed to achieve efficient and effective use of ASTA's information resources.

Scope of Information Technology Services

Information technology services at ASTA consist of the following:

Administrative Services

- Human resources
- Budgeting and fiscal review
- Stockholder relations
- Management reporting

Engineering Services

- Strategic planning and implementation
- Capacity planning
- Network design, maintenance, troubleshooting, and administration
- Server installations
- Contingency planning and backup

FIGURE CS 1.14 (CONTINUED)

Technology Services

- Technical support in the form of help desk and call management services
- User education and training
- Database management services
- Document management services
- System development and support
- World Wide Web access
- Computer graphics
- Hardware troubleshooting, upgrading, and replacement
- Antivirus and firewall services
- Systems administration and maintenance
- Systems audits

Information Technology Work Plan

ASTA management has identified several key projects to be completed during the next three-year period. Prior to beginning each project, a project management mechanism will be developed specifying the following:

- Required tasks
- Person(s) or organizations responsible for completion of the tasks
- Estimated amount of time required for each task

All projects will be managed using Gantt charts and network diagrams.

All projects with the exception of the knowledge-based RFP system and the skill set system will be accomplished with ASTA personnel resources. Project 6, the skill set system, will be developed by the student team, and project 7, the RFP system will be designed and implemented by KBS Consultants.

The projects and their estimated person months include the following. The first person listed is the project manager. Additional persons are support personnel.

Project	Project Manager(s)	Estimated Person-Months
1. Upgrade from Windows 95 to Windows XP	Sue Kim	0.2
2. Replace GroupWise e-mail system with an integration of Microsoft's Digital Dashboard and the ASTA relationship management system.	Elizabeth James Sue Kim	3.0
3. Implement the Outlook Telephony Interface, enabling the retrieval of e-mail from any Touch Tone telephone by calling a toll-free number.	Elizabeth James Sue Kim	2.5
4. Upgrade Word 97 to Microsoft Office XP. Add Excel and PowerPoint to the core training curriculum.	Elizabeth James Sue Kim	2.0
5. Deploy departmental-based intranet for library services and human resource information and services.	Yolanda Garza Sue Kim	4.0
6. Implement a Web-based skill set system.	Yolanda Garza, Sue Kim	18.0
7. Implement a knowledge-based system to determine personnel, production facility, and material, needs in response to RFPs.	Rick Gomez KBS Consultants	96.0

FIGURE CS 1.15

ASTA Problem Chain for Paper-Based "As Is" System

Symptoms

1. Difficulty in maintaining the skills inventory of employee knowledge and skills
2. Slow access of the skills inventory system
3. Errors in the skills inventory system
4. Difficulty in responding promptly to market opportunities
5. Lack of uniform support for the skills inventory system within the firm
6. Inability to enforce quarterly updating of skills inventory information

What is the problem (root cause)? Is there more than one problem?

Possible Problems

Symptoms 1, 2, 3: The manual nature of the paper-based skills inventory system

Symptom 4:

- Inability to quickly gather, process and disseminate information on market opportunities
- Inability to quickly formulate a strategy for responding to market opportunities

Symptom 5: Functional attitude of organizational units

Symptom 6: Lack of motivation by employees to comply with skills updating procedure

Problems (Root Causes)

Problem 1 : The problem is the manual nature of the paper-based skills inventory system.

Problem 2: The problem is unavailability of a responsive business intelligence system.

Problem 3: The problem is that organizational units have functional (rather than company) attitudes.

Problem 4: The problem is lack of discipline by employees in following policies and procedures.

Can these be collapsed into one or a few main problem areas?

Summary of Main Problems

Skills inventory system: The problem is the manual nature of the ASTA skills inventory system, making it slow, error prone, and difficult to maintain.

Market intelligence system: The problem is that ASTA does not have a system in place for responding to market opportunities.

Human resources: The problem is that employees are not motivated to support company programs and procedures.

FIGURE CS 1.15 (CONTINUED)

What should be the focus of the ASTA development team for the project?

Skills Inventory System

Objectives:
1. The skills inventory system should be computer based.
2. The skills inventory system should respond quickly to requests for information.
3. The skills inventory system should be accurate.
4. The skills inventory system should be easy to maintain

Performance criteria:
1. Requests for information concerning employee skills are filled within *15 minutes.*
2. All employees update their skills records at least *quarterly.*
3. Employees can update their skills inventory in *no more than 15 minutes.*
4. Employees update their skills inventory information from their *workstations.*
5. Employees update their skills inventory information by *changing only the data entries that need to be updated.*
6. The skills inventory system features a *user-friendly GUI front end.*

Market Intelligence System

Objective: The market intelligence system should provide management with current information in an easily retrievable form for the purpose of responding to market opportunities.

Performance criteria:
1. Market information should be stored in the system within two hours after becoming known to ASTA personnel.
2. Users should be able to retrieve market intelligence from their workstations.
3. The user should interface with the system using a user-friendly GUI.

Human Resources

Objective: Employees on all levels should place the well-being of the firm before that of their organizational units.

Performance criteria:
1. Employees always follow the company policies and procedures.
2. Employees will not make decisions or take actions that negatively affect the ability of the firm to meet its objectives.

CHAPTER 1

INTRODUCTION TO SYSTEMS DEVELOPMENT

LEARNING OBJECTIVES

- Know how the term *system* is used in the information systems field.
- Distinguish between the two basic classes of systems: physical and conceptual.
- Distinguish between open and closed systems, and open-loop and closed-loop systems.
- Understand the hierarchical nature of systems.
- Analyze a firm by applying the systems view.
- Understand what the information systems infrastructure is, and what major subsystems it contains.
- Use a functions/components matrix to relate system resources to the activities that are performed.
- Identify the keys to successful systems work.

INTRODUCTION

A system consists of several elements that work together to achieve an objective. Although systems can be classified in many ways, a fundamental subdivision recognizes two basic classes: physical and conceptual. Physical systems exist in a tangible form, and conceptual systems represent physical systems. The firm is a physical system, and management uses conceptual systems to manage the firm. An information system is a physical system, but its programs and data are conceptual systems, representing the physical processes and resources of the firm.

A system that interfaces with its environment is called an open system, and one that does not is called a closed system. Some systems have feedback loops and can control their own operations. These systems are called closed-loop systems. If a system does not have a feedback loop, it is called an open-loop system.

Systems exist on multiple levels, making it possible for anyone in a firm to perceive their organization in systems terms. The ability to view a firm as a system enables you to detect and solve problems that threaten the ability of the firm to operate as it should.

One way to view the firm as a system is to regard it as a network of physical resource flows, which are controlled by a conceptual system. The conceptual system consists of management, an information processor, and standards of performance. An intricate network of data and information flows exists, connecting management and the information processor with the physical system and the environment.

The diagram that shows how all of the system elements fit together is called the general systems model of the firm. Both managers and information specialists who develop systems can benefit from using this model as a blueprint of ideal system performance. All types of firms can be represented by the general systems model of the firm.

All of the business applications that are performed on the information system form the information systems infrastructure, which consists of five subsystems: the accounting information system, the management information system, decision support systems, office automation systems, and expert systems.

Conceptual systems are developed within a top-down framework that begins with enterprise modeling, strategic business planning, strategic information planning, and system development life cycles. Life cycle participants include users and systems developers who communicate in a chain-like fashion.

All information systems consist of information resources and perform basic functions of input, processing, output, storage, and control. The relationships between the resources and functions can be captured in a functions/components matrix.

If you want to do systems work, either as a systems developer or as a user, you must acquire the necessary knowledge and skills. This text will supplement the material that you have already learned and prepare you for a career in information systems.

What Is a System?

The term *systems age* could be used to describe our modern world, for this is truly the age of systems thinking. Each day, government officials talk about economic systems, military leaders talk about weapons systems, city planners talk about public transportation systems, and advertisers talk about shaving systems. We hear the word system so often that we scarcely pay attention to it, and we most likely fail to appreciate its full meaning.

The term is especially popular in the field of computing. Both government and industrial organizations use electronic computing systems to process their data, and the applications that the information systems perform are called systems—payroll systems, decision support systems, expert systems, and the like.

Any dictionary offers several definitions of the term *system.* However, the one capturing the meaning that is intended in the information system field defines a **system** as a group of elements that work together to accomplish an objective. The information system is a good example of a system because it is composed of thousands of electronic components and mechanical parts that are used in processing its data. In a like manner, the payroll system is composed of hundreds or thousands of processing steps that are built into the programs that compute the employees' pay. The same can be said for the decision support systems and expert systems. They all consist of many components that contribute to the achievement of specific objectives.

Physical and Conceptual Systems

Although there seems to be an infinite variety of system types, they can all be grouped into two basic classes: physical systems and conceptual systems.

A **physical system** is one consisting of tangible elements that can be seen and touched. An example is the firm. In this book we use the term **firm** to mean an enterprise of *any* type—governmental as well as industrial. The systems principles that are described here apply to all types of organizations. The elements of a firm are its build-

FIGURE 1.1

An Open System

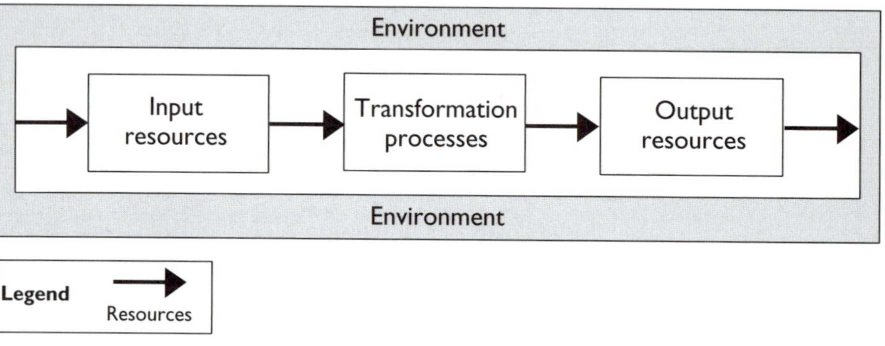

ings, employees, machines, materials, and money. All of these elements are applied so that the firm can meet such objectives as profit, return on investment, and market share.

A **conceptual system,** on the other hand, does not exist in a physical sense. It *represents* a physical system. The inventory system is an example. The data and information stored in the information system's storage units represent the physical inventory items that are located in the warehouse. The inventory system can print or display reports that contain information describing the inventory. Persons in the firm, such as managers, can view the reports to monitor the status of the inventory. In this way, a manager does not have to go to the warehouse to determine whether a particular item is in stock. Assuming that the report is accurate, the manager only has to view the report.

The same situation applies to the data and information that relate to other physical systems. The employee data and information represent the firm's employees, the customer data and information represent the firm's customers, and so on. The various files of information system data and programs can be viewed as conceptual systems representing physical systems. The data describes the physical resources of the firm, and the programs describe the processes that the firm performs on the resources.

The Relationship of the System to Its Environment

Physical systems and their accompanying conceptual systems exist in an environment. Systems theorists have coined two terms that describe the relationship of a system to its environment: open system and closed system.

An **open system** interfaces with its environment in some way. Since we have recognized that systems are composed of resources, it can be assumed that resource flows are the connections between a system and its environment. We define an open system as one that is connected to its environment by resource flows. All of the physical and conceptual resources flow into the firm from its environment, and then flow from the firm back to its environment, as shown in Figure 1.1. A business is a good example of an open system.

A **closed system** is one that is not connected to its environment by resource flows. Since a system relies on its environment for its life-giving properties, it cannot exist for long when these properties are taken away. For that reason, there are no truly closed systems. Scientists attempt to create closed systems for experimentation in laboratories, but these are special, artificial cases.

We are only interested in open systems.

The Ability of a System to Control Itself

Systems theorists have also coined terms that identify systems that can and cannot control their own operations. The terms for these systems are closed-loop systems and open-loop systems.

In order for a system to be able to control itself, it must contain a control mechanism. This mechanism receives information that describes the performance of the system and compares this information with the level of performance that the system is expected to attain. When the system does not perform as expected, the control mechanism issues signals that are intended to bring the performance in line with the desired level. This flow of information and signals between the system's output, control mechanism, and input forms a **feedback loop.** So a **closed-loop system** controls itself using a control mechanism and feedback loop and can adjust its operation to the desired level.

FIGURE 1.2

A Closed-Loop System

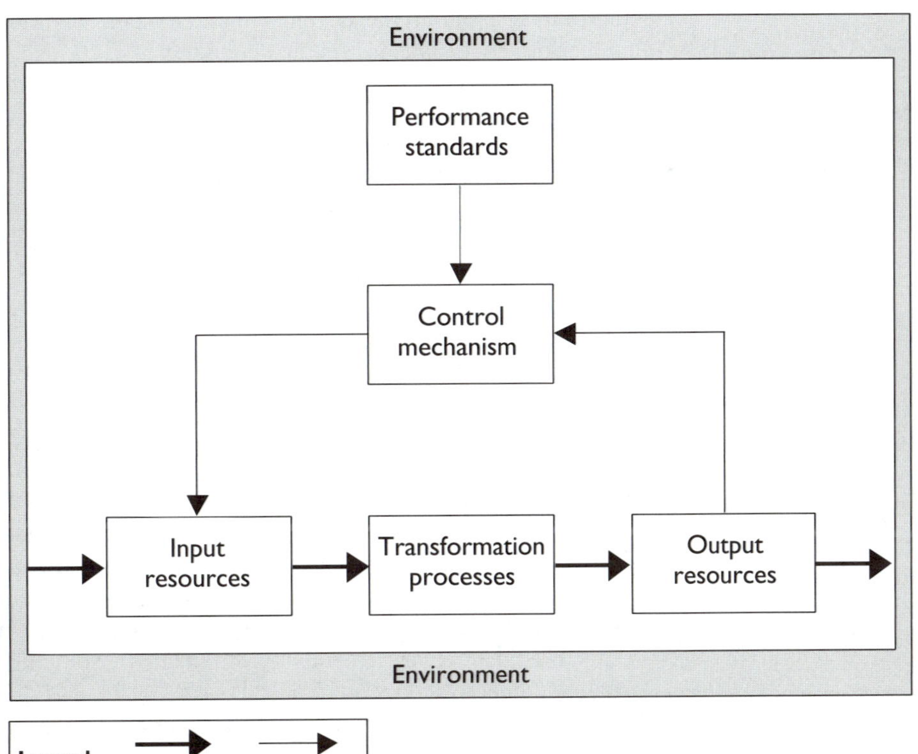

FIGURE 1.3

The Firm as a Closed-Loop System

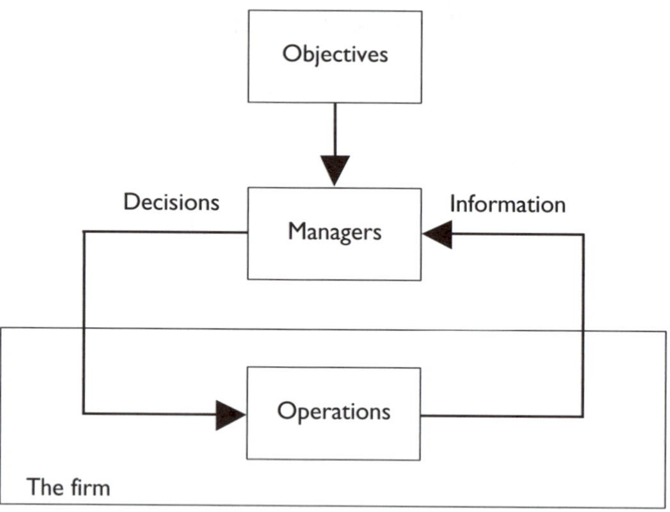

Figure 1.2 shows a system with a control mechanism, a flow of information from the system's output element to the control mechanism, and a flow of signals from the control mechanism to the system's input element. A component that contains the system performance standards is also included.

A thermostatically controlled heating unit is a closed-loop system. You control the operation of a heating unit by making adjustments to the thermostat. When the temperature drops below the set temperature, the thermostat issues a signal that turns the heater on so that the temperature will rise to the desired level. When that level is reached, the thermostat issues another signal that turns the heater off.

A firm is a closed-loop system. Managers achieve the same type of control by setting the objectives of the firm and then making decisions that cause the objectives to be met. This controlling action is diagrammed in Figure 1.3. Information that describes the firm's operations is compared with the objectives. When the operations do not measure up to the objectives, the managers make decisions that change the operations in some way. It is important to understand that the firm pictured in the figure is also an open system—its input resources come from the environment and its output resources go back to the same environment. *A firm is therefore both an open system and a closed-loop system.*

When a system has no control mechanism and feedback loop, it is called an **open-loop system.** Perhaps the feedback loop is missing altogether, or perhaps there is a gap somewhere that prevents the information and decisions from flowing as they should. Such a system has no ability to monitor its performance and make adjustments. If adjustments are made, they are made by something external to the system—usually another system.

Your automobile is a good example of an open-loop system. Although it includes much sophisticated circuitry, including possibly one or more special-purpose computer systems, it cannot drive itself. *You* must provide the control mechanism and feedback loop. You monitor the performance with your eyes and ears and the feel of the road, and you make the necessary adjustments with the steering wheel, gearshift lever, and brake and accelerator pedals. By itself, your car is an open-loop system, but you and your car together represent a closed-loop system.

System Levels

Systems can exist on several levels. The names **supersystem** or **suprasystem** are used for the highest-level system, and the name **subsystem** is used for a system within a system. For example, if you are studying the firm as a system, then the national economy is the supersystem, and the various departments within the firm are subsystems. However, if you next direct your attention at a lower level, such as at a department within the firm, then the department becomes the system, the firm becomes the supersystem, and perhaps sections within the department become subsystems.

Viewing the Firm as a System

Since a firm consists of multiple components working to achieve an objective, the firm can be viewed as a system. Such a view, called the **systems view,** is an especially effective way to analyze a firm or its organizational units for purposes of defining problems and achieving solutions. Systems theorists have taken several approaches to explaining the firm as a system, but one stands out as being especially well suited to systems development. It recognizes the ability of the firm to transform resources.

The Firm as a Transformation System

Richard J. Hopeman, a professor of production operations and management at Syracuse University in the late 1960s, recognized that a firm transforms its resources

Figure 1.4

The Firm as a Resource Transformation System

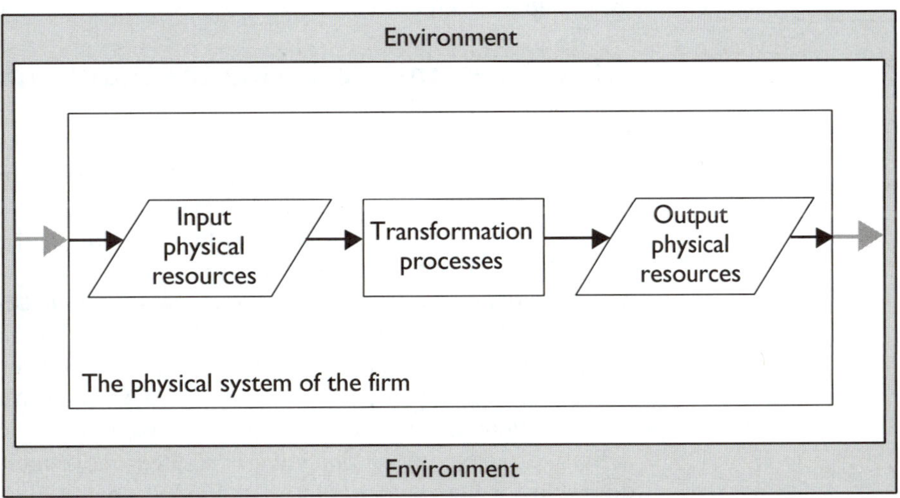

as the resources flow through it.[1] Figure 1.4 shows this resource flow. It is the task of the physical system of the firm to transform the input physical resources into forms needed by the environment. The figure shows the firm as an open system that interfaces with its environment.

As the resources flow through the firm, management seeks to maintain the flow at the proper rate. If the flow is too slow, the firm will not have enough resources to perform its necessary activities. For example, if a supplier is late in shipping raw materials, the production process will have to be delayed until the materials arrive. A resource flow that is too fast can have equally disastrous consequences. Take, for example, a high rate of personnel turnover that leaves the firm shorthanded in terms of experienced workers. The managers manage the resource flow for the purpose of achieving a **steady state,** which is a state of equilibrium produced by a balanced flow of input and output resources.

The Firm's Control Mechanism

The system in Figure 1.4 is an open-loop system that contains no means of controlling its own operations. Such control can be achieved by means of a conceptual system. Two elements in the conceptual system are management and an information processor, and they are added in Figure 1.5.

An **information processor** is any type of device, computer or noncomputer, that transforms data into information and makes information available to its users. As drawn in the figure, the information processor gathers data and information from the input, transformation, and output elements of the physical system. This data and information describes the current status of the firm. The information processor either provides the information to management immediately or stores it for future use.

The two-headed arrow connecting management and the information processor represents a two-way communications flow. Management both provides information to the information processor and receives information from it. For example, a manager enters decisions into the information processor for use in a mathematical model, and the information processor provides the manager with the model output. This addition of the information processor to the physical system enables management to remain current on the status of the physical system. The status can be up-to-the-minute when the data is gathered electronically and processed by the information processor immediately upon receipt.

Objectives and Performance Standards

It is not sufficient for management to simply know what is happening in the firm. Management must also know whether the activity is acceptable. In order to make this determination, management establishes standards of acceptable performance. The standards are set such that when they are satisfied, the firm will meet its objectives. A direct relationship therefore exists between the firm's objectives and its standards. The objectives tend to be rather broad statements of desired performance, and the standards are more specific. For example, a firm might have an objective of providing quality products, and a standard to support that objective would be a limit on the percentage of sold products that are returned by dissatisfied customers.

It is common for multiple standards to support an objective. In that way, the activity of achieving an objective is spelled out in multiple dimensions. It is also desirable for the standards to be expressed quantitatively so that it is easy to see whether they are met.

Information Flow: Controlling the System

Management can now evaluate system performance by comparing the output of the information processor with the standards. Figure 1.6 shows how management uses the standards to control the physical system of the firm. The information processor provides information that describes *actual activity*—what the system is accomplishing. The standards provide information that describes *desired activity*—what the system should accomplish.

For example, the management of a shoe factory might decide that a production rate of 900 to 1,100 pairs per day is the desired performance level. The 900 to 1,100 pairs represent a *performance range* that identifies both the lower and upper ends of an area of acceptable performance. Management is satisfied when performance remains within the range.

If the information processor reports that 875 pairs were produced yesterday, what action, if any, does management take? Management must determine whether the pro-

FIGURE 1.5

The Firm's Control Mechanism: Management and the Information Processor

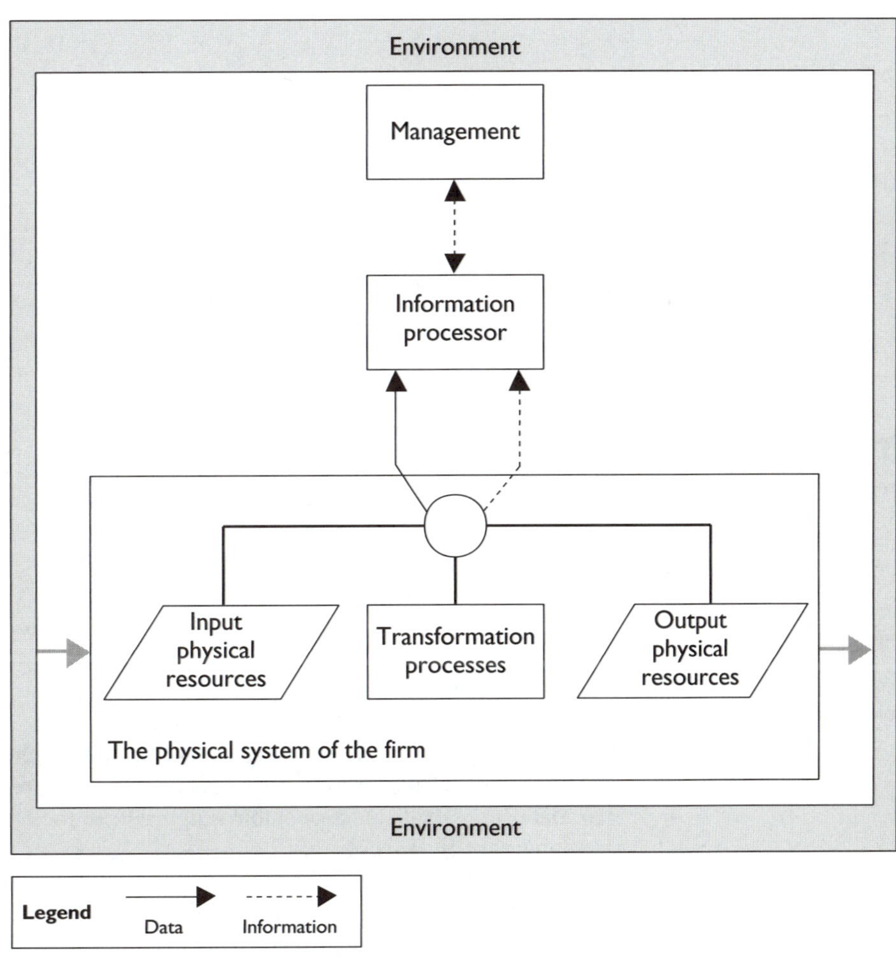

FIGURE 1.6

Using Performance Standards to Regulate Firm Activities

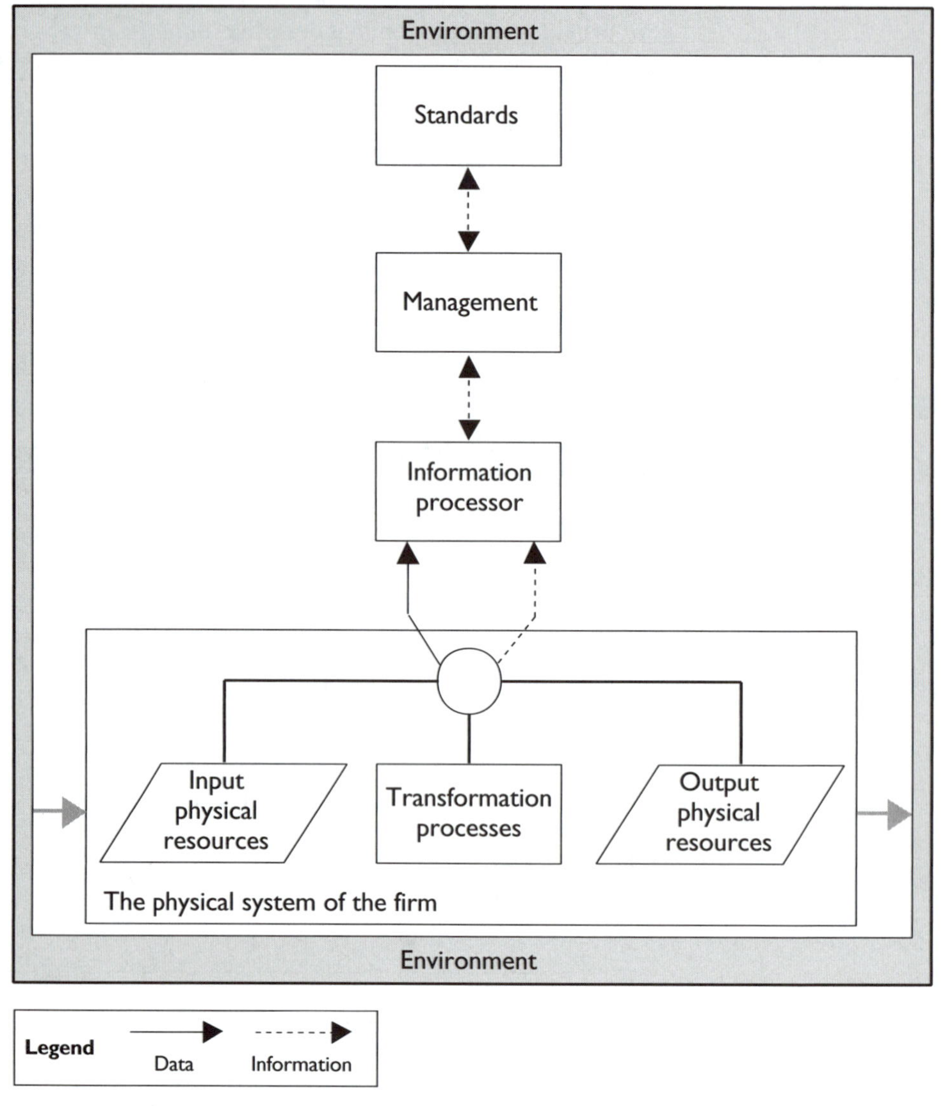

duction rate of 875 pairs is acceptable. If such a production rate lasts only a single day, management might regard it as a chance variation and do nothing. However, if the output continues for several days, management might decide that action is needed to raise the actual performance level. Management only becomes involved when performance is outside the acceptable range. The name of this management technique is **management by exception.**

If the performance standards are also made available to the information processor, as shown in Figure 1.7, it can relieve the manager of much of the monitoring activity. The information processor can compare the actual and desired performance and notify the manager when action might be needed. For example, the information processor can display a message on the manager's computer screen saying that yesterday's production fell below the acceptable performance range. You can see that the addition of the flow of standards information to the information processor facilitates management by exception.

Transmitting Decisions to the Physical System

When management determines that corrective action is in order, a communications network transmits decisions to the physical system so that changes can be made. Perhaps the problem is in the input area of the shoe factory, and management decides to add

FIGURE 1.7

Standards Information Flows to the Information Processor

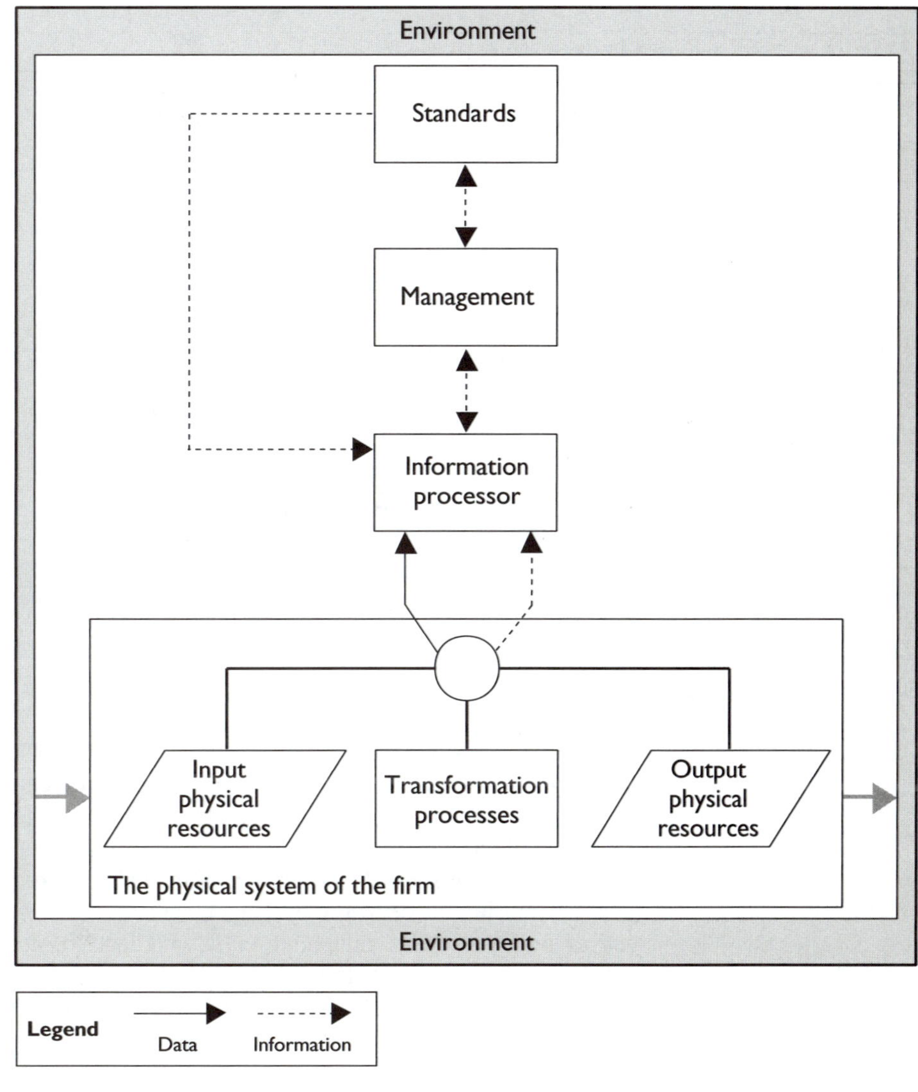

FIGURE 1.8

Decision Information Flows to the Physical System

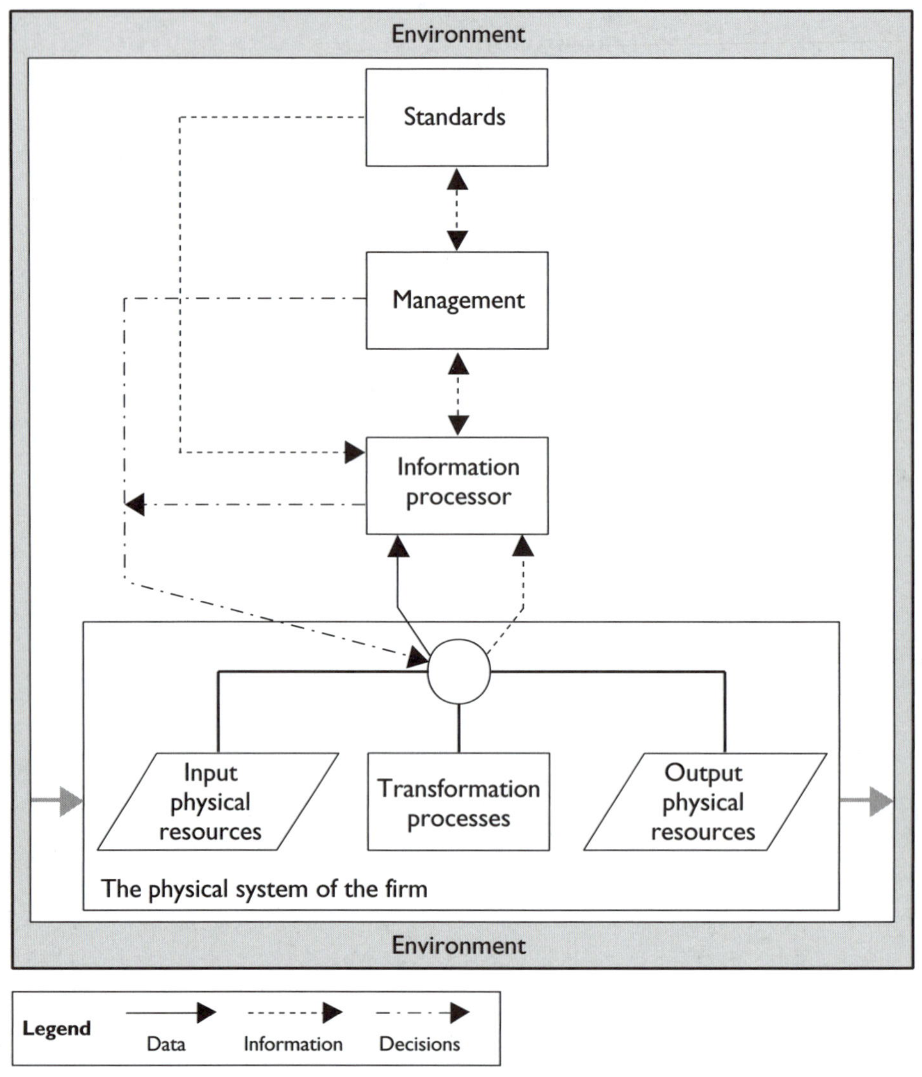

more buyers in the purchasing department. Or, the problem might be in the transformation area, and management decides to replace some aging production machines. The problem might also be in the output area, and management decides to use the information system to determine the best route for the delivery trucks to follow.

In transmitting the decisions, management uses a variety of communications media such as memos, letters, telephone calls, and face-to-face conversation. The arrow leading from management to the physical system in Figure 1.8 represents these conventional communications. The communications are directed to those lower-level managers and employees who are responsible for making the needed changes in the physical system.

The arrow leading from the information processor to the physical system via the flow of decision information from management in Figure 1.8 reflects the use of electronic media for decision communication. Management makes a decision and enters it into the information processor. The information processor then electronically relays the decision to the appropriate element of the physical system. Electronic mail and computer conferencing are examples of electronic communications media. The Internet has made it much easier for systems developers who are located around the world to communicate while developing global information systems.

Information Flows Directly to Management

It is not necessary for all information to flow to management through the information processor. Information can flow directly to management from the physical system. As an example, a clerk in the receiving department might notify an inventory manager by telephone, saying that a particular shipment has arrived. By the same token, some information can flow directly to management from the outside environment of the firm. A banker, for example, might send a newsletter to the vice-president of finance, warning of a projected downturn in the economy. These direct information flows are illustrated by the arrows in Figure 1.9 that lead to management from the physical system and the environment.

Conceptual Resource Flows

In addition to transforming physical resources to meet environmental needs, the firm also transforms conceptual resources for the same purpose. The environment provides the firm with data, the data is transformed into information, and the information is made available to the environment. For example, a manufacturing firm may conduct market research to determine the level of consumer interest in a new product and make the findings available to its retailers as a service.

The information processor performs the transformation of the conceptual resources. In Figure 1.10 on page 41, the information processor gathers data and information from the environment and transforms the environmental data into information. The information can be used internally by management as a way to remain current on conditions in the firm's environment.

The information processor also provides both data and information to the environment. An example of an outgoing data flow is data on social security deductions from employees' pay that is made available to the federal government. Management also has a responsibility to provide information to the environment. The president, for example, might make a phone call to the local mayor to pass along the news that the firm plans to expand its operations and offer more jobs to local residents.

The Model of the Firm as a System

Figure 1.10 is the **general systems model of the firm.** It is a graphic model that shows the intricate feedback loop and control mechanism that enables the physical system to maintain a steady state. The model illustrates how the standards, management, information processor, and communications channels work together to keep the physical system on course.

FIGURE 1.9

Information Flows to Management

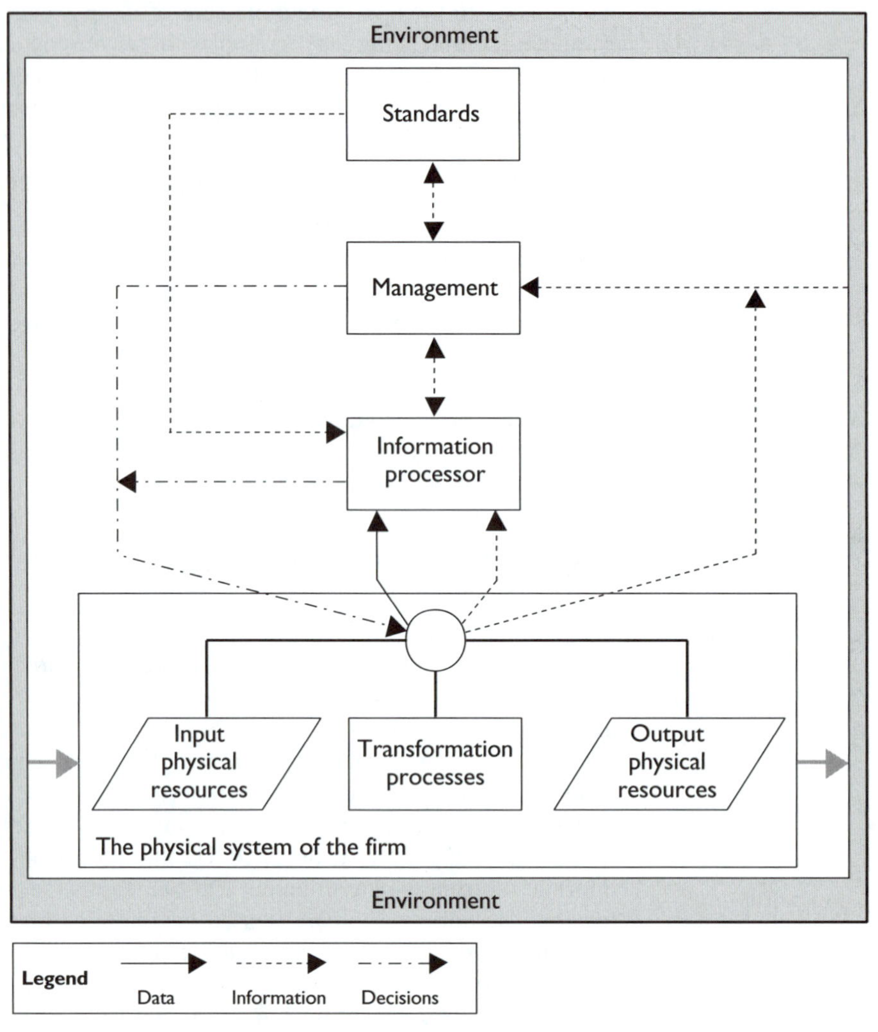

The Manager Uses the Model

When you are given the responsibility of managing an organizational unit, whether it is an entire firm or a subsidiary area within the firm, you must first evaluate that system. One way to take a systematic approach is to view the organizational unit as a system that should fit the pattern of the model. You compare the unit to the guideline, looking for the necessary elements. When the elements are missing or not performing as they should, you not only know that improvement is in order but also which parts of the system need attention. The systems view is a logical way to analyze your organizational unit.

The Systems Developer Uses the Model

A **systems developer** is a person who actively participates in the development of an information system, contributing specialized knowledge and skills. Some developers are information specialists, whereas others are members of the user area. An **information specialist** is a person whose full-time responsibility is to provide information systems to users in the organization. In most cases, the information systems are computer-based, but this is not a strict requirement. It is also not a requirement that the information specialists be assigned to the firm's information systems unit; they may be a part of a user group, such as marketing or finance.

There are several different categories of information specialist, each of whom contributes a special expertise. A **systems analyst** analyzes existing systems for the purpose of defining information needs, and then designs new or improved systems to meet those needs. When the user's system requires a change in the firm's collection of stored information system data, or its database, an information specialist

FIGURE 1.10

The General Systems Model of the Firm

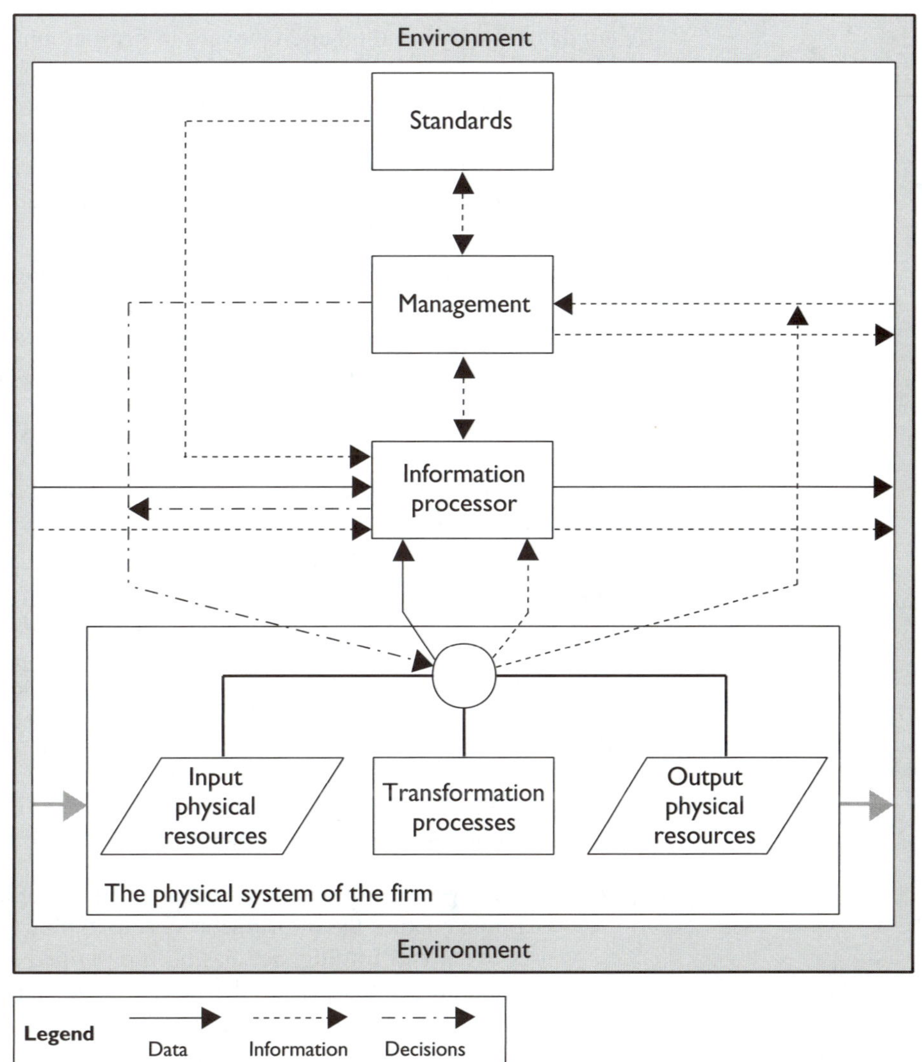

called a **database administrator,** or **DBA,** can be involved. Likewise, when the project deals with a system that communicates data from one location to another, a **network specialist** can participate. Other specialists include the **programmer,** who codes and tests the programs, and the **operator,** who runs the jobs on the information system.

If you become a systems developer, you will use the general systems model of the firm in basically the same way as the manager. The model serves as a guideline of how the system ought to function. When you spot defects, you know that those areas must be improved or replaced. The developer typically works with the conceptual framework represented by the standards, management, information processor, and communications network. As we can see from the model of the firm as a system, that conceptual framework can represent an intricate flow of data, information, and decisions. The complex nature of the firm's conceptual systems is a major reason why systems work is so challenging and rewarding.

THE INFORMATION SYSTEMS INFRASTRUCTURE

Every day, managers and other employees in firms around the world use information systems of various types. Each type is intended to perform a particular type of processing, and can be tailored to the specific needs of the firm's organizational units. The composite of all the computer-based conceptual systems of the firm provides the **information systems infrastructure.** Throughout the period of computer use in business, which began in the mid-1950s, the infrastructure has evolved to a composite of five subsystems.

- *Accounting information system*—The accounting information system (AIS) sometimes referred to as the **data processing system** or the **transaction processing system,** processes the firm's accounting transactions. Included within this system are the payroll system, the inventory system, and so on.

- *Management information system*—The management information system (MIS) consists of all conceptual systems that are designed to meet the general information needs of all managers in the firm or within organizational subunits. Examples are the executive information system, the marketing information system, and the human resources information system.

- *Decision support systems*—A decision support system (DSS) provides information to help a single manager or a small group of managers solve a particular problem or make a particular decision. Because the DSSs are tailored to individual managers, problems, and decisions, there are many DSSs in a firm.

- *Office automation systems*—An office automation system (OA) uses electronic circuits and devices to facilitate communications within the firm and between the firm and its environment. Popular examples are electronic mail, teleconferencing, and document retrieval.

- *Expert systems*—An expert system is an example of artificial intelligence (AI) that enables the information system to play the role of consultant to the user. **Artificial intelligence** has been described as the activity of providing information systems with the ability to display behavior that would be regarded as intelligent if it were observed in humans.[2] An expert system is programmed with the logic that an expert employs in solving a particular type of problem. The expert system solves the problem in basically the same manner as would the expert.

All information systems that have been developed to help can fit within these five categories. Each system is composed ules. Figure 1.11 illustrates how an accounting system called th consists of five modules, and a module can consist of one or more five main modules, or subsystems, in the example are order entry, in accounts receivable, and general ledger. Each of these systems consists ules. The submodules of the accounts receivable system are shown.

Information Systems and e-Business

The first information systems were focused on the needs of the firm. Then, when data communications technology was developed, firms began linking their systems with those of other firms. The transmittal of data from one firm's system to another firm is called **electronic data interchange (EDI).** EDI enables the participating firms (called business partners) to create an **interorganizational system (IOS).** These systems, which cross organizational boundaries, require that information specialists become especially knowledgeable about data communications hardware and software.

More recently, other technological innovations, the World Wide Web and the Internet, have further broadened the scope of these communications-oriented systems. With the advent of the Internet, firms can now establish electronic linkages with their customers. Customers can place orders for the firm's products using the Internet, and, in some cases, firms can use the Internet to deliver the products to the customers.

The activity of using the Internet as a marketing tool, called **electronic business,** or **e-business,** imposes an additional set of requirements on the information specialists who develop the systems. Today's information specialists must be able to use the software that enables a firm to engage in e-business. We address Web interface development in Technical Module H.

FIGURE 1.11

A System Structure

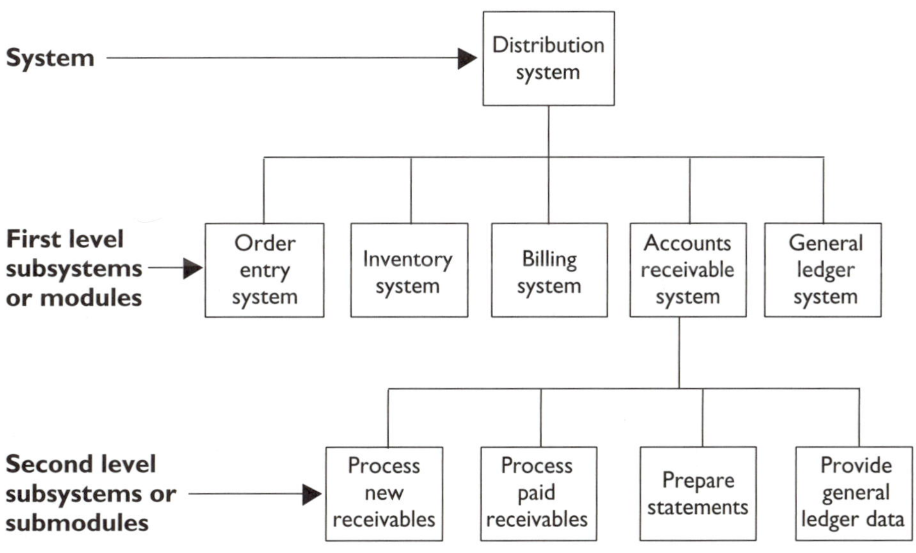

IGURE 1.12

Systems Development Planning Framework

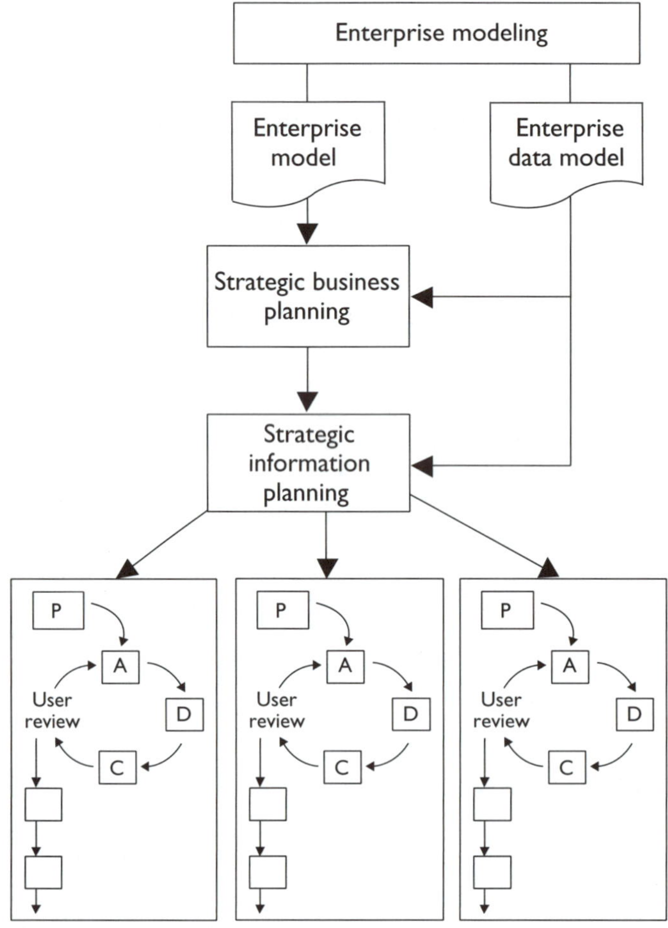

Development of Information Systems

Firms can follow various approaches in developing their information systems, but the efforts should support the strategic objectives of the firm. In meeting this requirement, the firm's executives engage in three layers of planning. From the top down, these layers are:

1. Enterprise modeling
2. Strategic business planning
3. Strategic information planning

With this framework in place, systems development projects are carried out. Figure 1.12 illustrates this top-down process. The three boxes at the bottom of the figure represent system development projects.

Enterprise Modeling

In many firms, the top-level executives comprise an **executive committee** that makes the key decisions concerning the firm's future operations. The executives include the president and the vice-presidents of the major business areas, such as marketing, finance, human resources, and information systems. The top executive in information systems often has the title of **chief information officer (CIO).**

The executives periodically engage in an introspective look at the firm and its position in its environment, a process that is called **enterprise planning** or **enterprise modeling.** The term **enterprise** refers to the entire organization. The formal written description that the firm's executives produce, using words and graphics, is called an **enterprise model,** and it describes the activities that the firm, or enterprise, should perform in the future.

As the executives develop the enterprise model, they can pay particular attention to the data and processes that will be required for the firm to meet its strategic objectives. When the firm takes an object-oriented approach to systems development, the enterprise model can include one or more class diagrams. Class diagrams are used in object-oriented development to model a system's objects, which are a firm's valuable resources. Figure 1.13 is a class diagram that identifies six important objects that are involved with filling customer sales orders. Each object is represented by a rectangle labeled with the object name, a list of the data attributes that describe the object in the middle, and a list of the operations that the object can perform at the bottom.

When a firm takes a data- or a process-oriented approach to development, the enterprise model can take the form of entity-relationship diagrams (ERDs) and data flow diagrams (DFDs). As described in the case study, this is the approach that the project team is taking at ASTA. The ERD in Figure CS 1.8 models the data, and the DFDs in Figures CS 1.11, CS 1.12, and CS 1.13 model the processes. Regardless of its format, the enterprise model is a blueprint of where the firm wants to be. It is like snapshot, capturing the status of the firm at some future point in time.

Strategic Business Planning

The enterprise model can provide the basis for the firm's strategic business planning. The **strategic business plan** is a formal statement that identifies the actions that the firm should take in order to achieve the status depicted by the enterprise model. For example, if the enterprise model specifies that the firm is to provide some new customer service in the future, the strategic business plan specifies how that service capability will be achieved.

Strategic Information Planning

A subset of the strategic business plan, called the **strategic plan for information resources,** identifies (1) the level of information resources that will be necessary in order for the firm to execute its strategic business plan and (2) how those resources will be applied. As an example, the strategic plan for information resources might recognize the need to install a new network next year and specify the major accomplishments leading to that installation. Both the strategic business plan and the strategic plan for information resources are like motion pictures, because they both define the sequences of processes required to achieve the status defined by the enterprise models.

FIGURE 1.13

A Portion of an Enterprise Model in the Form of a Class Diagram

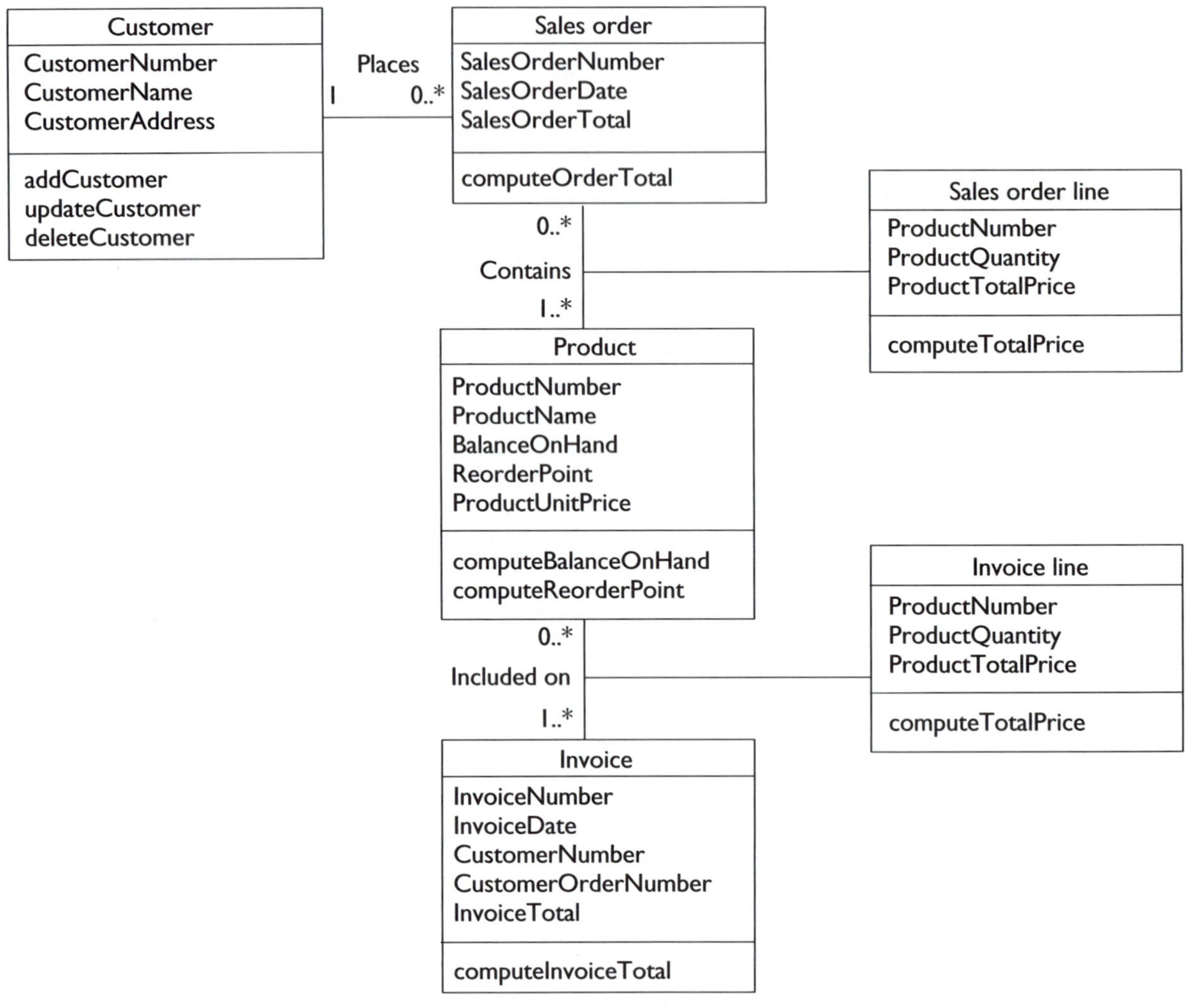

SYSTEMS DEVELOPMENT STAGES

The strategic plan for information resources specifies each of the information systems that the firm will require during the time period covered by the plan. The development and use of each system consists of a sequence of events called the system development life cycle. The **system development life cycle (SDLC)** is the evolution that a system undergoes from its inception to its end.

The organizations that developed the first information systems accomplished their task by trial and error-too much error, in many cases. The firms had no blueprint to follow. Over time, the keys to successful development were discovered and documented to represent a system development methodology. A **methodology** is a recommended way of doing something. One of the first SDLC methodologies was recognized by many firms as being especially effective and enjoyed a long-term popularity. This methodology, which is still used today in many firms, is called the **traditional system development life cycle** and consists of five stages.

- *Planning stage*—The problem is defined, and a plan is devised for developing a system to help in the problem solution.
- *Analysis stage*—The existing system is studied to understand its shortcomings so that the shortcomings might be overcome in the new system.
- *Design stage*—A design is prepared for the new system that specifies the hardware and software and how they are to be used.
- *Implementation stage*—The hardware, software, and data to be used by the new system are made available, and the firm puts the new system into operation.
- *Use stage*—The firm uses the new system, making relatively minor changes to it to increase its effectiveness.

At some point, it might become necessary to redevelop the system, perhaps to incorporate new technology. In that case, the cycle is repeated, beginning with the planning stage.

The traditional SDLC was the dominant methodology in the 1960s, 70s, and 80s. As systems became more complex, however, it became clear that the stages do not always follow one after the other. Sometimes, stages must be repeated. Newer methodologies were crafted, and today a firm has several from which to choose, such as prototyping, phased development, and rapid application development. We describe these methodologies in Chapter 3.

The methodology that provides the basis for this text is the phased development methodology. It includes a loop that is repeated for different levels and modules of the system, which were described in the previous section and illustrated in Figure 1.11. A diagram of the phased development methodology appears in Figure 1.14. The first stage is preliminary investigation, and then the next three stages are taken in sequence for each module. These stages consist of the analysis stage, design stage, and preliminary construction stage. As shown in the diagram, a user review comes after the preliminary construction stage. If the user does not approve the design, the three stages are repeated. The loop continues until approval is received. When the user approves of the module as designed, the final construction stage integrates all of the designed modules into an overall system. Finally, the system test and installation stage can begin.

The preliminary investigation stage compares to the planning stage of the traditional methodology. The analysis and design stages relate to the stages with the same names for the traditional approach. The implementation stage of the traditional approach is subdivided into the two construction stages of the phased development approach. The traditional approach includes a stage after implementation when the system is used, whereas the phased development approach does not. In the phased development approach, use is considered to be included in the system test and installation stage.

FIGURE 1.14

Phased Development Methodology

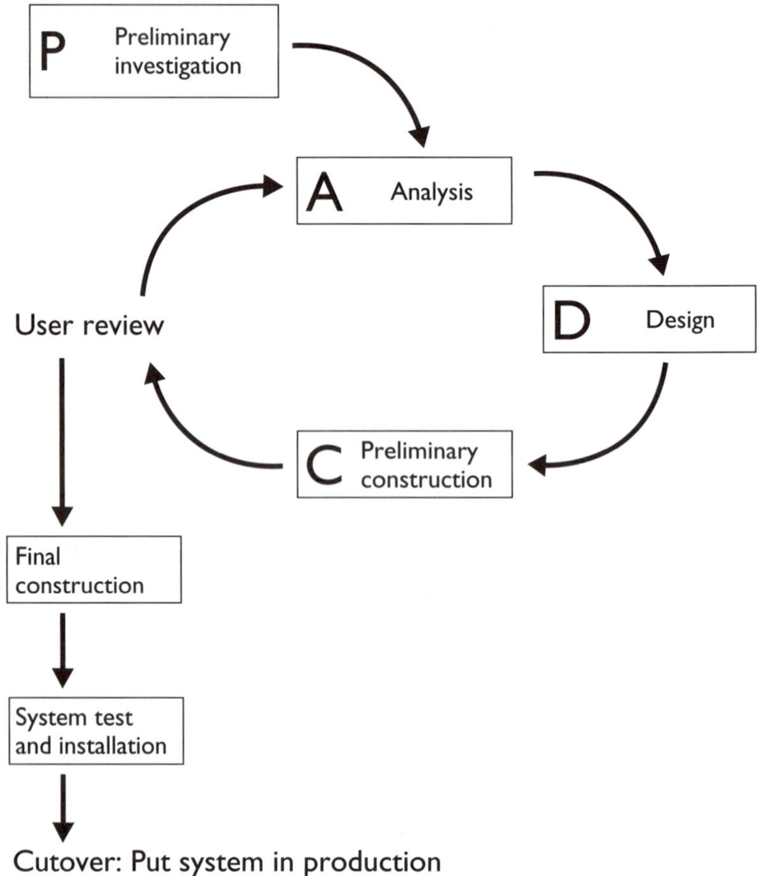

The Communication Chain

The system development life cycle can span months or even years, and during that time all of the people who are involved must communicate. The pattern of that communication is called the **communication chain,** and is illustrated in Figure 1.15. The user is on the left and the information system is on the right. The task is to communicate the information describing the user's problem to the information system so that the information system can produce problem-solving information that is communicated back to the user.

When information specialists are involved, they serve as intermediaries between the user and the information system. The key information specialist in this process is the systems analyst. He or she is like a police officer in the middle of an intersection directing traffic. In the case of the systems analyst, the traffic is the flow of communication among the user and information specialists. The systems analyst, assisted by the database administrator and network specialist, communicates with the user concerning the functional requirements of the new system. The analyst communicates with the programmer concerning the new system design. The programmer and operator communicate with each other concerning the operating instructions. Each of these communication links is accomplished both orally and in writing. The programmer communicates with the information system while coding the program, and the operator communicates with the information system while running the job.

The Project Team

The development of a new information system is such a large effort that the work is usually carried out by a project team. Figure 1.16 is a chart that shows a typical team composition. An important member is the *internal auditor,* who ensures that the conceptual system accurately portrays the physical system.

System Development Tools: The Functions/Components Matrix

A key tool in the systems development process is a thorough understanding of how the components and functions of the system relate to each other. Our definition of a system recognizes that it consists of multiple elements, or components. Although the form of these components will vary from one type of system to another, the basic information resources are the primary components of most systems.

Figure 1.15

The Communication Chain

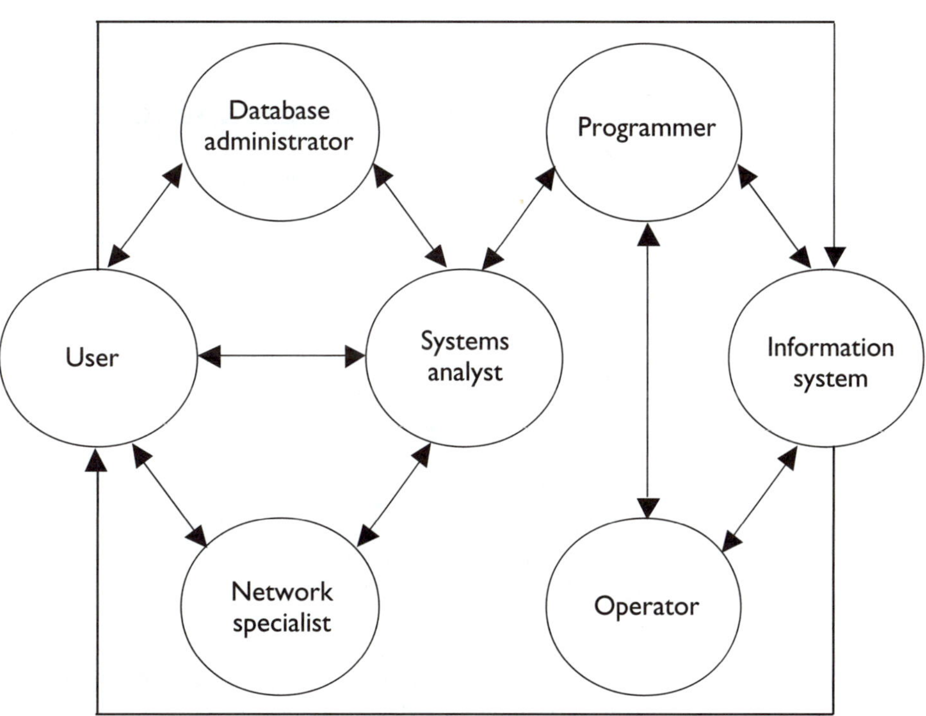

FIGURE 1.16

A Project Team

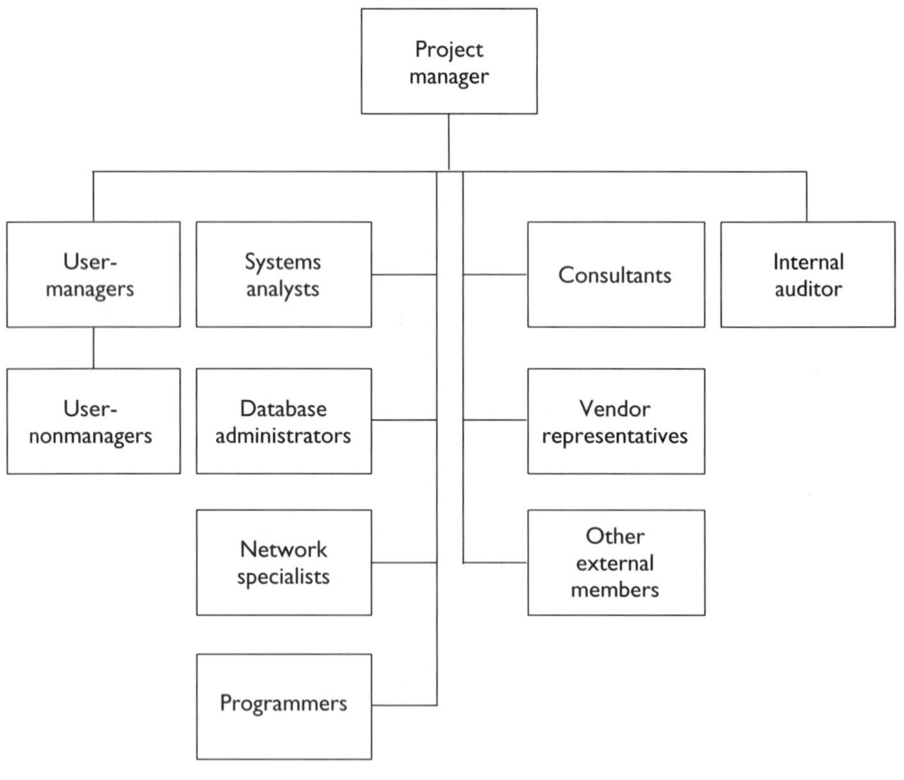

Information System Components

The **information system components** are the resources that comprise an information system. They include:

- People
- Data
- Information
- Software
- Hardware

Like all resources that are the responsibility of the manager, the information resources can be managed—an activity called **information management.** All managers in a firm have an information management responsibility, just as all have a human resources management responsibility, a financial management responsibility, and so on. As managers engage in information management, they must ensure that each of these components exist in the proper quantity and quality, and that they are used in an efficient and effective way.

Information System Functions

Any information system performs basic functions. All types of information systems, from the simplest system that enables a manager to retrieve a single data element from a database, to the most complex system that enables a manager to simulate some aspect of the firm's operations, perform five basic functions:

- Input
- Processing
- Output
- Storage
- Control

Data is entered into the system, where it is processed. The system can output the results of the processing in the form of processed data or information. The system can also store data and information for future use. All of these operations are controlled.

Functions/Components Matrix

A tool that developers can use in the process of developing an information system is the functions/components matrix. The **functions/components matrix,** or **F/C**

FIGURE 1.17

A Functions/Components Matrix with Selected Entries

	Input	Processing	Output	Storage	Control
People	Data entry operators enter sales order data				Control clerks generate sales order batch totals
Data	Customer number Item number Item quantity	Item extended price Sales tax Invoice total		Inventory master file Customer master file	
Information			Customer invoice Salesperson performance report		
Software		Update Inventory master file Prepare customer invoices		Oracle DBMS	Edit sales order data
Hardware	Workstations	Server	Printer	Magnetic disk unit	

matrix, matches the basic functions that any system performs with the components that are used to perform the functions. It is a valuable tool because it identifies what the system must do and the information resources that are required. An F/C matrix with selected entries from the following explanation is shown in Figure 1.17.

- *People*—The People row is used to identify processes that are performed manually and the people who perform them. When people perform input, processing, output, storage, or control functions, entries are made in the appropriate cells. For example, if data entry operators enter sales order data into a workstation, the entry "Data entry operators enter sales order data" is made in the People/Input cell. If control clerks batch sales orders and generate batch totals, the entry in the People/Control cell is "Control clerks generate sales order batch totals." You should be as specific as possible in terms of *who* performs the work and *what* work is performed.

- *Data*—The Data row is used to identify the data that are used in a system. When data are used for input or the other functions, entries are made in the cells. You enter names to identify data elements, records, or files. As an example of data elements that are input to a sales management system, the entries "Customer number," "Item number," and "Item quantity" would be entered in the Data/Input cell. Examples of data elements that are processed are "Item extended price," "Sales tax," and "Invoice total."

- *Information*—A distinction is made between data and information. Information is refined data, and it is specified on the Information row. Information most likely will appear as a system output, but it could be associated with any function. A good example of information output would be a report, such as the "Salesperson performance report" in the Information/Output cell. Another example is a document sent to an element in the firm's environment, such as a "Customer invoice."

- *Software*—Whereas the People row identifies functions performed by people, the Software row identifies functions performed by a computer-based system. In describing the software functions, you can use a verb and an object, or you can specify the program or software system being used. For example, you can enter "Oracle DBMS" in the Software/Storage cell to indicate that that system is used to manage the database. Most of the software will likely be entered in the Processing cell, using the "Update Inventory master file" and "Prepare customer invoices" entries in the figure as an example. It is also very common for control functions to be performed by software. Perhaps the software edits sales order data to detect errors. In this case, an entry is made in the Software/Control cell such as "Edit sales order data."

- *Hardware*—The Hardware row specifies the hardware that is used in performing each function. Some hardware, such as "Workstations," might be used only for input, and that entry is made in the Hardware/Input cell. Other hardware can be used only for output. An example is a printer. Still other hardware can be used only for storage, such as a magnetic disk unit. Other hardware, such as the server of a client/server network, can perform one or more of the listed functions. In the example, "Server" is entered in the Processing cell on the Hardware row.

Figure 1.18 is an F/C matrix that contains guidelines you can use to prepare F/C Matrices. F/C matrices are best suited to document systems at detailed, rather than summary, levels. You would use an F/C matrix for each of the lowest-level modules that are addressed as the analysis, design, and preliminary construction stages of the SDLC are repeated.

The Role of the Systems Developer

If you want to become a systems developer and be a success at it, you should acquire the knowledge and skills that are required. One feature of systems work that distinguishes it from many other professions is the fact that it demands such a wide variety of knowledge and skills.

Systems Developer Knowledge

A successful systems developer is knowledgeable in the areas of computer literacy, business fundamentals, systems theory, information use in problem solving, systems development, and systems modeling.

Figure 1.18

Functions/Components Matrix Guidelines

	Input	Processing	Output	Storage	Control
People	Person title + function	Person title + function	Person title + function	Person title + function	Person title + function
Data	Data elements, records, and files that are input to processing	Data elements, records, and files that are processed	Data elements, records, and files that are output from processing	Data elements, records, and files that are maintained in storage	Data elements, records, and files that are used for control
Information	Documents and other forms of information that are to be processed or stored	Documents and other forms of information that are processed	Records, files, documents, and other forms of information that are output	Records, files, documents, and other forms of information that are stored	Records, files, documents, and other forms of information that are used for control
Software	Complete programs that are used only to input data for further processing by another program	Processes (verb + object) and programs that process data	Complete programs that are used only to output data or information produced by another program	Programs or software systems that store data	Processes (verb + object) and programs that perform control functions
Hardware	Systems and such peripheral units as keyboard terminals and scanners that are used for input	Such systems as mainframes, servers, and workstations that process data	Systems and such peripheral units as printers and disk drives that are used for output	Such storage devices as disk drives and tape units that store data	Hardware includes control circuitry, but it is not specifically included on this form

- *Computer literacy*—The developer must know the fundamentals of information system processing in order to design computer-based systems. The term **computer literacy** is often used to describe this basic knowledge. The fundamentals include, as a minimum, an ability to program, knowledge of the various information system units and how they can be combined to meet particular needs, and a familiarity with the information system terminology. This is the type of literacy that is normally gained in an introductory computing course.

- *Business fundamentals*—Even when a developer works for a governmental or not-for-profit organization, he or she should be familiar with the fundamentals of business, such as economic influences, the nature of free enterprise, and accounting practices and terminology.

  These fundamentals apply to organizations of all types. With the trend to distributed information resources, it would be wise for the future systems developer to augment the business fundamentals with more specialized knowledge of the activities of the main business areas marketing, manufacturing, finance, and human resources. In addition, there is room for still more specialized knowledge that relates to particular industries such as health care, banking, and transportation. You cannot design systems for an organization unless you understand the activities of that organization.

- *Systems theory*—The systems view that we took earlier in the chapter of distinguishing between physical and conceptual systems is an example of systems theory. This theory applies to firms, their resources, and their procedures. The theory provides the pattern for the developer to follow in performing the analysis and design work. The theory tells the developer which elements must be present and how they must work together for the system to meet its objectives.

- *Information use in problem solving*—Modern systems work emphasizes the design of information systems that provide managers with problem-solving information. For the developer to design such systems, she or he must have **information literacy,** which is an understanding of how information is used in solving problems.

- *The systems development process*—The developer must have a thorough understanding of the top-down approach to systems development and the main systems development methodologies.

- *Systems modeling capability*—The systems developer should be able to model existing and new system designs using a variety of documentation tools. The main tools enable the developer to prepare data models, process models, and object models. We explain these tools in technical modules.

You will acquire much of the required development knowledge from this text. You will build on this knowledge as you continue your education and pursue your career.

Systems Developer Skills

Systems work uses many skills, but four stand out as being especially important. They are communications, analytical ability, creativity, and leadership.

- *Communications*—The systems developer must be able to communicate with other system development life cycle participants, as illustrated in the communication chain. During the early stages, most of the communication is in oral form. Then, as the problem becomes better defined, the developer transforms the oral communications into writing. The written documentation initially takes the form of informal notes and ultimately is refined in the form of proposals, reports, diagrams, and user manuals. Recruiters who visit college campuses invariably emphasize the importance of communications skills.

- *Analytical Ability*—The systems developer must be able to gather data on a problem area, sort through that data, and identify the cause. Some of the data may not relate to the problem, or may be distorted. Very often the users' personalities and company politics make it difficult to come to grips with the problem. In order for the developer to function in this environment, she or he must have an analytical ability. A person who enjoys working puzzles and using logic to solve problems should enjoy systems work.

- *Creativity*—An experienced developer is more likely to develop a good problem solution than is someone who is inexperienced. This is because solutions that proved successful in the past can be repeated. However, the developer should be able to apply creativity in developing new solutions when the situation demands. Systems theory provides the basis for developing creative solutions.

- *Leadership*—The systems developer plays a leadership role when working with users. The systems developer serves as a **change agent,** stimulating the user to implement systems that incorporate new technologies or methods. In a sense, the systems developer is a salesperson, convincing the user that the proposed system has the potential for solving the problem.

  The systems developer also has an opportunity to apply leadership skills when working with other information specialists. At first, these skills can be applied while the systems developer is still a member of project teams. Before long, the systems developer will be promoted to a management position, perhaps managing all of the systems developers in the firm. Leadership is the key to the developer's career advancement.

It is difficult to excel in all of these skill and knowledge areas. Even the most experienced systems developers continually work to keep their knowledge current and their skills sharp. You never stop learning as a systems developer, and this fact, combined with the ever-changing nature of the problems that you face, is the main reason that the work is so exciting.

One fact that works to the benefit of the developer is that the fundamental systems concepts do not change with the rapidity of technology. The concepts remain fairly constant over time. Therefore, when the developer builds a solid foundation of concepts, he or she can build each information system on that foundation. The foundation provides a starting point; it is not necessary to start every project with a clean slate.

In this text, we present the basic concepts that provide the foundation for systems work. Most of the basic concepts are presented in this and the next chapter.

PROJECT MANAGEMENT TOOLBOX

A Systems View of Project Management

A system development project can be viewed as a transformation process within the physical system of the firm. Management controls this process as the work evolves during the SDLC. Figure 1.19 is a modification to the general systems model of the firm, adapting it to the project management function.

Firms usually treat the development of an information system as a project. All but the smallest systems projects can involve large investments in resources over long periods of time and must be managed. **Project management** consists of all the actions that are taken to ensure that a project is carried out as planned. Therefore, it is important to establish a project management mechanism that includes the project plan, the project managers, and information flows.

Project Plan

The **project plan** identifies the tasks that are necessary to develop the system, identifies the person or persons who have responsibility to perform each task, and estimates the time required for each task.

Project Managers

The **project managers** are those users or developers who have responsibility for developing the project plan and making sure that it is carried out. The managers can exist in a hierarchy that ranges from the executive committee to the project manager.

Information Flows

The **information processor** facilitates the flow of information from the project team to project management, and the flow of decisions from project management to the project team, as shown in the general systems model. For example, in a global development project, project managers can exchange information in an Internet-based computer conference. Other information flows consist of narrative and graphical reports produced by the information processor, but many consist of face-to-face reports, such as scheduled meetings. In Technical Module D, we describe the reports and the scheduled meetings in greater detail.

SUMMARY

A system is a group of elements that work together to accomplish an objective. A physical system exists in a tangible form, and a conceptual system represents a physical system. A firm may be regarded as a physical system, as may its employee and machine resources. Managers use conceptual systems to manage physical systems.

A system that interfaces with its environment is called an open system. Closed systems exist only in such artificial environments as laboratories. A system that can control itself is called a closed-loop system. A business firm is an example of an open, closed-loop system.

Although systems can exist on many levels, names have been coined for only three. The system that is the subject of study is called the system. The system on the level immediately above is the supersystem or suprasystem. The system on the level immediately below is the subsystem.

One systems view emphasizes the transformation of resources as they flow through the firm. When the firm's management takes this view, they seek to achieve and maintain a steady state-a balanced flow of resources into and out of the firm.

FIGURE 1.19

A General Systems Model of Project Management

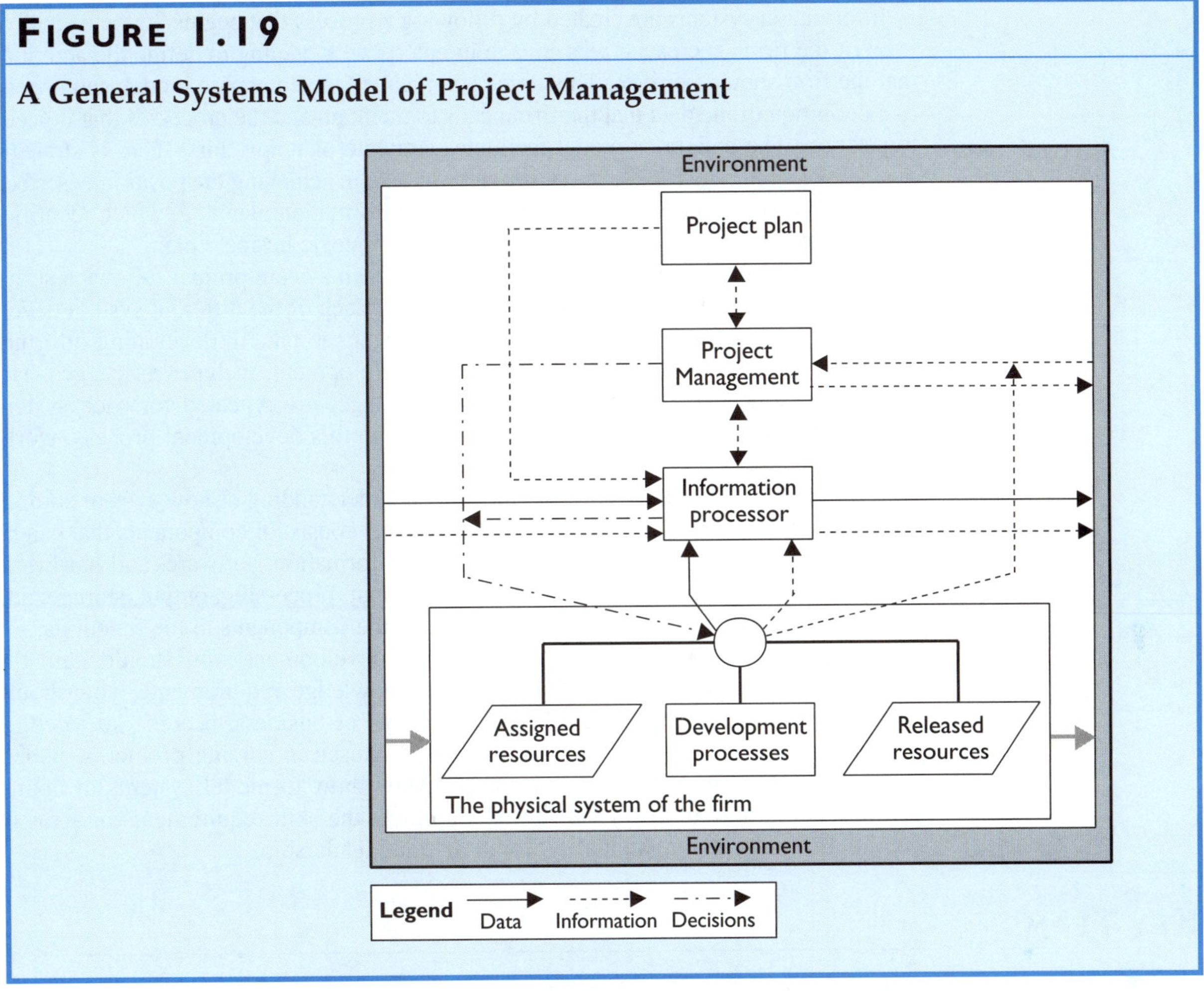

The graphic model that illustrates how the elements of a firm are integrated to form an open, closed-loop system is called the general systems model of the firm. It applies to all firms in a general way, and it illustrates the firm's operations as systems processes.

The value of the model of the firm as a system is its use as a guideline. The manager evaluates her or his firm in terms of the model. The model helps the manager identify weaknesses and the locations of these weaknesses. The systems developer uses the model in the same way, only applying it to the manager's system. The systems developer is a professional problem solver and uses the model as a means of coping with the intricate nature of flows of data and information through the information processor.

Business organizations use the information system in many different ways, but a framework consisting of five major subsystems can represent all of the uses. The framework is called the information systems infrastructure, and the subsystems are the accounting information system, the management information system, decision support systems, office automation systems, and expert systems. The first information systems had an internal focus. Developments in data communications and the Internet expanded this focus to include business partners and customers.

Information systems are created by following a process that begins on the executive level of the firm. The executives engage in enterprise modeling to define the activities that the firm should perform. This description, called the enterprise model, can consist of a definition of the data that the firm needs to maintain and the processes that it needs to perform. The enterprise model facilitates strategic planning. First there is strategic business planning, which spells out the steps to take in achieving the position described by the enterprise model. Then there is strategic information planning, which identifies the information systems necessary to support the strategic business plan.

With this organizational framework in place, each system project follows a series of steps called the system development life cycle. Each of the different system development life cycle methodologies prescribes the steps to take in developing information systems. One such methodology, phased development, includes six stages. The analysis, design, and preliminary construction stages are repeated for each system module. The systems developer plays a key role in this development process, working with the user.

A primary tool of systems development is an understanding of how system components and functions relate to each other. All systems consist of components that can be viewed as information resources: people, data, information, software, and hardware. All systems also perform the basic functions of input, processing, output, storage, and control. A functions/components matrix matches the components to the functions.

If you want to pursue a career in systems development, you should gain the required knowledge and skills. To meet the knowledge requirements, you should achieve computer literacy, learn the fundamentals of business, become knowledgeable in systems theory, know how information is used in solving problems, understand the system development process, and know how to model systems in both a graphic and narrative form. You should also meet the skill requirements in areas of communications, analytical ability, creativity, and leadership.

Key Terms

system
physical system
conceptual system
open system
closed system
feedback loop
closed-loop system
open-loop system
supersystem, suprasystem
subsystem
systems view
information processor
management by exception
systems developer
methodology
computer literacy
information literacy
information management
project management

Key Concepts

- A system is a group of elements with a common objective
- A conceptual system represents a physical system
- An open system interfaces with its environment
- A system can control itself
- Levels of systems
- Physical and conceptual resources flow to the firm from its environment, flow through the firm, and flow from the firm back to the environment

- Three elements comprise the conceptual system: management, an information processor, and standards
- The feedback loop in the firm as a controlled system consists of three media: data, information, and decisions
- The general systems model of the firm
- The information systems infrastructure
- The top-down process of systems development
- The system development life cycle (SDLC)
- The communication chain
- Information system components
- Information system functions
- The functions/components matrix

QUESTIONS

1. An ad for a razor with a replaceable double blade refers to it as a shaving system. Is it really a system? What are its elements? What is the objective?
2. What are the two basic types of systems?
3. What is an information processor?
4. What is the term for a system that interfaces with its environment? How is the interface achieved?
5. What term is used to describe a system that can control itself? That cannot control itself?
6. What elements are necessary if the system of the firm is to control itself?
7. What is the name of the highest system level? What is the name of a system within a system?
8. What function does an information system perform for management?
9. What two types of activity are compared to engage in management by exception? Where does the information on the two types of activity come from?
10. Are standards the same as objectives? Explain.
11. Why should standards be made available to the information processor?
12. To which elements in the physical system does the manager transmit decisions?
13. Management receives information directly from three main sources. What are they?
14. To whom does management provide information? Data?
15. Who uses the general systems model of the firm?
16. What is the information systems infrastructure? What are its five subsystems?
17. Which of the information systems infrastructure subsystems incorporates artificial intelligence?
18. Which of the information systems infrastructure subsystems emphasizes communications?
19. Which of the information systems infrastructure subsystems represents the firm's accounting system?
20. Which of the information systems infrastructure subsystems is intended to meet the general information needs of all the firm's managers?
21. Which of the information systems infrastructure subsystems is intended to meet the specific information needs of users working individually or in small groups?
22. What does the word enterprise mean? What does an enterprise model describe?
23. Explain the relationship between the strategic business plan and the strategic plan for information resources.
24. What are the two things that are identified in the strategic plan for information resources?

25. Which of the information specialists work directly with the user during the system development life cycle?
26. What are the basic functions that all information systems perform?
27. What are the basic components of all information systems?
28. What is the functions/components matrix and why is it a useful tool?
29. Name six types of knowledge that the systems developer should possess. Name four skills.

Topics for Discussion

1. Explain why your college or university is a system.
2. Is an information system a physical system, a conceptual system, or both?
3. Explain why a surgeon is a systems analyst. Do the same for a lawyer, a soccer coach, a professor, and a student.
4. Which is more important for a systems developer: computer literacy or information literacy? Which is more important for a manager?
5. Although this fact is not mentioned in the chapter, management attempts to speed the flow of certain physical resources through the firm, and slow down others. Which resources would be sped up? Which would be slowed down?
6. Would a firm ever be considered an open-loop system?

Problems

1. Read the Boulding article that is identified in the chapter bibliography, and write a paper titled "How Boulding's Systems Theory Relates to Business." Your instructor will advise you concerning format and length.
2. Read the Duncan article that is identified in the chapter bibliography, and write a paper titled "How Duncan's Systems Theory Relates to Business."
3. Write a paper titled "How I Can Develop the Four Systems Developer Skills While in College."
4. Complete an F/C matrix for the following system:

   Employees provide the departmental secretary with their time cards, which contain the hours worked for the week. The departmental secretary prepares a weekly time sheet that lists each employee, the total hours worked, and the hourly rate. The time cards are filed in a Time card history file.

   The departmental supervisor audits the time sheet and signs it if everything seems to be in order. If any of the figures are unacceptable, the sheet is returned to the secretary. The acceptable sheets from all of the departments are sent in the company mail to a clerical employee in the accounting department.

   The clerk uses the acceptable time sheets to calculate payroll earnings, which are written on the time sheets.

   Another clerk uses the time sheets to prepare the payroll checks, which are forwarded to the employees. After this operation, the time sheets are filed in a Time sheet history file.
5. Prepare an F/C matrix, using the following system description:

   A data entry operator in the information systems department keys the data from each time card into a keyboard terminal, and then files the time cards in a Time card history file. An information system program writes the entered data onto a Weekly time card file on magnetic disk. A prewritten sort program sorts the Weekly time card file by employee number (minor sort key) within department number (major key). A third program reads the Sorted weekly time card file on magnetic disk and prints a weekly payroll report. This report is filed in a Weekly payroll history file, which provides a printed record in the event that anyone wishes to audit the payroll activity.

The Sorted weekly time card file is also used to update the Employee payroll master file, on magnetic disk. This file maintenance program is the most complex of the system, computing the weekly regular and overtime earnings, the current and year-to-date gross earnings, social security tax, income tax, and net earnings amounts. The appropriate fields are updated in the employee master records, and an output file is written on magnetic disk that contains the most important computations for each employee. This output file, called the Weekly payroll file, is used to print the payroll checks, which are sent in the company mail to the employees.

Case Problem: Blue Bonnet Motor Homes

Blue Bonnet Motor Homes is located in Hempstead, Texas, on the outskirts of Houston. Hempstead is a small town, but Blue Bonnet derives most of its business from buyers who drive from Houston to take advantage of the low prices. Blue Bonnet claims in its television advertising to be the lowest-priced motor home dealer in the Houston area.

About three months ago, Blue Bonnet installed a personal computer to handle the inventory of motor homes. Previously a manual system had been used, but it was always causing problems. The salespersons would convince a customer to buy a certain style and color motor home, check the manual inventory records to ensure that the motor home was in stock, and then learn that the vehicle had already been sold. The manual inventory records did not accurately reflect the Blue Bonnet inventory.

The Blue Bonnet sales manager, Clarence White, convinced the owner, Henry Bailey, that the manual system should be thrown out and replaced by a computer. A PC was bought and installed, along with a prewritten software package designed especially for motor home dealerships. The person who had previously been keeping the manual inventory records, Carol Olsen, was trained to perform the data entry, and a systems developer, Jennifer Gordy, was hired to develop additional applications. Responsibility for the computer operation was given to Sunny Popp, the manager of the accounting department.

One bright summer day, Clarence walks into Henry's office.

Clarence: Henry, it's still happening. The inventory records still aren't right. We had a couple of situations yesterday where the computer said that we had the vehicles, but when we went out to the lot to get them they weren't there. We found out they had been sold. And the same thing just happened this morning. I thought you ought to know.

Henry: I'm glad you told me. This is pretty discouraging. We spend all that money on the computer and the people to operate it, and it's no better than the manual system. I'm going to talk to Sunny about this.

(Henry calls Sunny on the phone and asks her to come to his office. Sunny arrives within just a few minutes, and Henry explains what has happened.)

Henry: Sunny, do you have any idea what's going on? I thought that computers were supposed to be so accurate.

Sunny: I think I do. The salespersons aren't letting us know when they make a sale. When we receive a shipment of motor homes from the manufacturer, we immediately update our inventory records to show the new stock. But when the sales are made, the salespersons are either late in letting us know, or they forget to notify us altogether. The result is that the records show a vehicle as being in stock when it really isn't. As you know, the salespersons are supposed to fill out a Vehicle Sold slip and hand carry it to the computer room so that Carol can update the computer records. We decided on that procedure so that the computer records would be accurate up to the minute. If the salespersons would follow the procedure, I don't think we would have any problems.

(Henry thanks Sunny and she leaves. Henry then calls Clarence on the phone and explains what Sunny has said.)

Clarence: It sounds like Sunny is just trying to cover up for her own operation and put the blame on sales. Listen, Henry, our sales reps have more important things to do than fill out a bunch of paperwork. They're salespersons, not clerks. If we can't get this problem solved without turning our reps into paper shufflers, I'm going to tell them to just forget the sales slips altogether.

Assignments

1. Explain the Blue Bonnet situation in systems terms, using systems theory terminology.
2. What has caused the problem?
3. What should Henry do to solve the problem?

SELECTED BIBLIOGRAPHY

Boulding, Kenneth E. "General Systems Theory-the Skeleton of Science." *Management Science* 2 (April 1956): 197-208.

Duncan, Otis Dudley. "Social Organization and the Ecosystem." *In Handbook of Modern Sociology,* edited by Robert E. L. Faris, pp. 36-45. Chicago: Rand McNally, 1964.

Franz, Charles R. "User Leadership in the Systems Development Life Cycle: A Contingency Model." *Journal of Management Information Systems* 2 (Fall 1985): 5-25.

Hosalkar, A., and B. Bowonder. "Software Development Management: Critical Success Factors." *International Journal of Technology Management* 19 (Number 7,8, 2000): 760-772.

Ravichandran, T., and Arun Rai. "Total Quality Management in Information Systems Development: Key Constructs and Relationships." *Journal of Management Information Systems* 16 (Number 3, Winter 1999/2000): 119-155.

Scheer, August-Wilhelm, and Alexander Hars. "Extending Data Modeling to Cover the Whole Enterprise." *Communications of the ACM* 35 (September 1992): 166-172.

Soderquist, Klas., and Rajesh Nellore. "Information Systems in Fast Cycle Development: Identifying User Needs in Integrated Automotive Component Development." *R & D Management* 30 (Number 3, July 2000): 199-211.

NOTES

1. Richard J. Hopeman, *Systems Analysis and Operations Management* (Columbus, OH: Charles E. Merrill, 1969): 125-150.
2. Clyde W. Holsapple and Andrew B. Whinston, *Business Expert Systems* (Homewood, IL: Irwin, 1987): 4.

Case Study Installment 2
Advanced System Technology Associates

MANAGING THE ASTA PROJECT

The decision by Mel to outsource the market intelligence system to KBS consulting (incorporated in the new SPIR) made it easy for the team to scale down the scope of their project to include only the skill set system. Gary redrew his DFDs, deleting the Customers external entity on the context diagram, and process 3 on the figure 0 data flow diagram. This eliminated the need for the figure 3 data flow diagram. So, the team's process model included only the revised context and Figure 0 data flow diagrams.

THE TEAM'S PROJECT PLANNING MEETING

"Well, Rachel," Sean said as the team assembled for its first planning meeting. "You're the Gantt chart queen. What do we do now?"

Since she had come by her title honestly, it didn't take Rachel long to respond. "We definitely need a Gantt chart. We will also need a network diagram. Those are specified in the SPIR. We do the Gantt chart first, in a very detailed manner, listing every task that must be accomplished. When we are in agreement that the chart is correct, we can prepare a summary network diagram that identifies only the project phases. We can take both diagrams to every client meeting to keep Yolanda informed of our progress."

"Sounds reasonable," Sean said, looking around the group. "How do we start?"

Rachel pulled a copy of the phased development SDLC diagram from Chapter 1 of the text (see Figure 1.14) from her backpack and told the group that it would provide the basic framework. "We only have to flesh it out to fit the requirements of our project. As we think about each stage, we should check the textbook and see what it says about each one. We can shift things around and add more detail as necessary."

Kim decided to enter the discussion. "It seems like the most difficult thing will be to estimate how long it will take to perform each task. Identifying the tasks shouldn't be too difficult, and it should be pretty easy for us to make team assignments. But, we've never done this kind of thing before. Actual companies have a hard time estimating times. What do you think, Rachel?"

"You're absolutely right. There are probably a lot of approaches, but the most straightforward one would involve each one of us estimating the time required to accomplish the tasks that we are assigned. Of course there is always the chance that someone will pad their times but if we do it in a group session I think that the times will be our best estimates. If you agree that it is a good idea, I can put together a rough Gantt that we can add to in our next meeting."

Gary was the first to speak. "What do you think, team? Shall we let Rachel have responsibility for the Gantt?" Everyone nodded agreement.

"Well, what are the rest of us going to do, Gary?" asked Kim.

"In order to make good planning estimates, we have to be aware of any constraints that Mel and Yolanda might impose. Also, we have to be very clear on the project and system objectives, goals, and risks. As you know from class, there are forms that we can use for the goal analysis, and for the risk evaluation and reduction strategies."

"You're right about the objectives," Kim interrupted, "but we took a cut at those when we put together the problem chain. If you recall, we also came up with some performance criteria. I think we can do a better job now since we know so much more about ASTA's needs. Let me review what we've done and see if I can improve on it. I can also address the issue of constraints."

"Sounds good," Gary acknowledged. "Who wants to do the goals and risks?"

"I haven't contributed a whole lot to this discussion," Sean said. "I'll do the risk evaluation and reduction strategies."

Gary approved Sean's offer and volunteered to do the goal analysis himself. "Hey, wait a minute. Tracy, you don't have anything do you?"

"No, but I'll be happy to help anybody who needs it."

"I'm sure I'll need some help," Rachel answered. "You can help me with the Gantt."

With the project planning tools assigned, the team meeting broke up, with all of the members pledging to get right on their tasks.

FIGURE CS 2.1

Two Options for Phasing the ASTA Skill Set System Project

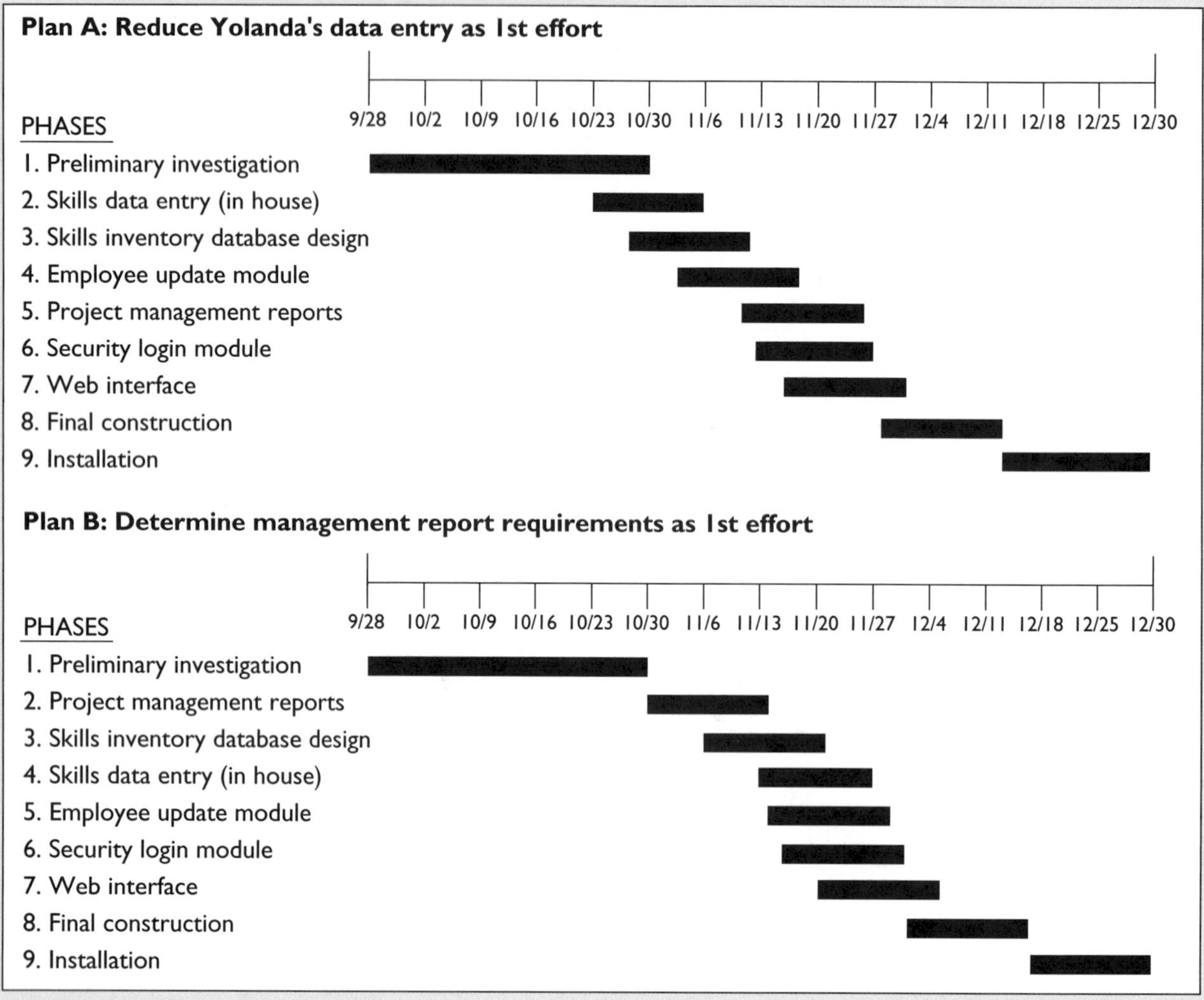

IDENTIFYING THE GANTT CHART PHASES AND ARRANGING THEIR SEQUENCE

The first thing that Rachel and Tracy did in plotting out the Gantt chart was to identify the project phases. Their first phase and last two came directly from the phased development methodology. The phases in between were the major modules of the ASTA system.

1. Preliminary investigation
2. Project management reports
3. Skills inventory database design
4. Skills data entry (in house)

5. Employee update module
6. Security login module
7. Web interface
8. Final construction
9. Installation

They had no sooner agreed that the nine phases represented a good way to subdivide the work when Tracy made an observation.

"OK, this is a good list and the sequence seems logical. But, it would be possible to perform some of these phases in a different order. For example, the way it is now, as soon as we do the preliminary investigation, we design the project management reports. This is a good way to be sure we know what the key users want so that we can be sure to design the database with all the information we need. This order will probably be fine with the project managers, but Yolanda might want us to first address the issue of application data entry—making it more efficient. Let me show you what I mean. I'll just plug in some estimated times." She sat down at her notebook and drew up the two abbreviated Gantt charts in Figure CS 2.1.

"I see what you mean," Rachel acknowledged. "We had better check with Yolanda and find out which sequence she wants us to follow. She's the main client contact and we should follow her suggestions." Rachel got on the phone and called Yolanda, who talked with Mel and called back a little later, asking the team to address the project management reports immediately following the preliminary investigation.

"This is a good lesson," Rachel said. "Since the phases can be performed in various sequences, it helps to know which one the client prefers."

Recognizing the Influences on the Project Plan

Tracy and Rachel then took a rough cut at identifying the tasks for each phase, referring to the textbook for the discussion of the phased development methodology, and applying what they understood about the project. They entered all of this data into a Microsoft Excel spreadsheet. They could have used other software, such as Microsoft Project, but they had seen charts printed from Excel and liked the appearance. Next, they contacted the other team members to arrange a meeting to complete the task list and assign each to one or more team members. The other team members were instructed to bring along the work that they had volunteered to do, so that it could be considered in doing the project planning.

The team met at the snack bar and Rachel spread the rough Gantt out on a table. "Before we get started with the details, I think that everyone should report on those factors that can influence our plan. Kim, why don't you go first?"

Influence of Constraints and Performance Criteria

Kim passed around a sheet of paper that identified the ASTA objectives, constraints, and performance criteria. See Figure CS 2.2. "I sort of beefed up the objectives a little bit, based on what we know about the users' needs now. I just made a few minor changes in the wording of the performance criteria. Since we hadn't addressed the constraints, I went back out to ASTA, and Elizabeth and Yolanda gave me that infor-

FIGURE CS 2.2

Objectives, Constraints, and Performance Criteria for the Proposed Skill Set System

Objectives

1. To allow employees to easily review and update their skill sets from workstations.
2. To allow employees and managers to browse others' skill sets from workstations.
3. To offer querying and reporting functionality to managers.
4. To create an intuitive, highly instructive graphical user interface.
5. To develop a system that is scalable and easy to update and maintain.
6. Ultimately, to develop a Web-based system.

Constraints

1. The skill set system must be completed and ready for cutover by December 5, (11 weeks).
2. The new skill set system must use the existing LAN consisting of a Dell server and workstations, running under Microsoft Windows NT. No new hardware will be purchased
4. In-house technical support has limited experience in systems development.

Performance Criteria

1. Requests for information concerning employee skills are filled within *15 minutes.*
2. All employees update their skills records at least *quarterly (the system will send a reminder to each employee).*
3. Employees update their skill sets in no more than *15 minutes.*
4. Employees update their skill sets from their *workstations.*
5. Employees update their skill sets by *changing only the data entries that need to be updated.*
6. Output will be displayed on the workstation screens, and *printed only upon request.*

mation. The constraints that will influence our planning are those relating to the hardware and software, and the time limit for the project. We'll have to keep the performance criteria in mind as we develop the system modules." Everyone seemed satisfied with the work that Kim had done.

Influence of System and Project Goals

Gary took a similar approach in explaining his goal analysis. See Figure CS 2.3. "I based this on the information we have gathered from the client. It's all pretty simple. We have to keep the functionality, maintainability, and flexibility goals in mind as we identify our design tasks. One point to not overlook is the lack of 100 percent client commitment by the project managers in sales and manufacturing or even all of those in R&D. That will undoubtedly add some time to everything that involves them."

Influence of System Project Risks

Gary had decided that it would be best for the entire team to agree on Sean's ratings for the risk evaluation form, so they addressed each one in order, coming up with the

FIGURE CS 2.3

Goal Analysis for ASTA's Skill Set System

Goal Analysis

This chart summarizes the issues for each of the major system development goals and our team's initial plans to meet each goal.

Goal	Context & Requirements Issue(s)	Action(s) to Meet Goal
SQ—Functionality (includes: reliability, clarity, efficiency, which includes user flexibility)	■ ASTA needs a faster, easier process for assigning teams ■ System should be user-friendly so employees can update their own information ■ System should be efficient to make best use of employees' time ■ System should have restricted access to employee info and updating capabilities	■ Create a GUI interface and involve employees in all divisions in JAD sessions to evaluate data entry clarity and effectiveness ■ Customize the data entry forms to be easy to read ■ Customize the data entry forms to include only necessary information ■ Require passwords for accessing and updating employee info
SQ—Maintainability	■ ASTA has no IT staff for development tasks ■ UT MIS team only available for 11 weeks so maintenance will be handled by ASTA staff	■ Construct software in modules with maximum commenting ■ Choose Microsoft Access because Rick knows it ■ Train Yolanda in Access ■ Provide clear documentation
SQ—Portability and Scalability	■ ASTA has experienced recent fast growth and could continue to grow quickly Note: The team cannot create the best system for growth in the short time allowed, so meeting this goal conflicts with meeting the next goal.	■ Choose Access because it is likely to be kept current with new operating systems and changes in storage; also, some tools that allow for more growth have the capability to convert Access dbs to their more robust databases
PM—Timeliness	■ Recent growth makes system urgent need for ASTA ■ UT team has only 12 weeks	■ Cut scope to top priority functions ■ Set and meet major milestone dates ■ Create detailed Gantt chart and monitor progress closely ■ Research package software solutions
PM—Cost	■ No cost information has been provided, but there is a clear potential for a high ROI if ASTA can staff more projects	■ Research cost restrictions ■ Sell the value of the system to ASTA project managers
PM—Client commitment	■ Mel, Yolanda, Elizabeth, and Sue are committed, but project manager interest interest is uncertain and staff in sales & marketing are not committed	■ Provide orientation sessions and feedback sessions to increase business-wide ownership of system ■ Involve Mel as project champion at key project points
OR—Efficiency	■ System will reduce tedious work for Yolanda ■ System automates team assignments	■ Design system for minimum redundant data entry and include hot keys for fast data entry ■ Design complete team assignment report function
OR—Effectiveness	■ Main goal of system is assist management decisions about accepting bids and assigning teams	■ Analyze reporting needs carefully ■ Design new reports as needed
OR—Competitive advantage	■ The system will help ASTA respond more quickly to RFPs and therefore increase market share and revenue	■ Design for quick response to market opportunities ■ Make optimum use of employee capabilities

FIGURE CS 2.4

Project Risk Evaluation Form

Factors Affecting Project Risk	Rating*	Comments
1. Characteristics of the organization a. Has stable, well-defined objectives?	+1	Mel has stated clear objectives for ASTA
b. Is guided by an information systems plan?	+1	Has a new SPIR
c. Proposed system fits plan and addresses organizational objectives?	+1	Aimed at clear statement of ASTA objectives
2. Characteristics of the information system a. Model available/clear requirements?	0	Existing system, but with new, improved processes
b. Automates routine, structured procedures?	0	Data entry simple, but assigning team members complex
c. Affects only one business area? (No cross-functional or interorganizational links?)	-1	Affects all business areas
d. Can be completed in less than three months?	+1	Scope has been limited to fit 12-week project time
e. Uses stable, proven technology?	+1	Standard database tools
f. Installation at only one site?	-1	Installation sites in Austin and Dallas
3. Characteristics of the developers a. Are experienced in chosen development methodology?	0	Team is familiar with phased development only from class projects
b. Are skilled at determining functional requirements?	0	Familiar, but not skilled
c. Are familiar with technology and information architecture?	0	Team knows Microsoft Access but not ASTA's infrastructure
4. Characteristics of the users a. Have business-area experience?	0	Yolanda and project managers know their processes well; others do not
b. Have development experience?	-1	No in-house development
c. Are committed to the project?	-1	Some are, some aren't
Total Points	+1	Indicates medium risk

* +1 = yes; 0 = maybe; -1 = no

results in Figure CS 2.4. If an item has potential risk, it is assigned a rating of a plus 1; if it is not risky, it is a minus one; if it is unknown or undetermined, it is a zero. The points are summed for an overall risk evaluation. A negative total is cause for concern. The ASTA point total was plus 1. "At least we aren't starting off in the hole," Sean said, causing everyone to laugh.

In a similar brainstorming series, the team came up with the risk reduction strategies in Figure CS 2.5.

Identifying Gantt Chart Tasks, Making Team Assignments, and Agreeing on Project Scope

With the influencing factors recognized, Rachel assumed the role of project manager and kept the discussion moving—addressing each phase and not moving on until team assignments had been made and an agreement had been reached on how long each task would take. Just as soon as someone would start to complain that the team was inexperienced in making the time estimates, Rachel would explain "We will be making changes to the Gantt throughout the project. The important thing is to get something down on paper to get us started."

Following this strategy, Rachel guided the team activity to the completion of the Gantt chart and was ready to close the meeting when Sean said he had a "serious concern."

"I've been sitting here trying to visualize how we are going to get all of this done this semester. I don't think we can do it. I'm especially concerned about the risk that

Figure CS 2.5

Risk Reduction

Factors	Risk Reduction Strategies
1. Organization	■ Carry out the strategic plan for information resources that supports the existing strategic business plan
2. Information system	■ Involve managers from all organizational units in feedback sessions on their project management needs to ensure that all components of the system are included and that there is strong ASTA buy-in ■ Use prototyping to fully develop requirements and to make sure that the system is complete before it is implemented company-wide ■ Research differences in two locations
3. Developers	■ Review existing systems to learn infrastructure and look and feel of purchased systems
4. Users	■ Conduct JAD sessions (to develop requirements and for feedback throughout the project life cycle) with users to achieve complete company-wide ownership of the system ■ Ask Mel Knowler to champion system at JAD sessions and send an e-mail to all ASTA employees

Gary identified of the client not being 100 percent supportive of the project. I'm speaking specifically of the functional managers. According to Gary, their attitude is going to slow down everything that they are involved with. Does anybody else have the same concerns that I do?"

Tracy and Kim were quick to voice their lack of confidence that the team can accomplish "everything that is in the Gantt." Seeing their support, Gary also indicated some doubt.

"Well, OK," Rachel said, "what do we do about it?"

Sean suggested that it would be easiest to completely cut out some aspect of the work, rather than try to trim everything down. That idea received approval and then the team looked over the Gantt to find the part that "could go." The part that stood out was the Web interface. Gary urged the team to keep in mind that "ASTA has only a static Web site—a few pages with their mission statement and contact information for each of their services. A Web-based skill set matrix needs to be part of a professional Web site if they are going to make it part of the application process. And none of us have much experience with Web connectivity for a database system. That one project at the end of our Advanced Programming class wasn't close to the size and complexity of the Web-based system we're planning for ASTA. Plus we have never worked with lots of users before."

The team discussed the feasibility of not doing the Web portion of the project, and just concentrating on developing a workstation-based system for internal use by the ASTA employees.

The team agreed that this would be a sound strategy and Sean and Gary volunteered to meet with Yolanda and tell her of their decision. They had the meeting, and Yolanda was at first obviously disappointed, but she quickly realized that the most important thing was to do a good job on the basic skill set system. She recalled that Mel only wanted the team to look into the possibility of a Web interface, and agreed that letting a follow-on Systems Development team add the interface next semester would be acceptable. She said that she would contact Eleanor and receive her commitment to provide the follow-on support.

Preparing the Gantt Chart and Network Diagram

Hearing of Yolanda's approval of the reduced project scope, Rachel and the other team members incorporated all of the planning suggestions and produced a Gantt chart. (The first part of the Gantt chart appears in Figure CS 2.6. You can retrieve the complete chart from the text Web site, www.wiley.com/college/mcleod). Although they had anticipated that eliminating the Web work would solve their scheduling problem, they were surprised to see that the remaining tasks required twelve weeks to complete, with the final date being December 12. "This isn't going to work," Sean said. "We've got to be out of here by the 15th—that's when the semester is over. Should we cut something else?" Otherwise, we have no slack time at all for any surprises.

The team discussed their dilemma and decided that more cutting was not the answer. There really wasn't anything else to cut. Rachel surprised the group by suggesting that they go with the plan as it is. "I believe that our time estimates are pretty conservative and we can shave off some time as we get into the work. If we stay on top of the situation each week, we should be able to bring it in line. I'm sure that everything will come out OK in the end."

With that assurance, the team agreed to not make any further refinements in the Gantt for the time being.

FIGURE CS 2.6

Gantt Chart for ASTA Skill Set System

Project Planning Documentation

System: Skill Set System for ASTA
Date: September 28, 2000
Chart Type: Gantt Chart

Assigned Task
Completed Task

Rachel Sanders, Gary Patel, Tracy Johnson, Kim Wu, Sean Patterson

Task		Activity	Assignment	Scheduled Time	Sept. 28	Oct. 6	13	20	27	Nov. 3
							Week Ending			
	Phase 1:	**Preliminary Investigation**								
	Analysis									
1	A-1	Hold first team meeting to prepare for initial contact	Team	9/28		*Team*				
2	A-2	Initiate contact with Yolanda Garza	Rachel	9/29 - 10/3			*Rachel*			
3	A-3	Meeting with Yolanda, Mel Knowler, Rick, Sue, Elizabeth	Team	10/4			*Team*			
4	A-4	Discuss ASTA background, business plan, org. culture	Team	10/4			*Team*			
5	A-5	Discuss ASTA current systems	Team	10/4			*Team*			
6	A-6	Discuss ASTA's information infrastructure	Team	10/4			*Team*			
7	A-7	Discuss functionality of proposed system	Team	10/4			*Team*			
8	A-8	Obtain Rick Gomez' ERD	Team	10/4			*Team*			
9	A-9	Obtain sample skills set matrix forms	Team	10/4			*Team*			
10	A-10	Plan and divide work for second team meeting	Team	10/4			*Team*			
11	A-11	Create ASTA organization chart	Sean	10/4			*Sean*			
12	A-12	Create ASTA's functions/components matrix	Rachel	10/4			*Rachel*			
13	A-13	Create ASTA's existing andproposed system components	Rachel	10/4			*Rachel*			
14	A-14	Information dimensions of the new ASTA skill set system	Rachel	10/4			*Rachel*			
15	A-15	Hold second group meeting	Team	10/5			*Team*			
16	A-16	Prepare agenda for second client meeting	Sean	10/5			*Sean*			
17	A-17	Conduct second meeting with Yolanda Garza, Sue Kim	Team	10/11				*Team*		
18	A-18	Plan and divide work for third team meeting	Team	10/11				*Team*		
19		**Analyze process flows**								
20	A-19	Create ASTA context diagram	Gary	10/12 - 10/14					*Gary*	
21	A-20	Create ASTA figure 0 diagram	Gary	10/12 - 10/14					*Gary*	
22	A-21	Create ASTA figure 3 diagram	Gary	10/12 - 10/14					*Gary*	
23	A-22	Create ASTA problem chain analysis	Tracy/Kim	10/12 - 10/14					*Tracy/Kim*	
24	A-23	Hold third group meeting	Team	10/15					*Team*	
25	A-24	Determine core problems based on problem chain analysis	Team	10/15					*Team*	
26	A-25	Prepare agenda for third client meeting	Sean	10/15					*Sean*	
27	A-26	Conduct second meeting with Yolanda Garza, Sue Kim	Team	10/18					*Team*	
28	A-27	Determine focus of system development and establish measurable criteria; goal analysis & risk evaluation	Team	10/18					*Team*	
29	A-28	Research existing ASTA infrastructure	Kim	10/19-10/22						*Kim*

FIGURE CS 2.7

Network Diagram

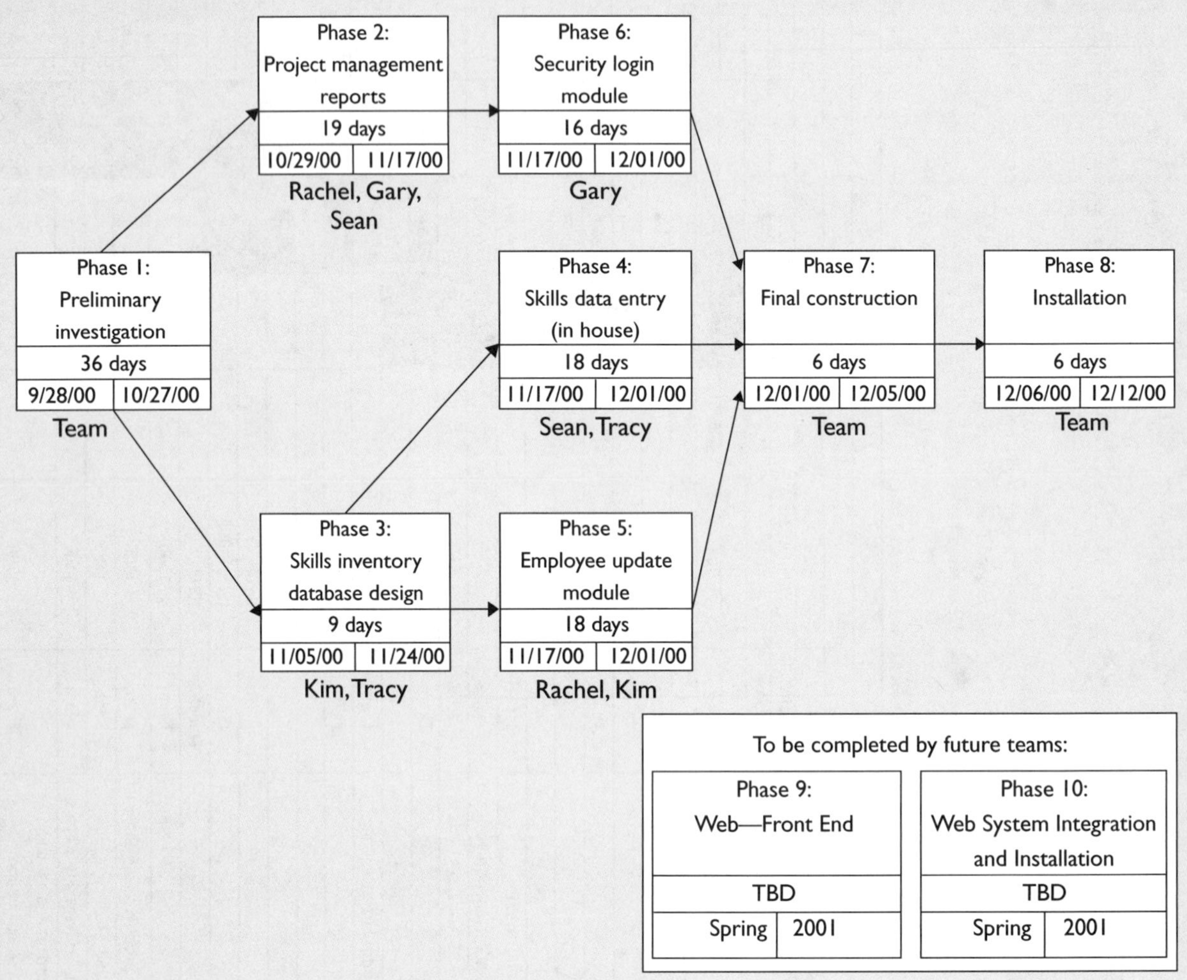

Rachel told the group that she would prepare the network diagram. Using the Gantt chart as a guide, the network diagram didn't take much time to complete. It appears in Figure CS 2.7. It is a good overview of the project, showing the phases and their linkages. The diagram makes it easy to see how the team will accomplish several phases in parallel.

REVIEWING THE PROJECT PLANNING TOOLS WITH THE CLIENT

At the next scheduled weekly meeting with Yolanda the team members followed the same order in reviewing their documents as they had followed in the Gantt chart planning meeting. Kim identified the objectives, constraints, and performance criteria, Gary talked about goal analysis, and Sean reviewed the risks and reduction strategies. Yolanda agreed that the lack of commitment by the project managers was a definite risk but promised to keep that point confidential within the company. Then Rachel and Tracy unrolled the Gantt chart on Yolanda's desk and she was really impressed with the long list of detailed tasks. She asked for a copy of the network diagram to put on her office wall.

In addition to getting the client's approval of the planning tools, the team previewed much of the first delivery report. That way, the client has seen much of the report content when it is presented and feels to have been a vital part of its preparation.

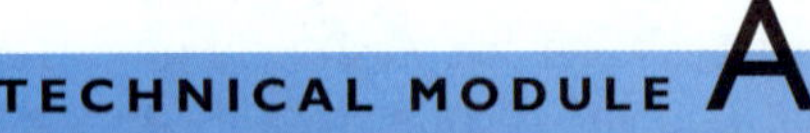

TECHNICAL MODULE A

DATA MODELING

An information system consists of both data and processes. In developing such a system, the developers must identify both the data and the processes and describe them with models. The models are typically a combination of narratives and graphics. In this technical module we describe the preparation of data models, which consist of entity-relationship diagrams and the data dictionary. We describe process modeling in Technical Module B.

GOAL OF THE TECHNICAL MODULES

The goal of the technical modules in this text is to provide you with an introductory understanding of the subjects discussed. The understanding should enable you to apply the technical material in a relatively simple system development project. In order to build upon this introductory knowledge, you should pursue sources that provide a more in-depth treatment, primarily those listed in the Selected Bibliography at the end of each technical module.

ENTITY-RELATIONSHIP DIAGRAMS

An entity-relationship diagram, or ERD, identifies the entity types within a system that are described with data, and the relationships among the entity types. The technique was introduced by Peter Chen in a 1976 journal article and has become the most popular tool for modeling data at a high level.[1]

An entity-relationship diagram is a good way to document the enterprise data model. But it is not restricted to use at the enterprise level; it can also be used on a smaller scale to document a *portion* of an enterprise's data, such as those used by a particular system or set of systems.

Entity Types and Entities

An **entity type** is something of such importance to the firm that it is described with data. It can be one of three things:

- An *environmental element* of the firm, such as a customer or supplier
- A *resource,* such as an account receivable, a product, or a salesperson
- An *information flow,* such as a sales order or an invoice

In order for something to be an entity type, it must occur multiple times. For example, the customer entity type occurs once for each customer. Each occurrence of an entity type is an **entity.**

Entity types are represented in an ERD with rectangles as shown in Figure A.1. The rectangles are labeled with the entity type names, which are usually singular nouns. The lines connecting the rectangles represent the relationships.

Relationships

A **relationship** is an association that exists between two or more entity types, and is illustrated with a labeled line as shown in the figure. In the first example, a relationship exists between a salesperson and a territory. A salesperson covers a territory. The salesperson and the territory are entity types, and the relationship is the act of covering the territory. This relationship is read as: "Salesperson *covers* territory." It can also be read in a reverse sequence: "Territory *is covered by* salesperson." In the second example, a customer places a sales order, and in the third example, an investor owns an investment.

There is considerable variation in how relationships are illustrated. Sometimes diamonds are superimposed on the lines, containing the names of the relationships. When plain lines are used, they can contain two labels. The label above the line represents the left-to-right relationship (such as "Covers"), whereas the label below the line represents the right-to-left relationship (such as "Is covered by").

Cardinalities

Different types of relationships can exist between the entity types. The term **cardinality** describes the number of times that each type occurs in the relationship. There are three basic cardinalities: one-to-one, one-to-many, and many-to-many.

FIGURE A.1

Examples of Entity Types and Relationships

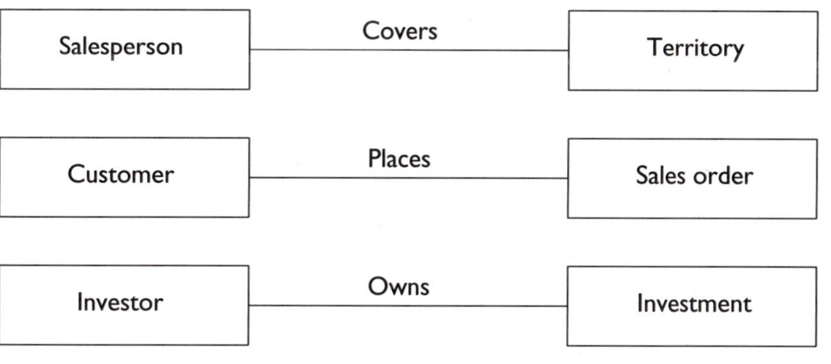

FIGURE A.2

Examples of Cardinalities

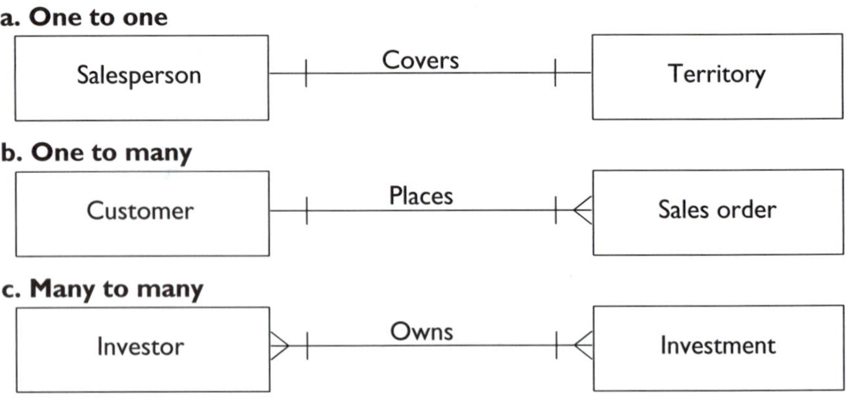

There are several different ways to show the cardinality on the ERD, but one that is supported by many Computer-Aided Software Engineering (CASE) tools is illustrated in Figure A.2. In this notation, a small cross mark on the relationship line means that the entity type exists only one time (the cross mark represents a "1"), and a cross mark plus a "crowsfoot" means that the entity type exists one or more (many) times.

In the example, all three basic cardinalities exist.

- One salesperson covers one territory, and one territory is covered by one salesperson. This is a one-to-one relationship.
- One customer places one or more sales orders, but a sales order is placed by only one customer. This is a one-to-many relationship.
- One investor owns one or more investments, and one investment is owned by one-or-more investors. This is a many-to-many relationship.

Optional and Mandatory Relationships

In the Figure A.2 examples, the entity types always participate in the relationships. For example, salespersons always cover territories, customers always place sales orders, investors always own investments, and investments are always owned by investors. These are the most likely relationships, but in the world of business, things seldom *always* occur. There are invariably exceptions. A firm may have customers in its Customer master file that never place sales orders, and a stock broker may have investors as clients who never own investments. As a way to handle these exceptions, relationships can be classified as optional and mandatory.

If an entity type can exist on its own or in a relationship with another entity type, it is called an **optional relationship.** On the other hand, if an entity type must always participate in the relationship it is called a mandatory relationship. The relationships in Figure A.2 are **mandatory relationships**—the entities always exist. Figure A.3 shows two examples of optional relationships. A small circle (think of it as representing the letter O for optional or zero for none) is placed on one end of the relationship line to indicate that the corresponding entity type *might not* participate. In the

FIGURE A.3

Examples of Optional Relationships

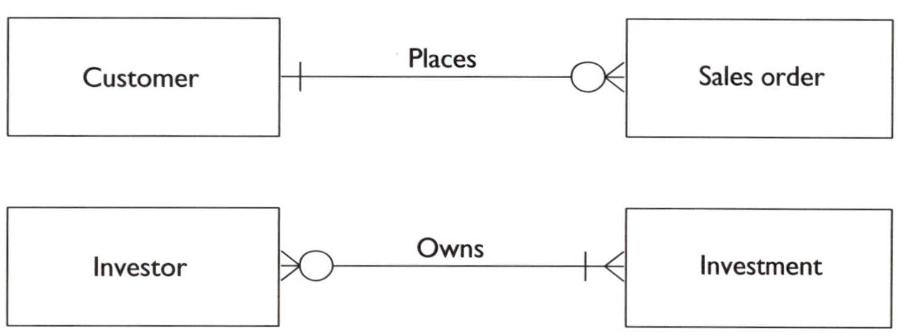

first example, customers place zero or more sales orders, and in the second, an investment is owned by zero or more investors.

When specifying the cardinalities, it is necessary that the developers conform to the firm's policies. Figure A.4a is an example of an ERD that does not match the firm's policies. According to the cardinalities, a salesperson covers one or more territories, and a territory is covered by one salesperson. The firm has four salespersons—John, Kathy, Jon, and Kim—and has three territories—Houston, Dallas, and Austin. John is assigned to Dallas, Kathy to Austin, and Jon to Houston. What is the problem here? Each territory has one salesperson assigned, as specified in the ERD. However, each salesperson does not have one or more territories. Kim doesn't have a territory. If it is acceptable for a salesperson to not have a territory, then the cardinalities should be expressed as in Figure A.4b.

FIGURE A.4

ERDs Must Reflect Firm Policies

a. Policies are not accurately reflected

b. Policies are accurately reflected

FIGURE A.5

Entities with Attributes

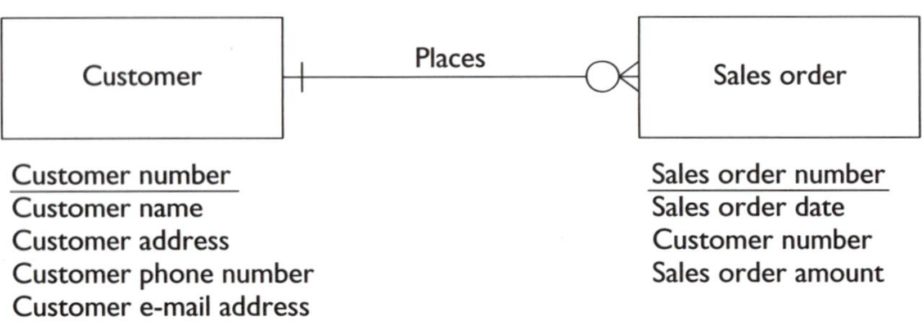

Attributes

Each entity has distinguishing characteristics, called **attributes.** For example, some attributes of a customer are name, number, address, and sales territory. The attributes are actually data elements that are maintained for the entity.

A particular *occurrence* of an attribute is called an attribute value. As an example, a customer name is ABC Company, customer number is 12872, and sales territory is 23. The attribute values are simply the values assigned to the attributes for the entity.

There are two types of attributes—identifiers and descriptors. An **identifier attribute** is the attribute that uniquely identifies the entity. The term **key** is also used. For example, the identifier or key of a customer entity type is the customer number. A **descriptor attribute,** on the other hand, provides information, but not identification. Examples are customer name, address, and sales territory.

In some cases, attributes are included in ERDs next to their entity types. In other cases, attributes do not appear on the ERD but are described elsewhere, as in the data dictionary. Figure A.5 is an example of an ERD with attributes. The accepted practice is to underline the identifier attributes.

The Development of the Entity-Relationship Diagram

If the ERD is to provide a basis for the enterprise data model, it is prepared as a part of the enterprise modeling process, and the work is most likely accomplished by a special task force. On the other hand, if the diagram represents the data of a single system, it is prepared by the project team. Either way, seven steps are required, and the developers and users play key roles.

Step 1: Identify the Entity Types

You identify those environmental elements, resources, and important transactions that you want to describe with data. A good starting point is provided by the existing master files. The Customer master file contains data about the customer entity type, the Inventory master file contains data about the inventory entity type, and so on. These particular master files identify environmental elements and resources. User interviews can confirm these designations and also identify important transactions that must be documented with data. Of the eight environmental elements of the firm that we identify in Chapter 2, customers and suppliers are almost invariably entity types.

Step 2: Identify the Relationships

Entity types are usually related in the manner of a subject and an object. One entity type is the subject and another is the object. A connecting verb describes the relationship.

Step 3: Prepare a Rough ERD

Sketch a rough ERD, and try to arrange the symbols so that the relationships read from left to right or top to bottom. Figure A.6 shows the appearance of the diagram at this point. A customer places zero or more sales orders, and a sales order is placed by one customer. A sales order specifies one or more products, and a product is specified on zero or more sales orders. A customer pays zero or more invoices, and an invoice is paid by only one customer. An invoice specifies one or more products, and a product is specified on zero or more invoices. Note that two many-to-many relationships exist—between sales order and product, and between invoice and product.

Step 4: Map Attributes to the Entity Types

Make a list of the attributes that will be maintained for each entity type, underlining the identifiers. Such a list appears in Table A.1. Multiple identifiers may be required for an entity type. For example, it might be necessary to identify an inventory item with both a product class and an item number. Identifiers that consist of multiple attributes are called **composite keys.**

Step 5: Perform a Data Analysis

A formal procedure exists for analyzing the attributes for each entity type and identifying the arrangement that represents the best logical database design. This process is called data analysis and it uses a technique called normalization to eliminate redundant elements and make the structure as flexible and efficient as possi-

FIGURE A.6

A Rough ERD

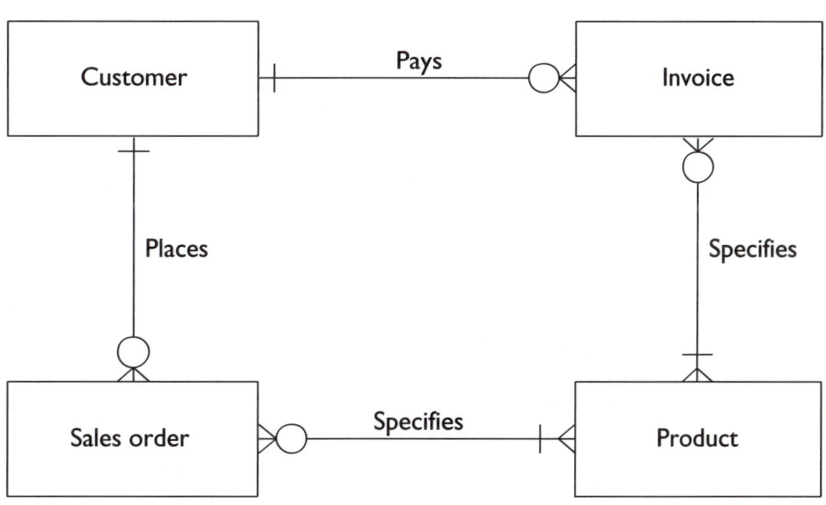

TABLE A.1

Initial Attributes for Each Entity Type

Sales Order Entity Type	Invoice Entity Type
<u>Sales order number</u>	<u>Invoice number</u>
Customer number	Customer order number
Sales order date	Invoice date
Product number (occurs n times)	Product number (occurs n times)
Product description (occurs n times)	Product description (occurs n times)
Product unit price (occurs n times)	Product unit price (occurs n times)
Product quantity (occurs n times)	Product quantity (occurs n times)
Product extended price (occurs n times)	Product extended price (occurs n times)
Total sales order amount	Invoice amount

Product Entity Type	Customer Entity Type
<u>Product number</u>	<u>Customer number</u>
Product description	Customer name
Warehouse location	Customer address
Product unit price	Sales territory number
Balance on hand	
Reorder point	
Order quantity	

ble. **Normalization** consists of converting the data to a series of normal forms—first normal form (1NF), second normal form (2NF), third normal form (3NF), and so on. You begin by putting the data into 1NF, then proceed to the higher levels in sequence. In most cases, 3NF is a far as you go.

First Normal Form When data is in first normal form, an entity type has no repeating elements. In order for something to be an entity type, it must have multiple occurrences. When an attribute exists more than one time for an entity type, the data must be normalized to remove that condition. When we mapped the data elements to the entity types in Table A.1, we identified repeating elements in two locations. These repeating elements are the ones that *occur n times.* They recognize that a sales order can specify multiple products that have been ordered, and that an invoice can specify multiple products that have been shipped. Figure A.7 illustrates the format for a typical sales order, which consists of a heading area, a body area with multiple lines, and a footing area where totals are printed. The multiple lines in the body area are where the products being ordered are listed.

The problem of repeating attributes can be solved by creating new entity types (sales order line and invoice line) to replace the many-to-many relationship with one-to-many relationships as shown in Figure A.8 on page 84. In this example, the two added entity types are highlighted in boldface but that technique is not ordinarily used in a diagram. The new relationships solve the problem of repeating groups. Now, multiple sales order lines exist, but each has only single product number, product quantity, product unit price, and product extended price attributes. Each sales order line and invoice line is an entity type. Table A.2 lists the attributes for each of the new entity types. Note that both are identified with composite keys.

FIGURE A.7

A Sales Order Form

Heading

Sales Order				
Sold to			Sales order no. Sales order date	
Product number	Product name	Product unit price	Product quantity	Product extended price
			Invoice amount	

Body

Footing

Second Normal Form Data is in second normal form when the descriptor attributes rely on the entire composite key for identification. We have two such situations, created when we added the sales order line entity type and the invoice line entity type. In the case of the sales order line, we assign a value to product description and product unit price if we know only the product number. This is because those attributes are included in the product entity. We do not have to know the sales order number. So, the product description and product unit price descriptor attributes can be removed from the sales order line entity type. However, we must know both the sales order number and the product number to assign values to product quantity and product extended price. So, those descriptor attributes remain in the sales order line entity

TABLE A.2

Additional Entity Type Attributes

Sales Order Line Entity Type	**Invoice Line Entity Type**
Sales order number	Invoice number
Product number	Product number
Product description	Product description
Product unit price	Product unit price
Product quantity	Product quantity
Product extended price	Product extended price

FIGURE A.8

Added Entity Types to Eliminate Many-to-Many Relationships

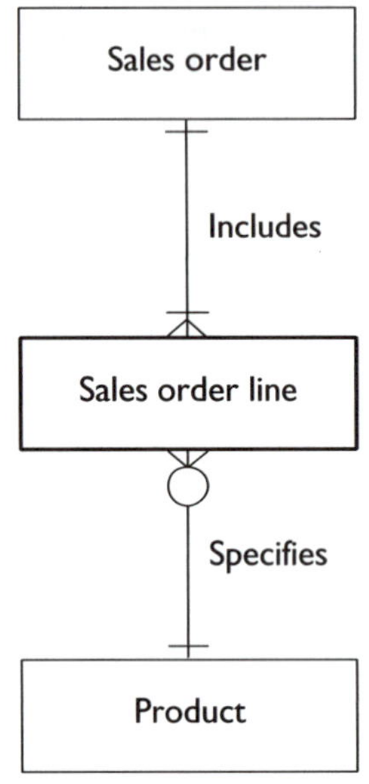

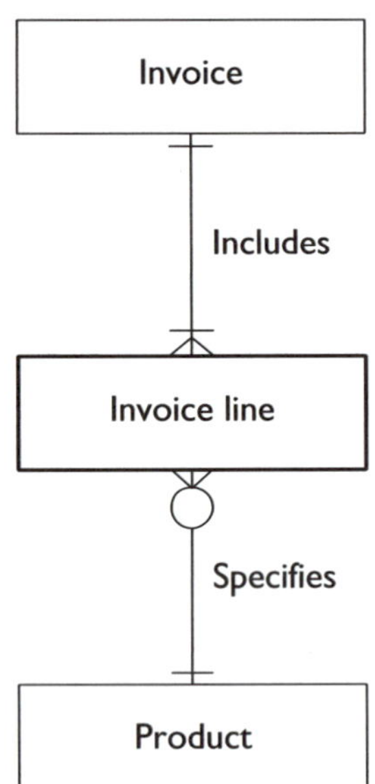

type. The same reasoning results in the removal of the product description and product unit price from the invoice line entity type. Table A.3 shows the new attribute lists.

Third Normal Form Data is in third normal form when descriptor elements are not dependent on other descriptor elements for the assignment of values. We have such a problem in both of the examples in Table A.3. The product extended price for the sales order line entity type can be computed from the product quantity (sales order line entity) and the product unit price (product entity). The solution is to eliminate the product extended price descriptor attribute. The same logic applies to the invoice line entity type. Table A.4 shows the normalized sales order line and invoice line entity types.

Two additional descriptor attributes are also removed during full normalization—these are total sales order amount in the sales order entity type, and invoice amount in the invoice entity type. Although these attributes are acceptable with the first three normal forms, they can be computed from other values in the database. Stored computed values can cause integrity problems during implementation.

TABLE A.3

Additional Entity Type Attributes in Second Normal Form

Sales Order Line Entity Type	Invoice Line Entity Type
Sales order number	Invoice number
Product number	Product number
Product quantity	Product quantity
Product extended price	Product extended price

The data analysis puts the data into its most efficient form for inclusion in a database. One of the problems with maintaining a corporate database is redundant data—the same data being maintained in different locations. By removing attributes from entities that do not necessarily have to be included in those entities, as we did when converting the data to second normal form, the redundant data is removed. Using those examples, if we ever need to know the product description or product unit price, we can obtain that data from the product entity type.

Step 6: Prepare a Modified ERD

Redraw the ERD, as shown in Figure A.9, reflecting the changes made in the data analysis. The diagram includes the identifier attributes for each entity type.

Step 7: Review the ERD With Others and Refine

The members of the task force or project team review the ERD with other users and perhaps the IS steering committee to ensure that it represents a true picture of the firm's data.

The ERD As a Blueprint for a Relational Database

Databases can have different types of data structures. The first databases featured a hierarchical or network structure, but were limited in terms of providing information that had not previously been specified. It is beyond the scope of this text to describe database structure. For an explanation, refer to a database textbook, such as *Data Management: Databases and Organizations,* 3rd Edition, by Richard T. Watson (2002, Wiley Higher Education). The database structure that is most popular today is the **relational structure,** which consists of multiple data tables that can be integrated

TABLE A.4

Normalized Entity Type Attributes

Customer Entity Type

Customer number
Customer name
Customer address
Sales territory number

Invoice Entity Type

Invoice number
Customer order number
Invoice date

Invoice Line Entity Type

Invoice number
Product number
Product quantity

Product Entity Type

Product number
Product description
Warehouse location
Product unit price
Balance on hand
Reorder point
Order quantity

Sales Order Entity Type

Sales order number
Customer number
Sales order date

Sales Order Line Entity Type

Sales order number
Product number
Product quantity

FIGURE A.9

A Modified ERD

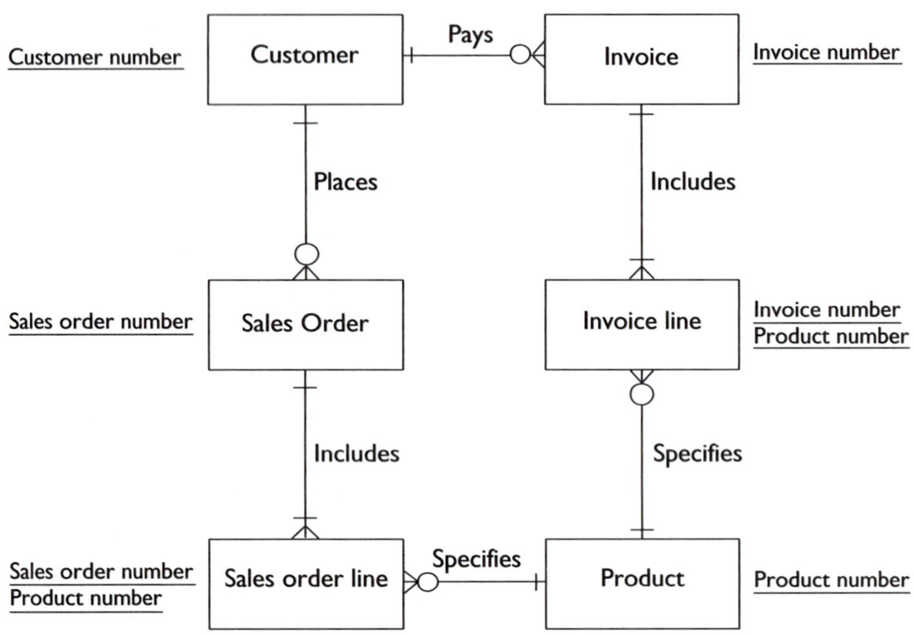

using their attributes. A main advantage of a relational database is that it is capable of providing information that has not previously been specified by users. This is a big advantage since users are not always able to tell developers exactly what information they will need in the future.

The relational database structure makes it possible to integrate table contents by using attributes in the tables. These relationships are called **implicit relationships** because the relationships are implied from the table contents. Prior to the relational structure, special attributes were incorporated into the hierarchical and network structures to accomplish the integration. These special attributes were called **explicit relationships.**

Figure A.10a illustrates how the contents of two tables can be integrated to produce a report, using implicit relationships. The salesperson table contains salespersons' numbers and names. The territory table contains salesperson's numbers and territory numbers. If a manager asked you to produce a report showing salespersons' numbers, names, and territories, you could do it using the data from the two tables. You would use salesperson number to link the contents of the two tables. You would obtain salesperson 112's number and name from the salesperson table and the territory number from the territory table. The logic that you would apply is exactly the same that a relational database management system applies in integrating table contents.

When this database was designed, the salesperson table was specified as an entity, the territory table was specified as an entity, and they were related by including salesperson number in both as identifier attributes. Figure A.10b shows the ERD. It is not necessary that only identifier attributes be used for the integration. Descriptor attributes can be used as well.

An Example of Implicit Relationships

Figure A.11 shows an ERD that documents the data involved in purchasing replenishment raw materials from a supplier. A buyer in the firm's purchasing department prepares a purchase order, which includes purchase order lines—each specifying a raw material to be ordered. A supplier fills the purchase order and prepares a supplier invoice, which includes supplier invoice lines—each specifying a raw material. The figure includes some attributes for the buyer, purchase order, and supplier entity types. The identifier attributes are underlined.

Assume that the manager of the purchasing department wanted to prepare a report showing the following data:

- Buyer number
- Buyer name
- Purchase order number
- Supplier number
- Supplier name
- Purchase order amount

The data from the buyer and purchase order entity types is integrated using buyer number. Data from the purchase order and supplier entity types is integrated using the supplier number. Buyer number and supplier number provide the implicit relationships.

FIGURE A.10

An Example of Implicit Relationships

a. Two tables

Salesperson	
Salesperson number	Salesperson name
112	Adams
128	Warren
153	Hanks
159	Francis
162	Wills
166	Grover

Territory	
Salesperson number	Territory number
112	1
128	3
153	2
159	1
162	1
166	2

b. The corresponding ERD

FIGURE A.11

An ERD of Purchasing Data with Selected Attributes

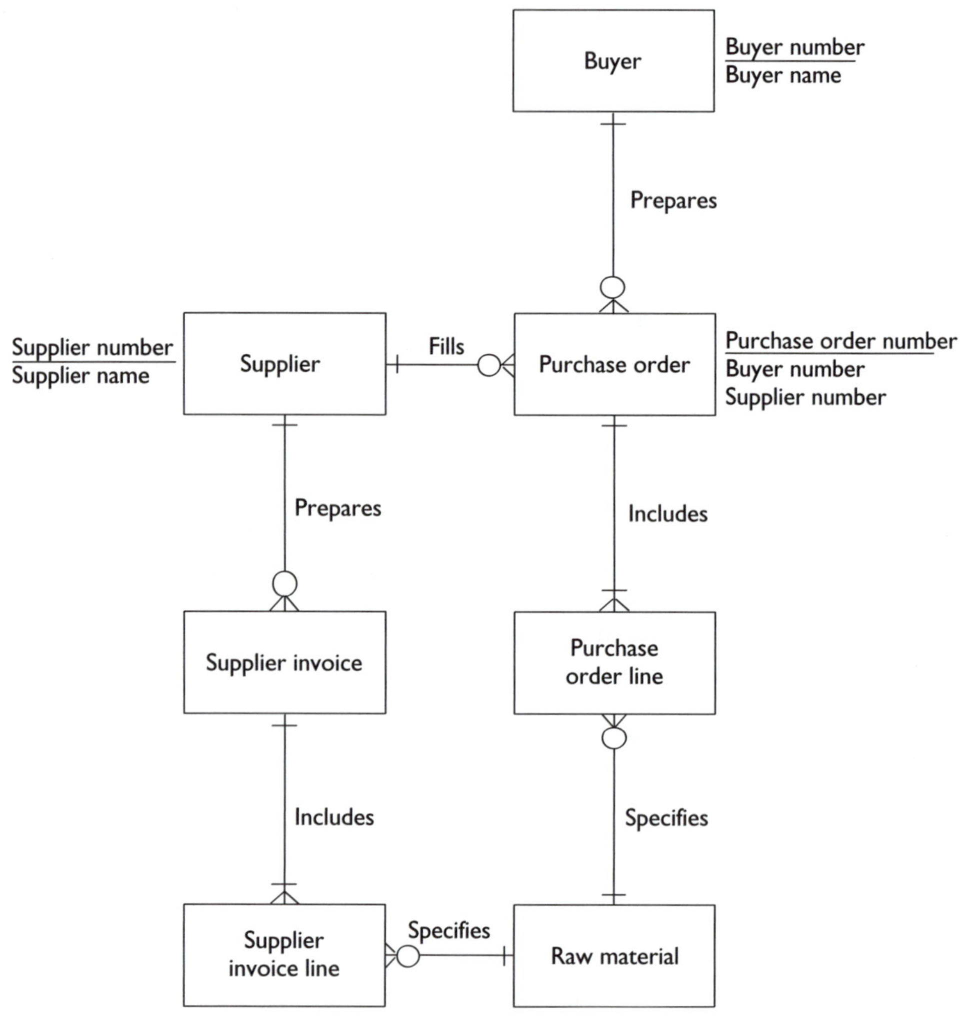

ERDs Show Data Relationships, Not Processes

It is important to note that the ERD in Figure A.11 does not show the purchase order being sent to the supplier, the supplier shipping the raw materials, or the supplier sending the supplier invoice to the firm. Those actions take place but they are all *processes* and are not included on an ERD. The ERD merely shows relationships among data entity types. Keep that point in mind as you prepare ERDs.

Putting the Entity-Relationship Diagram in Perspective

The popularity of the ERD as a systems development tool recognizes the important role played by the firm's data resource. With the data stored in the database, systems can be developed that provide virtually any information that users might need. The ERD can provide the basis for:

- The design of a relational database
- More detailed documentation of the firm's data with the data dictionary
- Documenting the processes with such tools as data flow diagrams and structured English

These capabilities explain the popularity of the entity-relationship diagram in the development of modern information systems.

The Data Dictionary

A **data dictionary** is a detailed description of the data in a firm's database. The first dictionaries were kept in three-ring binders, with each page describing a data attribute. For example, there might be a page for employee number and another page for employee name. System developers agreed on the characteristics of each attribute: the name to be used in programs, the type of data (alphabetic, numeric, or alphanumeric), the size of the field, the number of decimal positions if numeric, and so on. These characteristics were recorded in the data dictionary, which served as the reference guide for all of the developers as new systems were developed. Before these data standards were implemented, the situation could be chaotic. For example, one programmer used names of cigars, such as El Roi Tan and Dutch Master, to describe the attributes of the data for the programs that he wrote. Another programmer could look at the programs and not have the slightest idea of what they did. You can imagine what this did to program maintenance.

Data dictionaries became so popular that developers soon converted the binder pages to information system storage media. The conversion was facilitated by the development of software especially designed to manage the data descriptions. This software was given the name data dictionary system, or DDS. Some DDSs were stand-alone systems; others were contained in database management systems.

Today, a firm's data dictionary is maintained in the information system and is used by developers—information specialists and users alike. The data dictionary represents the detailed documentation of the firm's data resources. The data dictionary supplements the ERD, which provides the summary picture of the data. As today's developers take a top-down approach to system development, the ERD is prepared first, identifying the entity types and the attributes for each type. Then, each attribute is described in detail, producing the data dictionary.

An Example of a Data Dictionary Entry

Figure A.12 is a portion of a page from a data dictionary constructed in Microsoft Access. The example is from the tblCustomer entity type that provides data describing the firm's customers. The figure includes the detail for the identifier attribute—customer number (CustomerID). There are fifteen characteristics, such as Attributes (Variable Length), Description (Unique identification number for each customer), and DisplayControl (Text Box).

The bottom of the page includes information concerning the type of actions that are permitted by the database administrator and users. In the example, they can perform all of the actions listed—delete, read, insert, update, and so on.

FIGURE A.12

A Portion of a Data Dictionary

C:\Documents and Settings\McLeod\DataDictionary.mdb — Monday, September 18, 2000
Table: tblCustomer — Page: 1

Properties

Date Created:	9/18/2000 1:52:05 PM	GUID:	Long binary data
Last Updated:	9/18/2000 2:51:28 PM	NameMap:	Long binary data
OrderByOn:	False	Orientation:	0
RecordCount:	0	Updatable:	True

Columns

Name	Type	Size
Customer ID	Text	8

AllowZeroLength:	False
Attributes:	Variable Length
Collating Order:	General
ColumnHidden:	False
ColumnOrder:	Default
ColumnWidth:	Default
Data Updatable:	False
Description:	Unique identification number for each customer
DisplayControl:	Text Box
GUID:	Long binary data
Ordinal Position:	1
Required:	True
Source Field:	Customer ID
Source Table:	tblCustomer
UnicodeCompression	True

Group Permissions

Admins	Delete, Read Permissions, Set Permissions, Change Owner, Read Definition, Write Definition, Read Data, Insert Data, Update Data, Delete Data
Users	Delete, Read Permissions, Set Permissions, Change Owner, Read Definition, Write Definition, Read Data, Insert Data, Update Data, Delete Data

PUTTING DATA MODELING IN PERSPECTIVE

The ERD and the data dictionary can be used together. The ERD provides a summary graphic picture of the relationships between entity types and the data dictionary provides a detailed explanation of each entity type's contents.

The ERD is the newest of the data documentation tools and is the one that is currently experiencing the greatest surge in popularity. However, the ERD does more than simply document data. It provides the basis for data analysis. During enterprise modeling, the executives, assisted by information specialists, can use the ERD to conceptualize the data requirements that are necessary for the firm to meet its strategic objectives. During systems development, the developers can use the ERD to conceptualize the data that will be required of the system under study.

The ERD provides a graphic picture of the data resource, which shows the major groupings of data and how they are related. The ERD enables system developers to determine the data attributes that are needed and the logic of how certain ones are derived. The ERD is a powerful data design tool that can provide the starting point for the development of all of the firm's conceptual systems.

KEY TERMS

entity type
entity
relationship
cardinality
optional relationship
mandatory relationship
attributes
identifier attribute, key
descriptor attribute
composite key
normalization
relational structure
data dictionary

PROBLEMS

Prepare an ERD, including a list of attributes, for each of the following problems.

1. Customers prepare sales orders that specify the firm's products they want to purchase. Each customer is identified by a customer number, and each product by a product number. Each sales order is identified by a sales order number and can specify multiple products. Each product is described by a product name, unit price, balance on hand, reorder point, order quantity, and quantity on order. Each sales order describes both the customer and the products. Hint: Do not regard the firm as an entity type.
2. Modify the ERD in Problem 1 to include data involved with the ordering of replenishment products from the firm's suppliers. Buyers in the firm's purchasing department obtain products from suppliers by means of purchase orders. Each buyer is identified by a buyer number and described by name, e-mail address, phone number, and product line specialty code (each buyer specializes in one or more product lines, such as abrasives, solvents, and so on). Each supplier is identified by a supplier number and described by name, address, e-mail address, and phone number. Each purchase order can specify multiple products, is identified by a purchase order number, and describes both the supplier and the products. Hint: Do not regard the purchasing department as an entity.
3. The Woodstone Corporation owns a large apartment complex. The owners want to develop a database to keep track of each individual unit, the leases, the lessees (tenants who sign the leases), and workers who perform maintenance or housekeeping jobs on the units.

   For each worker, the worker id, name, address, phone number, and worker's specialty must be maintained. For each apartment unit, a unit number, number of bedrooms, number of baths, street rent, and street deposit must be kept. (Street rent and street deposit are the rents and deposits that will be charged for a new lease. These amounts may or may not be the same as the previous rent and deposit of the current lease for that unit.) A worker may work on many units, and the same unit may be worked on by many workers.

   Each lease contract has a unique lease number, rent, deposit, move-in date, and move-out date. A unit may not have more than one lease on it, and a lease is associated with exactly one unit. Lessees sign the leases. Each lessee is identified by his or her name. In addition, the occupation and the previous address of the lessee must be maintained. A lessee must be on at least one lease but can be on many leases. Similarly, a lease can be associated with many lessees but must be associated with at least one lessee.

   Lessees generate transactions. Each transaction is identified by a composite key consisting of the lessee's name and a transaction id. In addition, date, amount, and a description of the transaction is maintained. A lessee generates at least one transaction (at the time of signing the lease and paying the deposit) and at most, many. Each transaction is associated with exactly one lease.
4. Get-Well-Soon is a veterinary clinic owned by a few veterinarians in a small rural town. The vets would like to set up a database to keep track of their operations. These operations relate to the

clinic's employees, various animals the veterinarians attend to, the animals' illnesses, and the animals' owners.

Employees are categorized into two groups: doctors and staff. For each employee a social security number, name, address, phone number, and salary are maintained. In addition, a specialty must be kept for doctors, and a title must be kept for staff.

Each animal is identified by a unique id. In addition, the kind (such as horse), the gender, and the age of the animal is also maintained. If there is a birth, it is required that the mother be related to the offspring. An offspring has the same attributes as any other animal. Therefore, some animals are related to others through birth.

Doctors attend to the animals. A doctor may attend to more than one animal and an animal may be attended to by more than one doctor. For each attendance, the doctor's id (employee id), the animal id, the date of the visit, the diagnosis, the prescription, and the charge is specified.

For each owner of an animal, an account number, an address, a phone number, and the balance in the account is maintained. An animal must be owned by exactly one owner, but an owner may own zero or more animals.

SELECTED BIBLIOGRAPHY

Halpin, Terry, and Anthony Bloesch. "Data Modeling in UML and ORM: A Comparison." *Journal of Database Management* 10 (Number 4, October-December 1999): 4-13.

Rahayu, J. W., E. Chang, T. S. Dillon, and D. Taniar. "A Methodology for Transforming Inheritance Relationships in an Object-oriented Conceptual Model to Relational Tables." *Information & Software Technology* 42 (Number 8, May 15, 2000): 571-592.

Stoimenov, Leonid, Antonija Mitrovic, Slobodanka Djordjevic-Kajan, and Dejan Mitovic. "Bridging Objects and Relations: A Mediator for an OO Front-end to RDBMSs." *Information & Software Technology* 41 (Number 2, January 25, 1999): 57-66.

NOTE

1. Peter Chen, "The Entity-Relationship Model-Toward a Unified View of Data," *ACM Transactions on Database Systems* 1 (March 1976): 9-36.

TECHNICAL MODULE B

PROCESS MODELING

During the early years of business computing, system processes were documented with flowcharts. With the advent of structured programming in the 1980s, systems developers sought documentation tools that were more suitable to the hierarchical, structured format. The developers devised a number of tools, and the ones that received the most widespread adoption were data flow diagrams and structured English. We describe both tools in this technical module.

DATA FLOW DIAGRAMS

A **data flow diagram,** or **DFD,** is a drawing that shows how a system's environmental elements, processes, and data are interconnected. DFDs typically exist in a hierarchy, as shown in Figure B.1. A diagram on a lower level expands a process on the level immediately above, providing more detail. A DFD is a type of **decomposition diagram,** subdividing a system into lower-level systems, or subsystems.

The Context Diagram

The DFD on the highest level is called the **context diagram** because it describes the system in the context of its environment. The context diagram contains only a single, unnumbered process. In this case, the process represents the entire system. Figure B.2 shows the context diagram for an order entry system. The system is represented by the single circle, and its environmental elements are represented by squares. The system is connected to its environmental elements by arrows, which represent data flows. A **data flow** consists of one or more data elements that travel together and is labeled with a name that describes the element or elements.

The Figure 0 Diagram

The DFD on the second level in the hierarchy is the **figure 0 diagram.** It is called a figure 0 diagram because it shows the major processes contained in the single, unnumbered process of the context diagram.

Each process of the figure 0 diagram is numbered beginning with 1. In order to prevent a DFD from becoming cluttered, the general rule is to keep the number of processes to seven or less. This rule applies not only to the figure 0 diagram but to DFDs on the lower levels as well. Figure B.3 on page 97 shows the figure 0 diagram of the order entry system. The system contains three main processes. The first process screens sales orders and determines whether to accept or reject them. The second process prepares sales invoices, and the third prepares a rejected sales order report. Note that the figure 0 diagram includes all of the environmental elements from the context diagram, and that the data flows connecting these elements with the processes all have the same labels as in the context diagram.

This diagram contains a symbol not included in the context diagram. The symbol is an open-ended rectangle and it represents a **data store,** a place where data

FIGURE B.1

The Hierarchical Arrangement of DFDs

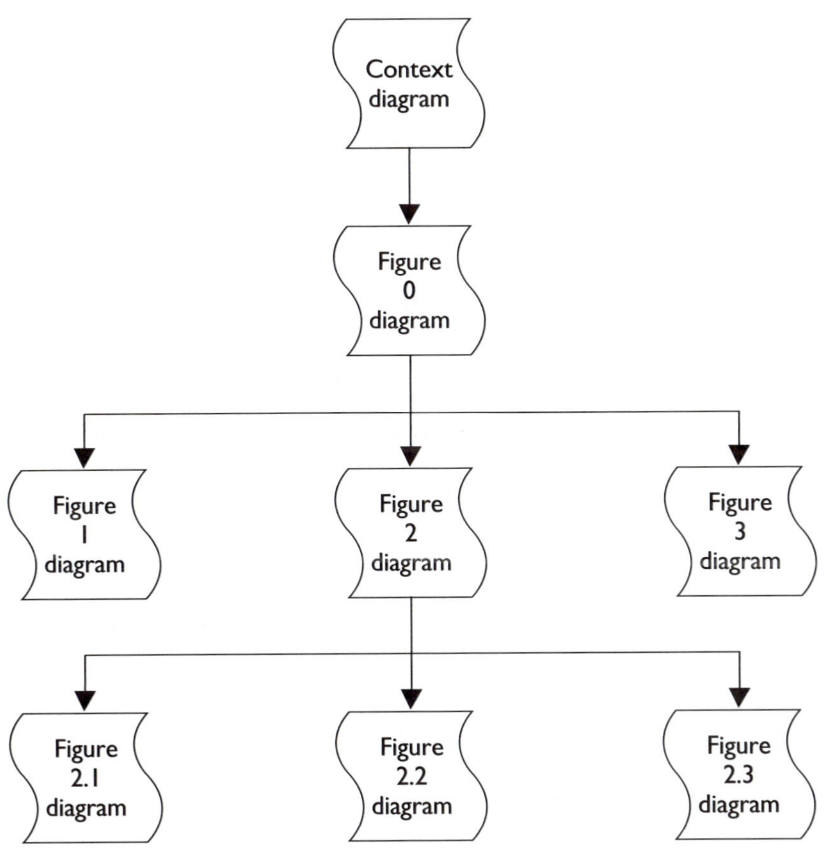

FIGURE B.2

A Context Diagram for an Order Entry System

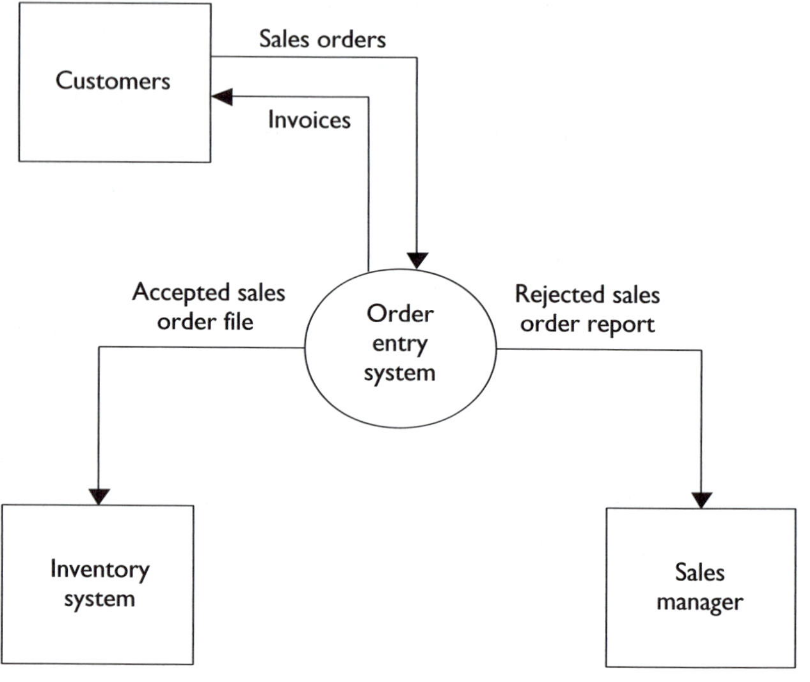

is kept. You can think of a data store as a file that is maintained in an up-to-date manner. In this system the data stores are master lists that contain valid item numbers and current prices.

Figure n Diagrams

On the next lower level you find DFDs with such names as figure 1 diagram, figure 2 diagram, and so on. The figure 1 diagram documents the major processes of process 1 of the figure 0 diagram; the figure 2 diagram documents process 2, and so on. We refer to the DFDs on this and lower levels as *figure n diagrams.*

Figure B.4 illustrates a figure 1 diagram. It documents the first major process of the order entry system—the screening of the sales orders. This system consists of two processes numbered 1.1 and 1.2. Process 1.1 verifies the item numbers on the sales orders by comparing them with those of the master item number list. Process 1.2 verifies that the customers have used the current prices by referring to the master price list.

Lower-level DFDs

The same top-down decomposition of the system structure can be continued to lower levels. For example, a figure 1 diagram can be subdivided into 1.1, 1.2, 1.3, and so on diagrams. In turn, a figure 1.1 diagram can be subdivided into 1.1.1, 1.1.2, 1.1.3, and so on diagrams. However, it is not necessary to document the same level of detail for all processes. Some processes can be adequately documented at a higher level in the hierarchy. The sort process in Figure B.3 is an example. Its documentation in the figure 0 diagram is sufficient.

The top-down process of documenting a system with DFDs continues until you reach a level of detail where the focus is on individual data elements. That level would likely come in the order entry system when you attempt to document the detail of process 1.1. For that task, you should use a documentation tool that is better suited to the detail, such as structured English.

Leveled and Balanced DFDs

When multiple DFDs are used in a hierarchy to document a system they are referred to as **leveled DFDs.** Leveled DFDs are developed in a systematic, top-down manner,

FIGURE B.3

A Figure 0 Diagram for an Order Entry System

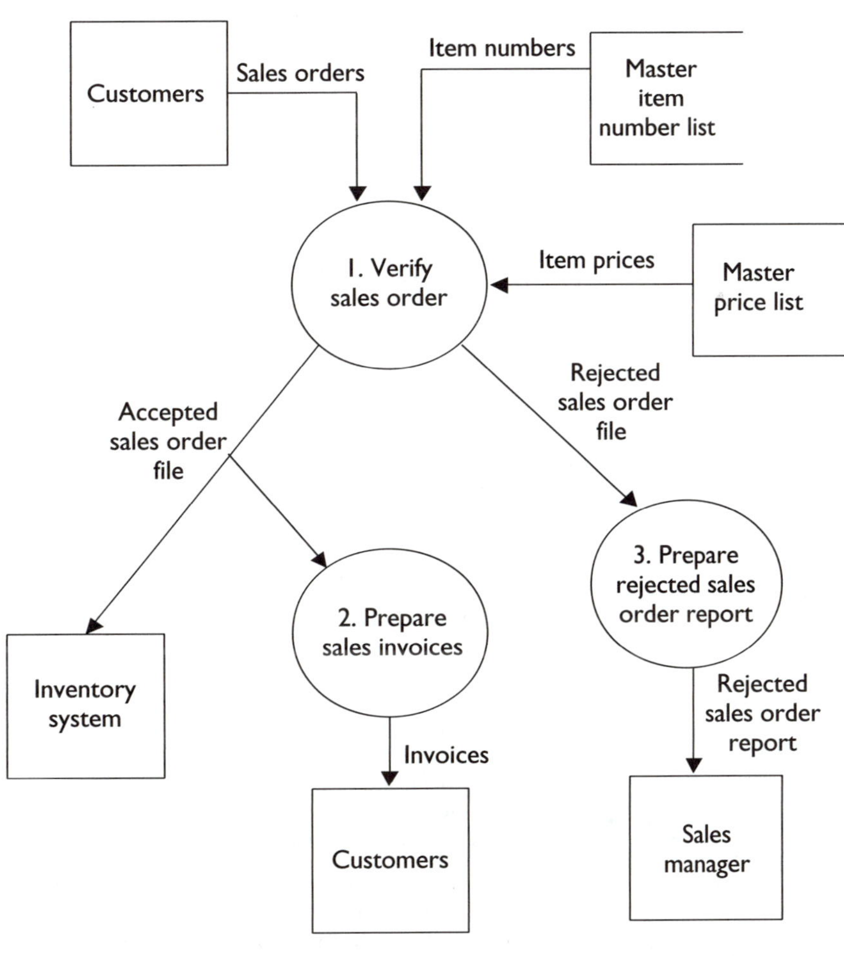

FIGURE B.4

A Figure 1 Diagram for Verifying Orders

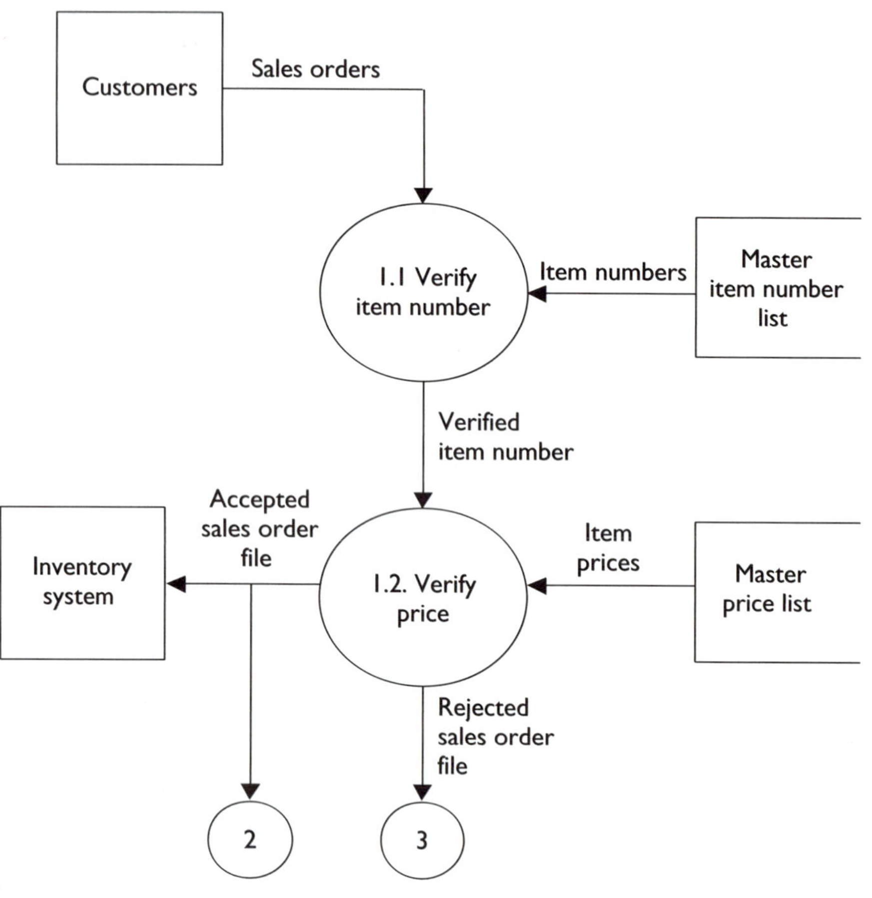

maintaining consistency from one level to another. This consistency can be seen in the process numbering—process 1, 1.1, 1.1.1, and so on. Consistency can also be seen in the data flow names that remain constant from one level to another. For example, the *Sales orders* data flow always represents the same grouping of data elements regardless of the level on which it appears. Leveled DFDs that have this top-down consistency in processes and data structures are called **balanced DFDs.** Your leveled DFDs should always be balanced.

Basic DFD Methodologies

There are two basic DFD methodologies, and they are distinguished by the shape of their process symbols. The **Gane-Sarson methodology** uses an upright rectangle with rounded corners. The **Yourdon-Constantine methodology,** on the other hand, uses a circle to document a process. We used Yourdon-Constantine for Figures B.2, B.3, and B.4.[1] Figure B.5 shows both types of process symbols.

Aside from the shape of the process symbols there is no real difference between the two methodologies. Gane-Sarson is probably preferred because the rectangle provides more space for labeling. Your choice of methodology is likely to be influenced by which one is supported by your Computer-Aided Software Engineering (CASE) tool. Some CASE tools allow you to select between the two methodologies.

DFD Symbols

DFDs consist of four basic symbols, which represent (1) processes, (2) environmental elements, (3) data stores, and (4) data flows. In addition, connector symbols can be used to connect one diagram to another.

Process Symbols

A **process** is a transformation of data. Data flows into a process, is transformed, and then flows out. In order for something to be a process, the output must be different from the input in some way. Process symbols are usually labeled with a verb and object, such as *Process accounting data* and *Edit sales orders.* However, upper-level processes can be labeled with system names when the processes are ordinarily regarded as systems. Examples are *Sales tracking system* and *Inventory system.* It is very common for the single process symbol of the context diagram to be labeled with the system name. The verb and object approach is common on lower levels.

FIGURE B.5

Process Symbols

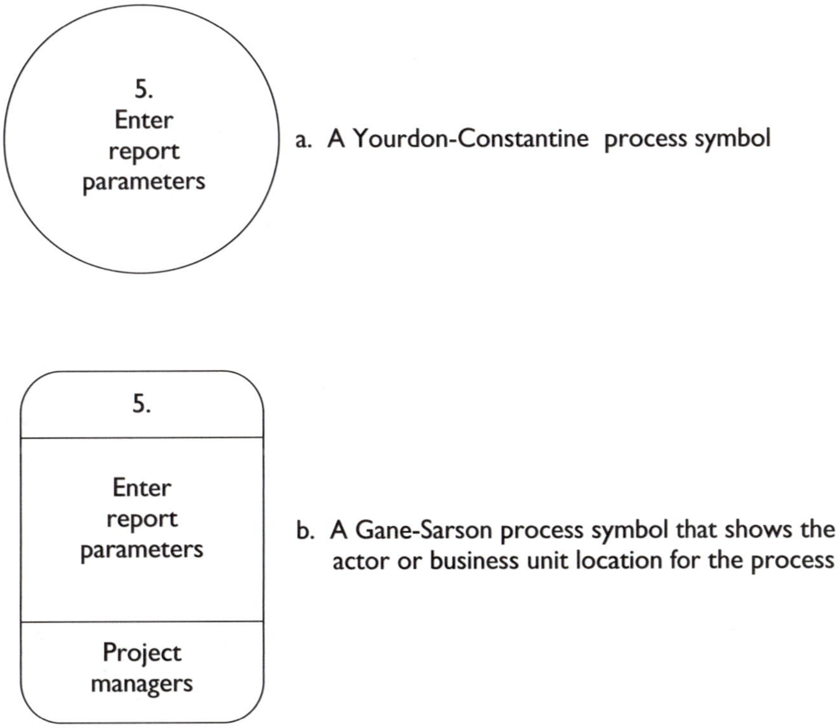

5.
Enter
report
parameters

a. A Yourdon-Constantine process symbol

5.
Enter
report
parameters
Project
managers

b. A Gane-Sarson process symbol that shows the actor or business unit location for the process

FIGURE B.6

Diverging and Converging Flows

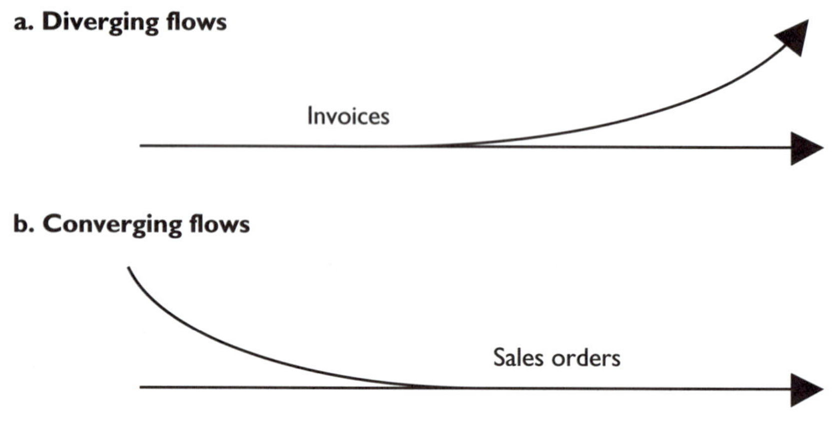

Environmental Element Symbols

Systems interface with persons, organizations, locations, and other systems. Each of these elements in the environment is called an *environmental element.* The names *entity* and *terminator* are also used. Each environmental element can be represented by a square or rectangle, and includes the name of the entity.

When we speak of the environment of a DFD, we are referring to external elements that interface with the *system.* This is different from the environmental elements of the *firm* that we described in Chapter 2.

Data Flow Symbols

A good way to think of a data flow is "data on the move." The data moves from an environmental element to a process, from one process to another, from a data store to a process, and so on. Therefore, data flows are represented with arrows. In most cases the data flow is one-way but two-headed arrows can be used. It is also possible to have diverging and converging flows, as illustrated in Figure B.6. Each data flow in a DFD is labeled with a *unique* name. However, when the same flow appears on more than one level the same name is used for each appearance.

The data flow arrows can take any of three forms. *Straight* lines are the shortest distance between two points. *Pipe* lines are straight lines that are always horizontal or vertical to the page, and contain only right-angle turns. We use pipe lines in Figures B.2 and B.4. *Curved* lines are also possible, as shown in Figure B.6. CASE tools typically allow you to select the line style.

Data Store Symbols

Whereas data flows represent data on the move, data stores represent data that is maintained in fixed locations. Think of a data store as "data at rest." Examples of data stores are master files of such resources as inventory and personnel data that are kept current, and history files that are held in archival storage. If a file is named a master file or a history file, it will always be a data store. Otherwise, it might be a data flow. Files are often used to communicate data from one location to another. So the name "file" does not distinguish between a data store and a data flow. Data stores are most often depicted with open-ended rectangles such as the ones in Figures B.3 and B.4. However, parallel lines and ovals can also be used, as illustrated in Figure B.7.

Some DFD experts maintain that a data store name should describe the data, rather than a form or a file. For example, a better name for an employee time card would be *Hours worked data,* and a better name for the Payroll master file would be *Employee payroll data.* This practice makes the DFD more generic but it also makes data naming more difficult. In addition, users are more familiar with form and file names and will more easily understand the documentation when those names are used. For these reasons, we suggest that you use form and file names for data stores when those names accurately describe the data.

Connector Symbols

You can make it easier for the viewer to follow the flow of data from one DFD to another by using connector symbols. A **connector symbol** is a circle that contains the number of the process *to* which a data flow is directed or the process *from* which a data flow comes. In Figure B.4 the circle with the number 2 connects the Rejected sales order file data flow to process 2. To follow the flow, you would next turn to the figure 2 diagram. The input data flow to the figure 2 diagram would be the Rejected sales order file, and it would originate with a connector labeled with the number 1, showing that it comes from process 1.

Tips for Using DFDs

Considerable flexibility is allowed in how you draw DFDs. We have seen this flexibility in the options that are available in choosing symbols for processes, terminators,

FIGURE B.7

Data Store Symbols

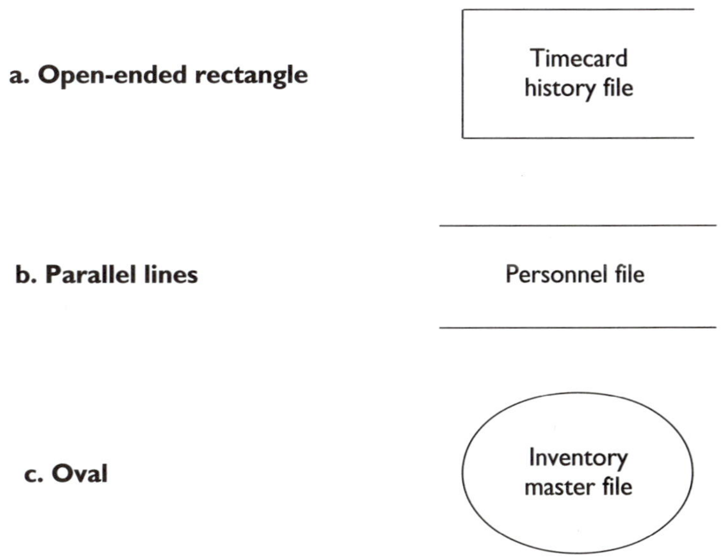

and data stores. However, once you decide on which symbols to use, or, more likely, your firm decides for you, you should consider the following tips.

- Although DFDs document a system in a top-down manner, it is frequently best to begin with a figure 0 diagram. At that level you identify the main processes and their linkages to each other and to the environment. When you are confident that the figure 0 diagram is a good picture of the basic system structure, you can complete the documentation by preparing the context diagram and lower-level DFDs. The context diagram is much easier to draw when you have a figure 0 diagram to serve as a guide.
- All environmental elements of the system should appear in the context diagram, in the figure 0 diagram, and in lower-level diagrams when they are involved with the data flow. Do not introduce a new environmental element on a lower-level DFD.
- Do not include data stores in context diagrams so those diagrams can remain as uncluttered as possible. Also, in the interest of simplicity, you might elect to not use data stores in a figure 0 diagram that contains a full page of processes and terminators.
- Do not use a process symbol to show that data is mailed from one location to another, or is filed away. In these cases, the form of the data is not changed. The data flow arrow is adequate for showing mailing and filing.
- When a process is documented with a lower-level DFD, all of the *connecting* data flows that have previously been defined on an upper level should also appear on the lower level, labeled *exactly* the same. See Figures B.3 and B.4 for an example. In Figure B.4, both of the data flows *(Sales orders* and *Item numbers)* entering process 1.1 are also inputs to process 1 in Figure B.3.
- When updating the records of a master file with transaction data, show a flow of master file records to be updated leading to the process, and another flow of updated master file records leading to the data store. Figure B.8 is an example.

Putting Data Flow Diagrams in Perspective

DFDs are a very natural way to document a system. The symbols and arrows are much like the notes you sketch on a note pad as you interview a user. The few symbols and the way that leveled DFDs allow the design to gradually unfold make DFDs especially appealing. However, DFDs are best suited to document systems on the higher hierarchical levels. For large, complex systems, they will also be supplemented with one or more other tools for the details. Structured English is a good way to provide the detail.

STRUCTURED ENGLISH

Information specialists who develop business systems have generally recognized that good documentation is important because the systems often have a life span of many years. The documentation is not only helpful in developing new systems but also in maintaining existing systems.

For many years information specialists relied on system and program flowcharts as their primary documentation tools. On the other hand, non-business information system users such as mathematicians and scientists have long done much of their own computing but their programs often do not have the life expectancy of business systems. A mathematician might create a program to perform a series of calculations and then never again use the program. In this setting the need for thorough documentation is not as great as in a business organization. For this reason, non-business users never felt a special loyalty to flowcharting and looked elsewhere for a more suitable tool. What they found was something that was given the name **pseudocode**—a narrative documentation that looks like information system code but is not. It is a shorthand way to jot down the main steps that must be performed.

The Origin of Structured English

Developers of business information systems recognized the merits of pseudocode but took issue with the fact that there were no guidelines. One programmer's pseudocode might look completely different from that of another programmer sitting at the next desk. Such individual differences in documentation were seen as a hindrance in a business setting. The information specialists saw a need for some standardization, which could provide a basis for control.

So information systems units in firms began to establish some pseudocode guidelines and the result was called structured English. **Structured English** is a shorthand way to document processes using a narrative that conforms to guidelines established within the firm in terms of structure and syntax.

A Structured English Example

Figure B.9 is an example of a program that is documented using structured English. The first line identifies the program name. Next, comes the driver module. The

FIGURE B.8

Updating a Master File

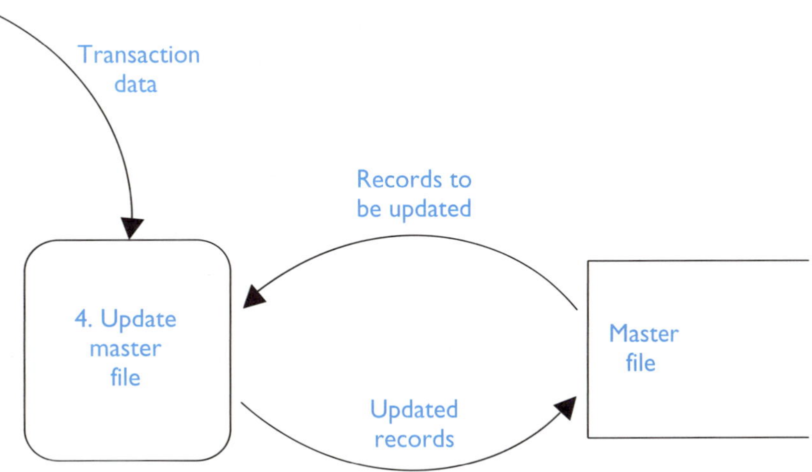

FIGURE B.9

Structured English Is Used to Model Process Detail

```
Verify Sales Orders
START
Perform Enter Sales Order Data
Perform Edit Sales Order Data
Perform Compute Order Amount
STOP
Enter Sales Order Data
   INPUT SALES.ORDER Data
Edit Sales Order Data
   Edit CUSTOMER.NUMBER by ensuring that it is a positive numeric field
   IF Edit Is Failed
      THEN WRITE REJECTED.SALES.ORDER Record
   END IF
   DO for Each Item
      EDIT ITEM.NUIMBER to ensure that it matches a number in the MASTER.ITEM.NUMBER.LIST
      IF Edit Is Failed
         THEN WRITE REJECTED.SALES.ORDER Record
      END IF
      EDIT UNIT.PRICE to ensure that it matches the price in the MATER.PRICE.LIST
      IF Edit Is Failed
         THEN WRITE REJECTED.SALES.ORDER Record
      END IF
      EDIT ITEM.QUANTITY to ensure that it is a positive numeric field
      IF Edit Is Failed
         THEN WRITE REJECTED.SALES.ORDER Record
      END IF
   END DO
Compute Order Amount
   IF no edit errors
      THEN DO for Each Item
               COMPUTE ORDER.AMOUNT = ITEM.QUANTITY *UNIT.PRICE
               COMPUTE ORDER.AMOUNT = ORDER.AMOUNT sum
      END DO
      WRITE ACCEPTED.SALES.ORDER Record
   END IF
```

driver module is that portion of a structured program that causes the submodules or subroutines to be executed in the proper sequence. The driver module is bounded by the words START and STOP. These words mark the logical beginning and end of the program.

Certain words are printed in uppercase, and there is quite a bit of indenting. Words in uppercase typically comprise *programming syntax,* such as INPUT, IF, THEN, END IF, and so on. Uppercase is also used to identify data that is defined in the *data dictionary.* Examples are SALES.ORDER and CUSTOMER.NUMBER.

Guidelines for Using Structured English

There are no generally accepted conventions for using structured English as there are for data flow diagramming. Rather, each firm decides on the format that its systems developers should use. However, the following guidelines give you some idea of a set that might be adopted. Most of these are tailored to structured programming.

- The structured format should consist of a driver module and subsidiary modules arranged in a hierarchy.
- The driver module should be bounded by the words START and STOP, which mark the logical beginning and end of the routine.
- The first line of each subsidiary module should be labeled with its name.
- Statements should consist of a verb and object, such as *Read sales order record* and *Print detail line.*
- The statements should be arranged in the same order as their processes are to be performed.
- Only the three structured programming constructs should be used. Figure B.10 illustrates these constructs, using program flowchart symbols. The sequence construct groups statements together that are executed one after the other. The selection construct represents IF/THEN logic, and the repetition construct controls looping.
- The contents of the selection and repetition constructs should be indented. In Figure B.9, the selection constructs begin with an IF statement, and end with an END IF statement. The word THEN is on a separate line, as is the word ELSE, when it is present. The repetition construct is bounded by DO and END DO statements.
- Uppercase should be used for all words that are typically found in a programming language—such as READ, COMPUTE, PRINT, IF, THEN, ELSE, and DO.
- Only data names that are described in the data dictionary should be used, and they should be printed in uppercase. Examples are PAYROLL.FILE, CUSTOMER-RECORD, and ITEM_NUMBER.
- You should keep in mind that you are *not* creating information system code and do not try to include every little detail. For example, in an information system program you might have to initialize main memory locations before proceeding with processing but in structured English you would not bother with such detail. The idea is to communicate the logic of a routine and not worry about how that logic will be implemented.

From this lengthy list of guidelines it is easy to get the idea that the term *structured* comes not from the hierarchical, modular design but from the high level of discipline that can be imposed. This is a good observation. Structured English is just like pseudocode, except for the rules.

Putting Structured English in Perspective

You can use structured English to document a system in a summary as well as a detailed fashion, but it is best suited to the detail. Structured English can provide the detail documentation that is not practical with DFDs. Therefore structured English and DFDs work together to provide all of the process documentation that is required.

Structured English is probably more appropriate for the programmer than the systems analyst. The systems analyst might not be expected to document systems in such

FIGURE B.10

Using Constructs of Structured Programming in Structured English

a. Sequence construct

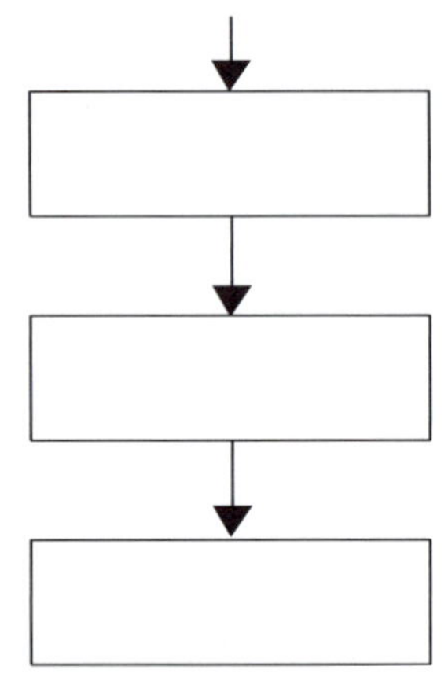

Perform Enter Sales Order Data
Perform Edit Sales Order Data
Perform Compute Order Amount

b. Selection construct

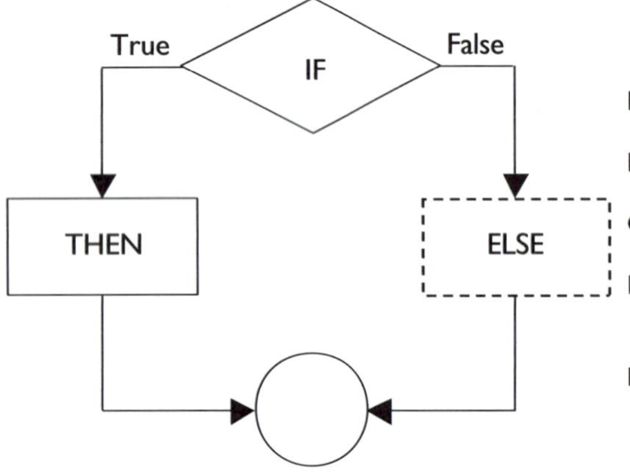

IF Edit Is Failed
THEN WRITE REJECTED.SALES.ORDER Record
END IF

Or

IF Edit Is Passed
THEN WRITE ACCEPTED.SALES.ORDER Record
ELSE WRITE REJECTED.SALES.ORDER Record
END IF

c. Repetition construct

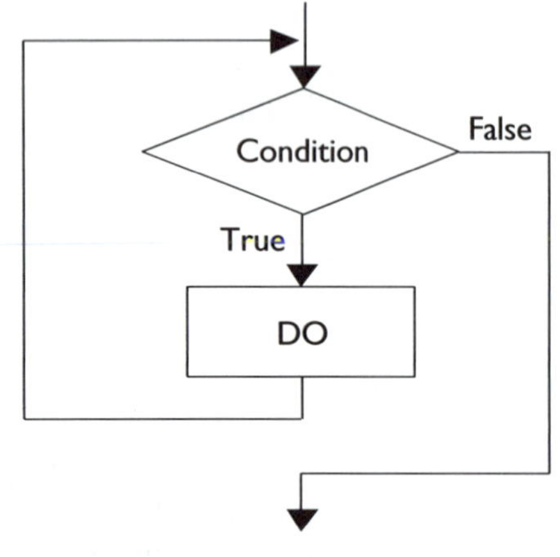

DO for Each Item
COMPUTE ITEM.AMOUNT = ITEM.QUANTITY * UNIT.PRICE
COMPUTE ORDER.AMOUNT = ORDER.AMOUNT Sum
END DO
WRITE ACCEPTED.SALES.ORDER Record

detail. Each firm must decide where to draw the line between the responsibilities of the analyst and those of the programmer.

KEY TERMS

data flow diagram (DFD)
decomposition diagram
context diagram
data flow
figure 0 diagram
data store
leveled DFDs
balanced DFDs
process
connector symbol
pseudocode
structured English

PROBLEMS

1. Draw a figure 0 diagram of the following procedure. Regard the employees as part of the system's environment. The transmittal of data from one location to another, without transforming it, is not a process.
   a. Employees provide the departmental secretary with their time cards that contain the hours worked for the week. The departmental secretary prepares a weekly time sheet that lists each employee, the total hours worked, and the hourly rate. The time cards are filed in a Time card history file.
   b. The departmental supervisor audits the time sheet and signs it if everything seems to be in order. If any of the figures are unacceptable, the sheet is returned to the secretary. The acceptable sheets from all of the departments are sent in the company mail to a clerical employee in the accounting department.
   c. The clerk uses the acceptable time sheets to calculate payroll earnings, which are written on the time sheets.
   d. Another clerk uses the time sheets to prepare the payroll checks, which are forwarded to the employees. After this operation, the time sheets are filed in a Time sheet history file.
2. Draw a context diagram of the system described in Problem 1.
3. Draw a figure 0 diagram of the following system used by a bank to open new checking accounts. Regard the customer and the new account department as elements in the system's environment. Also, regard each information system program as a separate process.
   a. The customer provides the bank with a completed new account application form.
   b. A data entry operator enters data from the new account application form into the information system, using a keyboard terminal. Label the output of this process *Entered new account data.*
   c. The information system edits the new account data and prepares an error listing of all applications that contain errors. The error listing is sent to the new accounts department. New account data that does not contain errors is written onto a magnetic tape file named New account file.
   d. The New account file is input to another computer program that adds the new account data to the Customer master file, on magnetic disk, and prints the transactions on a transaction listing. The listing is sent to the new accounts department.
4. Draw a context diagram of the system described in Problem 3.
5. Draw a figure 0 diagram of the following system that processes supplier receipts. Regard the suppliers and the purchasing department as part of the system's environment.
   a. When the firm receives shipments from suppliers, packing lists are enclosed in the cartons. A data entry operator keys the packing list data into the computer, and then files the packing lists in a Packing list history file.

b. The computer program obtains the corresponding records from the Outstanding purchase order file, on magnetic disk. The same program prints a report named the received purchases report, which is sent to the purchasing department through the company mail, and writes a Supplier payables file, on magnetic disk.

c. The Supplier payables file is input to another program that obtains supplier data from the disk-based Supplier master file and prepares checks that are mailed to the suppliers. The same program that prints the checks also creates a Supplier check history file, on magnetic tape.

6. Draw a context diagram of the system described in Problem 5.
7. Use structured English to document the following processes, which the departmental supervisor performs when auditing time sheets.

a. The supervisor examines the sheet and signs it if everything is in order.

b. If any figures are unacceptable, the supervisor returns the sheet to the secretary.

c. The acceptable sheets from all departments are sent in the company mail to the accounting department.

Selected Bibliography

Abdel-Hamid, T., and S. Madnick. *Software Project Dynamics* (Englewood Cliffs, N.J.: Prentice-Hall, 1991).

Madachy R. *Software Process Modeling with System Dynamics* (Washington, D.C.: IEEE Computer Society Press, 1997).

Note

1. For more information on the Gane-Sarson approach, see Chris Gane and Trish Sarson, *"Structured Systems Analysis: Tools and Techniques* (Englewood Cliffs, N.J.: Prentice-Hall, 1979). For more information on the Yourdon-Constantine approach, see Edward Yourdon, *Modern Structured Analysis* (Englewood Cliffs, N.J.: Yourdon Press, 1989).

TECHNICAL MODULE C

OBJECT MODELING

When the first computer applications were developed, during the 1950s and 60s, the emphasis was on the processes to be performed. Data took a back seat, with the programmers creating the files and record formats that were required by their programs. This situation of individuals, rather than organizations, determining data needs led to such inefficiencies as redundant files, out-of-date data, and files that would not balance. During the early 1970s, software vendors began to recognize the need for packaged programs that would manage a firm's data resources and developed database management systems (DBMSs). The database software enabled firms to shift emphasis from processes to data when developing systems. Firms could take a data-oriented approach, first defining the data needs for the entire organization and then developing the necessary programs to process the data.

OBJECTS AND OBJECT-ORIENTED PROGRAMMING

During the period of process- and data-oriented development, a movement began that would lead to a third major approach—combining data and processes into objects. An **object** is a valuable resource of the firm that the firm describes with data. Examples of objects are customers, inventory items, and salespersons. This movement toward objects began in 1967 at the programming level with an object-oriented (O-O) language named Simula-67. Next came a language named Smalltalk in the early 1980s, followed by such other languages as C++ and Eiffel.

Object-oriented programming quickly developed a strong following. The ability to subdivide large programs into objects meant that teams of only one-third the normal size could do the work, enabling the firm to spread its programming resources over more projects.[1] The smaller objects also made debugging much easier and facilitated reusability of code in multiple systems. The success of object-oriented programming called attention to the need for taking an object-oriented approach throughout the SDLC.

Object-Oriented System Development

As systems developers sought to apply the concept of integrated data and process objects to the early stages of the SDLC, a wide variety of approaches were identified.[2] Although the many books on O-O development that came on the market during the late 1980s and early 1990s created confusion as developers sought to follow the best approach, they identified a pool of core concepts.

Two O-O pioneers who made substantial contributions were Grady Booch (famous for Booch diagrams and operations) and James Rumbaugh (who originated object model technology, or OMT). They teamed up at Rational Software Corporation in 1994 and were joined by another pioneer, Ivar Jacobson. Together, these three developers combined their own core concepts and those of others to create what became known as the unified modeling language (UML). In November 1997, the Object Management Group (OMG) adopted UML as the standard object-oriented modeling approach. At long last, developers who wanted to pursue an object-oriented development had a single path to follow.

What Is UML?

The unified modeling language (UML) is a general-purpose visual language used to specify, visualize, construct, and document the artifacts of a software system.[3] The word "unified" means that it is applicable to all system development methodologies, to all SDLC stages, and to all applications (business and nonbusiness alike), and can be used with all implementation languages and platforms. It is intended to be supported by other visual modeling languages in the form of code generators and report writers.

Concept Areas

The UML object modeling tools consist of nine types of diagrams grouped into two major concept areas—system structure and system behavior. System structure focuses on the objects that comprise a system and their relationships, whereas system behavior addresses the dynamic nature of objects as they respond to events, perform actions, and transition to new states. The resulting diagram classifications are *structural* and *dynamic.*

Structural Diagrams

System structure is documented with use case diagrams, class diagrams, object diagrams, component diagrams, and deployment diagrams. These structural diagrams can be thought of as snapshots of the system—capturing features at a particular point in time.

- *Use case diagrams*—A use case diagram is prepared from a use case description or report, such as the one described in Chapter 5, and identifies the use cases that comprise a system and shows how the users interact with each.
- *Class diagrams*—A class diagram groups the objects of a use case into classes and shows the relationships among the classes.
- *Object diagrams*—An object diagram has the same general appearance as a class diagram but shows examples of objects at a particular point in time.

- *Component diagrams*—A component diagram shows the software and database components of a use case and the interfaces that connect them, along with linkages with the various users.
- *Deployment diagram*—A deployment diagram packages the software and database components with the hardware resources that they use (called nodes) and shows the communication links that connect the nodes.

These diagrams document the static nature of a system as it evolves through the development stages.

Dynamic Diagrams

The dynamic nature of a system is documented with sequence diagrams, statechart diagrams, activity diagrams, and collaboration diagrams. These diagrams are like videos of the system in action.

- *Sequence diagrams*—A sequence diagram illustrates how the object classes of a use case are linked by sequences of messages. A **message** is a communication of information from one object class to another that is intended to result in some kind of activity by the receiving class.
- *Statechart diagrams*—A statechart diagram, also called a state diagram, shows the various states of an object class as it evolves from its initial state to its final state.
- *Activity diagrams*—An activity diagram illustrates the high-level behavior of a use case. The system can consist of human workflows, software activities, or both.
- *Collaboration diagrams*—A collaboration diagram has the same general appearance as a class diagram but identifies the messages that comprise the linkages among the object classes. The direction of the message flow is shown, along with message numbers that indicate the sequence in which the messages are sent.

On the following pages of this technical module, we describe four of the diagrams in detail—use case, class, sequence, and statechart. We follow these detailed descriptions with summary descriptions of the remaining diagrams. The four types of diagrams that are described in detail provide the foundation upon which object-oriented systems are built.

Object-Oriented Methodology

We have recognized that UML is a visual language. It is a way to document the features of a system. This documentation must be implemented in order to put the system into production. Any methodology can be used to guide the development and implementation but one has been specially tailored to the task. It is the rational unified process, which consists of four stages or phases:

- Inception
- Elaboration
- Construction
- Transition

Each of these stages can be broken down into iterations. In this way, it is very similar to the phased development methodology that is emphasized throughout the text.

Use Case Diagram

During the preliminary investigation and analysis stages, the developers prepare written use case reports. Each use case describes how users interact with the system as it processes the users' transactions. Although the use case is essentially a "black box" view of the system, explaining what the system does rather than how it does it, the use cases can be revised as the development process moves from stage to stage to increasingly incorporate greater detail, technology, and implementation considerations.

A **use case diagram** is a graphic representation of the key features of the written use case reports that comprise a system, and consists of the features illustrated in Figure C.1 and listed below.

- The boundary of the system is defined with the rectangle.
- The system name can either be on top of the rectangle or inside.
- Each use case that is included in the system is illustrated with an oval and identified with its name, which is in the form of a verb and an object.
- The external entities with which the system interfaces are called **actors,** who are located outside the system boundary. Actors can be organizations,

Figure C.1

Use Case Diagram Format

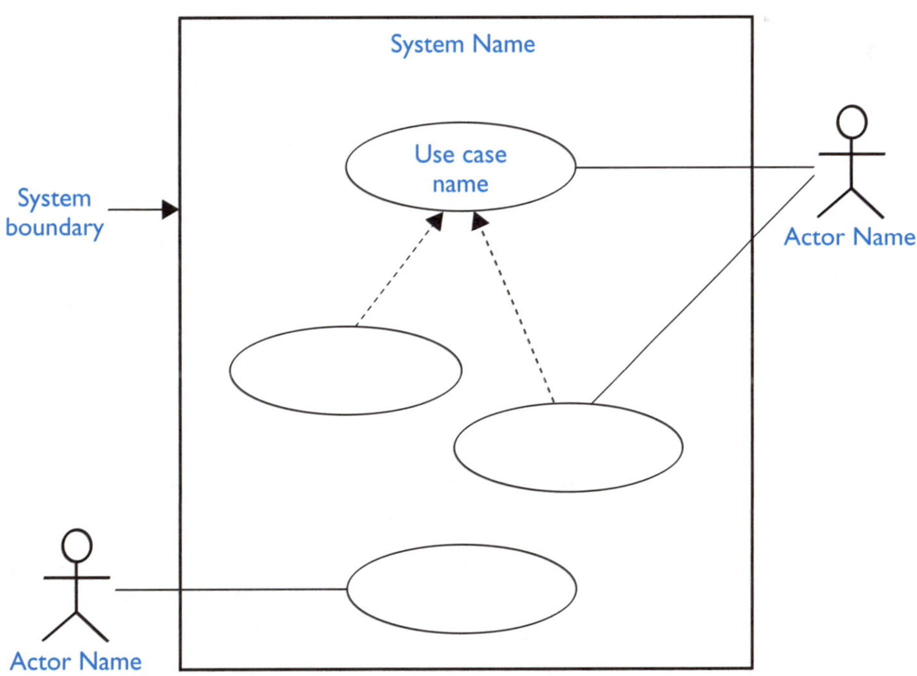

FIGURE C.2

The Process Customer Order Use Case Diagram

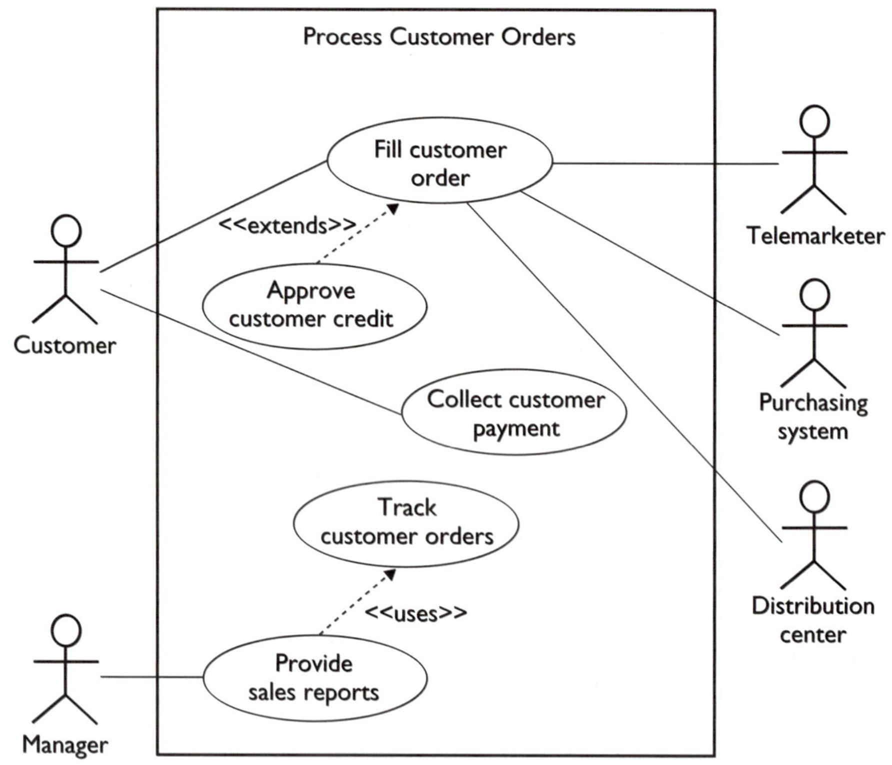

individuals, places, or other systems and are illustrated with stickfigures regardless of type. The actor names appear next to the stickfigures.

- Linkages between actors and use cases and between use cases are called **associations.** Associations that connect actors to use cases are shown with solid lines. Associations that connect use cases are shown with dashed-line arrows.

The purpose of the use case diagram is to provide a high-level view of a system. It is a good starting point for the object modeling effort.

Special Use Case Associations

It is not necessary that the use cases be connected; each can provide functionality in a stand-alone manner. There are times, however, when linkages exist, and they are illustrated with the dashed-line arrows.

- *Extensions*—In some situations, one use case augments the functionality of another. These types of associations are called **extensions.** Extensions are illustrated with an arrow labeled <<extends>>.

- *Uses*—Another situation arises when some functionality is shared by two or more use cases. Here, a separate use case is created for the common functionality and the original use cases make use of the shared use case. These types of associations are called **uses** and the corresponding arrows are labeled <<uses>>.

These special cases do not occur for all associations. When they are absent, the dashed-line arrows are unlabeled.

A Sample Use Case Diagram

Figure C.2 is a use case diagram of a system that processes customer sales orders and consists of five use cases.

- *Fill customer order*—In the Fill customer order use case, a customer places an order by telephone and a telemarketer gathers the required information and enters it in the customer sales order system. The system determines whether sufficient inventory exists. When it does, the distribution center is notified to ship the merchandise. When the product balance-on-hand reaches the reorder point, the purchasing system is notified to purchase replenishment stock.
- *Approve customer credit*—The Approve customer credit use case extends the Fill customer order use case by providing a credit check.
- *Collect customer payments*—The Collect customer payments use case maintains the accounts receivable and collects the customer payments.
- *Track customer orders*—The Track customer orders use case captures key data about each sale.
- *Provide sales reports*—The Provide sales reports use case uses the customer order data to prepare reports for management.

This example shows that associations need not exist between all use cases. It also shows how the actors can be organizations (such as customer firms), individuals (telemarketer and manager), other systems (purchasing), and places (distribution center).

FIGURE C.3

Class Diagram Format

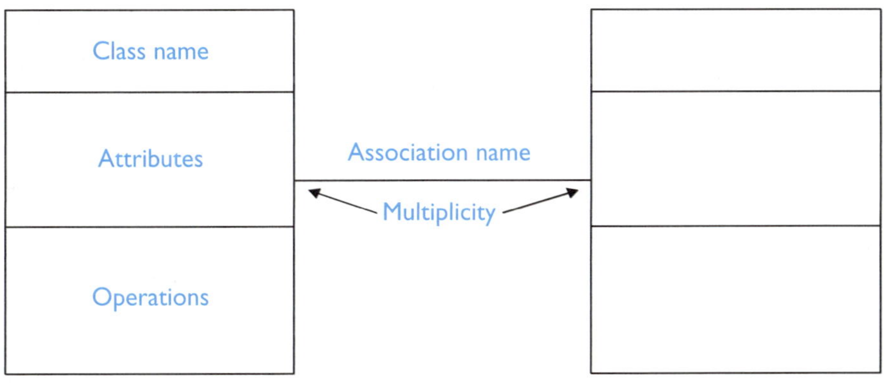

FIGURE C.4

A Unary Association

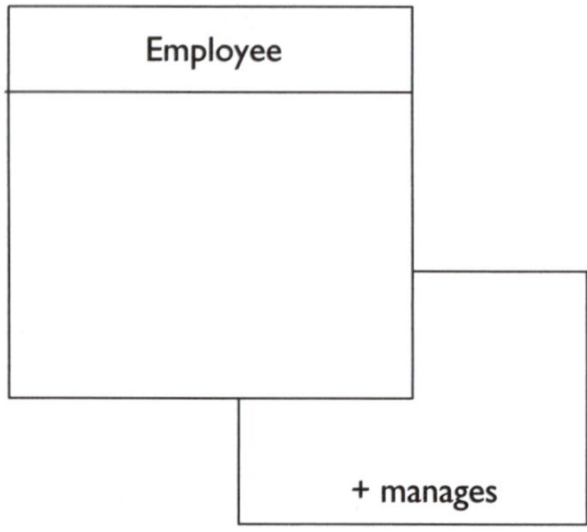

Putting the Use Case Diagram in Perspective

As the system developers work to gain an understanding of the user's system needs, they communicate to produce use case narratives or reports. With the reports approved by the user, they serve as the basis for the development process, which can follow a data, process, or object orientation. When an object orientation is to be followed, the contents of the narrative use cases are transformed to the graphical representation of the use case diagram. The starting point of object modeling is the use case diagram.

The ASTA team followed such an approach in modeling the ASTA skill set objects. They first prepared narrative use cases of the Search skill set and Request reports use cases (see Figures CS 4.4 and 4.5). Then, they prepared two use case diagrams—a high-level version (Figure CS 4.6) and a drill-down version on a lower level (Figure CS 4.7).

CLASS DIAGRAM

In a class diagram, similar objects are grouped in an **object class.** Each object is an instance of its class. For example, each of the firm's salespersons is an instance of the Salesperson object class. The object class therefore represents a group of objects that all exhibit a common structure and a common behavior.

The **class diagram** illustrates how the object classes of a use case are related. It is similar in appearance to an entity-relationship diagram (ERD), showing objects (rather than entities) and their relationships. However, the two diagrams are different in that the scope of the class diagram is much narrower—limited to the classes in a single use case rather than showing the entities in an entire system or enterprise. And, the class diagram identifies processes whereas the ERD does not. The different features of a class diagram are illustrated in Figure C.3 and listed below.

- Classes are illustrated with upright rectangles.
- The rectangle is subdivided into three parts. The upper part contains the class name. The middle part contains the attributes that describe the objects that

comprise the class (just as attributes in data modeling describe entity types). The lower part contains the operations that the objects can perform.

- Relationships among classes are also called associations and are shown with lines.
- The association lines are labeled with the name of the relationship.
- Each end of the association line contains an indication of how many times the class can participate in the relationship, called the multiplicity.

Class Associations

Class associations can be unary (one class related to itself), binary (two related classes, as in Figure C.3), ternary (three related classes), and n-ary (more than three classes related to each other). Binary associations are the most common, and unary associations are the most rare. A unary association is illustrated in Figure C.4. It shows how an employee (a manager) manages an employee (a subordinate).

Unary associations are labeled with a plus sign followed by the operation that one object performs on the other(s). Ternary and n-ary associations are illustrated with a diamond symbol that contains the name of the association, as pictured in Figure C.5

Aggregation and Generalization

There are two special forms of associations, and they are illustrated in Figure C.6. Figure C.6a illustrates an **aggregation association** where one superclass is composed of multiple subclasses. A **superclass** is a class that has subsidiary classes; a **subclass** is a class within a class. An example of an aggregation association is a

FIGURE C.5

A Ternary Association

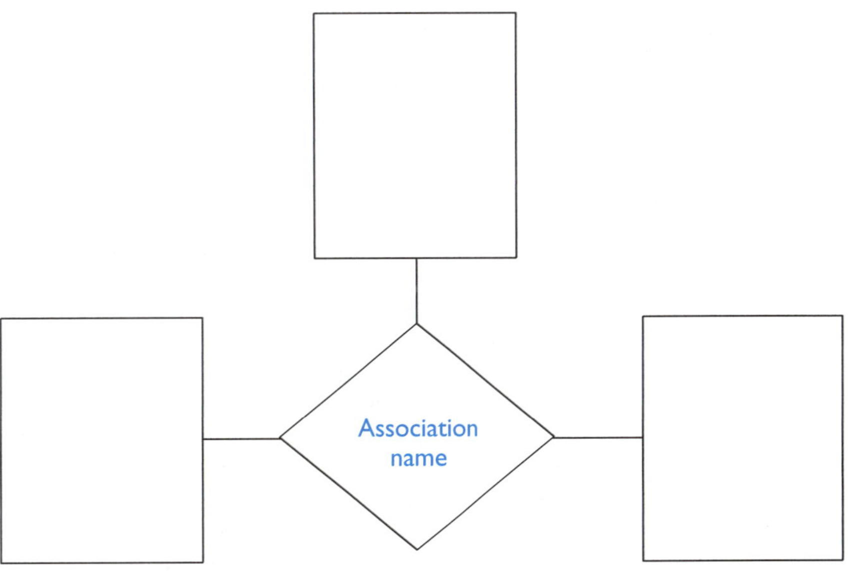

FIGURE C.6

Special Relationships

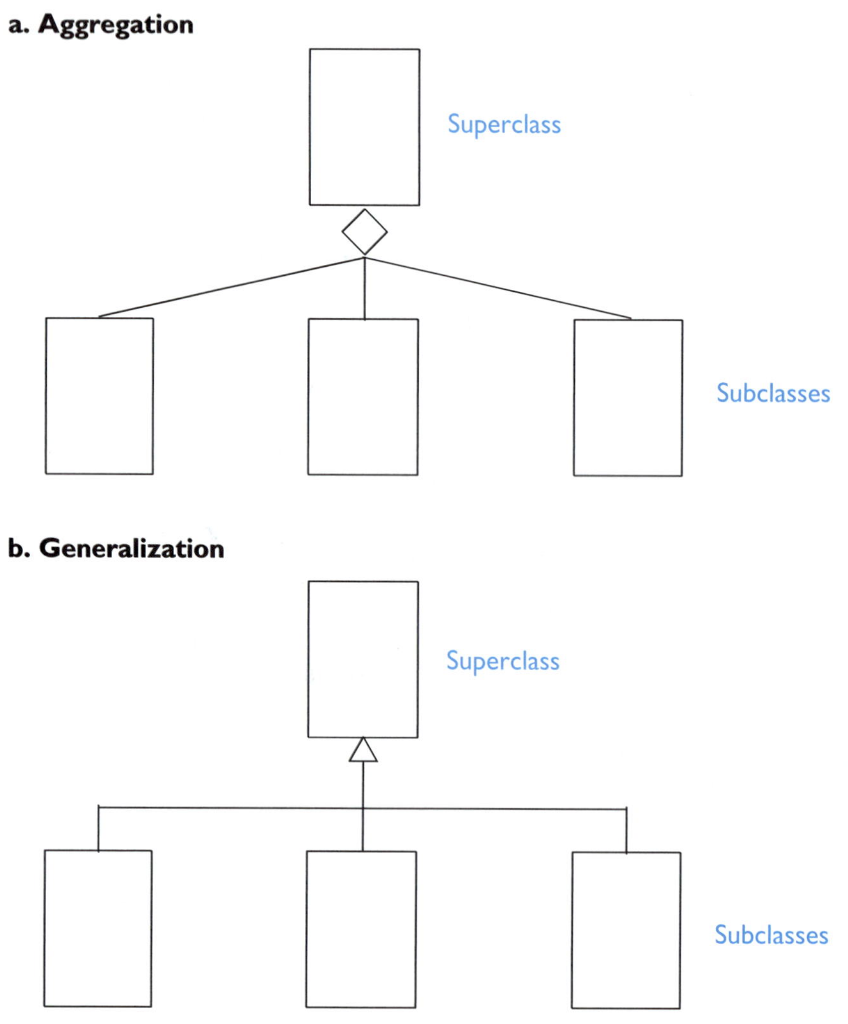

customer support team, which consists of sales rep, technical rep, and maintenance rep subclasses. A diamond is positioned at the point where the connecting lines from the subclasses attach to the superclass. The aggregation association represents a "whole-part" relationship, where the whole (the superclass) is composed of the parts (the subclasses). Another term that is used is "has-a," meaning that the superclass *has* a subclass.

Figure C.6b illustrates a **generalization association** where different types of an object class exist. This type of association has been described as a "is-a-kind-of" relationship, where the subclass is a *kind* of the superclass. An example is where there are different types of the superclass Customer-Profit seeking organization, Not-for-profit organization, and Government organization. A Profit seeking organization "is a form of" Customer. A hollow arrow connects the subclasses to the superclass.

TABLE C.1

Multiplicity Notation

Multiplicity	Explanation
1	One and only one
0..*	None or more
1..*	One or more
0..1	None or one
n..n	A continuous range, such as 2 to 4
n..n, n	A disjointed range, such as 1 to 6, 8

Multiplicity

The number of times that an object can participate in an association is called the **multiplicity.** Table C.1 shows the values that are used. A range is indicated with two values separated by two decimal points; the first is the minimum value and the second is the maximum. An asterisk indicates infinity.

In the case of a many-to-many association, it is necessary to create an additional class, called an **association class.** Figure C.7 shows a many-to-many association between customer order and product. A customer order can contain many (one or more) products, and a product can be contained on many (none or more) customer

FIGURE C.7

An Association Class

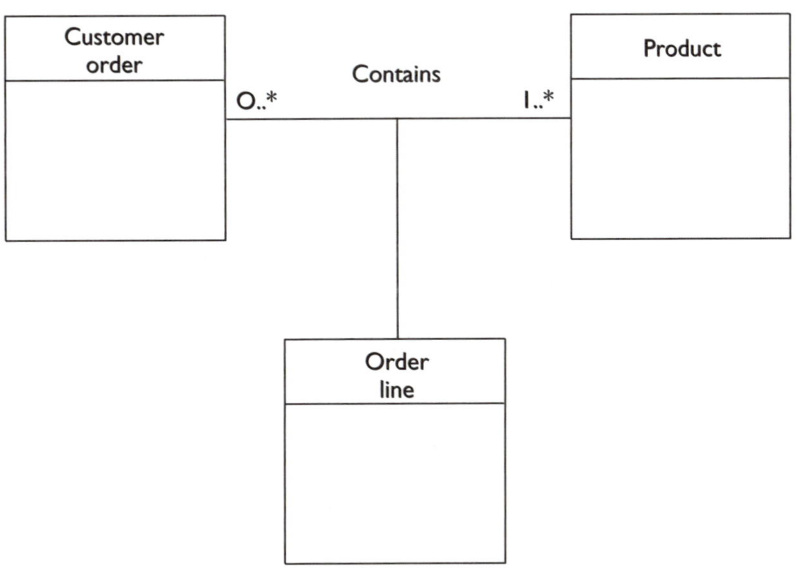

FIGURE C.8

Sample Attribute Names

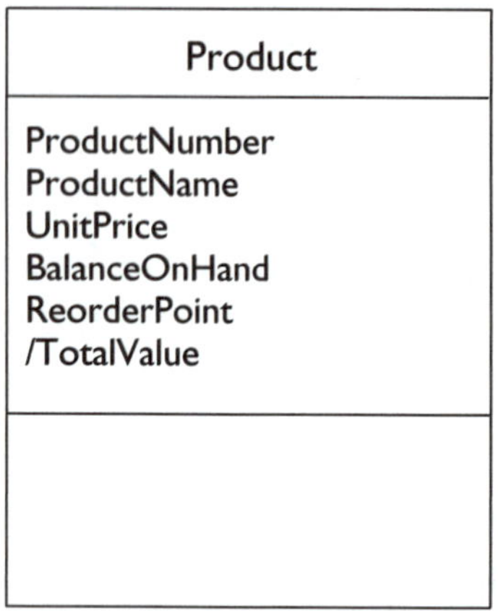

orders. In this example, an association class called order line is created. A customer order can contain multiple order lines but an order line can be contained on only a single customer order. Likewise, a product can be contained on multiple order lines but an order line can contain only a single product. In this example, the multiplicity for the order line is assumed to be 1.

Class Names

Each class is identified by a singular name such as Customer, Sales order, or Inventory item. Each instance of a class is unique; no two are the same. The software system assigns a unique identifier to each instance, which is usually hidden from the user.

Class Attributes

Attributes, or **properties,** are those data elements that can distinguish one instance of an object from another. Figure C.8 illustrates some attributes for the Product object class. A common naming format, shown here, is to combine attribute words without intervening spaces and to capitalize the first letter of each word.

Some attributes can be calculated from other attributes and are called **derived attributes.** These are identified with a diagonal (/) immediately preceding the name. An example in the figure is /TotalValue of the product inventory, obtained by multiplying the UnitPrice by the BalanceOnHand.

Class Operations

Operations, or **methods,** are the processes that a class performs. The operations are listed in the lower section of the object class symbol, as shown in Figure C.9. The operations in this example are typical; the first three (add, update, and delete) perform the basic functions of maintaining the class in a current status, the next two (compute) perform arithmetic operations on the class data, and the final one (answer) enables the class to answer queries. A common technique is to delete spaces between words, use a lowercase letter for the first character of the first word, and use uppercase letters for the first characters of other words. The operation name is followed by a set of parentheses. If a parameter exists for performing the method, it is included within the parentheses; otherwise the parentheses are positioned together, with no intervening space.

The operations list only identifies what operations are performed, not *how* they are performed. This hiding of details to the observer is called **encapsulation.** Operations are triggered by messages received from other objects. Messages are not shown on the class diagram, but appear on other diagrams.

Inheritance

One of the strengths of object modeling is that only the attributes and operations that are unique to an object are maintained by that object. Attributes and operations that are appropriate for a subclass can be obtained from a superclass, a concept called **inheritance.** For example, assume that a superclass and a subclass are associated as shown in Figure C.10. An open arrow leading to the superclass indicates inheritance.

The Employee class includes attributes and operations that are common to all employees. The Buyer class consists of employees in the purchasing department who make purchases from suppliers. The Buyer attributes and operations are only those unique to the buying function. The attributes and operations that are common to all employees are inherited from the Employee class.

A Sample Class Diagram

Figure C.11 is a class diagram for the Fill customer order use case. One customer can place many customer orders, and one telemarketer can enter data describing many customer orders. A many-to-many association exists between Customer order and Product, creating the need to add the association class named Order line. A

FIGURE C.9

Sample Operation Names

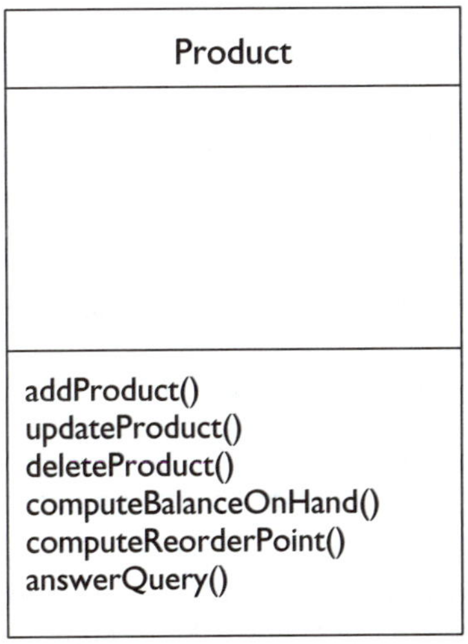

Product
addProduct() updateProduct() deleteProduct() computeBalanceOnHand() computeReorderPoint() answerQuery()

FIGURE C.10

Inheritance Illustrated

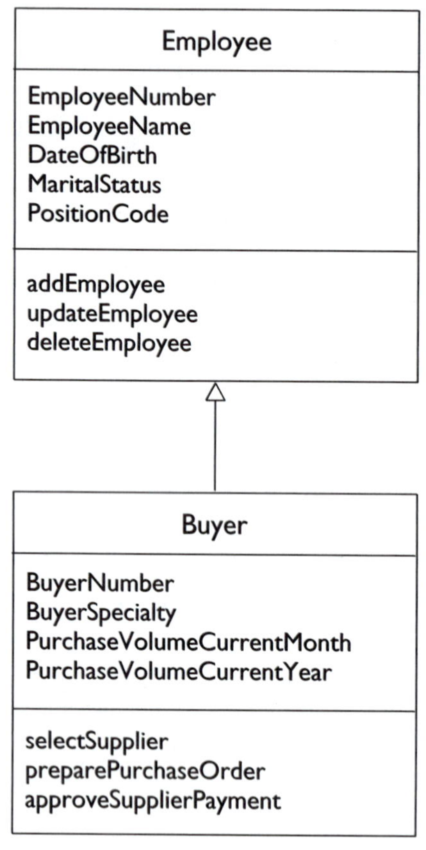

many-to-many association also exists between Product and Invoice, causing a second association class to be added for Invoice line.

Putting the Class Diagram in Perspective

The basic idea of object-oriented development is to express the components of the system as object classes, with each instance containing its own attributes and operations. The class diagram shows the object classes that are involved with a use case, along with the associations that exist among the classes. For each class, the diagram shows the attributes and operations. The diagram is a structural blueprint of the use case.

SEQUENCE DIAGRAM

Like the use case diagram, the **sequence diagram** is a dynamic model. It shows how the object classes of a use case communicate with each other by means of messages. Figure C.12 shows the symbols and how they are arranged.

Figure C.11

Class Diagram for the Fill Customer Order Use Case

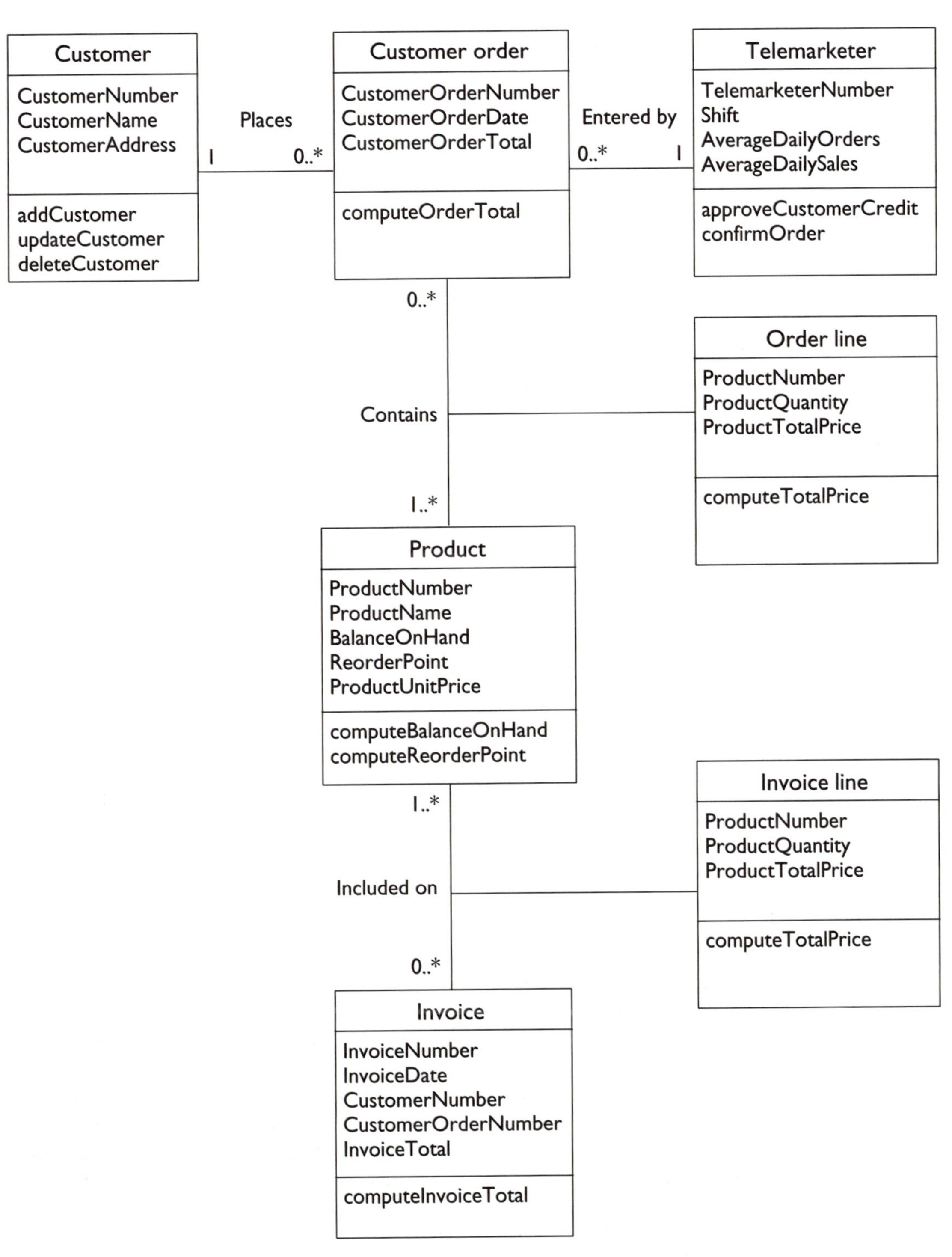
Customer
CustomerNumber
CustomerName
CustomerAddress
addCustomer
updateCustomer
deleteCustomer
Places
1
0..*
Customer order
CustomerOrderNumber
CustomerOrderDate
CustomerOrderTotal
computeOrderTotal
Entered by
0..*
1
Telemarketer
TelemarketerNumber
Shift
AverageDailyOrders
AverageDailySales
approveCustomerCredit
confirmOrder
0..*
Contains
1..*
Order line
ProductNumber
ProductQuantity
ProductTotalPrice
computeTotalPrice
Product
ProductNumber
ProductName
BalanceOnHand
ReorderPoint
ProductUnitPrice
computeBalanceOnHand
computeReorderPoint
1..*
Included on
0..*
Invoice line
ProductNumber
ProductQuantity
ProductTotalPrice
computeTotalPrice
Invoice
InvoiceNumber
InvoiceDate
CustomerNumber
CustomerOrderNumber
InvoiceTotal
computeInvoiceTotal

FIGURE C.12

Sequence Diagram Format

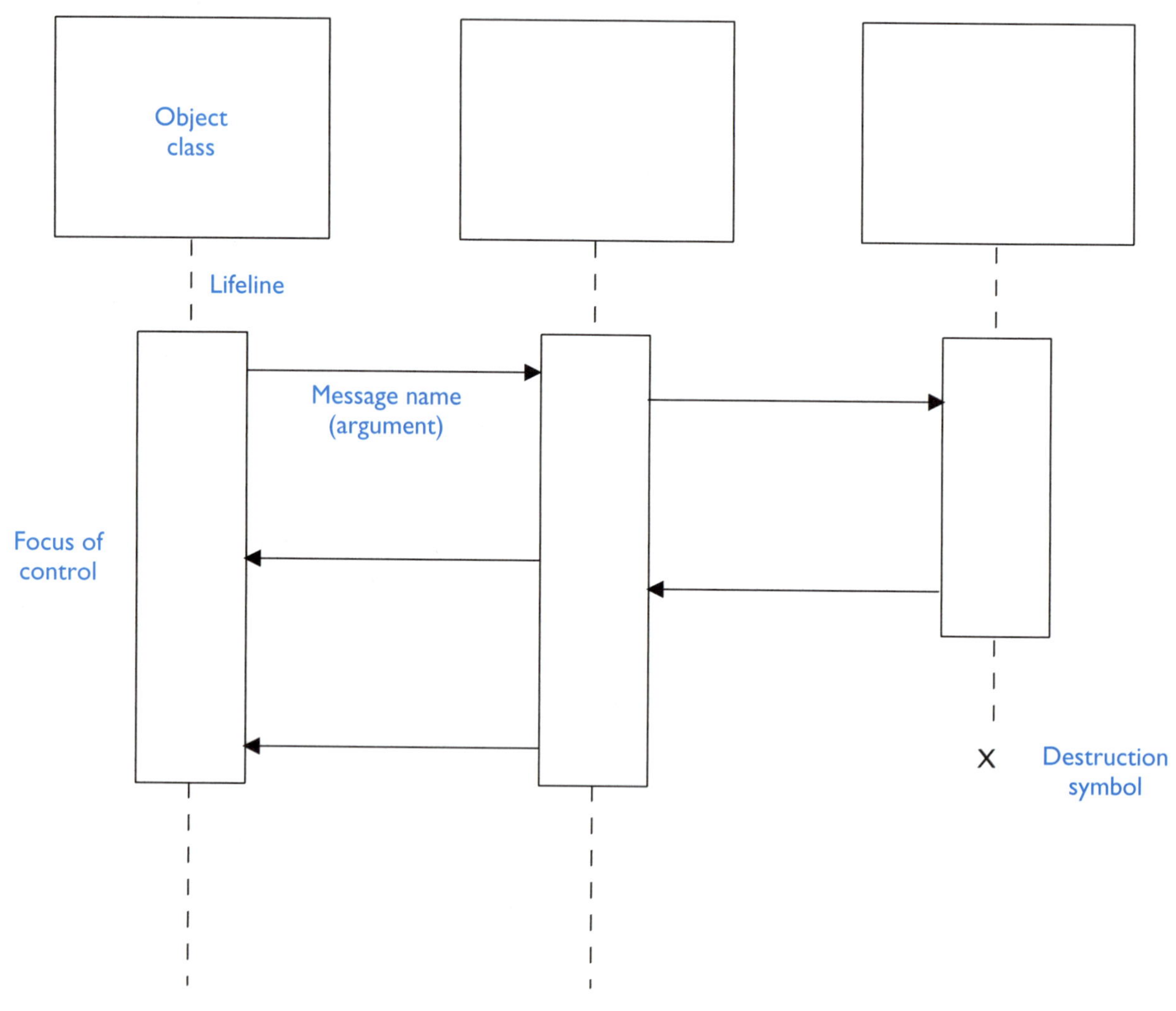

The object classes are arranged across the top of the diagram. The vertical dashed lines beneath the classes indicate their participation in the use case. The lines are called **lifelines.** They indicate that the objects are available to send and receive messages.

The lower portion of the diagram contains the messages that provide the communications among object classes. There are two basic kinds of messages. A **synchronous message** is one sent by a calling object that then suspends operation, waiting for a response. An **asynchronous message** is one sent by a calling object that does not wait for a response. The messages are illustrated with horizontal arrows and are listed in the order in which they are sent and received, reading from top to bottom. Each message is labeled with a message name, followed by any argument value or values in parentheses.

When an object class is sending or receiving a message, a vertical rectangle is positioned on top of the lifeline. This rectangle is named the **focus of control** or the **activation line** and it indicates that the lifeline is activated. If an object is destroyed during the use case, an X is attached to the end of the lifeline.

A Sample Sequence Diagram

Figure C.13 is a sequence diagram of the Fill customer order use case. The use case diagram (shown in Figure C.2) provides a good starting point to determine whether the external actors should be included as objects, and consider which databases will be required.

If the class diagram has been prepared prior to preparing the sequence diagram, the class diagram can be used as a basis for identifying the classes. These two diagrams may be prepared at the same time, refining one to reflect work done on the other.

The object classes that are selected for inclusion in the Fill customer order sequence diagram include customer, telemarketer, customer order, product, and invoice. The purchasing system and distribution center were identified as actors in the

FIGURE C.13

Sequence Diagram of the Fill Customer Order Use Case

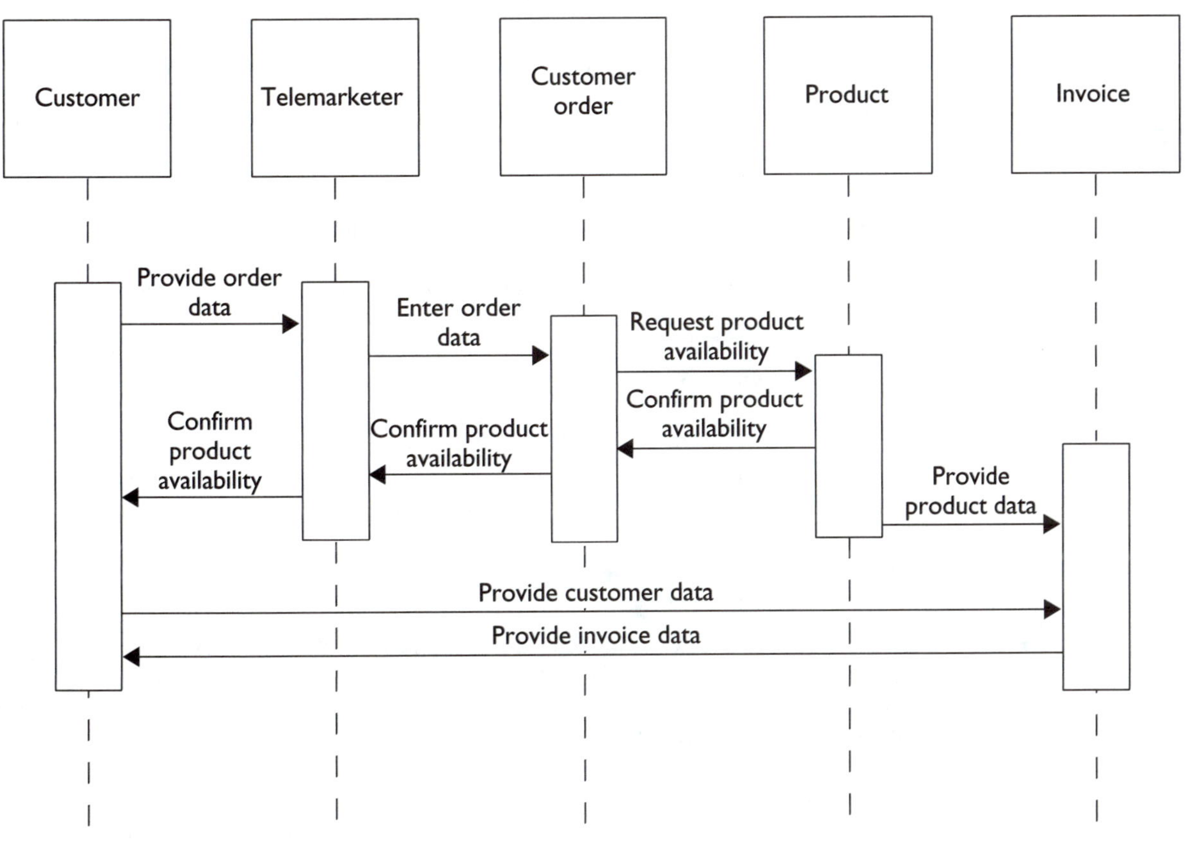

FIGURE C.14

Statechart Diagram Format

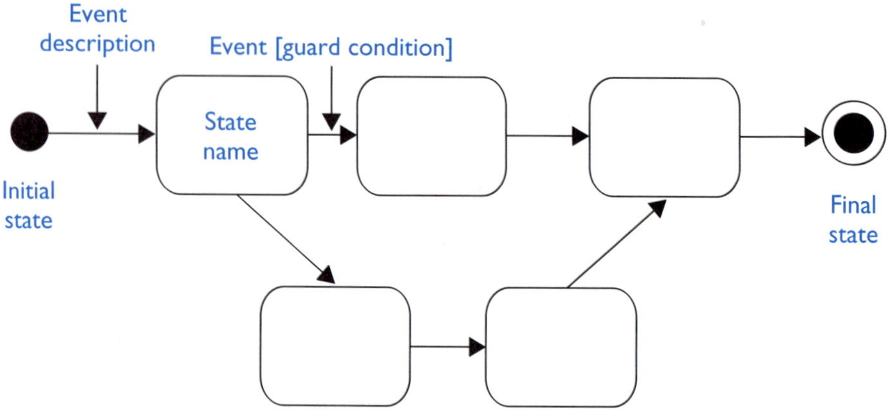

Figure C.2 use case diagram, however they are not objects since they do not have instances that are described with data.

Messages are transmitted in the top-to-bottom order shown.

- The customer provides order data to the telemarketer.
- The telemarketer enters the order data into the customer order.
- The customer order requests availability of the ordered product.
- The product confirms product availability to the customer order.
- The customer order confirms product availability to the telemarketer.
- The telemarketer confirms product availability to the customer.
- The product provides product data to the Invoice for use in preparing the invoice body.
- The invoice provides invoice data to the customer.

In order for an object to perform an operation, the operation must be specified in the operation area of the object, and a message must be received to trigger the operation.

Putting the Sequence Diagram in Perspective

Objects communicate with each other by means of messages. An object only performs its operations when requested to do so by a message. Therefore an important part of object modeling is to identify the messages that will link the objects. This identification is accomplished with the sequence diagram.

The sequence diagram and the class diagram provide the foundation for object-oriented system development, with the class diagram providing a static picture and the sequence diagram providing a dynamic picture of the objects and their communication linkages.

Statechart Diagram

A **statechart diagram,** also frequently called a **state chart,** is a dynamic model that shows the different states that an object assumes as the use case operations evolve. The state of an object is determined by its attributes and its associations with other objects. Figure C.14 shows the statechart symbols and their arrangement.

The beginning point of the diagram is called the **initial state,** and it is illustrated with a small, solid circle. The ending point of the diagram is called the **final state** and is illustrated with the same solid circle, within a slightly larger circle. Each state is shown as a rectangle with rounded corners, labeled with the name of the state. The events that trigger a state transition are shown as arrows labeled with the name of the events.

It is possible to integrate a certain amount of logic into the diagram to allow a transition only if a condition is true. This control is accomplished with a **guard condition,** which is a Boolean expression that is evaluated in a true/false manner as a prerequi-

Figure C.15

Statechart Diagram of the Customer Order Object

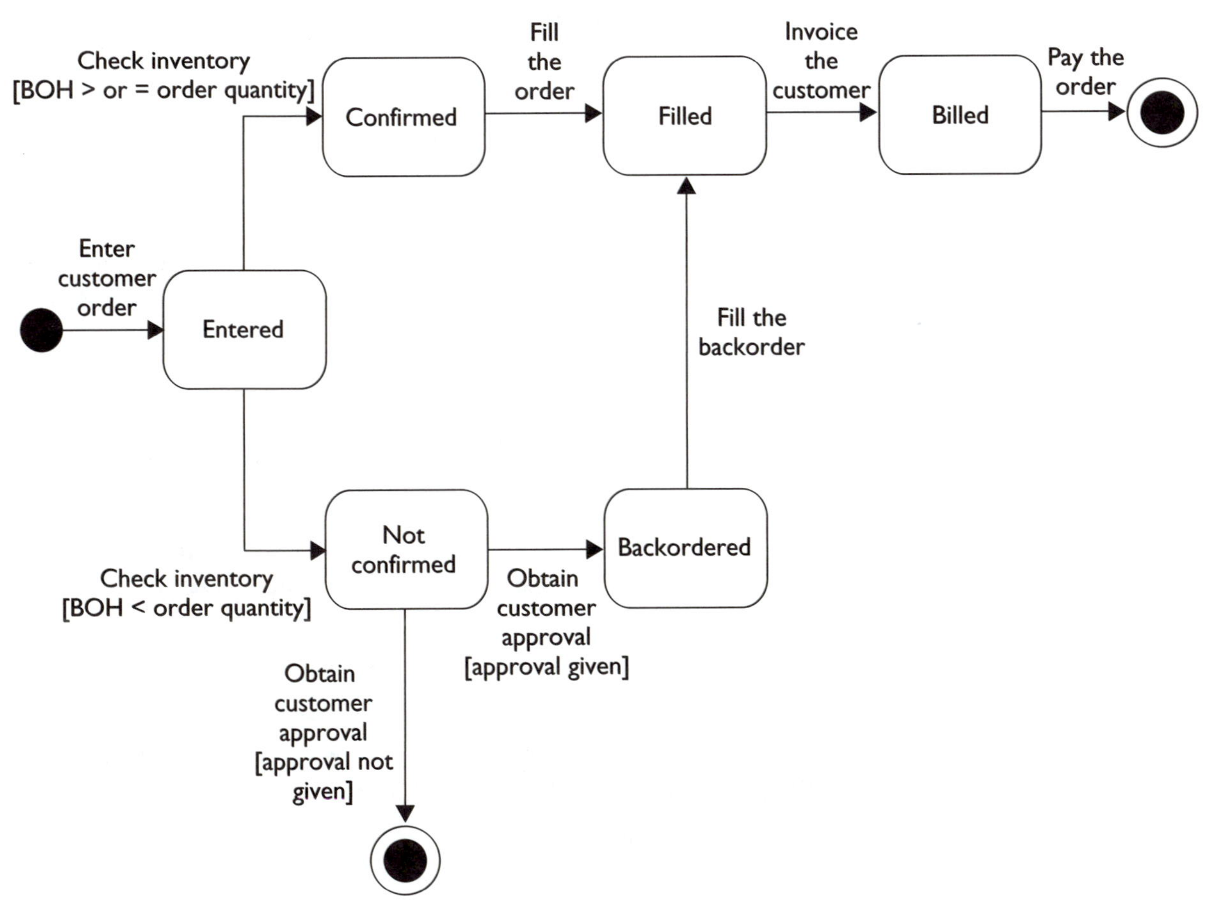

FIGURE C.16

Object Diagram of the Customer Order and Product Objects

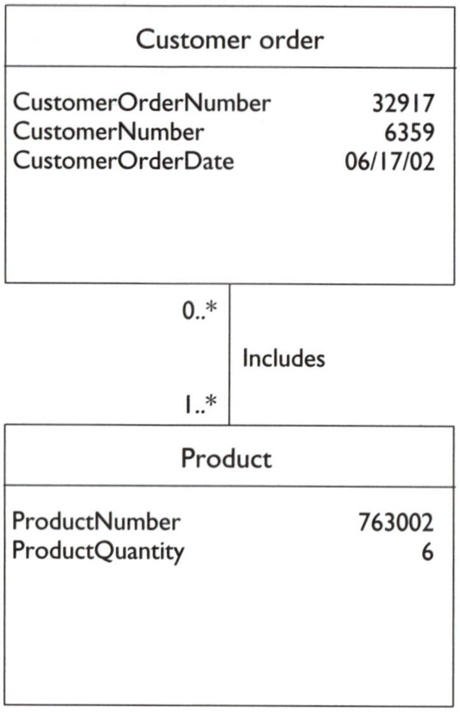

Customer order	
CustomerOrderNumber	32917
CustomerNumber	6359
CustomerOrderDate	06/17/02

0..* Includes 1..*

Product	
ProductNumber	763002
ProductQuantity	6

site for the transition to occur. For example, if a transition is labeled *enter order [amount > $1000]* the state is changed only if the amount is greater than $1000.

A Sample Statechart Diagram

Figure C.15 is a statechart diagram of the customer order object.

- The *initial state* signals the beginning of existence for the object when the customer order is entered. Then, the object state becomes *Entered.*
- A check of the Product balance-on-hand then reveals whether sufficient quantity exists to fill the customer order [BOH > or = Order quantity]. If so, the state becomes *confirmed.*
- However, if sufficient quantity does not exist [BOH < Order quantity] the state becomes *not confirmed.*
- When sufficient quantity does not exist and the customer approves backordering the object, the state becomes *Backordered.*
- When sufficient quantity does not exist and the customer does not approve backordering the object, the decision signals the end of the life of this particular object in this use case—its *final state.*

- When the backordered object is received from the supplier and the order is filled, the state becomes *Filled.*
- When the confirmed order is filled, the state becomes *Filled.*
- When the customer is invoiced, the state becomes *Billed.*
- When the customer makes payment, the payment signals the *final state.*

As you can see, the customer order object undergoes quite a few state changes during its life.

Putting the Statechart Diagram in Perspective

The statechart diagram is the second dynamic model that we have discussed, the other being the sequence diagram. Whereas the sequence diagram showed communication flows between multiple objects of a use case, the statechart diagram illustrates only a single object and shows how it undergoes changes as it is involved in the use case processing.

FIGURE C.17

Collaboration Diagram of Customer, Telemarketer, and Customer Order Dialog

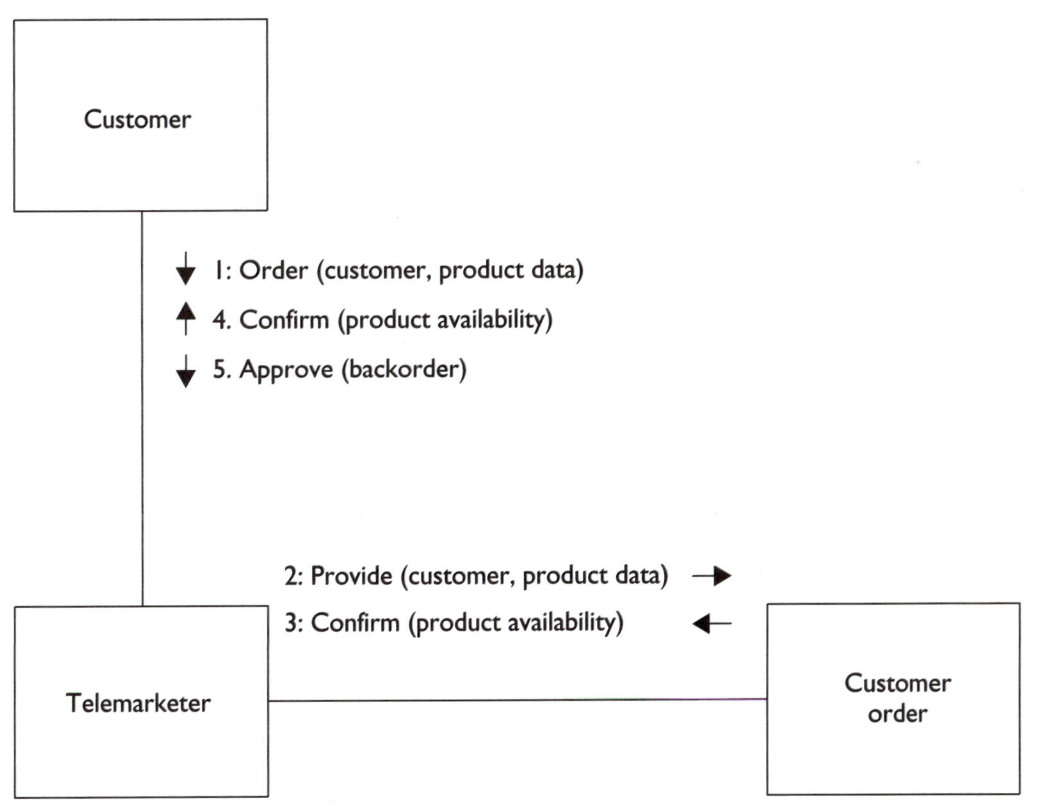

FIGURE C.18

Activity Diagram of Fill Customer Order Operations

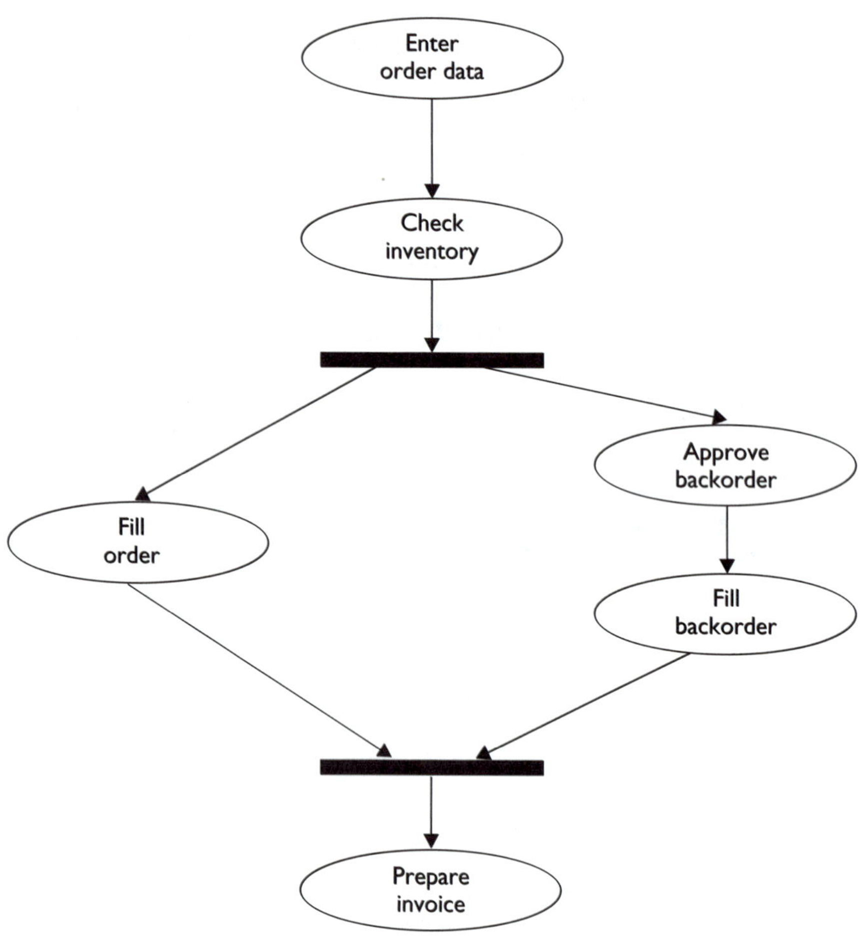

THE REMAINING UML DIAGRAMS

The four diagrams that we have discussed so far—use case, class, sequence, and statechart—are the ones most often described in systems analysis, design, and development textbooks. They represent a set that can provide the basis of development and construction using appropriate software.

There are five more diagrams that compose the UML object modeling set and we will provide brief definitions and examples. These additional diagrams include the object, collaboration, activity, component, and deployment diagrams.

Object Diagram

The **object diagram** is a snapshot of the status of an object at a point in time. It is a static diagram that includes sample values rather than definitions. Figure C.16 is an object diagram that shows sample values of Customer order and Product objects. The

FIGURE C.19

Component Diagram of the Fill Customer Order Use Case

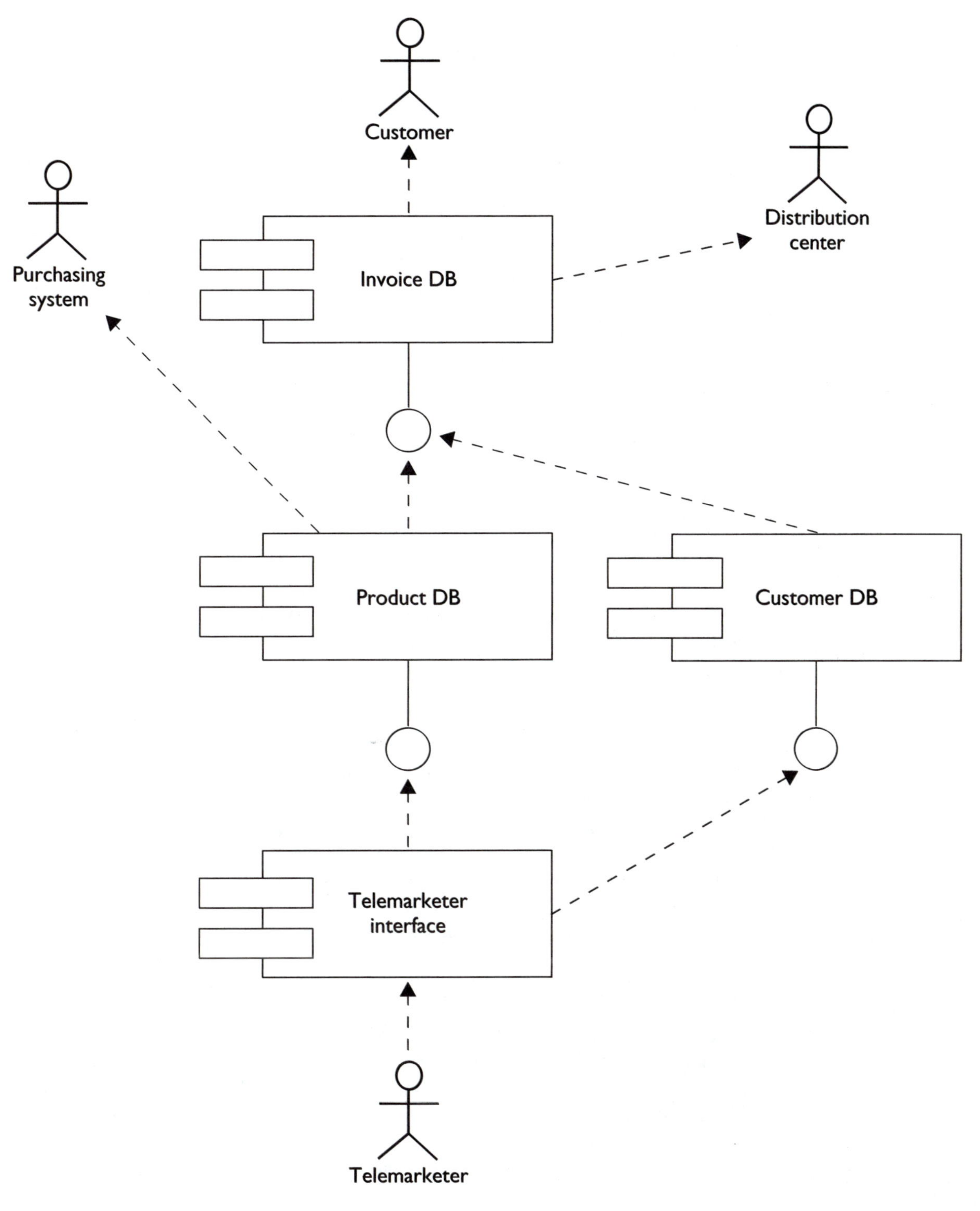

diagram provides an example of attributes for the two objects that must be specified at the point of order entry.

Collaboration Diagram

The **collaboration diagram** shows how selected object classes of the class diagram collaborate in processing a transaction. The Figure C.17 example depicts the dialogue between the Customer, the Telemarketer, and the Customer order. The diagram shows the object classes and the messages. The sequence of the messages is identified with sequential numbers. The messages are described in terms of the operation performed and the data properties involved (in parentheses). Arrows identify the direction of the message flow.

In the example, the customer provides order data, the telemarketer determines whether the product is available, and, if so, advises the customer of the order confirmation. When the product is not available, the telemarketer obtains customer approval to backorder the product.

Activity Diagram

An **activity diagram** is a dynamic model that is a version of the statechart diagram. Whereas the statechart diagram emphasizes the states of an object as the use case activity is carried out, the activity diagram emphasizes the activities, or processes. As shown in Figure C.18, the Fill customer order operations are illustrated with ovals in a top-down sequence. The ovals are defined with verbs and objects. Arrows show direction of the process flow, but are not labeled. Points where processes diverge (forks) and converge (joins) are illustrated with thick bars. This example shows that the inventory checking causes processing to diverge to one path on the left where orders are filled and a path on the right where backorders are filled. After filling, the two paths converge for the billing operation.

Component Diagram

Up to this point, all of the diagrams have been logical views of the system. The **component diagram** offers a physical view by illustrating the software components that comprise the system. The software components are illustrated with rectangles with two smaller rectangles superimposed on the left-hand side. Each component is a supplier of a service that is illustrated with the small circle below the component, connected with a solid line. When a component requests a service, that request is shown with a dashed arrow leading to the circle.

Figure C.19 is a component diagram of the Fill customer order use case. Beginning at the bottom, the telemarketer uses the telemarketer interface to enter order data, which is transmitted to both the product and the customer databases. When customer orders are filled, the product and customer databases provide data to the invoice database. The invoice database provides the customer with an invoice and also provides the distribution center with documentation necessary to fill the order. The product database also notifies the purchasing system when replenishment stock must be ordered.

Since the component diagram is a physical model, the Product, Customer, and Invoice object classes are shown as databases. The databases represent how the logic is implemented with technology.

FIGURE C.20

Deployment Diagram of the Fill Customer Order Use Case

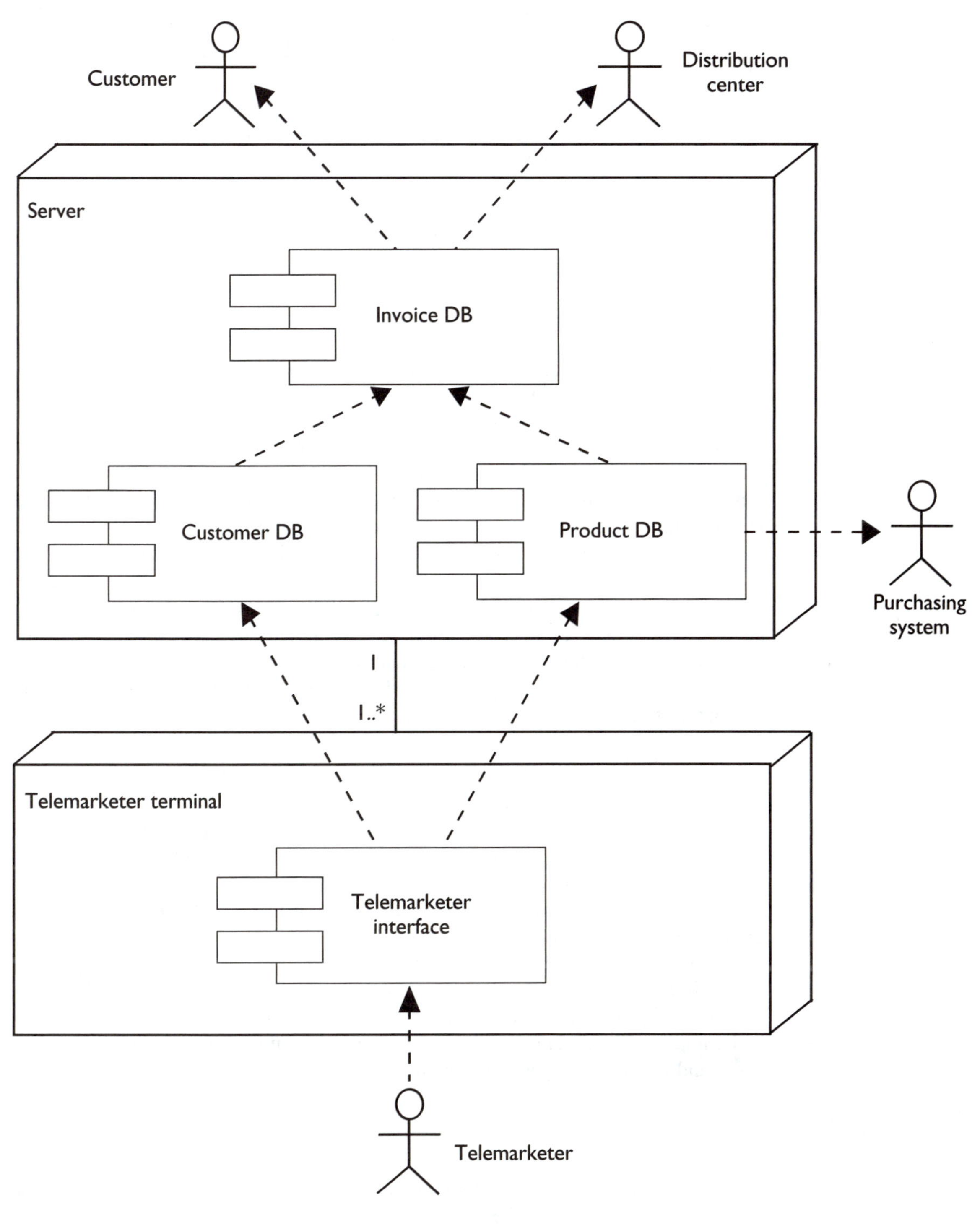

TABLE C.2

Categories of UML Diagrams

	Structural	Dynamic
Logical	Use case diagram Class diagram Object diagram Component diagram	Sequence diagram Statechart diagram Activity diagram
Physical	Deployment diagram	Collaboration diagram

Deployment Diagram

The **deployment diagram** shows the software components arranged in terms of nodes. A **node** is a run-time resource such as a mainframe computer, server, workstation, terminal, and storage unit.

The same symbols are used for the software components as in the component diagram and they are enclosed in larger three-dimensional box symbols that represent the run-time nodes. Solid lines connect the nodes and show the association multiplicities. Dashed arrows connect actors and software components.

Figure C.20 shows how the invoice, customer, and product databases are included in the server node, and how the telemarketer interface is included in the telemarketer terminal nodes. The example shows how the telemarketer interacts with the telemarketer interface, and that interface interacts with the product and customer databases, which are located on the server along with the customer database. The example also shows the associations among these databases and the customer, distribution center, and purchasing system.

Putting the UML Diagrams in Perspective

You can see that UML modeling provides a wealth of graphic views of a system in the form of its nine diagrams. Table C.2 shows that the diagrams can be logical or physical, and that they can document a use case or a portion thereof in either a structural or dynamic way. The influence of technology is incorporated in the physical diagrams but not the logical ones.

Compared to other data and process modeling tools, the diagrams provide relatively simplistic views of a system. A main reason is that the system is subdivided into use cases, objects, and operations, keeping the diagrams from becoming too cluttered and complex. The diagrams provide excellent communications media for the developers and users as the system is developed.

THE OBJECT MODELING PROCESS

One of the strengths of object modeling, unlike data modeling and especially process modeling, is the fact that the same tools can be used throughout the development process. When UML modeling is used, the diagrams are the tools. The diagrams are typically initiated in a sequential fashion and then are continually refined as more is learned about the system. Figure C.21 shows a typical initiation sequence and refinement span for the UML diagrams.

The use case diagram is begun in the preliminary investigation stage, based on the use case report. The class, sequence, and object diagrams originate in the analysis phase, with considerable shifting back and forth among all three as refinements are made. Compared to the other diagrams, the object diagram has a relatively short life span—it is used primarily to learn about complex data structures and identify the attributes that should be present at certain points in time. The five remaining diagrams—statechart, activity, collaboration, component, and deployment—can originate in the design phase. The deployment diagram is especially valuable in the system test and installation phase as the system is deployed in the form of software and hardware.

FIGURE C.21

Phasing of the UML Diagrams Over the SDLC

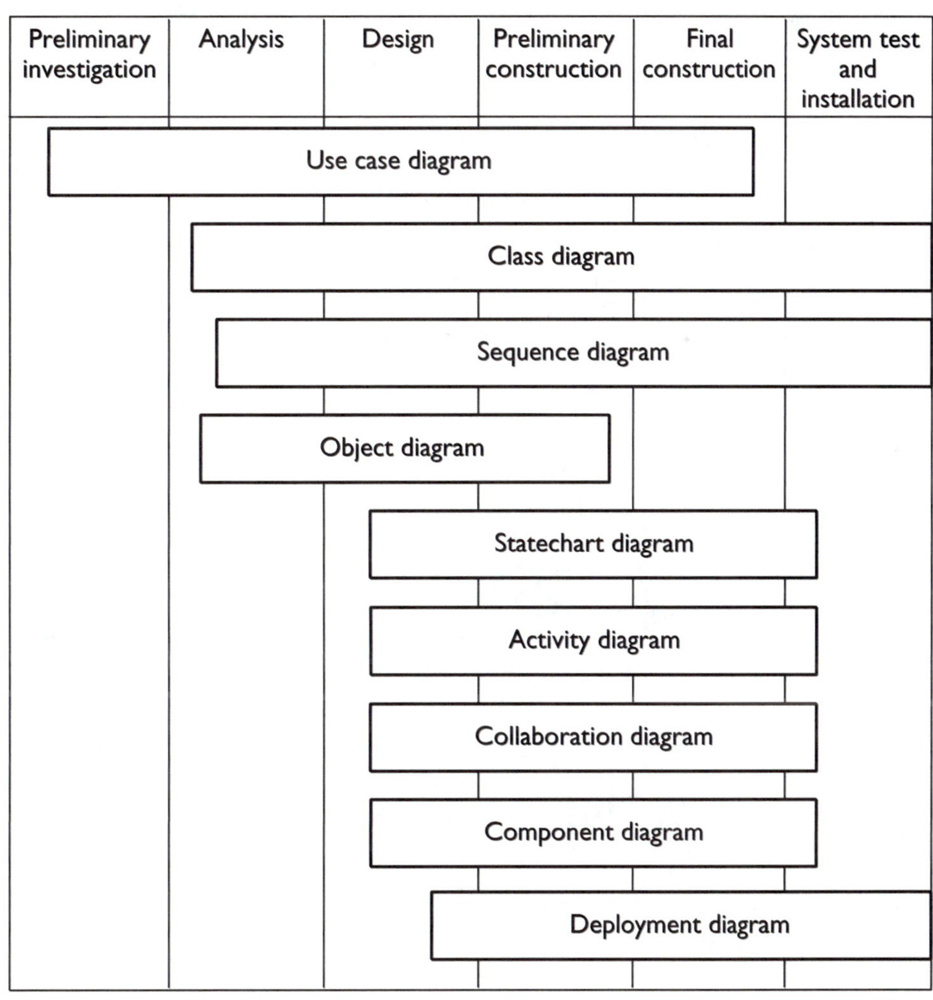

FIGURE C.22

A Class Diagram Prepared with Rational Rose

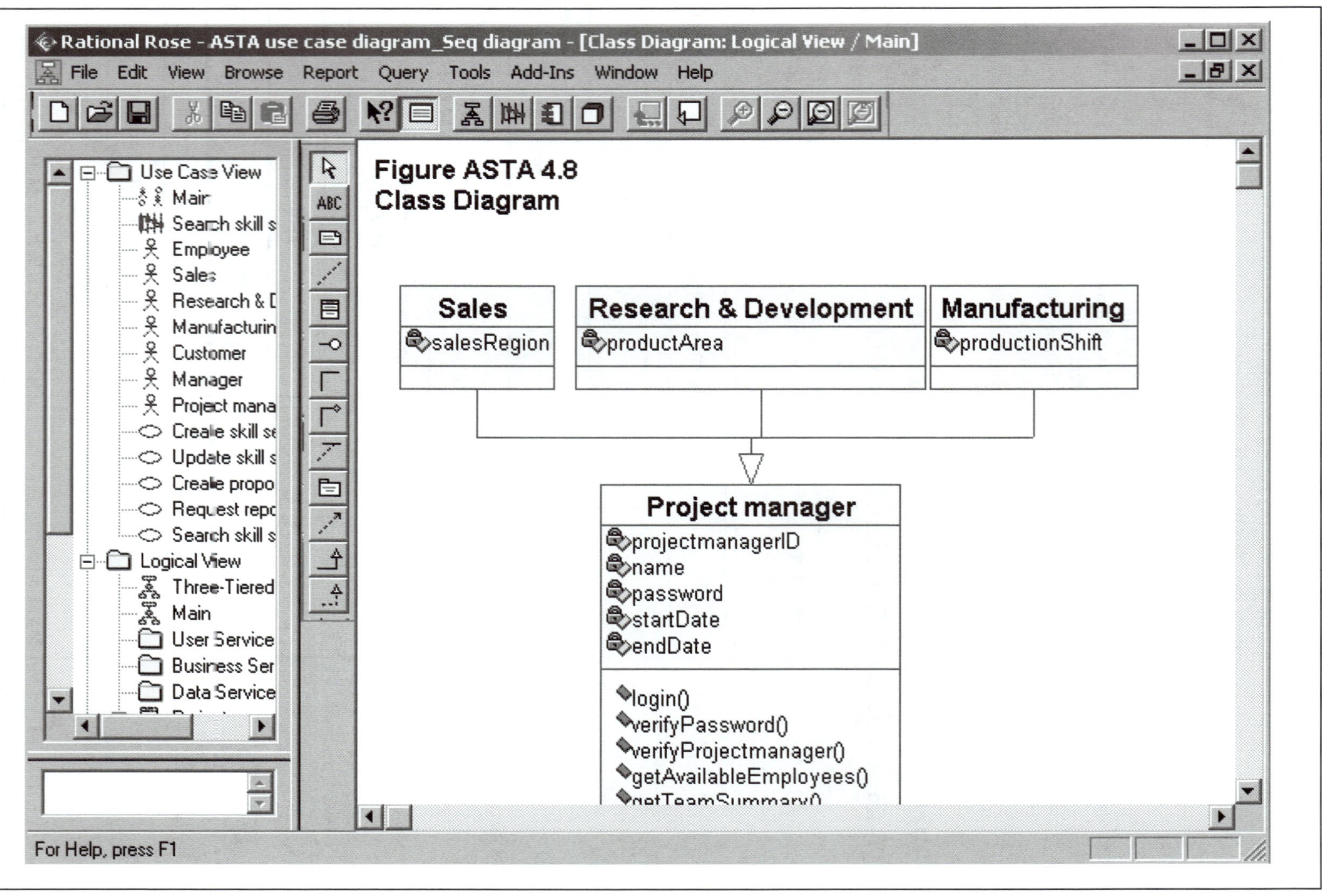
Rational Rose - ASTA use case diagram_Seq diagram - [Class Diagram: Logical View / Main]
File Edit View Browse Report Query Tools Add-Ins Window Help
Use Case View
Main
Search skill s
Employee
Sales
Research & D
Manufacturin
Customer
Manager
Project mana
Create skill se
Update skill s
Create propo
Request repo
Search skill s
Logical View
Three-Tiered
Main
User Service
Business Ser
Data Service
Figure ASTA 4.8
Class Diagram
Sales
salesRegion
Research & Development
productArea
Manufacturing
productionShift
Project manager
projectmanagerID
name
password
startDate
endDate
login()
verifyPassword()
verifyProjectmanager()
getAvailableEmployees()
For Help, press F1

Putting Object Modeling in Perspective

It was inevitable that the evolution of computer system development would lead to object modeling. First the processes were emphasized and then the data. The next logical step was to combine the two.

Along the way, certain innovations paved the way. Structured programming contributed the idea of subdividing a program into modules. Object oriented programming not only added the refinement of using objects as the basis for the modules, but also planted the idea of using objects as the basis for the entire system development process.

Although the evolution was more or less predictable, the road to achievement of widespread adoption of object modeling has been a rocky one. A major roadblock was the lack of a standard modeling approach, as recognized at the beginning of the technical module. Since there were no standards for so long, there was also an absence of computer-based development tools. Once the standards became set, the tools followed. An example is Rational Rose from Rational Software Corporation, which reduces the diagramming process to a click and drag operation. Figure C.22 is a Rational Rose screen shot that illustrates the ease with which a class diagram can be prepared. The availability of standards and good software development tools should go a long way toward overcoming any remaining obstacles to achieving the benefits that appear to be possible with the use of objects.

Key Terms

object
message
use case diagram
actor
association
object class
class diagram
multiplicity
attribute
operations
encapsulation
inheritance
sequence diagram
statechart diagram
state chart
object diagram
collaboration diagram
activity diagram
component diagram
deployment diagram

Problems

1. Draw a use case diagram of the following payroll system, which consists of three use cases—Create time sheet, Calculate payroll earnings, and Prepare payroll check.
   a. *Create time sheet*—Employees provide the departmental secretary with their time cards that contain the hours worked for the week. The departmental secretary prepares a weekly time sheet that lists each employee, the total hours worked, and the hourly rate. The time cards are filed in a Time card history file. The departmental supervisor audits the time sheet and signs it if everything seems to be in order. If any of the figures are unacceptable, the sheet is returned to the secretary. The acceptable sheets from all of the departments are sent in the company mail to a clerical employee in the accounting department.
   b. *Calculate payroll earnings*—The clerk uses the acceptable time sheets to calculate payroll earnings, which are written on the time sheets.
   c. *Prepare payroll check*—Another clerk uses the time sheets to prepare the payroll checks, which are forwarded to the employees. After this operation, the time sheets are filed in a Time sheet history file.

2. Draw a class diagram of the Create time sheet use case described in Problem 1.
3. Draw a sequence diagram of the Create time sheet use case.
4. Draw a statechart diagram of the Create time sheet use case.
5. Draw a use case diagram of the following demand deposit (checking) system used by a bank. Three use cases are involved—Open new account, Process checks, and Prepare monthly statement.
   a. *Open new account*—The customer provides the bank with a completed new account application form. A data entry operator enters data from the new account application form into the computer, using a keyboard terminal. The computer edits the new account data and prepares an error listing of all applications that contain errors. The error listing is sent to the new accounts department. New account data that does not contain errors is written onto a magnetic tape file named New account file. The New account file is input to another computer program that adds the new account data to the Customer master file, on magnetic disk, and prints the transactions on a transaction listing. The listing is sent to the new accounts department.
   b. *Process checks*—At the end of each day, customer checks are scanned by the optical character reader and the data is recorded on the Daily check file. The same procedure is followed for checks received from the clearing house. Checks on other banks are sent to the clearing house.
   c. *Prepare monthly statement*—At the end of the month, the Daily check file is input to the Prepare monthly statement program, which also uses the Customer master file to obtain customer data. The monthly statements are printed by the printer and mailed to the customers.
6. Draw a class diagram of the Open new account use case.
7. Draw a sequence diagram of the Open new account use case.
8. Draw a statechart diagram of the Open new account use case.
9. Draw a use case diagram of the following system that processes supplier receipts. The system consists of two use cases—Receive supplier shipment, and Prepare supplier check.
   a. *Receive supplier shipment*—When the firm receives shipments from suppliers, packing lists are enclosed in the cartons. A data entry operator keys the packing list data into the computer, and then files the packing lists in a Packing list history file. The computer program obtains the corresponding records from the Outstanding purchase order file, on magnetic disk. The same program prints a report named the received purchases report, which is sent to the purchasing department through the company mail, and writes a Supplier payables file, on magnetic disk.
   b. *Prepare supplier check*—The Supplier payables file is input to another program that obtains supplier data from the disk—based Supplier master file and prepares checks that are mailed to the suppliers. The same program that prints the checks also creates a Supplier check history file, on magnetic tape.
10. Draw a class diagram of the Receive supplier shipment use case.
11. Draw a sequence diagram of the Receive supplier shipment use case.
12. Draw a statechart diagram of the Receive supplier shipment use case.

Selected Bibliography

Brown, David William, An Introduction to Object-Oriented Analysis: *Objects and UML in Plain English,* 2nd. ed. (New York: John Wiley & Sons, Inc., 2002).

Booch, Grady, James Rumbaugh, and Ivar Jacobson, *The Unified Modeling Language User Guide,* (Reading, MA: Addison-Wesley, 1999).

Jacobson, Ivar, Grady Booch, and James Rumbaugh, *The Unified Software Development Process,* (Reading, MA: Addison-Wesley, 1999).

Rumbaugh, James, Ivar Jacobson, and Grady Booch, *The Unified Modeling Language Reference Manual,* (Reading, MA: Addison-Wesley, 1999).

Vessey, Iris, and Sue A. Conger, "Requirements Specifications: Learning Object, Process, and Data Methodologies." *Communications of the ACM* 37 (Number 5, May 1994), 102-113.

NOTES

1. Tom Moore and Phil Britt, "OOP Hits the Mainstream." *Enterprise Systems* XVI (June 2001), 30-31.
2. For an example of an early object-oriented approach, see Jean-Marc Nerson, "Applying Object-oriented Analysis and Design," *Communications of the ACM* 35 (September 1992): 63-74.
3. James Rumbaugh, Ivar Jacobson, and Grady Booch, *The Unified Modeling Language Reference Manual* (Reading, MS: Addison-Wesley, 1999), p. 3.

CHAPTER 2

SYSTEMS CONCEPTS

LEARNING OBJECTIVES

- Classify the elements in the environment of the firm.
- Differentiate between physical and conceptual resources.
- Identify the dimensions of information that contribute to its value.
- Explain how resources flow through the firm.
- Solve problems by following a problem chain.
- Use the systems approach to solve problems of all kinds.
- Define the linkage that connects problems, objectives, and performance criteria.
- Describe the resource constraints that influence systems design.

INTRODUCTION

In Chapter 1, we presented systems concepts that apply to systems of all kinds, and elaborated on how the firm can be viewed as a system. In this chapter, we continue our focus on the firm as a system by describing resources available to the firm, and the environment in which the firm functions.

The firm exists within an environment that includes customers, suppliers, competitors, government, financial community, local community, labor unions, and stockholders and owners. The firm is connected to these elements by resource flows. All of the resources flow from the environment to the firm and from the firm to the environment.

An enterprise or firm consists of resources. Some of the resources are physical in nature—personnel, material, machines, and money. Other resources, data and information, represent the physical resources and are called conceptual resources. Information is a valuable conceptual resource when it is accurate, timely, complete, and relevant.

In solving problems, it is important to distinguish between the problem cause and the problem symptoms. Medical doctors follow a chain of symptoms until it leads to the real cause. Business problem solvers can follow a similar chain. A systematic approach has been developed for solving problems of all types. This approach is called the systems approach, and it consists of ten steps grouped in three phases.

When a firm uses technology to solve a problem or to create an opportunity, objectives for the new system are established to ensure that it has the proper focus. These objectives can be restated in measurable terms to establish the performance criteria of the new system-what it must do in order to satisfy the user. As systems developers design the new system, they do so within certain constraints. Some constraints are imposed internally and some come from the firm's environment.

The systems approach provides the overall framework for solving problems. Definition and solution effort guide the problem solver along the problem chain.

THE ENVIRONMENT OF THE FIRM

In Chapter 1, we defined an open system as one that interfaces with its environment. In the general systems model of the firm, we explained how resources flow from the environment to the firm, and from the firm to its environment. The business environment can be very complex, but we present a model in Figure 2.1 that includes eight basic elements.[1] The eight elements in the figure are either organizations or individuals, and each affects the firm in some way.

- *Customers*—The firm's customers can be individuals, such as supermarket shoppers, and they can also be other firms, such as when Ace Hardware purchases electric drills from Black and Decker.

- *Suppliers*—The firm obtains its resources from suppliers. A supplier, also called a vendor, provides products and services to firms that use them in producing their own products and services. Suppliers are organizations just like the firm. In fact, the firm is one of the supplier's customers.

- *Government*—When we think of the government influence on business, we usually think in terms of the constraints-the requirements to report information and pay taxes. However, the government also provides a wide range of services, including roads and utilities. The government is especially helpful to small businesses, providing specialized expertise and guaranteeing loans. The government also makes available a wealth of data and information, often free of charge, so that businesses of all sizes can better understand the economy and their markets.

- *Financial community*—The financial community consists of those institutions that make money available to the firm or provide investment opportunities. Such institutions include banks, investment firms, insurance companies, credit unions, and any other organizations that have large accumulations of money.

- *Stockholders or owners*—A stockholder is one who invests in a corporation. When the firm is not a corporation, the owners are the proprietors or partners. A proprietor is the sole owner, whereas a partner shares the ownership with other persons. In most cases the proprietors and partners are the firm's top-level managers, but the money that they invest is their own-it is coming to the firm from the outside. The ultimate responsibility of the firm is to meet the investment expectations of its owners.

- *Local community*—The firm has a responsibility to be a good citizen of its local community, which is the city or town where it is located. The community provides support for the firm in the form of fire and police protection, cultural opportunities and education for the firm's employees and their families, and health care facilities. A large firm with widely distributed operations has

FIGURE 2.1

The Environment of the Firm

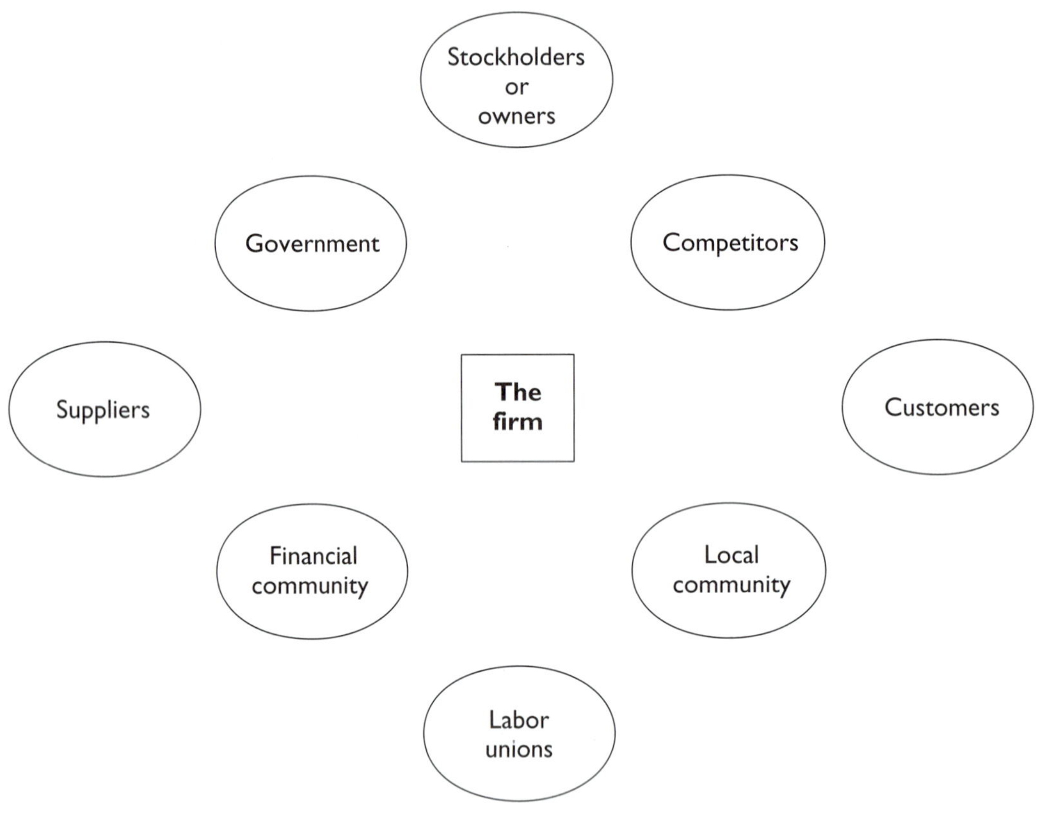

a local community that consists of many cities, perhaps in different states and even countries. The local community of today's multinational corporations includes the entire world.

The local community also serves as a source of the personnel resource. We assume that most of the firm's employees come to it from the local community. When employees come to the firm from employment agencies, colleges, and other organizations that provide human resources, these organizations are considered to be suppliers.

- *Labor unions*—Many industries are characterized by work forces that belong to labor unions. Management must work closely with the union officials in enacting policies that are mutually acceptable. Otherwise, the firm faces the threat of a strike or another kind of work stoppage that could cripple the firm.
- *Competitors*—The firm seeks to maintain a good relationship with the seven environmental elements that have been described. However, such an accommodating attitude is not directed at the competition. They are often seen as the enemy; their objective is to put our firm out of business. For that reason, the manager attempts to make life as difficult as possible for the competition, though in an ethical manner. The firm competes by offering products and serv-

ices superior to those of the competition or by offering products and services to their customers sooner than can their competition. Information technology is now a key resource for achieving and maintaining a competitive advantage.

SYSTEM RESOURCES

In Chapter 1, we recognized that the firm is a physical system. It consists of physical elements, which can be seen and touched. The elements of the physical system can be viewed as resources-physical resources. Management uses conceptual systems to manage the physical systems. The elements of the conceptual systems can also be viewed as resources-in this case, conceptual resources. Therefore, a system's elements are resources. *Physical systems are composed of physical resources, and conceptual systems are composed of conceptual resources.*

Physical Resources

There are many different physical resources that a firm can assemble but they can be classified into four basic types: material, machines, money, and personnel. These four types exist in all firms.

Material Resources

When we think of material resources, we tend to think of raw materials that are used in a production process. This is perhaps the best example, but we should also recognize that nonmanufacturing firms use materials. For example, banks obtain printed checks from printing companies, restaurants obtain food products from food wholesalers, and newspapers obtain newsprint from paper mills. The CD-ROM disks and paper forms used in an information system installation are examples of material resources.

Machine Resources

Some machines are designed to perform specialized functions and can be found only in certain types of organizations. Examples are machine tools used in a factory to transform the material resources into products and printing presses used to print and collate newspapers. Other machines perform basic functions that can be applied in a variety of situations. Good examples are pocket calculators, telephones, and computers. As with the material resources, we use the term machine in a broad sense, applying it to machines of all types. We also include the firm's buildings and land in this category.

Money Resources

Money is a unique physical resource in two respects. First, it is used to buy all the other physical resources. Second, money itself usually does not flow through the firm. Instead, something representing money, such as checks or electronic signals, is used. Only at the retail level does money actually change hands, and even there it is giving way to other forms of payment.

Personnel Resources

If you ask managers which of the physical resources is the most valuable, they will almost invariably reply, "My personnel." This is because the personnel apply the other physical resources to perform the activities of the firm. For example, the personnel use money to obtain materials, and then they use machines to perform operations on the material that transform it into finished products.

All firms are composed of combinations of these four types of physical resources, and it is the responsibility of management to manage the available resources to meet the firm's objectives.

Conceptual Resources

Conceptual systems represent physical systems and are composed of two types of conceptual resources: data and information.

Data

Data consists of detailed facts and figures such as customer numbers, unit prices, reorder points, and so on that *by themselves* are relatively meaningless to the user. Typically the data exists in such volumes that analysis is difficult. In order for the data to be meaningful, it must be transformed into information by an information processor. The information processor receives data from the physical system and from the environment. Humans are information processors, as are computers and other data processing devices. We included the information processor in the general systems model of the firm described in Chapter 1.

Information

The output of the information processor is **information,** which is processed data that is meaningful to the user. To many users, the output in the form of printed and displayed information *is the system.* They often leave all other aspects up to the developer, who must have a broader view.

Dimensions of Information

The value that information has for its user depends on four dimensions: accuracy, timeliness, completeness, and relevancy.

- *Accuracy*—The information system has earned a reputation for processing data in an accurate manner and producing accurate information. One important point concerning accuracy is that it is not always necessary to strive for 100 percent accuracy. When money is involved, such as the firm's payroll or its accounts payable, complete accuracy is desired. However, for many other applications, some degree of error can be tolerated. As an example, a report of projected sales revenues for the coming year is only intended to provide a marketing manager with a broad guideline for decision-making and is not expected to be accurate to the penny.

- *Timeliness*—The information system has also earned the reputation for producing timely information. Timeliness refers to the ability of information to give its user an understanding of the subject while it is still possible to act on that information. How fast is timely? The answer depends on the user's needs. It is not necessary that all information be made available in a few seconds or even a few minutes. As long as the user has time to take action based upon the information received, the system is considered timely.

- *Completeness*—Completeness is the ability of the information system to provide thorough information about a particular subject. In providing this information dimension, it is important not to go overboard and give the user more information than he or she can handle.

- *Relevance*—Information has relevance if it bears on the issue at hand. For example, if a manufacturing manager is interested in increasing production quality, a report showing the number of defects per thousand units produced would be extremely relevant. The relevance dimension imposes severe demands on the systems developer because users' interests are always changing. Systems developers must incorporate flexibility in their designs so that the systems can respond to changing user needs.

An important point concerning each of these four information dimensions is the fact that they all have their cost. Increases in accuracy and timeliness are achieved by increased investments in hardware and software. These costs escalate so rapidly as perfection is approached that users are usually willing to settle for something less. The cost of completeness and relevance is not as affected by the cost of the hardware and software but, rather, the cost of the system developers' time in precisely determining the user's needs. A key element in system development is finding the balance between what the user needs and what the user is willing to pay.

Resource Flows

We saw in the general systems model of the firm how resources flow through the firm. All of the physical resources originate in the environment and eventually return to the environment. Conceptual resources also flow to and from the environment, but some originate in the environment and some originate within the firm. Figure 2.2 shows the primary resource flows that connect the firm to its environment. The task of the manager is to establish the relationships with the elements in the environment that make the resources flow at the desired rate.

Personnel Flow

All employees come to the firm from its environment, are transferred from one area within the firm to another, and eventually return to the environment. The manager tries to expedite the flow of personnel *into* the firm, but once in the firm, the manager attempts to delay the flow of personnel *out* of the firm as long as possible. In this way, the firm has the benefit of the employees' services for the longest period possible.

Material Flow

A firm's materials represent a large investment. Once obtained, the manager wants to put the materials to use rather than let them sit idle. Therefore, the manager attempts to speed up the flow of material both into and out of the firm.

A good example of speedy flow is **JIT,** or **just-in-time.** The idea is that raw materials are scheduled to arrive at the plant "just in time" for the production process. Suppliers often locate a distribution center just across the street from a large customer's plant to ensure shipment without delay. By speeding up the material flow, firms that practice JIT have become tough competitors in the marketplace. The manager also attempts to speed up the material flow after the production process is finished. The sooner the customers receive their products, the sooner the firm receives its money.

FIGURE 2.2

Resource Flows in the Environment of the Firm

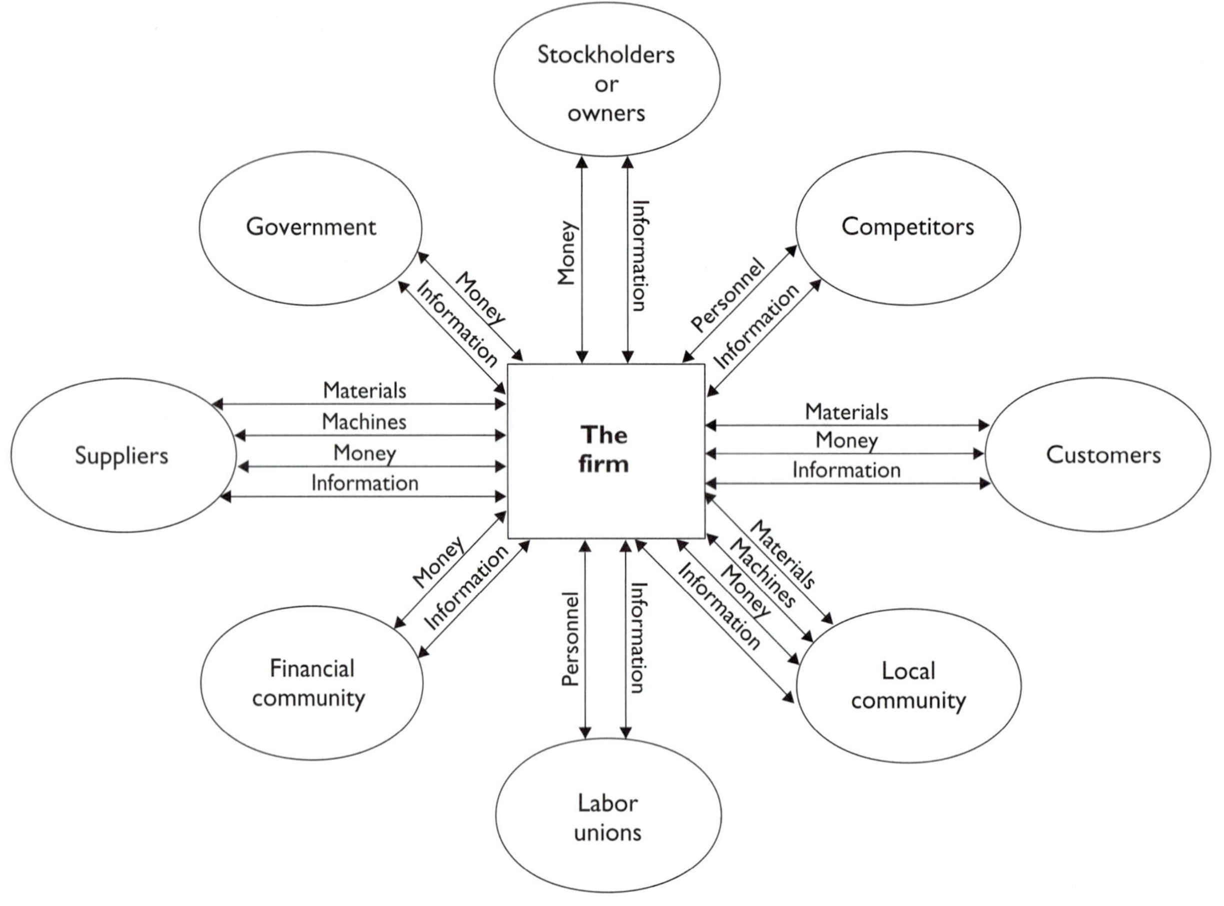

Machine Flow

The manager treats the machine flow exactly the same as the personnel flow. The flow into the firm is first expedited and then slowed down so that the machines can be used as long as possible. Maintenance is performed on the machines to prolong their useful life.

Money Flow

It comes as no surprise that the manager wants the money to flow into the firm as quickly as possible. Firms develop special systems to expedite this flow. Does the manager seek to expedite the money flow out of the firm? You might believe that the firm should hold on to its money as long as possible. However, firms want to put their money to work so that it earns even more money in the form of interest, dividends, and the like. This is accomplished by investing the money without delay. Applying this logic, the manager wants surplus money to flow out of the firm to an investment opportunity as soon as possible after it is received.

Data and Information Flow

The manager wants data to flow to the information processor as quickly as possible. This data flow originates both inside and outside the firm and can be expedited through the use of data communications networks. The manager also wants to expedite the flow of information from the information processor to the users as quickly as possible. The users can be both inside and outside the firm, and, again, data communications can be used.

USING SYSTEMS CONCEPTS TO SOLVE PROBLEMS

Now that we have addressed the fundamental systems concepts, we can see how these concepts can be used to apply technology to meet challenges. The term **problem** normally brings to mind something bad, and bad problems certainly occur in business. However, managers also react to opportunities. The manager wants to learn the cause of an opportunity in order to maximize its benefits. *Opportunities can be regarded as good problems.* The manager can follow the same general approach in reacting to good problems as to bad ones.

If you are to really solve a problem, you must identify its cause. Only by identifying the cause can you ensure that the same problem does not occur again if it is a bad problem or does occur again if it is a good problem. However, the cause is not always obvious. The cause is often obscured by one or more symptoms. A **symptom** is a condition that is produced by the problem.

Problem Chains

Medical doctors follow problem chains. When you have a medical problem, you go to a doctor. You have an ache or a pain that you want relieved. Actually, the ache or pain is not the problem, but a symptom. The doctor asks you questions and gives you tests that are aimed at clarifying the symptoms so that he or she can pinpoint the cause. In asking the questions and giving the tests, the doctor follows a problem chain that leads to the cause. A **problem chain** is a series of symptoms, one causing the next, that lead to the problem cause.

Assume, for example, that every year in July you have all the symptoms of a cold—a runny nose, watery eyes, and a sore throat. You need professional help and go to an eye, ear, nose, and throat doctor. She asks a series of questions that leads to the fact that you always visit your grandmother in July. More questions reveal that your grandmother has a fluffy Persian cat named Pete. The doctor suspects that you may be allergic to Pete and gives you some allergy tests. The tests confirm the doctor's suspicions. The runny nose, watery eyes, and sore throat are the symptoms, and your allergy to cats is the problem.

Now the doctor helps you solve the problem. One possible solution is to stop visiting your grandmother. Another is to take some allergy medicine. You decide to go the medicine route so that you can continue your trips to your grandmother's house.

Using Problem Chains to Solve Business Problems

Business problem solvers approach problems in the same way as do medical doctors. In fact, the business problem solver has the same responsibility as the doctor—that is, to keep his or her patient in good health. In the case of the business problem solver, the patient is the firm.

FIGURE 2.3

Problem Chain Analysis

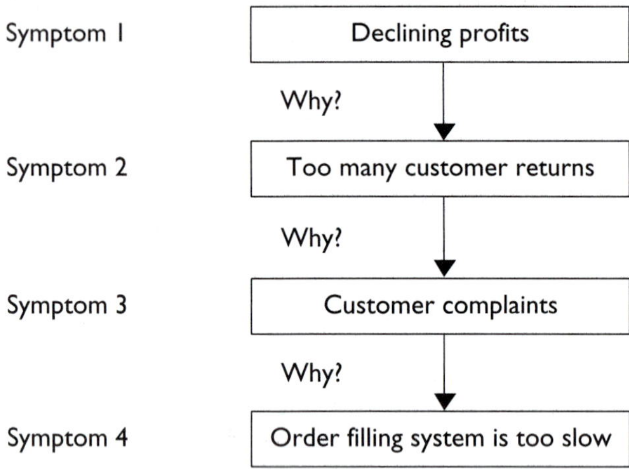

Take, for example, a sales manager who comes to work in the morning, accesses the sales management system on her workstation, and brings up a display of the latest quarterly income statement, which was produced overnight. The manager is shocked to see that profits are down. She studies the display and sees that revenues are at the normal level, but expenses are too high. The manager brings up another display that is a detailed breakdown of expenses and sees that the travel expenses are way out of line. Another display of travel expenses reveals that airline expenses have skyrocketed. The manager talks with several sales reps and learns that they had to increase their air travel in order to cover their territories. When asked why the high air travel expenses have not been incurred in the past, the manager learns that the territories have recently been realigned. The decision is made to realign the territories again, this time considering the impact on travel and expenses.

In this example, the low profits were not the problem. Neither were the high total expenses, the excessive travel expenses, nor the high airline expenses. All were symptoms of the real problem, which was the poor territory assignments.

Recognizing the End of the Problem Chain

How do you know when you have reached the end of the problem chain and identified the cause? The logic of the process is illustrated with the diagram in Figure 2.3. For each symptom, you ask the question: "Why?" For the answer, ask yourself, "Is this a problem that I should try to solve?" If the answer is no, you have only identified another symptom, and you repeat the question. When the answer is yes, you have identified a problem cause. The **problem cause** is the root condition that is the reason for an exceptionally good or bad influence on the situation under study. The term ***root cause*** is also used. In fact, the whole process of problem chain analysis is sometimes called **root cause analysis.**

An important consideration when recognizing the end of the chain is your ability to produce a solution. If the problem cause does not fall within your area of expertise, you should not attempt to solve it. Information specialists solve problems relating to conceptual systems. In Figure 2.3, if you decide to address symptom 4—order filling system is too slow—then it is no longer a symptom but is the root cause.

The ASTA development team followed the problem chain approach in identifying three problems to be solved. See Figure CS 1.15. Finding more than one problem often happens, especially when applying the chain in firms that have allowed problems to go unsolved. In the case of multiple problems, the team has to decide which one, or ones, to solve. At ASTA, the team felt best qualified to address the skills inventory system.

The Systems Approach

Information specialists have created an approach for solving problems in conceptual systems called the systems approach. The **systems approach** is the recommended procedure for the analysis and design of systems, characterized by defining the opportunity to be seized or the problem to be solved by the system, identifying and evaluating the possible system alternatives, selecting and implementing the best alternative, and finally, evaluating how well the system is performing. Our description of the systems approach consists of ten steps in three phases. These phases and steps are illustrated in Figure 2.4.

Phase I: Preparation Effort

Before you can begin to solve a systems problem, you should think in systems terms. Earlier in the text, we called this taking a systems view. The process of taking a sys-

Figure 2.4

The Three Phases and Ten Steps of the Systems Approach

Phase I. Preparation Effort

1. View the firm as a system.
2. Recognize the environmental system.
3. Identify the firm's subsystems.

Phase II. Definition Effort

4. Proceed from a system to a subsystem level.
5. Analyze system elements in a certain sequence.

Phase III. Solution Effort

6. Identify the possible solutions.
7. Evaluate the possible solutions.
8. Select the best solution.
9. Implement the solution.
10. Follow up to ensure that the solution is effective.

FIGURE 2.5

The General Systems Model of the Firm

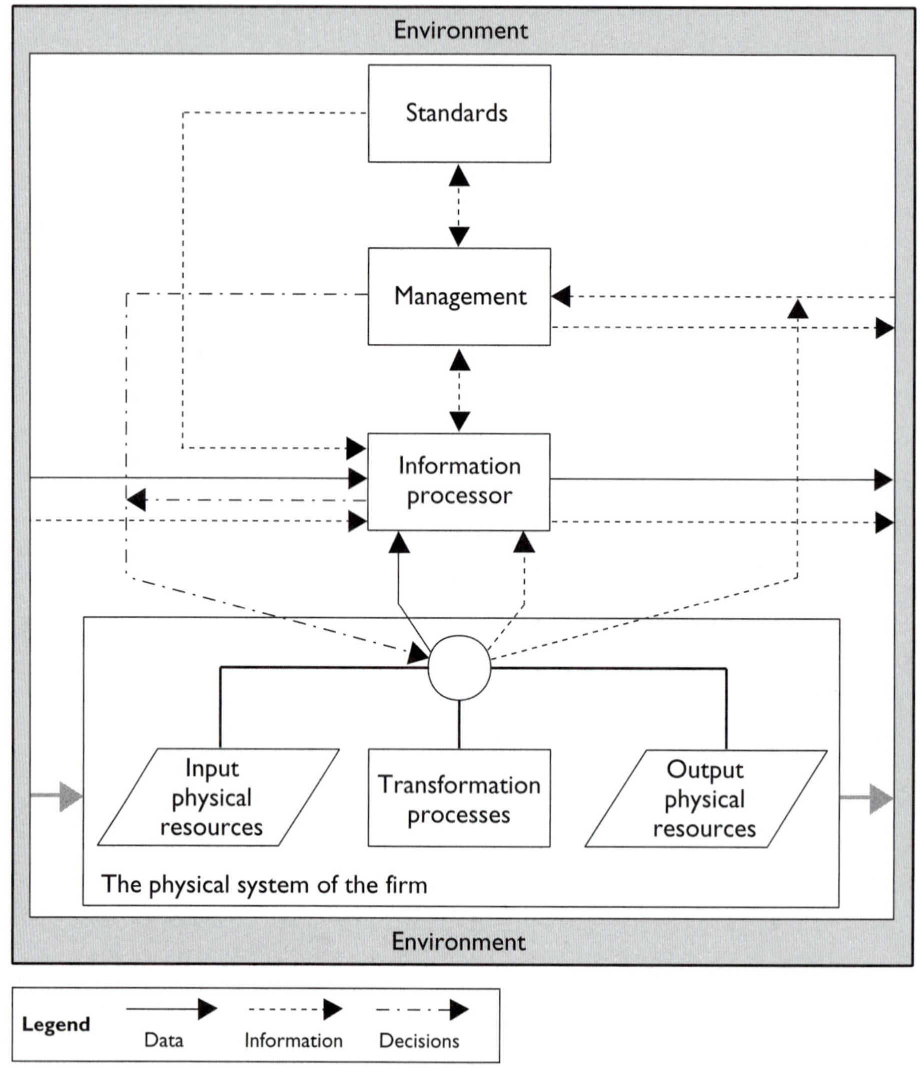

tems view is known as **preparation effort,** and begins in school by building a foundation of systems concepts. You build on this foundation after graduation, as you pursue your business career.

Step 1: View the Firm as a System

If you are going to help the firm solve a particular problem or meet a particular challenge, it is best to regard the firm as a system. Such a view is illustrated with the graphic model in Figure 2.5. This is the general systems model of the firm that we developed in Chapter 1. The system structure recognizes the importance of a conceptual information system that reflects the status of the physical system. The conceptual system consists of the three rectangles at the top, along with their associated data, information, and decision flows.

When you participate in projects to develop information systems, you should do so with the view of the firm as a system. Your information system should help management manage the physical system of the firm.

Step 2: Recognize the Environmental System

By viewing the firm as an open system, you recognize that it exists within an environment. Our earlier discussion of the firm's environment identified flows of both physical and conceptual resources between the firm and each of eight environmental elements. The resource flows are critical to the firm as it strives to meet its objectives. The systems that you develop should facilitate these resource flows.

Step 3: Identify the Firm's Subsystems

The firm as a system consists of subsidiary systems, or subsystems. *Each subdivision of the firm is a system,* which means the systems approach can be followed on any organizational level. You can develop a system for a lower-level organizational unit and use the same approach that you use on the top level.

Phase II: Definition Effort

Before you can solve a systems problem, you must define it. We use the term **definition effort** to describe the process of systems analysis that determines (1) what the problem or opportunity is, (2) where it is located, and (3) what caused it.

Step 4: Proceed from a System to a Subsystem Level

In defining the problem to be solved, it is always a good idea to start at the top of the organizational hierarchy and work your way down. This top-down approach recognizes that all of the firm's systems are intended to support the overall effort of the firm. Another reason to use the top-down approach is that it is easiest to do systems work by first gaining an understanding of the big picture, and then gradually narrowing your focus.

This approach does not mean that each systems development project begins with a study of the entire firm. Instead, it means that if you are expected to solve a problem for a particular organizational unit, such as the sales department, you first study that unit as a system in its environment. Once you study the sales department as a system, you focus on the next-lower system level, such as a regional sales office. Then, you proceed to a still lower level, such as a branch sales office. In your top-to-bottom study, your objective is to identify the level in the systems hierarchy where the cause of the problem is located.

Step 5: Analyze System Elements in a Certain Sequence

While you take the top-down approach, you examine the elements *on each level* in the sequence shown in Figure 2.6.

1. *Evaluate the standards.* You must first determine whether good standards exist for the system. If good standards do not exist, you cannot engage in problem solving until this deficiency is overcome. When good standards do exist, you proceed with the element-by-element analysis.

FIGURE 2.6

The Sequence for Analyzing the Elements of a System

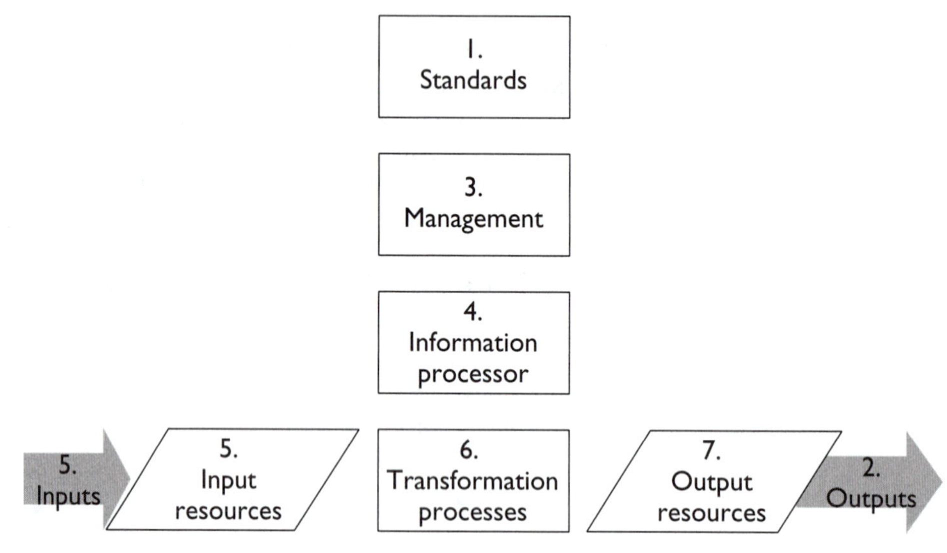

2. *Evaluate the outputs.* You determine whether the system is producing outputs that meet the standards. The outputs are the products and services that the system provides to its customers. If the outputs meet the standards, there is no problem to solve at this system level; the system is doing what it is supposed to do. However, if the outputs do not meet the standards, your task is to find out why. The answer lies somewhere in the remaining elements of the system.

3. *Evaluate management.* In most cases, the reason why the system is not producing the desired outputs lies with management. It is management who sets the policies and makes the major decisions. If the system is not working as it should, it might be because management made the wrong decisions, or perhaps failed to make any decisions at all. But, the key role of management in the firm's success does not mean that it is always to blame when things go wrong. For example, there might not be enough managers, and they might not have enough time to devote to all of their duties. This situation is typical in small, growing firms—especially in industries affected by rapid change.

4. *Evaluate the information processor.* In many cases, management cannot perform its functions because of a lack of information. If such is the case, then management must be provided with an adequate information processor. This step may be the last step in the problem-solving sequence for a systems developer. The reason is that the systems developer is concerned with the conceptual system, and element four is the final element in that system. However, if the problem is somewhere within the physical system, like in elements five, six, and seven, the manager or nonmanager problem solver continues with the analysis. Perhaps assistance is provided by a physical systems specialist, such as an industrial engineer.

5. *Evaluate the inputs and the input resources.* Perhaps the outputs of the system do not measure up because of the inputs and input resources. The inputs are the raw materials of the transformation processes. The firm's input resources are the resources that receive the inputs into the firm. Examples are receiving clerks, receiving inspectors, forklift trucks, and raw materials storage areas.

6. *Evaluate the transformation processes.* There are many possible causes of deficient output in the transformation element. Sloppy workmanship, worn-out machines, and poor working conditions are examples.

7. *Evaluate the output resources.* The cause of the problem might be the output resources, which make the transformed products available to the customers. Examples are finished goods storage areas, stock pullers, packers, and delivery trucks.

As soon as a problem element is encountered, the search halts on that system level, and the next-lower level system is addressed. Figure 2.7 illustrates this top-down process. In this example, assume that you are solving a marketing problem. The marketing division is the system under study. You examine the elements of the marketing system in the proper sequence until you determine that the information processor is the problem element. Marketing managers are not receiving the information that they need from their marketing research system.

You then turn your attention to the marketing research section on the next-lower level and subject it to the same element-by-element study. You evaluate its standards, outputs, and management. You find that the marketing research section is not providing the needed information because its management is not skilled in information system use. The problem cause resides in the management element of the marketing research system.

Phase III: Solution Effort

With the systems analysis completed, and with an understanding of the problem, you are now ready to solve the problem by developing a new or improved system. **Solution effort** involves all of the steps necessary to solve a problem that has been identified and defined. This is termed *systems design and implementation.*

Step 6: Identify the Possible Solutions

There is always more than one way to solve a problem, and the challenge is to identify all of the feasible alternatives. The more potential solutions you identify, the greater your chance of selecting the one that does the best job. This is perhaps the most difficult step of the problem-solving process. Experience plays an important role, but this does not mean that someone who is new to systems development cannot perform this step. All of the systems analysis knowledge that we identified in Chapter 1 can be applied in an innovative manner to identify creative solutions. Ideally, you want to reduce the total number of possible solutions to a reasonable number—for example, from two to six. An unreasonably large number of possibilities makes the evaluation difficult.

Step 7: Evaluate the Possible Solutions

All of the remaining solutions are evaluated using certain judgment standards called **evaluation criteria.** It is important that the evaluation criteria remain constant from

FIGURE 2.7

The Top-Down Approach of the Definition Effort

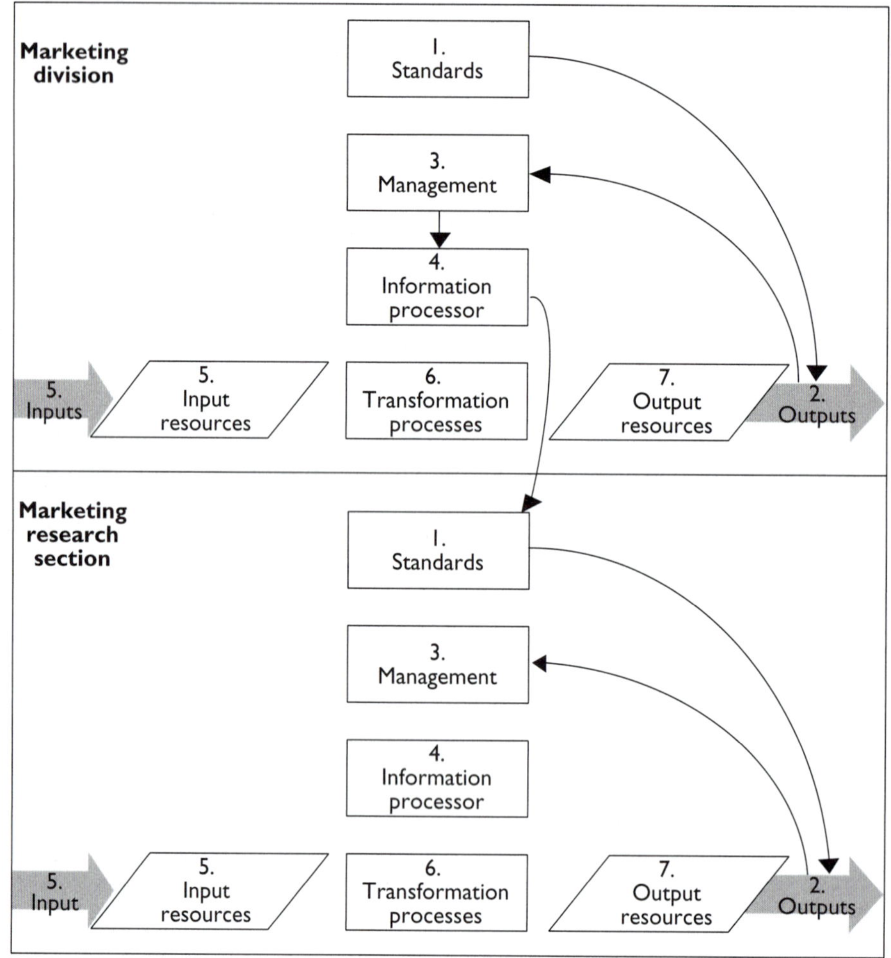

one solution to the next, in order for the evaluation to be fair.

The consideration of the evaluation criteria can be accomplished three different ways[2]:

- *Analysis*—a systematic evaluation of the advantages and disadvantages of each solution using quantitative data
- *Judgment*—a subjective evaluation of each solution by one or more problem solvers
- *Bargaining*—negotiations among several problem solvers

Ideally, the evaluation involves the analysis of quantitative data—specific prices, speeds, and so on. In the absence of such data, judgment fills the gap, and bargaining is always a consideration. Bargaining includes company politics, which play a more important role in systems development than one might expect.

Step 8: Select the Best Solution

The objective of the evaluation is to identify the best solution. Although this selection may consider multiple evaluation criteria, the process boils down to which solution best supports the firm in meeting its objectives.

Step 9: Implement the Solution

The design that exists on paper is converted to a system that consists of hardware, software, data, and personnel, and is put into use.

Step 10: Follow Up to Ensure That the Solution Is Effective

Some time after cutover to the new system, audits are conducted to ensure that the system is performing as intended. When users develop their own systems, it is their responsibility to conduct their own audits. When information specialists have participated in the development project, they conduct the audits. In some situations, internal auditors conduct the audits. The problem is not considered solved until the audits verify that the solution is working.

The systems approach begins in the classroom with preparation effort, includes definition effort to locate the problem cause in your firm's network of systems, and ends with solution effort that continues until you are assured that you did a good job.

Defining the System

System Objectives

Early in the development process, the user specifies the objective or objectives that the new system should accomplish in the form of functional requirements. The **functional requirements** are what the information system must do in order to meet the user's needs. There are any number of objectives that a particular system might be expected to achieve. However, since the objectives will be satisfied with an information system, one approach that you can use in identifying *types* of objectives is to use the four dimensions of information. The objectives can be stated in terms of these information dimensions.

Table 2.1 provides an example of an objective for each of the information dimensions. Note that the objectives are not all stated in quantitative terms. Specific measures are desired, but those can come later—during the analysis stage of the SDLC when measures of satisfactory system performance are defined. The objectives depend on the problem cause. For example, if the existing information system is not keeping the user current on the activity within the physical system, the objective, or objectives, of the new system would deal with timeliness.

The use of guidelines such as the information dimensions is an example of how the systems developer can make good use of systems concepts. Rather than wasting time by exploring every possible avenue and still running the risk of missing important items, the concepts provide a basis for a systematic search.

System Performance Criteria

After the existing system has been documented during the analysis stage, the next step is to define the system **performance criteria.** These criteria represent the standards

TABLE 2.1

Information Dimensions as a Basis for System Objectives

Dimension	Sample System Objective
Accuracy	The new distribution system will substantially reduce customer complaints arising from shipment of the wrong merchandise.
Timeliness	Warehouse managers will be notified not later than 8:30 AM of the volume of orders to be filled for the day.
Completeness	The program that determines whether to reject a customer's order because of poor credit will take into account, among other things, the customer's sales history for the past six months.
Relevance	The department head's report of excessive overtime hours for the week will include only those employees who regularly work overtime.

that the new system must satisfy in order to meet its objectives, which are jointly agreed upon by the user and the developers. There are a number of ways that the developer can approach this task. Following the same approach that we took with the system objectives, we can use dimensions of information.

For each dimension, the criterion must be stated in measurable terms. It is not sufficient to say that the new system "must process sales orders in an accurate manner." That might have been fine for the system objectives, but it is unacceptable for the performance criteria. The developer continues to question the user until they *both* agree to a criterion, such as: "Must fill 98 percent of the sales orders with the proper items."

The students developing the ASTA system have taken the first step toward establishing performance criteria with the identification of certain objectives for the information dimensions, as shown in Figure CS 1.6. However, these objectives are not in a measurable form. For each, the team must establish quantitative measures. For example, the objective of the RFP software making a decision "without delay" could be restated to making a decision "within ten minutes."

System Constraints

The ability of a system to accomplish its objectives is influenced by the constraints that are imposed on the design. Few systems projects are free from constraints of some kind. Any number of constraints can exist, and they can originate within the firm or in its environment.

Internal Constraints

Internal system constraints are limits on the performance of the system that are imposed by the firm's resources. A good way to come to grips with the internal system constraints is to think in terms of each of the resource types: personnel, material, machines, money, data, and information. The system will most likely be constrained in some way by a limitation on one or more of these resources. Table 2.2 lists examples of constraints for each of the six resource types.

External Constraints

External system constraints are requirements that are imposed on the system by elements in the firm's environment. These constraints can also be seen as restrictions on resources. For example, the firm might not be able to attract the desired number and types of systems developers because of a tight job market, or perhaps the firm cannot obtain the amount of financing that it needs from the financial community to construct new computing facilities. Also, suppliers might not be able to meet the firm's need for hardware or software within a specified time frame.

All of the constraints will not be known during the preliminary investigation stage, but the developer and user do their best to estimate them. The estimate provides the initial boundaries within which the system must operate and can be made more specific later as more is learned about the new system.

TABLE 2.2

System Constraints Caused by Limited Firm Resources

Resource	Sample Constraint
Personnel	The information services unit shall have no more than three full-time employees.
Material	Acquisition of supplies such as paper and CD-ROM disks will not exceed $1,000 per month.
Machines	No hardware upgrades will be permitted.
Money	The total annual budget for the computer operation is $375,000.
Data	Salespersons shall not spend more than 30 minutes per day entering sales order data.
Information	Preformatted screens for the executive information system will be updated at least daily.

FIGURE 2.8

Definition and Solution Effort of the Problem Chain

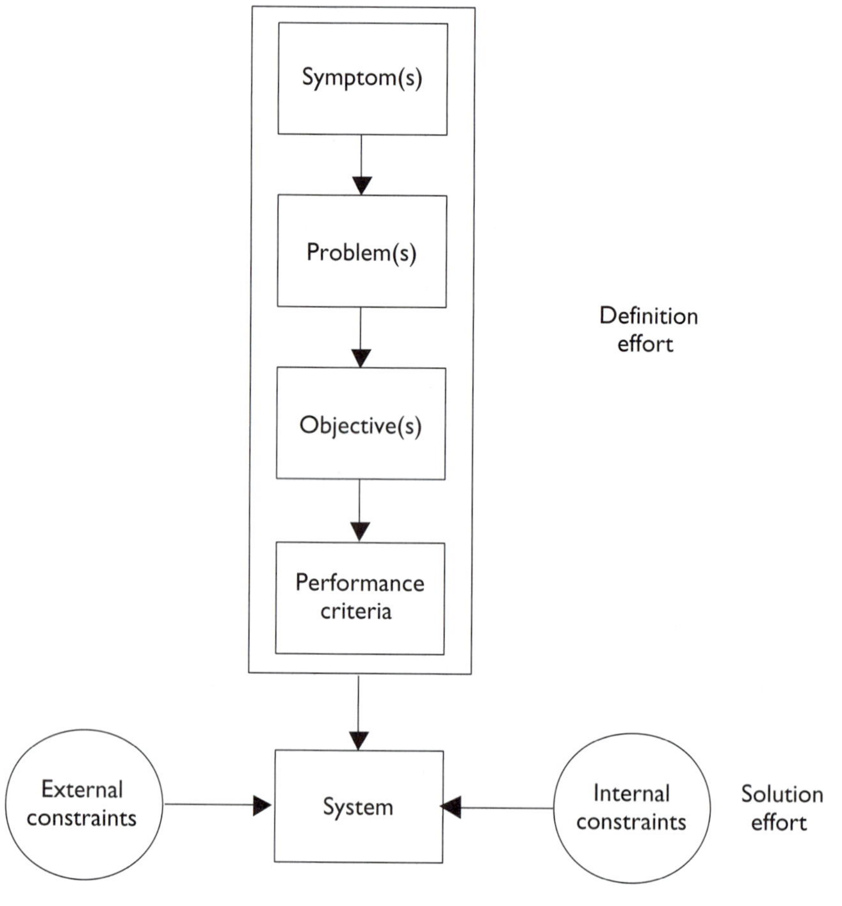

Using the Systems Approach to Follow the Problem Chain

There is a direct relationship among the existing system problem, new system objectives, and new system performance criteria. For each problem, there should be at least one objective, and for each objective, there should be at least one performance criterion.

For example:

Problem: The system takes too long to fill customer orders.

Objective: Fill customer orders faster.

Performance criterion: Fill all customer orders within 24 hours of receipt.

Figure 2.8 illustrates this linkage and shows that the problem definition and the setting of objectives and performance criteria come during the definition effort of the systems approach. Design and implementation of the new system, within the imposed constraints, comes during the solution effort.

Using Systems Concepts in Data and Object Modeling

Systems concepts can be used at practically every point during the SDLC when decisions must be made concerning the new system. The concepts provide useful frameworks that provide the starting point for identifying possible solutions and system components. A good example is in the identification of entities and objects. When the developers use a data-oriented approach, an important step is to identify the data entities. In a like manner, when the team follows an object-oriented approach, a step that is equally important is to identify the objects. In the case of both entities and objects, the developers must identify phenomena that occur multiple times and are of sufficient importance for the firm to maintain data to describe them.

Both entities and objects can be:

- Valuable resources
- Elements in the environment of the firm
- Important transactions

When deciding which resources are candidates for entities or objects, the four physical resources provide a starting point. As an example, material resources can be the firm's products and raw materials, machines can be production tools and company cars, money can be represented by accounts receivable and payable, and personnel can be salespersons and production workers. In a like manner, the eight environmental elements from Figure 2.1 provide a starting point. Customers and suppliers are invariably picked as entities and objects, and the other elements should also receive attention.

For the important transactions, the physical resources and environmental elements can be used again. Think of the types of transactions that can involve each. For example, personnel fill out time cards, factory workers fill out job tickets, customers place sales orders, and the firm places purchase orders with suppliers.

Putting Systems Concepts in Perspective

During this and the previous chapter, we have covered a number of systems concepts: physical and conceptual systems, open and closed systems, open-loop and closed-loop systems, system levels, viewing the firm as a transformation system, the general systems model of the firm, the environment of the firm as a system, physical and conceptual system resources, resource flows, and the systems approach. All of these concepts have one thing in common—they are all based on the notion of a group of elements working to accomplish an objective. Such a systems view is valuable to business problem solvers because the firm can be regarded as a system. The concepts describe how the system ought to function, and the performance of the firm can be compared to this ideal. The systems concepts are an organized way to get at the heart of problem solving with a minimum amount of trial and error. *The systems concepts form the basis for everything the systems developer does.*

Summary

Eight elements make up the firm's environment: customers, suppliers, stockholders or owners, labor unions, government, the financial community, the local community, and competitors.

PROJECT MANAGEMENT TOOLBOX

Project Management Must Be Alert to Environmental Constraints

In Table 2.2, we gave some examples of system constraints. All of the examples are internal constraints placed on the system. Constraints can also be imposed on the development project, and these can be imposed internally and by elements in the environment. Table 2.3 shows that five of the environmental elements can influence the flow of certain resources. Stockholders and the financial community can influence incoming money flows; suppliers can influence flows of machines, material, and personnel; and the local community and labor unions can also influence the personnel flow.

Money Constraints

If the scale of the project is massive, such as an e-business system intended to enhance the firm's competitive advantage, the consequences of a schedule or budget overrun could be disastrous. On the other hand, getting the system up and running as planned or, better still, ahead of schedule, could have a positive effect on the firm's stockholder relations. A similar effect could involve the financial community. If the project takes longer to complete than it should, it can delay the new system from reaching the break-even and payback points. These points are discussed in Technical Module F, which deals with economic justification. Also, a lengthy project decreases the net present value of benefits expected of the new system, a result that can have a negative influence on receiving management commitment to continue the project once it gets underway.

Machine and Material Constraints

If the new system will require additional hardware, the project plan must include selection of the vendor or vendors and scheduled delivery and installation. The systems approach can be used in vendor selection, with one of the evaluation criteria being the ability of each vendor to meet the specified delivery schedule. In a similar manner, attention must be given to selection of the vendors providing needed material, such as software, facilities, and supplies. As the scale of the project increases, the importance of vendor support increases.

A firm's physical resources can be seen and touched. They include personnel, material, machines, and money. Other resources, data and information, represent the physical resources and are called conceptual resources. The dimensions of information that contribute to its value are accuracy, timeliness, completeness, and relevance.

The managers of the firm manage the rate at which the resources flow from the environment, through the firm, and back to the environment. Management seeks to slow down personnel and machine flow and speed up material and money flow. Management also strives to speed up the flow of data and information between the firm and all of the environmental elements, except the competitors. The manager strives for only an incoming flow of competitive information.

In solving problems, it is important to distinguish between problem symptoms and the cause or causes of the problem. Medical doctors follow a chain of symptoms leading to the root cause. Business problem solvers follow this same problem chain. You know when you reach the end of the chain when you have identified a root cause and the solution of the problem falls within your area of expertise.

Information specialists have created an approach that is well suited to solving

TABLE 2.3

Environmental Constraints on Project Management

	Money	Machines	Material	Personnel
Stockholders	X			
Financial community	X			
Suppliers		X	X	X
Local community				X
Labor unions				X

Personnel Constraints

When additional personnel, either full- or part-time, are required to develop the system, these personnel can come from suppliers (such as consulting firms and employment agencies), the local community, and labor unions. When consulting help is needed, it might be necessary to evaluate several firms and select the best. When additional personnel are to come from the local community, it will be necessary to coordinate the acquisition with the firm's human resources unit, and when the personnel are members of a union, the acquisition and management must be coordinated with the firm's labor relations unit.

The time required to manage these environmental resource flows can be significant and must be considered when developing the project plan and monitoring performance.

business problems. It is called the systems approach, and consists of three phases of effort: preparation, definition, and solution. Preparation effort requires you to view the firm as a system, recognize the environmental system, and identify the firm's subsystems. In applying the definition effort, you proceed from a system to a subsystem level while analyzing the system elements in a certain sequence. Solution effort demands that you identify alternate solutions, evaluate them, select the best one, implement it, and follow up.

The new system is developed to accomplish particular objectives. The objectives are usually stated in broad, general terms and then are restated in measurable terms to establish the performance criteria of the new system—that is, what it will take to satisfy the user. As the system developers design the new system, they do so within constraints. The constraints, which represent restrictions on resources, can be imposed both internally and by elements in the firm's environment.

The steps of following the problem chain and establishing new system objectives and performance criteria are accomplished during the definition phase of the systems approach. The design and implementation of the new system within its constraints comes during the solution phase.

KEY TERMS

data
information
supplier, vendor
problem
symptom
preparation effort
definition effort
solution effort
evaluation criteria
performance criteria

KEY CONCEPTS

- Physical and conceptual resources
- The environment of the firm is a system consisting of eight elements, or subsystems
- The firm is connected to its environmental elements by resource flows
- Managers can follow the same problem-solving approach when reacting to opportunities as they follow when reacting to bad problems
- Problem chain analysis, root cause analysis
- The systems approach
- Systems view, systems orientation
- The systems approach can be applied on any system level
- Problems or opportunities, objectives, and performance criteria are connected logically
- All system constraints can be regarded as limitations on resources

QUESTIONS

1. Identify four physical resources.
2. Identify two conceptual resources.
3. What are the dimensions of information that contribute to its value?
4. Identify the eight environmental elements of a firm.
5. Which environmental elements could be individuals, as opposed to organizations?
6. What are two names that are given to organizations that provide the firm with materials and machines?
7. Which resource flows does the manager strive to speed up? To slow down?
8. Which of the physical resources usually does not actually flow through a firm?
9. Which of the physical resources would a manager likely believe to be the most important? Why?
10. Are data and information the same? Explain.
11. How does a problem solver know when the end of the symptom chain has been reached?
12. Which phase of systems approach effort is concerned with systems analysis? Systems design and implementation?
13. When following the ten steps of the systems approach, which two steps occur simultaneously?
14. Which system elements receive the attention of the information systems developer when solving problems?
15. Which system element represents the best bet of being the problem cause? Explain your reasoning.
16. Distinguish between inputs and input resources. Do the same for outputs and output resources.
17. Experience can contribute throughout the ten steps of the systems approach, but where does it play an especially important role?

18. As a general rule, how many alternatives should be evaluated? Why this number range?
19. What are three ways to evaluate alternatives?
20. Ideally, what fundamental feature characterizes the best solution?
21. Who conducts the new system audit?
22. Identify a theoretical system construct that can be helpful in identifying system objectives and performance criteria.
23. What is a common way to view both internal and external constraints?

Topics for Discussion

1. Why would an owner, who is president of the firm, be considered an element in the environment?
2. Is there an environmental element that would never constrain the firm in some way?
3. Can you think of a physical resource that does not originate or terminate in the firm's environment?
4. Do all of the data and information flows originate and terminate in the environment?
5. Where can politics enter into the systems approach? How can it influence the outcome?

Case Problem: Hoelscher, Nickerson, and Jones

You have just received your degree in information systems and have landed a job with Hoelscher, Nickerson, and Jones, one of the biggest firms in town specializing in commercial law. Hoelscher, as the firm is called, represents business firms in suits involving a wide variety of legal matters, such as trademark infringement, product safety, and pollution. You head for the office on your first day of work, making certain that you have your worn copy of the general systems model of the firm in your coat pocket.

Michael Hoelscher (Partner): Welcome to the firm. This is a big day for us. We've had our Dell desktops for about a year and have really been pleased with the results thus far. We subscribe to a legal information retrieval system. The database is in St. Paul and we retrieve abstracts and legal summaries using the desktops. Everything has gone so well that we decided to expand our applications, and that is why we hired you. We want you to conduct a thorough systems study of our operation and advise us on which applications should go on the computer next. We want to use the desktops as an information system to enable us to do a better job. Then, we can add the necessary resources—programmers, operators, and the like. Why don't you ask me some questions and we'll take it from there.

You: Great. You mentioned your desktops. Are you familiar with computers?

Mike: Pretty much so. I studied them at school and have learned a lot from my kids. We have a Mac at home, and I've diddled around with spreadsheets and the like. But I feel like an outsider here. Nobody else in the firm knows the least thing about computers. That's one reason I hired you. I wanted someone to talk to. (Mike smiles and you both laugh.)

You: Well, you can count on me for conversation. I love computers. Let me find out some more about the firm. (You remember what your professor said about the general systems model being a good guideline for evaluating a system and feel your coat pocket to make certain it is still there.) What is the size of your management team?

Mike: We really don't have managers as such. We have three partners, twelve other lawyers, and an office staff of six legal secretaries and four clerks. We also have an administrative assistant who helps the partners. We sometimes hire college students part-time to do various types of research.

You: O.K. (You are somewhat shocked that there are no managers. You wonder whether the general model is as great as your professor said it was.) What about performance standards? How do your people know what they are supposed to achieve?

Mike: We don't have formal standards. We just assume that all of the lawyers know that they are supposed to win their cases, and the secretaries and clerical personnel know that they are supposed to do high-quality work, keeping errors to a minimum.

You: Nothing in writing?

Mike: Not a word.

You: All right. Do you have objectives?

Mike: Well, we certainly want to stay in business. We want to return an investment to the owners, who are the partners. We want to provide a good place for our employees to work. We feel like we perform a service for the business community, providing legal service to those who need it. We would like to continue our growth, but we don't want to grow so fast that we lose our reputation as a firm that really cares for its clients and its people.

You: Those sound like good objectives. You say you want to use the desktops as an information tool. Exactly what do you mean by that?

Mike: As you can appreciate, our business is communications. We communicate with everybody—our clients, the district attorney, the jury, our sources of information, Washington, ourselves. All of this communication is now being done in person, on the phone, through the mail, by reading the paper and listening to TV and the radio, using e-mail, and so on. We will have to continue these ways, but we would like to take better advantage of electronics as well, such as using the Web. We would like to use the desktops to communicate better here in the office, and with our outside contacts as well. Most of our commercial clients have huge information system setups. We would like to be able to tie in with them.

At that moment, Mike's administrative assistant walks into the office, holding The Wall Street Journal. He excuses himself for interrupting and asks, "Mike, have you seen the article on air bags? I think it's relevant to the class action suit we're handling. Maybe we ought to talk about it." Mike excuses himself and you head to your office, holding on to your coat pocket all the way.

Assignments

Use the general systems model of the firm to evaluate your new firm.

1. Examine each element of the conceptual system individually and identify any associated problems.
2. Examine each flow of data and information in the model and explain how they can be improved with the desktops. It is not necessary that the desktops be applied to every flow.

CASE PROBLEM: PALOMAR PLASTICS

Palomar Plastics is located in Logan, Utah, and manufactures the clear plastic covers that protect information system keyboards from dust, dirt, and coffee spills. Palomar is a classic example of a company that recognized that problems can be good as well as bad. The booming information system industry created a need for protecting the vulnerable keyboards in an office environment, and Palomar seized the opportunity to satisfy the need.

Your name is Fred Feree, and you are a senior systems analyst at Palomar. You have just been asked by your manager, Walter Clark, to determine why customer credits are increasing. Each month, more and more customers are asking for credits against previous purchases. The credits are issued by the accounts receivable section of the accounting department, so you visit that section, talk with the supervisor, Amy Matula, and dig through a file of recent credit records. You learn that the main reason for the credits is poor product quality. The customers often are dissatisfied with the quality of the covers and want their money back.

You remember meeting someone several months ago named Amos Nash, who is the manager of quality control, and decide that he might be able to shed some light on the subject. You track Amos down, talk with him, and learn that he is aware of the situation. The problem, as Amos sees it, is low morale among the production workers. The workers just don't seem to try. You make appointments to talk with several production supervisors. The supervisors reveal that the workers are demoralized because of low pay. Although other companies in the area have increased worker salaries each year to compensate for the rising cost of living, Palomar has not. Some Palomar workers are making the same money today as they did five years ago.

Your first suspicion is that Palomar has had some financial difficulties that made it impossible to give raises to the factory workers. You check with Dale Barnett, manager of the accounting department, and she shows you the income statements for the past five years, revealing a substantial profit each year.

So why haven't the workers been receiving raises? The best person to answer that question is Ralph Burton, the vice-president of manufacturing. You make an appointment to see him, and get straight to the point. Ralph tells you that he knows of the morale problem but explains that one of his annual objectives is to keep manufacturing expenses to a minimum. Salaries are one of the major expense items, so he concentrates much of his attention there. You ask if the minimum expense objective is one that he established himself or one that was imposed on him. Ralph explains that the Palomar president, Rebecca Sandoval, establishes the annual objectives for each of the five vice-presidents, and their annual bonuses depend on the degree to which the objectives are met. You ask Ralph if you could see his list of objectives, and he gladly obliges. He hands you a list, and you examine each item. All look very reasonable. In fact, one specifies that Ralph should "achieve high quality production."

When you run out of questions for Ralph, you thank him for his time and assure him that you will copy him on all of your reports. As you walk back to your office, you say to yourself, "Whew, and to think that all of this started with excessive credits."

Assignments

1. Continue to assume that you are Fred, and write a memo to your manager, Walter Clark, advising him of what you have done. Include a problem statement based on the data you have gathered. Conclude the report with an identification of the next step, or steps, that you should take to complete your data gathering.
2. Now assume that you are Walter Clark. You want to give Fred some feedback on how well he has followed the systems approach. Make a list of the things he has done that indicate he has followed the approach. Make another list of things that indicate he has not.

SELECTED BIBLIOGRAPHY

Christiaanse, Ellen, and Jos Huigen. "Institutional Dimensions in Information Technology Implementation in Complex Network Settings." *European Journal of Information Systems* 6 (Number 2, June 1997): 77-85.

Frolick, Mark N., and Houston H. Carr. "The Role of Management Information Systems in Environmental Scanning: A Strategic Issue." *Journal of Information Technology Management* 2 (Number 3, 1991): 33-37.

Keon, Thomas L., Gary S. Vazzana, and Thomas E. Slocombe. "Sophisticated Information Processing Technology: Its Relationship with an Organization's Environment, Structure, and Culture." *Information Resources Management Journal* 5 (Fall 1992): 23-31.

Overton, Keith, Mark N. Frolick, and Ronald B. Wilkes. "Politics of Implementing EISs." *Information Systems Management* 13 (Number 3, Summer 1996): 50-57.

Sillince, John A., and Samar Mouakket. "Varieties of Political Process During Systems Development." *Information Systems Research* 8 (Number 4, December 1997): 368-397.

Wedberg, George H. "But First, Understand the Problem." *Journal of Systems Management* 41 (June 1990): 20-28.

NOTES

1. Hopeman, Richard J. *Systems Analysis and Operations Management.* (Columbus, OH: Charles E. Merrill, 1969): 79-81.
2. Based on Henry Mintzberg, "Planning on the Left Side and Managing on the Right." *Harvard Business Review* 54 (July-August 1976): 55-56.

CHAPTER 3

SYSTEMS DEVELOPMENT METHODOLOGIES

LEARNING OBJECTIVES

- Know the most popular system development methodologies and how they evolved.
- Identify the stages and steps of the traditional system development life cycle.
- List the potential strengths and weaknesses of prototyping.
- Understand the concept of rapid application development.
- Understand the phased development methodology and how it blends the strengths of other methodologies.
- Appreciate how methodologies facilitate understanding and communication.
- Use the systems approach in selecting the right methodology.

INTRODUCTION

The first two chapters provided you with a foundation of systems concepts. With that foundation in place, you can now apply those concepts in the development of information systems. In this chapter, we explain the primary methodologies that are used to guide systems developers.

A methodology is simply a recommended way of doing something. Methodologies that are applied to solve business problems exist within a hierarchy. Several of these methodologies are intended to guide the development of an information system. These methodologies typically consist of a series of stages called the system development life cycle, or SDLC.

The traditional SDLC methodology has provided the basis for information system projects since the beginning of the computer era. A dramatic modification that has received much attention is prototyping. Information specialists build a prototype, or model, of a new system to obtain a clearer understanding of users' information needs. Some prototypes eventually become production systems, whereas others serve as blueprints for systems that are then developed using custom programming. Even though the prototyping methodology offers some real strengths, there are some drawbacks.

One of the biggest influences on system evolution has been the information engineering methodology and its development component called RAD, for rapid application development. As the name implies, RAD is intended to develop systems quickly.

A fourth methodology is the one that forms the basis for the discussion of systems development in the remainder of this book. It is named phased development because it emphasizes subdividing a system into modules and executing a series of analysis, design, and preliminary construction phases for each module.

The primary goal of all of the methodologies is to provide a consistency within the firm for system development and to provide documentation that can guide future system development efforts.

The Evolution of Methodologies

A methodology is a recommended way of doing something. The physical and behavioral sciences created a methodology for guiding scientists as they conducted experiments in such disciplines as chemistry, physics, and psychology. This methodology was given the name scientific method and it consists of four steps.

1. Observe
2. Formulate a hypothesis
3. Predict
4. Test

For example, a research psychologist will *observe* that rats learn faster when physically handled. The scientist will then *formulate a hypothesis* that "Physical handling facilitates learning." This hypothesis enables the scientist to *predict*, "Rats physically handled will learn faster than those not physically handled." The scientist will then test the hypothesis by conducting an experiment. The scientific method worked so well that management scientists applied it to the solution of business problems and called it the *systems approach.* We described the systems approach in Chapter 2.

One system problem that has been a good application of the systems approach is the development of a new information system. The development consists of a series of stages, subdivided into phases and tasks, and is known as a system development life cycle. Several such system development life cycle methodologies have evolved. The principal ones are the traditional system development life cycle, prototyping, rapid application development, and phased development.

All of these methodologies exist in a hierarchy, as illustrated in Figure 3.1. The scientific method serves as the foundation, and the others are built upon it. The systems approach is the application of the scientific method to business problems in general, and the life cycle methodologies are applications of the systems approach to the business problem of system development.

The Traditional System Development Life Cycle

A **system development life cycle**, or **SDLC**, is the evolutionary process that is followed in developing and using an information system. Many people are involved and many separate steps must be taken. The process can become so complex that it is

FIGURE 3.1

The Evolution of Methodologies

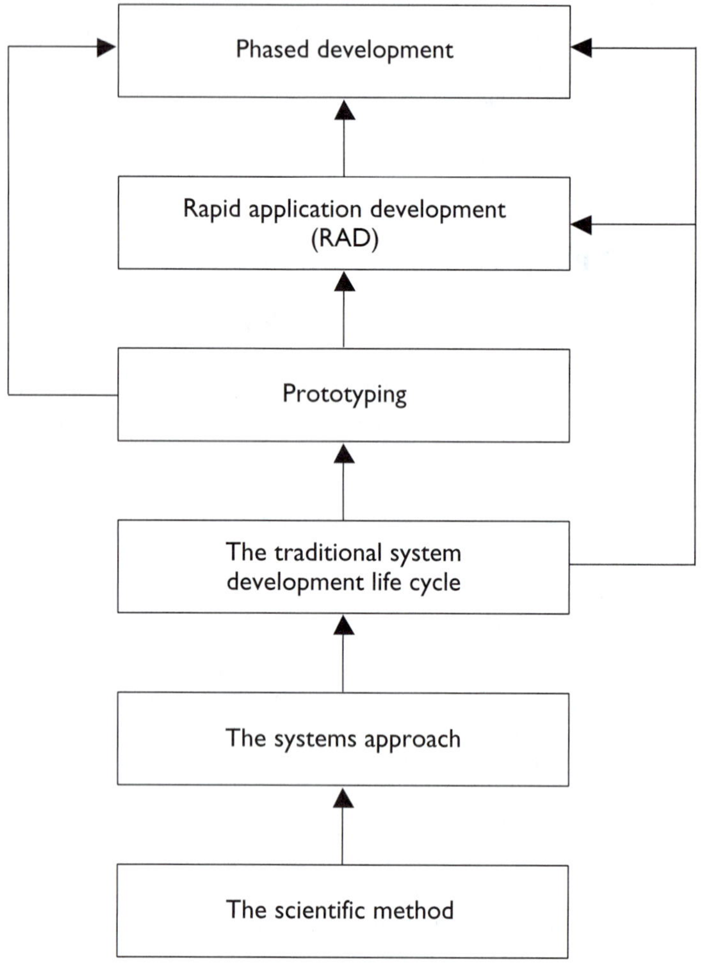

helpful to subdivide the work into stages. Firms that developed the first information systems concluded that a logical sequence of stages involved planning, analysis, design, implementation, and production.

Figure 3.2a illustrates these five stages as an orderly sequence. The traditional SDLC is also called the **waterfall cycle** since the basic idea is that one stage is performed, then the next, and so on until the process is completed. Figure 3.2b captures the idea that after a system is developed and used, the system eventually must be redesigned or redeveloped and the SDLC is repeated.

- *The planning stage*—The purpose of the planning stage is to react to a problem or opportunity signal and determine whether to embark on a system project. In Chapter 2, we recognized that problems can be good or bad, with opportunities regarded as good problems. During this stage, the user typically recognizes the problem or opportunity and works with the systems developer in defining it so that a system can be developed. The user and developer set the system objectives and identify any constraints. The developer conducts a feasibility study and prepares a study project proposal, which is either approved or disapproved by the firm's management. A **feasibility study** is a quick look to determine whether to continue the project. A **system study** is a thorough analysis intended to determine the objectives of the new system. Upon approval of the system study, management puts a control mechanism into place so that they can manage the project.

- *The analysis stage*—The purpose of the analysis stage is to gain a thorough understanding of the user's needs and prepare documentation that can serve as the basis for the system design. A project team is organized and it sets out to work with users to define their information needs and to define the system performance criteria. The project team prepares a design proposal, which is used by management in approving or disapproving progression to the design stage.

FIGURE 3.2

The System Life Cycle as a Sequence of Stages and a Repetitive Process

a. A sequence of stages

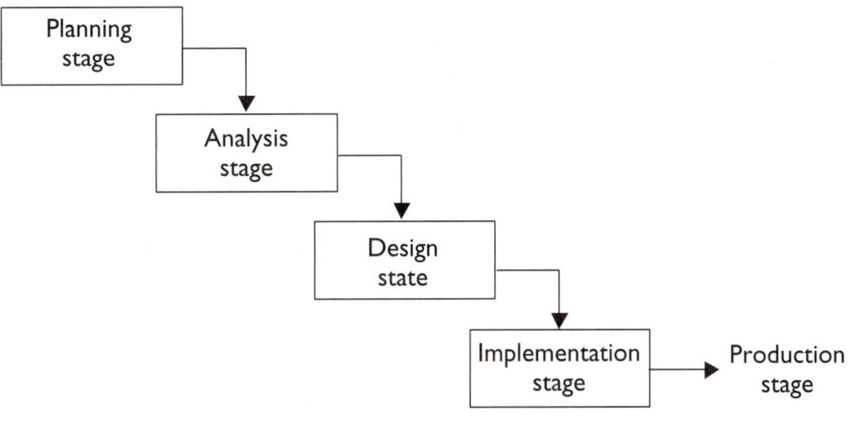

b. A repetitive process

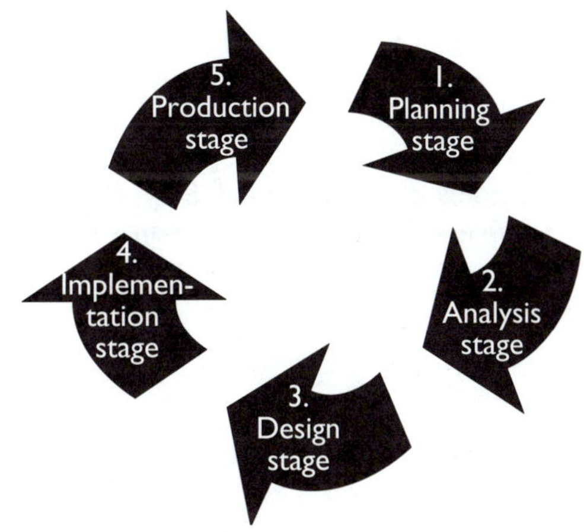

- *The design stage*—The purpose of the design stage is to determine the best way to meet the user's objectives. The project team prepares the detailed system design and then follows the systems approach in selecting the best system configuration—first identifying possible configurations and then evaluating them. The project team prepares an implementation proposal that is used by management to evaluate whether to continue the project.

- *The implementation stage*—The purpose of the implementation stage is to convert the design documentation into a functioning system. Programmers, representatives from the firm's information systems operations unit, and such other specialists as consultants and contractors join the project team to plan the implementation, obtain the necessary hardware and software, prepare the database and physical facilities, and educate users and others who will work with the new system. If custom software is required, it can be prepared by the firm's own programmers or outsourced to another firm specializing in software development. When the new system requires prewritten software, it can be obtained from software vendors. Management uses an implementation proposal as a basis for approving or disapproving **cutover,** the process of changing from the existing system to the new system.

- *The production stage*—In the production stage, the user uses the system to meet the objectives identified in the planning stage. For the period immediately following cutover to the new system, the project team members stay in close contact with the user to ensure that all is going well. Any difficulties that the user encounters are addressed and remedies are incorporated into the system.

Throughout the production stage, it is often necessary to modify the system so that it continues to meet the user's needs. These modifications are called systems maintenance. When maintenance is no longer effective, the firm's management may elect to have the SDLC repeated to develop an improved, and perhaps completely revolutionary, system.

Putting the Traditional System Development Life Cycle in Perspective

The traditional SDLC is heavily rooted in the systems approach. Like the systems approach, the SDLC consists of defining what you want to do, considering alternate solutions, implementing the one that appears to be best, and following up to make certain that it works. For most of the computer era, the traditional SDLC provided the most popular development methodology. However, users became impatient with the long-term process that could easily span several years. Newer methodologies were devised, with prototyping being among the first to gain a large following.

PROTOTYPING

The communication between the systems developer and user has always been a real challenge. The user has had a difficult time explaining exactly what the problem or opportunity is, what information is needed, how the information should be provided, and so on. The developers have had difficulty understanding and appreciating the user's job and needs.

Experienced developers decided that the communication problem could be reduced, if not completely eliminated, by using a technique that has proven effective in design engineering—prototyping. An automobile design engineer, for example, constructs a prototype of a new automobile. A **prototype** is a model that contains the essential elements of an object to be produced in the future, and is used as a pattern.

Information specialists follow the same approach by developing a prototype of a new information system. In the information systems field, the term prototyping describes the process of quickly building a model of the desired software system, which is used primarily as a communication tool to assess and meet the information needs of the user.

Prototyping can be the *only methodology* that is used in developing a system. This is possible when the system is relatively simple, such as one based on an electronic spreadsheet. A more common approach is to use prototyping *in conjunction with another methodology.* This occurs in large-scale projects, and multiple prototypes can be built. Prototyping can occur at any point in the SDLC.

Types of Prototypes

There are two types of prototypes. One, called an **evolutionary prototype**, eventually becomes the production system after a series of iterative changes based on user feedback. The evolutionary prototype eventually becomes an operational system. Figure 3.3 is a diagram that shows the sequence of events leading to final completion. When the user fails to approve the prototype, the analysis, design, and construction steps are repeated, incorporating the user's suggestions. When the user approves the prototype, it is installed as the production system.

The other type of prototype, called a **requirements prototype,** is a throwaway model that serves as the blueprint for the production system. It is used when the user has difficulty verbalizing exactly what the new system must do in order to meet her or his requirements. Figure 3.4 shows the sequence of events. The prototype must first satisfy the user, and then the production system is developed.

How Prototypes Are Built

Prototyping would not be possible if it were not for the software tools that permit quick delivery. The tools provide two basic prototyping environments—integrated application generators, and prototyping toolkits.

Integrated application generators are prewritten software systems that are capable of producing *all* of the desired prototype features—menus, reports, and screens that are linked to a database.

Prototyping toolkits consist of a collection of *separate software systems,* each capable of producing only a *portion* of the prototype features. Examples of such systems are report generators, screen generators, database management systems, and spreadsheets. Some CASE tools offer one or more of these capabilities. CASE—computer-aided software engineering—tools enable the computer to perform much of the development work. We describe CASE in Technical Module E. Table 3.1 lists some popular tools that can be used in prototyping the front end of the system (the user interface) and the back end (the database).

FIGURE 3.3

An Evolutionary Prototype

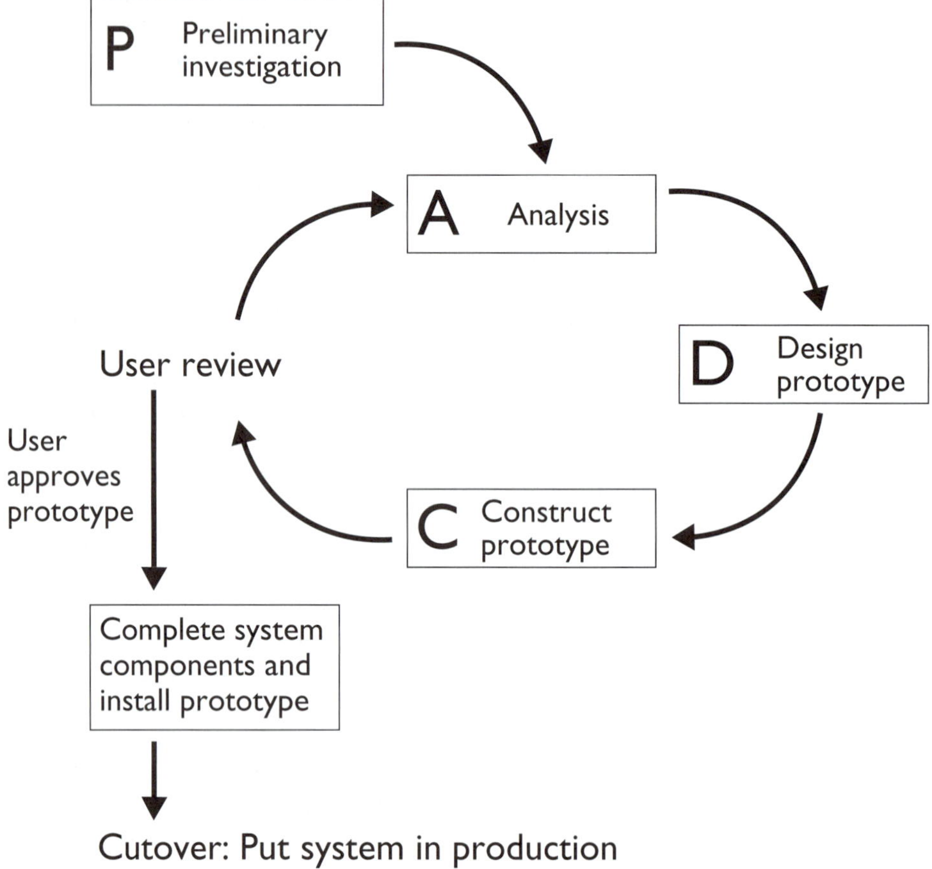

Prototyping Strengths and Weaknesses

Prototyping offers the following potential strengths:

- Communication between the user and the developer is enhanced.
- The user's needs are easier to determine.
- Errors in defining the new system requirements are detected earlier.
- The user plays a more active role in system development—in fact, some users may not provide much help or feedback without viewing a prototype.
- Less time and effort are required on the part of the developer and the user in developing the system.
- Implementation is much easier because the user knows what to expect.

These strengths reduce the cost of developing systems and the systems do a better job of meeting the user's needs.

It is easy to become so excited about prototyping that you lose sight of the fact that it has potential weaknesses:

- The haste to deliver the prototype may produce shortcuts in analysis, solution evaluation, testing, and documentation.
- The users may be so impressed with the prototype that they have unrealistic expectations about how long it takes to complete the production system.
- When an evolutionary prototype becomes the production system, it might not be as efficient as a system coded in a programming language.
- The computer-human interaction that characterizes certain prototyping tools may not reflect good design from a behavioral or physical point of view.

FIGURE 3.4

A Requirements Prototype

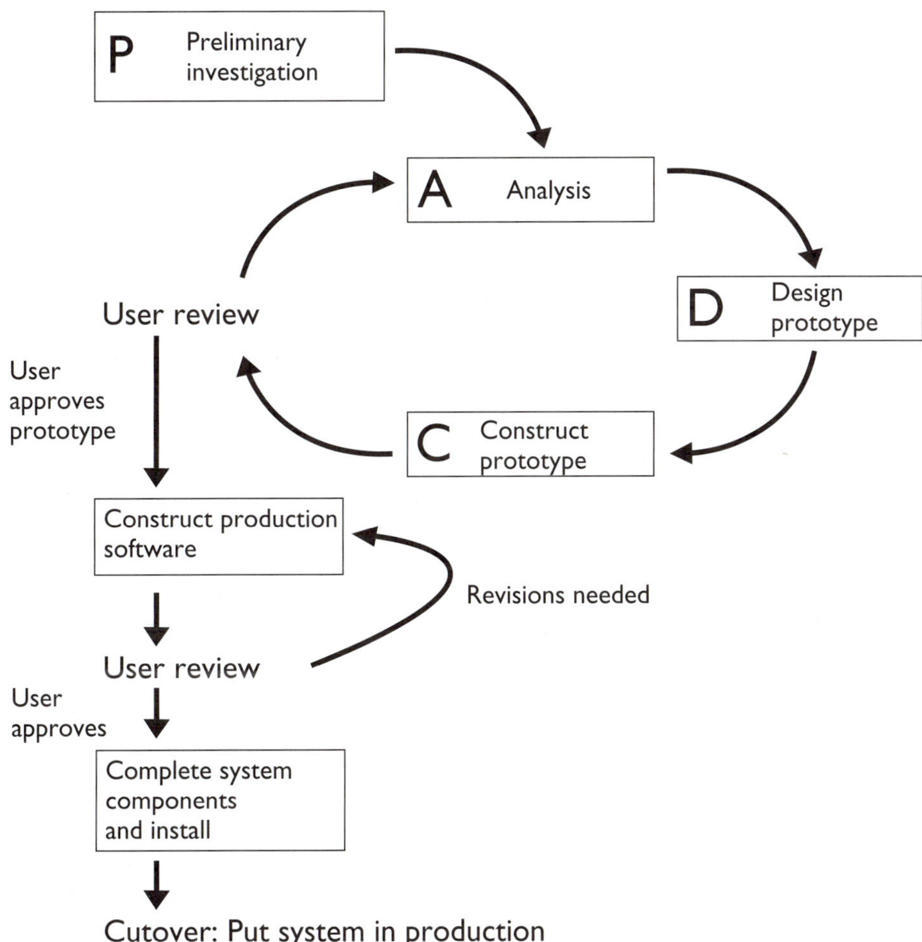

TABLE 3.1

Prototyping Tools

Front End/GUI For evolutionary and requirements prototyping	**Back End/Database** More complex stored procedures would be added after early phases to verify functions
Access	Access
Microsoft Explorer Netscape Browser	Access
Visual BASIC	MS SQL Server Access
PHP	My SQL
Java	JDBC
PowerBuilder	Oracle MS SQL Server Sybase SQL Server Informix
Front Page	

The CIO can implement controls to reduce the likelihood of these weaknesses when the prototyping is done by information specialists. The prototyping efforts of users, however, are much more difficult to control.

Putting Prototyping in Perspective

Prototyping was born out of necessity. System developers found it extremely difficult if not impossible to accurately define system requirements before design began. Users typically have only fuzzy ideas of what technology support they need; they are much more informative when presented with a sample and allowed to respond with suggestions for improvement. Of all the methodologies, prototyping has enjoyed the most success over the longest period of time. Today, it is regarded as a required ingredient in developing systems of all kinds.

RAPID APPLICATION DEVELOPMENT (RAD)

Information Engineering (IE) is a top-down methodology for developing systems that begins with enterprise planning and strategic planning for information resources. Systems are developed using RAD. **RAD,** for **Rapid application development,** is a life cycle strategy that is intended to provide much faster development and higher-quality results than those achieved with the traditional cycle. RAD consists of four stages:

- *Requirements Planning*—Users work with systems developers to identify business problems to be solved.
- *User Design*—Users play a big role in the non-technical design of new systems, assisted by systems developers.
- *Construction*—Systems developers use special software tools to build prototypes, which are reviewed by users. The reviews form the basis for refinements. This process is repeated until an acceptable system is produced.
- *Cutover*—The new system is quickly put into use, following thorough planning.

The RAD life cycle emphasizes speed. The time required to develop a new system is shortened but more effort is required of users. Figure 3.5 shows this higher level of effort and how it is shifted forward in the life cycle.

FIGURE 3.5

Effort Required by the Traditional Life Cycle and the RAD Life Cycle

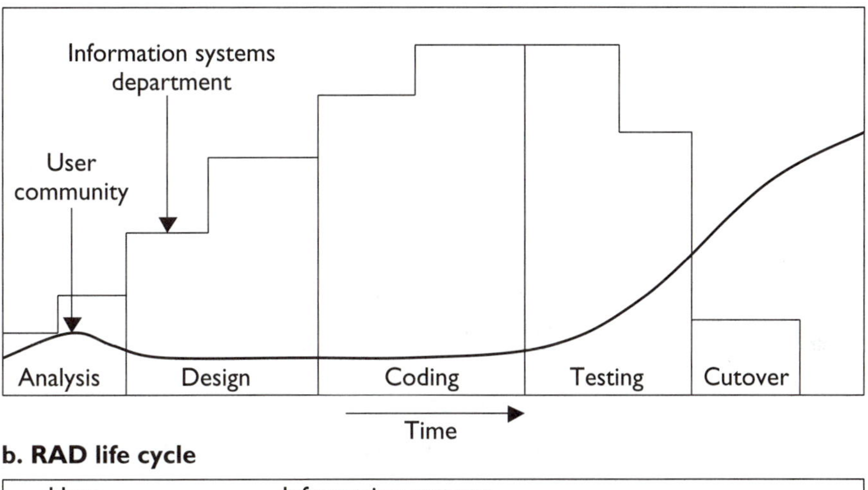

b. RAD life cycle

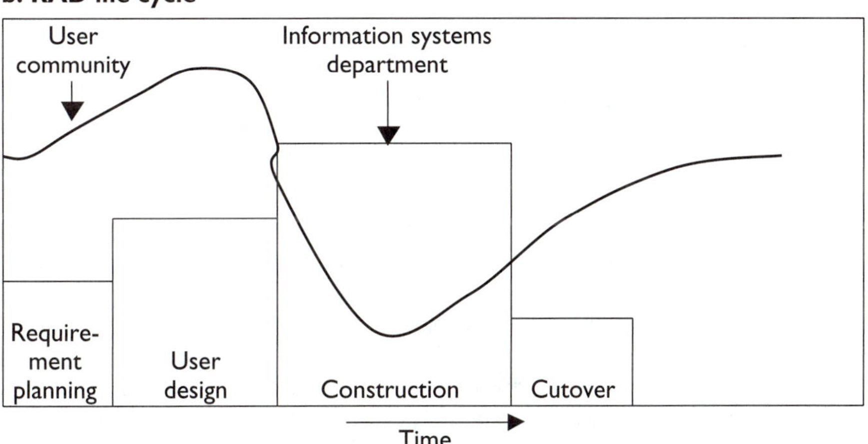

Source: James Martin, *Rapid Application Development,* Prentice Hall, New York, ©1991, page 127. Reprinted by permission of Pearson Education, Inc., Upper Saddle River, NJ.

FIGURE 3.6

The Phased Development Model

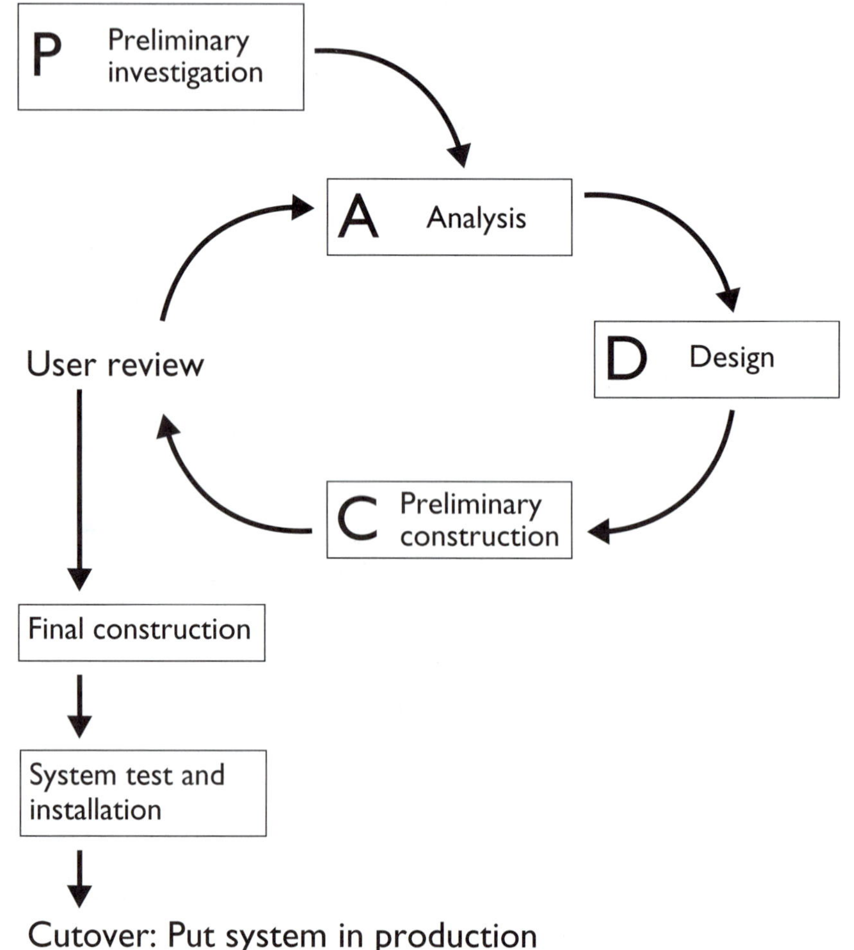

SWAT Teams

An interesting feature of RAD is the use of SWAT teams. SWAT stands for Skilled With Advanced Tools. A **SWAT team,** therefore, is a team of systems developers who are especially skilled in carrying out some particular aspect of system development. For example, one team might specialize in data modeling, another in front-end Web development, and still another in back-end coding. Each team performs only its specialty, moving from project to project. A systems project, therefore, can involve several teams. An e-business project might draw on combinations from SWAT teams expert in middleware connectivity, user interface design, database, and business-to-business communication. The SWAT approach recognizes the wide variety of specialized skills required to develop modern systems and the difficulty of single teams being expert in them all.

Putting RAD in Perspective

RAD grew out of the problem of too few developers to handle the increasing volume of systems projects. The solution was seen as the use of technology and a higher level of user involvement. RAD ties together a variety of modern tools to form a methodology that is well suited to the demands of modern systems work. RAD has enjoyed a solid record of success and is currently extremely popular.

PHASED DEVELOPMENT

The methodology that forms the basis for the remainder of this textbook is called phased development. **Phased development** is a derivation of the staged approach of the traditional SDLC, but it recognizes the need to incorporate the repetitive, looping nature of prototyping, and assumes the use of the modern-day software tools that form the basis for RAD. Figure 3.6 is a diagram that shows the six stages of phased development. The first stage is taken to initiate a project, and then the next three stages are repeated for each system module until each one meets with user approval. The development project concludes with the final two stages.

Preliminary Investigation

The purpose of the preliminary investigation stage is to determine whether to pursue a system development project, and, if so, to perform the necessary preparatory work. Four steps are involved.

Step 1: Perform Enterprise Analysis

The term *enterprise* has been adopted in the business field to capture the sense of modern global operations. In Chapter 1, we discussed enterprise planning and enterprise modeling as the top-down activities leading to the firm's strategic plan for information resources.

Before any work is done on a new project, the systems developer must acquaint himself or herself with the overall firm activity that relates to the potential project. The systems developer and the manager of the user area engage in enterprise analysis, viewing the firm in terms of the general systems model. The enterprise analysis should enable the systems developer and user to pursue the problem chain, sorting through levels of symptoms, and ending with a specific problem statement. In many cases, much documentation will already exist. This is especially true when enterprise analysis and modeling have already been performed. In many firms these efforts are performed on an annual basis.

Step 2: Specify System Boundaries, Determine System Objectives and Goals, and Evaluate Project Risk

With the problem defined, the systems developer and user can specify the system scope, determine what the system will be expected to accomplish, and recognize that certain risks should be addressed. It is especially important that the user and systems developer agree on the system boundaries. Otherwise, the project will be plagued by

FIGURE 3.7

A Use Case Defines System Boundaries

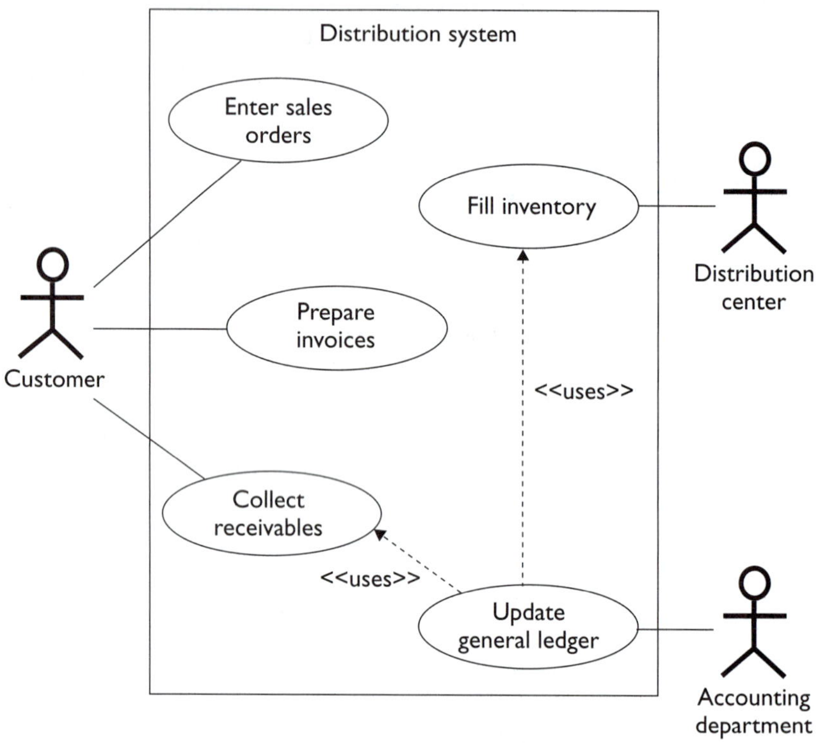

scope creep, where the user continually increases the demands on the new system as it is being developed. An effective tool that the developer can use for scope definition is the use case diagram. The example in Figure 3.7 uses a rectangle to identify the system boundary. The ovals within the boundary represent systems or processes. The stick figures outside the boundary represent persons, organizations, places, or other systems that interface with the system described within the boundary.

Step 3: Evaluate Feasibility and Obtain Approval to Proceed

Before allocating funds to the project, top management wants the assurance that the project and resultant system are feasible. The systems developer does most of the work in conducting feasibility analyses, obtaining any necessary data from the user. With all of the data compiled, the developer reports the findings to management and obtains permission to proceed.

The size and scope of the system determines the level of management approval that is required. For all but extremely small systems, top-level management approval is required. Most firms have an **information systems steering committee** that provides overall direction to the firm's information systems activities. The IS steering committee includes the CIO and other vice presidents and executives and is largely responsible for strategic information planning and monitoring the ongoing systems projects, as described in Chapter 1.

When the IS steering committee is convinced of the feasibility of the system and the project, it works with the project team to put into place a **project control mechanism.** The mechanism can take the form of the project plan, scheduled meetings, periodic reports, and such graphic techniques as bar charts. Some of these mechanisms have been incorporated into computer-based project management systems.

Step 4: Conduct JAD Sessions to Confirm Preliminary Findings

The final step of the preliminary investigation is a JAD session to confirm that the systems developers and the users are in complete agreement concerning the system needs. A **JAD (joint application design) session** is a group meeting of all persons involved with a systems activity to discuss the system and its requirements. JAD has become recognized as an especially effective way to obtain understanding among all project participants concerning the system features and requirements. When agreement cannot be reached, work is redone and another JAD session is scheduled. This process is continued until the manager of the user area and the project team leader agree that the system is well enough understood to proceed to the analysis stage.

With the control mechanism in place and the system focus agreed upon, the systems analysis can begin.

Analysis

The analysis stage is initiated with an announcement by management to the employees that a decision has been made to continue the development project based on the preliminary investigation. The announcement is best accomplished by a combination of written and oral media, such as group meetings. Some firms use videotapes or

FIGURE 3.8

Modular Structure of the Distribution System

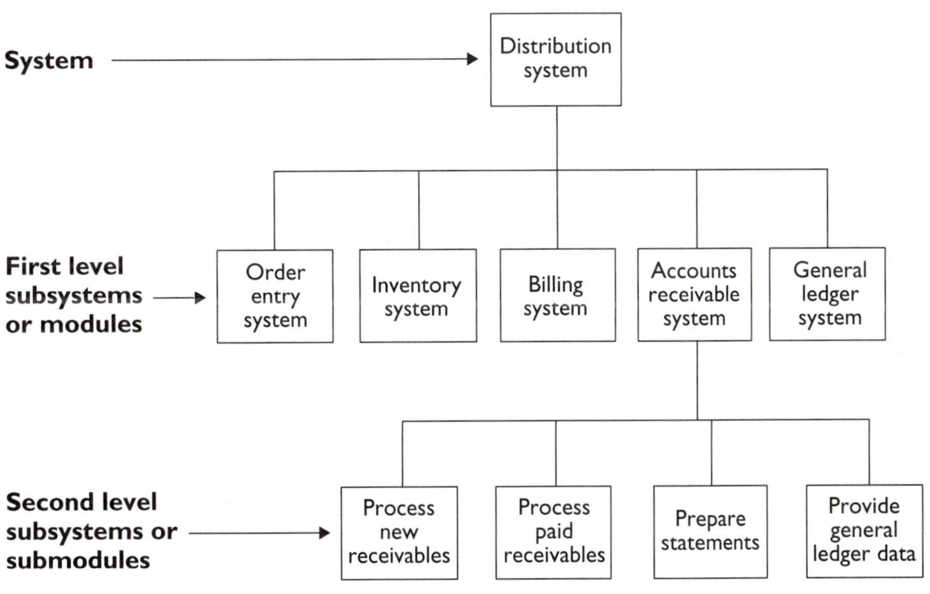

video conferences for large projects so that the announcements can be seen and heard by everyone who will be involved—even those in remote locations. A manager on the highest organizational level that is affected by the system makes the announcement. The president should announce system studies that affect the entire firm, vice presidents should announce studies that affect their areas, and so on down the line.

This stage and the next two of design and preliminary construction are performed in a repeating manner. The system is subdivided into modules—each one performing some part of the processing. Then, the modules are addressed individually in phases. A **phase** is a series of actions that are repeated until the designed system module meets user approval. This idea of repeating phases is the main characteristic of the phased approach.

The sequence in which the modules are addressed and the phases are performed is influenced by several factors. In some cases, a strict top-down direction is maintained. Using the hierarchy diagram of a distribution system in Figure 3.8 as an example, the analysis, design, and preliminary construction stages would first be conducted for the overall distribution system structure, and then for each of the five subsystems. Finally, the stages would be repeated for modules of the subsystems until a complete analysis has been completed.

Deviation from the top-down approach can be influenced by the priority of certain systems and subsystems. Management may insist that certain modules be addressed first. Questions to consider for ordering the phases are summarized in Figure 3.9. The analysis of the functional requirements of the new system will reveal the sequence to be followed in developing the modules. The two main activities of the analysis stage include the analysis of the user's functional requirements, and the documentation of those requirements.

Step 1: Analyze Functional Requirements

The existing system is studied for the purpose of understanding the functions that the new system must perform. A tool that facilitates this analysis is the functions/components matrix, which enables the systems analyst, user, and perhaps the database administrator and the network specialist to view a system in terms of its required processes and resources.

Step 2: Document the Functional Requirements

As the functional requirements of the new system are analyzed, the developers create written documentation in the form of narrative notes and graphic diagrams. The documentation describes both the processes and the data of the existing system. All of the documentation is maintained in a **project dictionary,** a collection of system documentation that the project team members create throughout the SDLC. The term **repository** is used to describe system documentation that resides in an electronic form, such as the project dictionary for a CASE (computer-aided software engineering) system.

The documentation is not merely the recording of the results of the analysis. Rather, the documentation facilitates the analysis. The two activities go hand-in-hand. The process of preparing the documentation enables the systems developers to synthesize the results of the analysis to form a well-ordered set of requirements.

Design

At this point, the systems developers and user understand the existing system and are ready to design a new, improved system. There are three main activities that occur in the design stage: the first two involve design and the third is related to documentation.

Step 1: Design New System Components

The project team designs the new system inputs, outputs, and storage, and specifies the processing to be performed by the hardware and software. When designing the inputs and outputs, special attention is given to user navigation. Since the system is expected to produce some type of outputs for the user, attention can first be given to that function. With the outputs specified, attention can then turn to processing, storage, and inputs. The functions therefore evolve based on the outputs. Figure 3.10 shows this reverse sequence.

Step 2: Design Interfaces with Other Systems

The system being designed will invariably interface with other systems. With the system functions designed, these linkages are then added. The developers can use

FIGURE 3.9

Questions to Consider for Ordering Phases

1. **What is urgent?** If the current billing subsystem in Figure 3.8 is error prone and costing the firm money, then the billing subsystem would be the logical third phase—after (1) preliminary investigation and (2) analysis and design of the overall distribution system.

2. **What could be a quick value added?** Planning to work on the error prone billing system might be the quickest value added, but it might be that the billing system problems require extensive redesign of the business processes and the organization of several business units. In this case the team might decide to start with a subsystem that could be completed and installed for a quick return on investment before starting the more complex billing system. Sometimes a good place to start is where it is easiest to impress the users and gain their confidence and support before tackling more disruptive subsystems.

3. **What is key to understanding requirements?** Completing report design is sometimes key to understanding the users' goals. In that case an early phase might be report design. The reports might be hand drawn and then created with word processing software in this early phase. The goal would be to learn the system requirements by creating a requirements prototype of just the reports before proceeding with any other portions of the system. Data entry is another aspect of the system that can be a good starting point if the end users have been unwilling or unable to provide much help defining requirements.

4. **What is key to determining broad design issues?** Analyzing, designing, and constructing a test database is sometimes the best phase to follow the preliminary investigation. Once the database is designed for the distribution system in Figure 3.8, for example, then a large team might be split into several smaller teams, each working simultaneously on a subsystem phase.

5. **What is key to the rest of development?** Are there other issues that might be important as the basis for later phases? For example, certain users might have a strong influence on system acceptance. The special needs of these "power centers" might be met first in order to gain their support.

FIGURE 3.10

New System Components Are Defined in a Reverse Sequence

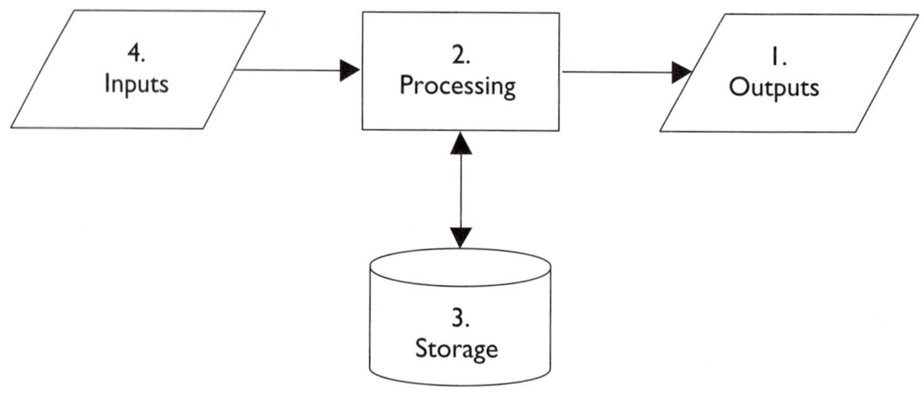

the F/C matrix to identify the linkages. They appear as entries in the input and output columns.

Step 3: Document the New System Design

The new system design is documented in terms of its data, processes, and perhaps objects. When a data-oriented approach is taken, the data model includes such tools as entity-relationship diagrams and the data dictionary. When a process-oriented approach is taken, the process model includes data flow diagrams, structured English, and other tools as required. When an object-oriented approach is taken, the object model includes such diagrams as class diagrams, sequence diagrams, and statechart diagrams. Use case diagrams are appropriate for all three approaches. The data modeling tools are explained in Technical Module A, the process modeling tools are explained in Technical Module B, and the object modeling tools are explained in Technical Module C.

Preliminary Construction

The new system modular design now exists in the form of some combination of models. The next step is to convert these models to a production system consisting of hardware, software, and data. This conversion is accomplished in the preliminary construction stage. At the end of this stage a production system module exists that can be subjected to user review.

Step 1: Construct New System Software Modules and Test Data

When the new system is to use custom software, the code can be prepared by the firm's programmers or it can be outsourced. This custom code can be prepared using programming languages or CASE. Many of the CASE tools have a **code generator** that produces computer code directly from the design documentation.

Whereas large computer-using firms with large staffs of information specialists once invariably opted for developing their own custom software, the practice today is definitely one of making use of prewritten software whenever possible. Rather than prepare custom code, firms assemble the combination of prewritten software that meets their needs.

Regardless of how the software is obtained, the programs are entered in the software library, and program documentation is added to the project dictionary. Test data is prepared to subject the new software to thorough tests to ensure that it will meet the user's needs.

Step 2: Demonstrate to Users and Project Sponsors

The project team demonstrates the new system module to its intended users and to such project sponsors as the IS steering committee. When the users and sponsors are not completely satisfied with the demonstration, they specify what will have to be done in order to make the module acceptable. In that case, the analysis, design, and preliminary construction stages are repeated. This repeating continues until the users and sponsors approve of the design of each module as demonstrated. The project team can then proceed with the final construction.

Final Construction

During final construction, all of the modules of the new system are assembled and made ready for installation. Figure 3.11 illustrates two major points concerning final construction. First it shows the iterative analysis, design, and preliminary construction phases for each module prior to final construction. Each module is documented with a functional delivery to the user. Second, it shows how the five construction activities span the SDLC stages. For example, the activity of planning and administering the education program begins prior to final construction and continues through system test and installation. Each of the five final construction activities is described below.

- **Plan and prepare the physical facilities.** When additional hardware is acquired, work is often required to prepare the computing facility. This work is similar to any construction project, and is performed by one or more contractors. For big changes, work must begin early.

- **Plan, obtain, and install the development environment hardware.** Information specialists provide purchase order details for any new hardware that is required. For large orders they prepare a **request for proposal,** commonly known as an **RFP.** The RFP is sent to hardware vendors, asking them to submit bids. Much detail concerning the design and implementation is included so that the vendors will clearly understand the demands that will be placed upon the hardware. Each vendor who wishes to bid responds with a **proposal** that describes its products and services, and explains why it should be selected. When large orders are involved, vendors supplement the written proposal with formal oral presentations to the IS steering committee and the project team. Once the hardware vendor selection has been made, orders are placed, and the hardware is installed.

- **Obtain software tools, and code or purchase application software.** Programmers plan the acquisition effort for development tools and then prepare custom code. The firm can also purchase application software or follow

FIGURE 3.11

Installation Activities Begin in the Analysis Phase

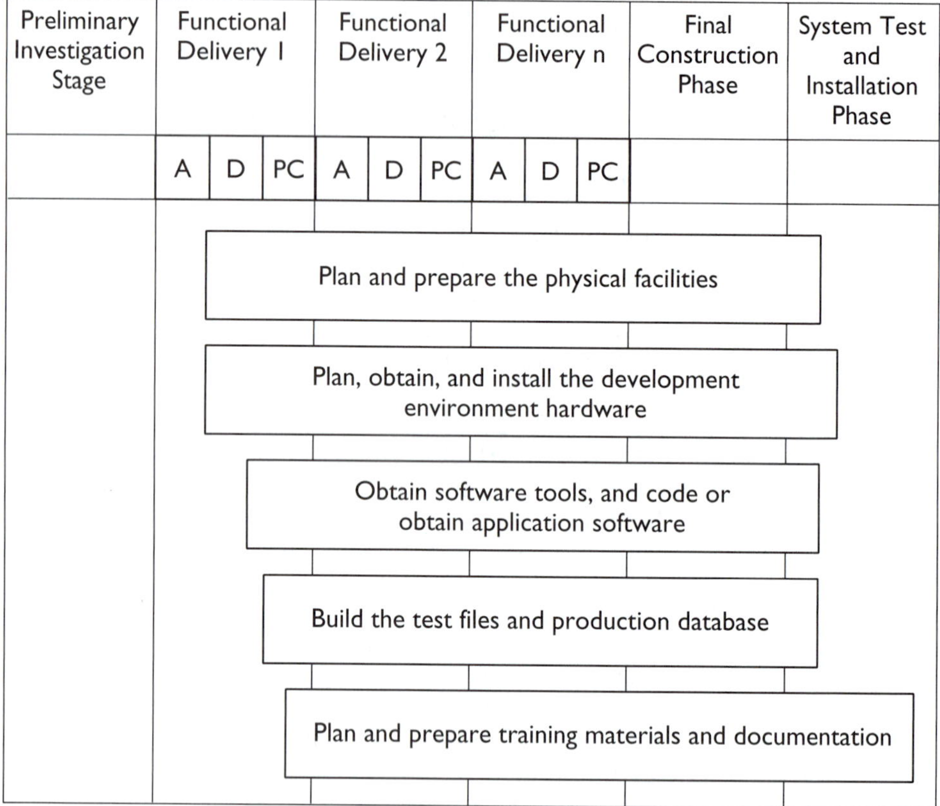

a combination of custom and prewritten code. In the event that production software is purchased, the process that was followed in obtaining hardware is followed for the software—preparing software RFPs, evaluating the software vendors' products, and installing them in accordance with the implementation plan.

- **Build the test files and production database.** Developers create test files to use while coding and testing their software. Database administrators plan for the preparation of the database and then accomplish the preparation.

- **Plan and prepare training materials and documentation.** Planning for the education and training program should begin early in the SDLC even though the sessions will not take place until shortly before cutover to the new system. The education and training can be performed by special education teams, in the case of large firms, or by such information specialists as systems analysts in smaller firms. Analysts are a good choice for this assignment because they have good communication skills and know the system inside and out. Similarly, other user materials and system materials are planned as development progresses.

Final construction concludes with the project team completing the documentation for the project dictionary. This documentation will be important in maintaining and redeveloping the system in the future.

System Test and Installation

The new system is almost ready for installation. Before that occurs, a final system test is required. Installation occurs and then user feedback is obtained to verify acceptability.

Step 1: Design and Perform the System Test

The testing performed up to this point has consisted of tests to ensure that the hardware and software components function as specified. The system test includes the other components as well—people, facilities, procedures, data, and information. The purpose of the system test is to ensure that the complete system will perform satisfactorily once it is turned over to the users.

Step 2: Install Components

Installation of the new system involves replacing the components of the existing system with those of the new one. For example, additional personnel are added to assist existing personnel in performing the functions of the new system. The users begin performing the procedures of the new system.

Step 3: Conduct a User Acceptance Test

The systems developers and possibly members of the firm's internal auditing unit and consultants conduct one or more reviews for the purpose of ensuring that the new system meets its objectives. In some instances, it is necessary to conduct a formal acceptance test to demonstrate the ability of the system to meet all of the system objectives and satisfy the performance criteria.

Putting Phased Development in Perspective

The main strength of phased development is its top-down, modular approach. The existing system is analyzed and the new system is developed in a modular fashion. The top-down focus provides the best opportunity for the new system to meet its objectives, and the modular approach is aimed at ensuring that all of the system modules work together as intended.

Phased development is an SDLC methodology. The stages carry the project through installation and the firm begins to use the system. The system test and installation stage will last as long as the system performs satisfactorily. At some point, it will be necessary to redevelop or scrap the system.

Putting the System Development Life Cycle Methodologies in Perspective

In Chapter 2 we identified the systems approach as the basic systems methodology in the computing field. In this chapter we have described four methodologies for developing and using information systems. All of these methodologies are adaptations of the systems approach. This and the previous two chapters provide you with a good methodological foundation upon which to build your systems career.

PROJECT MANAGEMENT TOOLBOX

Using the Systems Approach to Select the Right Methodology

Early in the project—in fact, as early as possible—the methodology to be followed must be selected. This selection will form the basis for the project plan. The systems approach can provide the framework for this important decision. Essentially, this involves taking the following steps:

1. Understand the main organizational unit where the system will be used.
2. Understand the environment of this organizational unit.
3. Understand subunits within the organizational unit.
4. Define the system to be developed.
5. Identify candidate development methodologies.
6. Evaluate the candidate methodologies.
7. Select the methodology to use.

Understand the Organizational Unit

Use the general systems model of the firm (Figure 1.10) as a blueprint. The organizational unit can be the firm, a major division, a department, or a lower-level unit. Understand the flows of data, information, and decision flows. Pay particular attention to environmental flows.

Understand the Environment

Use the environmental model (Figure 2.1) as a checklist to address the environmental flows identified in Step 1.

Understand the Subunits

Use organization charts of the unit to identify subunits. Identify the units that are directly involved with both internal and environmental flows of data, information, and decisions.

Define the System

Using information gathered during the preliminary investigation stage, define the system to be developed in terms of the system:

- Scope
- Risk
- Complexity

System scope defines the organizational units and environmental elements that will be involved with the system—supplying input and receiving output.

System risk captures the importance of the system in terms of the contribution it can make to the firm if the system is successful, and the consequences if it is unsuccessful. For example, an e-business system has much higher risk than does a system to determine the ideal location of inventory items in the warehouse. Another element of system risk is the extent to which new technology is to be employed. Using new, unproven technology can be extremely risky.

System complexity generally varies by type of system in the information system infrastructure described in Chapter 1. Office automation and accounting information systems tend to be the simplest, management information systems can be moderately complex, and decision support systems and expert systems can be of maximum complexity. System complexity recognizes the degree to which the problem is understood and the degree of success in previous efforts to solve it. With this understanding of the system, attention can turn to the project.

TABLE 3.2

Evaluation of Alternate Development Methodologies Based on *System* Characteristics

System Characteristics	Traditional SDLC	Prototyping	RAD	Phased Development
Scope	Small, medium, or large scope	Small or medium scope	Small, medium, or large scope	Small, medium, or large scope
Risk	Low risk	Medium risk	Medium to high risk	Medium to high risk
Complexity	Little or no complexity	Medium to great complexity	Medium to great complexity	Medium to great complexity

Define the Project

In a similar manner, define the project in terms of:

- Scope
- Risk
- Time constraints

Whereas system scope is concerned with system users, project scope is concerned with system developers. A project that involves developers scattered over a wide area is much more difficult to manage than one that involves developers in one location. Project risk addresses the issues of both user support and developer capability. Are the users supportive of the system effort, and can they be expected to work together? Do the developers have experience in using the development tools that will be required? Time constraints relate to the length of time that the developers will have to complete the systems work. At this point, project management understands the environment in which the system will function, and the basic characteristics of the system and the project.

Identify and Evaluate Candidate Methodologies

The four SDLC methodologies that we described in this chapter may not all be candidates, based on characteristics of the system and the project. Table 3.2 shows how the methodologies compare in terms of the system characteristics. In terms of system scope, prototyping is generally limited to systems of small or medium scope, whereas the other methodologies can handle projects of any scope. The traditional SDLC is best suited to low-risk projects with little or no complexity. The other three methodologies can handle higher levels of risk and complexity.

Table 3.3 shows how the methodologies stack up when faced with certain project characteristics. Again, prototyping is limited in terms of project scope, and the traditional SDLC is ideal when there is little project risk. Prototyping is best suited when time constraints are tight.

Select the Right Methodology

When the project involves a relatively simple, low risk system and there are no tight time constraints, the traditional SDLC is an attractive choice. When system scope is limited but time pressures are tight, prototyping has much appeal. RAD and phased development can be evaluated against each other for risky and

TABLE 3.3

Evaluation of Alternate Development Methodologies Based on *Project* Characteristics

Project Characteristics	Traditional SDLC	Prototyping	RAD	Phased Development
Scope	Small, medium, or large scope	Small or medium scope	Small, medium, or large scope	Small, medium, or large scope
Risk	Low risk	Medium to high risk	Medium to high risk	Medium to high risk
Complexity	Few or no time constraints	Very tight time constraints	Moderate to tight time constraints	Few to moderate time constraints

complex systems. Because a major objective of RAD is speedy development, the phased approach is best suited when time constraints are few or moderate.

The two tables greatly simplify the factors that influence methodology choice. Perhaps after gathering the data on the system and project, the project management team and the users can gather in a JAD session for the purpose of applying the expertise and judgment that influence the final choice.

Methodology Goals

The main goal of all methodologies is to ensure that consistency exists in the firm's many systems development efforts. The methodologies represent proven approaches that fit the needs of the firm. The consistency can be seen in system requirements specifications, system design specifications, and the system test plan.

- System requirements specifications document the user's needs and are expressed in terms of the new system objectives and performance criteria. These specifications are created during the preliminary investigation and analysis stages.
- System design specifications document the new system design in terms of data and processes. These specifications make use of data, process, and object modeling techniques and first emerge during the analysis stage. They are finalized during the design stage.
- The system test plan specifies the rigor that will be followed in testing the new system software and hardware. The testing comes during the preliminary construction, final construction, and system test and installation stages of the SDLC.

The documentation that is produced by each methodology enables the systems developers to better understand the system and to communicate among themselves. The documentation also facilitates communication among all stakeholders—users and project managers on each organizational level, including the IS steering and executive committees. The methodologies provide a common language that enables everyone who is involved in the project to work together.

Summary

Methodologies are recommended ways of doing things. They exist in a hierarchy, with the scientific method providing the basis for methodologies that guide system development.

The staged evolutionary process that an information system follows is called the system development life cycle, or SDLC. When a system reaches the end of its production stage it can be scrapped or it can trigger redevelopment.

Since the SDLC is based on the proven logic of the systems approach, there have been few changes over the years in terms of the logical sequence of tasks that are performed—planning, analysis, design, implementation, and production. However, there have been some refinements. One of the first to earn a large following was prototyping. There are two basic kinds of prototypes. Evolutionary prototypes eventually become production systems whereas requirements prototypes provide the basis for the development of production systems. Everything considered, prototyping is a prescribed system development methodology. But, it has its weaknesses, most of which result from lack of control.

Information engineering (IE) makes maximum use of information system-based techniques and is intended to achieve development speed without sacrificing quality. The development portion of IE is called RAD, for rapid application development. RAD consists of a four-stage life cycle, heavy user involvement, and SWAT teams. An outgrowth of IE is the phased development methodology, which consists of six stages, three of which are repeated for each system and subsystem module.

An understanding of these methodologies is a fundamental knowledge for anyone who develops information systems. The understanding enables you to make contributions during systems development that achieve consistency in the firm's system requirements, design, and testing efforts

Key Terms

feasibility study
system study
systems maintenance
prototype
Information Engineering (IE)
evolutionary prototype
requirements prototype
SWAT (skilled with advanced tools) team
scope creep
information systems steering committee
joint application design (JAD) session
project dictionary
repository
request for proposal (RFP)
proposal
cutover

Key Concepts

- The system development life cycle (SDLC)
- The repeating nature of the SDLC
- Prototyping
- Information engineering (IE)

- Rapid application development (RAD)
- Phased development

QUESTIONS

1. What is the relationship between the systems approach and the SDLC?
2. Why subdivide the system development life cycle into stages and steps?
3. What is a feasibility study?
4. What purpose does a project control mechanism serve? Give three examples of such mechanisms.
5. What is meant by performance criteria?
6. What are the two types of prototypes? Which type does not have to be maintained? Why?
7. How does a SWAT team differ from a project team?
8. In what major way does phased development differ from the traditional SDLC?
9. Which phased development stages are repeated in an iterative manner?
10. What factors can influence the sequence in which the modules are constructed when following the phased development methodology?
11. Where is all of the system documentation maintained?
12. Who prepares an RFP? Who prepares a proposal?
13. What are the goals of methodology?

TOPICS FOR DISCUSSION

1. A set of house blueprints is an example of a methodology, and a carpenter uses various tools in applying that methodology. What are some other examples of everyday methodologies and corresponding tools?
2. How could an IS steering committee ensure that prototyping projects do not skip over problem definition, alternative evaluation, and documentation?

PROBLEM

1. Assume that you have decided to replace your laser printer with a printer that serves as a printer, a copier, and a fax machine. Conduct research and identify three manufacturers of the combination unit. (Hint: Computer and office equipment stores usually have these machines on their shelves.) Prepare a one-page letter that can be sent to each manufacturer, serving as an RFP. You are primarily interested in the cost of the printer, the printing speed, the copying speed, the cost of replacement toner cartridges, and the term of the guarantee. Make copies of the three letters.

CASE PROBLEM: SPLASHDOWN (A)

You have just been hired as a systems analyst by Spashdown, a large water park near NASA, on the outskirts of Houston. On your first day, the systems analyst manager, Mildred Wiggins, explains that one of the important decisions in a system development life cycle is whether to use prototyping. Mildred explains that job requests come in from users every day and, for each, the prototyping decision must be made. She thinks that some type of printed form would make the decision easier. Since she knows that you are an expert in prototyping, she asks you to design the form. She wants the form to list the factors that go into the decision and, for each, to include a five-point scale. She gives you a sheet of paper that lists the six factors as she sees them.

1. There is a *high risk* involved—the problem is not well structured, there is a high rate of change over time, and the data requirements are uncertain.
2. There is considerable *user interaction*—the system features online dialog between the user and the user's workstation.
3. There are a *large number of users* and agreement on design details is difficult to achieve without hands-on experience.
4. The system must be *delivered quickly* and is expected to have a short life span.
5. The system is *innovative,* either in the way that it solves the problem or its use of hardware.
6. The user's *behavior is unpredictable* in relation to the system due to lack of experience with such a system

As an example of the scale that addresses user interaction, Mildred makes a sketch:

1. The amount of online dialog between the user and the information system is:

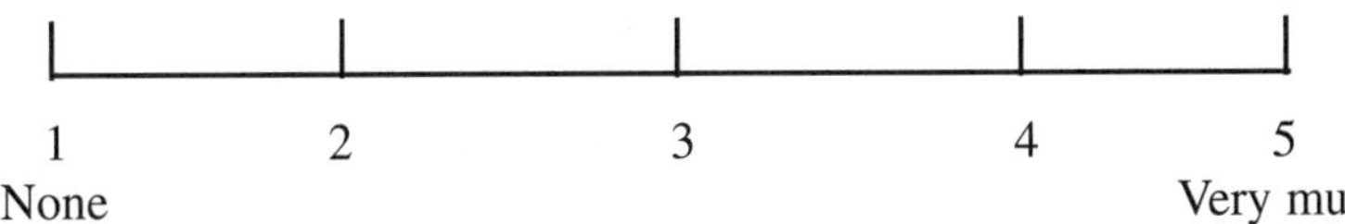

The scale points have values ranging from 1 to 5. The developer who must make the prototyping decision will circle the scale points that best describe a potential application. The scale points for all of the factors will be added together, producing a total. Design the form so that a high total indicates a good prototyping prospect.

After you design the form, Mildred wants you to test it out on three prospective applications. You interview the people who submitted the job requests, and obtain the following information:

Cash Flow Model: The controller wants to implement an electronic spreadsheet on his PC to show the flow of money into and out of the firm. This is a common application, with all firms doing the job a standard way. The controller is currently performing the calculations using pencil and paper. However, he is in no big hurry to make the switch since he feels comfortable with the manual system, and nobody else is involved.

Sales Commission System: The sales manager wants to implement a system for computing salespersons' commissions according to a new formula that he heard about on his last trip to California. The formula takes into account each salesperson's Zodiac sign. Before the sales manager can give the go ahead to use the new system, it must be approved by all six marketing managers at headquarters. The mainframe information system program will make the computations, and print the results in the form of a monthly sales commission report. The sales manager is anxious to get the system on the air because he was recently transferred from the shipping department and has no experience in computing sales commissions. Although commission accounting is usually cut and dried, this approach contains some gray areas that have not yet been explored.

Job Openings System: The director of human resources wants to create an Intranet system that employees can use from their workstations to retrieve lists of current job openings in the company. It will be strictly a database retrieval application—no computations. Most of the firm's 1200 employees regularly use a database in their daily work. The director wants the system in place no later than 30 days from now, just prior to negotiations on the new union contract.

Assignments

1. Design the form that Mildred has requested. Use your word processor or similar software. Be as inventive as you can in the form layout. Print a blank copy.
2. Make three additional copies of your form, and complete them using the findings of your data gathering.

3. Prepare a memo to Mildred, advising her of your forms design efforts, and your recommendations concerning the three jobs. Do you recommend prototyping, and, if so, how strong is your recommendation? Attach the blank form, followed by the three completed forms.

SELECTED BIBLIOGRAPHY

Barlow, John F. "Putting Information Systems Planning Methodologies Into Perspective." *Journal of Systems Management* 41 (July 1990): 6ff.

Borger, Egon, and Wolfram Schulte. "A Practical Method for Specification and Analysis of Exception Handling—A Java/JVM Case Study." *IEEE Transactions on Software Engineering* 26 (Number 9, September 2000): 872-887.

El Louadi, Mohamed; Yannis A. Pollalis; and James T. C. Teng. "Selecting a Systems Development Methodology: A Contingency Framework." *Information Resources Management Journal* 4 (Winter 1991): 11-19.

Gavurin, Stuart L. "Where Does Prototyping Fit In IS Development?" *Journal of Systems Management* 42 (February 1991): 13-17.

Khalifa, Mohamed, and June M. Verner. "Drivers for Software Development Method Usage." *IEEE Transactions on Engineering Management* 47 (Number 3, August 2000): 360-369.

Li, Eldon Y. "Software Testing in a System Development Process: A Life Cycle Perspective." *Journal of Systems Management* 41 (August 1990): 23?31.

Martin, James. Rapid Application Development (New York: Macmillan, 1991).

Skarke, Gary; Dutch Holland; Bill Rogers; and Diane Landon. *The Change Management Toolkit* (Houston, TX: WinHope, 1995).

Sullivan, Tom. "Merant Takes ASP Approach to Application Development." *Infoworld* 22 (Number 38, September 18 2000): 22.

Willis, T. Hillman, and Debbie B. Tesch. "An Assessment of Systems Development Methodologies." *Journal of Information Technology Management* 2 (Number 2, 1991): 39-45.

TECHNICAL MODULE D

PROJECT PLANNING AND CONTROL

Firms have traditionally treated the development of an information system as a project. One or more of the system development life cycle (SDLC) methodologies discussed in Chapter 3 guide the developers through the project. The developers are usually organized into one or more project teams, which can include members of the firm's IS unit, representatives of the user area where the system is to be applied, and such other members as consultants and outsourcers.

PROJECT MANAGEMENT AND THE PROJECT MANAGEMENT MECHANISM

Project management consists of all the actions that are taken by the firm's managers to ensure that the project meets three basic objectives—functionality, timeliness, and cost effectiveness. The project is expected to produce a system that meets the user's functional requirements, and the project is expected to be completed within the allotted time, at a cost not to exceed the budgeted estimate.

Project management is facilitated by a **project management mechanism** that consists of project managers, the project plan, a system of scheduled meetings and reports that enable the managers to monitor actual progress compared to the plan. In the following sections, we first discuss each of these management elements. We then provide tips for creating useful reports. In the final section we describe a quantitative estimating technique that can be used for project cost management.

PROJECT MANAGERS

Managers who are involved in managing a project exist in a hierarchy. This hierarchy, beginning at the highest management level and working down, consists of:

- The firm's executive committee
- The firm's IS steering committee
- Management in the user area and the firm' IS unit
- The project team leader or leaders

The executive committee includes the president and vice presidents and other executives who have the responsibility to develop and carry out the firm's strategic business plan. The IS steering committee includes some of the members of the executive committee plus other top-level managers who have the responsibility to develop and carry out the firm's strategic plan for information resources. Managers in the user area ensure that the system meets the needs of their area and allocate their own personnel to participate in the development. Managers in the firm's IS unit allocate and manage the IS resources that are assigned to the project. The project team leader has the responsibility to provide day-to-day management of the members of the team. Some teams can have more than a single leader, and some projects may involve more than a single team.

The Project Plan

The **project plan** consists of a list of all of the activities or tasks that must be performed during the process of developing the system. The responsibility for performing each activity is assigned to one or more persons, and an estimate is made of the amount of time required to perform each one.

Since a project typically includes many activities, perhaps hundreds, the accepted practice is to group them into stages and phases. In Chapter 3, we identified the stages of the traditional system development life cycle and the phased development methodology. In addition to the SDLC stages, the project activities can be organized in terms of phases that relate to modules of the system being developed.

Figure D.1 illustrates a typical way to subdivide the project when using the phased development methodology. The project begins with the preliminary investigation phase. This is the first stage of the phased development methodology. Then, the next phases are based on the system being developed. Each phase represents a subsystem module, such as Web interface and database. The number of subsystem modules varies by system. Upon completion of the subsystem modules, the next phase is final construction, followed by system test and installation. The two final phases are the final stages of the phased development methodology.

You will notice that each phase is identified with the lettering A-D-C-R. These letters represent analysis, design, construction, and review. Each phase consists of analysis, followed by design, then construction, and finally review activity.

1. *Analysis*—Determining the user requirements of this phase
2. *Design*—Determining how you are going to meet the user requirements for this phase
3. *Construction*—Creating the user deliverables for this phase
4. *Review*—Reviewing the deliverables for this phase with the user

The structure identified in Figure D.1 forms an excellent starting point for a project plan. It is only necessary to fill in each phase with the detailed analysis, design,

FIGURE D.1

An Example of the Phases of Phased Development

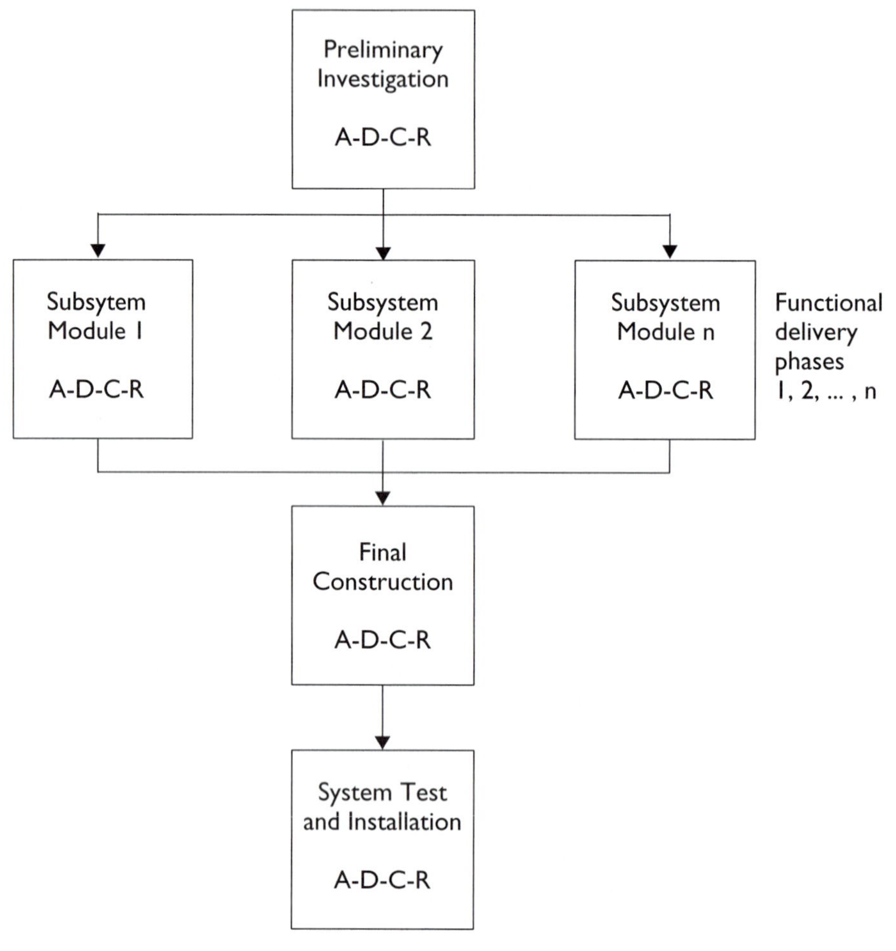

construction, and review activities that are required. With the project plan in place, the various levels of project managers use it to monitor the development process.

SCHEDULED MEETINGS

Project managers schedule periodic meetings to discuss the progress of the project as it evolves through the planned stages and phases. The highest-level group of managers are members of the IS steering committee that meets periodically to monitor project progress. Early in the SDLC, the meetings may be held once a month. As the cutover date approaches, the meetings occur more frequently, such as once each week. During a meeting, the steering committee chairperson directs the discussion. The project team leader is always in attendance, and she or he may invite team members when their expertise is needed. The steering committee chairperson will also invite such other persons as consultants and vendor representatives as they become involved in the project. On a lower organizational level, the project leader follows a similar approach in scheduling and conducting meetings of the project team.

Reports

Once the project team is formed, the project leader has the responsibility of preparing reports, usually weekly, that keep the management levels advised concerning the team's progress. Since a firm can have many projects ongoing at any one time, and each manager's time is valuable, the reports should be as brief as possible, straight to the point, and easy to read. Three types of reports are prepared—narrative, graphic, and tabular.

Narrative Reports

Narrative reports provide the basic framework for the discussions in the scheduled meetings. The reports address three topics:

1. Progress since the last report
2. Any problems that must be resolved
3. Tasks to be performed during the coming reporting period

The reports provide a written record of the project team's activity. The reports provide a good chronology of problems that were encountered and solutions that were implemented. Such a record can be valuable in the future as similar systems problems are encountered. Copies of the reports should be distributed prior to the meetings so that the attendees have an opportunity to read them over and prepare for the discussion.

Graphic Reports

The project participants recognize the value of graphics as a means of effectively communicating information. Two graphic techniques that have enjoyed widespread use are Gantt charts and network diagrams.

Gantt Charts

Henry L. Gantt, a management consultant who practiced his trade around 1900, is credited with the idea of using a bar chart to schedule work. The chart is typically called a **Gantt chart,** although some software tools refer to it as a **project work plan.** Each activity to be performed is listed down the left-hand side. Horizontal bars show when the work will be performed. Figure D.2 shows the basic format. In this example, there are ten activities. A time scale is provided for each activity, which identifies the planned start and completion dates. The time scale can be based on months, weeks, or days.

The main limitation of the Gantt chart is the fact that it fails to show the interrelationships between activities. Perhaps one cannot begin until another is completed. One way to achieve the interrelationships is to arrange the activities in the form of a network diagram.

FIGURE D.2

A Gantt Chart

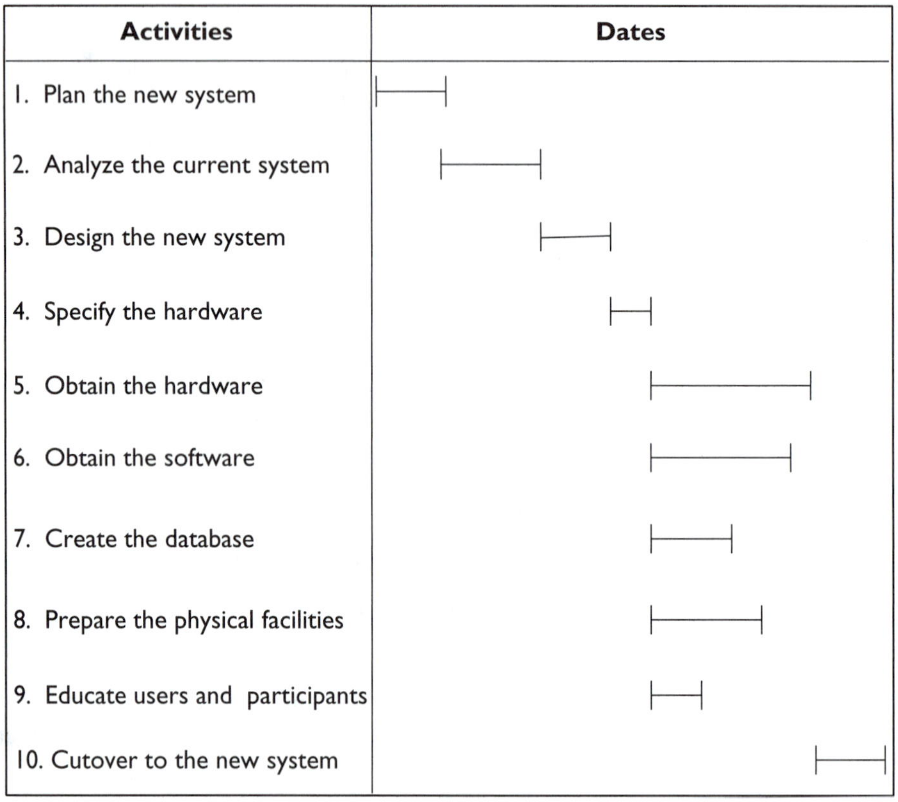

Activities	Dates
1. Plan the new system	
2. Analyze the current system	
3. Design the new system	
4. Specify the hardware	
5. Obtain the hardware	
6. Obtain the software	
7. Create the database	
8. Prepare the physical facilities	
9. Educate users and participants	
10. Cutover to the new system	

Network Diagrams

A **network diagram** is a pattern of interconnected arrows that represents work to be done. Figure D.3 portrays the same project plan as the ten-activity Gantt chart in a network form. Perhaps you have heard a network diagram referred to as a CPM diagram or PERT chart. They are the two basic network diagram formats and they differ in how they compute the activity times.

A **CPM (critical path method)** diagram uses a single time estimate for each activity. The estimate is the best that can be made using the available information. A network typically represents a maze of paths, but all of them may not require the same amount of time to complete. The most important path is the one that requires the *most amount of time.* This path is called the critical path because it determines the overall time of the project.

A **PERT (program evaluation and review technique) chart** uses *three* time estimates-an optimistic, a pessimistic, and a most likely. The formula below is one that is often used and it shows how the most likely estimate has the greatest influence.

$$\text{Activity time} = \frac{T_p + 4T_m + T_o}{6}$$

Where: T_p = pessimistic time
T_m = most likely time
T_o = optimistic time

For example, if Tp = 1.2, Tm = 4.0, and To = 5.0, the activity time would be:

$$\frac{1.2 + 16.0 + 5.0}{6} = \frac{22.2}{6} = 3.7$$

The appearance of a PERT chart is the same as that of a CPM diagram. Both reflect single times for each activity. In the case of PERT, the single times are computed from the three estimates.

Tabular Reports

The tabular arrangement of information is the classical report format. The information is displayed in the form of rows and columns. Certain information can be communicated in the most effective way in this form. Figure D.4 is an example of a tabular report used for project management. This report is a summary report that identifies major milestones. A **milestone** is an activity that, when accomplished, can represent

FIGURE D.3

A Network Diagram

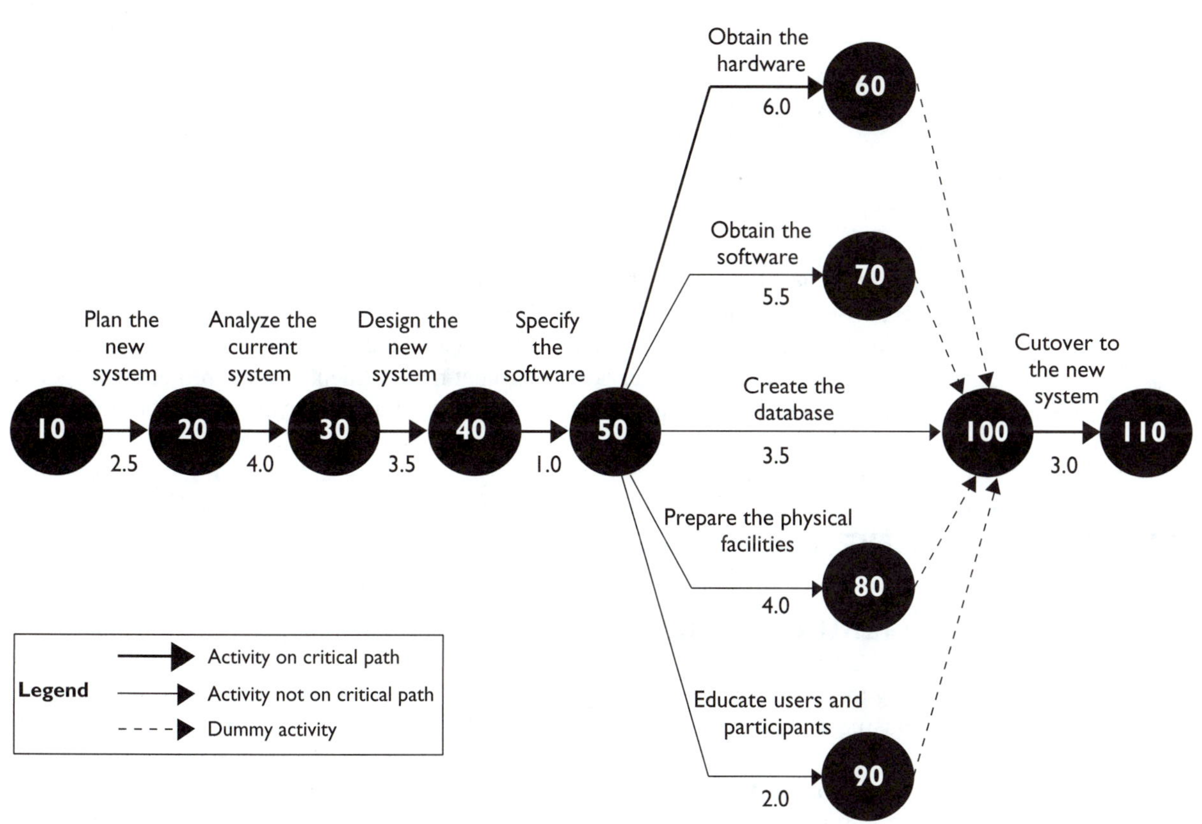

FIGURE D.4

A Portion of a Milestone Summary Report

Phases and Milestones	Week	Ending Date
Phase 1: Preliminary Investigation & Analysis		
Conduct initial sessions with clients	Week 1	October 6
Investigate background information		
JAD session with client and users	Week 2	October 13
Document existing systems		
Create problem chain		
Analyze system objectives, constraints, and scope		
Establish a project control mechanism		
JAD session with client for requirements	Week 3	October 20
Present prototype and system plan		
Receive feedback and approval		
Revise system plan and user interface	Week 5	November 3
Phase 2: Design System Database		
Analyze software and security requirements		
Design and construct HTML template		
Design and construct prototype Web site structure		
Client validation of proposal	Week 6	November 10
Phase 3: Marketing Module		
Analyze marketing strategy		
Develop marketing section		
Review development with client	Week 6	November 10

measurable progress in the development process. A milestone should represent an activity where there can be no question whether it has been accomplished. Excellent milestone activities are user deliverables that come at the end of stages or phases.

This concludes the overview of project management and the project management mechanism. The remainder of the technical module will be devoted to providing more detail on Gantt charts and network diagrams, plus the use of quantitative project cost estimating techniques.

TIPS FOR CREATING USEFUL REPORTS

Gantt Chart Techniques

Figure D.5 is the beginning portion of a Gantt chart for a project to develop an e-business Web site. The heading identifies the project, provides a legend for the shading of the bars, and lists the project team members. The body provides the detail for each activity.

In this example, the system developers decided to use the pattern in Figure D.1 for the basic structure. Phase 1 is a combination of the first two phased development

FIGURE D.5

A Gantt Chart Prepared with Spreadsheet Software

Project Planning Documentation

System: Online Career Labs Supplemental Web Site
Date: October 27th
Chart Type: Gantt Chart

Assigned task
Completed task

Team #2:
Person 1 Person 3 Person 5 Person 1/Person 2/Person 5 = "1/2/5"
Person 2 Person 4 Person 3/Person 4 = "3/4"

Task		Activity	Assignment	Scheduled Time	Oct 6	13	20	27	Nov. 3	10	17	24
	Phase 1: Preliminary Investigation											
	Analysis											
1	A-1	Initiate contact with project sponsors (schedule meetings)		10/2 - 10/2		*Person 4*						
2	A-2	Informal meeting with client (introductions & organization summary)		10/4 - 10/4		*Team*						
3	A-3	Hold group meeting to prepare for initial contact		10/8 - 10/8			*Team*					
4	A-4	Conduct initial meeting with client sponsors (Susan and Susan)		10/9 - 10/9			*Team and Client*					
5	A-5	Hold meeting with lab members		10/9 - 10/9			*Team and Client*					
6	A-6	Hold team meeting to assess information		10/15 - 10/15				*Team*				
7	A-7	Conduct JAD session with client to investigate system needs		10/16 - 10/16				*Team and Client*				
8	A-8	Investigate background information		10/16 - 10/16				*Person 4 and Client*				
9	A-9	Document the career lab system		10/16 - 10/16				*Person 2*				
10	A-10	Create a problem chain		10/17 - 10/17				*Person 1*				
11	A-11	Investigate hardware alternatives		10/17 - 10/17				*Person 5*				
12	A-12	Analyze system objectives, constraints, and scope		10/17 - 10/17				*Person 1*				
13	A-13	Analyze available resources, benefits, and feasibility		10/16 - 10/21				*Team*				
14	A-14	Analyze documentation needs		10/20 - 10/31						*Team*		
15	A-15	Assign specific documentation roles to team members		10/31 - 10/31						*Team*		
16	A-16	Analyze project risk		10/10 - 10/31						*Person 3/Team*		
17	A-17	Hold group meeting to assess all information		11/5 - 11/5							*Team*	
	Design											
18	D-1	Prepare and submit preliminary system proposal		11/6 - 11/6							*Team*	
19	D-2	Get initial approval from user sponsor		11/6 - 11/6							*Team*	
20	D-3	Design steps to reduce risk		10/17 - 10/17				*Person 3*				
21	D-4	Investigate feasibility of project objectives		10/16 - 10/31						*Team*		
22	D-5	Put a project control mechanism (Gantt chart) into place		10/16 - 10/31						*Team*		
23	D-6	Design documentation standards for project		10/27 - 10/31						*Team*		
	Construct											
24	C-1	Begin to put risk-reduction strategies into place		10/20 - 10/31						*Team*		
25	C-2	Prepare prototype of proposed system components		10/24 - 10/31						*Team*		
26	C-3	Produce and present documentation for initial proposal		10/20 - 10/31						*Team*		
	Review											
27	R-1	Conduct JAD session to confirm preliminary findings		10/20 - 10/31						*Team*		
28	R-2	Revise plan as needed		10/15 - 11/2						*Team*		

methodology stages-preliminary investigation and analysis. Phases 2, 3, and 4, which are not shown, are subsystem modules unique to the system being developed.

Each activity is assigned a sequential task number, which is listed at the beginning of the row. In addition, each activity has a unique code. The codes represent a **work breakdown structure,** which is simply a method of uniquely identifying each activity or task in a project. In this example, the work breakdown structure uses the letters A, D, C, and R to identify those particular types of activity. These are only examples; the coding scheme can vary from one firm to another.

The activity descriptions are expressed as a combination of verb and object, which is the recommended technique. In this example, using a Microsoft Excel spreadsheet, the scheduled times are next identified, followed by the persons who are assigned to do the work. This sequence can be reversed, the team assignments coming before the times. The word *team* recognizes that an activity is accomplished by the entire team. The scheduled time identifies the scheduled beginning date followed by the scheduled ending date. The time duration for the activity is illustrated with a bar. Shading identifies whether the activities have been completed. A popular project management software tool is Microsoft Project. In addition to preparing the Gantt chart, it can also prepare a network diagram from the same file.

Hints for Identifying Gantt Chart Activities

As the size of the project increases, the identification of Gantt chart activities becomes more intimidating. "Where do we start?" If you follow these hints, it is not so difficult.

- Subdivide the project into the stages of the SDLC methodology. Select the ones that appear relevant to your project. When using the phased development methodology, good candidates are preliminary investigation, final construction, and system test and installation.
- Subdivide the project into submodules of the system being developed. Each submodule represents a phase. Popular submodules are Web interface, database, and reporting modules. Others can take the form of processes that meet user requirements, organizational units, management levels, and so on.
- Subdivide each phase into the A-D-C-R grouping. For each one, think in terms of the deliverables that the user will expect. Refer to Chapters 6, 7, and 8 for descriptions of activities involving analysis, design, and construction.
- When the entire team is to work together on a phase, the identification of activities can be accomplished in a group meeting. When only selected team members are involved, those persons can meet together.
- Once the entire Gantt chart is roughed out, the entire team can review it in a meeting.

By subdividing the project into small subsets, the planning has a much sharper focus and you can expect accuracy to improve.

Network Diagram Techniques

Each arrow in a network diagram represents an activity. The activities are performed in a left-to-right sequence, and you cannot begin an activity until all of the activities leading to it have been completed. Figure D.6 is an example of a simplified network diagram of the activities that are performed during a pit stop at an Indianapolis 500 automobile race.

Activities and Nodes

This particular format for a network diagram is called an **activity-oriented diagram.** The important information is specified in the activities. Each activity is labeled with a brief description plus an estimate of the amount of time that will be required. In the Indy diagram, the estimates are in seconds.

At the beginning and end of each arrow is a circle, called a **node.** The purpose of the nodes is to provide a unique identification to each of the activities. If you were referring to the first activity of the Indy diagram, you could identify it as activity 10-20.

FIGURE D.6

A Network Diagram of an Indianapolis 500 Pit Stop

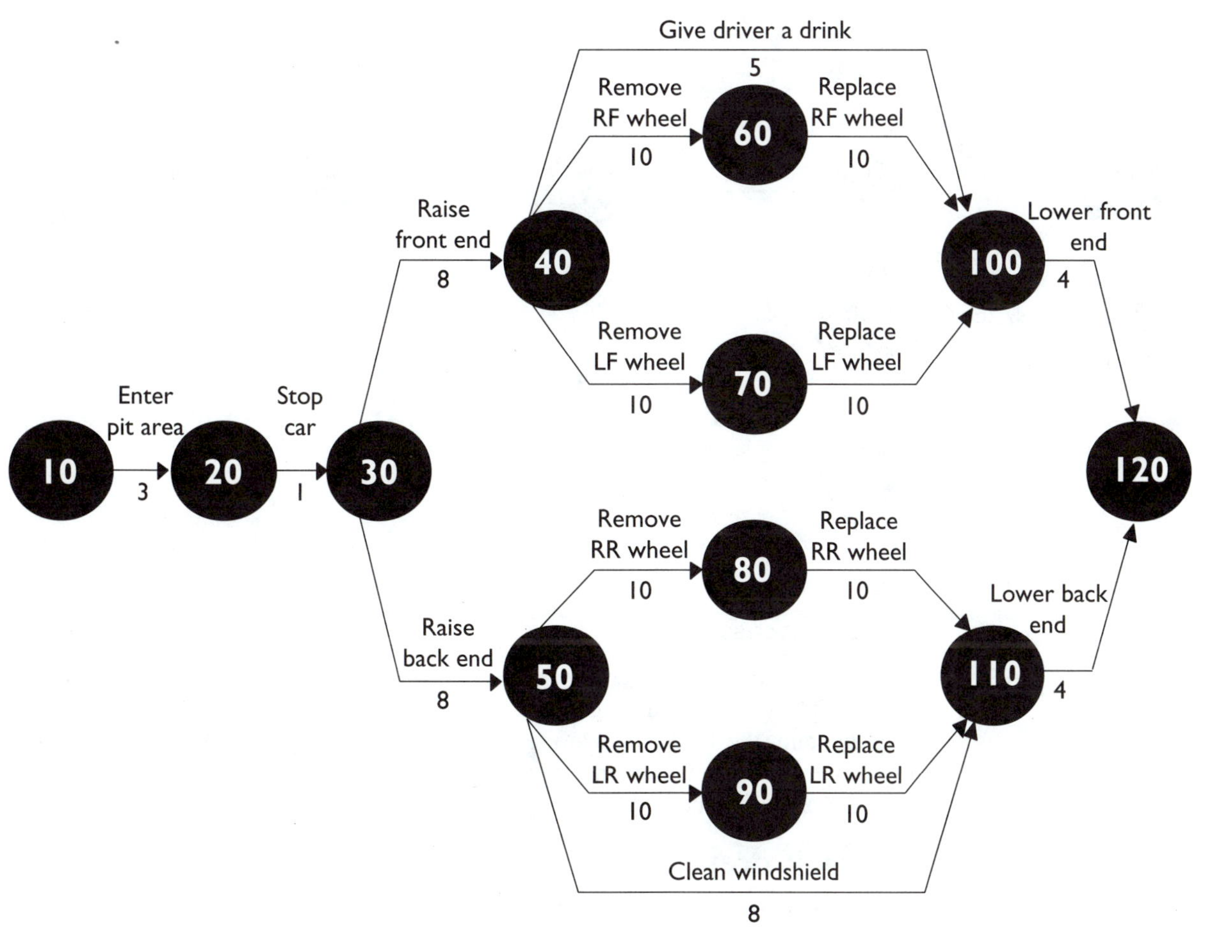

FIGURE D.7

The Network Diagram for Banking System Analysis (expressed in working days)

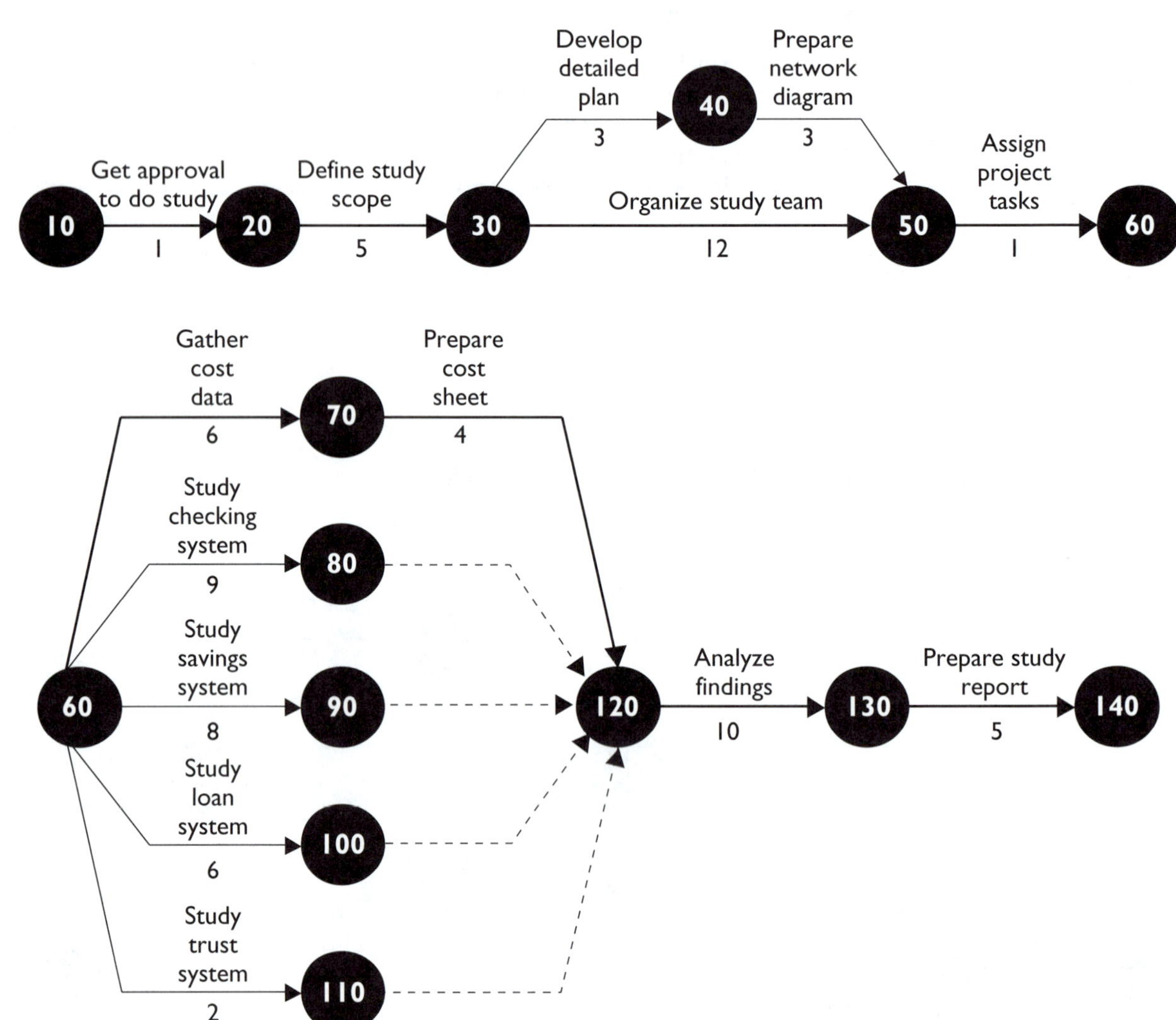

Serial Processes

The pattern of the network arrows reveals the manner in which the work is performed. When single arrows are arranged in a series, such as activities 10-20 and 20-30 in the Indy diagram, the work is performed serially-one activity after the other. In a serial arrangement, the same person, or persons, can accomplish all of the activities, moving from one to the next.

Parallel Processes

When more than a single activity can be performed at a time, the arrows can be arranged in parallel, as shown in the Indy diagram between nodes 30 and 120. The important point to remember about parallel processes is that separate resources are required.

Dummy Activities

You will often see a network diagram with unlabeled activities. They are usually represented by dotted lines. These are dummy activities. A **dummy activity** does not represent work to be done but is included so that each activity will have a unique pair of node numbers. The diagram in Figure D.3 includes four dummy activities to connect the five parallel activities to the final activity of cutover.

The Critical Path

Figure D.7 is a network diagram of an analysis of a banking operation, with the time expressed in working days. The critical path is highlighted with a heavy line. The critical path contains no **slack,** or excess time. Conversely, activities *not* on the critical path *do* contain slack. An activity not on the critical path can be delayed by an amount of time not exceeding the amount of slack for the *path.* Such a delay will not affect the project time. In the Figure D.7 example, activity 40-50 can be delayed as long as six days without affecting the project completion date.

Early and Late Dates

Each activity can be described in terms of early and late dates. The **early start date** is the earliest that an activity can begin. The **late start date** is the latest that an activity can begin without affecting the overall time of the project. In the same manner, the **early completion date** is the earliest that an activity can be completed and the **late completion date** is the latest that an activity can be completed without affecting project time. Figure D.8 shows the early and late dates for the banking analysis project.

Activities on the critical path have early and late dates that are the same. For activities not on the critical path there is a difference, and the difference is the amount of slack on the path.

Detailed and Summary Reports

All three types of reports—narrative, graphic, and tabular—can display information in either a detailed or summary fashion. Figure D.9 is an example of how a network diagram can be used to provide a summary overview of a project.

This diagram was prepared using Microsoft Project and uses a slightly different way to describe the activities than was presented above. This is a **node-oriented diagram.** The important information is included in the nodes, which are illustrated with rectangles. The upper portion of a rectangle identifies the activity (in this case, a project phase). The middle layer identifies the activity number on the left and the time increment on the right. The letter d refers to days. The bottom layer identifies the scheduled start date on the left and the scheduled completion date on the right.

In this example, phases 1, 10, 11, and 12 cannot be overlapped with other phases. They are performed serially. However, phases 3, 5, 7, and 9 can be performed while phases 2, 4, 6, and 8 are being performed. This pattern can easily be seen in a summary report.

Project Cost Management

In addition to managing systems projects to ensure that they develop systems that meet the user's functional requirements, and that the development proceeds on

FIGURE D.8

Early and Late Dates for the Banking Project

Nodes		Activity	Estimated Time (Days)	Early Start Date	Early Completion Date	Late Start Date	Late Completion Date
10	20	Get approval to do study	1	0	1	0	1
20	30	Define study scope	5	1	6	1	6
30	40	Develop detailed plan	3	6	9	12	15
30	50	Organize study team	12	6	18	6	18
40	50	Prepare network diagram	3	9	12	15	18
50	60	Assign project tasks	1	18	19	18	19
60	70	Gather cost data	6	19	25	19	25
60	80	Study checking system	9	19	28	20	29
60	90	Study savings system	8	19	27	21	29
60	100	Study loan system	6	19	25	23	29
60	110	Study trust system	2	19	21	27	29
70	120	Prepare cost sheet	4	25	29	25	29
120	130	Analyze findings	10	29	39	29	39
130	140	Prepare study report	5	39	44	39	44

Note: The dates are the number of days from the beginning of the project.

schedule, many firms also manage the project costs. Project cost management consists of four activities:

- Resource planning
- Cost estimating
- Cost budgeting
- Cost control

The starting point is resource planning. This is accomplished with such tools as the Gantt chart and network diagram. With that planning base, estimates can be made of the cost to carry out the project. If management feels that the cost is justifiable, a budget can be established for the project, and then cost controls consisting of a cost reporting system can be put into place.

Some firms use quantitative techniques in making the cost estimates. In this section, we describe such a technique used by a Texas computer manufacturer. This particular company uses the Microsoft Solutions Framework (MSF) for their SDLC methodology, which consists of five stages-envisioning, planning, development, deployment, and stabilization. Although the names are different from those of the phased development methodology, the logical sequence of development activity is the same.

The estimating method used by the computer company involves estimating the number of days that will be required for each SDLC stage. A **person day** is the time of a person working an entire day (8 hours). Then, the person days are converted to person hours so that an hourly cost rate can be applied.

FIGURE D.9

A Project Summary in the Form of a Network Diagram

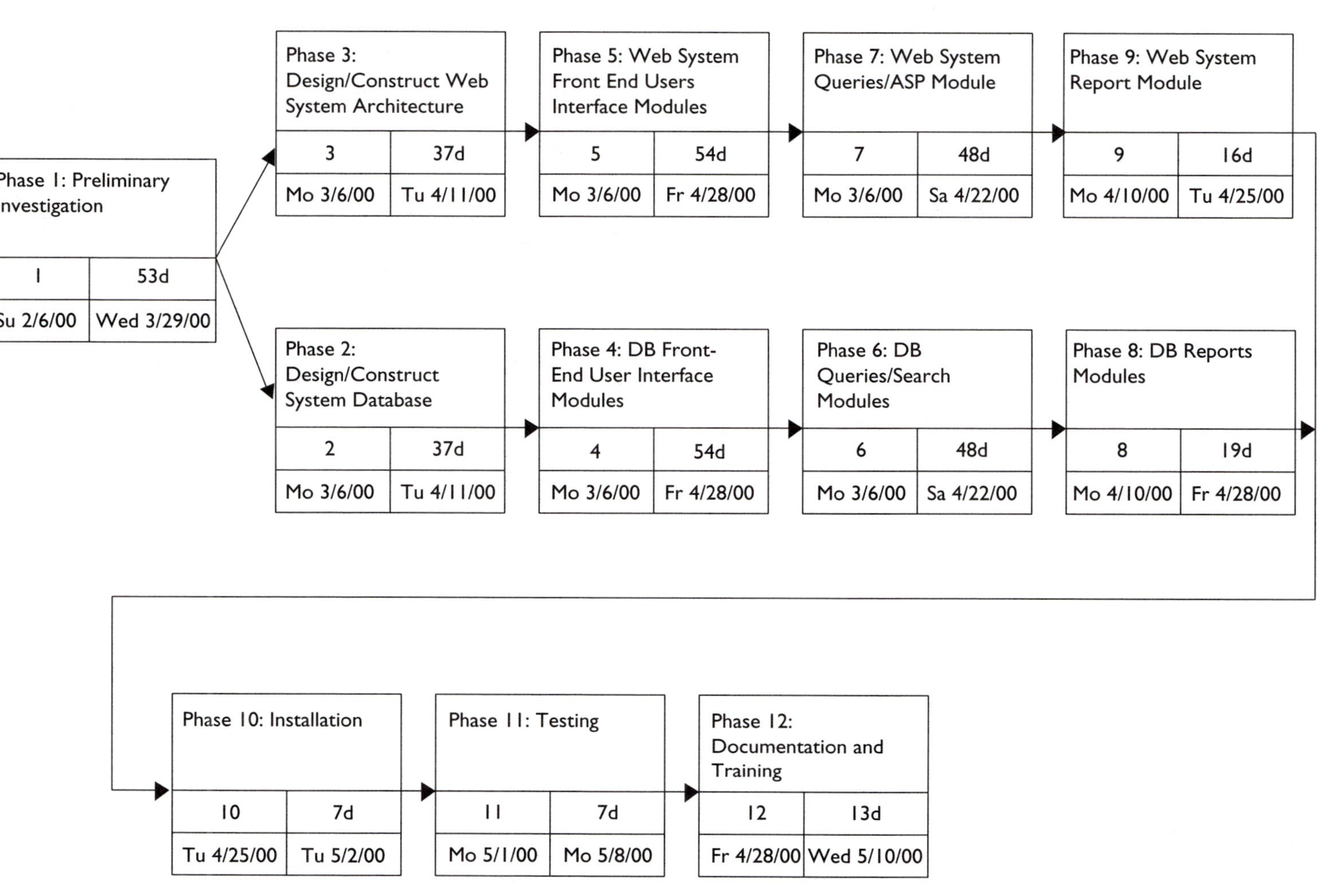
Phase 1: Preliminary Investigation
1
53d
Su 2/6/00
Wed 3/29/00
Phase 3: Design/Construct Web System Architecture
3
37d
Mo 3/6/00
Tu 4/11/00
Phase 5: Web System Front End Users Interface Modules
5
54d
Mo 3/6/00
Fr 4/28/00
Phase 7: Web System Queries/ASP Module
7
48d
Mo 3/6/00
Sa 4/22/00
Phase 9: Web System Report Module
9
16d
Mo 4/10/00
Tu 4/25/00
Phase 2: Design/Construct System Database
2
37d
Mo 3/6/00
Tu 4/11/00
Phase 4: DB Front-End User Interface Modules
4
54d
Mo 3/6/00
Fr 4/28/00
Phase 6: DB Queries/Search Modules
6
48d
Mo 3/6/00
Sa 4/22/00
Phase 8: DB Reports Modules
8
19d
Mo 4/10/00
Fr 4/28/00
Phase 10: Installation
10
7d
Tu 4/25/00
Tu 5/2/00
Phase 11: Testing
11
7d
Mo 5/1/00
Mo 5/8/00
Phase 12: Documentation and Training
12
13d
Fr 4/28/00
Wed 5/10/00

TABLE D.1

Estimation of Total Person Months

Stage	Percent of Project	Estimated Construction	Person Days	Required Resources	Adjusted Person Days	Total Person Months
Envisioning	.10		27	3	9	0.45
Planning	.25		68	3	23	1.15
Development	.35	95	95	3	32	1.60
Deployment	.10		27	3	9	0.45
Stabilization	.20		54	3	18	0.90
Totals	1.00		271		91	4.55
Total Project Days:		271				

Estimation of Person Months

Table D.1 shows the format of the Excel spreadsheet that is used to determine the person months. The SDLC stages are listed down the left-hand margin and the first column contains the estimated effort required for each stage. These percentages are based on historical project data.

The company uses a mathematical model (feature point estimating techniques) to estimate the number of days that will be required for the development stage, which includes all of the software construction and unit testing. Experience has shown that it is easier to estimate software construction based on project characteristics than it is to estimate the other stages.

In this example, the mathematical model determined that 95 person days of construction would be required for the development stage. The estimated effort (35%) required for the development stage and estimated size of the construction (95 days) are used to determine the total project days (271) required to complete the project. This figure is then extrapolated to produce the estimated person days for the remaining stages. For example, the 27 person hours of envisioning was computed by multiplying 271 times 10% (project effort for the envisioning stage).

The required resources column identifies the minimum number of persons who will be assigned to the project. In this example, the company will use three teams to develop the system-a business team and two teams of developers from the firm's IS unit. The business team consists of persons from the user area who provide expertise concerning the functional requirements of the system being developed. The assumption is that at least one person from each team will be allocated to the project at all times.

The number of person days for each stage is then divided by the required resources (3) to produce the adjusted person days (the numbers are rounded). These person days are converted to person months by dividing the days by 20 (the number of working days per month). At the conclusion of this step, the company has an estimated number of person days required for each stage, and duration of the project (4.55 months).

Resource Allocation by Project Stage

The next step is to normalize the estimated number of person days to a calendar and estimate the total number of hours that will be required for each stage. For this estimate, the company uses an Excel spreadsheet to assign the team members to the project by week. Table D.2 shows the layout, which has the appearance of a Gantt chart.

The project stages are listed down the left-hand side, and the numbers of workweeks are arrayed across the center. In this example, the project work is expected to last 19 weeks, and is to be performed by the three teams. The digits in the workweeks columns indicate the number of team members required to work on the project.

The three normalized columns on the right-hand side contain totals of the person weeks, days, and hours that are required for each phase. The **normalized person weeks** are a sum of the number of person weeks required for that particular phase, and the **normalized person days** are calculated by multiplying the weeks by 5. The **normalized person hours** are calculated by multiplying the number of person weeks on each row by 40. For example, during the envisioning stage, two weeks of effort (80 hours) will be required of the business team. The same number of hours (80) will be required of the two other teams as well. The estimated person days and weeks are obtained from Table D.1. Notice that once the project effort is normalized to calendar weeks, the total number of person days required for the project may change and truly

TABLE D.2

Estimation of Person Days and Hours

		Work Weeks																			Normalized Person		
MSF Phase	Team	1	2	3	4	5	6	7	8	9	10	11	12	13	14	15	16	17	18	19	Weeks	Days	Hours
Envisioning	Business	1	1																				80
	Team 1	1	1																				80
	Team 2	1	1																		6	30	80
Planning	Business			1	1	1	1	1	1														240
	Team 1			1	1	1	1																160
	Team 2			1	1	1	1														14	70	160
Development	Business									1	1	1	1										160
	Team 1					1	1	1	1	1	1												240
	Team 2							1	1	1	1	2	2	2							20	100	400
Deployment	Business													1	1	1							120
	Team 1														.5	.5							40
	Team 2														1	1					6	30	80
Stabilization	Business																1	1	1	1			160
	Team 1															1	.5	.5	.5	.5			120
	Team 2																1	1	1	1	11	55	160
Weekly resource TOTAL		3	3	3	3	4	4	3	3	3	3	3	3	3	2.5	3.5	2.5	2.5	2.5	2.5	57	285	2280

TABLE D.3

Estimation of Project Cost

Group	Person Hours Required for each Stage							
	Envisioning	Planning	Development	Deployment	Stabilization	Person Hours	Hourly Costs	Total Cost
Business	80	240	160	120	160	760	$35.50	$26,980.00
Team 1	80	160	240	40	120	640	$75.00	$48,000.00
Team 2	80	160	400	80	160	880	$75.00	$66,000.00
						2280		$140,980.00

reflect the level of effort required for the project. At the conclusion of this step, the company has an estimated number of person hours that will be required from each team for each stage.

Estimation of Project Cost

The number of normalized person hours is then totaled, producing the total person hours for each team. Table D.3 shows this calculation. The person hours are then multiplied by the hourly costs of the members of each team to determine total cost. In this example, the business representative is charged at a rate of $35.50 per hour, and team members from IS are charged at $75.00 per hour.

At this point, the company has an estimated cost for the number of resources required to complete the project. If the project required additional resources such as hardware, software, consultants, and so on, the costs for these resources would have to be estimated and included in the total cost of the project. If resource estimates are quantified prior to the project, management can make a fact-based decision on whether to approve the project. Management could well decide that the expected benefits from the system do not warrant the estimated cost.

If the project is approved, the budgeted costs can be allocated by stage to provide cost budgets for each stage. As the project evolves, management can measure how well the teams are meeting their budgets.

PUTTING PROJECT PLANNING AND CONTROL IN PERSPECTIVE

Although project management software and quantitative estimating techniques make extremely valuable contributions to planning activities for project management, they are not the key to successful on-time project completion. The key is the attention that the various levels of management and the members of the project team devote to the planning process. These planners must invest the necessary time in determining the tasks that will be performed, identifying their interrelationships, obtaining the necessary resources and making staff assignments, and estimating the amount of time that each task will require. Once this is done, software enables the plan to be updated quickly and easily, and provides management with information that is needed to monitor the plan. Keeping the team on track will require all of the communication skills the team can bring to the project and following the tips we have provided throughout the text.

KEY TERMS

project management mechanism
project plan
Gantt chart, project work plan
network diagram
CPM (critical path method) diagram
PERT (program evaluation and review technique) chart
milestone
work breakdown structure

PROBLEMS

1. Draw a network diagram of a project plan using the phased development methodology. Assume that the first project phase is preliminary investigation, and that the analysis, design, and preliminary construction phases are each conducted on four system modules-accounting system, finance system, human resources system, and marketing system. After the system modules are completed, the last two phases are final construction and system test and installation.
2. Determine the critical path for a the project in problem 1 using the following activity times:

Preliminary investigation	3 weeks
Accounting system	
Analysis	1 week
Design	1.5 weeks
Preliminary construction	2 weeks
Finance system	
Analysis	.5 weeks
Design	2 weeks
Preliminary construction	3 weeks
Human resources system	
Analysis	1.5 weeks
Design	2 weeks
Preliminary construction	4 weeks
Marketing system	
Analysis	.5 weeks
Design	5 weeks
Preliminary construction	1 week

Final construction	3.5 weeks
System test and installation	4 weeks

Write a memo to your instructor, identifying the activities on the critical path and explaining your logic.

3. Use the project estimating worksheet provided on the companion Web site to compute the total people months, using the following percentage of project estimates:

Envisioning	.15
Planning	.25
Development	.25
Deployment	.20
Stabilization	.15

The estimated construction time for the development phase is 30 days. Assume that the project team consists of 4 people who will work on each phase.

SELECTED BIBLIOGRAPHY

Fioravanti, F., and P. A. Nesi. "Method and Tool for Assessing Object-Oriented Projects and Metrics Management." *Journal of Systems & Software* 53 (Number 2, August 31, 2000): 111-136.

Gordon, Phillip. "Track Projects on the Web." *Informationweek* (787, May 22, 2000): 88-89.

Khirallah, Diane Rezendes. "Keep IT in Line With Business Goals." *Informationweek* (791, June 19, 2000): 119.

Lee, Jin Woo, and Soung Hie Kim. "Using Analytic Network Process and Goal Programming for Interdependent Information System Project Selection." *Computers & Operations Research* 27 (Number 4, April 1, 2000): 367-382.

Yourdon, E. "Success in e-Projects." *Computerworld* 34 (Number 34, August 21, 2000): 36.

TECHNICAL MODULE E

COMPUTER-AIDED SOFTWARE ENGINEERING

CASE, for **computer-aided software engineering,** is a philosophy for using the computer to model a firm, its activities, and its development of information systems. CASE originated in the early 1980s, growing out of the CAD (computer-aided design) software that had been so successful in increasing the productivity of design engineers.

THE VALUE OF CASE IN SYSTEM DEVELOPMENT

As the SDLC unfolds, work is done using one or more CASE tools, and the outputs are stored in a repository, as shown in Figure E.1. A **repository** is an electronic storage of all of the system documentation such as details of data elements, data structures, data flows, process logic, and object classes. The term **central encyclopedia,** or simply **encyclopedia,** is also used. During the analysis stage, the systems developer uses CASE to prepare use case diagrams, data models, process models, and object models. The diagrams and models reside in the repository.

The diagram in Figure E.1 shows the repository in a client/server network. The central repository is maintained by the server and a local repository is made available to the client workstation. Toolsets are used in preparing the various CASE outputs. Figure E.2 is a partial list of the outputs. These outputs provide more than a graphics capability; they can automatically generate some or all of the follow-on products that lead to a production system. The process models can be used to generate executable code, and the entity-relationship diagrams and class diagrams can be used to develop a data structure for such a database management system as Oracle or Sybase. Once the system goes into production, changes are accomplished by updating the documentation and regenerating the software and data structure. This is much more efficient than making changes to the code and database.

Categories of CASE Tools

There are many CASE tools on the market, ranging from those designed for use on client/server or Web-based systems to those tailored to personal computers. As an aid in positioning each tool in the SDLC, four categories have been established: upper CASE, middle CASE, lower CASE, and integrated CASE.[1]

Upper CASE Tools

An **upper CASE tool** is one that is used either prior to the SDLC or during the preliminary investigation stage for strategic planning for information resources and enterprise modeling. Examples of upper CASE tools are Visio Pro from Microsoft,

Figure E.1

The Role of the Repository in CASE

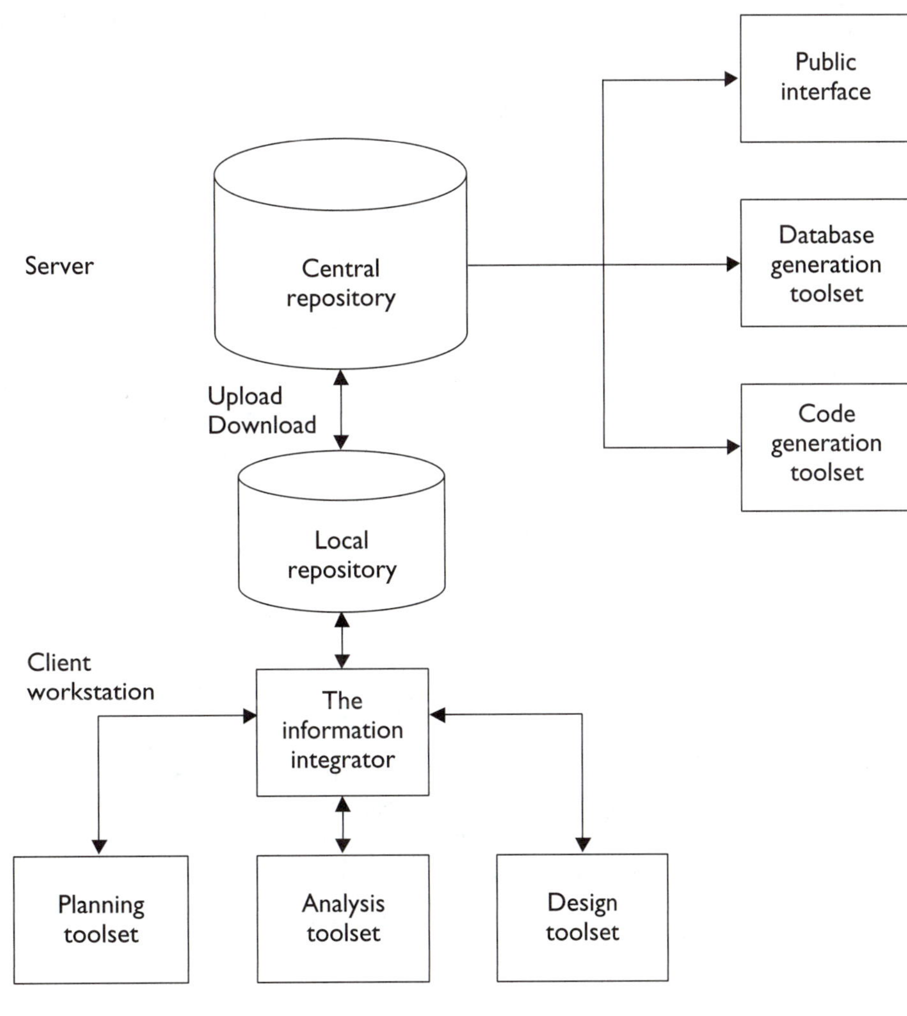

FIGURE E.2

Some System Documentation Prepared by CASE

1. Data repository reports, which are complete or partial listings of all the data elements and structures contained in the system.
2. Various diagrams, including, but not limited to:
   - Leveled sets of DFDs, serving as both logical and physical models of the existing and proposed system
   - System architecture
   - Structure charts
   - Entity-relationship diagrams
   - Organization charts
   - Hierarchy charts
   - Dependency diagrams
   - Action diagrams
   - Menu structure diagrams
3. Various project management tools, including, but not limited to:
   - Network diagrams such as PERT charts or CPM diagrams
   - Milestone schedules
   - Work breakdown charts
   - Gantt charts
   - Budgets
   - Tracking charts
4. Source and object code listings
5. Consistency checking reports
6. Requirements specifications

SmartDraw from Knowledge Based Systems, Visible Analyst Workbench from Visible Systems Corporation, and ERwin from Platinum Technology.

Middle CASE Tools

A **middle CASE tool** is one that is used during the analysis and design stages to document the existing and new systems. Examples are Visible Analyst Workbench, Analyst/Designer Toolkit from Yourdon, and ProcessAnalyst and DataArchitect from Powersoft. Figure E.3 is a sample DataArchitect entity-relationship diagram.

Lower CASE Tools

A **lower CASE tool** is used during the construction and installation stages to help the programmer develop, test, and maintain program code. Examples are TELON from Computer Associates International, ERwin, and Rational Rose from Rational Software Corporation.

Integrated CASE Tools

A firm can use a combination of upper, middle, and lower CASE tools to provide the coverage that it needs throughout the SDLC or it can use an **integrated CASE tool,** or **I-CASE tool,** that supports the firm's strategic planning and all SDLC stages. Popular examples of integrated CASE tools are the COOL product line from Computer Associates, Information Engineering Workbench from Ernst & Young, and KEY from Computer Associates International.

Using CASE to Manage Projects

I-CASE tools not only support phased system development but also provide a project management capability. All projects, regardless of their intended purpose, have the following characteristics:

- They are unique within an organization and have defined start and end points.
- They have a work scope that can be decomposed into definable tasks.
- They have a budget.
- They require the use of resources.
- They often cross organizational boundaries.

Figure E.3

A DataArchitect Entity-Relationship Diagram

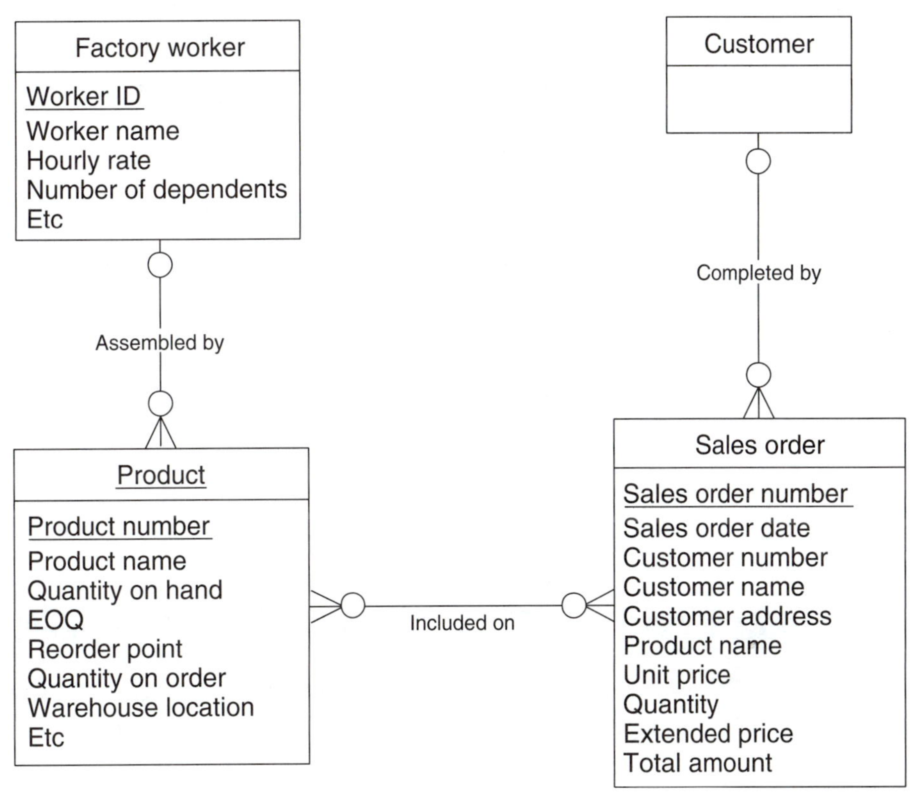

FIGURE E.4

A COOL:Gen Dependency Diagram

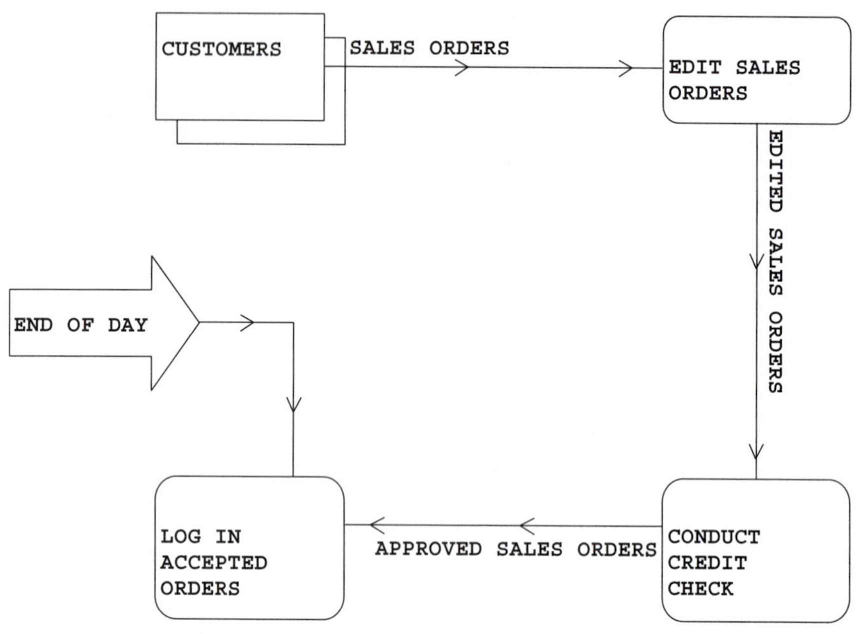

Projects require management of scope, time, human resources, costs, quality, and communications. Over the years, various tools, such as those listed below, have been developed for use in project management.

- Budgets
- Forecasting, analysis, and corrective action routines
- Work breakdown structures
- Network diagrams and Gantt charts
- Performance tracking graphics

Many CASE tools incorporate these project management capabilities to varying degrees. However, if the CASE tool that the firm is using does not provide the needed support, it is possible to purchase additional software that aids in the management task. This approach loses the feature of integration, but is much more productive than foregoing the use of software-based management tools altogether.

THE IMPACT OF CASE ON THE SYSTEM DEVELOPMENT LIFE CYCLE

The impact of CASE on the SDLC is not as straightforward as you might expect. In general, once organizational use of CASE tools has matured, the development time is greatly reduced. However, some CASE requirements may actually lengthen the life cycle stages.

One aspect of development that CASE tools encourage is an iteration of the phases, such as that of the phased development methodology. This iterative cycling may increase the length of certain phases, a situation that is especially true when users are involved in the cycling in order to enhance requirements definition or design specifications. Upper-CASE tools can also require an emphasis on the early phases of development that an organization might have previously neglected. This emphasis will likely result in better systems, but might also serve to lengthen the life cycle.

Preliminary Investigation

CASE tools provide a methodology and the tools for understanding the informational and procedural needs and goals of a target system. In this stage, the most important aspect is the completion of an information requirements assessment. Users and developers work together to determine which features will be required by the target system and perhaps to develop an additional list of desired but not mandatory features.

Systems Analysis

One of the tasks of analysis is to model the existing system in order to understand what it does, what it does well, and what it does not do well. In addition, the analysis stage also generates user interface requirements and standards, system performance criteria, target hardware and software environment requirements, and perhaps, most importantly, data requirements.

CASE tool outputs from the analysis stage may include decomposition diagrams, dependency diagrams, decision trees and tables, subschema data models, and data flow diagrams. Figure E.4 is a sample COOL:Gen dependency diagram. A dependency diagram is very similar to a DFD.

Systems Design

All systems should adhere to proven guidelines, which are intended to make the systems easier to develop and maintain. Since maintenance can represent as much as 50 percent of system costs, it is important to make the maintenance task as easy as possible to accomplish so that enhancements and adjustments can be made in a timely manner with as little effort as possible.

The logical design can take the form of a leveled set of DFDs that are used to communicate the proposed system to users, who must approve the design. Then, the DFDs, along with other process and modeling documentation such as hierarchy charts, ERDs, and a complete data dictionary, are made available to those persons who will have responsibility to implement the systems. CASE products support the completion of all these design outputs. Figure E.5 is a sample COOL:Gen hierarchy chart and Figure E.6 on page 223 is a sample COOL:Gen action diagram.

Preliminary and Final Construction

Of all the implementation stage activities, CASE is especially helpful in coding, documenting, testing, and educating.

- *Coding*—When the CASE tool has a code generation capability, this step requires very little time.
- *Documenting*—The automatic documentation capability of CASE tools ensures that the documentation is done, is done correctly, and stays current with the code.

FIGURE E.5

A COOL:Gen Hierarchy Chart

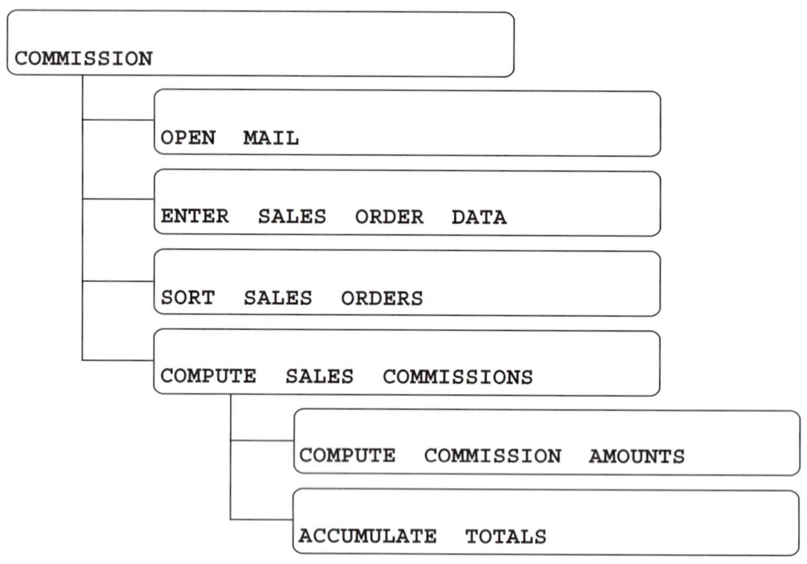

- *Testing*—Use of CASE reduces module testing to an almost negligible level. However, system testing, the testing of complete systems, and integration with other systems is still needed.
- *Educating*—Heavy user involvement throughout the SDLC reduces the amount of user education necessary prior to cutover. In addition, using CASE tools to generate code ensures consistency in the user interface, which also reduces not only the time required for education but also its necessity.

These advantages can clearly be seen during construction, but they also reappear once the system goes into production, when maintenance and business process redesign become necessary.

System Installation

Many of the advantages of using CASE tools rather than relying on traditional techniques for system development come during installation. Because CASE requires and encourages heavy user involvement in the development process, installation is not as difficult due to user familiarity with the system.

CASE ACHIEVES CONSISTENCY IN SYSTEM DESIGN

One of the problems encountered in traditional analysis with non-automated tools is lack of consistency among documentation and software products. Leveled DFDs are not balanced, or the structured English does not match the program code, for example. Almost all CASE tools offer support for consistency checking.

Consistency checking ensures that the diagrams and data repository entries are complete, do not violate any methodological rules, and are consistent within and among diagrams.

Most CASE tools allow consistency checking for single diagrams or for the entire project. When each diagram is completed, it should be checked for consistency. The same holds true for the project. Consistency checking should be conducted on the whole project as the first phase of system testing. After the inconsistencies have been addressed, then testing with live and test data can be conducted.

Consistency checking can detect, but is not limited to, the following types of errors:

- Unnamed or unnumbered modules and other constructs
- Dangling modules, which have no inputs, outputs, or both
- Incorrectly placed control structures such as looping structures
- Lack of balance, such as a data flow that appears on several DFD levels, with different names and perhaps showing the data flowing in different directions
- Lack of appropriate keys on data structures
- Lack of data normalization in database designs

FIGURE E.6

A COOL:Gen Action Diagram

```
BAA Action Block: CALCULATE_SALES_COMMISSION
Action Block Description:

┌─ CALCULATE_SALES_COMMISSION
│     IMPORTS:
│     EXPORTS:
│     LOCALS: ...
│     ENTITY ACTIONS: ...
│
│   ┌─ READ EACH invoice
│   │  SET local_sales_total ief_supplied total_currency TO
│   │  local_sales_total ief_supplied total_currency + invoice amount
│   │
│   │  ┌─ IF invoice amount IS GREATER THAN 1000
│   │  │  SET local_commission_total ief_supplied total_currency TO
│   │  │  local_commission_total ief_supplied total_currency + 100 +
│   │  │  (invoice amount - 1000 * .15)
│   │  │
│   │  ├─ ELSE
│   │  │  SET  local_commission_total ief_supplied total currency TO
│   │  │  local_commission_total ief_supplied total_currency +
│   │  └─ invoice amount * .10
│   └─
└─
```

FIGURE E.7

A Rational Rose Class Diagram

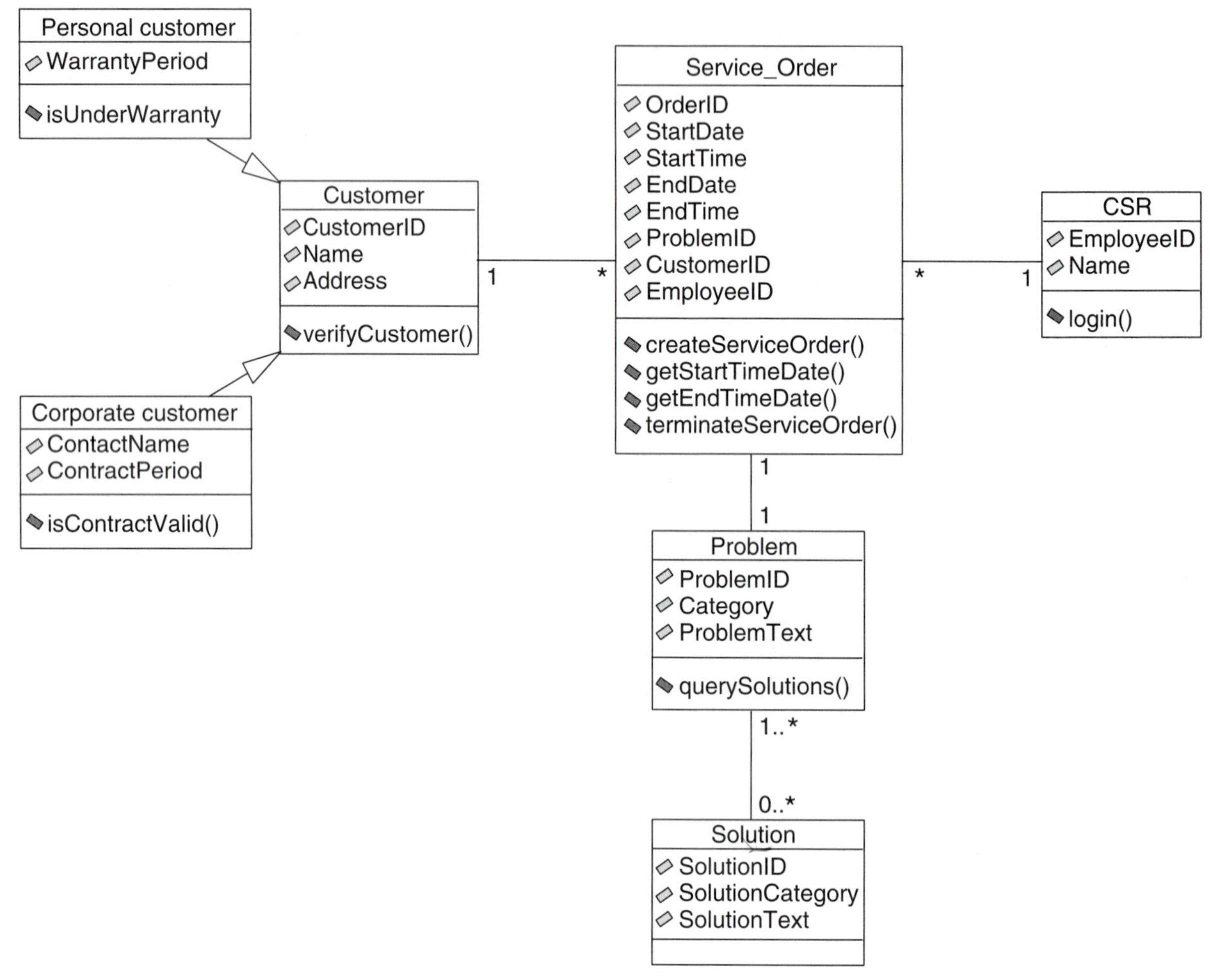

- Lack of a data repository entry for a data store that appears on a DFD
- Lack of a DFD for an entry that appears in the data repository

When the project team takes advantage of the ability of a CASE tool to achieve consistency in system design, the likelihood is increased that the resultant system will meet the user's needs.

CURRENT TRENDS IN CASE TOOLS

CASE tools have undergone significant changes since their introduction. The changes have come about in terms of the modeling tools that are used for development and the hardware platforms that are supported for the developed systems.

Evolution in Modeling Tools

The first CASE tools supported data and process modeling, enabling developers to model a system's data with entity-relationship diagrams and data dictionaries, and to model processes with DFDs, dependency diagrams, hierarchy charts, and action diagrams. More recently, CASE tools have been developed to support object modeling. The Rational Rose CASE tool, for example, prepares all of the UML diagrams described in Technical Module C. Figure E.7 is a sample Rational Rose class diagram, Figure E.8 is a sample Rational Rose sequence diagram, and Figure E.9 is a sample Rational Rose statechart, or state, diagram.

Evolution in Supported Hardware Platforms

The first CASE tools were designed to support development of mainframe systems. These were then adapted to client/server systems and to PCs. Today, the CASE tools are being designed and reengineered to support development of e-business systems.

FIGURE E.8

A Rational Rose Sequence Diagram

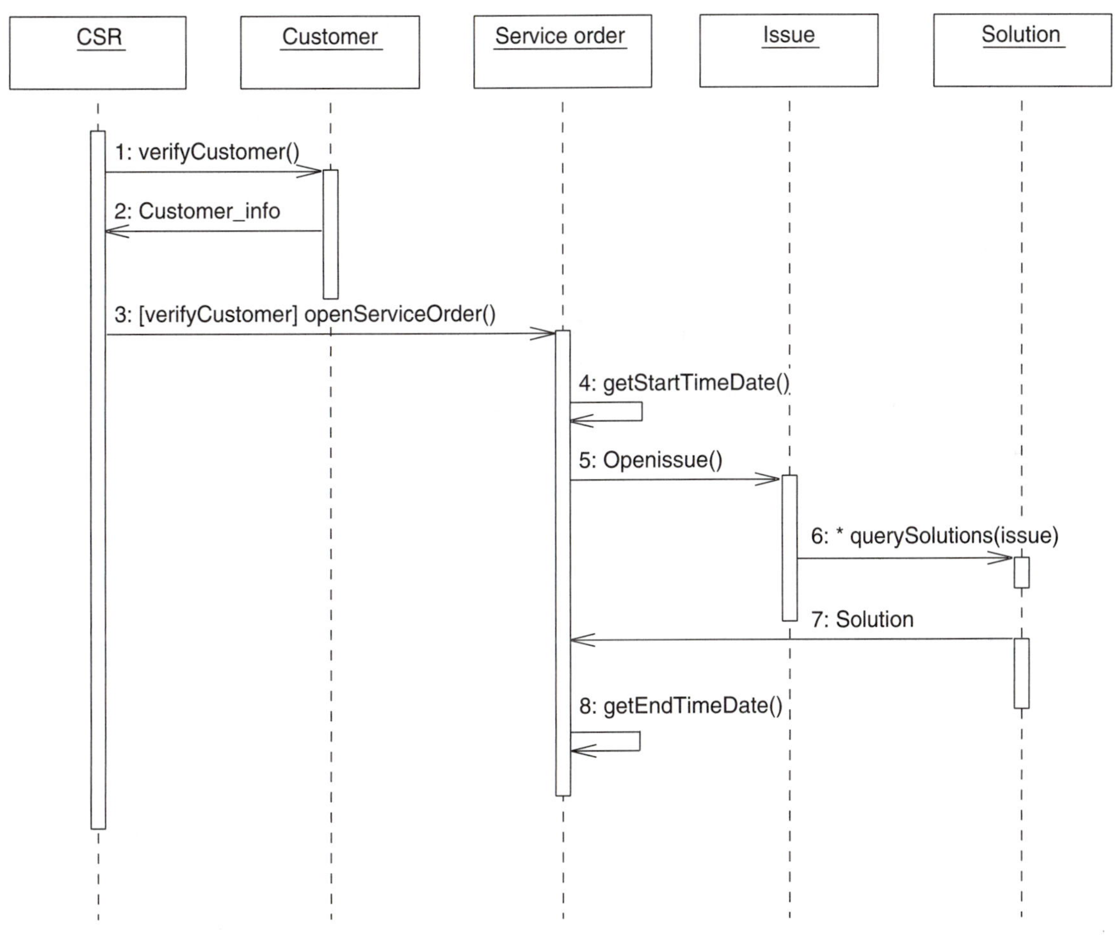

FIGURE E.9

A Rational Rose Statechart Diagram

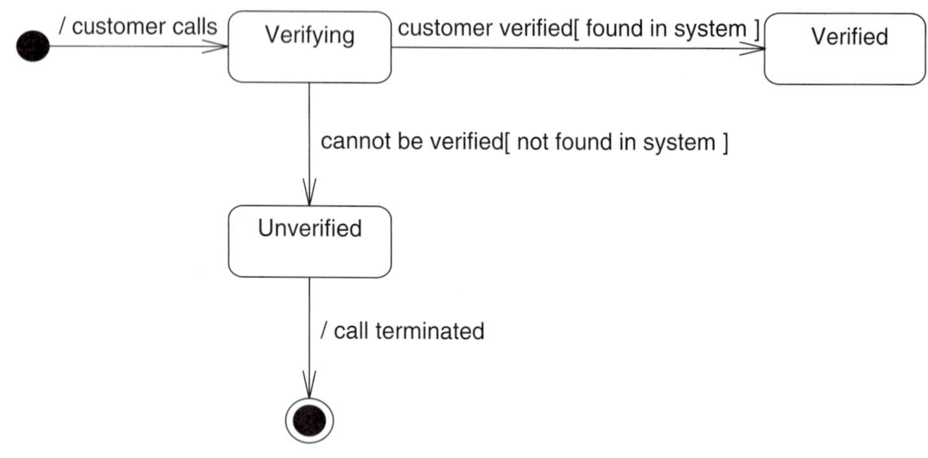

The COOL:Gen product of Computer Associates is a good example of this trend. Version 6.0 provides a 100 percent Java server solution that allows users to utilize Web/application servers on any platform ranging from NT through Linux and UNIX to MVS. In addition, the COOL:Gen applications can integrate with Jasmineii, the Computer Associates e-business platform, to facilitate the development of intelligent e-business solutions.

Putting CASE Trends in Perspective

It is clear that CASE vendors will continue to make improvements so that their products support development of systems that are evolving in terms of complexity and scope. With the current and projected shortage of systems developers, it is difficult to conceive of a future where CASE will not be the primary system development technology.

KEY TERMS

repository, central encyclopedia
upper CASE tool
middle CASE tool
lower CASE tool
integrated CASE tool
consistency checking

PROBLEMS

1. Use a CASE tool to solve the data modeling problems at the end of Technical Module A.
2. Use a CASE tool to solve the process modeling problems at the end of Technical Module B.

SELECTED BIBLIOGRAPHY

Dean, Douglas L.; James D. Lee, Mark O. Pendergast, Ann M. Hickey, and Jay F. Nunamaker, Jr. "Enabling the Effective Involvement of Multiple Users: Methods and Tools for Collaborative Software Engineering." *Journal of Management Information Systems* 14 (Number 3, Winter 1997/1998): 179-222.

Gisselquist, Richard. "Engineering in Software." *Communications of the ACM* 41 (Number 10, October 1998): 107-108.

Jarzabek, Stan, and Riri Huang. "The Case for User-Centered CASE Tools." *Communications of the ACM* 41 (Number 8, August 1998): 93-99.

Lai, Vincent S. "A Contingency Examination of CASE—Task Fit on Software Developer's Performance." *European Journal of Information Systems* 8 (Number 1, March 1999): 27-39.

Saiedian, H., and R. Dale. "Requirements Engineering: Making the Connection Between the Software Developer and Customer." *Information & Software Technology* 42 (Number 6, April 15, 2000): 419-428.

Wohlin, Claes, and Bjorn Regnell. "Strategies for Industrial Relevance in Software Engineering Education." *Journal of Systems & Software* 49 (Number 2, 3, December 30, 1999): 125-134.

NOTE

1. This classification is from Michael Lucas Gibson, "The CASE Philosophy," *BYTE* 14 (April 1989): 209ff.

PART II

SYSTEMS DEVELOPMENT

CHAPTER 4

PRELIMINARY INVESTIGATION

LEARNING OBJECTIVES

- Know what can trigger a system project.
- Explain how business process redesign is accomplished by means of reverse engineering and forward engineering.
- Describe how a firm goes about strategic planning.
- Identify the necessary components of the strategic plan for information resources.
- Follow the systems approach in conducting an enterprise analysis.
- List good sources of information when conducting an enterprise analysis.
- Identify the factors that influence system constraints.
- Use the major system development objectives and goal analysis to help identify objectives, constraints, and project scope.
- Evaluate project risk.
- Describe the multiple dimensions of system and project feasibility.
- Define project scope based on goal analysis, risk evaluation, and feasibility analysis.
- Explain what a JAD session is and why it is a useful information-gathering technique throughout the system development life cycle.

INTRODUCTION

Now that we have built a foundation in systems concepts and systems development methodologies, we are ready to begin a systems development project. In this chapter we describe all of the important activities that must be performed before systems analysis begins—the activities of the preliminary investigation stage.

Users inside and outside of the firm often trigger a systems project by making known their information needs. Other triggers include new technology, direction provided by a firm's strategic plan, and the need for business process redesign, or BPR. BPR consists of reverse engineering followed by forward engineering. The firm can be guided by a strategic business plan, and each business area can also have its own strategic plan. The term strategic plan for information resources, or SPIR, has been coined to describe the strategic plan that guides the use of all the firm's information resources.

The system life cycle begins with preliminary investigation. This stage includes (1) enterprise analysis, (2) a definition of system objectives, constraints, goals, risks, and scope, (3) feasibility analysis, and (4) confirmation of initial functional requirements. The systems approach, using the general systems model of the firm and the environmental model, provides a good framework for conducting the enterprise analysis.

The ability of a system to meet worthwhile goals can be facilitated through a formal consideration of system quality, project management, and organizational relevance. Risks can be avoided or minimized by considering characteristics of the organization, the information system, the developers, and the users, and by pursuing specific risk reduction strategies. In conducting a feasibility study, the systems developers consider five dimensions—technical, economic, legal and ethical, operational, and schedule. A joint application design (JAD) session is a good vehicle for achieving agreement among all of the systems developers and key users concerning major issues and system features.

PROJECT TRIGGERS

A system development project can be triggered by user needs, technology, and strategic direction.

User Needs

There are two main groups of users—external and internal. **External users** exist within the environment of the firm and include such entities as customers, suppliers, and the government. These external users rely on the firm's information system to provide necessary information relating to such activities as the firm's sales, purchases, and tax payments. Information may be mailed to external users (such as monthly reports to bank customers) or accessed by telephone (such as bank customers transferring funds among accounts) or provided in a wide variety of ways on the organization's Web site. **Internal users** are members of the firm and can exist on any organizational level. Internal users need information to perform their duties.

Both external and internal users can trigger a system development project by recognizing that they have unmet information needs. Perhaps the existing system is deficient in some way or perhaps a need is seen for an entirely new system. The firm must be sensitive to the needs of the external users and respond with new or improved systems. Within the firm, lower-level managers, such as supervisors and department heads, often report the needs of the internal users to upper-level managers who make the needs known to top management.

Many firms have a formal procedure to follow in evaluating users' needs, which includes a **project request form** that the user or a user representative fills out to describe what computer support is needed. When the firm has an information systems steering committee, that group evaluates the request and decides whether a system project is in order. If so, the committee forwards the approved request to the information systems unit and one or more information specialists are assigned to work with the users in learning more about the users' needs.

Technology

Information technology, in the form of new hardware and software, evolves so rapidly that it offers new possibilities for solving problems and capitalizing on opportunities. Although users sometimes become aware of new technology sooner than do the infor-

FIGURE 4.1

Business Process Redesign

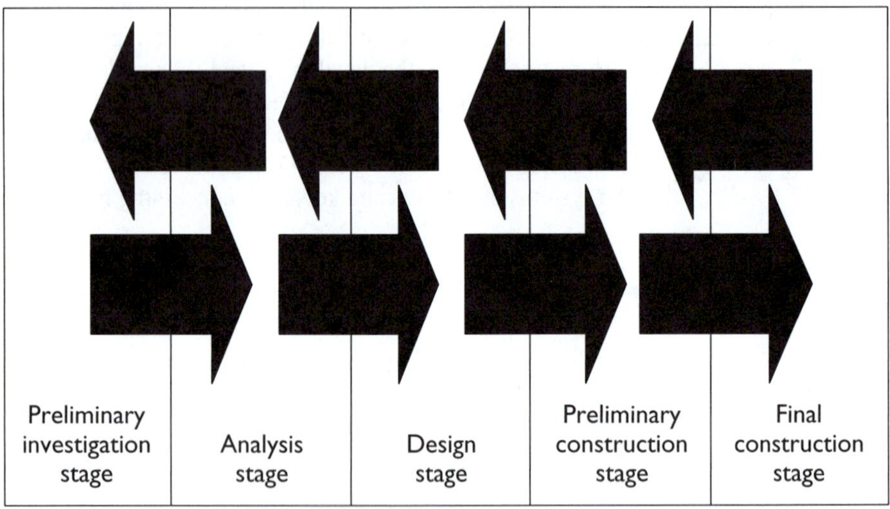

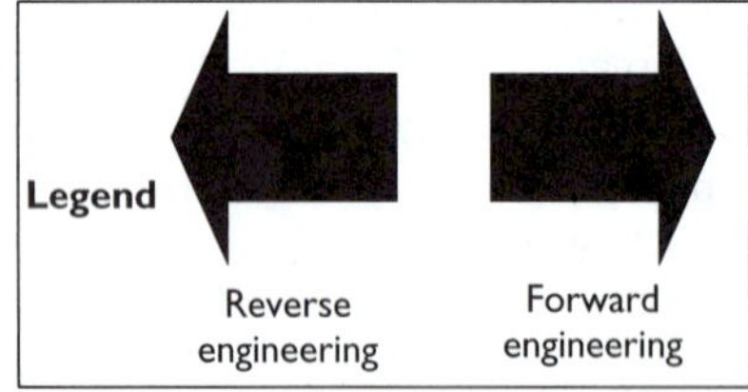

mation specialists, it is the specialists' responsibility to remain current on leading-edge technology.

Strategic Direction

The stimulus for a systems development project can come about as a part of a long-range plan that schedules the firm's information system activity a year or more into the future. Both user needs and technology are *push catalysts;* something happens that pushes the project along. Strategic direction is a *pull catalyst;* the project comes about as a result of a pre-existing strategic plan. In the sections below, we describe how firms establish strategic direction.

Business Process Redesign

Many firms are beginning to question the ways in which they perform their basic processes. In some cases, when the processes were originally designed, they were constrained by forces that no longer exist. For example, many systems were designed during the early years of the computer when such systems were severely limited in terms of speed, capacity, and adaptability. Today's executives want to redesign these systems to take full advantage of existing technology. This redevelopment of existing physical and conceptual systems, *without being constrained by their current form,* is called **BPR,** which stands for **business process redesign** or **business process reengineering.**

Although the systems developers want to be free from constraints, they do not ignore how the existing system works. The developers want to salvage the usable portions of the existing system, but one of the problems that they face is understanding what the system was originally intended to do. This task is made difficult by the lack of good documentation. One way to solve the problem is to recreate the documentation and this can often be accomplished with reverse engineering.

Reverse engineering is the process of analyzing a system to identify the elements and their interrelationships, and to create documentation on a higher level of abstraction than currently exists. The objective of the reverse engineering is to achieve an improved understanding of the system. Once this understanding is achieved, the new system can be developed by following the SDLC methodology in the normal fashion, a process called **forward engineering.** Figure 4.1 shows the reverse and forward engineering processes.

Each time you backtrack to an earlier life cycle phase while performing reverse engineering, you produce documentation on a higher system level. For example, the object code from the construction stages can be reverse engineered to produce the process models (flowcharts, DFDs, and so on) of the design stage. These models can, in turn, be used to identify the problem definition, functional requirements, and system objectives of the analysis and preliminary investigation stages. This understanding can provide the basis for redeveloping the system by forward engineering. Special reverse engineering software has been developed to facilitate the backtracking process.

Figure 4.2 shows how legacy code is reengineered to produce code for new platforms. The reverse engineering process uses the legacy code to produce the requirements specifications of the new system, which are technology independent. In other words, they apply to any technology. These specifications are the inputs to the forward engineering process that converts the requirements specifications into the design specifications for the new platforms. These specifications are technology specific in that they provide the physical details of the new platform code. As systems developers conduct the enterprise analysis, one of the key decisions is whether to treat the project as a BPR effort.

Strategic Business Planning

Firms formulate strategies that guide operations for one or more years into the future. Separate strategies can be developed for the firm as a whole, and for each of its major business units. Information systems is often considered as a major business unit.

The Strategic Business Plan

Many firms have an **executive committee** that consists of the top-level managers who make the decisions that have long-term, strategic implications. The executive committee consists of the president and vice presidents of the business areas—usually finance, human resources, information systems, marketing, and manufacturing. The committee meets periodically, perhaps monthly, to address strategic issues. The executives engage in formal strategic planning on perhaps a quarterly

FIGURE 4.2

Reengineering of Legacy Code

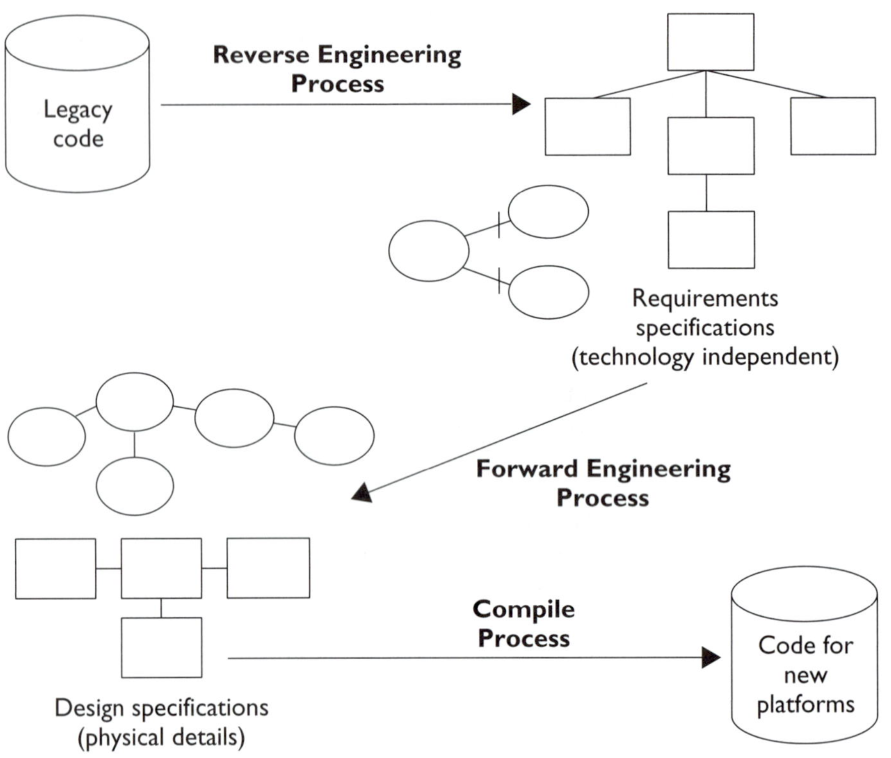

or annual basis. The planning process considers both environmental and internal influences as pictured in Figure 4.3.

- *The environment influences the plan*—An organization exists to serve its environment. Firms provide products and services to their customers, and provide a return on investment to their owners and stockholders. The environment also imposes constraints. Competitors seek to take customers away from the firm, the government enacts legislation to ensure legal and ethical business practices, and so on.

- *The plan influences the firm's resources*—Once the strategic business plan is in place, the resources that will be required to meet the strategic objectives must be acquired.

- *The firm's resources influence the plan*—The executives do not select business strategies without first considering the ability of the firm to successfully achieve them. For example, the executives know that a strategy of adding a new product line requires adequate production facilities and a knowledgeable sales staff.

A reciprocal relationship therefore exists between the strategic business plan and the firm's resources. The two-way arrow in the figure illustrates this relationship. The executives consider these internal and environmental influences and draft the overall plan that will guide the firm in the future, called the **strategic business plan.**

Strategic Plans for the Business Areas

A firm is not restricted to a single strategic plan. Each of the business areas can develop its own strategic plan to support the plan of the firm. For example, there can be a strategic marketing plan, a strategic manufacturing plan, a strategic plan for information resources, and so on.

The executives *work together* to develop the business area plans as illustrated in Figure 4.4. For example, the strategic plan for information resources is developed by the chief information officer (CIO) working with the other executives and with managers in information systems. The term **SPIR,** for **strategic plan for information resources,** has been coined to describe the guidelines for future development and use of the firm's information resources so that they support the strategic objectives of the firm.

The Strategic Plan for Information Resources

The SPIR content can vary considerably from one firm to the next but it should answer two basic questions:

- What systems should be developed in the future?
- What resources are needed for these systems?

These questions can be addressed by specifying the information illustrated by the matrix in Figure 4.5. The systems to be developed will fall within the five categories of the information systems infrastructure, and the resources required for each can be classified in terms of the five components of the functions/components matrix. For example, if the firm decides to implement a marketing information sys-

FIGURE 4.3

Influences on Strategic Business Plan Development

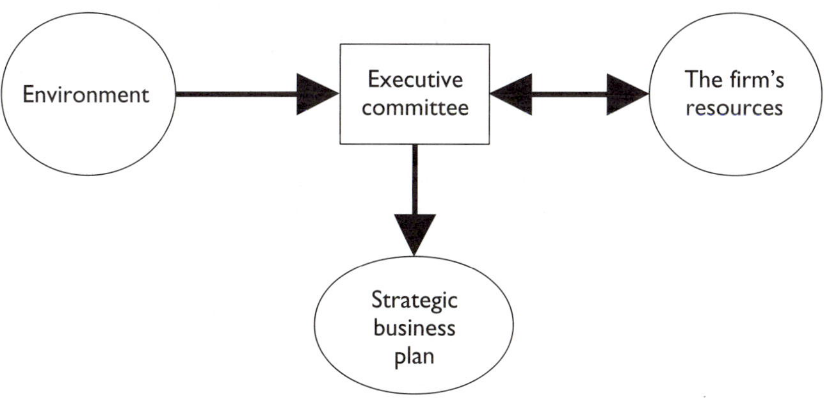

FIGURE 4.4

Cooperation in Developing Strategic Plans for Business Areas

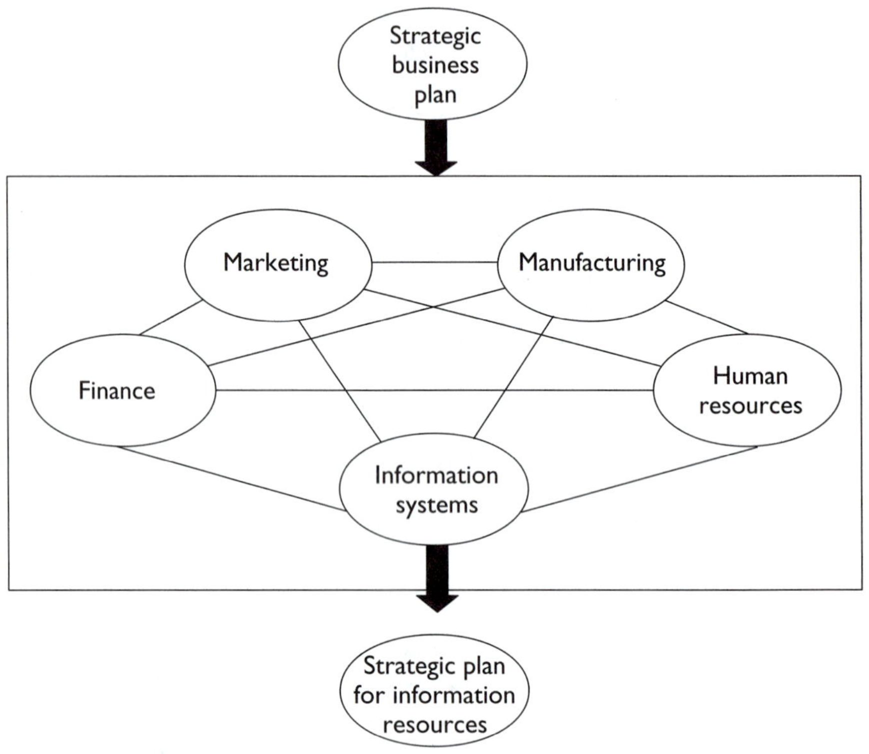

tem, it is a type of management information system, and it will require some combination of the component resources.

For each of the information systems, estimates are made of the level of information resources that will be required. These resources include the components people, data, information, software, and hardware. Attention to personnel resources focuses on both the users and the information specialists, specifying the numbers and types that will be required to develop the projected systems. Note that the answers to the resources question will provide a high-level summary of how the systems will be developed. For example, the information specialists who will be the developers should be identified as contract developers or consultants, or the personnel to be included in the in-house information systems group should be identified. Similarly the software tools and hardware specifications will indicate whether current systems platforms will be used or whether new technology will be acquired.

Putting Strategic Planning in Perspective

The strategic plans for the firm and its information resources provide a positive, stabilizing influence on systems work. The plans minimize the likelihood of wasted effort by the information specialists and the users in developing misdirected systems. All of the systems support the firm's strategic objectives. This is the organizational framework within which all information systems work is performed. Information specialists and users alike should understand the setting since it both imposes constraints and provides opportunities. The firm looks to the information systems for support in achieving the strategic objectives. All information systems, whether developed by information specialists or users, should be designed to meet this expectation.

The SPIR provides the basis for all of the firm's system development projects. It serves as a timetable, specifying when each project will occur. As the projected start date rolls around, the project team initiates the appropriate methodology. If the firm pursues a phased development approach, the preliminary investigation stage is initiated.

The Preliminary Investigation Stage

Figure 4.6 shows the preliminary investigation stage as the first stage of phased development. There are two reasons for conducting the activities in this preliminary stage. The first is to determine whether to pursue the development of a system. When a justification is found for the project, the second objective is to learn

FIGURE 4.5

Identifying the Information Resources Needed for Each Information System

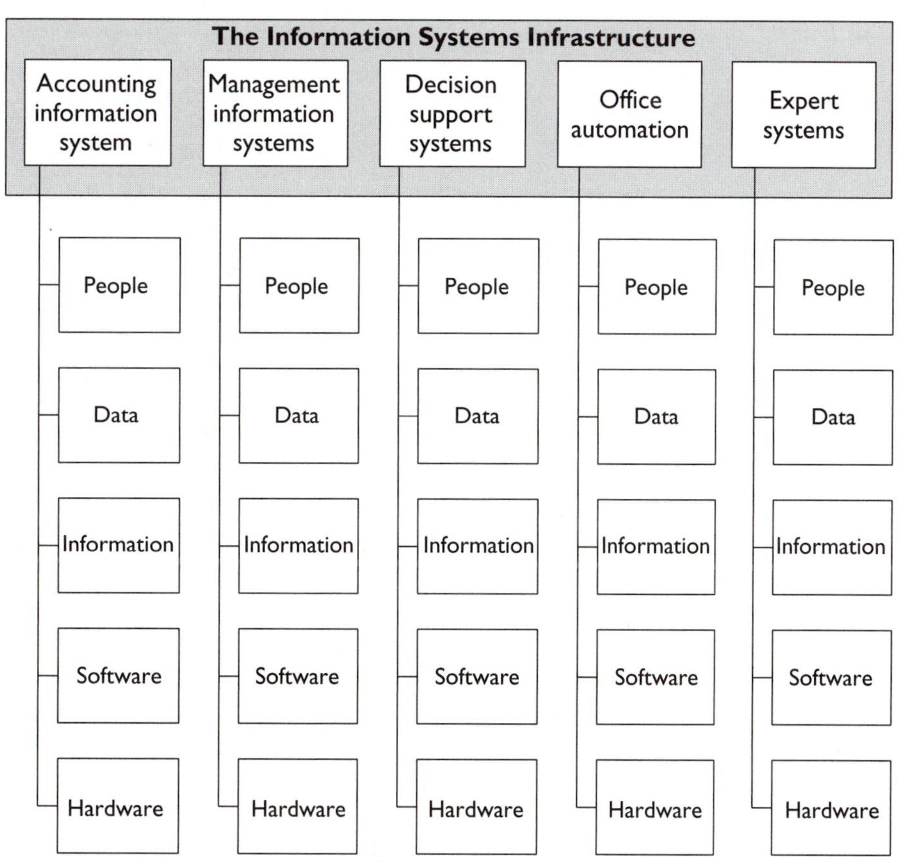

FIGURE 4.6

Preliminary Investigation Phase Overview

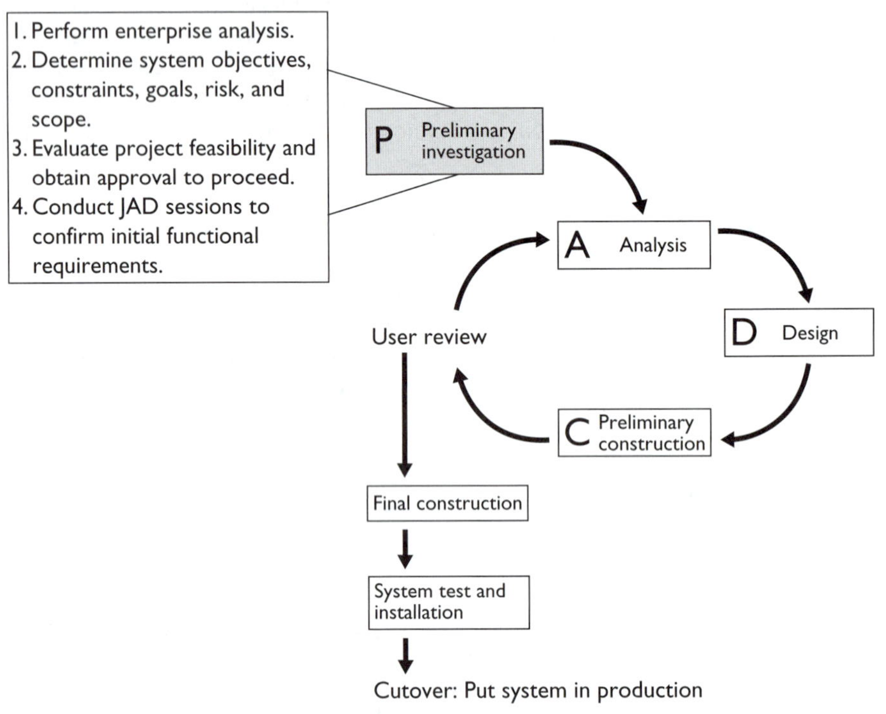
1. Perform enterprise analysis.
2. Determine system objectives, constraints, goals, risk, and scope.
3. Evaluate project feasibility and obtain approval to proceed.
4. Conduct JAD sessions to confirm initial functional requirements.
P Preliminary investigation
A Analysis
D Design
C Preliminary construction
User review
Final construction
System test and installation
Cutover: Put system in production

as much as possible about the setting in which the project will be conducted. This stage consists of four steps.

1. Perform an enterprise analysis.
2. Determine system constraints, objectives, goals, risk, and scope.
3. Evaluate project feasibility and obtain approval to proceed.
4. Conduct JAD sessions to confirm initial functional requirements.

With this stage completed, the project team can begin the development of the new system by performing, in an iterative manner, the analysis, design, and preliminary construction of each of the new systems modules as illustrated by the loop in Figure 4.6.

STEP 1: PERFORM ENTERPRISE ANALYSIS

A good way to perform enterprise analysis is to follow the systems approach. This approach can be followed for solving problems of all kinds but it is especially effective for solving systems problems. Our description in Chapter 2 grouped the steps into three types of effort, or phases.

- Preparation effort
- Definition effort

- Solution effort

As you begin a systems project, the preparation effort should be accomplished early in the SDLC, during the preliminary investigation stage. This preparation effort is termed enterprise analysis. **Enterprise analysis** is the study of the firm in its environment for the purpose of understanding the firm's mission and objectives, its responsibilities to its environmental elements, and the level of its resources. With this understanding, the project team can then tackle the project, which can range from one with broad scope, such as a venture into e-business, to one with very narrow scope, such as redevelopment of a payroll system. The important point is that an enterprise analysis is the way to begin *any* type of system project.

Preparation effort consists of three steps—view the firm (the enterprise) as a system, recognize the environmental system, and identify the firm's subsystems.

View the Firm as a System

The first step of preparation effort is to view the firm in systems terms. This can be done by using the general systems model in Figure 4.7 as a template. Address each of the system elements and ask questions that reveal how the firm measures up to the model of a closed-loop, open system.

- *Standards*—Does the firm know where it is going? Does it have a mission statement, strategic business plan, objectives, and standards of performance to use in ensuring that its objectives are being met?

- *Management*—Does the firm have a strong management team? Are there enough managers and do they have the right knowledge and skills? Is the appropriate organizational structure in place, and do the units work together to help the firm meet its objectives?

- *Information processor*—Does the firm have a good system for gathering data both internally and from the environment, and converting that data into information? Is the information being made available to all management levels and units within the firm, and to environmental elements that should receive it? If the system is computer-based, are the hardware and software current, and do the information specialists have the right knowledge and skills?

- *Input physical resources*—Is the firm obtaining the physical resources that it needs to accomplish its objectives?

- *Transformation process*—Is the transformation process efficient?

- *Output physical resources*—Do the firm's outputs meet the needs of the environmental elements that receive them?

With a good understanding of the system elements, you can turn your attention to the flows of data, information, and decisions.

- *Data flows*—Is the firm receiving input data that it needs from its internal operations and the environment? Is it providing output data that the environment needs?

- *Information flows*—Is the information processor transforming data into useful information for use by the environment and internal users?

FIGURE 4.7

The General Systems Model of the Firm

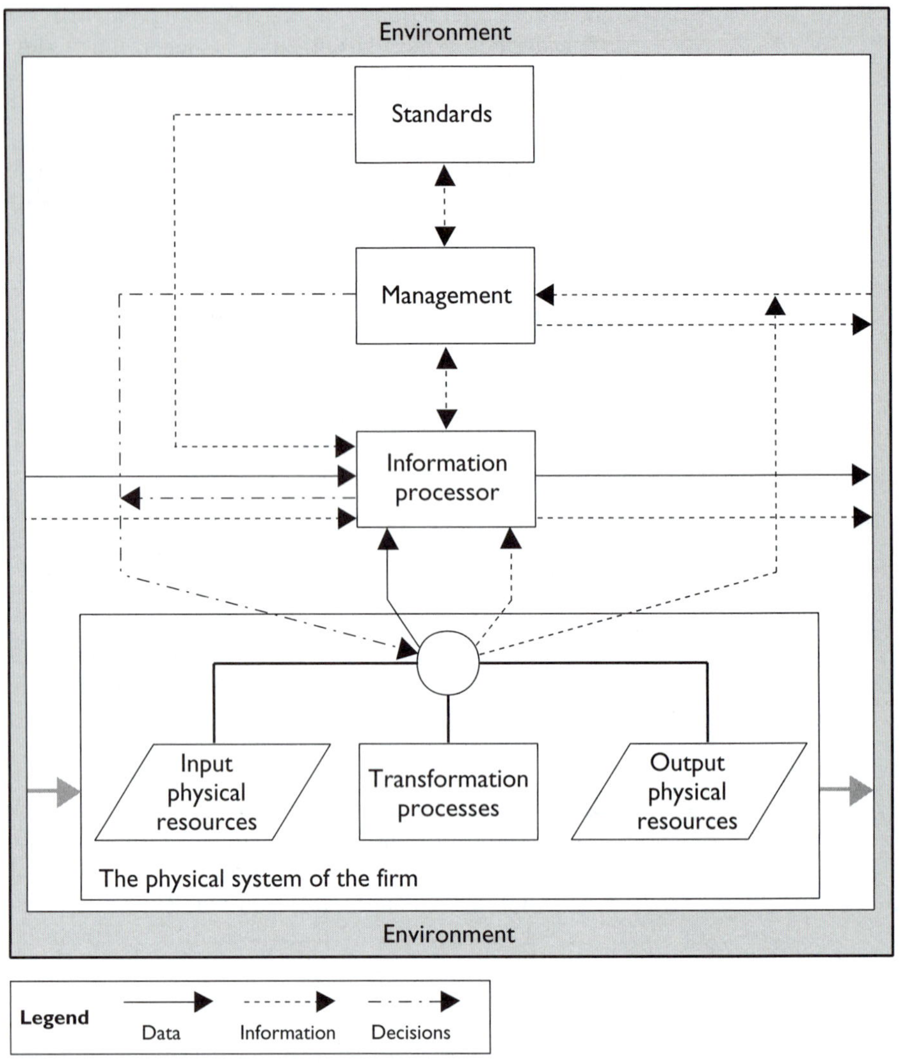

- *Decision flows*—Are management decisions being communicated to the parts of the physical system where the decisions will be applied?

With an understanding of the system elements of the firm and how they are linked by flows, you can expand the scope of the enterprise analysis to include the environment.

Recognize the Environmental System

We have described the firm's environment as consisting of the eight elements pictured in Figure 4.8. We also described the linkages that connect the firm with these elements as resource flows. The physical resources include personnel, materials, machines, and money. The conceptual resources take the form of data and information. The task of the firm's management can be viewed as making sure that the proper resources flow at the proper speeds.

Table 4.1 shows the primary resource flows for each of the environmental elements. *The legal and ethical feasibility of the system being developed demands that the project team understand the environmental resource flows.* This is a major objective of enterprise analysis.

- *Personnel flows*—According to the table, personnel flow into the firm from labor unions, the local community, and such suppliers as employment agencies, colleges, and trade schools. Personnel can flow from competitors as long as the flow is conducted in an ethical way. For example, it would be unethical to lure a competitor's key employees as a way of obtaining competitive advantage.
- *Material flows*—Materials should flow into the firm only from suppliers and should flow out only to customers in the form of the firm's products.
- *Machine flows*—Machines should be obtained only from suppliers, but may flow from the firm to the local community as scrap when the machines are no longer useful, and may flow back to suppliers as trade-ins on new machines.

FIGURE 4.8

The Environment of the Firm

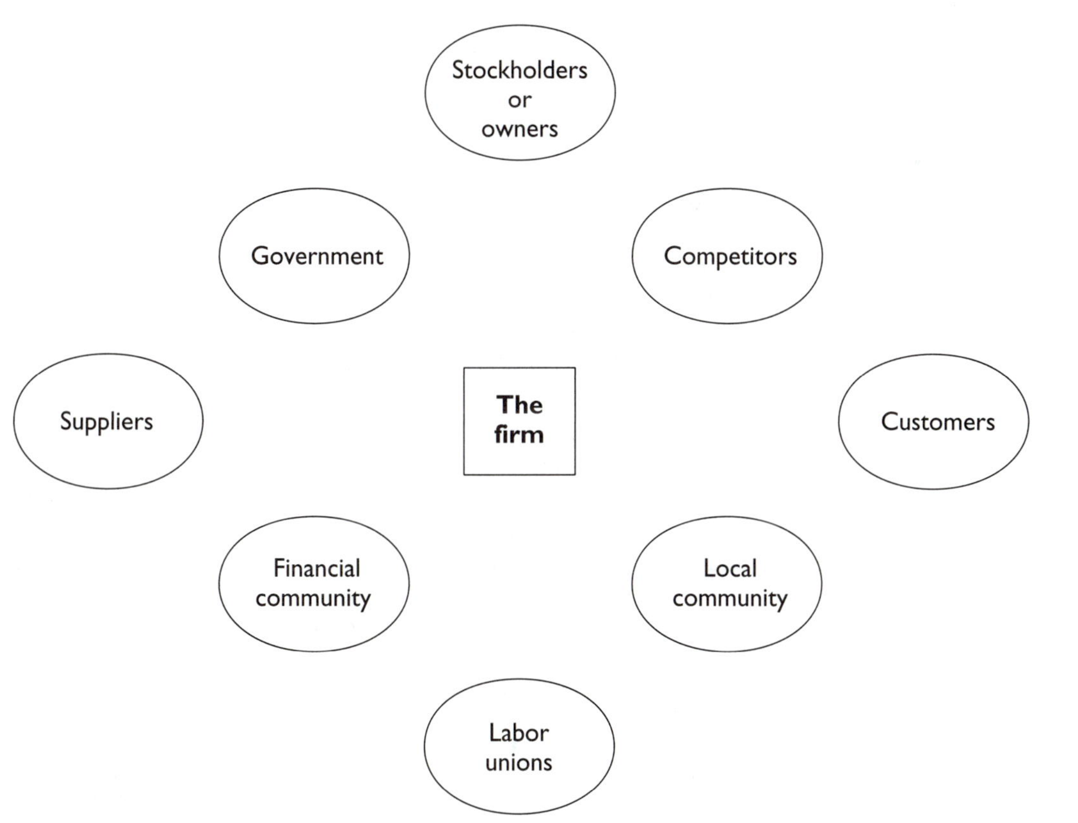

TABLE 4.1

Primary Environmental Resource Flows

Environmental Element	Personnel Flows	Material Flows	Machine Flows	Money Flows	Data and Information Flows
Stockholders or Owners				X	X
Government				X	X
Suppliers	X	X	X	X	X
Financial Community				X	X
Labor Unions	X				X
Local Community	X		X	X	X
Customers		X		X	X
Competitors	Ethical only				Incoming only

- *Money flows*—As the table shows, the money flow is the physical flow that connects the firm with most of its environmental elements. Money can flow to and from all of the elements except labor unions and competitors.
- *Data and information flows*—The table shows that data and information flows can connect the firm to all eight elements. However, the flow that connects the firm to its competitors should be only incoming. The firm seeks to remain current on its competitors' activities and make it as difficult as possible for competitors to monitor the firm's performance.

Since the information system being developed can influence the flows of the physical resources, it is important that the project team members understand all of the flows. For an e-business system that will allow such suppliers as grocery wholesalers to directly stock a retailer's shelves, research on material flows, suppliers, and relevant data and information will be extensive. For an internal accounting system this activity will be a quick check to determine whether there are any environment elements to investigate further.

Identify the Firm's Subsystems

The third and final step of preparation effort is to focus on the way that the firm is organized into subunits. Traditionally, the organization has been based on such *business units* as finance, human resources, and information systems. These units can be found in firms of all types but the names of other units can be tailored to particular types of firms. A life insurance company will, for example, have units with such names as underwriting, policy issue, and claims.

Firms are often organized into units based on their *product line.* General Motors follows this practice with its divisions—Chevrolet, Buick, Oldsmobile, and so on. Other firms organize based on *geographic areas* with such unit names as western region, European operations, and United Kingdom subsidiary. Firms can also organize based on their *customers* with units assigned to serve government, health care, aerospace, and the like.

Sources of Information for Enterprise Analysis

As you conduct enterprise analysis, you should take advantage of any available information that sheds light on the firm and its environment. You should conduct searches for existing information, and supplement the findings with efforts aimed at obtaining new information. The following potential sources exist.

Organization Charts

An especially valuable tool for identifying the firm's subsidiary units is the organization chart. We included an organization chart in the ASTA case for the entire small company, and a generic organization chart of a large project team in Chapter 1. See Figure CS 1.3 in the ASTA case, and Figure 1.16 in Chapter 1.

One of the first requests that the team should make of the managers of the user areas is for an organization chart that shows the position of the unit within the firm and its hierarchical structure. If you have to redraw the user's chart or draw a new one for any reason, you should follow these guidelines:

- *Use a rectangle for each position.* Label the rectangle with the title of the position and the name of the person filling the position. It is also a good idea to include the person's phone number and e-mail address.

- *Arrange the rectangles in a hierarchy.* If there is a board of directors, it usually is at the top, with the president immediately below. All of the vice presidents are listed on one row below the president. Arranged below each vice president are all of the positions that report to him or her.

- *Show responsibility relationships.* Use lines to connect the positions. For staff positions, such as a strategic planning group reporting to the board of directors, use dashed lines.

- *Only document the organizational unit(s) involved in the study.* It is not necessary to show the structure of the entire firm. For example, if you are doing a study in the marketing department, you only need an organization chart showing marketing and how it fits into the overall structure. Be sure that the chart shows all of the necessary detail for the study area.

The chart will be extremely valuable in identifying organizational boundaries (constraints) and key personnel. However, you should be aware that the charts do not always identify power centers and informal relationships that can be just as important to the success of a systems project as those on the chart.

Policy and Procedure Manuals

Many firms have their manuals in a computer form, facilitating retrieval of those portions that relate to the system being studied.

FIGURE 4.9

A Workflow Diagram

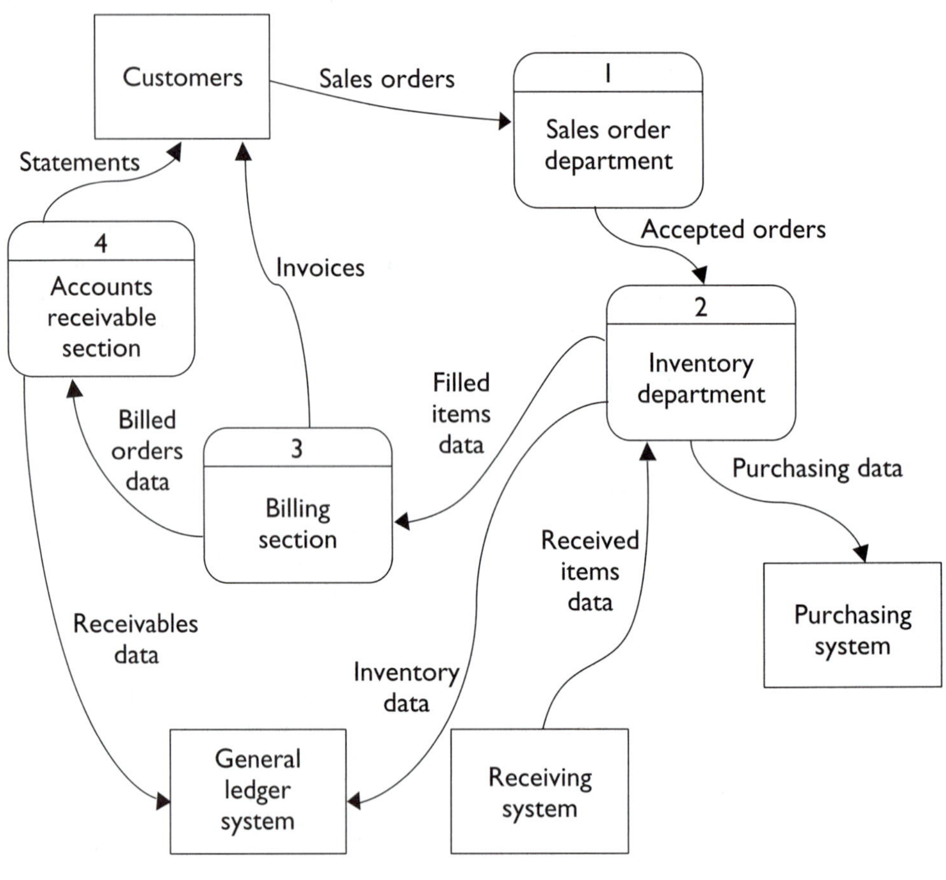

Existing System Documentation

Existing systems should be documented with data, process, and object models. Data models include entity-relationship diagrams, record layout forms, printer spacing charts, and screen layout forms. Process models include system and program flowcharts, data flow diagrams, and workflow diagrams. A **workflow diagram** is a high-level DFD that specifies the organizational units performing the processes. An example appears in Figure 4.9. Object models can include class diagrams, use case diagrams, and statechart diagrams. Good documentation should be expected for newer systems but does not always exist for legacy systems.

News Stories

Articles frequently appear in newspapers and magazines that report on the firm's activities. This information can be obtained from the firm's public relations department or from the Internet. If the firm has a newsletter or news magazine, it should be especially helpful.

Executive Speeches

Copies of speeches that executives have made to such groups as stockholders meetings can be obtained from the executives or their executive secretaries.

Executive Interviews

The firm's executives can be an especially rich source of information, and can most likely identify other sources.

With this understanding of the firm in its environment, the resource flows, and the subsidiary structure, the project team has taken the first step of the preliminary investigation of conducting an enterprise analysis.

An Example of Enterprise Analysis

Enform Technology is a Houston, Texas based firm that develops information systems for its clients. It conducts an enterprise analysis for each and views the process as the linkage shown in Figure 4.10.

Organizational Strategy

A firm's organizational strategy consists of a hierarchy of guidelines. The hierarchy begins at the top with the executives' vision, and then proceeds to the mission statement, the strategic business plan, goals, objectives, and finally to the operational-level action plans. On lower organizational levels, the strategy spells out how to accom-

FIGURE 4.10

Overview of Enterprise Analysis

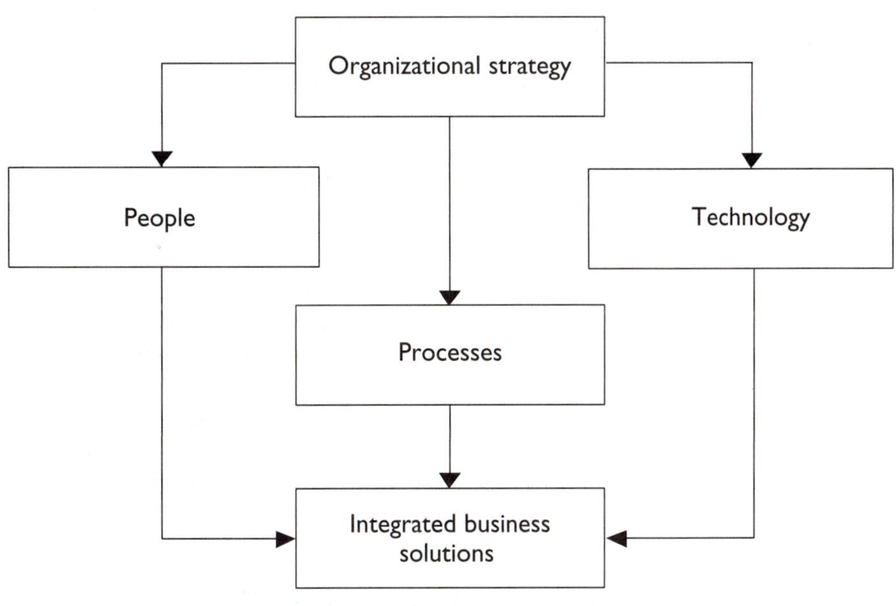

plish the strategy for the firm. The organizational strategy is implemented using people, processes, and technology.

- *People*—When evaluating a firm's human resources, attention is given to the firm's corporate culture, the focus of the organizational model, and the employees' competencies, capabilities, and skill sets.
- *Processes*—The firm's processes can be modeled using such tools as data flow diagrams. These processes can be analyzed to detect inefficiencies and redundancies, which can be removed through redevelopment, business process redesign, and automation.
- *Technology*—A firm's information technology exists in the form of toolsets, infrastructure, and direction.

Integrated Business Solutions

The objective of enterprise analysis is to determine the necessary people, processes, and technology to create integrated business solutions for enterprise challenges. When enterprise analysis indicates weaknesses in processes or technology, the weaknesses may be overcome by developing a new system or redeveloping an existing one.

Step 2: Determine the System Constraints, Objectives, Goals, Risk, and Scope

The enterprise analysis provides a systems view of the firm. This understanding enables the project team to specify what the system will and will not encompass, what it will and will not be expected to accomplish, and what risks can threaten a successful implementation. This is the second step of preliminary investigation.

System Constraints Define the System Scope

Systems are usually aimed at particular subsets of the firm's activities. These subsets can impose limitations on the **scope** of the system, which is the definition of the area within which the system is to be applied and the development project is to be focused. It is important to stay within these constraints, or imposed limitations, otherwise resources will be spent on unnecessary tasks. The limits of a system can be based on organizational units, business resources, and processes.

- *Organizational constraints*—Some systems are intended to support the entire enterprise. An example is a data warehouse that generates a variety of enterprise wide reports and allows managers to select reports from a menu of possibilities or use ad hoc report-building features. Other systems support organizational subsystems. Examples are marketing information systems, financial information systems, and human resources information systems. Boundaries of these systems are fairly specific, as they are defined on the organization chart. However, as one unit interfaces with another, the boundaries often blur.
- *Resource constraints*—The systems view of the firm encourages the development of systems to support particular resources. As an example,

many firms have built systems to facilitate the material flow. Such systems are examples of supply chain management and are called materials management systems, logistics systems, or distribution systems. They manage the flow of materials from suppliers, through manufacturing, through marketing distribution channels, to customers. In addition to materials, other resources that lend themselves to this approach are money, human resources, and information.

- *Process constraints*—The first information systems were designed to facilitate processes. This influence still exists, and stimulates projects to reengineer such processes as order filling, inventory management, billing, and accounts receivable.

The system constraints influence what the system can be expected to accomplish.

System Objectives and Goals

An **objective** is a condition or situation to be attained that is of major importance. Objectives are usually stated in broad terms meaningful to users. Examples of objectives of information systems are cost reduction, cost avoidance, increased revenues, increased productivity, and improved decision making.

- *Cost reduction*—Early information systems reflected a philosophy of **cost reduction**—to reduce operating costs, primarily clerical costs. The flaw in this reasoning became obvious to management when they realized that the personnel whose work had been converted to the computer were being reassigned rather than terminated.

- *Cost avoidance*—Although the computer has not been especially effective in reducing the size of the workforce, it has been able to delay the need to hire more employees of the same type in the future. Firms have been able to avoid costs rather than reduce them-an economic justification called **cost avoidance.** Cost avoidance reflects a more realistic attitude toward the impact of information systems than does cost reduction.

- *Increased revenues*—Whereas management first viewed the computer in terms of its potential impact on costs, recent emphasis has been on revenues. Modern information systems are expected to increase revenues by increasing productivity and sales. One example would be to create a Web site for direct sales. This will increase costs for the organization. The objective will be to offset these increased costs with an even greater increase in revenues, since the manufacturer will be able to sell directly to the customer without sharing revenues with wholesalers or retailers.

- *Increased productivity*—As early systems were being applied to achieve cost reduction, it became clear to management that they could also increase productivity. For example, early inventory systems printed out picking tickets with inventory items listed in a sequence that minimized picking time by the warehouse stock clerks. A more current example is the use of a knowledge-based system by a stockbroker, enabling her or him to handle many more clients than doing the work without system support.

- *Improved decision making*—Investments in information systems, decision support systems, and expert systems are being made with the assumption that the information they provide will result in better decisions. The better decisions will enable management to solve problems and seize opportunities.

Identifying the objectives for a system development project is an important and often time-consuming activity. One approach is to perform problem chain analysis, a process explained in Chapter 2. What starts out as an identification of a couple of problems or symptoms may lead to a list of changes that are needed in people, processes, and technology to create or improve the integrated systems of the entire enterprise, as shown in the ASTA case example in Figure CS 1.15. The team identified three main problems—the skills inventory system, the market intelligence system, and human resource issues. In their problem chain analysis they listed specific objectives and measurable performance criteria for each of these three problem areas. The time constraints for the project team and the ASTA organizational boundary constraints caused the ASTA clients and developers to limit the project scope to just the skills inventory system.

Determining the right objectives for the system itself, the product that will be the result of the development process, is a critical early step in preliminary investigation. But a modern systems developer must think more broadly about the development process and how the system (the product) matches the organizational situation and broader organization strategies and goals.

System Development Goals

An experienced developer will immediately think about issues like maintaining the system in the future, scalability of the system for company growth, and keeping users happy and committed to what may be a long development process. For inexperienced developers we recommend a formal goal analysis process to focus attention on a series of nine general goals in three areas that must be met for every system development process. These goals are:

System quality

- Functionality
- Maintainability
- Portability, Scalability

Project management

- Timeliness
- Cost
- Client commitment

Organizational relevance

- Efficiency (operations)
- Effectiveness (decision making)
- Competitive advantage

Going through this checklist of goals will increase the chance of success from the early step of defining objectives through analysis, design, and construction.

Figure 4.11 is a form called a **goal analysis form** that lists the nine goals to be met by a system and its development project. The center column lists notes that relate the goals to the firm, and the right-hand column lists actions necessary to meet the goals. The purpose of the form is to focus the project team on those system and project characteristics that contribute to a successful effort. The sample includes entries for an Internet-based insurance sales system. The goals are geared to satisfying Gail Torres, the owner of this home-based insurance business. Gail has been successful supporting herself for a year with completely manual record keeping. After working with a CPA on taxes for her first year of business she realized that she needed to take advantage of a computer for financial record keeping. A friend suggested that she also increase her sales by creating a Web site for her business. As a small business, she knew she could not hire a full time staff member for information systems development and support, so she followed her CPA's advice to purchase a small business accounting package and hire an independent information systems consultant that the CPA had found to be reasonably priced and sensitive to the priorities of small businesses.

System Quality (SQ) The first three goals relate to system quality. **Functionality** is the users' view of how they would like a new system to function. It is influenced by what the existing system does and does not do. **Maintainability** is the ability to keep the system on target in meeting users' needs. The software changes over the life of a system can be more expensive than initial development. Developers must design systems and choose tools that make these changes ("maintenance") easy. A key concern for any system is whether the organization will be able to maintain the system or whether the firm should buy software or negotiate for services of an application service provider rather than attempt in-house custom development. Note that in the example in Figure 4.11 this is a major concern for the home-based business Torres Insurance. **Portability** is the ability of the system to adapt to a changing environment. Portability is often called **scalability** when the issue is adapting to growing data storage or increased transaction processing.

All systems should meet the three system quality goals. The ASTA team defined major objectives including a Web interface for the system to meet the goal of maximum availability for all users, especially job applicants who could fill out the skills inventory matrix as part of their application process from their home. As the goal analysis in Figure CS 2.3 indicates, maintainability was such a concern for the ASTA team that Web deployment was eliminated since no one at ASTA had experience with Web development. Portability was also a concern since ASTA had more than one office and growth made scalability an issue for choice of tools.

Project Management (PM) The next three goals are focused on development process issues. **Timeliness** is the ability to implement the system on schedule. **Cost** is the ability to stay within cost constraints. **Client commitment** captures the notion that user support is necessary for a successful project. The development process will be important for user satisfaction. All projects should meet these goals. For the ASTA project, development time was such a tight constraint that several original system objectives were eliminated from the initial project scope.

Organizational Relevance (OR) The system should meet the needs of the organization. **Efficiency** has been defined as "doing the job right" whereas **effectiveness** is "doing the right job." Efficiency goals are at the operational level of a business. Effectiveness is a measure of whether the system supports management decision-making. The goal of **competitive advantage** gives the firm some type of edge over its competitors. All projects will not meet all three of these goals, but they represent a set that should be considered as specific system goals are identified.

Based on the goal analysis shown in Figure 4.11, Gail and the consultant agreed on the summary of objectives, constraints and scope shown in Figure 4.12.

FIGURE 4.11

A Goal Analysis Form

Torres Insurance: Goal Analysis for a Quoting Web Site and Customer Tracking System

	Context & Requirement Issue(s)	Action(s) to Meet Goal
System quality (SQ): functionality	■ Gail needs a Web site with quote prices to attract customers and a sales history database to keep up with information ■ Easy-to-use functionality ■ All processes are currently manual ■ Currently Gail has no reports or methods to track trends	■ Interview and observe Gail to determine her computer skills and her current processes ■ Create a system to track customers and generate reports ■ Create an attractive Web site with quoting capabilities and methods to notify Gail of new potential customers
SQ: maintainability	■ Gail has no in-house IT support ■ No automated systems are currently in place	■ Use simple format without bells and whistles ■ Train Gail on how to use and maintain system ■ Choose widely-known, well-documented, and inexpensive development tools
SQ: portability/ scalability	■ Minimal expansion expected for Gail's business ■ Web site and database capabilities should not be restrictive	■ Commercial server can easily handle expected Web site traffic ■ Access can handle amount of data to be stored in the database for at least 5 years
Project management (PM): timeliness	■ There is no specific deadline, but the sooner the site is available, the sooner benefits are possible	■ Design basic system and Web site in phases with immediate use possible for initial information (static) website
PM: cost	■ Maximum budget: $20,000 for development ■ Continual outlay for Web site hosting should not exceed $1,200 the first year	■ Plan carefully to avoid scope creep ■ Use inexpensive tools ■ Research options for reliable, inexpensive Web-site hosting
PM: client commitment	■ Gail wants systems ■ Gail is eager to learn ■ Gail is very cooperative	■ Observe Gail's processes to ensure new system meets needs ■ Create easy-to-use database with on-line help and documentation with clear examples
Organizational relevance (OR): effectiveness (decision making)	■ Manual processes slow and repetitive ■ Gail's current process limits how many clients she can service ■ Gail needs to reply to initial client inquiries more quickly	■ Web site will speed up correspondence process ■ Design thorough verification checks to ensure good data
OR: efficiency (operations)	■ Gail needs improved information for decision making	■ Provide meaningful reports and statistics from information in database ■ Satisfy potential customers with instant quotes; send Gail instant email notifications with information on site visitors
OR: competitive advantage	■ Potential for reaching more clients ■ Potential for handling clients more efficiently and therefore increasing percentage of contacts that result in initial and repeat sales	■ Web site will reduce customer time spent on filling out application ■ Checking processes and reports will improve Gail's service and accuracy

Project Risk

As top management evaluates whether to pursue a systems project, attention is given to risk. A risky project offers a higher likelihood of failure than does one with little or no risk. Four categories of factors influence risk and are listed in the **project risk evaluation form** in Figure 4.13. They are characteristics of the organization, the information system, the systems developers, and the internal and external users. The sample includes entries for Web site development for Torres Insurance.

Each of these four categories can be evaluated by asking a series of questions. The questions are listed in the left-hand column below the characteristics. In making the evaluation, the systems developer assigns a numeric score. If the risk does not exist (the answer is positive), the score is +1. If it does exist, it is a -1. If it is not certain whether the situation exists, the score is 0. For the basic four-category form, there are fifteen possible scores, providing a total score range from -15 (extremely risky) to +15 (no risk). Explanatory comments are entered in the right-hand side of the form.

Note that the risk evaluation for the Web site and customer tracking system for Torres Insurance shows two categories of users: internal (Gail) and external (visitors to her Web site). Another example of risk evaluation with two user categories

FIGURE 4.12

Project Objectives, Constraints, and Scope

Torres Insurance: Quoting Web Site and Customer Tracking System

Objectives

- To increase customers by increasing potential customer awareness of Gail's business by creating an on-line presence.
- To create a professional-looking Web site to gather prospective customer contact information and provide immediate insurance policy quotes.
- To decrease the time required for Gail to respond to a potential customer's initial inquiry to 15 minutes for a single quote.
- To allow Gail to access information on Web site visitors from any computer with access to the Internet.
- To provide an accurate customer tracking system for tracking policies sold, client information, details on direct mailing, and insurance company information.
- To provide reports on sales data to increase Gail's decision-making effectiveness.

Constraints

- *Budget:* Initial development costs must be no more than $20,000.
- *Maintainability:* The quoting Web site and customer tracking system will have no in house IT support.
- *Maintainability:* Gail has no experience in Microsoft Access or Microsoft FrontPage, the development tools selected for the project. Therefore, all of the components must be easy to maintain and use.

Scope

- The customer tracking functions will include information on clients, policies sold, insurance companies that Gail deals with, and direct mailings. The system will produce canned and ad hoc reports and statistics to assist Gail in making knowledgeable decisions.
- The online quoting functions will calculate instant quotes based on available policies from TransAmerica. The system will also gather contact information from potential clients and notify Gail of site visits by sending email messages to her. There will be a secure, password-protected Web site provided for Gail to view reports on site visitors and their contact information.

FIGURE 4.13

A Project Risk Evaluation for Torres Insurance

Factors Affecting Project Risk	Rating*	Comments
1. Characteristics of the organization a. Has stable, well-defined objectives?	0	Torres Insurance does not have a written mission statement, but Gail's goals and focus on a narrow objective (term life policies at reasonable costs) are clear.
b. Is guided by a strategic plan for information resources (SPIR)?	-1	Gail sees no need for a strategic plan for information resources because of her small business.
c. Proposed system fits plan and addresses organizational objectives?	0	Project is key to increasing sales by streamlining process and reaching more customers.
2. Characteristics of the information system a. Model available/clear requirements?	-1	There is no documentation for Gail's existing process.
b. Automates routine, structured procedures?	0	Tracking clients and providing quotes are structured routines, but increasing visibility through the Web site is not routine.
c. Affects only one business area? (No cross-functional or interorganizational links?)	+1	Potential implementation is throughout the entire organization, but since there is only one user, the accounting, marketing, and customer's service roles are unlikely to cause confusion or contention.
d. Can be completed in less than three months.	+1	Scope is estimated to be 10 weeks.
e. Uses stable, proven technology?	+1	Chosen tools are well proven.
f. Installation at only one site?	+1	Single user but Web hosting site will be at a separate location.
3. Characteristics of the developers a. Are experienced in chosen development methodology?	+1	Consultant has developed systems for small businesses for 5 years and is experienced in the phased development methodology chosen.
b. Are skilled at determining functional requirements?	+1	Yes. See above.
c. Are familiar with technology and information architecture?	+1	Consultant has chosen development tools and operating environment to match this small business environment.
4. Characteristics of the internal user (Gail Torres) a. Have business-area experience?	0	Gail understands her current process but has only vague ideas about how to improve processes.
b. Have development experience?	-1	No experience working with any developer.
c. Is committed to the project?	+1	Yes and has adequate time for working with developer to provide feedback.
5. Characteristics of external users a. Have business area experience	0	Gail has found that most of her clients know little about insurance options.
b. Have relevant computer experience	0	Current clients are older and most are not Web users.
Total	**5**	

* +1 = yes; 0 = maybe; -1 = no

would be Procter & Gamble's data warehouse. All the users are internal—only employees of P&G have access to the system. Some P&G users are part of a user group that works with P&G systems developers to define major enhancements to their data warehouse, but most of the thousands of users of the data warehouse have never been involved with the evolving development of the system and so would be a similar user category to the external Web users in Torres Insurance's risk evaluation in Figure 4.13. (The total score range for this variation of the form with two user categories is -17 to + 17.)

The total score provides the project team and management with a measure of the risk of the project. With this understanding, strategies can be devised to reduce the risk. A separate form, a **risk reduction strategies form,** can be used to address the strategies. Figure 4.14 provides a sample for the Torres system, with entries for all risks that received a rating of -1 or 0. For example, a rating of -1 was applied to the fact that Torres has no SPIR. This was addressed in the risk reduction strategies form by recommending that an SPIR be developed.

There are strategies that can be directed at each of the risks, and they vary from one project to the next. Table 4.2 lists some of the more common strategies. JAD sessions and prototyping are especially useful risk reduction strategies.

STEP 3: EVALUATE FEASIBILITY AND OBTAIN APPROVAL TO PROCEED

Thus far, the project has not been too costly, involving only selected user personnel working primarily with the systems developer. However, if the project continues,

FIGURE 4.14

A Risk Reduction Strategies Table for Torres Insurance

Factors	Recommended Risk Reduction Strategies
1. Organization	Develop a brief strategic business plan and information resources plan for next five years to help focus this project on immediate needs and create a design compatible with future expansion for Torres Insurance.
2. Information system	Use prototyping to identify requirements alternatives and be sure that Gail understands the proposed system design and processes
3. Developer	No identified risks for this factor.
4. Internal User	Use prototyping to identify requirements alternatives and be sure that Gail understands the proposed system design and processes. Keep processes and reports simple.
5. External Web Users	Provide clean information, obvious links, and step-by-step instructions. Research levels of computer sophistication among current clients. Ask selected clients to provide feedback on the site several points during development in return for thorough insurance analysis.

TABLE 4.2

Possible Risk Reduction Strategies

Risk	Reduction Strategy
Poorly defined objectives	Develop a strategic business plan.
No SPIR	Develop a strategic plan for information resources
System not focused on organizational objectives	Conduct a JAD session with managers from the organizational unit.
System requirements are unclear	Engage in requirements prototyping.
Unstructured system procedures	Document the procedures with such a top-down structured tool as DFDs.
Multiple business areas involved	Conduct a JAD session with managers from the organizational units.
Project estimated at longer than 1 year	Subdivide the project into smaller projects.
System uses unproven technology	Use evolutionary prototyping to prove the technology as the design evolves.
Multiple system sites involved	Implement the system with a pilot installation or a phased approach.
Developers inexperienced in methodology	Enroll developers in classes taught by experienced instructors.
Developers unskilled at determining functional requirements	Train developers in use of the systems approach.
Developers unfamiliar with information technology architecture	Enroll developers in computer classes or use packaged self-study courses.
Users have little business area experience	Enroll users in such courses as those offered by industry associations.
Users have little system development experience	Conduct on-site classes in system methodologies.
Users are uncommitted to the project	Conduct JAD sessions with committed top-level mangers present.

many more personnel will become involved and the cost will jump. Before management commits to a big cash outlay, it wants to be assured that it is the right thing to do. The systems developer provides this assurance by conducting one or more feasibility studies. This is the third step of the preliminary investigation.

A **feasibility study** is an abbreviated form of systems analysis that is intended to determine whether a system project should be pursued. The systems developer wants to learn only enough about such a solution to justify going on, and this can be accomplished with personal interviews and record search. The interviews are limited to persons in the manager's area who are especially knowledgeable about the problem or opportunity. The records search may involve digging through some of the unit's files to gather data that the interviews fail to yield or to substantiate the interview findings.

When conducting the feasibility study, the systems developer is concerned with five feasibility types—technical, economic, legal and ethical, operational, and schedule.

Technical Feasibility

During the early years of the computer, managers tended to be skeptical of its abilities to solve their problems. The managers were concerned about **technical feasibility**—the availability of hardware and software to do a particular job. Today, hardware is available to do practically any job that the user wants done. The only question is whether the user can afford it. The same situation applies to the other aspect of technical feasibility—software. It is possible to create information systems to do practically any job but the question that management must answer is whether it wants to incur the expense.

Economic Feasibility

The type of feasibility that has always been of most importance to management has been **economic feasibility**—the ability of a system to pay for itself in monetary terms. Management does not want to spend a dollar unless it receives more than a dollar in return. In order to provide management with the economic justification that it wants, the systems developer conducts a **cost-benefit analysis**—a study of the costs and benefits that will be incurred in developing and using an information system. We describe economic justification in detail in Technical Module F.

Legal and Ethical Feasibility

Very few laws have been passed in the United States to regulate computer use. Most of the legislation has been aimed at computer use by the federal government. Therefore, the systems developer who works for the government has a greater responsibility in evaluating the legal feasibility of a new system than does a developer doing the same work in private industry.

The legislation aimed at private industry deals primarily with credit information. Therefore, the systems developer working in private industry runs the greatest risk of violating the law when designing systems that maintain credit and personal information in the database. Systems that fall in this category include financial and human resource information systems. The systems should be designed so that the information is always kept current, is kept secure, and is made available to only those persons who are authorized to view it.

Whereas systems developers have always been aware that their systems must fit within legal frameworks, the concern for complying with moral and ethical guidelines is much more recent. Many professional organizations such as the Association for Computing Machinery (ACM) have established codes of ethics that are meant to guide information specialists. The same types of codes have been developed by firms.

Operational Feasibility

Operational feasibility relates to the ability of the people working within a system to do their job in a prescribed manner. The basic premise is the fact that no system, regardless of the soundness of its design from a technical standpoint, can succeed if it does not have the support of its personnel resource. Without question, one of the most frequent causes of system failure is a lack of cooperation from the system's users and participants.

Schedule Feasibility

The above types of feasibility all relate to the system being developed. The final type deals with the development process. **Schedule feasibility** is concerned with whether the system can be put in place by the time that it is needed. The best way to achieve schedule feasibility is to engage in effective project management. Project management and scheduling are discussed in detail in Technical Module D.

Putting System and Project Feasibility in Perspective

Most of the questions relating to system and project feasibility cannot be answered in a detailed way during the preliminary investigation stage. The systems developer is only able to make estimates but those estimates are necessary if management is to make a sound decision concerning continuation. Later, as more is learned about the system and its development, management will expect the developer to update the feasibility evaluations.

Step 4: Conduct JAD Sessions to Confirm Initial Functional Requirements

As the preliminary investigation stage draws to a close, the project team has gathered all of the information and data that will provide the basis for the remainder of the SDLC. Before proceeding to analysis, design, and construction, the team should ensure that the users and upper levels of project management understand the findings and approve continuation of the project. This assurance can be obtained by conducting one or more JAD sessions.

JAD stands for **joint application design** or **joint application development.** It is a formal approach to systems design in a group-decision support system setting. It is currently a very popular way to obtain agreement and understanding among users and members of the project team concerning the important elements of a system project.

Throughout the computer era, one of the biggest challenges of information specialists has been communication with users. The communication can involve one information specialist such as a systems developer conducting a personal interview with one user. Or the communication can involve multiple information specialists or users engaging in an informal setting called a **brainstorming session.**

Brainstorming works well because it brings together the people who are involved in a system project and provides an opportunity for an open discussion and, ultimately, an agreement. The session might address a problem or a definition of user needs, a consideration of possible system designs, or any other unanswered questions. Brainstorming has been so successful in bridging the communications gap between users and information specialists that efforts were made to improve its effectiveness by incorporating three elements. The end result is JAD.

- One of the most important JAD elements is the **facilitator,** the person who provides direction to the discussion and creates a climate that enables the group to reach a consensus.

- Another important element is the recognition that a written record should be maintained of the session discussion. A person called a **scribe** maintains a record of everything that is said, and publishes a written report. More than a single scribe may be required.

- A third important element is an **executive sponsor** who is a top-level manager from the user area who kicks off the session and is present for the conclusion.

This person's presence conveys to the group the fact that the topics being discussed are very important and must be addressed in an open manner.

These persons support the discussions by the representatives of the project team and the user area. The facilitator and executive sponsor are especially critical in ensuring that the session meets its objectives.

A JAD session can last for a few hours or a few days, depending on the amount of material to cover. The session can be held in a conference room or any type of facility that enables the participants to interact and view visual aids. A simple, yet effective, arrangement consists of chairs in a circle to encourage participation, and a flipchart easel, overhead projector and screen, chalkboard, or some combination to provide for visual display. The facility can be made more elaborate by providing one or more PCs and computer-generated displays.

The Three Phases of JAD

JAD is performed in three phases. First, planning must be done. Then, the session is held. Finally, the results are documented.

- *Planning for the session*—The project team prepares for the JAD session by identifying the other participants, selecting the site, making certain that all of the required equipment is available, and establishing an agenda.
- *Conducting the session*—The key to a good JAD is the facilitator. This person ensures that all participants contribute their ideas, that the session is not monopolized by the most vocal participants, that the discussion stays on track, and that disagreements are settled. It is not necessary that the facilitator be an expert on the application area. Rather, she or he must be skilled in conducting a group session in a stimulating manner.
- *Documenting the results*—When the scribes deliver the detailed written record of the session, the task of the project team is to prepare a **specification document** that summarizes the agreement—the problem statement,

FIGURE 4.15

An Outline of a Specification Document

1. Management Objectives
2. Scope and Limits
3. Business Questions the System Will Answer
4. Information Required to Answer the Questions
5. Interfaces with Other Systems
6. Issues
7. Data Element Specifications
8. Screen Layouts and Report Layouts
9. Menus
10. Processing Rules
11. Operating Procedures
12. Performance Criteria and Operational Requirements

PROJECT MANAGEMENT TOOLBOX

Tips for Preliminary Investigation

In the preliminary investigation stage the team establishes the development process procedures that will launch the team toward success or failure. While the development team performs enterprise analysis, determines system objectives, and completes the other activities of the preliminary investigation stage, relationships are being established with:

- The executive sponsor
- Internal end users (or their representatives)
- Representative external users
- Vendors supplying technology
- Computer support personnel who will maintain the production system
- Development team members
- Development team superiors

For large teams working with diverse groups, like those illustrated in Figures 1.15 and 1.16, establishing these relationships will be critical for success and may be quite time consuming. A half-day of team building exercises might be valuable once the team is chosen and before the first series of meetings to define the project beyond the initial problem statement or first list of objectives.

For smaller projects the development team might be two or three developers who know each other from years of working together with the same group of users. But this is an unusual situation; due to changes in organizations (promotions, transfers, resignations, and so on) at least one of the developers or users is likely to be new to the others on the development team.

Avoid the beginners' misperception that since the users want this system, they will:

- Provide thorough information without much help from developers
- Allow plenty of time to answer developers' questions and review developers' suggestions
- Manage the development process

Typical users are busy and unfamiliar with development tasks, so many of the tips below provide a way to increase participation by busy users who think that developers can guess what is needed from a few general requests.

Timeliness

1. Set regular meetings with users who will provide information. One or more of these may be a formal JAD session.

performance criteria, system design, implementation schedule, and so on. Figure 4.15 identifies sections that might be included in such a document.

Placement of JAD in the System Life Cycle

JAD can be used by the firm's top executives during preliminary investigation, and then used throughout each subsequent SDLC stage. When used as one of the analy-

2. Set regular meetings with the development team to discuss technical issues and monitor progress.
3. Make good use of meeting time with users and developers by:
   - Assigning a team member to create agendas and e-mail them to all participants before meetings
   - Writing clear lists of questions and e-mail them to participants before meetings when appropriate
   - Bringing copies of diagrams and screen printouts to meetings to allow participants to mark changes clearly

Cost

1. Create rough estimates early as part of the feasibility study to determine whether the benefits expected for the system justify the costs.
2. Alter the project scope to keep the cost well below the projected benefits, including paying attention to maintenance and scalability issues relevant to the findings of the team's enterprise analysis and goal analysis.
3. Keep technical and user management informed about cost/benefit information from the first rough estimates through all the changes in the estimates as the scope becomes better defined.

User Commitment and User Satisfaction

1. Gain the users' respect and trust by:
   - Listening carefully
   - Communicating in clear, jargon-free language
   - Showing prototypes that reflect users' requests
2. After meetings e-mail minutes to participants with a summary of the tasks to be completed by the next meeting.
3. When completing the goal analysis, notice any conflict or contradictions between the user sponsor and end-users. Meeting all three sub-goals for organizational relevance is the best way to establish good relationships with all stakeholders. If this project is driven by the user sponsor's goals for increasing revenues by gaining competitive advantage or improving management decision making, research the possibility of improving operations performed by end-users. Similarly, if the main driver of the project is streamlining operations to avoid costs or reduce costs, research the possibility of improving management decision-making. Whenever the main goal is to streamline operations to reduce user frustrations, be clear that there are competitive level advantages of reducing costs or increasing revenues by increasing customers.

sis activities, JAD can facilitate the definition of the user's information needs. During one of the iterative design phases, JAD can be used to obtain feedback concerning how the evolving design is meeting the defined needs. During preliminary and final construction, JAD can provide an opportunity to gain user approval of system modules and the overall system, respectively. During system test and installation, JAD can be used for such tasks as approving test plans and deciding on cutover strategy. A firm that is totally committed to JAD will likely use it on all management levels, and at several stages throughout the development process.

Putting Preliminary Investigation in Perspective

All of the stages of the SDLC are important but there is no question that the first one, the preliminary investigation stage, is most important. The enterprise analysis positions the system within the context of the firm and its environment. Management and the project team work together to identify objectives, establish goals, address risks, and determine system scope. Management evaluates feasibility and provides the team with approval to proceed. The success of the project rests largely on the quality of work done during preliminary investigation.

Summary

System projects can be triggered by user needs, technology, strategic direction, and business process redesign (BPR). Business process redesign involves reverse engineering and forward engineering in order to analyze the existing system and define the new system. The strategic direction is provided by the firm's strategic plans. The long-range plan that the executive committee develops is called the strategic business plan. As the executives develop this plan they are aware of the resources that they have available. Once set, the plan influences the acquisition of additional resources that are needed to meet the plan.

Once the strategic business plan is set, similar plans are made for each business area. The business area plan for information systems is called the strategic plan for information resources. The SPIR is developed by the vice president of information systems, or CIO, working closely with executives in the other business areas. One way to organize the strategic plan for information resources is to specify the information resources required by each of the types of systems in the information systems infrastructure.

Phased development begins with preliminary investigation, a stage that consists of four steps. The first, enterprise analysis, can be taken by viewing the firm as a system, recognizing the environmental system, and identifying the firm's subsystems. As the systems developer conducts the enterprise analysis, he or she seeks out all available information—organization charts, policy and procedure manuals, news stories, executive speeches, and executive interviews.

The second step of preliminary investigation is to specify system constraints, determine system objectives and goals, and evaluate system and project risk. The firm's organizational structure, resources, and processes can influence system constraints that will determine the scope of the objectives that will be met by the system.

Many types of objectives can be identified for a new system, but five appear fundamental—reduce costs, avoid costs, increase revenues, increase productivity, and improve decision making. The cost reduction objective guided early systems efforts but has largely been replaced by the others. Much current interest is aimed at making improved decisions as a way of solving problems and taking advantage of opportunities, and thereby increasing revenues. Objectives should be broad statements that are meaningful to users.

Goal analysis can be used to focus attention on goals relating to system quality, project management, and organizational relevance that might not be immediately apparent to users, but are very important to the success of the project.

Management realizes that all projects will incur a certain amount of risk. A project risk evaluation form can be used to evaluate four categories of risk—the organization, the information system, the developers, and the users.

The third step of preliminary investigation consists of a feasibility analysis. There are five types of feasibility—technical, economic, legal and ethical, operational, and schedule. Technical feasibility considers whether needed hardware and software are available. Economic feasibility is concerned with justification of an information system in monetary terms. Legal feasibility is concerned with laws that deal mainly with computer use by the federal government and credit reporting. Ethical considerations focus on individuals' right to privacy and accuracy of information maintained about individuals. Operational feasibility relates to the abilities and attitudes of the system users and participants—how well they can be expected to support the system. Schedule feasibility considers the time required to implement the system. When management is convinced that the proposed system and its project are feasible, it establishes a control mechanism to be used in managing the remainder of the project.

The last step of preliminary investigation is centered around a JAD session aimed at confirming the initial functional requirements. Keys to a good JAD session are the facilitator and executive sponsor. The sessions are planned, are conducted, and are then documented in the form of a specification document. JAD can be used throughout the development process to gain agreement on key project issues.

With the preliminary investigation accomplished and the project control mechanism in place, the SDLC is ready to move to analysis activities, the subject of the next chapter.

Key Terms

- project request form
- business process redesign (BPR), business process reengineering
- reverse engineering
- forward engineering
- executive committee
- strategic business plan
- strategic plan for information resources (SPIR)
- enterprise analysis
- workflow diagram
- scope
- objective
- functionality
- maintainability
- portability, scalability
- feasibility study
- cost-benefit analysis
- JAD (joint application design) session
- facilitator
- scribe
- executive sponsor

Key Concepts

- The top-down influence of a firm's strategic plans on system development
- The reciprocal relationship between the firm's strategic plan and its resources
- Strategic planning for information resources (SPIR)
- The systems approach can provide a format for conducting enterprise analysis
- Business process redesign (BPR) is a combination of reverse engineering followed by forward engineering
- Management, in its desire to increase profits, has shifted its focus from decreasing costs to increasing revenues
- Project scope is determined by identifying all objectives and then limiting the project objectives to those that are within constraints and do not lead to unreasonable risk of successful completion
- The dimensions of feasibility—technical, economic, legal and ethical, operational, and schedule

QUESTIONS

1. Name three ways that a project can be triggered.
2. Which formal group in the firm has responsibility for strategic planning? Who belongs to the group?
3. What is the relationship between the environment and the strategic business plan?
4. What is the relationship between the firm's resources and the strategic business plan?
5. Who develops the strategic plan for information resources?
6. Who are the people who are considered to be information resources?
7. What are the other information resources?
8. What is the relationship between the strategic business plan and the strategic plan for information resources?
9. Identify two conceptual models that can be useful in conducting an enterprise analysis.
10. List four ways that a firm can organize its subsystems.
11. What is the main difference between business process redesign and repeating the SLC when a system becomes outdated?
12. Why would a firm engage in reverse engineering?
13. What are three types of system constraints?
14. Explain the difference between cost reduction and cost avoidance.
15. What are the three major goals for all information system projects?
16. What is the current emphasis in information system justification?
17. List four categories of factors that can add to the risk of a project.
18. Which element of the firm's environment has been the focus of most legislation concerning computer use?
19. Identify two applications that are exceptionally susceptible to legislation concerning computer use.
20. Who leads a JAD session? What capabilities should that person have?
21. Give an example of how JAD could be used in each of the stages of phased development. Refer to the description of each stage in Chapter 3.

TOPICS FOR DISCUSSION

1. An information link between the firm and the government is an incoming flow of economic and legislative information. What are some examples of an outgoing flow to the government?
2. If you were a systems developer, how would you know whether to spend a lot of time conducting a cost-benefit analysis?
3. If a systems developer continually conducts feasibility studies indicating that systems projects should *not* be pursued, isn't that a bad reflection on the developer's abilities?

PROBLEM

1. Assume that you are a systems developer and your boss asks you to design a questionnaire that can be sent through the company mail to all employees who are currently using PCs. Design the questionnaire so that you can determine the level of the user's capabilities and his or her future needs. The questionnaire should include information about the individual, such as department, position, and degree of computer and information literacy. Also include questions about computer use, such as how often, and the purpose. The questionnaire responses will provide a basis for developing a SPIR that addresses user needs.

CASE PROBLEM: ANDERSON'S

Anderson's is one of the leading department store chains in northern California, consisting of its headquarters in San Francisco, eighteen retail stores, and three distribution centers that provide merchandise to the stores. A data center is located at the headquarters and is linked to local area networks in each of the stores and distribution centers. The Anderson's top-level managers include Bill Glass, president; Harold Hall, director of information systems; Chung Kim, vice president of marketing; Charlie Sims, vice president of finance; Alice Wingate, vice president of administration; and Beth Yardley, director of human resources. Eight years ago, a management consultant studied Anderson's strategic planning system and recommended that an executive committee be formed. This was done, with the membership limited to the president and vice-presidents. The committee wasted no time in developing the initial strategic plan, spanning the period five to ten years into the future. Each year, during September through November, the plan is revised. At the same time, the executives engage in management control—deciding how to implement the strategic plan.

Most of the strategic planning and management control discussions take place during the committee's weekly meeting. It is early September, and the committee is meeting in Bill Glass's office.

Bill Glass (president): One of the items that we must address is how to implement our decision last year to go mail-order. As you know, we decided to publish catalogs on a quarterly basis, distribute them on a national scale, and fill the orders from a new distribution facility in Oakland. We decided on this new venture with the idea of gaining at least a five percent share of the mail-order market. Are we going to be ready? Chung?

Chung Kim (vice president of marketing): Well, I don't think we will have any trouble assembling the marketing resources that we need. The mailing list will not be a problem either. We have access to one of the most complete lists on the market. It is the one of people who have made catalog purchases in the past. If anybody doesn't believe me when I say it's a good list, may they be hit on the head with all the catalogs I receive each week. (Everybody laughs.)

Charlie Sims (vice president of finance): What about the mail-order distribution center staff, Chung? Will they be ready?

Chung Kim: No sweat. We've got such a good reputation as an employer that staffing won't be a problem. I've been working very closely with Beth (Yardley, director of human resources). We meet every week and look at the situation concerning marketing personnel. We're confident that we'll be able to assemble a top-flight staff. I've told her to follow the same procedure we did when we opened the San Jose distribution center.

Bill Glass: That sounds good. Does she have a plan underway?

Chung Kim: She sure does. Everything is written down—headcounts, schedules, interview dates, the works.

Bill Glass: Excellent. Charlie, do you see any problems getting the financing to build the new building and buy the equipment we need?

Charlie Sims: None at all, Bill. Our credit rating is tops with every lending institution in the area. I can see only clear sailing.

Bill Glass: Great. Chung, what about our inventory of stock? Will we be able to offer the same quality of merchandise that we sell in our stores? And, I don't want a lot of backorders. We've got to be able to fill the orders quickly. If we don't, the whole thing goes belly up.

Chung Kim: I don't anticipate any problems at all, Bill. The buyers who will order merchandise for the mail-order distribution center, for the most part, will have several years experience with the company. It's the promotion-from-within policy that Beth and I agreed to. And practically all of our suppliers are large-scale operations. They will be able to keep us supplied with what we need.

Bill Glass: They will as long as the computer tells the buyers that it is time to order. Which brings up a question to you, Alice. What about computer support? Harold (Hall, director of information systems) reports to you.

Alice Wingate (vice president of administration): I don't see any problem there. When I told Harold last year about our decision to go mail-order, he was pretty upset. I expected that. That's just his style. He's always complaining that he doesn't have enough people.

Chung Kim: Harold has his hands full. He's been working on my marketing information system for over two years now. I don't think he's ever going to get finished. He claims he doesn't have enough programmers.

Charlie Sims: I've had the same experience with the budgeting model that he's doing for me. Harold has good people but they're just overworked. You have to be patient.

Bill Glass: Well, we can't be patient when it comes to the mail-order distribution center. When it goes on the air, the information system will have to be in place. Alice, have you given Harold any kind of idea of what level of computer support we will need?

Alice Wingate: I've told him what we decided-that the mail—order distribution center will be operated just like the ones for our stores. That's about all he should know, isn't it?

Chung Kim: (Interrupting) Well, the systems aren't exactly the same. In the stores, the orders are entered into the point-of-sale terminals. Everything is automatic. In the mail-order center, the orders will be keyed in by my order takers. The mail-order operation is going to be pretty new from an information system standpoint.

Bill Glass: That's an important point. Alice, I want you to get with Harold and make certain that he understands just what we expect of him.

Alice Wingate: Right, Bill. That's what strategic planning is all about, isn't it?

Assignments

1. In what way is Anderson's doing a good job of strategic business planning?
2. In what way is Anderson's not doing such a good job?
3. Should Beth Yardley be a member of the executive committee? What about Harold Hall? Support your answers.
4. Suppose that Bill Glass decides to add only one person to the executive committee. Whom would you recommend? Beth or Harold? Support your answer.
5. Assume that Bill Glass is against enlarging the executive committee. What recommendations would you make to him to solve any problems that exist with the current membership?

Case Problem: Splashdown (B)

You are a systems developer and your boss, Mildred Wiggins, asks you to design a form to be used in evaluating system feasibility. She tells you that Splashdown doesn't regard all of the feasibility types as having the same amount of influence on the decision to develop a system. She hands you a piece of paper with the following weights written on it:

Technical feasibility	.10
Economic feasibility	.40
Legal and ethical feasibility	.10
Operational feasibility	.25
Schedule feasibility	.15
Total weight	1.00

Mildred also wants you to rate a prospective system on each of the feasibility types using the following point values:

Good performance	5 points
Fair performance	3 points
Poor performance	1 point

For example, if a system does a good job of satisfying its economic feasibility, the developer awards it 5 points. That process is repeated for each of the feasibility types. Then, each point value is multiplied by its weight, and the weighted values added. A system will be evaluated as a system development opportunity according to the following total weighted point values:

Good	3.01—5.00
Fair	2.01—3.00
Poor	1.00—2.00

Mildred asks you to get on with the form design, and, when you are finished, to try it out on two managers who have requested projects. One is Flora Henry, the director of corporate financial planning, and the other is Emma Ward, the president's executive secretary.

You go back to your office and use up about half of a yellow pad, making rough sketches of the form. You want it to be very user friendly so that the developer only has to (1) briefly describe the application, (2) enter the five ratings, (3) make the weight and total calculations, and (4) write a brief explanation at the bottom. The form should be self-explanatory—identifying the weights, the meaning of the rating points, and the meaning of the ranges of total points.

You finally come up with a form that you like and decide to test it out on Emma. You go to the executive suite and she explains that the members of the executive committee—the president and four vice presidents—want to implement an electronic calendaring system. The executives can use their workstations to check each other's calendars when they want to schedule a meeting. You ask Emma if the system can be justified economically, and she replies: "No question about it. When you consider how valuable an executive's time is, if the system saves only a few seconds a day, it's justified." You then ask if anyone else in the firm will have access to the executives' calendars, and she explains that their secretaries will, plus all managers in the firm, plus quite a few people outside the firm who frequently make appointments. You make a note of that on your yellow pad, and continue the line of questioning: "Will there be any confidential or personal information included in the calendars?" Emma assures you that there will not. Finally, one last question: "When does the system have to be up and running?" Emma smiles, and says "Yesterday." You look puzzled, and she explains "No, I'm just kidding. The executives would like to have it within 90 days." You jot that down, say good-bye, and head for Flora Henry's office.

Flora wants to implement a new competitor forecasting subsystem for the MIS. She wants to be able to use economic indicators to project the annual revenues for all the other water parks in the country. She tells you that it has never been done before, but, if it works, it could give Splashdown a real competitive edge. The system would use existing hardware, and the forecasting program would be written in Sybase Inc.'s PowerBuilder, a language that none of the programmers in information systems know anything about. You ask who the system users would be, and Flora says that they would include all of the forecasting analysts in the financial planning unit, and that they are all checked out on their terminals. You follow up with the big question about economic justification and Flora says: "Believe it or not, it's expected of us. Eileen (Jacobs, the vice president of finance, and Flora's boss) told me that the only way we could get the system approved would be if we displaced two of our forecasting analysts." You ask Flora whether that is likely to happen, and she says: "I'm not sure. The forecasting analysts have gotten wind of Eileen's requirement, and they're all pretty upset. I think they'll fight it tooth and nail." You write all that down, and then explain that you are concerned about not breaking any computer laws or violating anyone's rights. Flora assures you that there is "no sweat." It will use data that is available in commercial databases that Splashdown can purchase for a reasonable price. You sense that Flora is getting a little impatient, so you ask your last question concerning the schedule. Flora surprises you by saying that she would like cutover five weeks from now, when the new fiscal year begins. That way, the displaced analysts' salaries will be taken out of her budget.

Having filled the remaining pages of your yellow pad, you decide to call it a day and take a dip in the company pool.

Assignments

1. Design the form that Mildred has requested. Use your word processor to print a blank copy.
2. Make two additional copies of your form and complete them using the findings of your data gathering.
3. Prepare a memo to Mildred, advising her of your forms design efforts and your recommendations concerning the two systems. Do you recommend implementation for either or both and, if so, how strong is your recommendation? Attach the blank form, followed by the two completed forms.

SELECTED BIBLIOGRAPHY

Gupta, Yash P., and T. S. Raghunathan. "Impact of Information Systems (IS) Steering Committees on IS Planning." *Decision Sciences* 20 (Fall, 1989): 777-793.

Hammer, Michael. "Reengineering Work: Don't Automate, Obliterate." *Harvard Business Review* 68 (July-August 1990): 104-112.

King, William R. "Strategic Planning for Information Resources: The Evolution of Concepts and Practice." *Information Resources Management Journal* 1 (Fall 1988): 1-8.

Lederer, Albert L., and Vijay Sethi. "Critical Dimensions of Strategic Information Systems Planning." *Decision Sciences* 22 (Winter 1991): 104-119.

Pearlson, Keri E. *Managing and Using Information Systems: A Strategic Approach.* (New York: John Wiley and Sons, Inc., 2001).

Roetzheim, William H. "Estimating Project Risk." *Information Executive* 3 (Winter 1990): 47-50.

Sabherwal, Rajiv. "The Relationship Between Information System Planning Sophistication and Information System Success: An Empirical Assessment." *Decision Sciences* 30 (Number 1, Winter 1999): 137-167.

Salmela, H., A. L. Lederer, and T. Reponen. "Information Systems Planning in a Turbulent Environment." *European Journal of Information Systems* 9 (Number 1, March 2000): 3-15.

Teo, Thompson S. H., and James S. K. Ang. "Critical Success Factors in the Alignment of IS Plans With Business Plans." *International Journal of Information Management* 19 (Number 2, April 1999): 173-185.

TECHNICAL MODULE F

ECONOMIC SYSTEM AND PROJECT JUSTIFICATION

The systems developer has the responsibility of showing management that money spent on an information system is not only a good investment but it is as good as, or better than, other investments that management could make. Management seeks an **economic justification,** or support for the notion that the monetary value of the information system or information system project is greater than the cost.

COST-RELATED JUSTIFICATION STRATEGIES

During early years of computing, management sought to justify expenditures by means of a **cost reduction strategy.** That is, the costs of the information system were expected to be less than those of the noncomputer systems that were replaced. When it became evident that the costs of the displaced resources were seldom reduced, but merely shifted to other areas, management turned to a **cost avoidance strategy.** This strategy, popular today, reflects an intent to postpone future costs, such as those of increasing personnel, by implementing computer-based systems.

THE DIFFICULTY OF ECONOMIC JUSTIFICATION

In Chapter 1, we described the information systems infrastructure as consisting of different types of systems. The economic justification of data-oriented systems, such as the accounting information system (AIS), is usually easier to achieve than that of the information-oriented systems, such as the management information system (MIS), decision support systems (DSS), and expert systems. It is difficult to economically justify the information-oriented systems because of the difficulty of placing a monetary value on information.

Of the data-oriented systems, the one that has realized the most success in terms of economic justification is inventory. It is relatively easy to prove that the inventory investment is reduced by means of the information system. Money previously invested in inventory can be invested in other, more profitable ways.

The Responsibility of the Developer for Economic Justification

The systems developer must be alert to management's requirements in terms of justifying the information system or information system project and strive to satisfy those requirements. When management insists on an economic justification, the systems developer must examine the feasibility of that justification.

When the justification cannot be made, the project should be scrapped. In no case should the developer indicate that an economic justification exists when, in fact, it does not. It is *not* the responsibility of the developer to prove the justification. Rather, the developer is responsible for conducting the analysis and reporting the results to management. Then it is management's responsibility to decide whether to proceed with the project. In this setting, as in all others dealing with systems development, the developer recommends and the manager decides.

Economic Justification Methods

Several methods have been devised to provide the basis for establishing some, or all, of the economic justification. The most popular methods include break-even analysis, payback analysis, and net present value.

Break-Even Analysis

Although a new system may not be justified based on a cost savings or reduction, management still wants to know how the cost of the new system will compare with the cost of the existing one. In most cases, the new system will have lower operational costs due to the use of new technology. The new technology allows the new system to process larger volumes, with greater accuracy, than older technologies. However, high developmental costs can delay the realization of the operational benefits from the new system.

Break-even analysis compares the monthly costs of both the existing and new systems, and identifies the month when the costs are equal. When you want to conduct a break-even analysis, you assemble the cost data on the two systems as shown in Table F.1. You then use this data to construct a graph similar to the one in Figure F.1. The graph contains two cost lines, one for the existing system and one for the new. The point where the cost of the existing system is equal to that of the new system, where the lines intersect, is the **break-even point.** The cost of using the existing system rises each year as it handles the increasing business volume. The cost of the new system is very high in the beginning, reflecting the developmental costs, but eventually falls and then has a smaller annual rate of increase than the existing system. The time prior to the break-even point is the **investment period** of the new system, and the time after is the **return period.** The firm invests in the new system so that it may enjoy the return.

The strengths of break-even analysis are its ability to compare the costs of the existing and new systems, and its inclusion of developmental costs. The main weakness is

TABLE F.1

Break-Even Analysis Compares the Costs of the Existing and New Systems

Year	Month	Existing System Costs	New System Costs	Difference
1	1	8	28	+20
1	2	8	29	+21
1	3	9	30	+21
1	4	9	31	+22
1	5	9	33	+24
1	6	10	34	+24
1	7	10	34	+24
1	8	10	32	+22
1	9	10	30	+20
1	10	10	28	+18
1	11	11	27	+16
1	12	11	24	+13
2	1	11	23	+12
2	2	11	21	+10
2	3	11	19	+8
2	4	11	18	+7
2	5	12	16	+4
2	6	12	13	+1
2	7	12	12	0
2	8	12	11	-1
2	9	13	10	-3
2	10	13	9	-4
2	11	13	9	-4
2	12	13	8	-5

the fact that it considers only costs and ignores the benefits. Its popularity is based, in part, on the fact that it is generally easier to compute costs than benefits. Therefore, break-even analysis is appropriate for all of the subsystems of the information system infrastructure.

Payback Analysis

Once management is convinced that the new system compares favorably to the existing one in terms of costs, the next question is how long it will take for the new system to pay for itself. Payback analysis can provide the answer. **Payback analysis** determines how long it will take for the cumulative benefits of the new system to equal its cumulative costs. The point in time at which the new system benefits and costs are equal is the **payback point.** The length of time required to reach the payback point is the **payback period.**

The payback concept is illustrated with the graph in Figure F.2 and the data in Table F.2. The annual costs in the table are averages of the costs in Table F.1. The computation of the payback period uses the formula:

$$PBP = Y + \frac{C}{V}$$

Where: PBP = Payback period

Y = The last year that the cumulative benefits of the new system were negative

C = The cumulative benefits of the new system for the last year that they were negative

V = The absolute value of the cumulative benefits of the new system for (1) the last year that they were negative (disregard the negative attribute of the value), and (2) the first year that they are positive

Using the data in the table, the payback period is computed as:

$$PBP = 4 + \frac{4}{4 + 12}$$

$$= 4 + \frac{4}{16}$$

$$= 4.25 \text{ years}$$

or 4 years and 3 months

Payback analysis is a more robust method of economic justification than is break-even analysis. This is because payback analysis incorporates not only the costs of the existing and new systems but also projects the point at which the new

FIGURE F.1

Break-Even Analysis

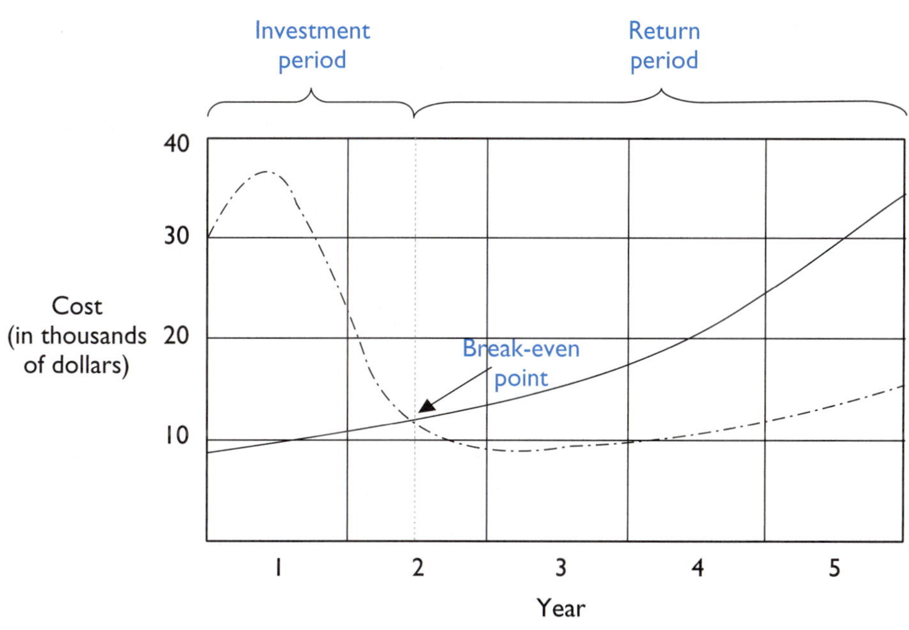

FIGURE F.2

Payback Analysis

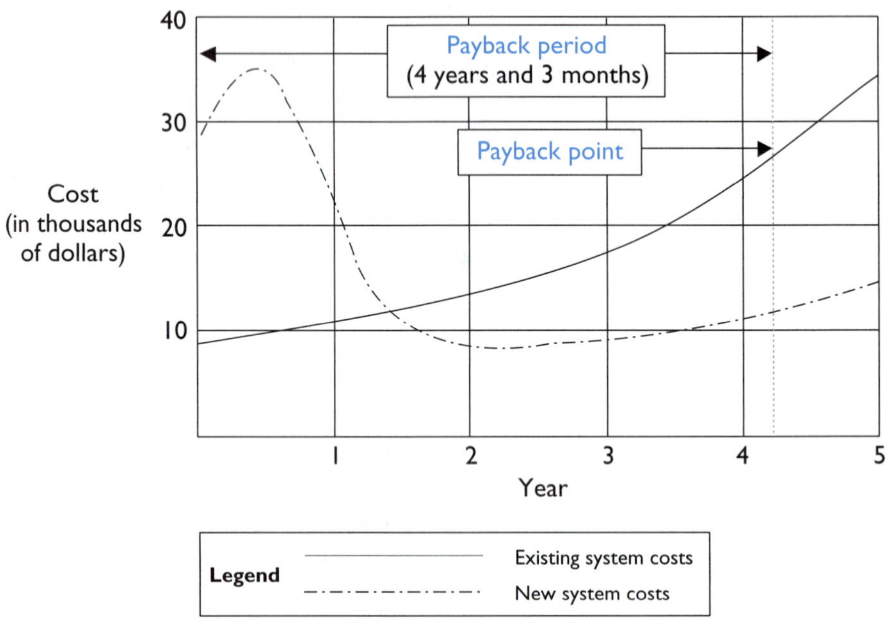

system development costs will be recovered. The payback point identifies to management when the new system will begin to have a more positive effect on the firm's cash flow than will a continued use of the existing system.

However, payback analysis is not without its limitations. Note from Table F.2 that the new system benefits are calculated by subtracting the new system costs from the existing system costs. This is a rather narrow view of benefits in that it ignores the value of the new system's output. For example, the value of a marketing information system is not based on its lower costs than a previous system but, rather, on the problem-solving information that it can provide. Another limitation of payback analysis is the fact that it fails to recognize the time value of money. This limitation can be overcome with another cost-benefit method called net present value.

Net Present Value

If you invest $100 for five years at an interest rate of 12 percent, compounded annually, the investment will increase in value as shown below.

Year	Investment Value at End of Year
1	$112.00
2	125.44
3	140.49
4	157.35
5	176.23

Another way to look at the interest influence is to take a value, such as $100, at some time in the future, say five years, and compute the amount necessary to invest now in order to have the $100. The computation is made using the formula:

$$\text{Discount percent} = \frac{1}{(1+I)^{n}}$$

Where: I = Annual interest rate

n = Number of years in the future

The computations are made for each of the five n values at a given interest rate. For an annual interest rate of 12 percent, the discount percentages are:

1 year = 0.8929

2 years = 0.7972

3 years = 0.7118

4 years = 0.6355

5 years = 0.5674

The percentages are multiplied times $100.00, and the results are those illustrated in Table F.3.

The table shows that the *present value* of $100 one year from now is $89.29, for two years from now it is $79.72, and so on. The concept is called the **present value of money,** and it recognizes that existing money has greater value than future money. The reason is that existing money can be invested now to produce increased value in the future.

This same approach can be used to determine the **net present value (NPV)** of a new system by computing the present value of both the benefits and the costs.

TABLE F.2

Payback Analysis Is Concerned with the Cumulative Benefits of the New System

	Year 1	2	3	4	5
Existing system costs	9	12	15	22	29
New system costs	30	13	8	11	13
New system benefits	-21	-1	+7	+11	+16
Cumulative benefits	-21	-22	-15	-4	+12

Note: Annual costs and benefits in thousands of dollars.

Y C V

TABLE F.3

Interest Decreases the Present Value of a Future Amount

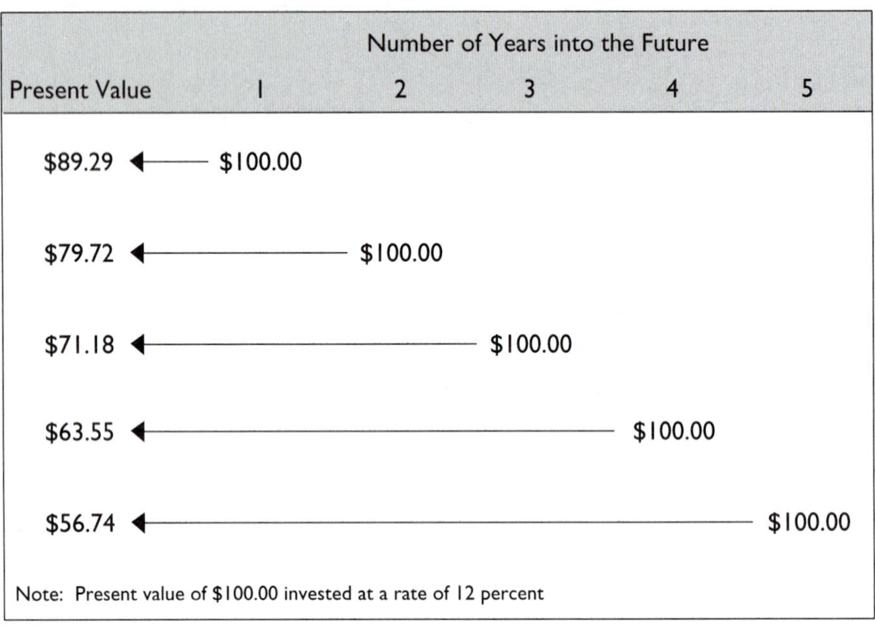

	Number of Years into the Future				
Present Value	1	2	3	4	5
$89.29 ←	$100.00				
$79.72 ←		$100.00			
$71.18 ←			$100.00		
$63.55 ←				$100.00	
$56.74 ←					$100.00

Note: Present value of $100.00 invested at a rate of 12 percent

This computation is shown in Table F.4. The data is the same as that used for payback analysis in Table F.2. The only difference is that Table F.4 discounts the future benefits computed by payback analysis. Whereas payback analysis looks at new system benefits in terms of current dollars, NPV discounts those dollars to reflect the fact that they are future money.

The discounted benefits for each of the five years are shown, as are the cumulative discounted benefits. At the end of the fifth year, the cumulative discounted benefits are $1,500 (cumulative benefits of minus $7,600 through year 4 plus the benefits of $9,100 in year 5). You can see that the process of discounting the benefits produces two dramatic changes. First, it reduces the cumulative benefits for the five-year period from the $12,000 in Table F.2 to the $1,500 in Table F.4. Second, it prolongs the payback period from the 4 years and 3 months computed earlier to 4 years and 10 months.

NPV makes economic justification more difficult but management might insist on its use. This is especially true when management is considering alternate ways of investing in the future. For example, the firm might be able to realize a greater profit by investing in a certificate of deposit (CD) than an information system project. Management could invest $851.10 in a CD today at an interest rate of 12 percent to produce the same $1,500 value five years from now that is produced by the system project. The present value of the CD is computed by multiplying its value five years from now times the discount percent for the 12 percent interest rate: $1,500 × 0.5674 = $851.10.

When you consider the amount of effort required by the system project, its substantial development expense, and the often traumatic effect that the implementation can have on the firm, the CD represents a very attractive alternative. However, management still might decide to go with the system project, recognizing that it will produce noneconomic value such as providing the firm with a greater ability to achieve competitive advantage.

A Cost-Benefit Analysis Model

The break-even, payback, and net present value formulas can easily be incorporated into a mathematical model that the developer and manager can use to make the required calculations. Figure F.3 is an example. In designing mathematical models for use in evaluating the impact of management decisions, it is common practice to provide the user with an ability to easily change the scenario, or setting, in which the calculations are made. This technique makes it possible to use the model for a variety of situations.

In the Figure F.3 model, the user enters the scenario data in the two large upper rectangles, labeled Costs and Benefits. Data is entered into each of the smaller rectangles with the heavy borders. The user can enter data that describes the estimated monthly hardware, software, personnel, data, and facility costs during both the development period and the production period when the system is used. In a like manner, the user enters the anticipated monthly benefits, the length of the development period, the annual interest rate, and projected annual changes in production costs and benefits.

With the scenario data entered, the model makes the computations necessary to produce the projected costs and projected benefits in the two large rectangles. Then, the user determines the last year that the NPV of Cumulative Net was negative, and enters that year number in the heavy-bordered rectangle at the bottom. The model then computes the payback period. The user can use the model to play the what-if game, changing such data values as estimated costs and benefits and interest rates to see the effect of the changes.

Table F.4

The Net Present Value of the New System

	Year				
	1	2	3	4	5
Existing system costs	9	12	15	22	29
New system costs	30	13	8	11	13
New system benefits	-21	-1	+7	+11	+16
Discount percent	0.893	0.797	0.712	0.636	0.567
Discounted benefits	-18.8	-0.8	+5.0	+7.0	+9.1
Cumulative discounted benefits	-18.8	-19.6	-14.6	-7.6	+1.5

Discounted PBP = $4 + \frac{7.6}{9.1}$ = 4.83 years, or 4 years and 10 months

Note: Annual costs in thousands of dollars; annual interest = 0.12

Economic System and Project Justification

FIGURE F.3

Cost Benefit Analysis Model

DECISIONS

COSTS (Monthly):	Development	Production
Hardware	$2,000	$750
Software	$6,000	$500
Personnel	$25,000	$2,500
Data	$7,500	$400
Facilities	$4,000	$250

BENEFITS (Monthly):	$14,000
Scenario Values:	
Development Period (Months):	8
Interest Rate (Annual):	6.0%
Projected Changes (Annual)	
Production Costs:	5.0%
Production Benefits:	3.0%

PROJECTED COSTS:	Year 0	Year 1	Year 2	Year 3	Year 4	Year 5
Hardware	$16,000	$9,000	$9,450	$9,923	$10,419	$10,940
Software	$48,000	$6,000	$6,300	$6,615	$6,946	$7,293
Personnel	$200,000	$30,000	$31,500	$33,075	$34,729	$36,465
Data	$60,000	$4,800	$5,040	$5,292	$5,557	$5,834
Facilities	$32,000	$3,000	$3,150	$3,308	$3,473	$3,647
Annual Costs	$356,000	$52,800	$55,440	$58,212	$61,123	$64,179
NPV of Annual Costs	$356,000	$49,811	$49,341	$48,876	$48,415	$47,958
NPV of Cumulative Costs	$356,000	$405,811	$455,153	$504,029	$552,443	$600,402

PROJECTED BENEFITS:	Year 0	Year 1	Year 2	Year 3	Year 4	Year 5
Annual Gross	$0	$168,000	$173,040	$178,231	$183,578	$189,085
NPV of Annual Gross	$0	$158,491	$154,005	$149,646	$145,411	$141,296
NPV of Cumulative Gross	$0	$158,491	$312,496	$462,142	$607,553	$748,849
Annual Net	($356,000)	$115,200	$117,600	$120,019	$122,456	$124,907
NPV of Annual Net	($356,000)	$108,679	$104,664	$100,770	$96,996	$93,338
NPV of Cumulative Net*	($356,000)	($247,321)	($142,657)	($41,887)	$55,110	$148,447

Enter the last year that the NPV of Cumulative Net* was negative (Enter 0, 1, 2, 3, or 4):	3
PAYBACK PERIOD in Years (Based on NPV Values):	3.43

One closing comment concerning mathematical modeling is in order. The user must frequently enter data values that are at best only estimates. It is often difficult or impossible to determine some values with exact precision. For this reason, the user applies considerable judgment in evaluating the outputs of the model.

Putting Economic Justification in Perspective

Management will not invest in an information system or an information system project without the assurance that the decision will benefit the firm. As managers become more knowledgeable of the capabilities and limitations of information systems, they recognize that much of the justification for information system use cannot be measured in dollars and cents. Like so many decisions made by top management, the one to invest in an information system can be a largely subjective one, based on faith. Management has faith that the systems developers will be able to develop and implement a good system.

Before management gives the go-ahead based on faith, however, they might insist on an economic analysis. In this case the systems developer must be prepared to make the economic justification calculations that we have described. As with the other tools in the developer's toolkit, the ability to use the economic justification tools are the mark of a professional systems developer.

Key Terms

break-even analysis
break-even point
payback analysis
payback point
net present value

Problems

1. Use payback analysis to compute the payback period for the new system, using the data below. Write a one-page memo to your instructor, explaining your findings.

Annual Costs in Thousands of Dollars

	Year				
Existing system costs	12	15	19	25	32
New system costs	27	11	12	15	19

2. Use the figures in problem 1 to compute the net present value of the investment. Assume an annual interest rate of 10 percent. Use the formula for calculating the discount percent given earlier. What effect does the discounting of the benefits have on the payback period? Write a one-page memo to your instructor explaining your findings.
3. Use the cost-benefit analysis model on the companion Web site (www.wiley.com/college/mcleod) to see the effect of changing the interest rate and the projected changes in production costs and benefits. Use the same scenario data from Figure F.3 but use 8 percent for the interest rate, 4.0 percent for the production costs, and 6.0 percent for the production benefits. Write a one-page memo to your instructor explaining the effects of the changes.

SELECTED BIBLIOGRAPHY

Dewhurst, R. F. J. *Business Cost-Benefit Analysis.* London: Roland Frederick James, 1972.

Hilton, Ronald W. *Managerial Accounting.* 4th ed. Boston: Irwin McGraw-Hill, 1999.

Marshall, David H. and Wayne W. McManus. *Accounting: What the Numbers Mean.* 4th ed. Boston: Irwin McGraw-Hill, 1999.

Martin, Merle P. *Analysis and Design of Business Information Systems.* 4th ed. Englewood Cliffs, NJ: Prentice Hall, 1995.

Stedman, Craig. "ERP Costs More than Measurable ROI." *Computerworld* 14 (April 5, 1999): 6.

Case Study Installment 3
Advanced System Technology Associates

ANALYZING THE ASTA SYSTEM

It was the end of the fifth week of the client project, and Rachel had called the team together to review their progress and map out a direction for the next few weeks. As usual, the team convened in the snack bar and Rachel used the entire table surface for the Gantt chart.

"It looks like we have done everything that we had planned for Phase 1, preliminary investigation, except evaluating the ASTA network. Tracy, you and Kim were supposed to do that last week. Is it done?"

Kim spoke up. "It sure is. Tracy evaluated the server and network, and I audited the workstations. It looks like we've got a good network to build our system on. Everything checked out OK."

Having received the answer that any Gantt chart queen would want to hear, Rachel turned the team's attention to the next step. "That's great. That means we've reached that portion of the phased development methodology where we are looping through analysis, design, and preliminary construction. We'll do that loop for each of the main system modules. The modules that we take on first are Phase 2, project management reports, and Phase 3, the skills inventory database. We can do those in parallel since I'll be working with Gary and Sean on the reports and Tracy and Kim are assigned the database. How do you guys think we should start?"

COMPLETING THE FIRST DELIVERY REPORT

One of the advantages of having a "take charge" team leader like Rachel who tends to the details is that it gives the other team members a chance to keep the big picture in mind. Kim had been thinking about the first delivery report that is due next Friday, and thought it was time for the team to start putting it together. "I checked out the first delivery report specs on the Web site, and we have a lot of the things already. We've got the organization background, org chart, objectives, constraints, scope, goals and risks, components of the existing and proposed system, the system diagrams, Gantt and network diagrams, and sample client documents. But, we still need a project overview, a requirements summary, a planning overview, major milestones, and some input/output and programming standards. And we need them by Friday."

"Well, we definitely need them by Thursday, and really ought to have them by Tuesday," Rachel added. "I'm glad you're on top of the delivery, Kim. I've been spending all my time thinking about the client work and this report has really slipped up on me. Who is going to do all of these things? I need some volunteers."

Gary waved his hand at Kim to get her attention. "Kim, you said *project* overview." I looked at the delivery specs also, and it mentions system overview as well. You know that list of report contents is only a suggested guideline. I'd like to do a *system* overview. I keep going back to those DFDs I did before the RFP portion was farmed out to the consultants, and before we decided to postpone the Web work until next semester. I'd like to draw a graphic that shows all of those original components, segmented in terms of who will do them. I think it would give the client a good dynamic picture of the overall system and when all the pieces will fit together."

Rachel asked if anyone else had any other ideas for the project or system overview, and when nobody showed any sign of life, she gave Gary the go-ahead. "Sean, do you want to volunteer for something?"

"I've got a similar idea for the requirements summary. I'd like to view the requirements in terms of the part of the system that the user sees—the screens. As you all know," Sean said as he rose from his seat and curtsied to each team member, "I developed those wonderful screen prototypes that Mel and Yolanda fell in love with." Everyone shouted for him to sit down, which he did, while continuing. "I'd like to show one of the screens at the top of the page and then explain below how it meets the system requirements. I've seen that done before in some sample reports that were passed around in class."

Rachel asked the group if they liked Sean's idea (which they did), and then told Sean to "get on with it." She then volunteered to do the planning overview and the milestones since she was so familiar with the Gantt. "That leaves the I/O and programming standards. Kim, neither you nor Tracy has anything."

"Well, since I brought up the whole issue of getting the report ready, I'll take a cut at the standards," Kim said.

"Excellent," was the response from the Gantt chart queen. "I think standards will really help us. My team in Advanced Programming never was organized. We did a lot of last-minute programming. Lots of the screens looked like they came from different teams. And we had a hard time making changes in the last couple of days because it turned out that two team members hadn't commented code or followed naming conventions. What a nightmare. But, not this time, right? Let's meet again on Tuesday and see where we stand. If anyone is having trouble, we can bail 'em out."

"Well, I'm not going to leave this meeting without something to do," Tracy said. We started off by talking about working on the first two system modules. I'd like to contribute something to that effort."

"Anything specific?" Gary asked.

FIGURE CS 3.1

System Overview

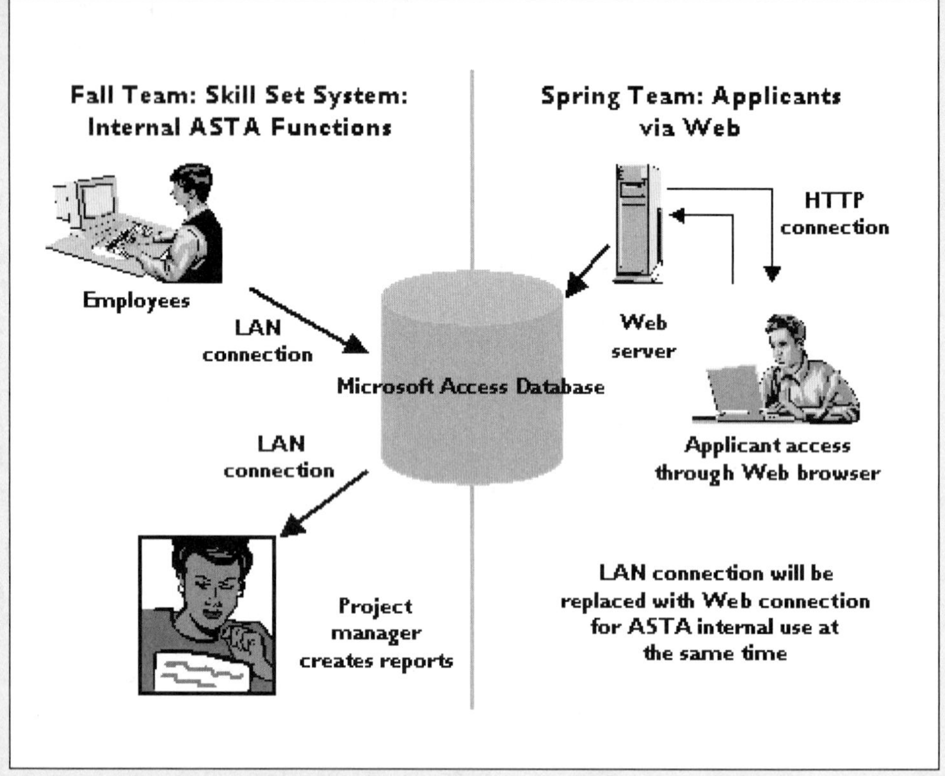

"Well, yes. We're reaching a point in the project where we are going to have to start interviewing people. I think it's important that we make maximum use of their time, and ours as well, by planning ahead exactly what information we want to obtain. I think we should design an interview checklist form that we can use to plan each interview and also record what we find out. We're supposed to include client meeting agendas in the delivery appendix. An interview checklist would not only serve that purpose but also provide a planning capability."

"Sounds good to me," Gary said, looking at the other team members. They all indicated approval, so Tracy was to design an interview checklist to bring to the Tuesday meeting.

ASSEMBLING THE FIRST DELIVERY REPORT

Tuesday rolled around faster than the team would have liked. For the first time, the project was beginning to cut into the team's sleeping habits. The Cowboy Programmers assembled around the snack bar table, a little less perky than usual.

"Let's see what we've got," Rachel commanded. "Here's the report outline we agreed on, and the sections that we've already done. All we need are the items that we assigned last Friday. Let's take them in the order in which they will appear in the report. Gary, do you have the system overview?"

"Here it is. It's kind of an adaptation of the figure 0 DFD I drew, only using some neat graphic symbols, and segregated into the two work areas—us this semester, on the left, and another Systems Development team next semester, on the right." Gary passed the copy that appears in Figure CS 3.1 around for everyone to see. It received universal approval.

"OK, Sean. The requirements summary?"

"Sure, Rachel, the screens with the system specs below." See Figure CS 3.2. "Everybody like it?" Everybody loved it.

"Great. Moving right along, here's the planning overview that I did. I just tried to describe the highlights of each project phase—identifying the major work to be done and who is to do it." See Figure CS 3.3 on page 286. Rachel had produced copies for everyone and passed them around.

"I took the major milestones from the Gantt." Everybody cheered at the mention of the magic word. "Here they are." See Figure CS 3.4 on page 288.

Only one item remained—the input/output and programming standards. "Kim, do you have the standards?"

"Well, actually, no," Kim replied. "I've started them but still have some work to do. I'll have them by tomorrow. Promise."

"As soon as you get them you had better e-mail them to everyone on the team so we can check them over. I don't want to include anything in the report that hasn't been reviewed by the whole team." With those orders given, Rachel set another meeting for the next day to assemble the report.

Presenting the First Delivery Report

At the meeting the next day, Rachel began assembling all the report sections and realized she didn't have everything. "Kim, when are you going to send us all the input/output and programming standards you promised yesterday?"

"Oh, here are my copies. I wondered why none of you gave me any feedback. I guess I forgot to e-mail them to all of you. Sorry." Kim said as she pushed her copies to the middle of the table for everyone to see." Refer to Figures CS 3.5 and CS 3.6 on pages 289 and 290, respectively.

"Kim, these look good. Thanks." Rachel said as everyone else was nodding agreement. "But listen everyone. If you don't hear from anyone when you ask for feedback, check to make sure the rest of us received it. I'll look more carefully at Kim's input/output standards. Tracy, will you review the programming standards? We want to be sure we are starting the functional delivery phases with our overall design in place so none of us have to live through an end-of-semester nightmare."

With all of the first delivery sections present and accounted for, Rachel passed them around for everyone to approve. Copies were made—one to turn in to Ray on Friday, one for the client, and one for each team member. An appointment was made with Yolanda to present the report the next Tuesday, which the team did. Rachel kept the discussion moving. As she identified each section, the team member or members primarily responsible for it explained it briefly. Yolanda turned the pages of her report as the team explained its contents. Occasionally, she would interrupt to ask a question, but there were no big hang-ups. Yolanda said that she would read the report and let the team know if she had any questions or suggestions. She also said that she would let Mel see it. Rachel offered to give Mel a presentation, but Yolanda said that she didn't think that would be necessary.

As the team walked to their cars, Sean said, "Well, check off delivery number one."

FIGURE CS 3.2

Requirements Summary

Figure 1: Search Skill Set

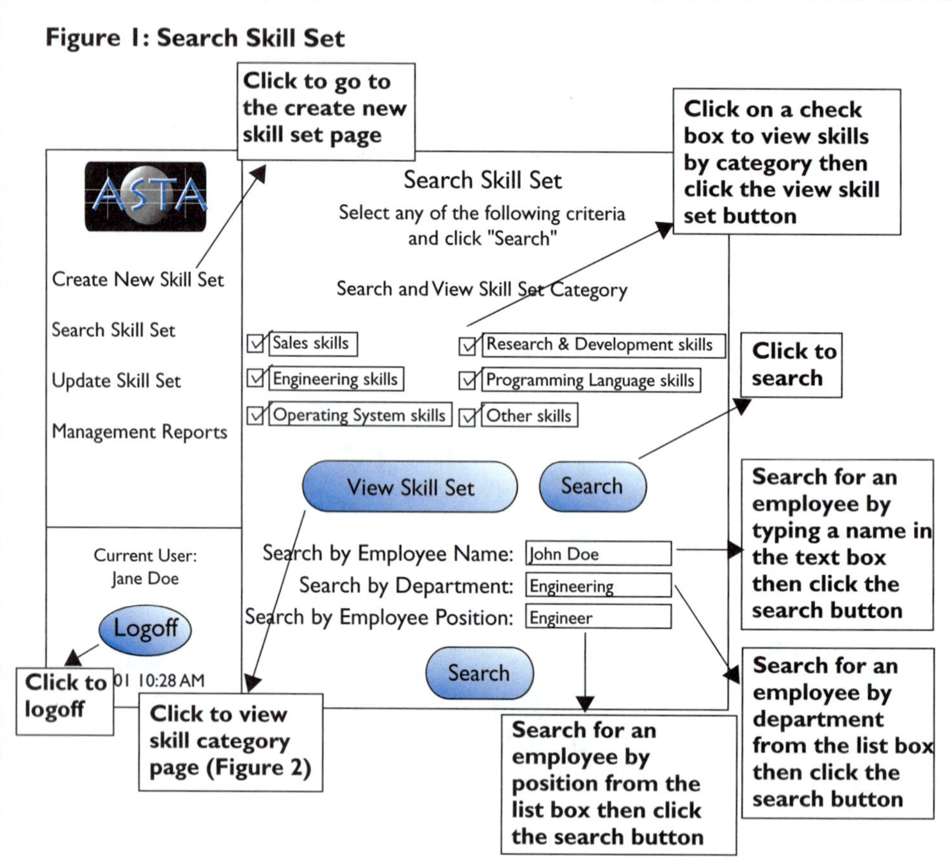

1. Search Skill Set

a. Users can view skill categories of their choice by selecting the check boxes. Users can view categories by sales skills, engineering skills, research and development skills, programming language skills, operating system skills, and other skills.

b. Any combination of the six categories can be selected; the query checks to see which are null.

c. Once the users make their selections of categories, the next step is to click the View Skill Set button. The system will then display a second screen for each of the checked boxes. See Figure 2.

d. The users also have the option to search by an employee name, department, or a position.

e. When the user clicks on the search button, the database is queried and returns the results.

f. The users can change their menu selections anytime by clicking on the options on the left. The users have four different options to choose from.

FIGURE CS 3.2 (CONTINUED)

Requirements Summary

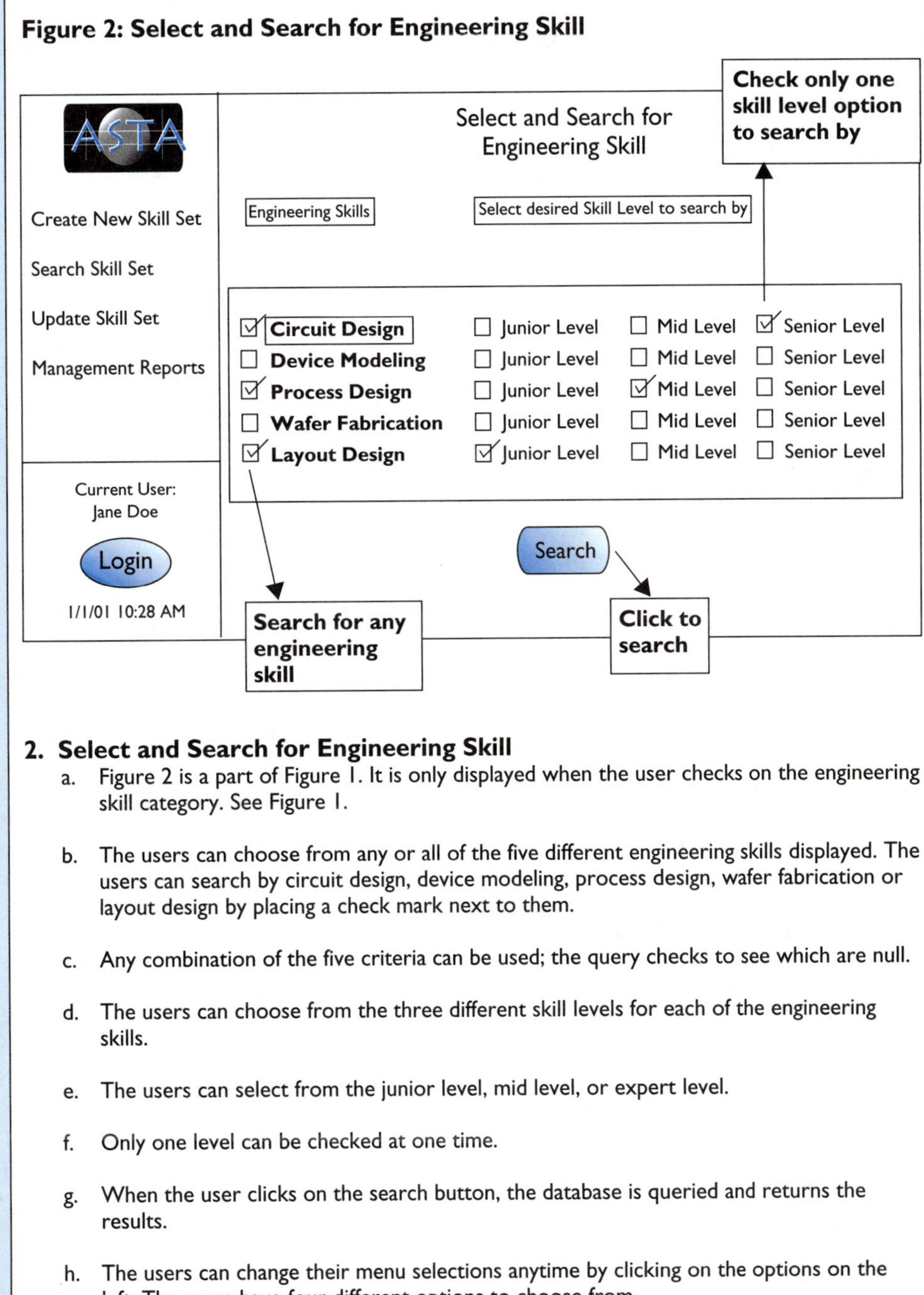

2. Select and Search for Engineering Skill

a. Figure 2 is a part of Figure 1. It is only displayed when the user checks on the engineering skill category. See Figure 1.

b. The users can choose from any or all of the five different engineering skills displayed. The users can search by circuit design, device modeling, process design, wafer fabrication or layout design by placing a check mark next to them.

c. Any combination of the five criteria can be used; the query checks to see which are null.

d. The users can choose from the three different skill levels for each of the engineering skills.

e. The users can select from the junior level, mid level, or expert level.

f. Only one level can be checked at one time.

g. When the user clicks on the search button, the database is queried and returns the results.

h. The users can change their menu selections anytime by clicking on the options on the left. The users have four different options to choose from.

FIGURE CS 3.3

Skill Set System Planning Overview

Planning Overview

As a means of ensuring that the ASTA team meets its project objectives, an 8-phase plan has been devised. The phases consist of the following:

1. Preliminary investigation
2. Project management reports
3. Skills inventory database design
4. Skills data entry (in house)
5. Employee update module
6. Security login module
7. Final construction
8. Installation

After completion of the first phase (preliminary investigation), the team is subdivided into groups so that multiple modules can be worked on at the same time. While Rachel, Gary, and Sean are working on Phase 2 (project management reports), Kim and Tracy will be working on Phase 3 (the skills inventory database design). After Phase 2 is completed, Gary can work on Phase 6 (the security login module). After Phase 3 is completed, Sean and Tracy can work on Phase 4 (skills data entry) while Rachel and Kim are working on Phase 5 (the employee update module). When Phases 4, 5, and 6 are completed, the team can address Phases 7 (final construction) and 8 (installation) in sequence. The plan for accomplishing each phase is described below. Descriptions in past tense indicate accomplished phases. Descriptions in future tense indicate planned activities.

Preliminary Investigation

After initial meetings with the client, the team gathered information about the ASTA organization, current systems, and information infrastructure. We discussed the functionality of the proposed system and obtained sample skill set matrix forms. We created an organization chart, F/C matrix, compared existing and proposed system components, and defined the information dimensions of the new system. Gary prepared data flow diagrams, and Tracy and Kim performed a problem chain analysis. Tracy evaluated the server and network capacity, and Kim audited the existing workstations. Kim revised Rick Gomez's ERD, and Tracy and Sean created a menu hierarchy and screen prototypes. A client meeting with Yolanda and Sue confirmed the accuracy of the preliminary investigation. The team presented the first delivery report to Yolanda.

Project Management Reports

Rachel and Gary will analyze the report requirements of the new system, Sean and Gary will design the reports, and Sean will construct prototypes of all reports. Rachel, Gary, and Sean will review the prototypes with the users, and Sean will construct the reports. The reports will be reviewed with Yolanda and revised as necessary. This phase will conclude with a review with Mel Knowler, Yolanda, and the project managers.

Skills Inventory Database Design

Tracy and Kim will analyze the data storage and retrieval requirements, and the hardware and software requirements. Kim will refine the ER diagram as necessary, and construct the final ER diagram. Kim will install the Beta version on Yolanda's PC and the project managers' PCs. Kim will test the Beta database and reports, and refine as necessary.

Skills Data Entry (In House)

Sean will analyze the data entry requirements and design an interface. Sean and Tracy will then construct the data entry module, and, accompanied by Rachel, will review the module with selected users. Sean and Tracy will make any required changes, and the entire team will review the second delivery report with Mel Knowler. Sean and Tracy will then install Beta 2 on Yolanda's PC, and test and refine as necessary.

FIGURE CS 3.3 (CONTINUED)

Skill Set System Planning Overview

Employee Update Module
Rachel will analyze the employee update requirements and design an employee update interface. Kim will then assist in a unit test of the employee update form. Rachel and Kim will review the update form with selected users and revise as necessary.

Security Login Module
Gary will analyze the security requirements and design a security login interface. He will then construct and unit test the security login form, and review it with Yolanda and Sue. Gary will make any necessary revisions.

Final Construction
Rachel will prepare the system test specification forms, and then the entire team will conduct the tests and document the results. Rachel and Gary will put together the users manual, and Kim, Tracy, and Sean will assemble the developers manual. Yolanda will use e-mail to notify the ASTA employees who will participate in the training program. Rachel and Gary will design the training sessions, make the arrangements, and conduct the sessions. The entire team will conduct a post-implementation evaluation with Mel and Yolanda.

Installation
Yolanda will bring on board data entry temp employees who will enter the production data. Kim and Tracy will install the database and modules on the server, and test the production database. Kim will check the workstations for use with the system, and Rachel and Gary will conduct a user acceptance test. The team will refine and debug the system as necessary and review the final delivery report with Mel Knowler and Yolanda.

PREPARING FOR THE CLIENT INTERVIEWS

Not content to sit back and enjoy the fruits of meeting the first major project deadline, the team pressed on—meeting two days later to plan for the client interviews. Tracy produced the interview checklist shown in Figure CS 3.7 on page 291.

"This is really geared to the project managers," Tracy explained. "I thought it would be a good idea to preprint each form for each manager to be interviewed, including some information pertinent to that person. For example, in this version, we would be interviewing the R&D manager and we include some background information that might help guide the interview. I've got time estimates for each item on the agenda—adding up to a one-hour interview."

"Tracy, you said that the form could be used to record the findings. I don't see them anywhere."

"Kim, they would go on the back. I left it blank to give us as much flexibility as possible."

"Would they be handwritten or typed?" Tracy asked.

"I think handwritten would be best—done right after the interview when the information is fresh on our minds."

Sean asked, "Tracy, what happens if the person we interview heads off in some other direction and doesn't follow the agenda?"

"We need to be flexible—maybe make some notes on the front side that we are deviating from the plan and then later make the notes on the back."

"I really like it," Gary said. "I might not have asked all of these questions. It forces us to plan ahead and we can give more time to thinking through the

FIGURE CS 3.4

Major Milestones

Phases and Milestones	Week	Ending Date
Phase 1: Preliminary Investigation		
Revise Rick Gomez's ERD	2	October 6
Prepare screen prototypes	3	October 13
Review Phase 1 findings with Yolanda Garza	4	October 20
Audit existing workstations	5	October 27
Phase 2: Project Management Reports		
Arrange contacts and review with project managers	6	November 3
Design reports	7	November 10
Construct reports	8	November 17
Review reports with client	8	November 17
Phase 3: Skills Inventory Database Design		
Analyze hardware requirements	7	November 10
Refine ER diagram for proposed system	7	November 10
Construct final ER diagram	8	November 17
Review final ER diagram with client	8	November 17
Install Beta version on client workstations	8	November 17
Refine and debug database	9	November 24
Phase 4: Skills Data Entry (In House)		
Analyze data entry requirements	8	November 17
Design data entry interface	8	November 17
Construct data entry module	9	November 24
Review delivery 2 with Mel Knowler	9	November 24
Install Beta 2 on Yolanda's PC	9	November 24
Refine and debug Beta 2	10	December 1
Phase 5: Employee Update Module		
Analyze employee update requirements	8	November 17
Design employee update interface	9	November 24
Construct and test employee update form	9	November 24
Review employee update form with users	10	December 1
Phase 6: Security Login Module		
Analyze security requirements	8	November 17
Design security login interface	9	November 24
Construct and test security login form	9	November 24
Review security login form with users	10	December 1
Phase 7: Final Construction		
Refine and debug system	11	December 5
Design and construct users manual	11	December 5
Design and construct developers manual	11	December 5
Plan and design training sessions	11	December 4
Conduct training sessions	11	December 5
Phase 8: Installation		
Refine and debug system	12	December 10
Review client delivery 3 with Mel Knowler	12	December 10
Obtain feedback from Mel Knowler and users	12	December 10
Conduct post-implementation evaluation	12	December 12

FIGURE CS 3.5

Input/Output Standards

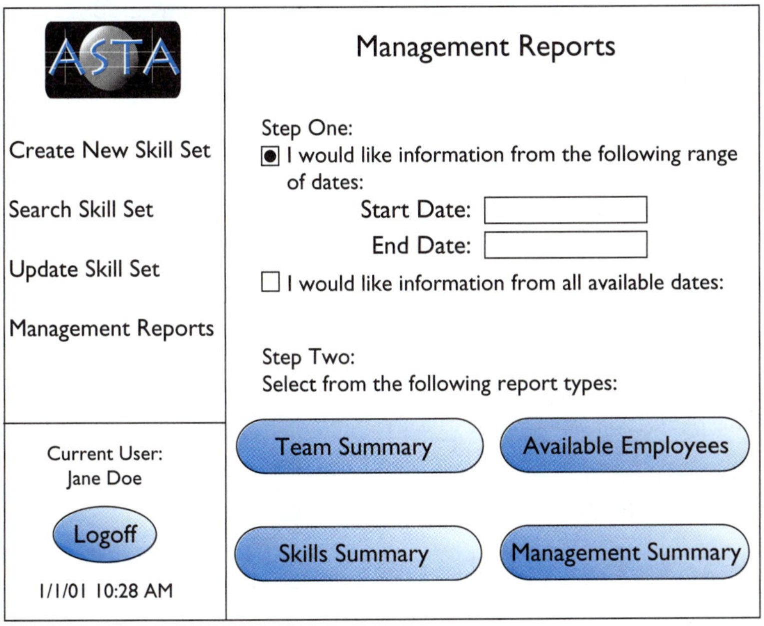

Form Standards

1. The font will always be Tahoma.
2. All screens will have white background and have the ASI logo in the top left corner. All text will be black.
3. All buttons will be blue.
4. Every page should have a title.
5. The ASTA title on the form should be 24 points or larger and must be a graphical icon.
6. All data entry fields and their labels will be 12 pt. font. The labels will be bold and white, while the data entered will be black.
7. All screens will be maximized, and the contents of a form should fit within one screen.
8. Navigation buttons should be used consistently.
9. There should be no scroll bars.
10. Text boxes should be large enough to view the data inside them.
11. Dates should be in the DD-MM-YY format.
12. All data should be lined up so it is easy to read.
13. Every page should have four options on the side for users to change selection.
14. Every page must display the current users name and the current date.
15. Every page must display the ASTA graphical icon.
16. Every page must have a logoff button.

Button Standards

1. Logoff buttons must be included on every page.
2. All buttons are oval shaped and blue.
3. Tool tips must be used for every button.
4. All buttons must have black texts.

Reporting Standards

1. All printable reports are printed in portrait or landscape format.
2. All titles are Tahoma 14pt bold.
3. All reports must have the ASTA logo.
4. Body of the report must be Tahoma 12pt black.
5. Background color should be white.

FIGURE CS 3.6

Programming Standards

Code Standards

1. Clearly comment all code.
2. Indent lines for readability.
3. Include author name and date for all code pages.

Control Naming Standards

1. A name prefix should be used to indicate the type of control. (e.g., cmdSearchSkillSet, or txtName—see Control Naming to the right).
2. Controls should not have the same names as the fields in tables. For example, the table field LastName might be shown in the form control txtLastName. The form control should not be named LastName.
3. Tool tips should be given for every important control.
4. No spaces or symbols (other than the underscore) will be used in naming any Access objects or fields.
5. The title bar name (caption property) should be related to the task and is coordinated with references to the task in forms or menus.
6. A frm prefix should be used in the name of the form (see Object Naming to the right).
7. All button names should begin with cmd (see Control Naming on right).
8. Buttons should not be abbreviated, but spelled out (e.g., cmdSearch, not cmdsear).

Variable Naming Standards

1. A prefix should be used such as int or str to indicate a variable's type (see Variable Naming to the right).
2. Names should not be abbreviated, but spelled out (e.g., strLastName, not strLN, strLastNam, or strLName).
3. It is acceptable to use short, meaningless names to reference temporary results (e.g., intI in a For/Next loop is acceptable as in: For intI = 1 to 20, no need to to use intCounter as in: For intCounter = 1 to 20).
4. All component words within variable names should be catenated and capitalized.

Table Standards

Tables must adhere to the four rules of normalization.

1. Field uniqueness (Data fields represent unique information, with no compounds and no repeating fields.)
2. Primary keys (Every table must have a primary key.)
3. Functional dependence (Data fields must be unique to key fields.)
4. Field independence (Changes to data fields must not affect *any* other data fields.)

Table Name Standards

1. Table names must be prefixed with tbl.
2. Names of tables should be spelled out; names should not be abbreviated.
3. Plurals are not acceptable. (Names like tblEmployee and tblEmployees are unacceptable.)
4. There should not be any spaces in table name, as in tblEngineering Details.

Field Naming Standards

1. Field type as a prefix cannot be used for a field.
2. Names should be spelled out whenever possible, and do not use plurals.
3. An ID suffix should be used for keyed fields, especially with auto numbers or serial numbers.
4. Blanks between words in field names should be avoided.

Naming Conventions

Object Naming

Object	Prefix
Form	frm
Table	tbl
Query	qry
Report	rpt
Module	mod

Control Naming

Control	Prefix
Command button	cmd
Combo box	cbo
List box	lst
Text box	txt
Label	lbl
Frame	fra
Subform/report	sub
Check box	chk
Line	lin
Option button	opt
Option group	grp
Toggle button	tgl

Variable Naming

Data Type	Prefix
Integer	int
Long	lng
Single	sng
Double	dbl
Currency	ccy cur
String	str
Variant	var
Date	dat dte
Boolean	bln
Object	obj

FIGURE CS 3.7

Interview Checklist

Personal Interview Checklist

Interviewer:	**Interviewee:**
Place:	**Date:** **Time:**
Objectives: User requirements of new system	**Background Information:**

Agenda

Introduction — 5 minutes

Introduce yourself.
How long have you been with ASTA?
Where were you before?

Background on Project — 10 minutes

Do you have any experience with the current skill set matrix?
Are you having any problems with it? If so, what are they?

Topic Questions: User Requirements — 45 minutes

How much time do you spend using your workstation?
Do you use Web-based systems? If so, do you like them?
How often will you use the new skills system?
When would you most use the skills system?
What kind of information would you like the new system to have?

information that we need. I think this is a real contribution, but I would like to suggest something in addition that I think will help also."

Having captured everyone's interest, Gary passed around two sheets that contained what looked like cartoons. "Now we're talking," Sean said, "Something that even I can understand," as everyone laughed.

Trying to restore order, Gary explained the first one. "This is a drawing of the current system." See Figure CS 3.8. "As we ask the managers about their involvement with the current system we can give them this to look at. I think this really helps the managers appreciate all the work that Yolanda has been doing with the current manual system. They should realize that there is no way she can speed up enough to match ASTA's growth with this process."

Everyone seemed to like what Gary had done. Especially Sean, who said, "I think I've got it. Then, when we ask about the new system, the manager looks at the other one." Refer to Figure CS 3.9. The general feeling was that the "cartoons" would help relieve any tension that might exist between the manager and the team member, facilitating an information flow.

FIGURE CS 3.8

Cartoon of Existing System

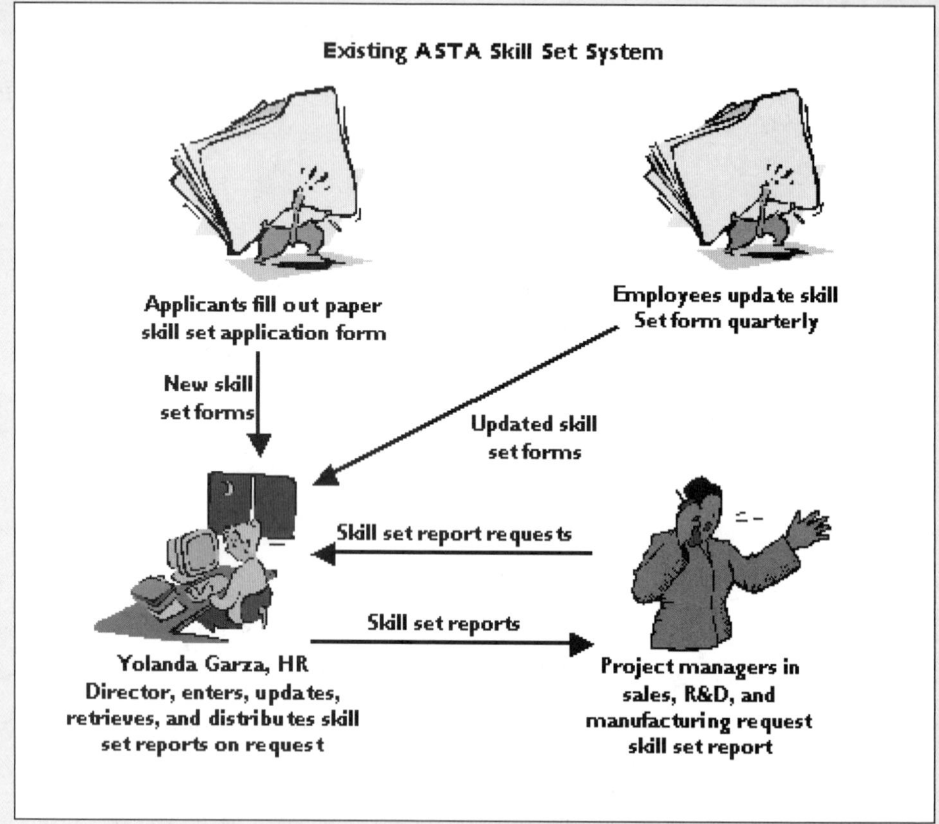
Existing ASTA Skill Set System
Applicants fill out paper skill set application form
Employees update skill Set form quarterly
New skill set forms
Updated skill set forms
Skill set report requests
Skill set reports
Yolanda Garza, HR Director, enters, updates, retrieves, and distributes skill set reports on request
Project managers in sales, R&D, and manufacturing request skill set report

Content that the team recognized the value of the graphics, Gary added "Also note that the graphic for the proposed system shows that it is on the Web and that applicants will key in their own skills data. This is what ASTA can look forward to after two semesters of team projects. We will finish the internal functions for the skill set system this semester. Then next semester another team can add the enhancements. This will be another chance to emphasize the two semester time frame for Yolanda and the project managers."

"Good idea," Rachel acknowledged. "I think these documents are a good way to show how much work we are doing this fall even though we won't be able to accomplish all of ASTA's original requests. They are a good foundation for conducting the analysis. Now let's do it."

FIGURE CS 3.9

Cartoon of Proposed System

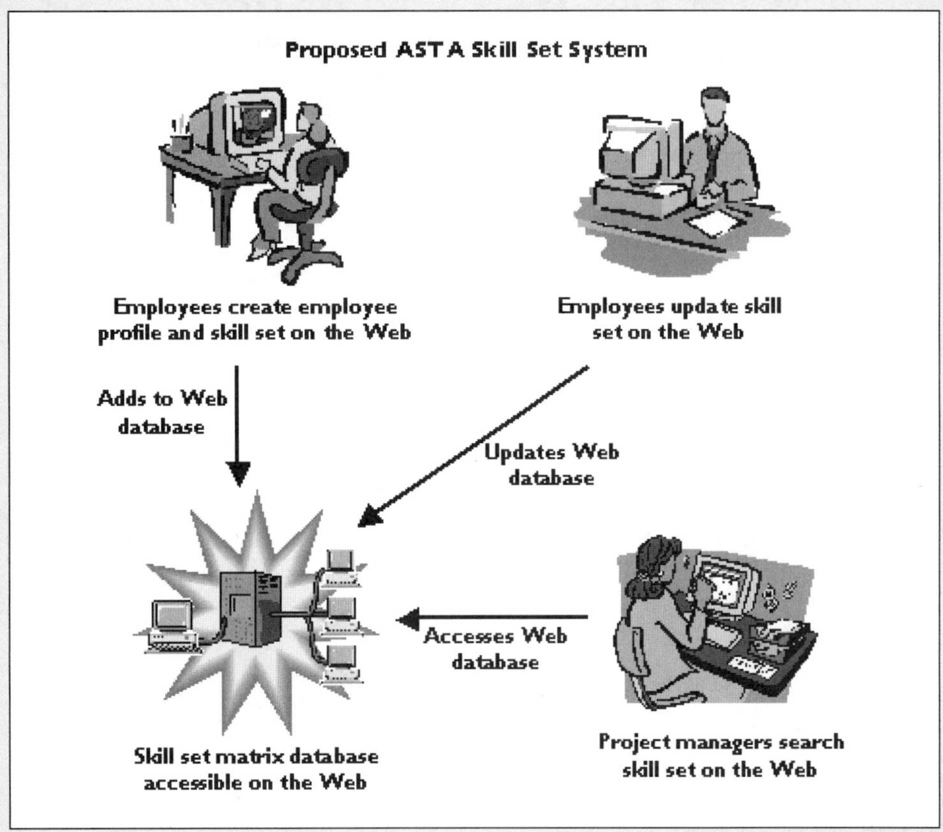

CHAPTER 5

SYSTEMS ANALYSIS

LEARNING OBJECTIVES

- List the basic steps of systems analysis.
- Identify the more popular process and data modeling tools.
- Conduct an effective in-depth personal interview.
- Describe the different types of surveys and the strengths and weaknesses of each.
- Describe techniques for designing questionnaires.
- Explain the nominal group technique for obtaining consensus among group members.
- Understand the role of observation in analysis.
- Conduct effective searches of records that shed light on the details of the existing system.
- Document each system module with a functions/components matrix and a use case.
- Manage the analysis phases of a project.

INTRODUCTION

Having completed the preliminary investigation phase of the project, as described in Chapter 4, the project team has defined the boundaries of the system, has determined the objectives and goals, and has an understanding of the potential project risks and how to cope with them. With this foundation, the team can now begin systems analysis, which is the series of activities that are performed to determine the requirements of the new system. This determination is made in a series of analysis phases and will provide the basis for the design of the new system.

Each repeated analysis phase consists of two steps. The first is to analyze the functional requirements. This is accomplished by gathering data and information concerning the existing system and analyzing that data. The second step is to document the functional requirements. These two steps comprise the system study.

The systems developer uses a variety of data and information gathering techniques while conducting the system study. He or she analyzes the existing system documentation, conducts in-depth personal interviews, conducts surveys, convenes group collaborative sessions, observes the existing system in operation, and searches through existing system records.

Existing system documentation includes data flow diagrams, structured English, flowcharts, Warnier-Orr diagrams, and action diagrams that serve as process models. The documentation also includes data models in the form of layout forms, the data dictionary, and entity-relationship diagrams. Object models such as class diagrams document both processes and data.

The most effective way to determine functional requirements is by conducting in-depth personal interviews with key users. When there are a large number of users they can be surveyed, using personal, telephone, and mail surveys. When collaboration among users is necessary in order to reach agreement on their functional requirements, the users can employ what is known as the nominal group technique (NGT) or engage in one or more JAD sessions. When the individuals and groups do not provide all of the information needed, or it is appropriate to verify the findings, a good technique is to observe the users in action. When these methods fail to provide all of the needed data and information, the developer can engage in record search.

As the developer analyzes the gathered data and information, it is documented using a variety of techniques that define the requirements at both a high level and in detail. The documentation from each iteration of the analysis process is added to the project dictionary.

BASIC ANALYSIS STEPS

During preliminary investigation, the systems analyst was the information specialist who played the key role, perhaps assisted by a database administrator and a network specialist. Large projects require multiple analysts, DBAs, and network specialists. This arrangement of information specialists and users working together as systems developers continues during the analysis phase.

Figure 5.1 positions the systems analysis phase in the phased development methodology. This is the first phase of the three that are repeated for each system module. The other two are design and preliminary construction.

Systems analysis consists of two basic steps.

1. *Analyze functional requirements*—The systems developer gathers data and information that specify the functions that the users will require of the new system. If an existing system is being replaced or improved, some of the data and information may exist in the form of documentation prepared by previous project teams. Such documentation is supplemented by efforts to obtain additional information so that the developer can have a complete picture of the users" requirements.

2. *Document functional requirements*—As the requirements are being understood, they are documented so that they can serve as a basis for the development of the system during the remaining phases of the project. The documentation facilitates the analysis.

The term **system study** is used to describe the activity of analyzing the existing system and documenting the functional requirements of the new system. The system study is one of the most important parts of the SDLC, and during the early years of business computing, no time limits were imposed. The idea was to do the most thorough job possible. Gradually, both information specialists and users came to the conclusion that less time could be spent in analysis with no ill effects on the quality of the new system. The reasoning was that the existing system was to be replaced so there was no reason to document it in an elaborate way. The thorough documentation was simply adding unnecessary time to the project.

So, a new view of systems analysis evolved. This view recognizes that systems analysis is important but no more time and effort should be devoted to it than is

FIGURE 5.1

Analysis Phase Overview

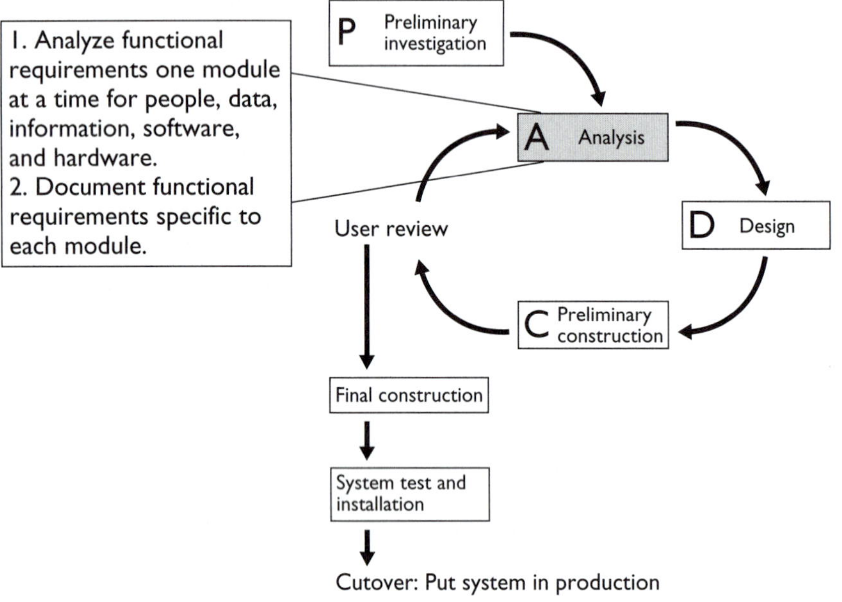

required to obtain a clear understanding of the new system requirements. This view is the dominant one today.

ANALYZE FUNCTIONAL REQUIREMENTS

As the systems developer takes the first step of systems analysis, he or she determines the functional requirements by using some combination of the following data and information gathering methods:

- Analyze existing system documentation
- Conduct in-depth personal interviews
- Conduct personal, telephone, and mail surveys
- Convene group collaborative sessions
- Observe the existing system in operation
- Search through existing system records

The developer will use all of the methods for a project involving a complex system or for a project for a global organization, and will use some subset on simpler projects or those involving only single locations. All of these data and information gathering methods require that the systems developer interface with users. However, before the developer begins the gathering, top management of the user area makes an announcement to the personnel. The announcement advises them of the study and asks for their cooperation.

Analyze Existing System Documentation

It is rare when the systems developer develops a brand new system from scratch. In most cases the task is to replace or improve an existing system and the chances are good that some form of documentation already exists—at least in the form of printed reports produced by the system. When the system is computer-based, the documentation may include such graphic documentation as data models, process models, and object models. For very old systems, the most emphasis was placed on processes, and those models are likely to be the most complete. When database management system software became available, more attention was devoted to data models, and they are included in the documentation package of more recent systems. Only systems that have been developed during the past few years can be expected to provide documentation in the form of object models.

The potential documentation for existing systems includes:

- Reports and screens
- Data flow diagrams (DFDs)
- Structured English
- Flowcharts
- Warnier-Orr diagrams and action diagrams
- Layout forms
- The data dictionary
- Entity-relationship diagrams (ERDs)
- Object diagrams

Each of these types of documentation is described briefly below.

Reports and Screens

The information component of the existing system is documented in the form of reports and screens that the system produces. The systems developer can gain a sense of the scope of the existing system and obtain a way to check the completeness of other information by compiling copies of these reports and screens. Users are the best source of this information.

Data Flow Diagrams

A detailed description of data flow diagrams is included in Technical Module B. This section summarizes the material in the technical module. A **data flow diagram (DFD)** uses only four sets of symbols to document the processes and data of a system within its environment. It documents the *processes* with circles or rectangles, and documents the *data repositories* with open-ended rectangles. *Data flows* are documented with arrows. The elements in the *system environment* are represented with squares.

DFDs document a system at various levels of detail. The DFD that describes the system in the most summary fashion is called a **context diagram** and is illustrated

FIGURE 5.2

A Context Diagram for an Order Entry System

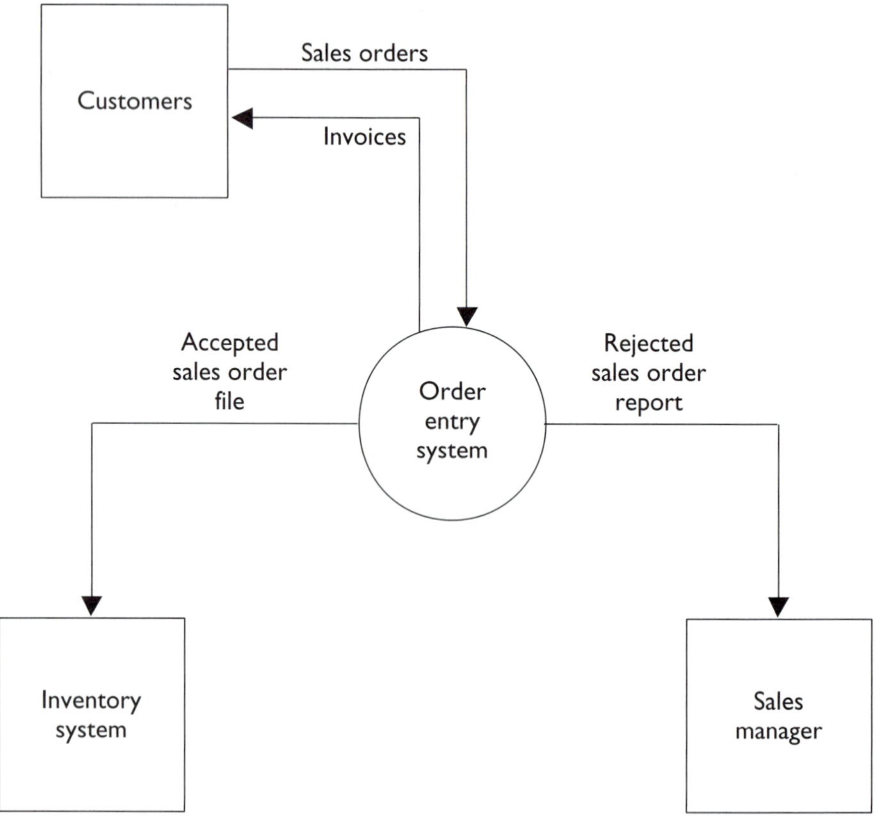

in Figure 5.2. The single process symbol in the center represents the entire system. The flows of data from and to the system environment are represented with arrows.

We can explode the single process symbol of the context diagram to show the major processes. This produces the **figure 0 diagram** in Figure 5.3. It is called a figure 0 diagram because the DFD on the next higher level, the context diagram, does not contain a numbered process. A DFD name refers to the number of its higher-level process.

Each of the processes in the figure 0 diagram can then be documented with its own DFD. This top-down documentation continues until only the detailed processes remain. For example, if you determine that additional detail is required for process 3, you would prepare a figure 3 diagram that shows those processes.

Structured English

DFDs are best suited to document systems on the higher hierarchical levels. They must be supplemented with other tools for the details, using such tools as structured English and pseudocode. We explain the details of structured English in Technical Module B. **Structured English** is a narrative in a shorthand form, which looks like computer code but is not. Earlier versions of structured English were called **pseudocode.** An example of structured English appears in Figure 5.4. This structured English explains the logic and arithmetic that is performed in step 1 of the figure 0 diagram in Figure 5.3.

Flowcharts

There are two types of flowcharts—system and program. Figure 5.5 illustrates a system flowchart. A **system flowchart** is a diagram that uses symbols to show how the major processes and data of a system are interconnected. The processes can be performed manually, with the aid of such key-driven machines as calculators and cash registers, and with computer-based information systems. The flowchart symbols indicate the types of technology that are used. The information system processes are illustrated with rectangles. Each rectangle represents a single program. You can see that the system in Figure 5.5 consists of three information system programs—processes 2, 3, and 4. Each processing step is numbered.

The upper shape in the figure is used to illustrate any type of printed *document.* In this case, it represents the Sales orders that provide input to the system. The two cylinder-like

FIGURE 5.3

Figure 0 Diagram for an Order Entry System

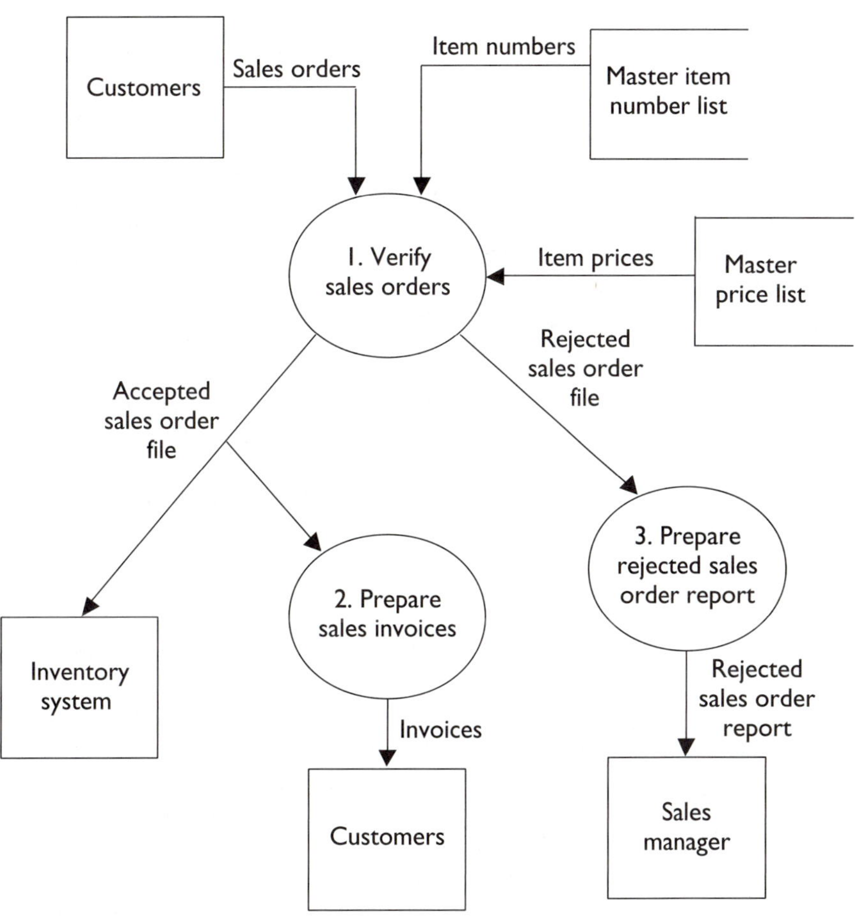

FIGURE 5.4

Structured English

```
Verify Sales Orders
START
Perform Enter Sales Order Data
Perform Edit Sales Order Data
Perform Compute Order Amount
STOP
Enter Sales Order Data
  INPUT SALES.ORDER Data
Edit Sales Order Data
  Edit CUSTOMER.NUMBER by ensuring that it is a positive numeric field
  IF Edit Is Failed
    THEN WRITE REJECTED.SALES.ORDER Record
  END IF
  DO for Each Item
    EDIT ITEM.NUMBER to ensure that it matches a number in the
     MASTER.ITEM.NUMBER.LIST
    IF Edit Is Failed
      THEN WRITE REJECTED.SALES.ORDER Record
    END IF
    EDIT UNIT.PRICE to ensure that it matches the price in the MASTER.PRICE.LIST
    IF Edit Is Failed
      THEN WRITE REJECTED.SALES.ORDER Record
    END IF
    EDIT ITEM.QUANTITY to ensure that it is a positive numeric field
    IF Edit Is Failed
      THEN WRITE REJECTED.SALES.ORDER Record
    END IF
  END DO
Compute Order Amount
  IF no edit errors
    THEN DO for Each Item
        COMPUTE ITEM.AMOUNT = ITEM.QUANTITY * UNIT.PRICE
        COMPUTE ORDER.AMOUNT = ORDER.AMOUNT sum
      END DO
      WRITE ACCEPTED.SALES.ORDER Record
  END IF
```

symbols on the left-hand side are used to document *magnetic disk storage.* Such storage is typically used for master files and for intermediate files that communicate data from one program to another, such as the Rejected sales orders file that is used to prepare and print the rejected sales orders report. The symbol used for process 1, labeled *Enter sales order data,* is used to illustrate an *online keying operation.* Here, the symbol indicates that someone enters data into a keyboard terminal or workstation.

System flowcharts are usually prepared by systems analysts. The responsibility to document the programs within the system falls to the programmers and they may use a more detailed type of flowchart called a program flowchart. A **program flowchart** is a diagram that uses interconnected symbols to show the detailed processes performed by a single information system program. Figure 5.6 is a program flowchart of the program in step 4 of the system flowchart in Figure 5.5. This program flowchart conforms to the rules of structured programming.

A feature of flowcharting that distinguishes it from other tools is the fact that the flowcharts document the system in *either* a summary *or* a detail fashion. The system flowchart provides the summary and the program flowchart provides the detail. There is no ability for producing documentation between the two extremes. This inability creates two problems for the systems developer. First, it makes it difficult to take a top-down, structured approach since the developer cannot gradually reveal the detail. Second, it makes it difficult to communicate designs to users. A user might understand the system flowchart but get lost in the detail of the program flowchart. Most program flowcharts are considerably more complex than the one shown in Figure 5.6.

FIGURE 5.5

A System Flowchart

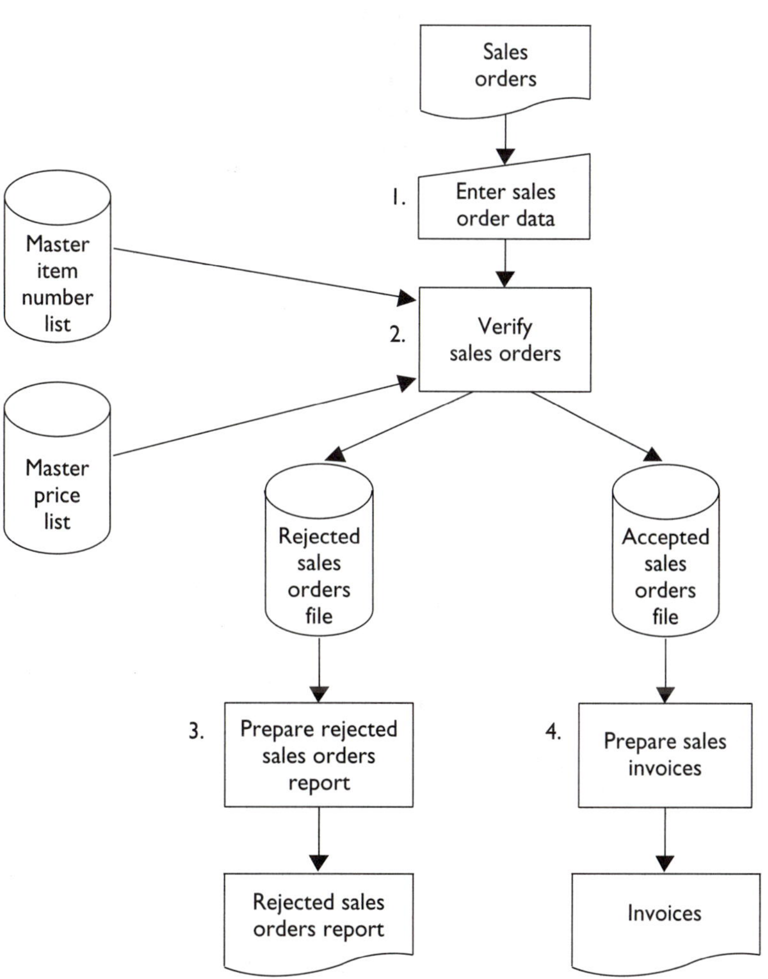

FIGURE 5.6

A Program Flowchart

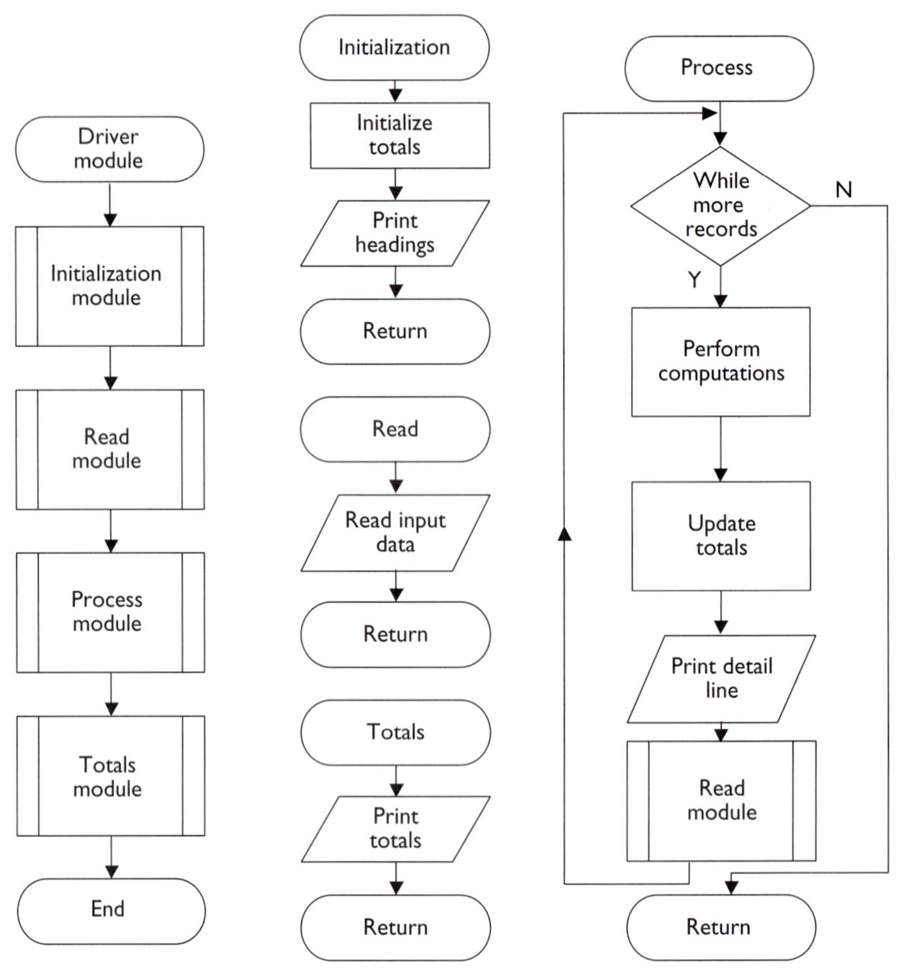

Warnier-Orr Diagrams and Action Diagrams

A process modeling tool that is capable of documenting a system at all levels is Warnier-Orr. In a **Warnier-Orr diagram,** pictured in Figure 5.7, the processes are described with process statements arranged in brackets. Each statement consists of a verb and object.

The system is identified at the left, and the leftmost bracket encloses the major processes. Each of these processes can then be documented in lower levels of detail, using additional brackets and moving from left to right. The format is that of an organizational chart, turned on its side.

At the lowest level of detail, the descriptions can be similar to structured English or information system code. The documentation therefore evolves in a gradual manner from the overall system to the detailed processing statements.

Because of space limitations, it is usually necessary to draw several Warnier-Orr diagrams to document an entire system from top to bottom. For that reason, the diagram in the figure does not include all of the details that are possible. However, the example diagram documents the same sales order process that we have documented with DFDs and flowcharts.

The Warnier-Orr diagram in the figure illustrates both the sequence and the repetition constructs of structured programming. Arranging the statements in a top-to-bottom manner specifies that they will be executed in that sequence. The numbers and letters in parentheses beneath each statement indicate the number of times the statement will be executed. The number 1 indicates that the statement is executed only one time, whereas the n indicates a variable number of times.

Warnier-Orr diagrams were perhaps the best process modeling tool of the era before DFDs came along. The Warnier-Orr diagrams failed to achieve widespread use because vendors of CASE software elected to support DFDs rather than Warnier-Orr.

FIGURE 5.7

A Warnier-Orr Diagram

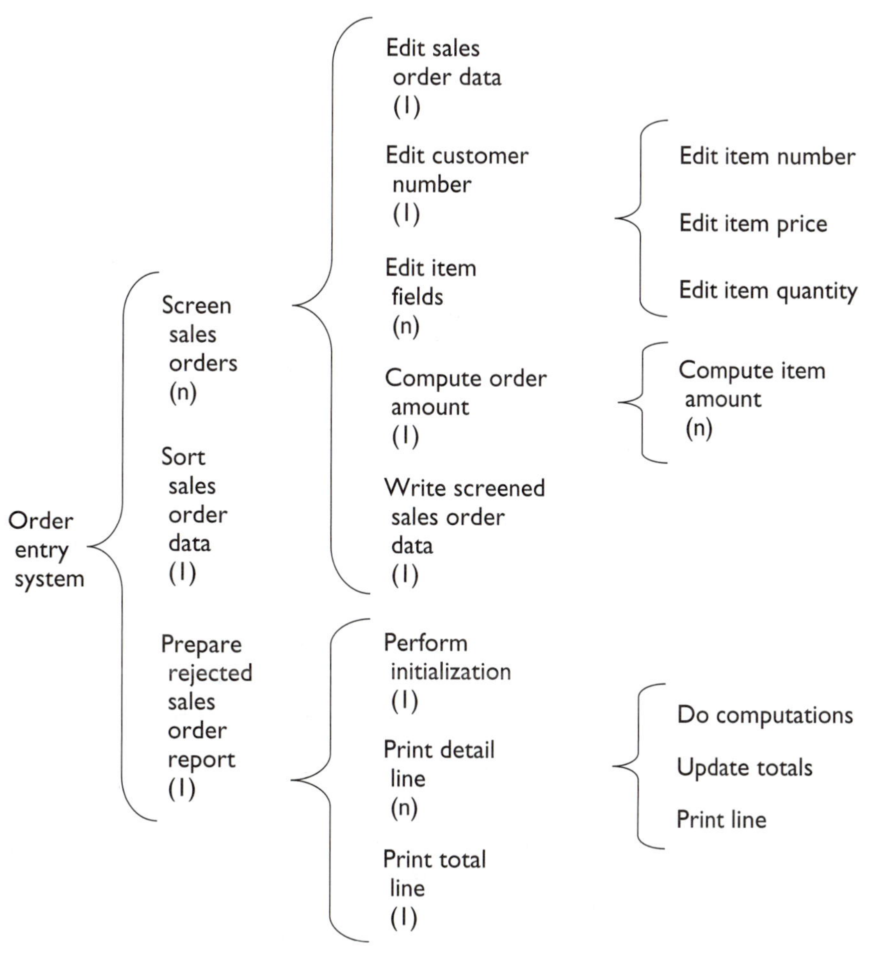

FIGURE 5.8

An Action Diagram with Nesting

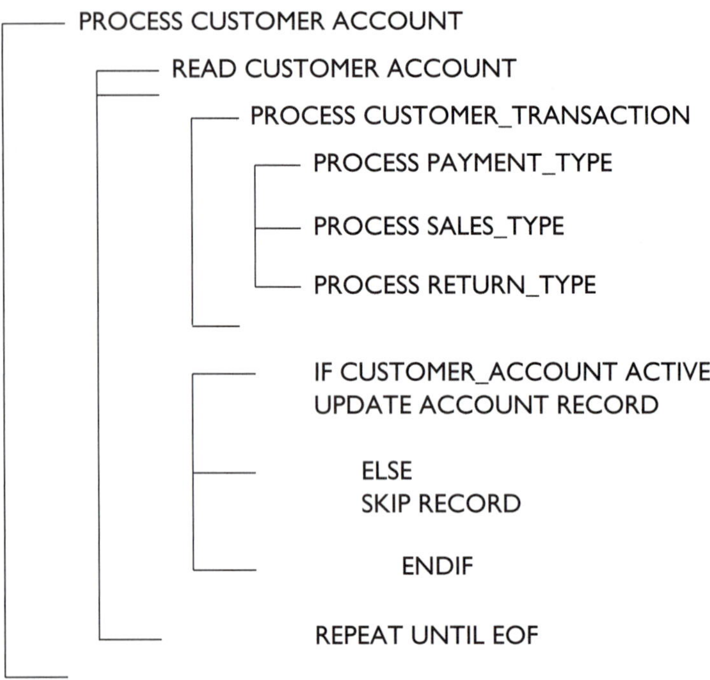
PROCESS CUSTOMER ACCOUNT
READ CUSTOMER ACCOUNT
PROCESS CUSTOMER_TRANSACTION
PROCESS PAYMENT_TYPE
PROCESS SALES_TYPE
PROCESS RETURN_TYPE
IF CUSTOMER_ACCOUNT ACTIVE
UPDATE ACCOUNT RECORD
ELSE
SKIP RECORD
ENDIF
REPEAT UNTIL EOF

Some CASE tools include a tool called an action diagram. An **action diagram** is like Warnier-Orr in that it uses brief narratives enclosed in brackets to describe processes, but unlike Warnier-Orr, it is usually aimed at only the lowest level of detail. Figure 5.8 is an example.

As you analyze existing documentation, the DFDs, flowcharts, Warnier-Orr diagrams, and action diagrams can be valuable sources for learning about the processes of the existing system. To learn about the data, you may find the documentation in layout forms, the data dictionary, or entity-relationship diagrams.

Layout Forms

The early systems developers documented the records of the data files with record layout forms such as the one pictured in Figure 5.9. A **record layout form** shows the data elements that comprise a record. The form typically includes multiple layers, each with a capacity of 100 characters. One or more layers are used to identify the locations of the data elements in a large record. The example in the figure is of an inventory master record of 82 characters, so the first layer is adequate to show all of the elements.

During the early years of computing, when the emphasis was on the processes rather than the data, record layouts provided the only documentation of data maintained in files. Similar forms, called **printer layout charts,** were used to document the positioning of data on lines of a printed document. Still other forms, called **screen layout forms,** were used to position the data on a screen. Printer and screen layout forms are still in use.

When firms began to recognize the value of data as an information resource, more attention was given to data documentation, which led to today's data dictionary and entity-relationship diagrams.

The Data Dictionary

A **data dictionary** is a detailed description of all the data used in a system. The descriptions are likely to be stored in a CASE repository or in the data dictionary system (DDS) of a database management system (DBMS). Prior to electronic storage, the dictionaries were maintained in a hardcopy form. Figure 5.10 is an illustration of a form used to document a single data element. You may find such forms in the documentation of legacy systems.

We provide more information on electronic-based data dictionaries in Technical Module A: Data Modeling.

Entity-Relationship Diagrams

An **entity-relationship diagram,** or **ERD,** identifies the entities within the system that are described with data, and the relationships between the entities. ERDs are discussed in detail in Technical Module A. There are many conventions that are followed in ERD documentation, but the entities are usually represented with rectangles. The relationships can be represented with diamonds as shown in Figure 5.11.

In this example, letters and numbers are included next to the rectangles to show how many entities are involved in a relationship. A 1 means that the entity occurs only a single time, a 0 means it *can* occur zero times, and an M means "many." Some diagrams, such as the one in the figure, also include the data elements, or attributes, next

FIGURE 5.9

A Record Layout Form

Application *Inventory* By *Ron Whatley* Date *3/18/01* Job No. *01-0012*

File Name										
Inventory master	*Product number*	*Product name*	*Warehouse location*	*Unit price*	*Reorder point*	*Order quantity*	*Balance on hand*	*Back-order quantity*	*Quantity on order*	
File Name										
File Name										

5 10 15 20 25 30 35 40 45 50 55 60 65 70 75 80 85 90 95 100

FIGURE 5.10

A Data Element Dictionary Entry Form

DATA ELEMENT DICTIONARY ENTRY

Use: To describe each data element contained in a data structure

DATA ELEMENT NAME:	*Unit sales price*
DESCRIPTION:	*The retail sales price for one unit of an item in the product line*
TYPE OF DATA:	*Numeric*
NUMBER OF POSITIONS:	*7*
NUMBER OF DECIMAL PLACES:	*2*
ALIASES:	*Sales price* *Price*
RANGE OF VALUES:	*00000.50 – 08999.99*
TYPICAL VALUE:	*None*
SPECIFIC VALUES:	
OTHER EDITING:	*Nonnegative*
DETAILS:	

to the entities. The underlined entries are the entity keys that identify the entity. For example, the customer number identifies all of the data that describes one occurrence of the customer entity.

The ERD and the data dictionary are used together. The ERD provides a summary graphic picture of the relationship between entities and the data dictionary provides a detailed narrative explanation of each entity's contents.

Object Diagrams

Systems developed during the past few years may incorporate an object-oriented design. In such designs, the system data and processes are organized into objects. The objects are similar to the entities in an entity-relationship diagram, packaged with the processes that use the data. Figure 5.12 provides an example of an **object class diagram,** which identifies the object classes and shows their communications linkages.

There can be considerable variation in how object-oriented systems are documented since much of the work was accomplished prior to the advent of the Unified Modeling Language, which has been adopted as a standard. We describe object modeling in Technical Module C.

Putting the Existing System Documentation in Perspective

Today, firms put great emphasis on documentation of new systems in the form of process, data, and object models. Such has not always been the case. Many legacy systems have little or no documentation. This means that when you reengineer those systems you very often have to start from scratch. The more recent the system development effort, the greater likelihood that good documentation exists—at least in large firms with project management mechanisms. Good documentation provides a starting point for analyzing system requirements, but even when such documentation exists,

FIGURE 5.11

An Entity-Relationship Diagram

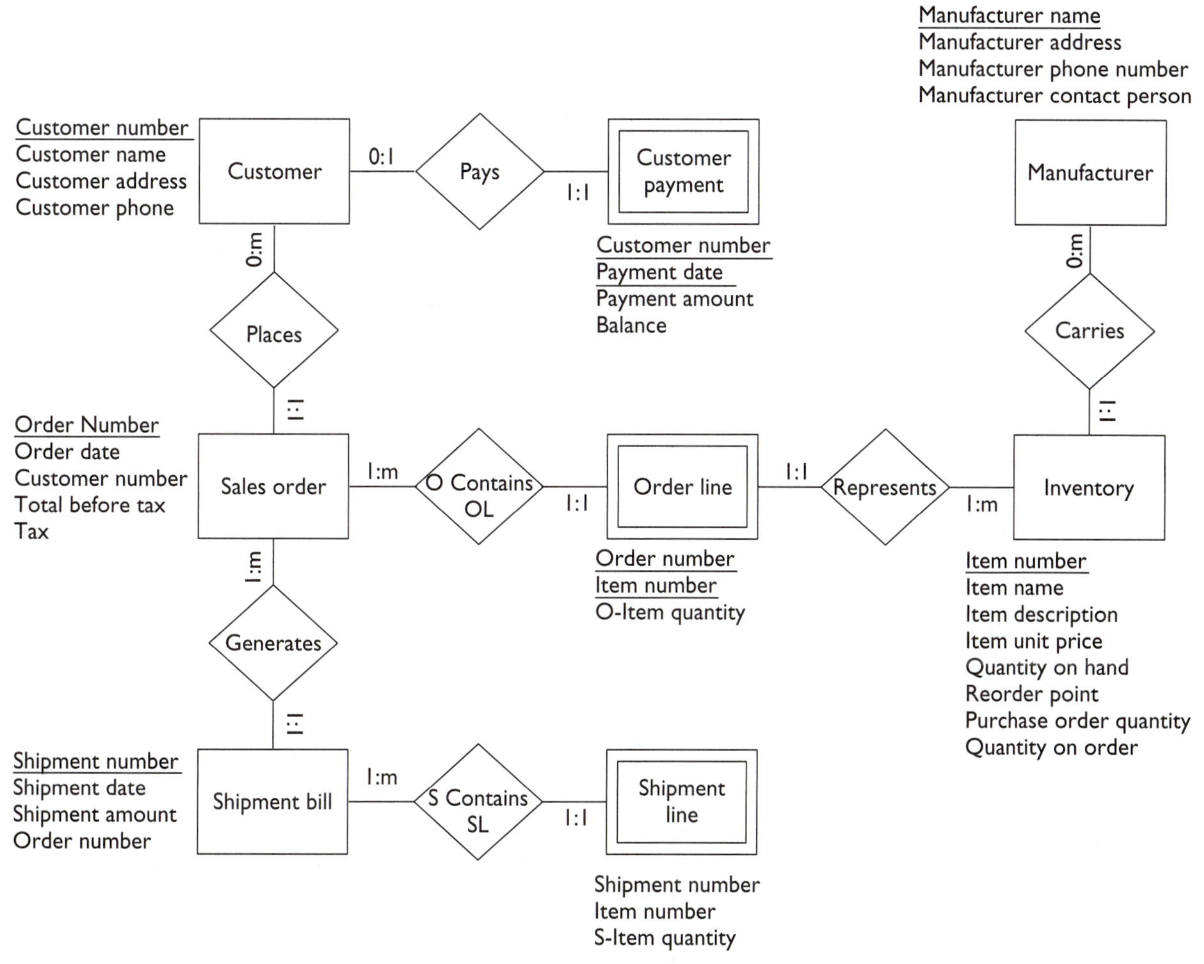

FIGURE 5.12

Class Diagram for Ordering Replenishment Stock

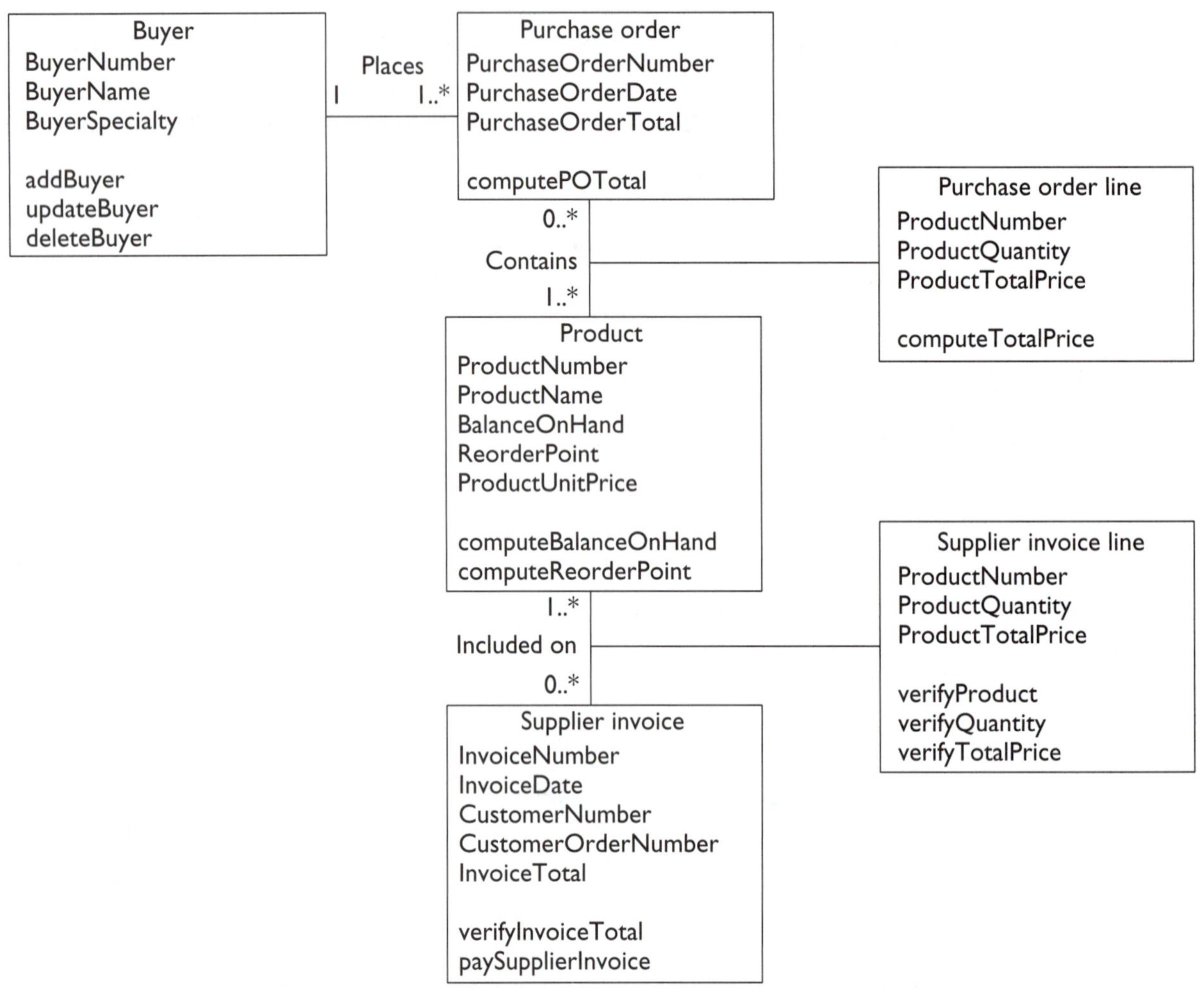

it should be supplemented with special data-gathering aimed at defining users' needs. The users are the best source of this information, and the information can be derived by interviews, surveys, group sessions, and observation. Additional information can be gathered by searching through records in the user area.

Conduct In-Depth Personal Interviews

An **in-depth personal interview** is a face-to-face session involving a person who asks questions and another person who answers them. In a development project, the systems developer asks questions and the user answers them. The developer conducts the interview in a setting that is best suited to gathering the data, usually in the user's office or work area. Here, the user feels the most comfortable and, as the user talks, the developer takes notes.

In most cases, more than one interview is required—spread over several days or maybe even weeks. The first meeting is not intended to provide all of the data. Rather, it is mainly a get-acquainted session. It is important that a bond of trust and mutual respect be established between the user and the systems developer, and the first meeting sets this tone.

Structured and Unstructured Interviews

The questioning can take either of two forms—structured or unstructured. In a **structured interview,** the developer prepares a list of questions ahead of time and makes an effort to stick to that sequence. An **unstructured interview,** on the other hand, begins with no formal plan and follows a path that is determined largely by the user's answers.

The factor that determines whether a structured or unstructured interview will be used is the developer's knowledge of the problem area. When the knowledge is limited, the unstructured interview is most appropriate. As the user answers each question, the developer learns more about the problem area and this increased knowledge provides the basis for more questions. When the developer is already an expert in the problem area, the structured interview is the way to go. The developer can draft a list of questions in advance and follow that sequence.

Tips for Conducting In-Depth Personal Interviews

Here are a few tips that contribute to an effective interview:

- *Make an appointment.* Always make an appointment, either by telephone or in person, with the user. Give the user a brief idea of why you want to conduct the interview. Then be on time.

- *Dress properly.* You should dress in a manner that does not distract the user. A good guideline is to dress in such a way that when you have left, the user cannot remember what you were wearing. Neither over-dress nor under-dress.

- *Always have a written agenda and use a question list.* A list of the topics you want to cover and the questions you want to ask will ensure that you get the information that you need and you do not waste the user's time or your own. The user will appreciate the fact that you are prepared.

- *Be flexible.* If the user says or does anything to indicate that your line of questioning is leading nowhere or in the wrong direction, then you should adapt your questions to fit the situation. This even applies to a structured interview. Break off the planned line of questioning and see where the new path will lead. For example, if a user says "We don't always do it that way," you have to pick up on that and ask "How do you do it the other times?" You might obtain some information that you never knew existed. Also, in being alert to the user, keep in mind that a person can communicate in ways other than words. **Body language**—facial expressions and gestures—often reveals a person's inner feelings.

- *Use a tape recorder whenever possible.* When you make the appointment for the interview, ask the user if there are any objections to using a tape recorder. Usually, there are none—especially at upper-management levels where there is little fear of criticism from higher levels for passing along information that should not be passed along. Assure the user that you will not make the tape available to anyone outside the project team without first obtaining permission. By using the tape recorder, you will not have to worry about taking notes and the tape will provide an accurate record not only of *what* is said but *how* it is said.

- *Validate the responses.* You are never certain whether the user is giving answers that reflect the true situation. You should conduct data validation by comparing the gathered data with other, related data. For example, if you ask an executive how many telephone calls she receives each day and she replies "About forty," validate the response by asking her secretary to keep a log for a couple of weeks. People are not always completely accurate when it comes to their perceptions. It is always a good idea to validate responses. This applies to *any* type of data gathering technique.

When to Use an In-Depth Personal Interview

The in-depth personal interview is the best way for the developer and the user to jointly define the new system requirements. However, a major drawback is the high cost in terms of the amount of time that is required. For that reason, the developer only uses the technique with key people in the user's area—the manager and employees who are on the inner circle of the problem area.

Conduct Personal, Telephone, and Mail Surveys

Whereas the in-depth personal interview asks different questions of a limited number of persons, a **survey** asks the *same* questions of a *large* number of persons. The person asking the survey questions is the **surveyor,** and the person answering them is the **respondent.** In a systems study, the systems developer is the surveyor and the user is the respondent.

Surveys are increasing in importance as a data gathering method because of the trend to global systems. Surveys provide the systems developer with a way to gather data from users and participants hundreds or thousands of miles away, and keep data gathering costs to a minimum. There are three types of surveys—personal, telephone, and mail.

Personal Survey

The personal survey is conducted by personally interviewing the respondents. Since more respondents are involved than in an in-depth interview, the length of the personal survey interview is usually much shorter.

The setting for the personal survey interview is the same as for the in-depth personal interview—the user's office or work area. The questions are printed on a form called a **questionnaire.** The developer reads the questions and writes the user's answers in the appropriate spaces on the questionnaire.

Objective and Subjective Questions Although the personal survey interview is always structured, the questions can be either objective or subjective. An **objective question** is one that can be answered only in certain, predefined ways. Examples are like the true-false and multiple-choice questions that are found on exams, but rather than asking a true-false question, the developer asks a question that can be answered "yes," "no," or "I don't know" or "I'm not sure."

Multiple-choice types of questions are difficult to ask in a personal interview because the respondent usually likes to view all of the choices before answering. This difficulty can be overcome by making a card that contains the list of possible answers and showing it to the user as the question is asked.

The main advantage of objective questions is that they make it easy to conduct a computer analysis of the responses. The main limitation is that the format often forces the user to respond with an answer that she or he would not ordinarily give, leaving the wrong impression. This limitation is overcome by another type of personal survey interview question, called the **subjective question.** It is also called an **open-ended question** because it permits the respondents to answer any way they like. For example, the developer asks: "How do you feel about the existing system?" The questionnaire contains several blank lines where the developer records the answer.

Tips for Designing Personal Survey Questionnaires Most of the in-depth personal interview tips also apply to the personal survey interview. You should make an appointment, dress properly, and be alert to the user. In addition, you should keep these points in mind:

- *Keep the questionnaire short.* By designing the questionnaire so that the questions can be answered in no more than, say, twenty minutes, you conserve not only the user's time, but yours as well. Plus, you make certain that the data analysis does not get out of hand.
- *Ask the easy questions first.* You should begin with questions that are easy for the user to answer. If you begin with the more difficult ones, the user may decide not to participate, and you are left with a blank questionnaire. The likelihood of the user not cooperating lessens once the questioning begins.
- *Understand the importance of proper question sequence.* The answer to one question can influence the answer to another. For example, if you ask the user to list the weaknesses of the existing system, and then ask how the user feels about the existing system, you can imagine what the response will be. Ask for general feelings first, and then follow up with specifics.

When to Use a Personal Survey The personal survey is second only to the in-depth personal interview in effectiveness. Once the developer has used the in-depth personal interview for the key people in the user area, he or she will use the personal survey for others who can be contacted in a face-to-face manner.

Telephone Survey

In some cases, it is impossible to meet with users personally. A good alternative is the telephone. The same general survey rules apply to a telephone survey but the developer does not have as much control. A telephone respondent can more easily terminate the session than in a personal interview. You know that from experience with telemarketers when you say "I'm not interested" and hang up.

Tips for Conducting Telephone Surveys The same tips that are used in designing personal survey questionnaires also apply to the telephone. The tip to keep the questionnaire short is even more critical. Telephone questionnaires that keep the respondent on the line for more than five or ten minutes should be used only in special situations. In addition, you should design the questionnaire for easy administration. This can be accomplished by using the information system to display the questions on the screen as they are asked. The respondent's answers can be keyed into the information system to facilitate analysis.

When to Use a Telephone Survey The telephone survey provides a good way to establish a two-way dialog with persons in remote user areas. It ranks second only to the two forms of personal interviews in effectiveness.

Mail Survey

When the cost of a telephone survey is too great, a mail survey might be a good alternative. The questionnaire can be sent to the respondent using a postal service, company mail, or e-mail.

Tips for Designing Mail Survey Questionnaires The main problem with the mail survey is the potentially low response rate. To keep the response rate as high as possible, consider the following:

- *Keep the questionnaire short.* The questionnaire length is more critical for the mail survey than any other type because the entire length is obvious to the respondent when the envelope is opened or the e-mail is received. Ideally, the questionnaire should occupy no more than a single page or screen.

- *Personalize the mailing.* For e-mail, use a format that does not include a long list of names. Write a short paragraph at the beginning of the e-mail about the purpose. For postal or company mail, enclose the questionnaire in an envelope addressed to a named person, not a title. Include a short cover letter or memo that explains the purpose of the survey. Ideally the e-mail, letter, or memo should be from someone in upper management who has responsibility for the area being surveyed.

- *Use the telephone or e-mail for follow-up.* If you have not received the completed questionnaire after a couple of weeks, follow up with a telephone call or e-mail message. Offer to send a second questionnaire if one is needed.

In addition to these techniques for achieving a higher response rate, you should keep the following suggestion in mind for increasing the effectiveness of the questionnaire.

- *Consider the use of scales.* Ratings scales offer a good way for users to express their opinions. One type of scale, called a Likert scale, consists of five points that are labeled with descriptors or numbers. The scale follows a statement and the respondent checks the appropriate point on the line. For example:

The system provides me with valuable problem-solving information.

Strongly Agree	Agree	Indifferent	Disagree	Strongly Disagree

When to Use a Mail Survey If you cannot ask questions of the respondent either in person or over the telephone, the next best choice is the mail survey. It is relatively inexpensive, and much valuable data can be gathered. In fact, you might be able to obtain data by mail that you could not gather in person. People are often more open in their written responses than in the ones they give in person or over the telephone. Consider the mail survey as a way to gather data on sensitive issues. Assuring the respondents that they will remain anonymous will help.

Convene Group Collaborative Sessions

The first information and decision support systems were designed to help individuals solve problems and take advantage of opportunities. It did not take systems developers long, however, to realize that business problems and opportunities were seldom handled on an individual basis. Rather, they were the combined efforts of groups. The first formal evidence of this realization was seen in **group decision support systems (GDSS)** or **group support systems (GSS)** that applied the DSS concept to relatively small groups such as committees or task forces. The popularity of this approach spread and gave birth to similar approaches with the names **computer-supported cooperative work (CSCW)** and **electronic meeting systems (EMS).** The common thread of all of these approaches is the fact that an information system is employed. Participants assemble in a room equipped with workstations that are used to enter views, perceptions, and observations, which can be displayed on a large screen by a **facilitator** who directs the session toward the desired objectives. The participants can vote on alternative solutions and the information system tabulates the votes and displays a ranking, which is further evaluated by the participants. This process continues until agreement is reached. One or more **scribes** take notes during the session to produce a permanent record.

GDSS, GSS, CSCW, and EMS are all forums for stimulating group collaboration. A **group collaborative session** is a meeting of persons for the purpose of achieving agreement on a discussion topic for which diverse opinions may exist. Examples of group collaborative sessions include JAD, the nominal group technique, and focus groups.

JAD Sessions

The JAD sessions that we have described as an effective data-gathering technique throughout the SDLC are a form of group collaborative session. JAD sessions were discussed in detail in Chapter 4. An elaborate JAD facility could include one or more information systems used to gather and display information from the participants. JAD can be an effective analysis strategy to gain agreement among multiple users concerning their functional requirements.

Nominal Group Technique

A similar collaborative approach that can be used is the **nominal group technique (NGT),** which is a group interview technique developed to facilitate meeting procedures and to maximize individual contributions by minimizing the inhibitions caused by pressures from peers or superiors. NGT aids idea generation and discussion by separating ideas from specific personalities. It focuses the group's attention on the problem or opportunity and encourages tolerance of conflicting ideas. NGT also encourages participation and brainstorming by discouraging censure and promoting free and creative thinking. It assumes that the more ideas that are generated, the greater the likelihood that superior ideas will surface.

NGT consists of six steps:

1. Individuals generate ideas during or before the meeting.
2. Individuals' ideas are listed in round-robin fashion.
3. The group discusses the ideas, possibly adding ideas to the list.
4. Each group member ranks the listed ideas.
5. Individual rankings are compiled to form a group ranking.
6. The group ranking of ideas is discussed. If the group ranking is unacceptable, Steps 3 through 5 are repeated.

You can see the similarity between NGT and an information system-based GDSS session where participants vote on their inputs. You can also see the similarity between NGT and JAD in that both do not necessarily rely on an information system to facilitate the discussion. Unlike both GDSS and JAD, NGT does not require a facilitator. Rather, in most cases, a user acts in a role of keeping the process moving from one step to the next. It is possible that the systems developer can serve in this capacity but it is much better if the whole process is under the control of the users. The systems developer can be present during the session and actively participate when he or she believes it is appropriate.

Focus Groups

A collaborative technique that has been around for quite a while is the focus group, which is a meeting of persons who are either interested in a particular subject, or are expert in it, or both. As an example, textbook publishers frequently assemble instructors from various colleges for the purpose of voicing their needs and suggestions concerning textbooks.

Such focus group sessions have been popular because they are so simple to set up, but they have not enjoyed much use in systems development—until now, anyway. However, a type of project that is demanding the type of information inputs that a focus group can provide is the development of Web-based systems. The problem with Web-based system development is the fact that many, or perhaps all, of the users are unknown to the firm until they decide to use the system. The users are not employees of the firm or its suppliers or customers who can be interviewed, surveyed, or observed. Take an e-business system, for example, where the firm's customers order the firm's products over the Internet. The system developers must develop a Web interface that can be used with no training and by following only a bare minimum of instructions. One way to obtain feedback from such potential users is to arrange for focus group sessions, where the developers can present mock-ups or prototypes and gather reactions and suggestions.

Such focus group sessions have the same objective as a test market for a consumer product, such as a new soft drink or dishwasher soap. The manufacturer introduces the product into a tightly controlled market to gauge response. The Web developers use the focus groups to test market their Web designs.

Any type of collaborative session—JAD, NGT, or focus group—can be an effective way to achieve group consensus concerning functional requirements.

Observe the Existing System in Operation

The earliest professional systems analysts, industrial engineers, pioneered data gathering by means of observation. **Observation** is the viewing of activity as it occurs.

Tips for Gathering Data and Information by Observation

When using observation, you should:

- *Be as inconspicuous as possible.* The secret to obtaining good data is to do so without influencing the work process. When employees know they are being observed they tend to work faster, do more important jobs, demonstrate greater interest, and so on. Find a chair outside the main work flow and don't take notes. As soon as you get back to your desk, write down what you saw.

- *Observe a representative work flow.* Observe long enough to cover periods of both heavy and light activity so as to acquire a feel for the fluctuation in workload.

You should always be alert to what is going on during the entire time that you are in the user area. Follow the above tips when conducting observation in a formal way.

When to Use Observation

Users are often too busy to provide as much information as developers need. Observation is a way to save users time since they can continue their duties while you observe. Also, the users may have been following the same work process for so long that they are on "automatic pilot" and go through the motions without thinking. It is difficult for these users to verbalize what they do and how they do it.

In addition to its ability to gather information that cannot be gathered any other way, observation is excellent for validation. Also, it provides a better understanding of the setting in which the employees do their work than does any other data gathering technique. The setting often explains *why* things happen as they do.

Observation also enables the developer to remain in the area for a longer period, increasing the opportunity for being accepted as "one of us." This objective can be achieved by following one of the cardinal rules of data gathering: *It is always better to work in the user area than in your office.* By being on site, the user develops an appreciation for the amount of time and effort that you are putting into the study and is more likely to respect your recommendations.

Search Through Existing System Records

The final data gathering method is **record search** and is without a doubt the most unglamorous part of systems work. For an example of the need to do record search, assume that a unit has had difficulty keeping up with the daily volume of sales orders. On certain days the volume is too great to handle. On other days there is much idle time. A record search can be conducted of the file of sales orders for the past several months and the number of orders for each day can be tabulated. This data provides a clear picture of the fluctuation in transaction volume that the new system will be expected to handle.

When you see the need to conduct a record search, design a special data-gathering form that is tailored to the specific type of data that is being gathered. In the example of determining the daily volume of sales orders, a form such as the one in Figure 5.13 could be designed.

When to Use Record Search

Use record search when users cannot provide all of the data through interviews, surveys, and observation, and when there is a need to validate findings from the other techniques.

Putting Analysis Activities in Perspective

The analysis activities make or break the project. There is probably no greater challenge in business than being asked by a user to solve a problem that he or she has not

FIGURE 5.13

A Special Form Designed to Facilitate Record Search

DAILY SALES ORDER VOLUME									
Date			Day of week	Volume	Date			Day of week	Volume
Yr	Mo	Da			Yr	Mo	Da		
0 1	0 1	0 4	M O N	155					
		0 5	T U E	78					
		0 6	W E D	82					
		0 7	T H U	111					
		0 8	F R I	93					
		1 1	M O N	165					
		1 2	T U E	89					

been able to solve or meet a new business opportunity that is exciting, challenging, and only vaguely defined. The methodology of the systems approach provides the framework for you to meet this challenge, and the data and information gathering techniques are applied within this framework. These techniques are important tools of systems analysis and design—just as important, or more so, than the tools for documenting functional requirements.

DOCUMENT FUNCTIONAL REQUIREMENTS

The second and final step of the analysis phase is to document the functional requirements. The documentation accomplishes two main objectives. First, it enables the systems developer to understand the existing system. Second, it enables the developer to communicate the details of the system to others—the users and other members of the project team who will develop the system.

All of the documentation is entered into the project dictionary, which includes all of the media that have been accumulated from the preliminary investigation phase and each iteration of the analysis phase. Table 5.1 provides an example of the content. Sections 1 through 5 contain material gathered during preliminary investigation. The

Section 6 material is gathered during the analysis phase and content is added as each system module is analyzed. The development plan in Section 8 originated during preliminary investigation and is refined with information learned during the analysis iterations. All of this material is augmented in Section 7 with documentation provided by functions/components matrices and use cases.

Functions/Components Matrices

The functions/components (F/C) matrix was described in Chapter 1 and illustrated in Figure 1.18. Such a matrix can be prepared for the existing system that captures its processes and how they are performed. During design, another matrix can be prepared for the new system. The two matrices can provide the developers and users with snapshots that vividly illustrate the system changes.

TABLE 5.1

Contents of the Project Dictionary Created During Analysis Activities

1. Problem Definition
2. System Objectives
3. System Goals
   - 3.1 Goal Analysis Form
4. System Constraints
5. System Performance Criteria
6. Existing System Documentation
   - 6.1 Process Models
     - 6.11 Data Flow Diagrams
     - 6.12 Structured English
     - 6.13 System Flowcharts
     - 6.14 Program Flowcharts
     - 6.15 Warnier-Orr Diagrams
   - 6.2 Data Models
     - 6.21 Layout Forms
     - 6.22 Data Dictionary
     - 6.23 Entity-Relationship Diagrams
   - 6.3 Object Models
7. New System Functional Requirements
   - 7.1 Functions/Components Matrices
   - 7.2 Use Cases
8. Development Plan
   - 8.1 Project Risk Evaluation Form
   - 8.2 Risk Reduction Strategies
   - 8.3 Gantt Charts
   - 8.4 Network Diagrams
   - 8.5 Milestone Report
9. Appendix
   - 9.1 System Reports and Screens
   - 9.2 I/O and Programming Standards
   - 9.3 Interview Notes and Tapes
   - 9.4 Working Papers

Use Cases

A **use case** is a step-by-step narrative description of all of the processes that are performed by a system. The processes include those performed by the information system and by people. The description provides a "black box" view of the system, addressing the inputs and outputs but not the details of the processing.

General Guidelines for Preparing Use Cases

In preparing use cases, three general guidelines should be followed[1]:

1. Segment the system into separate processes by numbering each one.
2. Show alternative courses of action separate from the main course.
3. Identify related use cases of systems that interact with the one being described.

There are different formats for use cases. Figure 5.14 is one format that consists of narrative statements in a sequential list.[2] The sequence of the narrative conforms to the sequence in which the processes are performed. This example describes the processing that is performed to fill a customer sales order. The processing is performed by the information system, data entry operators, and order clerks. The use case also refers to processes performed by inventory stock clerks, shipping clerks, and mail clerks—processes that are described by related use cases. Note that the sequence of normal events is described first, followed by alternative events.

Another use case format is called the **ping-pong format** because it shows how the dialog between the information system and the user goes back and forth. The ASTA project team used such a format in documenting the create skill set, search skill set, and request reports use cases. See Figures CS 4.3, CS 4.4, and CS 4.5.

Use cases can also be documented with graphics. A use case diagram shows the associations that can exist among several use cases that comprise a system, and the linkages between the use cases and actors in the system's environment. The ASTA team prepared two such diagrams. Figure CS 4.6 is a high-level diagram, and Figure CS 4.7 is a drill-down diagram that shows additional detail for one of the high-level use cases.

An important point to remember about use cases is that they are a good way to begin the documentation of a system, regardless of whether you plan to use data and process modeling, or object modeling, techniques.

Putting the Analysis Phase in Perspective

The analysis phase is where the systems developer gets the chance to apply her or his communications and analytical skills. Preliminary investigation got the project underway but it is the analysis phase where the real work begins. The analysis phase probably will not be the lengthiest stage of system development, since that honor will probably go to the design phase. The developer does not want to spend unnecessary time in analysis, but recognizes that the key to a good project is a clear understanding of the user requirements. For this reason, the developer will devote as much time to analysis as is necessary to obtain this understanding.

FIGURE 5.14

A Use Case

Use Case Name: Customer Makes Purchase
When a customer mails a sales order, this use case is initiated by the data entry operator.

Sequence of Normal Events
The *Main menu* is displayed on the screen, waiting for a menu selection.

- *The data entry operator selects "Process Sales Order" from the Main menu.*

The Process Sales Order menu is displayed on the screen, waiting for a customer number.

- *The data entry operator keys in the customer number and the system verifies that the number is valid.*
- If the number is valid, *the system completes the invoice header.*
- *The system prompts the operator to enter an item number.*

Waiting for an Item Number

- *The operator keys in the item number for the first item on the sales order.*
- *The system prompts the operator to enter an item quantity ordered.*

Waiting for Quantity Ordered

- *The operator keys in the quantity ordered.*
- For each item ordered, *the system creates an invoice item line, consisting of item number, item name, quantity ordered, unit price, and extended price (quantity ordered times unit price).*
- *The system prompts the operator to enter another item number or to signal the end of the sales order.*
- If another item number is entered, *the system creates another invoice item line.*

Waiting for the End of Order Indicator

- When the operator signals the end of the order, *the system creates an invoice footer by calculating and printing the total invoice price.*
- *The system prints the invoice in four parts (original, picking ticket, packing list, and shipping label).*

Distribute Invoice Copies

- *The order clerk separates the invoice copies.*
- *The order clerk puts the invoice Part 1 copies in the mail room mail box.*
- *The order clerk puts the invoice Part 2, 3, and 4 copies in the stock room mail box.*

Complete Order Filling

- *The inventory stock clerk uses the invoice Part 2 copy as a picking ticket to fill the order.* (See Fill Customer Order use case.)
- *The shipping clerk uses the invoice Part 3 copy as a shipping label and the Part 4 copy as a packing list to pack the order.* (See Ship Customer Order use case.)
- *The mail clerk mails the invoice Part 1 copy to customer.* (See Mail Customer Invoice use case.)

Alternative Events
An invalid customer number is entered

- *The system displays an error message and prompts the operator to try again.*
- If three successive attempts to validate the customer number fail, *the system prompts the operator to mark the sales order for manual verification.*

An invalid menu selection is entered

- *The system displays an error message and prompts the operator to try again.*

The sales order does not include the customer number

- *The operator selects a command button and the system displays a pop-up screen and prompts the operator to enter the customer's phone number.*

Waiting for Phone Number

- *The operator enters the customer's phone number.*
- *The system matches the phone number with the appropriate customer record and creates the invoice header.*
- If no match is found, *the system displays an error message, and prompts the operator to mark the sales order for manual verification.*

The item number is invalid.

- *The system prompts the operator to enter the item number again.*
- If three successive attempts to validate the item number fail, *the system prompts the operator to mark the sales*

PROJECT MANAGEMENT TOOLBOX

Management of the Project's Analysis Phase

An expression that is often heard in relation to the analysis phase is "It's where the rubber meets the road," capturing the notion that the success of the project rests largely on how well the user's requirements are understood. If this phase is so important—and it is—it should be managed with care. Since the two basic steps of the analysis phase are to (1) analyze functional requirements, and (2) document functional requirements, it makes sense to aim project management at these two activities.

Managing the Analysis of Functional Requirements

The chapter identified six methods that can be used to gather information for defining functional requirements. Management of this task focuses on ensuring that all possible sources of information are tapped. This can be accomplished by including tasks within the analysis phase for each system module to address each information gathering method. Table 5.2 captures this idea. The Gantt chart can include the six activities, with specifications of who is to do the work and when it is to be done.

Managing the Documentation of Functional Requirements

The right-hand column of the table identifies the documentation that project managers can use to ensure that each information source was utilized. For example, as proof that the project team gathered information by personal interview, the team can provide interview plans, interview notes, and use cases developed from the interview information. Of course, all six information sources will not always be used due to unique characteristics of the project. In those cases, project management will not require that documentation. The ASTA team recognized the value of planning its interviews and developed an

TABLE 5.2

Information Gathering Matrix

Activity	Who?	When?	Documentation
Analyze existing documentation			Process models Data models Object models
Conduct personal interviews			Interview plans Interview notes Use cases
Conduct surveys			Questionnaires Follow-up e-mails and telephone records Survey reports
Convene group sessions			Session plans Scribe notes Use cases
Observe existing system			Use cases
Search system records			Data recording forms

interview checklist. See Figure CS 3.7. The checklist lists topics to be covered in the interview, and includes space for recording the findings.

All of the documentation listed in the table can be used to develop functions/components matrices for each module phase. For example, if the system consists of Web interface, database, and reporting modules, at least one functions/components matrix will be developed for each. Some of the information sources are better suited than others for providing contents to certain matrix cells, as shown in Table 5.3.

Documentation of the existing system and personal interviews can provide material for all cells. Whereas this blanket contribution is possible from the other information gathering methods as well, the table contents show where the sources are most likely to contribute.

The Output/Data and Output/Information cell contents are highlighted in the table, recognizing that they are the best source of information on the user's functional requirements. Most systems have the requirement of producing information or data to meet the user's needs.

To summarize the project management of functional requirements analysis and documentation, the Gantt chart should include tasks aimed specifically at each of the information gathering methods for each system module, and project management should insist on evidence that each method applicable to the project was carried out.

TABLE 5.3

Analysis Phase Functions/Components Matrix

	Input	Processing	Output	Storage	Control
People	Documentation Interviews Observation	Documentation Interviews Observation	Documentation Interviews Observation	Documentation Interviews Observation	Documentation Interviews Observation
Data	Documentation Interviews Surveys Observation Records	Documentation Interviews Observation Records	**Documentation Interviews Surveys Groups Observation Records**	Documentation Interviews Observation Records	Documentation Interviews Observation Records
Information	Documentation Interviews Observation Groups	Documentation Interviews	**Documentation Interviews Surveys Groups Observation Records**	Documentation Interviews Records	Documentation Interviews
Software	Documentation Interviews Observation Records	Documentation Interviews Records	Documentation Interviews Observation Records	Documentation Interviews	Documentation Interviews
Hardware	Documentation Interviews Observation	Documentation Interviews Observation	Documentation Interviews Observation	Documentation Interviews Observation	

SUMMARY

The systems developer defines the functional requirements of the new system by analyzing existing system documentation, conducting in-depth personal interviews and surveys, convening collaborative group sessions, observing users in action, and searching through records. The surveys can be conducted in person, over the telephone, and through the mail. The documentation might be slim when the existing system has been in use for a long time. Likewise, it might not be possible to gather all of the required information from individuals using interviews or surveys, and such group sessions as JAD and NGT might be appropriate. Observation not only saves users' time, it often yields information that users are unable to supply. Record search is necessary to quantify information gathered by the other means.

As the systems developer understands the functional requirements, they are documented using process, data, and object modeling techniques, in addition to functions/components matrices. All of the documentation is maintained in the project dictionary.

Documentation is important in the development and use of business systems because of their typically long life cycles. We have seen in this chapter how the documentation enables the systems developer to understand the existing system. With this thought in mind, the project team places a high priority on documenting the new system. Today's new system will become the existing system that is maintained, redeveloped, or reengineered tomorrow.

With the requirements of the new system defined and documented, the project team can design the new system, the subject of the next chapter.

KEY TERMS

system study
data flow diagram (DFD)
structured English
system flowchart
program flowchart
Warnier-Orr diagram, action diagram
data dictionary
entity-relationship diagram (ERD)
object class diagram
in-depth personal interview
structured interview
unstructured interview
survey
objective question
subjective question, open-ended question
group collaborative session
nominal group technique (NGT)
observation
use case

KEY CONCEPTS

- A developer only spends the amount of time in systems analysis that is necessary to identify the requirements of the new system
- Gaining an understanding of the new system requirements by using a variety of information and data gathering techniques
- The importance of existing system documentation in systems analysis
- The best information concerning requirements comes from users, gathered by means of interviews, surveys, group collaborative sessions, and observation
- The project dictionary provides a written record of the SDLC as it unfolds

QUESTIONS

1. Why is a systems analysis conducted?
2. What are the two steps of the analysis phase?
3. What types of documentation can provide information on the processes of the existing system? What types of documentation provide information on the data?
4. What is a good tool to use in conjunction with DFDs to document a system's processes?
5. What are the two types of flowcharts?
6. Identify a documentation tool that displays a system's hierarchical structure in a left-to-right manner?
7. How are the ERD and data dictionary used in combination?
8. What distinguishes an in-depth personal interview from a personal survey?
9. Which of the data gathering techniques involve a respondent?
10. Distinguish between a structured and unstructured interview.
11. Which of the data gathering techniques involve the use of a questionnaire?
12. Distinguish between an objective and a subjective question.
13. Which data gathering technique might be the best for gathering sensitive data? Explain your answer.
14. In what kind of survey would you use a Likert scale?
15. In what way is the NGT similar to a GDSS? In what way do they differ?
16. In what way is the NGT similar to JAD? In what way do they differ?
17. What are the two objectives of system documentation?
18. When is analysis documentation added to the project dictionary?

TOPICS FOR DISCUSSION

1. Which data gathering technique would most require validation? Are there any that would require none?
2. Assume that you are a systems developer, and the user with whom you have been working during the analysis phase tells you: "Why don't you go ahead and figure out the functional requirements by yourself." What should you do?

PROBLEMS

Technical Module B (data flow diagrams and structured English) provides the necessary techniques for working the following problems.

1. Prepare a figure 0 diagram of the following procedure. A clerk opens the mail and selects out all customer payments. Each payment consists of a payment document and a check. The payment documents are sent to the data entry department. The checks are sent to the cashier's office. All other mail is placed in a Suspense file. A data entry operator keys the payment document data into a keyboard terminal. After the keying operation, the payment documents are filed in the Payment history file. The information system sorts the payment records into customer number sequence, and writes them onto magnetic disk as a Payments file. The Payments file is used to update the Accounts receivable master file (on magnetic disk). At the same time, a payments report is printed by the printer. The payments report is used by the supervisor of the accounts receivable section.
2. Repeat problem 1, only draw a context diagram.
3. Prepare a figure 0 diagram of the following procedure. Sales orders are received from customers. A

clerk in the order department batches the orders in groups of 25, and uses a desk calculator to accumulate batch totals for each batch. The totals include: (1) number of orders, and (2) total order amount. The desk calculator prints the totals on a paper strip that is held for use later in the procedure. The batches of sales orders are given to a data entry operator who keys the data into the information system. After the keying operation, the sales order batches are filed in the Sales order history file. The information system generates the same totals as the order department clerk, and prints the totals on a Batch totals report. During the same operation, the information system writes the sales order data onto a Suspense file that resides on magnetic disk. A control clerk compares the batch totals computed by the order department clerk with those computed by the information system. No action is taken when the totals balance. However, when they do not balance, the control clerk identifies the cause of the imbalance and makes any necessary corrections to the error batches, which are removed from the Sales order history file. For example, numbers are rewritten to make them more legible. The corrected error batches are sent to the data entry operator for reentry. The desk calculator strips and the Batch total report are filed in a Batch totals history file.

4. Repeat problem 3, only draw a context diagram.
5. Prepare a figure 0 diagram of the following procedure. Consider the work of the employees in creating their time cards to be part of the payroll system—not the environment. Therefore, the payroll system will not be triggered by an environmental input.

   Each day, each employee writes the number of hours worked on her or his time card. At the end of the week, each employee totals the hours worked, using a pocket calculator, and writes the total at the bottom of the card. The cards are given to the supervisor, who uses a desk calculator to verify the total figures on each of the cards. If a card contains an error, the supervisor corrects it. All of the cards for each department for each week are forwarded to the information systems department where the data is keyed into a keyboard terminal. After the keying operation, the time cards are placed in a Time card history file. The information system writes the data on a Weekly payroll transactions file, on magnetic disk. The information system, using a program named Update payroll master file, then reads from the Transactions file and obtains the appropriate master record from the Employee master file, on magnetic disk. The information system computes the regular, overtime, and total earnings, using data from both the transaction and master files. The master record is updated to reflect the new year-to-date totals. During the same operation, a summary of the payroll transactions is written on a magnetic tape as a Payroll summary file. Using a program named Print weekly payroll summary report, the information system then reads from the Payroll summary file and prints a weekly Payroll summary report for the manager of the payroll department.
6. Repeat problem 5, only draw a context diagram.
7. Use structured English to document the Update payroll master file program described in problem 5.

CASE PROBLEM: MIDCONTINENT INDUSTRIES

Midcontinent Industries manufactures garden tools. Of the firm's 425 employees, between 275 and 350 are assigned to the manufacturing division. The number depends on the season of the year. The largest production volumes come in the fall. Although Midcontinent has an information system, very few of the systems are completely computerized. The hourly payroll system is a good example of an integration of information system and manual processing.

The Hourly Payroll System

Everyone in manufacturing, except the managers, is paid an hourly rate. Each week, each hourly manufacturing employee is given a time card. As the employees come to work in the morning and leave in the afternoon, they insert their time cards in time clocks that are installed at the plant entrances. The time clocks print the date and the time of day on the cards for both arrival and departure. The time of day is based on a twenty-four hour clock; for example, 1:30 PM is printed as 1330.

On Friday afternoon, as the employees leave for the weekend, they compute the hours that they worked that week. Using pocket calculators, the employees subtract the time in from the time out, and then subtract another hour and a half for the lunch hour and two fifteen-minute coffee breaks. The remainder is the number of hours worked for the day. Finally, the employees total the daily hours to arrive at the weekly hours. The employees sign their time cards and give them to their departmental secretaries.

Departmental Secretaries Check the Time Cards

The departmental secretaries check the employees' time cards against their lists of department employee names to ensure that there is a card for each employee. When a time card is missing, the secretary locates the employee and obtains the card. When a card cannot be found, the secretary fills out a new card for forty hours and the employee is paid for that amount of time. Next, the secretary scans each card to ensure that all fields have been filled in for daily and weekly hours. When necessary, the secretary fills in the missing data. When the secretaries have finished their operation, they bundle the verified time cards together and give them to their department managers.

Department Managers Approve Overtime

The department managers scan the cards, looking for those with overtime. Employees with forty or more hours are eligible for overtime pay—one and a half times the regular hourly rate for all hours worked over forty. When the manager approves an employee's overtime, the manager signs the card. When the manager cannot recall a need for the employee to work overtime, the manager writes a "40" above the employee's figure, and signs the card. The employee with the disapproved overtime is paid for forty hours. If the employee can later show that overtime was actually worked, overtime pay is computed by a separate system. After signing the overtime cards, the department managers bundle all of the cards together, and send them to the information systems department through the company mail.

The Information System Performs Weekly Payroll Processing

A data entry operator in the information systems department keys the data from each time card into a keyboard terminal, and then files the time cards in a Time card history file. An information system program writes the entered data onto a Weekly time card file, on magnetic disk. A prewritten sort program sorts the Weekly time card file by employee number (minor sort key) within department number (major key). A third program reads the Sorted weekly time card file, on magnetic disk, and prints a weekly payroll report. This report is filed in a Weekly payroll history file, which provides a printed record in the event that anyone wishes to audit the payroll activity.

The Sorted weekly time card file is also used to update the Employee payroll master file, on magnetic disk. This file maintenance program is the most complex of the system—computing the weekly regular and overtime earnings, the current and year-to-date gross earnings, social security tax, income tax, and net earnings amounts. The appropriate fields are updated in the employee master records, and an output file is written on magnetic disk that contains the most important computations for each employee. This output file, called the Weekly payroll file, is used to print the payroll checks, which are sent in the company mail to the employees.

The Information System Performs Monthly Payroll Processing

The Weekly payroll files are maintained until the end of the month and are then used to prepare a monthly report. First, the weekly files are merged, using a prewritten merge program. Then, the Merged weekly payroll file is used to print the monthly payroll report, which is sent to the president in the company mail.

Assignments

(Note: Technical Module B provides the detailed understanding of DFDs and structured English that will be useful in performing these tasks.)

1. Draw a set of data flow diagrams that document both the weekly and monthly hourly payroll procedure. Use the following guidelines:
   a. Draw a context diagram and a figure 0 diagram. The context diagram should reflect that the daily hourly payroll system provides the time cards and that the employees receive the checks. In drawing the figure 0 diagram, regard all of the weekly information system processing as process 1, and the monthly processing as process 2. Connect the weekly and monthly processes with a data store.
   b. Draw a figure 1 diagram of the processing performed by the weekly system. Assume that the processing begins with the computation of daily and weekly hours by the employees. Show the weekly work performed by the (1) employees, (2) secretaries, (3) managers, and (4) information system. Document the processes of the employees, secretaries, and managers with single symbols. Do not include the detailed payroll computations in documenting the processes of the file maintenance program. Also, do not include the special payroll system that corrects errors when employees are paid for only forty hours although they worked overtime.
   c. Draw a figure 2 diagram of the processing performed by the monthly system.
2. Use structured English to document the processes required to update the Employee master file. Include reading the record to be updated, performing all of the necessary computations, and writing the updated record back to the file.
3. Draw an F/C matrix that shows the processing described above in the section "The Information System Performs Weekly Payroll Processing."

SELECTED BIBLIOGRAPHY

Bui, Tung. "Building Agent—Based Corporate Information Systems: An Application to Telemedicine." *European Journal of Operational Research* 122 (Number 2, April 16, 2000): 242-257.

Kim, H., Y. Ko, and J. Seo. "Implementation of An Efficient Requirements—Analysis Supporting System Using Similarity Measure Techniques." *Information & Software Technology* 42 (Number 6, April 15, 2000): 429-438.

Nakamori, Y., and Y. Sawaragi. "Complex Systems Analysis and Environmental Modeling." *European Journal of Operational Research* 122 (Number 2, April 16, 2000): 178-189.

Orr, Ken; Chris Gane, Edward Yourdon, Peter P. Chen, and Larry L. Constantine. "Methodology: The Experts Speak." *BYTE* 14 (April 1989): 221ff.

Saunders, Paul R. "Effective Interviewing Tips for Information Systems Professionals." *Journal of Systems Management* 42 (March 1991): 28-31.

Stevens, W. P.; G. J. Myers, and L. L. Constantine. "Structured Design." *IBM Systems Journal* 2 (Number 2, 1974): 115-39.

Volkner, P., and B. Werners. "A Decision Support System for Business Process Planning." *European Journal of Operational Research* 125 (Number 3, September 16, 2000): 633-647.

Warnier, Jean-Dominique. *Logical Construction of Systems*. New York: Van Nostrand Reinhold, 1981.

Yourdon, Edward, and Larry L. Constantine. *Structured Design: Fundamentals of a Discipline of Computer Program and Systems Design.* Englewood Cliffs, N.J.: Prentice-Hall, 1979.

NOTES

1. From Sandra Donaldson Dewitz, *Systems Analysis and Design and the Transition to Objects.* (New York: McGraw-Hill), 1996, 332.
2. This format follows that in Dewitz, 430-431.

TECHNICAL MODULE G

EVALUATION OF SYSTEMS SOLUTIONS

Choices are critical in every stage of the system development life cycle. For example:

- What is the best scope for the project?
- What is the best platform for implementation?
- Should we buy application software or create custom software?
- If we purchase application software, what is the best available software to meet project goals?
- If custom development is chosen, should end users or technical specialists create the software?

EVALUATION TABLES FOR TWO TO FOUR SOLUTIONS

When choices among a few possible solutions are difficult, the systems approach can be followed in making the selection. First, the choices are identified; then they are summarized in a way that helps clarify the issues for users; and finally the best is selected. An **evaluation table** is a quick way to create a summary for discussions among developers and users. The example in Figure G.1 illustrates the standard rows with columns for three possible solutions for a new bug tracking system for Casper Manufacturing. The final column for the "client decision" allows users to create a fourth solution that emerges from the discussion and best fits the users' objectives and constraints.

Susan Whittier, a developer in the IT Division of Casper Manufacturing, created the evaluation table in Figure G.1 to highlight early concerns she had about the scope of her executive sponsor's project request. Susan started the project with great enthusiasm. The vice president for technical support asked her to use her Web skills to create a new bug tracking system for complaints about the custom-developed sales system and other in-house systems that his unit supported. Her Web-enabled system should also include all the functions of the current IT help desk support system since he thought availability on Casper's intranet would improve user access tremendously.

FIGURE G.1

Sample Solution Evaluation Table

	Solution 1: Proceed with Initial Scope	Solution 2: Alter Scope to accommodate User Feedback	Solution 3: Alter Scope to Accommodate User Feedback and Supplement Current Systems	Client Decision
Key Features	Create a single bug tracking system that includes all the current functions of the bug tracking system and the IT help desk system	Enhance the existing bug tracking system. Leave the current IT help desk system as it is	Create a new bug tracking system independent of the IT help desk to help track bugs within the department Research needs by interviewing the IT help desk staff as well as users of the in-house systems	
Advantages	Will improve IT service to users due to better bug tracking and IT help desk information Integrated system using research from all current users of both systems will be the most efficient for all users	Least costly for development resources Custom enhancement of tracking system driven by user feedback Purchased software for IT help desk is already paid for so no additional funds are needed IT help desk knows the current system well and prefers not to change their process	Will improve IT service to users due to better bug tracking system Replaces only the bug tracking system, which is a relatively simple system that can be recreated quickly with a reasonable resource expenditure	
Dis-advantages	Most expensive to develop Proven and established systems already in use Political concerns with questioning IT help desk methodology	Users will continue to keep track of information in two applications at once Continued maintenance overhead for developers supporting applications	Users will have to keep track of information in two applications at once Additional maintenance overhead for developers supporting applications	
Questions	Is a business need not being met by the current systems?		Do the managers need this information?	

Susan began her preliminary investigation by interviewing sales personnel (the end users) and IT help desk personnel who currently supported the custom developed systems. She learned that few users supported the creation of a new bug tracking system. All of them had ideas about enhancements, but none of them wanted to learn a new system that would just be a little easier to access or "whatever the VP wants." Susan was afraid to tell the vice president directly that she thought the project would fail due to lack of end-user support. Instead she created the evaluation table in Figure G.1 to convey the suggestions made during the interviews. To create the table she identified possible scopes for the project based on the initial proposal by the vice president and the suggestions of the end users. She then summarized the key features of each solution, as well as its advantages and disadvantages. This table formed the basis of discussion for a reconsideration of the scope of the project. As the developer, Susan completed the first two steps of the evaluation process: identify possible solutions and summarize key issues. She presented her summary table to the vice president for the third step: select the appropriate solution based on this information or request that Susan repeat the process by considering additional solutions and gathering more information. When he insisted Susan continue with his initial request, she decided a risk evaluation would be an important task before her next review meeting.

Our second example of an evaluation table illustrates a way to present milestone lists when time and budget constraints force a review of the project scope. Figure G.2 is an evaluation of an orders tracking system for Casper Manufacturing.

Chul Lee was a new program manager at Casper Manufacturing. He wanted a system to manage the allocation of customer orders to the firm's manufacturing sites in several locations worldwide. The firm's program managers currently used their own methods—spreadsheets or word processing—to keep track of orders from customers, as well as specifications to complete these orders at manufacturing sites that promised the quickest completion and delivery. Most program managers wanted to keep their individual "systems" so there was little support among the user group for a single system. Chul's boss refused to approve a development budget since she did not want to force program managers to change their processes. She sympathized with Chul and thought that business process redesign would be a good idea. However, she thought company wide process changes would be too difficult at this time. All the program managers were too busy with the growth of Casper's product line and increased orders. Chul was unwilling to give up on process improvement, so he contacted a local university. He hoped that an IS student team might develop an initial system that would convince the established program managers that a company wide system would have great advantages over the current ad hoc processes.

The student team assigned to the project was shocked by the magnitude of the initial request. Chul wanted a complete system using an Oracle back end to be compatible with current in-house systems at Casper. After the student development team's first meeting with Chul and two other program managers, they created the table in Figure G.2 to show three alternate definitions of project scope. They wanted to be clear that additional development resources would be necessary to achieve their clients' initial choice. In the last row of their table they included a question about hiring an intern as a low cost way to continue their work. One student offered to continue in a paid part-time position. They also suggested the possibility of bringing in a contract developer or an in-house developer to complete the project. The high-level milestones presented with the table helped the program managers grasp the extent of the project and focus on the question of whether to increase development resources.

After a long discussion of the development team's solutions, the program managers decided that the best choice was Solution 1: Oracle back end with simple reports

FIGURE G.2

Sample Solution Evaluation Table with Milestone List

	Solution 1: Oracle Back End w/ Simple Reports	Solution 2: Limited Scope of Data with Prototype GUI	Solution 3: Proceed with Initial Scope and Requirements	Client Decision
Key Features	Good relational database model Test completeness with manufacturing sites and products	Prototype of portion of system	Oracle back-end with functioning GUI	
Advantages	Foundation for GUI implementation and future modifications Able to fit within time constraints of team	Prototype to show user groups Model data flow Show how system parts will be integrated	Functioning system	
Dis-advantages	Not fully complete No functioning front end	Incomplete back end Incomplete front end All elements of system not analyzed thoroughly	Will not fall within time constraints Lack of continuity in development Phases may be cut short due to time constraints	
Questions	Will this be sufficient? How important is GUI design?	Which functions need to be demonstrated?	Could firm hire a part- time intern to start in March or April & continue team's work?	

Milestones

Solution 1: Oracle back end w/ simple reports	**Target Completion Date**
1. Gather and analyze all requirements	3/12
2. Create E-R diagram of database relationships	3/26
3. Implement E-R diagram	4/23
4. Create queries & present for review of process	5/7
leaves one-week slack until final deadline for course	5/12

Solution 2: Limited scope of data with prototype GUI	**Target Completion Date**
1. Determine data to model	3/12
2. Gather requirements about data to be modeled	3/26
3. Implement database model	4/17
4. Design front end prototype	4/23
5. Code front end & present for review of process	5/7

Solution 3: Proceed with initial scope and requirements	**Target Completion Date**
1. Gather and analyze all requirements	3/12
2. Create E-R diagram of database relationships	3/26
3. Implement E-R diagram	4/23
4. Create queries	5/7
5. Design front end displays and reports	5/21 (past end date)
6. Code front end, test, train program managers, install	6/30

as a first step. If this was successful, they could approach their supervisor once again for resources to complete the system.

Evaluation Worksheets for Many Solutions

When many solutions are available, the systems approach is even more helpful in arriving at a choice that fits the requirements. The evaluation tasks are:

1. Identify the possible solutions
2. Determine the criteria
3. Evaluate the possible solutions
4. Select the best solution(s)

The process is similar to the evaluation of a few solutions, but each step will take longer. Several of the steps are likely to be repeated. The creation of an **evaluation worksheet** and identification of numeric weights and ratings helps speed the elimination of a large number of solutions. Our illustration will be the purchasing of application software, since the process for this choice is often long and detailed. The same process may be applied to all choices facing users and systems developers.

Purchasing application software that has already been tested and tried in many organizations reduces the risk of developing custom software that fails to meet users' requirements, saves development resources, and allows an organization to reap the benefits of a new system much faster than if the software was analyzed, designed, and built from scratch. Purchasing software does not eliminate the development process: all the main tasks of preliminary investigation and analysis must take place. Some design and construction tasks are also required. But much of the detailed work of analysis, design, and construction can be eliminated.

Step 1. Identify the Possible Solutions

If purchasing application software is considered viable, the first step after preliminary investigation is to identify available software packages to purchase to meet the objectives, constraints, and scope identified in preliminary investigation. For common business processes, a wealth of information is available. Seven sources of information to aid the process of identifying candidates for purchase are:

- *Internet research*—Popular search engines will lead you to a variety of sites. Examples of sites that have sections specializing in software research are www.cnet.com, www.zdnet.com and www.gartner.com.
- *Software vendors and their Web sites*—Demonstration versions of software or introductory tutorials are available for many software products.
- *Other organizations with similar needs*—This is the best resource for evaluation if a noncompetitor will share information.
- *Trade magazines and trade organization Web sites*—Industry specific resources often have articles and advertisements for software designed for their industry's needs.
- *Computer magazines*—They often include software product reviews for the most popular categories of software.

- *User groups*—These are great sources of public-domain software and users' opinions of software products; check computer journals, Yellow Pages, or the Internet for groups in your area.
- *Consultants*—Insist on references or choose a consultant based on other users' recommendations.

Quickly compiling a list of solutions speeds the evaluation process.

Step 2. Determine the Criteria

Any criteria can be used in making the evaluation; they will vary from one situation to another. If there are more than a half dozen possibilities, it is best to take a phased approach. Identify those first-cut criteria that are absolutely essential to purchase of the software. For example, a small company might choose to eliminate all software packages that cost more than $50,000 in their first evaluation of possible packages. A company with cash flow problems caused by errors in their accounts receivable software might consider three criteria for evaluating new accounts receivable software.

- Contract terms for payment after proven savings in accounts receivable processing
- Immediate installation with training available by vendor technical specialists to eliminate current problems as soon as possible
- Compatibility with current information architecture to minimize installation difficulties

Only software that met those initial first-cut criteria would be evaluated further.

Once the possibilities are reduced to about a half dozen, more detailed criteria are considered. An evaluation worksheet is illustrated in Figure G.3. The evaluation criteria are based on the categories of goal analysis conducted during the preliminary investigation phase. These categories are:

- System quality (SQ)
- Project management (PM)
- Organizational relevance (OR)

System quality includes functionality (SQ-FN), maintainability (SQ-M), and portability and scalability (SQ-P/S), as explained for goal analysis in Chapter 4. Project management includes time-to-develop (PM-T), cost (PM-C), and client commitment (PM-CC). Organizational relevance includes efficiency (OR-EFCY), effectiveness (OR-EFCT), and competitive advantage (OR-CA). The company with cash flow problems mentioned above has already determined organizational relevance. The criteria chosen for Figure G.4 are for the evaluation of software packages and vendors that have already met their first-cut criteria.

Step 3. Evaluate the Possible Solutions

Each evaluation criterion is given a weight ranging from 1 to 10 based on its relative importance, with 1 meaning *unimportant* and 10 meaning *critical to success.* Each alternative product is then evaluated on each criterion by assigning a raw score ranging from 1 for *poor* to 10 for *good.* The raw scores are multiplied by their criterion

FIGURE G.3

Evaluation Worksheet with Sample Criteria based on the Goal Analysis Categories

Evaluation Criteria	Weight*	Package 1		Package 2	
		Raw Rating**	Weighted Rating	Raw Rating**	Weighted Rating
SQ-FN: Completeness of functionality					
SQ-FN: Supports multiple users					
SQ-FN: Ease of learning					
SQ-FN: Ease of use					
SQ-FN: Quality of user interface					
SQ-FN: Adaptability to varying user levels					
SQ-FN: Quality of user documentation					
SQ-FN: Retrieval speed and memory requirements					
SQ-FN: Production environment stability					
SQ-M: Ability to customize					
SQ-M: Ease of maintenance					
SQ-M: Vendor support and services					
SQ-P/S: Compatibility with existing platforms and systems					
SQ-P/S: Ability of system to grow with company expansion					
PM-T: Installation and training					
PM-T: Development speed					
PM-C: Cost					
TOTAL SCORES					

* Weight from 1 (unimportant) to 10 (highly critical to success)
** Raw rating from 1 (poor) to 10 (good)

weights to obtain weighted scores, which are then summed. (If you use spreadsheet software the weighted scores and totals can be automatically generated by your spreadsheet.) The use of these criteria is only one approach but it should have value as a starting point. It is only logical that the software enable the firm to meet the goals that are established for the system.

The quantitative evaluation of software products is a semi-structured decision—some parts can easily be quantified and some cannot. Some items that the developers may consider when making the final software selection decision are:

- The vendor's financial stability
- Documentation
- Technical support

These items are grouped together as the last SQ-M criteria in Figure G.4, but are likely to be considered in more depth for the final two or three best software choices. When you select a vendor, you want to be assured that it will remain in operation for at least as long as the expected life of the system. You also want to purchase products that are well documented to make it easier to use them and perhaps modify them as needed. Also, you want to select a vendor with a good reputation for always being available to provide support when difficulties are encountered. If the firm has previously purchased products from a vendor, the evaluation of the documentation and technical support is based on this past history, as well as the sample documentation provided for the new purchase.

The developers, users, and project sponsors give much attention to the determination of the evaluation criteria since they influence the vendor choice. The criteria are selected that best fit the particular situation. For example, the vendor characteristics of financial stability, documentation, and technical support could be incorporated into the evaluation worksheets for either the first level of evaluation or a second, more detailed evaluation, or the final evaluation of possible software purchases.

FIGURE G.4

Evaluation Worksheet for CRM Software for Torres Insurance (page 1 of 5)

		Package 1		Package 2	
Evaluation Criteria	**Weight***	**Raw Rating****	**Weighted Rating**	**Raw Rating****	**Weighted Rating**
PM-C: Cost of software	10	8	80	5	50
PM-C: Cost of hardware upgrades	10	10	100	4	40
SQ-M: Vendor support and services, especially Help Line	9	3	27	9	81
SQ-FN: Good business practices followed	9	5	45	9	81
SQ-FN: Ease of use	9	8	72	7	63
SQ-FN: Quality of user tutorial for database set up & use	7	0	0	5	35
SQ-FN: Quality of user documentation	7	5	35	6	42
SQ-FN: Ease of learning	5	7	35	5	25
SQ-FN: Retrieval speed	3	5	15	8	24
SQ-FN: Memory requirements	3	10	30	7	21
SQ-FN: Supports multiple users	3	0	0	8	24
SQ-P/S: Ability of system to grow with Gail's expansion	8	3	24	5	40
TOTAL SCORES	83		463		526

* Weight from 1 (unimportant) to 10 (highly critical to success)
** Raw rating from 1 (poor) to 10 (good)

Step 4. Select the Best Solution(s)

After completing the worksheets, the developers then meet for the purpose of making a selection. Perhaps the meeting can take the form of a JAD session. For the first round of evaluations, the choice may be to select the five to eight products that meet the initial first-cut criteria. The developers then repeat tasks 2 and 3: determine more detailed criteria and evaluate each of the finalists or semi-final choices on these criteria. The developers may write a request for proposal (RFP) and distribute this to the five to eight vendors that meet the initial first-cut. In that situation the detailed criteria are included as specifications in the RFP. (A discussion of the process for RFPs and vendor responses is included in Chapter 8 along with outlines for a typical RFP and vendor proposal in Figures 8.5 and 8.6.)

The final two or three choices are evaluated on the basis of a series of performance tests or benchmarks. A vendor who has responded to an RFP might perform the testing, but the tests should always be based on user specifications determined in the preliminary investigation. The users and project sponsors make the final choice based on research conducted and summarized by developers.

Evaluation of Solutions for Customer Relationship Management (CRM)

In Chapter 4 we introduced you to Gail Torres, an independent insurance agent and owner of Torres Insurance. To automate her financial record keeping and create a Web site to increase sales, Gail hired an IT consultant recommended by her CPA. The consultant recommended an accounting package for small businesses, like Torres Insurance. He installed it, set up the chart of accounts for Torres Insurance, and trained Gail to use it. He also recommended a custom-developed Web-based system to provide insurance premium quotes to customers and aid Gail in tracking sales. The goal analysis for this system and the identification of the objectives and scope for Torres Insurance are presented in Figures 4.11 and 4.12. A risk evaluation and a table of the risk reduction strategies for Torres Insurance are presented in Figures 4.13 and 4.14. It is clear from these preliminary investigation tasks that a major risk for this one-person business is managing and maintaining a custom system since Gail has no computer skills beyond word processing. After talking with her CPA once again, Gail decided to research purchasing software for customer relationship management (CRM). The CPA explained that CRM is the term for software that provides a wide range of functions that help companies reach customers and stay in contact with them. "There are inexpensive CRM packages now available," the CPA continued, "that can track customers and sales for Torres Insurance."

Step 1. Identify the Possible Solutions

Gail began her research on the Internet, using a few tips she learned from the IT consultant. When she entered "customer relationship management" in a popular search engine, she was surprised to find 5,050 links. She next tried www.techrepublic.com. Most of the 452 vendors listed on this site for CRM seemed to offer services beyond the needs or resources of her small firm. At this point she worked out a second contract with the IT consultant who had installed the accounting software. This contract specified that he would help her evaluate CRM packages as well as complete the installation and training process for the CRM package chosen.

Step 2. Determine the Criteria

To determine criteria, the IT consultant first reviewed the objectives, constraints, and scope they had identified earlier, expanding those objectives and requirements focused on customer tracking functions. Together they identified two first-cut criteria: price and the stability of the vendor. Gail wanted a product that would be supported or upgraded for at least the next five years.

The IT consultant identified five CRM packages that cost less than $500 per computer user. He and Gail then identified more detailed criteria and created a worksheet to evaluate all five packages. They weighted each of the criteria in order of its importance to Torres Insurance. Figure G.4 is one page of the evaluation worksheet and shows the evaluation of the top two packages.

Cost was included again as a criterion since initial costs for the software ranged from a little more than $100 to almost $500. Cost of hardware upgrades to meet the package specifications also varied. Since Gail had little business experience, one highly weighted criterion was the quality of the business processes followed by the software.

Step 3. Evaluate the Possible Solutions

The IT consultant obtained test versions of the software and sample documents from all five vendors, either by downloading them from the vendor Web site or by contacting the vendor. Gail rated each alternative product on ease of use, quality of the user tutorial, quality of user documentation, and ease of learning. The IT consultant rated the packages on all the other criteria.

Step 4. Select the Best Solution(s)

After entering the ratings in the worksheets and calculating the total weighted ratings they focused their selection on the two products with the highest total scores. (See Figure G.4.) Gail noted that Package 1 was less expensive and easier to learn because it had fewer features. She selected Package 2 because it had the highest total score and, considering the differences in these top two products, she thought this would be the best choice for growing her business and improving her business processes while still staying within her financial constraints.

Putting the Evaluation of Possible Solutions in Perspective

Evaluation of possible solutions is a key task repeated many times throughout the system development life cycle. Often the evaluation will be a quick verbal exchange among experienced developers. If the developers understand the users' requirements and the organization's strategic plan for information resources, their quick brain storming of possibilities and mental review of criteria may lead to the right selection with little effort. If the evaluation is based on a limited or incorrect perception of system objectives, constraints, and requirements and the organization's current infrastructure and strategic plan, the final selection will probably be a poor one. No amount of researching the choices or systematically weighting criteria and rating the options can lead to the right solution unless the process is based on a foundation of clear information about the system objectives, constraints, and requirements and the organization's current infrastructure and strategic plan.

Key Terms

evaluation table
evaluation worksheet

Problems

1. Review preliminary investigation research for Gail Torres that is summarized in Figures 4.11, 4.12, 4.13, and 4.14. Should Gail Torres develop custom software for a Quoting Web Site and Sales Tracking System or purchase application software for these functions? Create an evaluation worksheet to answer this question. Identify one alternative as "Custom Development" and the other alternative as "Package Software." List at least six criteria relevant to this question in the first column of your worksheet. Choose appropriate weights and rate custom development and purchased software in the raw ratings columns. Multiply the weights and raw ratings to fill in the weighted ratings columns. Total your weighted scores and write a short answer to the question based on your total scores. (Note that this is an evaluation of approaches to creating the software component of the system, not an evaluation of specific packages.)
2. A chain restaurant with three locations and 150 staff members wants to purchase software to handle customer orders, create customer checks, and track sales. They currently have no information technology staff, but instead rely on a CPA for their payroll, record keeping, and tax reporting. Create an evaluation worksheet to compare vendors offering hardware and software that would network the three locations and provide the basic restaurant functionality they require. Identify two possible vendors as "Vendor 1" and "Vendor 2." Use the goal analysis categories to list at least fifteen criteria relevant to comparing vendors. Choose appropriate weights so that your worksheet is complete up to the point of actually identifying and rating specific vendors.

Case Problem: Charter Oak Insurance Company

Charter Oak Insurance Company is a major player in the Insurance business in the USA with branches in all major cities. Their main data center is located in Patterson, New Jersey, and the annual IS budget is in the $120 million range. There are about 600 full-time IS staff members and they are routinely augmented by consultants who enable the permanent staff to quickly gain competency in such emerging areas as client/server technologies and object-oriented methodologies. The consultants are usually about twice as costly as full-time staff but Ken Rosenthal, the Charter president, figures that it is a price worth paying to avoid continually retraining his staff on the newer technologies.

Most computer applications perform such accounting functions as policy issue, premium billing, and claims payment. Charter is in the process of considering Web-enabled versions of the accounting systems.

Existing System Architecture

The hardware is largely based on IBM mainframes and PCs. The system configuration consists of one IBM 3090 mainframe (which is located at the main data center in New Jersey), 25 IBM AS/400 mainframes (one at each branch office), and over 1800 PCs.

The systems use a 3-tier client/server approach that consists of front-end PC's, back-end AS/400s that act as servers, and the IBM 3090 that serves as the host. The implementation is distributed and is spread over the AS/400s at various locations across the country. IBM's SNA communication protocol is used for communication between the different layers of the architecture.

Charter has fourteen major application systems, totaling about 8 million lines of COBOL code. These systems have been developed over many years and are customized to the specific needs of the company. Studies indicate that on a daily basis, about 1200 employees use their PCs for 8 hours daily, 5 days a week.

Even though Charter is operating in a client/server environment, their applications are deeply rooted in COBOL. Even the user interfaces are written in COBOL. These systems provide much flexibility but maintenance and enhancement are very difficult as the user requirements change and new user requests are received. Overall, the IS department operates in a very professional manner with standards for practically everything—user interface, coding, maintenance, and documentation. Proof of the professional status of the IS division is the ISO 9000-3 quality certification that was awarded in 1998.

Information Systems Organization

Carol Skudera is vice president of information systems in charge of three key systems: the adjuster workstation system (AWS, about 700,000 lines of COBOL), the producer billing system (PBS, about 650,000 lines of COBOL) and the credit reinsurance and recovery system (CRRS, about 330,000 lines of COBOL). Mary Jane Faulkner, an assistant vice president reporting to Carol, has responsibility for managing the AWS and PBS systems with about 40 IS staff reporting to her. Bob Hackett is another assistant vice president reporting to Carol, who manages the CRRS system with the assistance of his IS staff of about 16.

Preliminary Planning for New Systems Architecture

Ken, Carol, Mary Jane, and Bob have had several meetings and have come to the conclusion that they should either rewrite their applications or purchase software to make full use of the newer technologies, especially Web technology and component-based development approaches. They envision that the new systems will provide significant benefits in terms of reducing redundant data entry and enhancing user satisfaction. The new systems should have better designed user interfaces, greater functionality than the present systems, and be easier to maintain.

Description of Systems to be Replaced

AWS is the system that handles the worker's compensation line of business. It electronically captures all information needed to settle a claim, and is comprised of fourteen different modules.

The PBS is an accounts receivable system that facilitates the collection, payment, and analysis of producer premiums and commissions. The agents who sell the policies are called producers. The PBS is comprised of eighteen different modules.

The credit reinsurance and recovery system (CRRS) identifies those claims for which reinsurance is available and provides a user interface that can be used to work on claims, and create proofs of loss, loss advices, and forms for recovering the losses. The CRRS consists of 23 different modules.

All three systems are broadly divided into online and batch functions.

Assignment

Assume that these steps of systems development have been completed:

1. Initial research has been conducted on functionality of all three systems, including extensive user interviews.
2. PBS has been chosen as the first system to be redeveloped, since it has the greatest potential for an early return on investment. This is because the data center that key enters hand-written applications will be eliminated.
3. Ten software packages have been selected for consideration.

Review the evaluation worksheet in Figure G.3 as the basis for an evaluation of software packages for Charter Oak Insurance Company. Your task is to consider the criteria and determine whether they are suited to supporting the software decisions that will have to be made. Are there criteria that should not be considered? Are there additional criteria that should be added?

Assume that you are a consultant, hired to assist Carol in making the software selection decision. Write a memo to her that includes your revised version of Figure G.3, and explain why your evaluation worksheet should be the basis for a software evaluation for Charter Oak Insurance Company.

SELECTED BIBLIOGRAPHY

Beath, C. M., and G. Walker. "Outsourcing of Application Software: A Knowledge Management Perspective" *Proceedings of the 31st Annual HICSS,* Vol. VI, January 1998, pp. 666-674.

Ameen, David A. "Evaluating Alternative Computer Acquisition Strategies." *Journal of Systems Management* 41 (September 1990): 15-20.

Nelson, P., W. Richmond, and A. Seidman. "Two Dimensions of Software Acquisition" *Communications of the ACM,* July 1996, Vol. 39, No. 7, pp. 29-35.

CASE STUDY INSTALLMENT 4

ADVANCED SYSTEM TECHNOLOGY ASSOCIATES

DESIGNING THE ASTA SYSTEM

It is the end of Week 7 of the ASTA project, and the team is still in the analysis, design, and preliminary construction loop. They have been through the loop twice-once for the project management reports module and once for the skills inventory database design module. Those modules were completed a little ahead of schedule. This put the team on track in terms of completing the project by the end of the semester, which is nice since the team members want to spend the holidays wrapping up something other then a term project. The Gantt was rerun with the new times and everything was due to be finished by Week 12.

With the second delivery report due at the end of next week, the team finds itself once again juggling several balls. In addition to completing the delivery report, Sean and Tracy are trying to finish the skills data entry module, Rachel and Kim are working on the employee update module, and Gary is working solo on the security login module. Once these modules are completed, the team is out of the loop and can concentrate its efforts on final construction and installation.

Pinpointing Their Position on the Gantt

The team has been meeting every Friday in the snack bar since the project began and they have assembled once again. The Gantt chart is in its regular place, as is Rachel, using it as a checklist of items to discuss.

"Sean and Tracy," Rachel asks, "Where are you in data entry? Have you finished construction? That was supposed to be done last week."

"That's finished," Tracy explained. "We are going to review it with several users next week and then install a Beta version on Yolanda's machine to give her the opportunity to test it out."

"Speaking of Beta versions, Yolanda and the project managers really like the Beta of the database. Tracy, you and Kim really did a good job."

"Thanks, Rachel," Kim said. "Let me tell the group how our work with the employee update module is going. I can see that question coming. We've determined the update requirements and have designed the interface. We're set to construct it, starting this weekend, right after we finish working on the second delivery."

"This all sounds very good," Rachel said. "We're in good shape to get on with final construction. As soon as Gary finishes the security login module, we have clear sailing. But, the rest of us can get started even if Gary is still tied up. Gary, how much longer?"

"I can't say for sure, Rachel. It's taking a little more time than I anticipated. I'm really not supposed to review it with Yolanda and Sue for another week, but I should be able to beat that. Give me a couple more days and I should be finished."

Planning the Second Delivery Report

Satisfied that the team was on course, Rachel folded up the Gantt chart and pulled the second delivery report requirements out of her backpack. "Let's see what we are going to have to do to get the report ready by next Friday." The Cowboy Programmers pulled out their copies of the report specs and Rachel continued, "We need a status report. That is very important. I can do it since it's based on the Gantt. The next section is revised planning. We've been able to stick to the Gantt really well. I'll rerun the Gantt showing the week that we picked up during phases 2 and 3. As usual, any time we update the Gantt, I'll e-mail a copy to Yolanda."

Rachel continued, "The big items are a users manual and a developers manual. We have a lot of things for the developers manual—all the documentation that we produced for the first delivery goes in. So, we're in good shape there. Looking ahead in the Gantt—Kim, you and Tracy and Sean have the responsibility for putting the developers manual together. Actually, all we need for the second delivery is a table of contents."

Tracy looked at Sean and Kim. "We might as well do the TOC right after the meeting." Sean and Kim, as well as Rachel, put their seal of approval on Tracy's suggestion.

Attention then turned to the users manual. Gary decided to take charge. "I'm really not as bad off as everyone thinks. While you guys do the developers manual, I can whip out the users manual TOC. When do we need it by, Rachel?"

"The report is due Friday. Let's shoot for Tuesday."

With a good idea of what should go in the second delivery report and who would provide it, the developers manual group got together, and Gary headed back to his apartment, promising to work on the users manual.

FIGURE CS 4.1

Developer Manual Table of Contents

Developer Manual Table of Contents

ASSEMBLING THE FIRST DELIVERY REPORT

At the Tuesday meeting, Rachel followed the sequence of the report. She began by asking Tracy if she ran off copies of the developers manual table of contents (which she had), and Tracy passed them around the table. See Figure CS 4.1. It received a lot of support. The team liked the idea of a system overview followed by the various technical sections. It seemed well organized.

Rachel then asked Gary for the users manual TOC, which he held up for the rest of the group to see. "Well what do you know? I didn't go back to the apartment to go to sleep the other day after all." Figure CS 4.2 shows the fruits of Gary's work.

"But that's not all, folks," Gary said in his Porky Pig voice. Since Gary was running Sean a tight race for Team Clown, nobody was surprised at Gary's imitation. "I'd like to make an announcement. I just accepted a job offer from one of the Systems Development clients last semester—Virtual Realty." All the other Cowboy Programmers and the Gantt Chart Queen expressed their congratulations. Gary continued "The only problem, and it's really not a problem at all, is that they are big on object-oriented development, using UML. I'd really like to get some experience in using it before going to work. I checked out the object modeling technical module in the textbook and I think I can put together some of the diagrams using ASTA data. In addition to the data modeling ERD and the process modeling DFDs, it would round out the picture. And, since OO is supposed to be the coming thing, it might be of real value to anybody who continues to work on this system. I can't have the diagrams in time for the second delivery, but we can certainly put them in the final delivery. What about it?"

Everybody was sort of stunned by Gary's proposal. It was the first real break from the development strategy that the team had followed since the beginning of the project. Not fully seeing how Gary's UML diagrams would fit in with everything else, the team told him to "give it a try and see what you come up with."

Hoping that the meeting was over and there were no more startling announcements, Rachel collected all of the second delivery documents that had been discussed and said that she would have the report put together by Thursday. She asked that the team reassemble at the same place for the purpose of reviewing it before copies are made.

FIGURE CS 4.2

Users Manual Table of Contents

Users Manual Table of Contents

FIGURE CS 4.3

Create Skill Set Use Case

Use case name:	**Create skill set**
Description:	**Covers creating skill matrix for employees**
Prerequisites:	**Create employee**
Associations:	**Main menu**
Principle Actor:	**Employee**

Employee	**System**
1.0 Employee logs on with a password 1.0-B Employee logs on as a new employee	2.0 System verifies employee and prompts user to enter additional information 2.0-B System recognizes employee as a new employee and provides password
2.1 Employee enters name, phone number, e-mail address, and skill level	2.1 Go to 3.0
3.0 Employee creates new skill set matrix	4.0 System displays system time, date, and user name on the screen
5.0 Employee requests to create skill set	6.0 System creates and saves employee profile and skill set
7.0 Employee requests to see main menu	8.0 System displays main menu
9.0 Employee logs off	10.0 System logs employee off

PRESENTING THE SECOND DELIVERY REPORT

At the Thursday meeting, Rachel passed around the report for everyone to give a final check. Copies were made, and an appointment was made with Yolanda to present the report the next Monday. Yolanda said that Mel would be present as planned, so the team brought along his copy as well. Rachel followed the same section-by-section approach that she used for presenting the first report. Both of the clients liked what they saw and were excited about the prospects of having their skill set system in just a few more weeks. Being the leader of a project-oriented company, Mel could appreciate the speed with which the team was meeting its challenge and told them to keep up their good work.

As the team walked to their cars, Sean said, “Well, check off delivery number two.”

ADDING OBJECT-ORIENTED DOCUMENTATION

A couple of weeks later, at the team meeting, Gary showed the team the UML documentation that he had prepared.

“This turned out to be a much bigger job than I thought. At first, I was thinking of about three diagrams, but I've ended up with eight.”

One word described the team reaction: “Wow.”

"The place to start was the use case. I have three narrative ones and two graphic ones. Here's one for creating the skill set." See Figure CS 4.3. "This is called a ping pong format, where the actions of the user and the system go back and forth. The numbers tell the sequence."

"There's also one for searching the skill set." See Figure CS 4.4

"And, here's one for requesting reports." See Figure CS 4.5.

"And, as you know from the class lecture on UML, there's a use case diagram. Here is what I came up with." See Figure CS 4.6 on page 349.

"I call this my high-level use case diagram. You can see the use cases—the ovals—create the skill set, update it, and search it, and two using use cases—create proposal and request report. The three stick figures all pointing to the project manager show the types of managers. Now, it's possible to show more detail for one of these use cases by drilling down to a lower level. That is what I've done with this one." Gary passed around Figure CS 4.7 on page 350. "This shows the detail for searching the skill set."

Once we have the use cases, we have a really solid foundation for the UML diagrams. Here's the class diagram. The three classes at the top are generalization associations—the three types of project managers that you can have." See Figure CS 4.8 on page 351. "Each class includes an identification of its attributes and the operations it performs."

FIGURE CS 4.4

Search Skill Set Use Case

Use case name:	**Search skill set**
Description:	**Covers searching skill set**
Prerequisites:	**Create project manager**
Associations:	**Main menu**
Principle Actor:	**Project manager (Sales, Research & Development, Manufacturing)**

Project Manager	**System**
1.0 Project manager logs on with a password	2.0 System verifies project manager 2.1 System verifies password 2.1-B System denies entry 2.2 Go to 3.0
3.0-B Project manager logs off	
4.0 Project manager selects search criteria 4.1 Project manager enters name as search criterion 4.2 Project manager selects department as search criterion 4.3 Project manager selects position as search criterion 4.4 Project manager selects specific skills as search criteria	6.0 System matches search criteria 6.0-B System does not match search criteria 7.0 System displays search results 7.0-B System displays error message 7.1 Go to 4.0 9.0-B System logs project manager off
5.0-B Project manager requests system to search	
8.0 Project manager logs off 8.0-A Project manager returns to main menu	

FIGURE CS 4.5

Request Reports Use Case

Use case name:	**Request reports**
Description:	**Covers creating reports for managers**
Prerequisites:	**Create manager**
Associations:	**Main menu**
Principle actor:	**Manager**

Manager	**System**
1.0 Manager logs on with a password 1.1 Go to 3.0 3.0 User logs off 4.0 Manager creates customized reports based on his/her criteria 4.1 Manager inputs start and end dates and requests to see information based on the dates 5.0 Manager selects report type 5.1 Manager requests to view team summary report 5.2 Manager requests to view skill summary report 5.3 Manager requests to view management summary report 5.4 Manager requests to view available employee summary report 7.0 Manager logs off	2.0 System verifies manager 2.0-B System cannot verify password 2.1 Go to 3.0 2.2 System displays system time, date, and user name 6.0 System displays requested report 8.0 System logs manager off

"And then we take the three object classes and they form the basis for the sequence diagram." See Figure CS 4.9 on page 352. "The arrows represent messages flowing from one class to another.

"And, here's one that I really like." Sean cheers and everyone else (including Gary) laughs. "It's the statechart diagram. It shows the various states that an object can assume. This shows the various states of a skill set—created, updated, deleted, and finally archived." See Figure CS 4.10 on page 353.

Nobody could believe that Gary had done so much in such a short time. "That's what the motivation of getting a job can do for you," Gary explained.

The Gantt chart queen could see the value of the added documentation. "These are really good. We definitely should include them in our final delivery report. And, I think we should include them in our final report presentation. All of the project managers will be there and this will add a lot of emphasis to what we've done. It should be clear that we are trying to be as thorough as possible."

This plan met with the approval of the Cowboy Programmers and the meeting was adjourned. The team set out to address the final two phases of the project—final construction and installation.

FIGURE CS 4.6

High Level Use Case Diagram

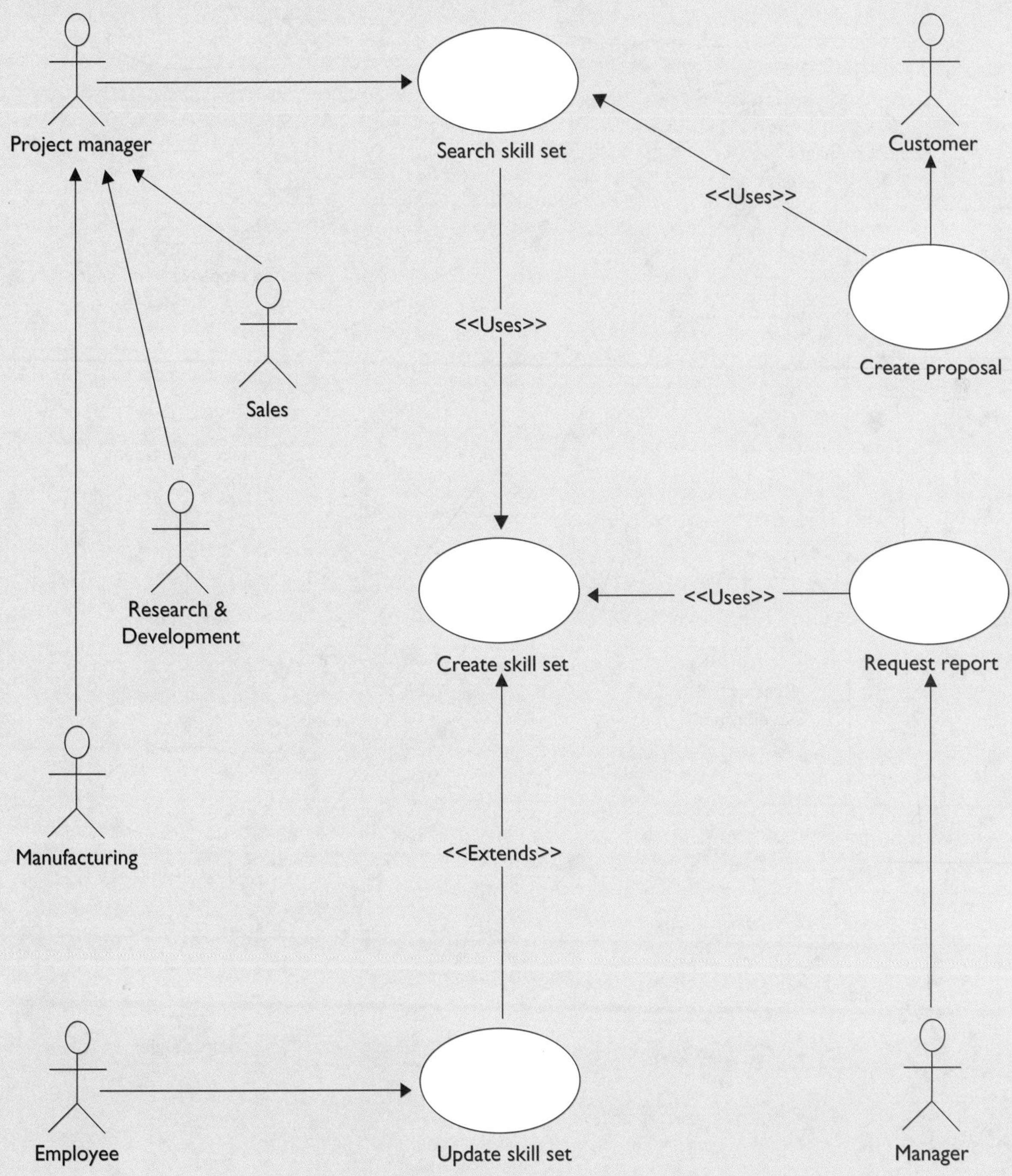

FIGURE CS 4.7

Drill Down Use Case Diagram for Search Skill Set

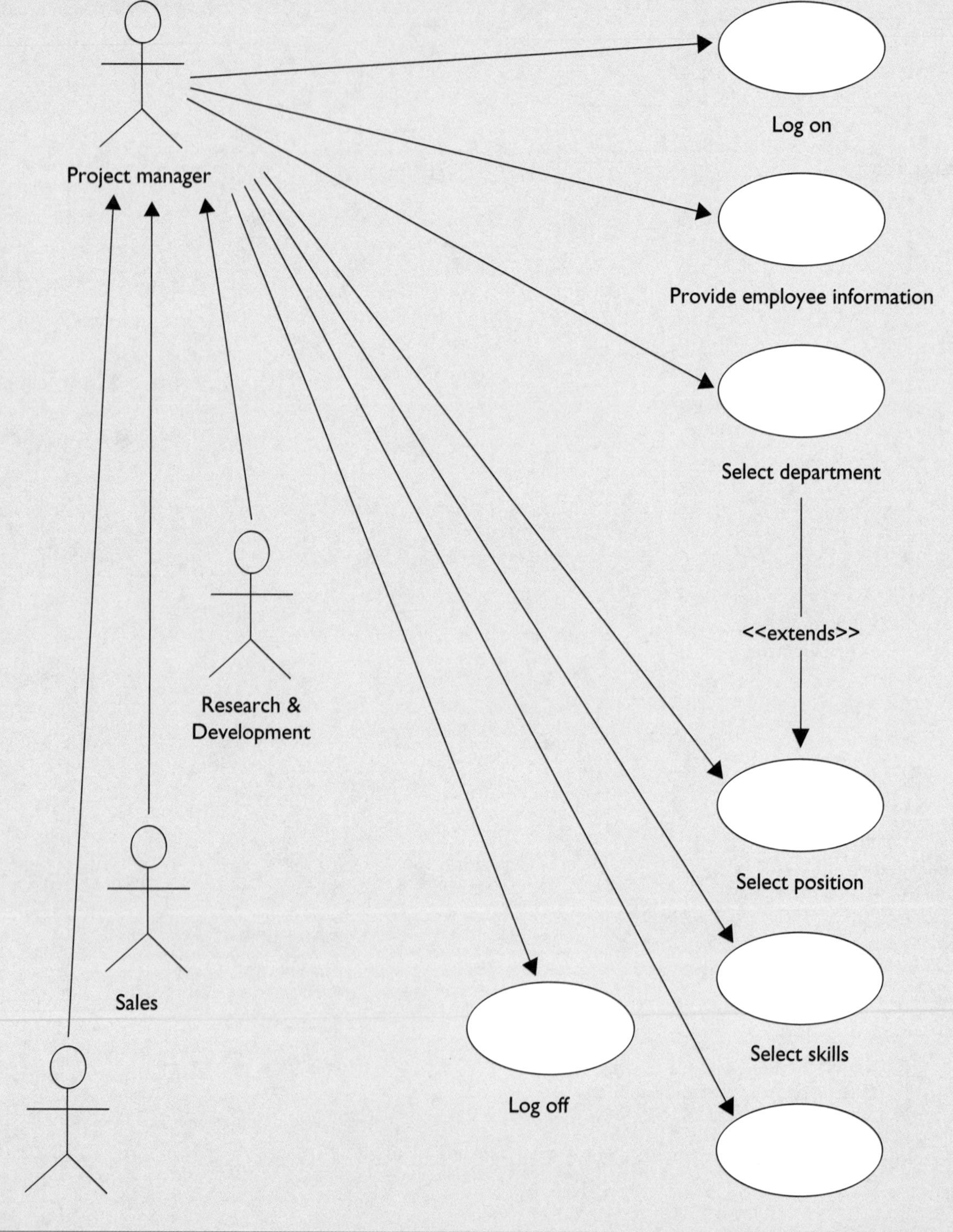

FIGURE CS 4.8

Class Diagram

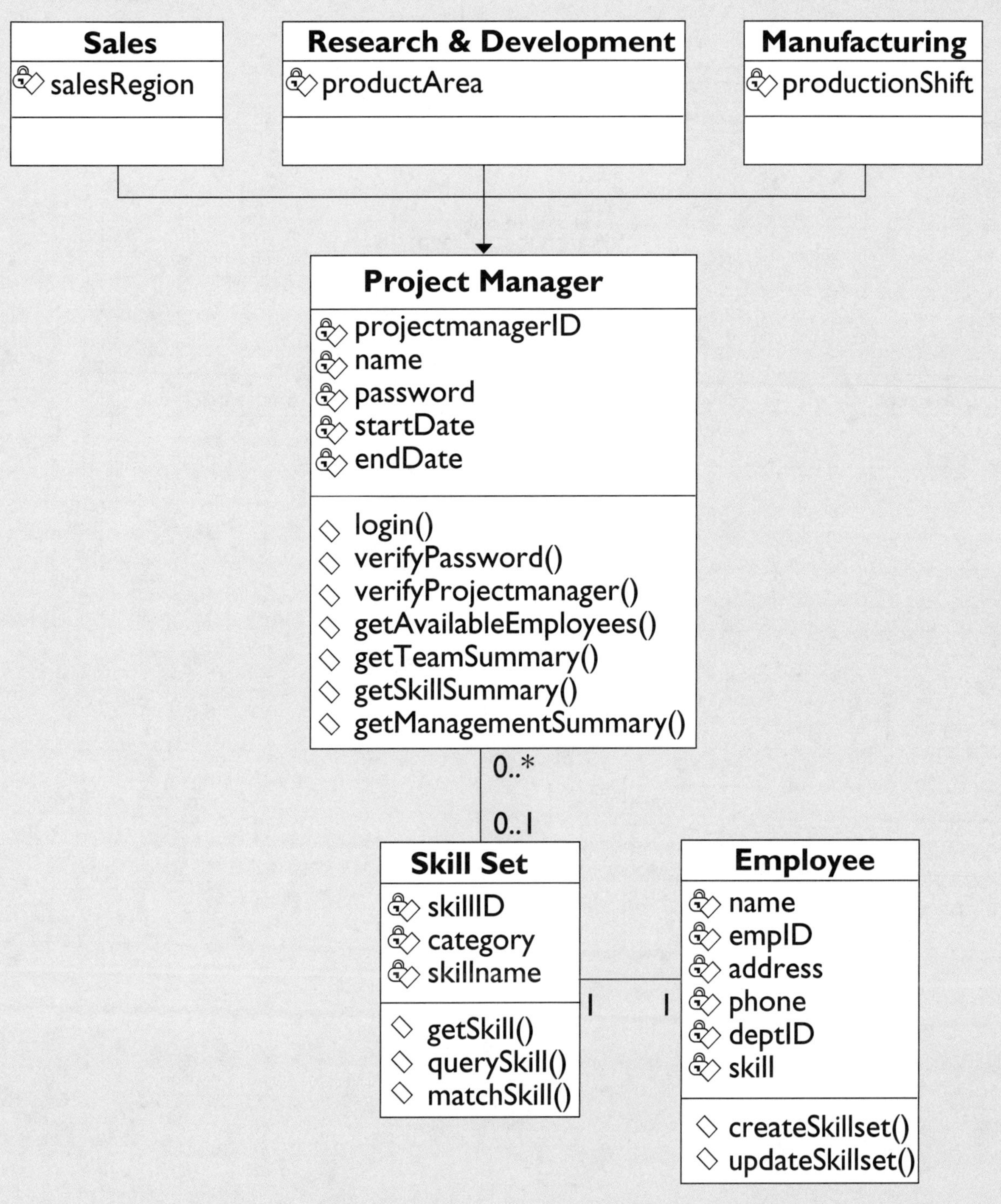
Sales
salesRegion
Research & Development
productArea
Manufacturing
productionShift
Project Manager
projectmanagerID
name
password
startDate
endDate
login()
verifyPassword()
verifyProjectmanager()
getAvailableEmployees()
getTeamSummary()
getSkillSummary()
getManagementSummary()
0..*
0..1
Skill Set
skillID
category
skillname
getSkill()
querySkill()
matchSkill()
1
1
Employee
name
empID
address
phone
deptID
skill
createSkillset()
updateSkillset()

FIGURE CS 4.9

Sequence Diagram

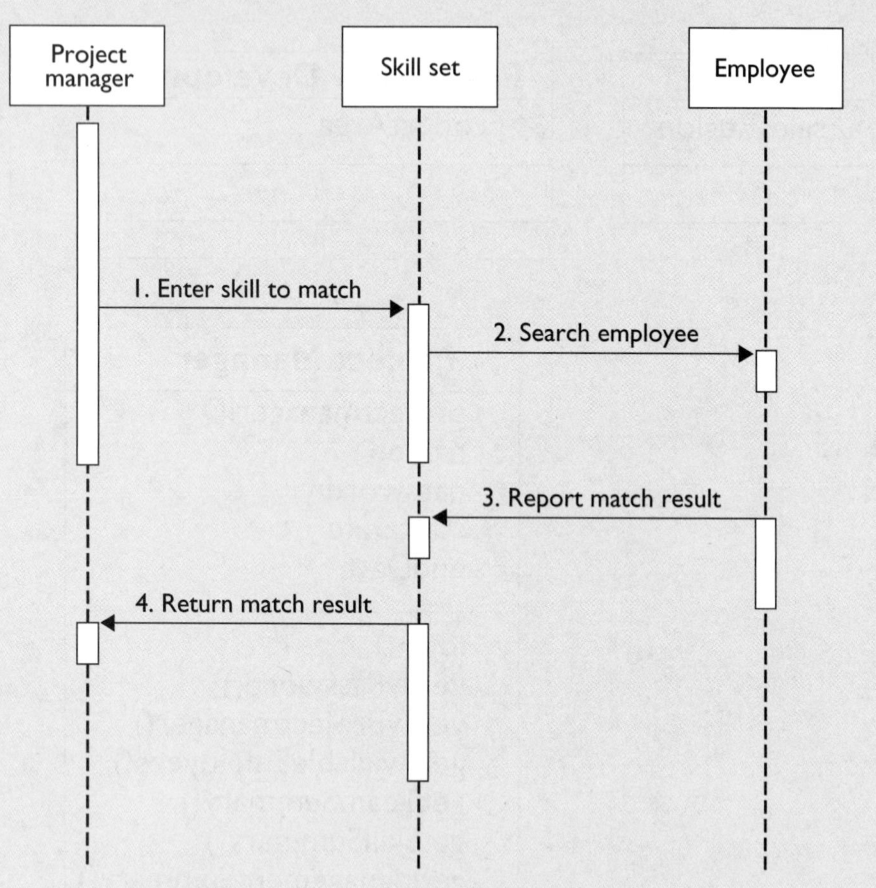

FIGURE CS 4.10

Statechart Diagram

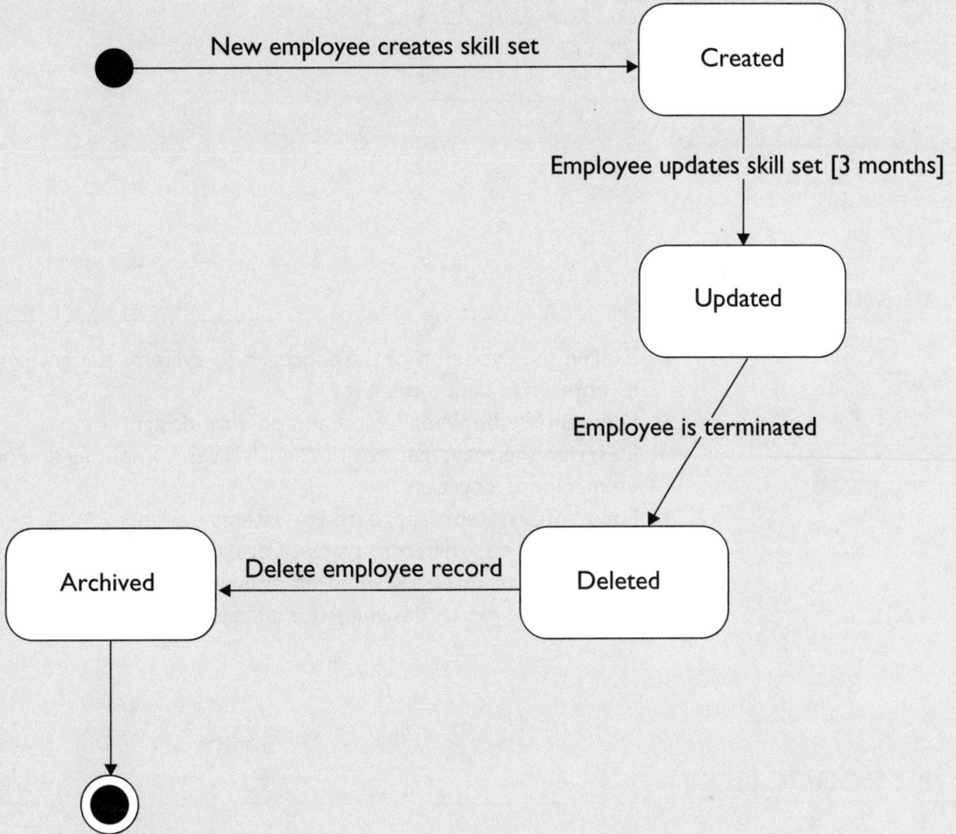

CHAPTER 6

SYSTEMS DESIGN

LEARNING OBJECTIVES

- Explain the evolution of the approach to systems design, from document preparation to enterprise data modeling.
- Differentiate between logical and physical design.
- Describe the main features of client/server computing and how it can be implemented in varying degrees.
- Follow the systems approach to systems design.
- Describe the six different types of design and how to approach each one.
- Know how to make a structured evaluation of alternate system configurations.
- Identify the keys to designing the different types of information systems.

INTRODUCTION

In the last two chapters we focused on issues and techniques for the preliminary investigation and analysis stages of the system development life cycle. In this chapter, our focus is design stage activities. The design activities follow those of analysis and precede those of preliminary construction, as these three phases are repeated for each system module.

The design task consists of three steps—design the system components, design interfaces with other systems, and document the design. The designs of early information systems featured an approach emphasizing the preparation of output documents but current sentiment favors an enterprise-wide approach featuring a central database, called a data warehouse.

There are two basic types of system design—logical and physical. Logical design is the specification of the processing and the data that are necessary to transform system input into output. Physical design is the specification of technology-specific details for the acquisition and assembly of the information resources that are necessary to accomplish the transformation.

Early computer architectures featured mainframe computers with users gaining access by means of terminals—mainframe computing. This configuration evolved to one where users have the option of performing computations on their own workstations or on a central server—client/server computing. Client/server designs are being adapted to the Internet to gain greater scalability, maintainability, and global access with Web-based system development.

The systems approach lends itself to systems design. Alternate configurations can be identified and evaluated, and the best one selected. For each configuration, it is necessary to engage in six types of design effort—user interface, data, procedure, software, system interface, and system control. Once the alternative configurations have been designed, they can be evaluated quantitatively to provide a structured basis for the selection of the one to be constructed.

Each type of system in the information infrastructure has its own characteristics that call for special knowledge and skill. In addition, developers should take advantage of all human and software resources that can contribute to good design.

DESIGN TASKS

The placement of design activities in a loop with analysis and preliminary construction, as shown in Figure 6.1, is a key feature of the user-driven phased development process. After the user requirements are analyzed for a portion of the system, a solution is designed and then constructed so that users can review the solution and provide feedback before continuing with the analysis, design, and construction of the next portion of the system. Each of the repeated design stages consists of three steps:

1. Design new system components.
2. Design interfaces with other systems
3. Document the new system design.

In the systems analysis stage we recognized that the documentation of the new system functional requirements is accomplished *concurrently* with the analysis of the requirements. The same holds true here. Design documentation is not an afterthought, but is an integral part of design.

THE EVOLUTION OF APPROACHES TO SYSTEMS DESIGN

During the relatively brief history of the computer, four basic approaches have been followed in designing information systems. The approaches have emphasized document preparation, problem solving, the database, and, most recently, the enterprise data model.

The Document Preparation Approach

The early *accounting information systems* were developed in a two-step fashion. First, each system, such as inventory and billing, was designed with an emphasis on the processes that transform input into output. Then, all of the systems were integrated by linking the inputs and outputs. The designs reflected an output emphasis on such accounting documents as income statements, invoices, and payroll checks. Since the systems were designed separately, each one tended to be an island, with its own data files.

The Organizational Problem-Solving Approach

Beginning in the mid-1960s, firms implemented *management information systems* on an organization-wide basis, but there was no grand plan for integrating the separate

FIGURE 6.1

Design Phase Overview

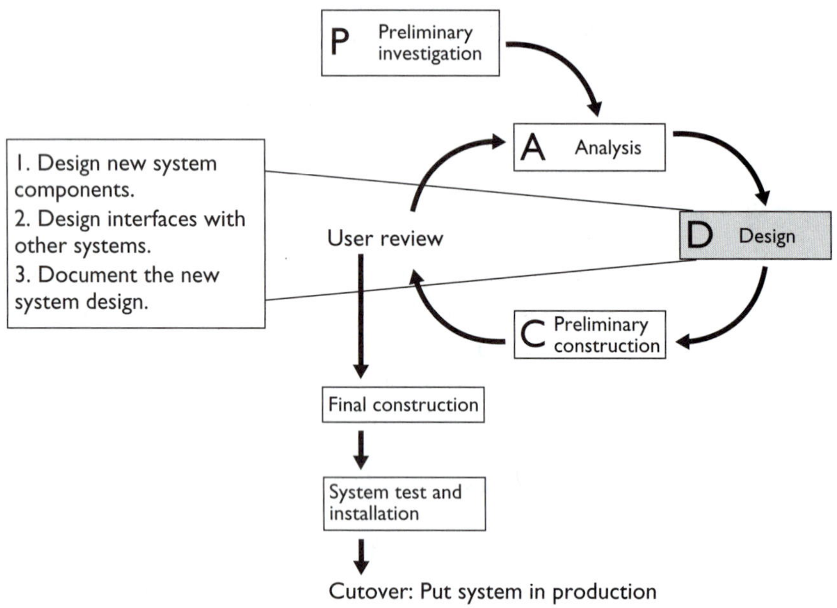

systems. As a result, the development process continued the same bottom-up emphasis on processes. Separate data files, often incompatible, were typical.

The Organizational Database Approach

During the early 1970s, two events occurred that had a dramatic effect on systems design. One was the availability of *database management system (DBMS)* software that permitted the creation and maintenance of a database that could be shared by users throughout the firm. The DBMS signaled the beginning of a shift in emphasis from processes to data. The other influence was a refocusing of system scope on specific problems of individual managers—the *decision support system (DSS)* approach.

The key feature of the DSS era has been the organizational database that applies a top-down constraint on the design of separate systems. The database provides a much-needed vehicle for the integration of the systems.

The Enterprise Data Model Approach

An emerging approach to systems design that is achieving widespread attention today shifts emphasis from the users' data resource to that of the organization. The idea is simple: If all of the firm's data is stored in a data warehouse, there is no limit to the support that the firm's information systems can provide.

We introduced this approach in Chapter 1 and illustrated it with Figure 1.12. Management engages in a modeling effort to develop an **enterprise model,** which is a high-level description of the firm—its objectives, resources, and how the resources will accomplish the objectives. Information specialists then prepare an **enterprise data model** that defines the firm's data resources. The basis for the data model is an entity-relationship diagram supported by data dictionary descriptions, or by class diagrams if an object-oriented approach is taken. Enterprise data modeling represents a step beyond providing a data resource to meet individual problem solvers' needs by also meeting the needs of the organization.

Putting Contemporary Systems Design in Perspective

Many firms today are following the systems design approach that has characterized the DSS era. These firms make available a database to meet the needs of their managers in solving problems and seizing opportunities. More and more firms are beginning to engage in enterprise modeling but it is a massive undertaking. Both approaches represent modern, top-down strategies for applying the computer, and are likely to continue to represent the mainstream design philosophies in the foreseeable future.

Logical and Physical System Design

There are two basic types of systems design—logical design and physical design.

Logical Design

Logical design is the determination of the steps that the system will follow in transforming the input data into the output information that is needed to solve a problem or react to an opportunity. The emphasis is on only the steps, and not on the technology that will be used in accomplishing the steps. The logical design is accomplished during the design stage of the system development life cycle, with the developers experienced in analysis playing the key roles. The analyst uses the systems methodologies and tools and produces entries in the project dictionary that document both the data and the processes of the new system.

The logical design task is essentially one of modeling the new system. In our discussion of systems analysis in Chapter 5, we saw that the developer gathers data and information in various ways, and assembles a set of documentation that provides a complete description of the functional requirements of the new system. The developer has the same modeling responsibility in the design stage, only this time the assignment involves documenting the *new* system.

Basically, two features of the new system must be documented—its data and its processes. The developer prepares a **data model** to document the data to be used by the new system, and a **process model** to document the processes. If an object-oriented approach is taken, an **object model** documents both data and processes.

Physical Design

Logical design is a technology-independent activity defining what the new system will accomplish. **Physical design** includes all of the activities that convert the logical design into a system consisting of hardware, software, data, information, and personnel that work together for the system to meet its objectives. For an object oriented approach this will include preparing component diagrams and deployment diagrams.

FIGURE 6.2

The Evolution in Computer Architectures

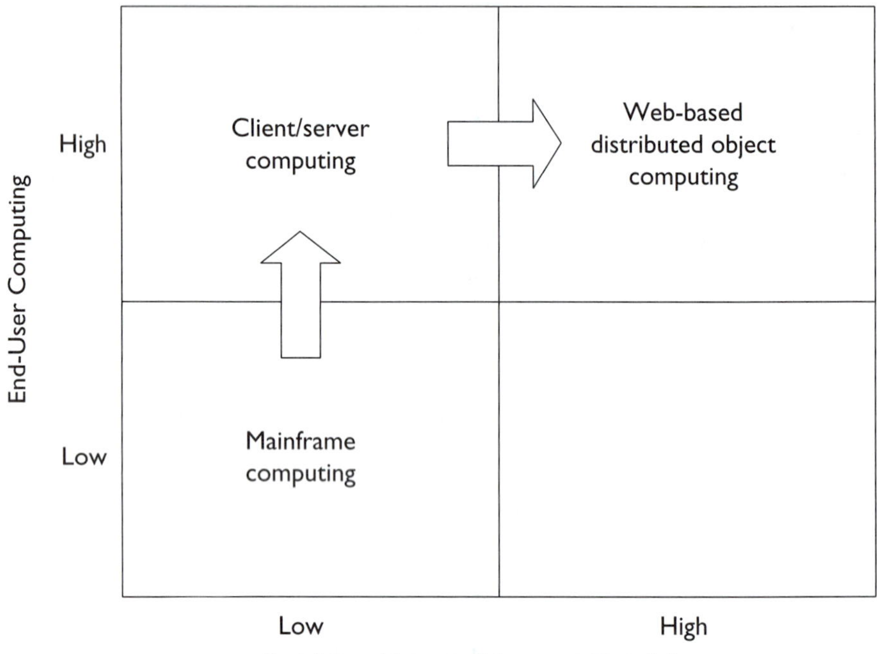

Source: Adapted from Ming Fan, Jan Stallert, and Andrew Whinston, "The Adoption and Design Methodologies for Component-based Systems Enterprise Systems." *European Journal of Information Systems* 9 (2000) 25-35. Reproduced with permission.

EVOLUTION OF BASIC COMPUTER ARCHITECTURES

From its beginning in the mid 1950s, the computer era has been marked by an almost exponential increase in the productivity of hardware and software. Computer architectures have evolved in two directions during this period, as illustrated in Figure 6.2. First, architecture evolved in terms of the level of support that is provided for **end-user computing**—computing performed by users themselves rather than by information specialists. Initially, there was little or no end-user computing, and this use of the computer is now called *mainframe computing*. Subsequently, the trend was to a high degree of end-user computing, a use that has been given the name *client/server computing*. Currently, another trend is underway—Web-based distributed object computing. This trend is producing systems that have higher degrees of scalability, maintainability, and global access.

Mainframe Computing

The term **mainframe** was coined early in the computer era to describe the large hardware systems that were used by such industry giants as the Fortune 500 firms. The term mainframe also became used to describe how the computers were used. In **mainframe**

computing, all processing was done centrally, on the very large computer, which also maintained a central database. In this setting, diagrammed in Figure 6.3, users in outlying locations used keyboard terminals to transmit input data to the headquarters mainframe and receive information output. The data was transmitted by means of communications networks, usually consisting of telephone lines.

Client/Server Computing

The breakthrough that shifted the focus of business computing away from the mainframe was the development of microcomputers, commonly called PCs for personal computers. Rather than interface with the mainframe using terminals, users could use their PCs. This approach was given the name **client/server computing,** which involves use of a centrally located computer, called the **server,** that is linked to a network that includes user workstations, called **clients.** Users can use their PCs to accomplish much of their own computing, but can use the server for the types of processing that it performs best. Figure 6.4 shows this configuration.

Client/server systems can be implemented in varying degrees, based on the division of tasks between the client and the server. The tasks include:

FIGURE 6.3

Mainframe Computing

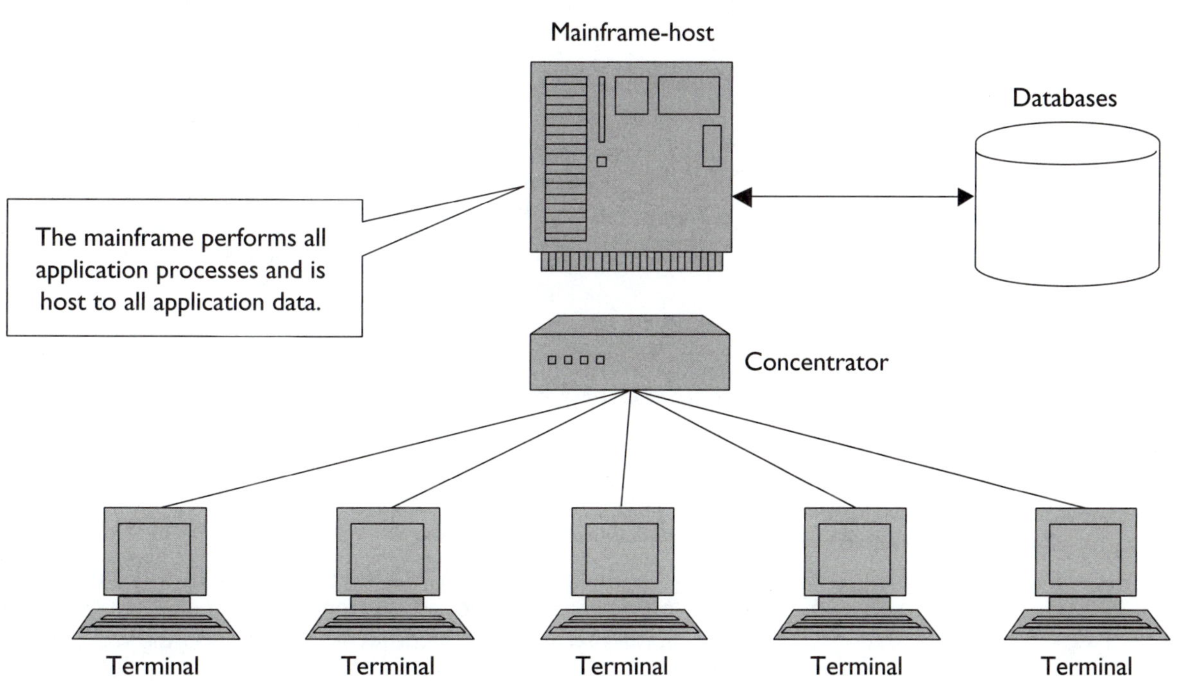
Mainframe-host
Databases
The mainframe performs all application processes and is host to all application data.
Concentrator
Terminal
Terminal
Terminal
Terminal
Terminal

Source: Sandra Donaldson Dewitz, *Systems Analysis and Design and the Transition to Objects,* McGraw-Hill, ©1996, page 144. Reproduced with permission of The McGraw-Hill Companies.

FIGURE 6.4

Client/Server Computing

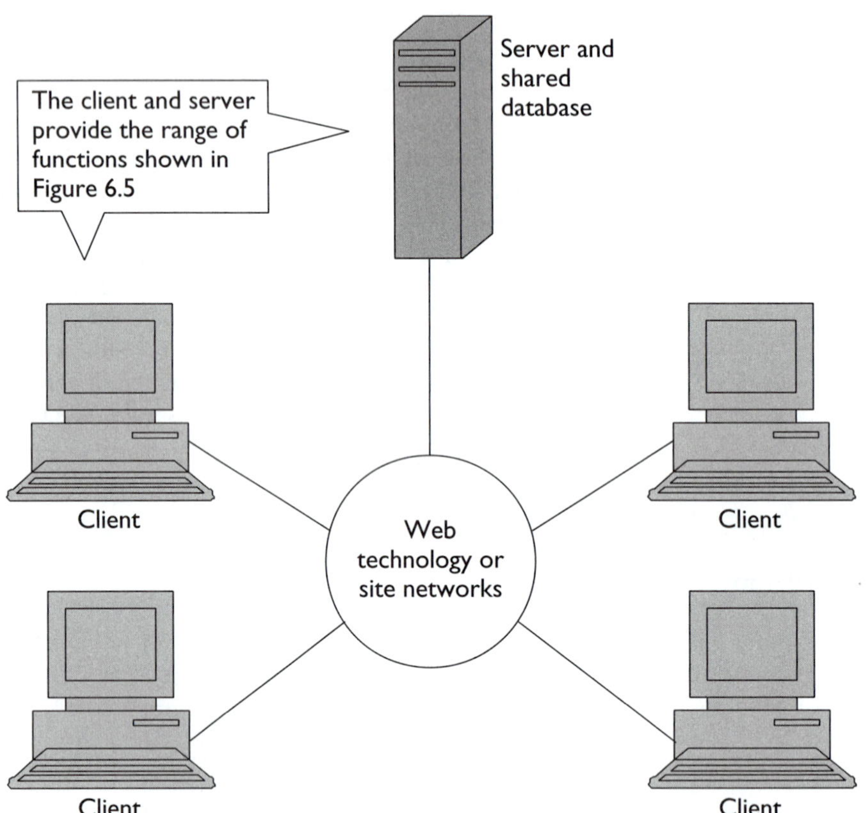

Source: Adapted from Sandra Donaldson Dewitz, *Systems Analysis and Design and the Transition to Objects,* McGraw-Hill, ©1996, page 144. Reproduced with permission of The McGraw-Hill Companies.

- *User interface*—How the user and the system exchange data, instructions, and information
- *Function*—The processing of the user's data
- *Data access*—The storage of the user's data

Figure 6.5 shows five client/server environments based on the division of these tasks. The environments range from the configuration on the left, called a **thin client,** where very little capability exists at the client level to the one on the right, called a **fat client,** where the client has most of the capabilities. A thin client (distributed presentation) has control over only its user interface; the server also retains some control over the user interface. A fat client has control over the interface, the function, and a portion of the data access. Note that no environment gives total data access privilege to the client.

Web-Based Distributed-Object Computing

Two innovations have accounted for the refinement in the end-user capability of client/server computing that has resulted in **Web-based computing.** One is the Internet, and the other is the use of objects to model data and processes. The Internet provides an avenue for users located anywhere in the world to access the firm's information systems. This global access increases the challenge for developers to create systems that are easy to use with no documentation and little learning time. The rapidly changing business environment forces organizations to change their systems faster than ever before, especially those Web-based systems that give them a competitive advantage. The use of objects to model data and the associated processes contributes to the ability of systems to change with environmental changes (scalability) and adapt to new business rules (maintainability).

FIGURE 6.5

Range of Application Partitioning for Web-Based Distributed-Object Computing

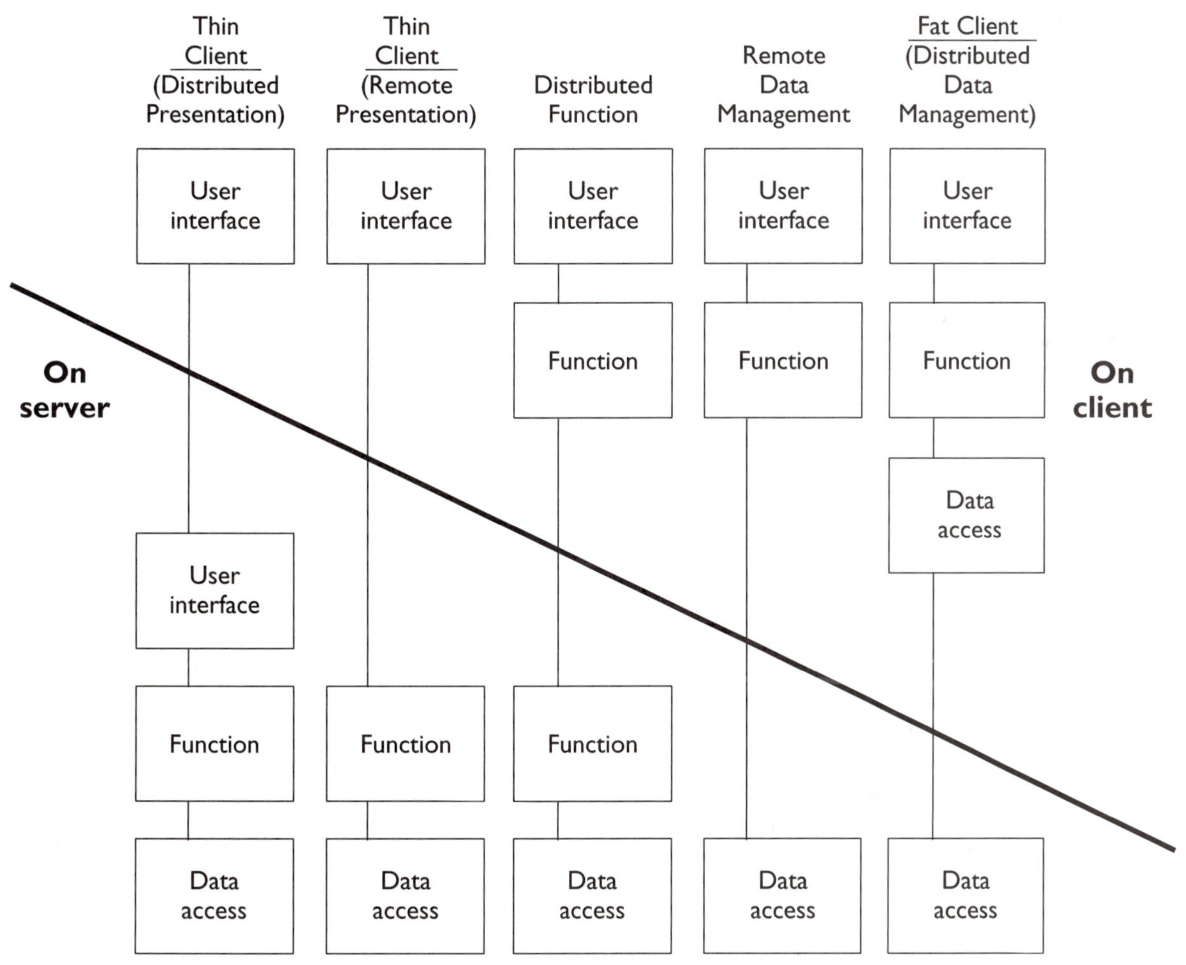

At the time this book is going to press there is some talk that the client/server era ended with the beginning of the Internet era. We have chosen to treat Internet systems as a special case of client/server environments, with several clients connected by a local area network or thousands of clients accessing software and data over the Web. In either case, developers must analyze user characteristics and user needs and then design and implement the appropriate system to be successful.

The Systems Approach to Design

In Chapter 2 we presented the systems approach as a basic framework for solving problems of all kinds, and pictured its three major efforts—preparation, definition, and solution—in Figure 2.4. Definition effort encompasses the preliminary investigation and systems analysis stages of the system development life cycle, whereas solution effort encompasses the remaining stages. The first three steps of solution effort represent system design.

- Identify the possible solutions.
- Evaluate the possible solutions.
- Select the best solution.

We will use this framework to describe the design task. The basis for systems design is the documentation that was prepared during the analysis stage, which includes use cases, data and process models, perhaps object models, and the F/C matrix. The use cases are prepared at a broader level during preliminary investigation and at a detailed level during each of the iterations of analysis while creating the functional deliveries for the users.

Identify the Possible Solutions

The first step of identifying alternate solutions is the identification of alternate system configurations that each have the capability of satisfying the functional requirements. This is perhaps the most difficult part of system development. It is a real test for the developer's analytical ability and creativity. Certainly, the experienced developer has an advantage since he or she can recall strengths and weaknesses of configurations that have been used in the past. Knowledge of systems theory is a good supplement for the needed experience. By taking a systems view, the analyst has the best chance of identifying all of the system configurations that should be considered.

For each configuration, six separate types of design are involved. The types are illustrated in Figure 6.6, but the task does not necessarily have to be as intimidating as the figure suggests. It is not necessary that each system *component* be unique from one configuration to the next. For example, multiple configurations being considered for a DSS might all include a GUI interface.

- *User interface design* is concerned with how the user interfaces with the system on both input and output. This design considers not only the input and output devices but also how the devices are used.
- *Data design* includes the determination of the data that will be required to produce the system output, and the devices that will be used to store the data.

- *Procedure design* includes the determination of the functions that the users and system will perform to produce the system output.
- *Software design* includes the specifications that will guide programmers in the construction of software during the preliminary and final construction stages.
- *System interface design* is concerned with how the system being designed will interface with other systems. The interfaces include both input and output capabilities.
- *System control design* considers the types of controls that must be built into the system to ensure that it performs as intended.

As shown in the figure, both software design and system control design encompass all of the other efforts. Each type of design must conform to the software standards, and controls must be built into all components of the system where they are needed.

These types of design are described in the following sections. As they are described, keep in mind that they are performed *for each functional delivery or*

FIGURE 6.6

System Design Efforts

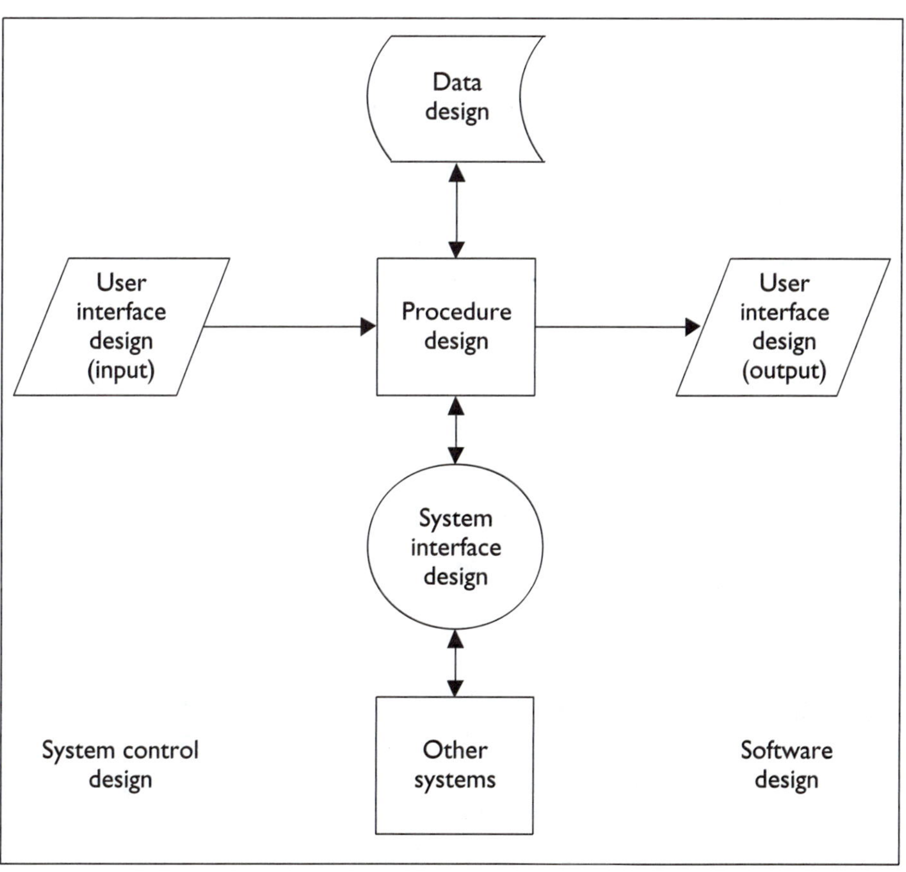

FIGURE 6.7

Five Types of Design Performed on Each Configuration of a Sample Module

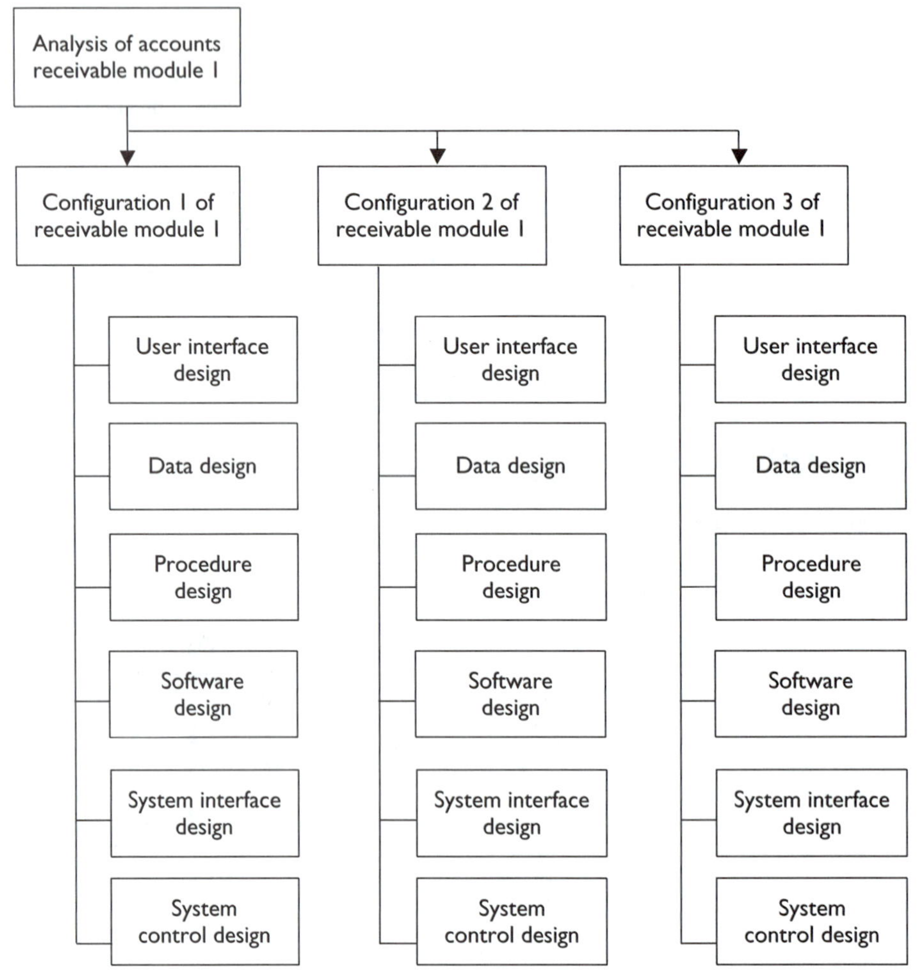

module of the new system as they are applicable and also keep in mind that they are performed on *each of the alternate system configurations*. Figure 6.7 illustrates the mechanics of this process, using three modules of an accounts receivable system as an example.

USER INTERFACE DESIGN

In the most basic terms, the computer/user interface consists of how data is entered into the system and information received from it.[1] Some interfaces handle both input and output. An example is the graphical user interface, or GUI. We devote Technical Module H to graphical user interface design and will not cover that material here.

Input Design

In Chapter 3 we recommend a reverse sequence for system design, beginning with output, then processing, and then input. When the system features an interactive dialog with the user, both input and output should be jointly addressed first.

The design of system input is influenced by (1) the volume of data, (2) who is responsible for data entry, and (3) whether the data entry can be designed to take place "on location" in the store or manufacturing site or wherever the most immediate data entry is possible. One of the main advantages of a Web-based system is that the customer, sales representative, and other users can directly enter data. This saves the organization significant data entry expenses, but the developer has the increased responsibility of designing input forms and procedures that are easy to understand with little or no instruction. And software must be designed in situations such as online customer ordering to handle data entry from millions of users located worldwide with no training in a particular application or interface.

Input Device Choices

One of the main input design choices is the hardware device that will be used for entering data and commands. Possible choices include online key-driven units, special-purpose terminals, voice input devices, push-button telephones, magnetic ink character recognition devices, and optical scanners.

Online Key-Driven Units

When applied to hardware, the term **online** means that the device is connected to the computer. Examples of online key-driven units are keyboard terminals, PCs, and handheld devices, including cell phones and personal digital assistants (PDAs). Although most data input is accomplished by means of the keyboard, many users prefer to use a **pointing device,** such as a mouse for a PC or a stylus for a handheld device.

Special-Purpose Terminals

Some terminals are designed to minimize the amount of keying required by the operators. McDonald's, for example, uses terminals that represent each of their products with a single key; you order a large fries and the clerk enters the transaction with a single keystroke. Other special terminals are ATMs and scanners that read data from the magnetized strip on the back of credit cards.

Voice Input

You can enter data into the computer by speaking commands and data into a microphone or telephone.

Push-Button Telephone

You can also use the telephone to enter numeric data from a remote location and receive audio responses from a distant computer. For example, a sales representative who is making a sales call on a customer can use the pushbuttons of the customer's phone to enter such data as a request for an inventory status report. The salesperson's central computer retrieves the data and prepares an audio response that the salesperson can hear over the telephone.

Magnetic Ink Character Recognition

The specially shaped characters at the bottom of checks are printed in magnetic ink, and **magnetic ink character recognition (MICR)** input devices read the data into the computer. MICR was conceived as a way to relieve the input bottleneck in banks. An **input bottleneck** is the inability of key-driven data entry devices to keep pace with the faster speeds of computer processing and output.

Optical Character Recognition

Optical character recognition (OCR) devices called **scanners** read data that is printed in ordinary ink. Some scanners read machine-printed characters, some read hand-printed data, some read barcodes, and some read pencil marks, such as those you make on true-false and multiple-choice exams. The scanners at supermarket checkout counters are examples of OCR, as are the cash registers in department stores that feature reading wands.

Source Document Design

A **source document** is a paper form that provides the input data to a system. It is usually a printed form and can be completed by someone inside the firm (such as an employee completing a time card) or someone outside the firm (such as a customer completing a sales order form). The entry of data on the source document can be accomplished by hand or by some device such as a typewriter or printer.

The source document data can be entered into the system by a data entry operator who reads the data from the source document and keys it into the computer. Or the source document data can be read by an MICR reader or an OCR scanner.

Tips for Designing Source Documents

By following these tips the source documents that you design will have the best opportunity to contribute to the efficiency and accuracy of system input.

1. *Provide for a natural forms completion pattern.* When filling out a form, persons usually enter data in a left-to-right, top-to-bottom sequence, and that format should be reflected in the form design. This sequence is typical of Western cultures but may not be followed in other cultures.

2. *Make the fields the right size.* The areas that are reserved for various data elements should be large enough to contain those elements. Fields to be completed by hand should identify the character spacing, ideally with a box for each letter.

3. *Use carbon sets to provide multiple copies.* When more than a single copy is needed, use a **snap-apart form** that contains multiple copies attached to a binding stub at the top or side. Each copy should be in a special color, with its use, such as "Customer copy," identified. The sets can use interleaved carbon paper or the forms can be printed on **NCR paper.** NCR stands for "no carbon required."

   Regardless of the type of paper used, reserve the top copies of the forms set for the most important uses such as customer copies and warehouse picking tickets. This design ensures that the most important copies will be the most legible. For sets with many copies, such as eight to twelve, use thin paper to improve the legibility of the bottom copies.

4. *Design mail documents to fit envelopes.* How many times have you tried to enclose a document in an envelope that is too small? When source documents must be mailed they should be designed to fit in the envelopes when properly folded, and the firm's name and address should show through the window.

5. *Test forms usage before printing.* Give a sampling of users the opportunity to use the form before printing large quantities. Use desktop publishing or word processing software to produce forms prototypes. As the users go through the motions of using the prototypes they often see the opportunity for improvements. Continue prototyping until the form is acceptable to the users.

   Rely on the local sales representatives of forms companies for help in designing source documents and other printed forms. The reps are both knowledgeable and cooperative, and they can provide sample forms and perhaps even forms design handbooks.

Putting Input Design in Perspective

Accounting information systems feature large volumes of data, which can be entered by means of MICR or OCR, or by data entry operators using keyboard units. The operators have good typing skills, therefore, the key-driven units represent a practical approach. For order entry systems on the Web, customers directly enter their own data, saving the seller redundant data entry expenses.

The information-oriented systems, such as data warehouse and CRM (customer relationship management) systems, usually feature a large volume of user-computer dialog. In these systems, the input design must consider whether the computer program or the user will direct the dialog. A **program-directed dialog** is one where the program specifies the nature of the user's response. The three most common forms are menus, form filling, and prompting. In a **user-directed dialog,** the user determines the sequence of the processes. This can be accomplished by use of a command language or by direct manipulation using a pointing device.

Users vary in their preferences for particular types of dialog. One way to address this variability is to use prototyping to tailor system dialog to specific users. Another is to design systems so that users can select the dialog type that they prefer.

Output Design

The computer provides information to users in three basic ways: reports, outputs from simulations, and communications.

Reports

Reports have always been the most popular way to represent computer output. They can be printed on a printing device or displayed on a screen. The two basic types of reports are periodic and special. A **periodic report** is prepared according to some schedule, such as weekly or monthly. The names **repetitive report** and s**cheduled report** are also used. A periodic report is triggered by the passage of time. A **special report** is one that is triggered by a request or an event. An example of a request is when a human resources manager queries the database to produce a list of employees with over ten years of service. An example of how an event triggers a special report is an accident that causes lost production time and causes a lost time report to be prepared. Another example of an event is an exception to planned performance, such as

FIGURE 6.8

Types of Reports

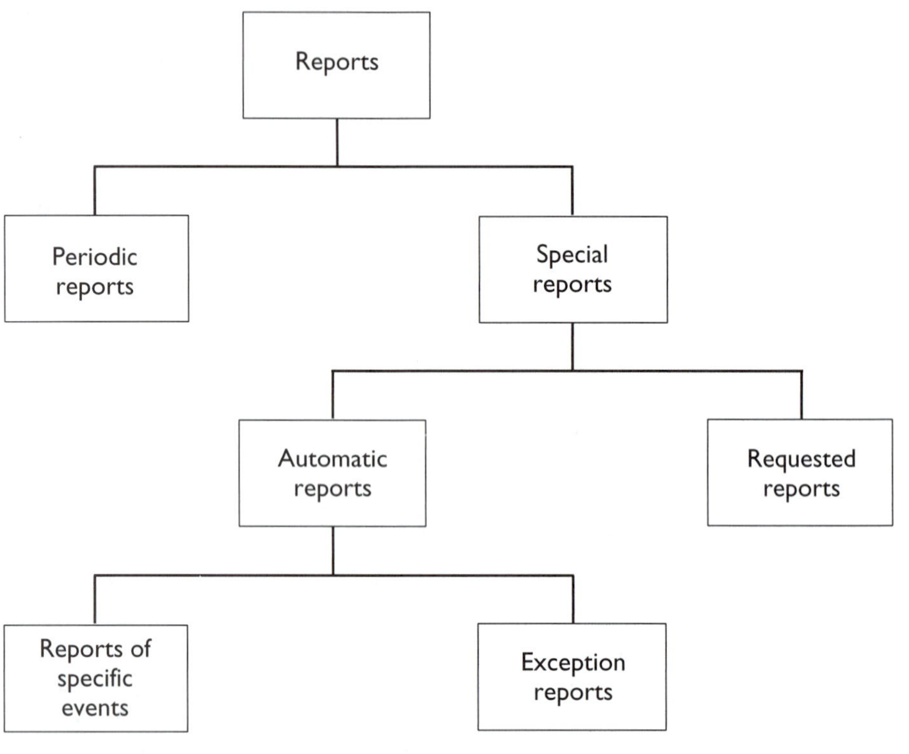

when sales exceed the projected level. The term **exception report** is used to describe a special report that can be used to practice management by exception.

Figure 6.8 is a hierarchy diagram that shows the classification of report types. Each type can portray its contents in either a printed or displayed form, and in a tabular, graphic, or narrative manner.

- *Printed and Displayed Reports*—Before computer screens became popular, reports were always printed on paper. Such output is called **hardcopy.** The popularity of computer screens has shifted much of the output from hardcopy to a displayed form. Users prefer the speed and convenience of the displays, along with the vivid colors.

- *Tabular, Graphic, and Narrative Reports*—The traditional report format arranges the words and numbers in the form of rows and columns, forming a table. Such an arrangement is called a **tabular report.** A report that represents information pictorially is called a **graphic report.** When information is communicated in the form of sentences it is called a **narrative report.**

Recently, there has been interest in combining the tabular, graphic, and narrative presentations. The narrative offers a brief explanation of the tabular and graphic information. This technique has been especially effective in executive information systems.

Outputs from Simulations

Developers of early information systems were quick to recognize the ability of the computer to represent business phenomena in the form of mathematical formulas. Any representation of a phenomenon, or entity, by means of one or more mathematical formulas is a **mathematical model.**

A mathematical model can represent a particular entity, such as the flow of cash through the firm or fluctuations in the level of inventory. A manager or other decision maker can subject the model to certain influences to see what the effect of the changes might be. Model output can be printed or displayed. Some models have the capability of displaying output in full motion. A model that simulates a production line in a factory can show the products flowing down the line.

Communications

When we explained the general systems model of the firm in Chapter 1 we recognized the need for the manager to communicate decisions to the physical system. This communication can be facilitated by such office automation applications as electronic mail, word processing, or teleconferencing. OA can communicate problem-solving information *to* and *from* the user.

Report Design

Systems developers have been designing reports since before the computer was invented. Therefore, proven guidelines exist. Graphical reports are a more recent display option, but the developer does not have to start out from scratch. Research has produced guidelines that, like those for tabular reports, should be considered.

Tips for Designing Tabular Reports Tabular reports include three main areas as shown in Figure 6.9. The **headings area** is at the top and identifies the report and its contents. The **body** is in the middle and contains the rows and columns of data. The **footings area** is at the bottom and includes page and final totals. Within the body, it is common practice to locate **coded data** such as dates and item numbers on the left-hand side, **descriptive data** such as names in the center, and **quantitative data** such as quantities and amounts on the right-hand side.

Follow the tips below to make your tabular reports more effective.

1. *Use a layout form to design the report.* When designing a report, use a **layout form** that provides for both horizontal and vertical spacing. If you cannot obtain a report layout form, you can use graph paper or any paper with a grid.

2. *Provide complete identifying information.* Unless there are reasons to the contrary, you should include the following information in the headings area: report title, time period covered by the report, report preparation date and time, and column headings. Executive information systems frequently identify the name and telephone extension of the person in the firm who is expert on the report data so that the executive can follow up if necessary.

3. *Incorporate management by exception.* Management by exception can be built into a report three different ways:

- *Only print the report when an exception occurs.* A good example is a report showing employees who worked overtime the previous week.

FIGURE 6.9

Basic Design of a Tabular Report

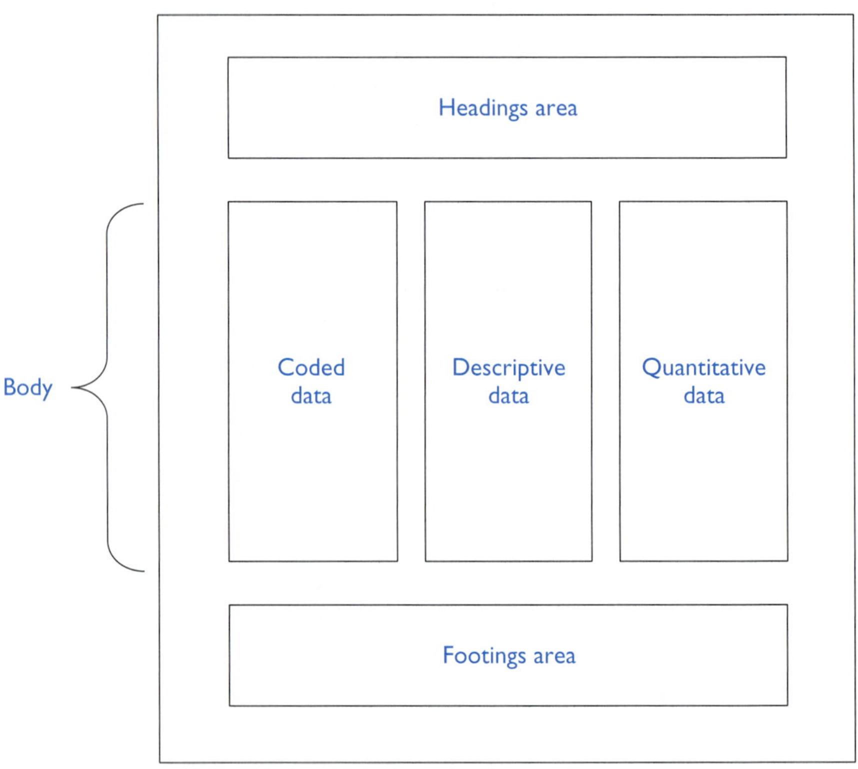

- *Print exceptions in special columns.* A good example is an aged accounts receivable report that uses columns to show the age of each receivable—30 days, 60 days, 90 days, and so on.
- *Use variance columns to highlight exceptions.* A standard report format shows actual performance, expected performance, and the variance in separate columns. The user scans the variance column to see exceptions that demand follow-up action.

Tips for Designing Graphic Reports When designing reports for users who prefer graphics, consider the following tips.[2]

1. *Use line and bar charts to summarize data.* Line charts enable quick decisions, and bar charts facilitate understanding and readability.
2. *Use line and bar charts to show trends over time.* Use groups of lines and bars, as shown on the left-hand side of Figure 6.10, rather than single lines and bars.
3. *Use grouped bar charts to illustrate parts of a whole.* The human eye does the most accurate job when reading grouped bars with a common baseline. Neither segmented bar charts nor pie charts offer this capability.

4. *Use grouped line and bar charts to illustrate patterns.* Segmented charts are not so effective for showing such a pattern as the change in annual sales.

5. *Use horizontal bars to show relationships.* Users tend to overestimate the length of vertical bars.

6. *Use single-variable bar charts to illustrate data points.* Research has not supported the effectiveness of graphics over tabular data for portraying single values. Include the actual data values at the end of the bars for added precision.

These guidelines are expected to apply to users in general. Use prototypes to identify the types of graphs that particular users prefer.

FIGURE 6.10

Sample Graphic Report Formats

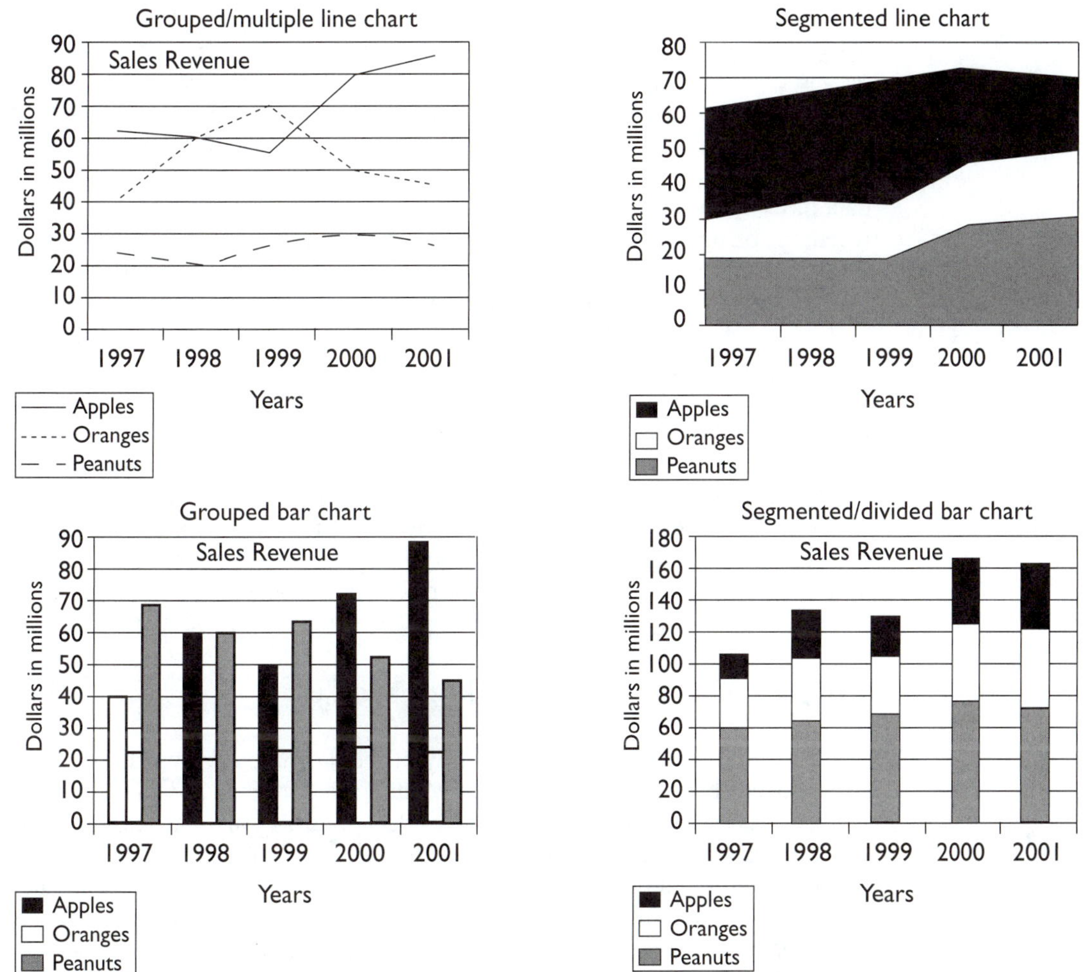

Source: Sirkka L. Jarvenpaa and Gary W. Dickson, "Graphics and Managerial Decision Making: Research Based Guidelines," *Communications of the ACM*, 31 (June 1988), page 770. Reprinted with permission.

Putting Output Design in Perspective

The task of the user and the developer is to match the form of output to the problem-solving situation. Reports are effective for distilling large volumes of data into information, mathematical models enable the manager to simulate the possible effect of decisions, and communications facilitate exchange of information with others. These three forms of computer output are combined with non-computer information to provide support that decision makers need to take advantage of opportunities and solve problems.

Users may not be very clear on the details of the system that they need, but they have strong preferences concerning how they will interface with the system. This is an excellent place to use prototyping. The visual pictures created in phased development are ideal for giving the user a sense of confidence that their requirements are being met.

DATA DESIGN

Once the output is determined, data storage must be designed. The most common situation is adding functions to an existing system or creating a new system that depends on one or more existing systems. In both cases developers must verify that all of the data elements are present in the current data model (or models). If all of the necessary data is not included in an existing model, the model must be redesigned. For a new system, the process of database design must start with an examination of the logical data model. Since the relational database model has become the de facto standard in recent years, this design process will most likely require entity-relationship modeling described in Technical Module A. For an object-oriented approach, designers will complete class diagrams, as explained in Technical Module C.

A major physical design task in a client/server environment or distributed computing environment is determining where the data is stored. The first consideration is whether all the data will reside on a server or whether data will be split between clients and servers, as shown for the "fat client" in Figure 6.5. If any data will reside on a server, a series of decisions may be required to allocate storage across a complex server farm. A **server farm** is a large collection of servers in one or more locations. Or, the design step may be a simpler process of testing whether the current single server for an application can handle any increased capacity. If the available server space is inadequate, then specifications must be completed to purchase or lease additional servers.

Putting Data Design in Perspective

Data design is the primary responsibility of the database administrator (DBA) or an experienced developer who has a background in data structures, data design, and technology issues including data integrity, data security, and processing efficiency. Physical data design details are outside the scope of this text. In considering each alternate configuration, the DBA will determine the available servers, their adequacy, and how the data will be allocated among the necessary servers as well as the more basic task of database design. The DBA and other developers use such data modeling tools as ERDs, the data dictionary, and class diagrams to document the physical data design. A network specialist will help the DBA and other developers determine server capacity and allocation of data among servers, unless there is only a single server or if the DBA is responsible for data storage design and allocation among servers.

PROCEDURE DESIGN

In the simplest development environment, a user will create a system with relatively simple database software, such as Microsoft Access or FileMaker by FileMaker, Inc., for personal use. The procedures are likely to mimic the same steps followed by the user using word processing and a calculator. The series of steps might seem quite complex to an outsider, but no instructions need to be written nor any user training conducted since the developer and user are the same individual. At the other extreme a large team of developers may create a data warehouse to be used worldwide by a global company or a Web-based customer order system with hopes that millions will use the system. In both cases the goal of procedure design is to create procedures that will make the system easy-to-use and reliable within the project constraints for budget and time. In the simplest case the user-developer knows what will be easy for personal use. At the other extreme, developers taking a user-driven phased development approach must work with users who represent a wide range of computer skills and reasons for using the system to create procedures that will make the system successful. In both the simple and extreme situations, procedure design will be based on the analysis of procedures. In the simple situation, this will probably be in the user-developer's head; in more complex situations, the analysis documents created by the team will be the basis for procedure design. If a structured development approach is taken, then each of the process bubbles in the detailed data flow diagrams will require procedure design. In an object oriented approach each use case will require procedure design.

One of the most important decisions for each process bubble or use case will be to determine what will be batch processing and what will be online processing. We will discuss this decision as an example of procedure design trade offs.

Batch Processing

In **batch processing,** transaction data is accumulated in a batch of, say, 25 documents, and all of the transactions in the batch are processed through each sequential step of the procedure. Figure 6.11 is a DFD that illustrates this approach. The two small circles are connectors, providing the connection from the bottom of the left-hand column to the top of the one on the right. The numbers identify the "to" and "from" processes.

Sales transactions are entered into the computer in step 1. The data is used to update three master files. A **master file** is a file that represents an important resource or an element in the firm's environment. The master files in the flowchart include the Inventory master file, the Customer master file, and the Salesperson master file. The Inventory master file is maintained in item number sequence, the Customer master file in customer number sequence, and the Salesperson master file in salesperson number sequence. Before each master file can be updated, the transaction file must be sorted into the master file sequence. The sorting occurs in steps 2, 4, and 6, and the files are updated in steps 3, 5, and 7.

The main advantage of batch processing is efficient computer use. For example, airline capacity reports by city of origination, city of destination, or a particular month or day are valuable for strategic planning for airlines. Generating these reports as a batch at a particular time (daily for some reports, weekly for others, monthly and quarterly for other reports) is the most efficient way to supply information to financial analysts, schedulers, food service managers and others who need this information. Payroll processing is another example; entering weekly payroll data as a batch at the end of each weekly payroll is an efficient use of information systems and workers' time.

FIGURE 6.11

Batch Processing

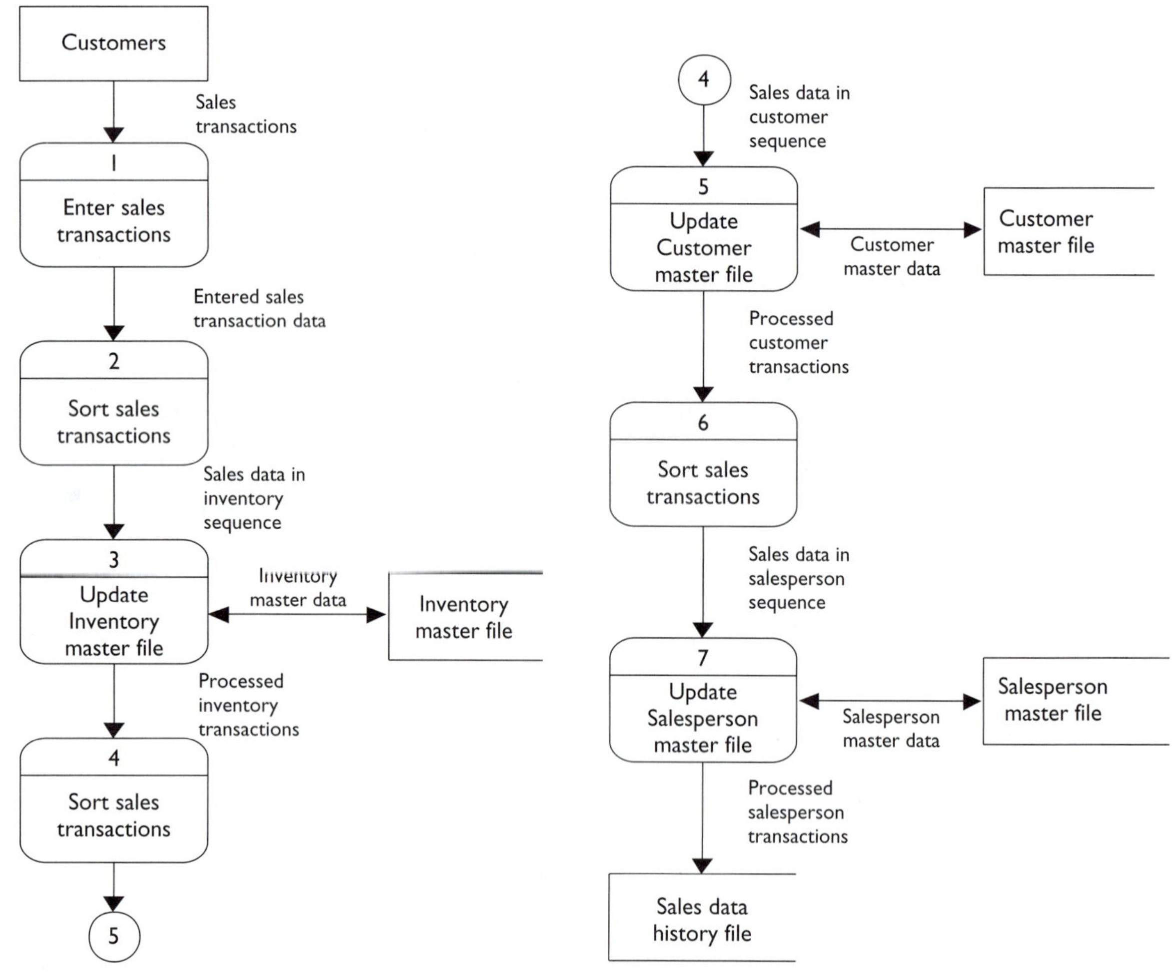

A major limitation of batch processing is that it requires redundant procedures. A student filling out a scan sheet with courses they wish to take, must mail or deliver this scan sheet to a central office where the scan sheet is scanned by a clerk to add to a transaction file of class registration requests. If a student directly enters course registration numbers using a telephone for registration data entry or a Web-based registration system, then no intermediate procedure is required to update a master file for course registration.

A second major limitation of batch processing is the fact that it does not provide current data. The master files are current only immediately following file updating. As the firm continues to do business, the files do a less and less effective job of reflecting the status of the physical system. In some cases, such as mid-week payroll totals, the lack of timeliness does not justify entering the data on an hour-by-hour basis. In other situations a current database is so important to many modern computer applications, systems designers have shifted almost exclusively from batch to online processing or a combination of both. An example of combining both is the airline industry reporting example where some reporting procedures will be standard periodic batched reports. These will be supplemented by decision support capabilities that allow analysts to create their own reports online.

Online Processing

When the master files are updated as each transaction is entered, the technique is called **online processing.** (The term *transaction processing* is often used to describe the separate handling of transactions. We do not use this term since it is also used to mean the firm's accounting information system.) Figure 6.12 shows how the same three master files can be updated online. Data for a single transaction is entered into the computer and, while the transaction data is in main memory, all three master files are updated. Then, another transaction is entered.

A special type of online system that controls the physical system is called a realtime system. Realtime means "right now," and a **realtime system** is one that controls one or more processes as they occur. The key word is *control.* Take, for example, a point-of-sale system used by a department store to enter data into terminals as sales are made. If the data simply updates the inventory and other files, it is an online system. If, on the other hand, the data is used to conduct a credit check to determine whether the sale will be made, the system is a realtime system. The system controls the firm's sales activity.

Determining whether online processing or batch processing is best will depend on user characteristics and user needs as well as project constraints for budget and development time. If potential customers are widely spread and would be motivated to search for and use a Web site for ordering, then an online Web-based ordering system makes sense, as it does for personal computers. If potential customers are unlikely to realize they might want a special rock and roll CD or exercise equipment, a phone ordering system advertised on television might be the best approach. In phased development the general procedures are determined in preliminary investigation and then the details for procedures are analyzed, designed, and constructed in iterative phases focusing on functional deliveries that the users or user representatives review.

Putting Procedure Design in Perspective

As the process of designing a new computer-based system unfolds, many decisions concerning system alternatives must be made. However, few affect system performance more than the choice between batch and online. This choice of procedures is *a fundamental design decision* because of the ultimate influence that it has on (1) how the users interact with the system and (2) information value. Once the decision is made to use batch or online, the design of the application software can proceed. The developer uses object-oriented modeling techniques or process modeling tools such as DFDs to document the procedure design.

SOFTWARE DESIGN

An advantage of phased development is that the rapid iteration of analysis-design-construct-review activities increases the chance that the final system will have the required functions. A disadvantage is that design may be left out. With visual development environments, "painting" the user interface screens is constructing software

FIGURE 6.12

Online Processing

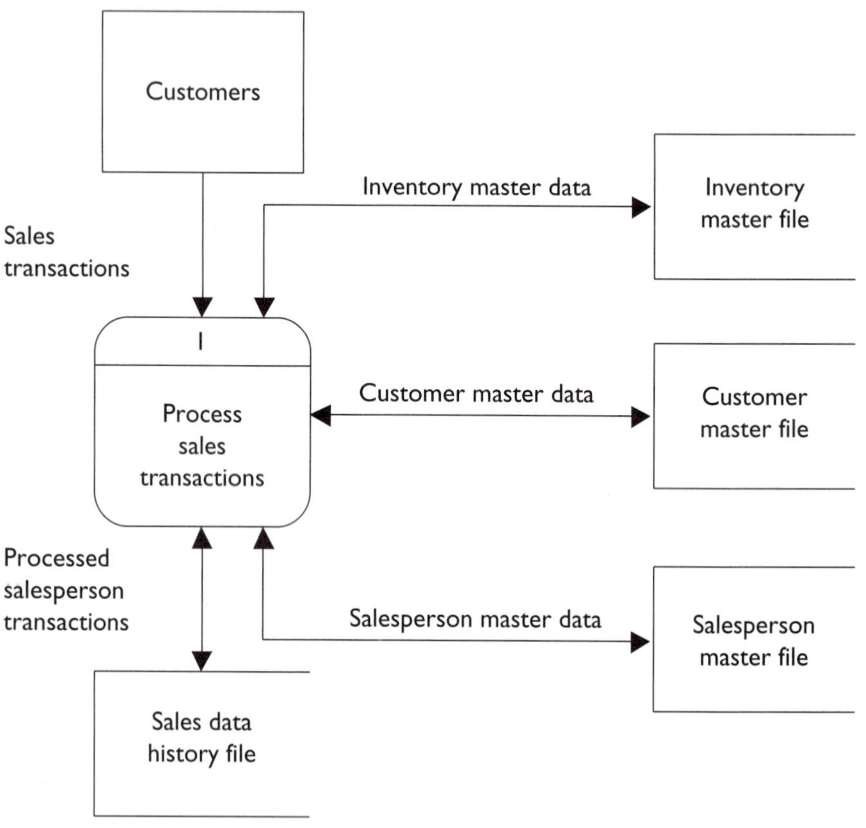

so user interface design and user interface construction happen in the same step. Here, developers may be tempted to leave out critical software design steps, working out the design of each function mentally. This lack of specifications makes it difficult to coordinate team members or adhere to organizational standards. The result is likely to be a series of final prototypes that work well in each individual developer's sandbox with a small test data set, but leads to a conversion nightmare in creating a production system that runs efficiently. Any enhancements required in the future are likely to be a maintenance nightmare.

For a single-user system developed for use on a single client PC, the accomplishment of the analysis-design-construction loops may be largely unplanned and informal. In this case, the cost of design errors is likely to be small. For systems to succeed in a more complex environment, five software design strategies are critical.

- Determine which functions will reside on the client and which will reside on the server for the production system. (Options are illustrated in Figure 6.5.) Create a version of the menu hierarchy chart that identifies the location of each function. A network specialist or developer experienced with multi-tier systems of the type planned by the team should lead this early physical design activity of determining where functions will reside.

- Adopt strict naming conventions for all software modules (or pages or classes or applets or whatever the appropriate term is for the software tools chosen for each layer of development). For Web-based systems, adopt path rules so that the conversion of the system from the development environment to the production environment does not require renaming files or rewriting links. Links should be relative so that any server specification may be handled with current virtual storage processes rather than depending on hardware-specific links.

- Adopt and enforce software design principles that include limit modules or objects to simple routines performing single, small functions. Combined with a good design for naming modules and a good, well-documented module hierarchy, the practice of cohesive, single-function routines will make changes easier during development and post-production maintenance.

- Adopt and enforce programming principles that include clear commenting, field naming standards, indentation, and spacing for easy reading and changing.

- Create templates and class libraries (or code libraries) that comply with all design decisions. Require all developers to use these as a way to save construction time and enforce design standards. The result will be design consistency that makes the system easier to use and maintain.

By completing these software design strategies early, system developers will save time in the preliminary construction, final construction, and system testing stages as well as in post-implementation maintenance.

Putting Software Design in Perspective

From a project manager's perspective, the key to successful software design is involving a knowledgeable technical expert early so that the overall design is in place at the time of the first analysis-design-construction iteration. When the team is formed in the preliminary investigation phase this expert (or experts) should be included on the team or identified as an available resource. Developers responsible for coding should understand the design principles we have outlined and be committed to high quality design. Technical training, if needed, should include design strategies as well as any necessary language skills.

System Interface Design

Very seldom will a single system handle all of the processing that is required. Invariably, one system will interface with one or more other systems and they will share the processing workload. Figure 6.13 is a DFD that shows several subsystems of a distribution system—order entry, inventory, billing, accounts receivable, and general ledger. In addition, the inventory system interfaces with the purchasing system and the receiving system. The data flows show how these systems are linked together. Each of these linkages is a system interface. When linked systems are developed by more than one project team, they must work together to ensure that the interfaces are compatible.

When the systems exist in a single location, the linkages can be accomplished by some type of secondary storage, such as magnetic disk. When the systems are in different locations, the linkages can be accomplished by data communications.

FIGURE 6.13

The Distribution System

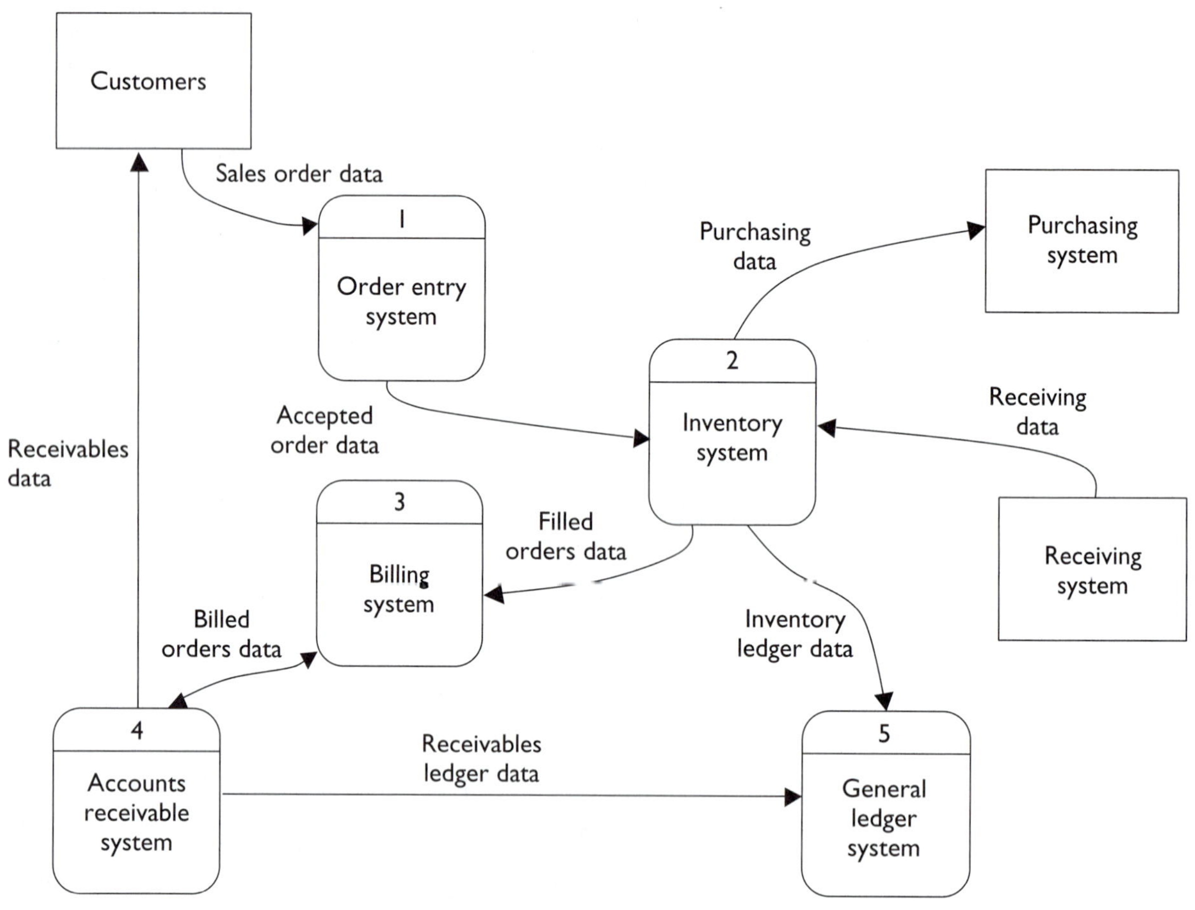

Putting System Interface Design in Perspective

One advantage of taking a top-down, modular approach to system design, such as that of phased development, is that the system interfaces are determined early in the system development life cycle. The system linkages are defined prior to the detail design work for each module. However, in many cases, one system or module is already in production, and the developers of the new system or module must tailor it to fit. Interface design forces the developers to look beyond their system to the environment in which their system functions.

SYSTEM CONTROL DESIGN

System control design includes the routines and procedures that are incorporated into information systems to ensure that the data is processed correctly. Design controls have two main objectives—information integrity and compliance.

- *Information Integrity*—The condition that exists when the firm's data accurately represents its physical systems is called **information integrity.** It is achieved by controlling both data and processing. **Data controls** ensure that the data flows properly through the system, from its point of origin to its destination. **Processing controls** ensure that the data is processed in the desired manner.

- *Compliance*—Constraints are applied to an information system by management and elements in the firm's environment. The system must be in **compliance** with these constraints. Management constraints come in the form of policies, procedures, and performance criteria. Environmental constraints come in such forms as government laws and regulations, plus standards from professional accounting and auditing organizations.

System control design begins with an identification of the risks that can threaten the ability of the system to achieve information integrity and compliance. When a risk is identified, the next step is to identify one or more controls that will either prevent the risk from occurring or minimize the damage should the risk materialize.

The Risk Matrix

A good way to address risks in a systematic fashion is to organize them in the form of a matrix. In a **risk matrix,** the processes of a system are listed along the left-hand side and the various *types* of potential risks are listed across the top, as shown in Figure 6.14.[3] In this example, the risks are those that threaten the information integrity of an order entry system—guarding against incomplete data, inaccurate data, and unauthorized transactions. The potential risks are entered into the appropriate cells as they relate to each process.

The Control Matrix

Once the risk matrix has been prepared, the task is to identify one or more controls that can be directed at each risk. These controls can also be displayed in a matrix form. In a **control matrix,** the cells contain controls that can be applied to the risks in corresponding cells of a risk matrix. Figure 6.15 identifies potential controls for the order entry system. These controls are then incorporated into the system design.

The Concept of Controls for Each System Element

There are so many potential control techniques that can be incorporated into modern information systems that the developers must approach their task in a systematic way. Otherwise, the likelihood of control imbalance is high, with some areas being over-controlled and other areas under-controlled.

One technique that can contribute to a balanced application of controls is to view them in terms of the system elements that they affect. Figure 6.16 on page 382 is a DFD that shows eight system elements that are found in all information systems in some combination.[4] The task of the developers is to incorporate as many controls into each element as is necessary to reduce the risks to the desired level.

1. *Transaction origination*—Users originate transactions of various types. For example, customers order the firm's products, employees work a certain num-

FIGURE 6.14

A Risk Matrix

System Elements	Risks		
	Incomplete data	Inaccurate data	Unauthorized transactions
1. Log in sales orders	Missing data ■ Customer number ■ Customer order number ■ Customer order date	Wrong data ■ Customer number ■ Customer order number ■ Customer order date	No customer
2. Edit sales order data	Missing data ■ Item number ■ Quantity	Wrong data ■ Item number ■ Quantity	
3. Conduct credit check			Bad credit rating or credit limit exceeded

ber of hours, and managers make decisions to be entered into a mathematical model. The transaction data is typically recorded on a source document. The main control objective for this element is to ensure that all transaction data is completely and accurately recorded. An example of a transaction origination control is the requirement that department supervisors sign employees' time cards before the cards are sent to information services.

2. *System input*—Next, the transaction data is entered into the system. The main control objective is to ensure that the input is accomplished in both a complete and accurate manner. This is where data validation occurs; each entered data element is checked against such predetermined characteristics as the type of data, field size, and range of numeric values. Another example of a system input control is the use of pre-numbered source documents to guard against loss or misuse. This second system element can be combined with the first when there are no source documents and the transaction data is entered directly into the system. An example of this form of system input is the taking of sales orders over the telephone by an order clerk sitting at a keyboard terminal.

3. *Input data communications*—The input data communications element exists when system input occurs some distance from the location of the processing. In this situation, controls are implemented to ensure that data is completely and accurately transmitted from the sending nodes to the central computer, with no loss of security. An example of an input data communications control is the use of hardware and software that detects electronic transmission errors.

4. *Data processing*—The transaction data enters the system either from the system input element or input data communications. The control objective is to

ensure that the data is completely and accurately processed. An example of a data processing control is a program module that compares entered item numbers against a master list to ensure that the numbers are those of the firm's products.

5. *The database*—Database controls have the objective of ensuring that the database is an accurate reflection of the physical resources and activities that it represents, and that its contents are made available to only authorized users. An example of a database control is the use of a user directory that identifies those persons who are authorized to retrieve data.

6. *The software library*—The **software library** is the collection of all the firm's computer programs. An example of a software library control is the policy of maintaining master copies of all approved programs in a vault, and periodically comparing all production programs to those master copies. This policy is intended to detect instances when programs are illegally modified after they become operational.

7. *Output data communications*—The data processing output must be transmitted by means of output data communications when the output occurs in

FIGURE 6.15

A Control Matrix

System Elements	Risks		
	Incomplete data	Inaccurate data	Unauthorized transactions
1. Log in sales orders	Telephone customer for missing customer order number and order date	Sight verify log entries	Check customer number against master list
2. Edit sales order data	Use item description to look up missing item number in master list Telephone customer for quantity	Check item number against master list Conduct reasonableness check on quantity	
3. Conduct credit check			Obtain current credit rating from credit bureau Compare updated accounts receivable amount with credit limit

FIGURE 6.16

Controls Are Designed into System Elements

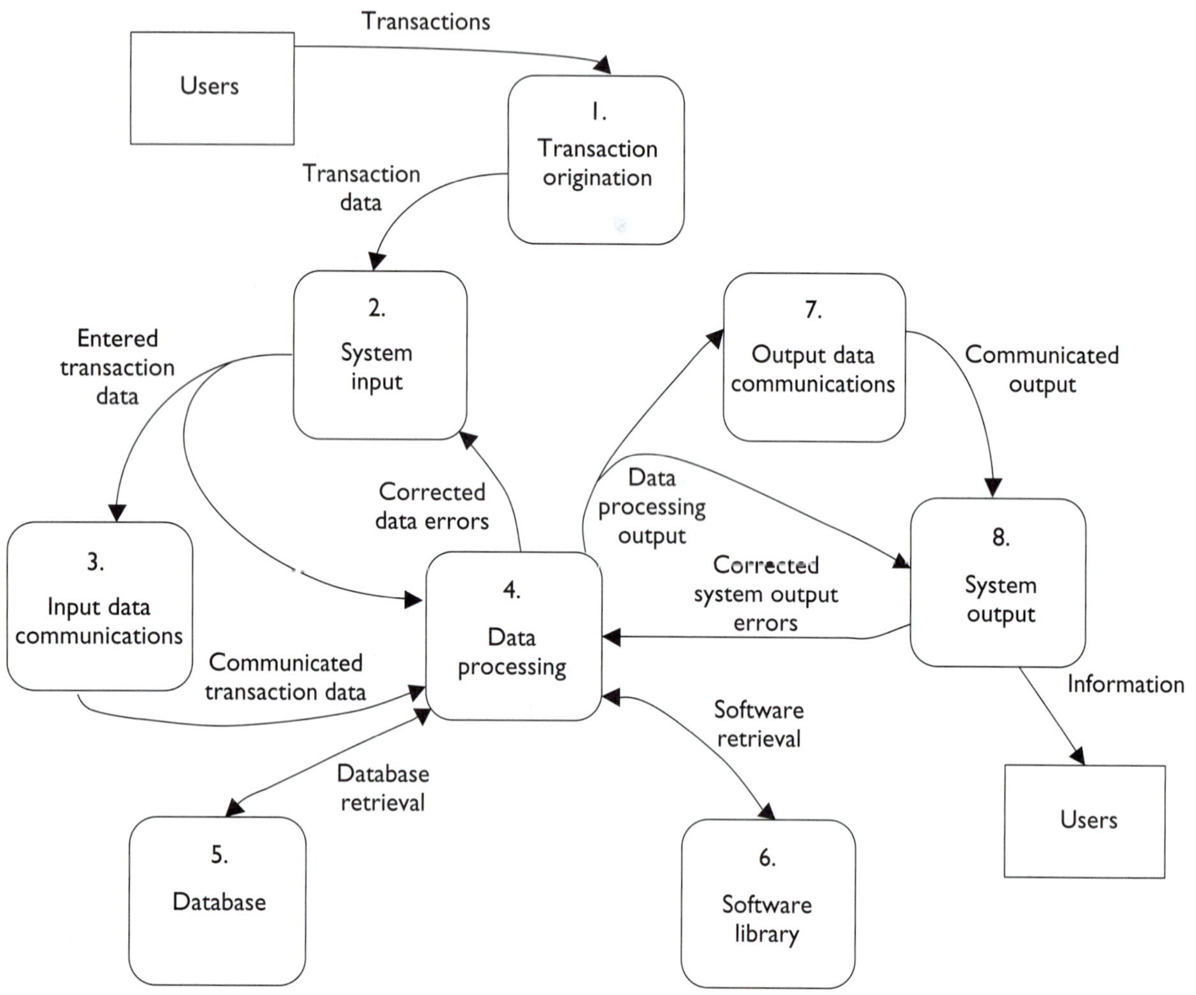

a location that is remote from the processing. For example, the computer in Des Moines prints out a picking ticket in a warehouse in Cedar Rapids. The same controls can be used for output data communications that are used for input.

8. *System output*—System output controls are intended to guarantee that the results of the processing are reported to only those persons who are authorized to receive them. An example of an output control is a requirement that a user send a special e-mail message to confirm receipt of a report.

Each of the eight system elements can be further subdivided into processes, and controls built into each process.

Putting System Control Design in Perspective

It would be possible to design a system without any controls. That would certainly reduce the design costs but could result in high costs of unacceptable performance once the system goes into production. For that reason, the functional requirements of the new system will likely include a good set of controls. That is why the right-hand column of the F/C matrix is devoted to controls.

When we identified the makeup of the project team and illustrated it in Figure 1.16, we included an internal auditor. This person should be able to contribute to the development effort in many ways, but none is likely to be more important than to provide expertise in system control design.

Putting the Identification of Possible System Configurations in Perspective

We have just completed a description of the types of design that go into a new system. At this point, there should be no doubt in your mind about design being a mammoth effort. Such would be the case even if we were talking about only a single system. But, you have to keep in mind that *each* alternate system configuration should receive this effort so that it can receive a proper evaluation.

One strategy that can be followed, however, in keeping the design effort to a reasonable level, is to keep the number of possible solutions to a reasonable number, say two to six.

Evaluate the Possible Solutions

With the possible solutions identified, the developers next identify the measures that will be used to evaluate the ability of each to satisfy the functional requirements. These are the **evaluation criteria.** There are no strict rules to follow in identifying the criteria; they depend on the user's needs. One possibility is to choose criteria that relate in some way to the dimensions of information value that we identified in Chapter 2—accuracy, timeliness, completeness, and relevance. Another possibility is to choose criteria based on the nine goals that we focused on in goal analysis in Chapter 4 and are the basis of evaluations of software tools in Technical Module G.

The persons who are responsible for evaluating the alternatives rate each one on each criterion. This can be accomplished in a completely subjective way, with each person simply rank ordering the alternatives. Or, a more disciplined approach is to quantify the evaluation as illustrated in Figure 6.17. In this example, each criterion is weighted based on its relative importance, and each is rated on a scale that ranges from very good to very poor. A rating of very good receives 10 points, good receives 8, and so on. The ratings of all of the persons evaluating the particular system configuration are averaged, and a total score is computed.

The letter P in the figure stands for probability. The probability measures the likelihood of the alternative receiving the associated rating on the criterion. For example, the illustrated possible system configuration has a 20 percent chance of performing very good in terms of its input efficiency. The letters EV stand for expected value. The expected value is computed by multiplying the probability times the rating points. For example, the EV for very good input efficiency is 2.0 (.20 times 10).

FIGURE 6.17

A Quantitative Approach to the Evaluation of a Possible Solution

Ratings for System Alternative I													
Criteria	Weight	Very Good (10)		Good (8)		Average (6)		Poor (4)		Very Poor (2)		Total Points (total EV)	Total Weighted Points (weight x total EV)
		P	EV	P	EV	P	EV	P	EV	P	EV		
Input efficiency	.20	0.2	2.0	0.6	4.8	0.2	1.2	0	0	0	0	8.0	1.60
Responsiveness	.35	0.2	2.0	0.7	5.6	0.1	0.6	0	0	0	0	8.2	2.87
Currency of information	.25	0	0	0.2	1.6	0.2	1.2	0.3	1.2	0.3	0.6	4.6	1.15
Disaster recovery capability	.20	0	0	0.7	5.6	0.3	1.8	0	0	0	0	7.4	1.48
Total points												28.2	7.10
Maximum points												40.0	10.00

Legend: P = probability; EV = expected value

All configurations are rated in the manner illustrated in the figure, and the configuration with the highest total weighted score is the prime candidate for selection.

Putting the Quantitative Evaluation of Possible Solutions in Perspective

All project teams do not follow a quantitative process such as the one illustrated in the figure. However, the approach has value because it forces the participants to agree on the criteria and to consider the impact of each on the selection. The quantitative approach lends a certain amount of discipline to a process that can be very subjective.

SELECT THE BEST SOLUTION

With the evaluation of each alternative completed, the next step is to select the best. This is the point in the process where the cohesiveness of the project team is put to test since participants tend to support the alternatives that will best benefit their units.

However, the team is motivated to reach agreement because it knows that the choice should *not* be left to the MIS steering committee. The committee has neither the time nor the tools for making such a choice. The project team is in the best position to select the system configuration for implementation, and then submit their choice to the MIS steering committee for approval.

Putting the Use of the Systems Approach for System Design in Perspective

The almost infinite number of possible system designs that can be directed at a single problem or opportunity demands that some framework be used to guide the evaluation. The systems approach is ideal for this task. The identification of the alternate systems is the key. Once that is accomplished, the evaluation and selection of the best can be fairly automatic. By considering the alternate choices for each system component, the developers have the greatest opportunity of coming up with the best system design.

Putting Systems Design in Perspective

At the beginning of the chapter, we identified the three steps of systems design as (1) designing the new system components, (2) designing interfaces with other systems, and documenting the new system design. These three tasks were accomplished during the step of the systems approach where the developers identified the alternate solutions. For each solution, design efforts were directed at the user interface, data, procedure, software, system interface, and system control. As those design efforts occurred, the documentation was prepared.

This concludes the description of the design process. The following section supplements the discussion of the design process with a set of tips to keep in mind when designing each of the systems in the information infrastructure.

Design Tips for the Information Infrastructure

The design requirements placed on a system depend on its type. A system that performs the firm's accounting functions demands a different design expertise than does an enterprise system that facilitates the firm's basic functions, such as a marketing information system, a group support system used by the corporate planning committee, or an expert system used to approve credit sales. Listed below are the types of design knowledge and skill that each system demands.

Accounting Information System

There are three keys to the design of the accounting information system:

- A good understanding of accounting fundamentals
- A good understanding of the information needs of elements in the firm's environment
- An ability to design databases that mirror or improve the firm's operations

An Enterprise System

The keys to the design of the enterprise system are:

- An understanding of organizational structure—how firms are organized, the activities of the various organizational units, and the information needs of persons in each unit

PROJECT MANAGEMENT TOOLBOX

Project Management Tips for Design

Each new hardware and software development brings with it new challenges in systems design. There is so much more to know about design today than just a few years ago that it is impossible for one individual to know it all. The snowballing effect of innovations in technology explains the trend to more specialization in the form of database and network specialists, as well as SWAT teams.

Four suggestions appear to be especially appropriate for the project team faced with the challenge of remaining current on systems design.

- Consider purchasing well-tested software for any application that is not unique to your organization.
- Seek the help of technology specialists *early,* both inside and outside the firm. Adhere to their recommendations and to company standards for the development process and the target production environment. Create or update standards if no current standards exist.
- Use prototyping as a means of improving communications with the user by arranging vendor demonstrations of purchased software or frequent reviews of custom developed software in each phase of development.
- Make maximum use of CASE tools or visual development environments that not only remove much of the drudgery from design and documentation but can do a better job.

By taking advantage of existing human and software resources, the systems that you design have the greatest opportunity of meeting the needs of the users and your organization.

- An understanding of management functions and roles
- An ability to design periodic reports that reflect the four dimensions of information
- An ability to design databases to facilitate the preparation of special reports
- An ability to design complex mathematical models using programming languages or special modeling languages.
- An understanding of group dynamics—how people interact in a group setting while solving problems—and how to influence this interaction so as to achieve the best results with appropriate system functions.

The accounting information system knowledge and skill boil down to understanding and facilitating the firm's operations, whereas the enterprise system knowledge and skill deal with how to support the information needs of the firm's problem solvers and decision makers.

SUMMARY

The design stage of phased development consists of three steps-design new system components, design interfaces with other systems, and document the new system design. This process has evolved from one that focused attention on the documents that the system would produce, to one that emphasized organizational problem-solving, and then to one that emphasized the organizational database, and most recently to the one that is currently in the spotlight-the enterprise data model approach.

There are two basic types of design-logical and physical. The design stage of the system development life cycle is concerned with logical design, and the design is documented with data and process models. Physical design identifies the technology that is required to convert the logical design to a production system. Both logical and physical design have been carried out on an evolution of computer architectures. First there was mainframe computing, followed by client/server. Today, the movement is toward Web-based distributed-object computing.

When alternate system configurations are identified, each must be documented in terms of six types of design—user interface, data, procedure, software, system interface, and system control.

Design of user input interfaces is concerned with the hardware units and the types of dialog. The units include online key-driven devices, special-purpose terminals, voice input, push-button telephones, MICR, and OCR. When input data is recorded on a source document rather than entered directly, the form should be designed to facilitate preparation and data entry. User-computer dialogs can be program-directed or user-directed.

Design of user output interfaces encompasses reports, outputs from simulations, and communications. Reports can be periodic, special, or exception. They can be printed or displayed, and prepared in a tabular, graphic, or narrative form.

Data design is the responsibility of the DBA, who assists with database design and makes decisions about the allocation of data among available servers or recommends purchasing additional servers. The DBA and other developers on the team model the data using ERDs, the data dictionary, and class diagrams.

Procedure design selects between batch or online processing and then makes use of such modeling techniques as DFDs and object oriented tools.

System interface design recognizes that systems seldom operate independently, but invariably link up with other systems. One way to ensure that the systems interface in the required manner is to take a top-down design approach.

System control design has dual objectives of information integrity and compliance. Creating risk matrices, and then creating matching control matrices can facilitate the design. Controls can be incorporated into eight elements that exist in systems of all types-transaction origination, system input, input data communications, data processing, the database, the software library, output data communications, and system output.

Once each of the selected possible solutions has been subjected to this design detail, they are evaluated—a process that can be accomplished in a structured or unstructured manner. A structured approach includes use of probabilities and expected values to compute a score for each solution. Decision makers consider the scores in making the selection of the best solution to construct in the next phase.

Each system in the information infrastructure demands a unique set of knowledge and skills. In addition, some general design tips can be employed—purchase application software when possible, seek the help of specialists, use prototyping, and select CASE tools or visual development tools for custom systems.

After each portion of the new system is analyzed and designed, the next step is preliminary construction, the subject of the next chapter.

Key Terms

mainframe computing
client/server computing
Web-based computing
magnetic ink character recognition (MICR)
optical character recognition (OCR)
information integrity
periodic report, repetitive report, scheduled report
special report
exception report
batch processing
online processing
realtime system
information integrity
compliance

Key Concepts

- Systems design has evolved from a document approach to an enterprise approach
- The difference between logical and physical design
- The variety of client/server environments, influenced by the degree to which the user interface, function, and data access are shared between the client and the server
- Use of the systems approach as a framework for systems design
- System design can be subdivided into efforts aimed at the user interface, data, procedure, software, system interface, and system control
- Use of risk and control matrices to identify system points where controls should be implemented
- System elements provide a good basis for achieving a balance in system controls
- Each type of system in the information infrastructure demands a unique set of design knowledge and skills

Questions

1. What are the three steps of the design task?
2. When is documentation of the new system design prepared?
3. Explain the difference between the organizational database approach and the enterprise data model approach.
4. What is the difference, if any, between the enterprise model and the enterprise data model?
5. What data modeling tools would be used in preparing the enterprise data model?
6. Distinguish between logical and physical design.
7. How do you distinguish between a fat client and a thin client?
8. When you take the systems approach to systems design, which systems approach steps do you take?
9. Name the six types of design that go into systems design.
10. What is meant by the term input bottleneck?
11. How can you tailor dialog to a particular user's preferences?
12. What triggers a special report?
13. What are the main tasks of the database administrator in database design?
14. Who is primarily responsible for data design?
15. What is the main disadvantage of batch processing?
16. Is an online system the same as a realtime system? Explain.
17. What is the fundamental process design decision?

18. When one system must interface with another system, how is the interface accomplished?
19. What are the two objectives of system control design?
20. How is information integrity achieved?
21. How are a risk matrix and a control matrix related?
22. What is the name given to the piece of paper that is used to enter transaction data into a system?
23. The chapter explains a control that can be built into the software library. Give another example.
24. What is the value of a quantitative evaluation of alternatives even if the evaluators do not automatically select the one that makes the best showing?
25. What are the design keys that are important for both accounting information systems and enterprise systems?
26. What two types of software should the developer consider when engaging in systems design?

Topics for Discussion

1. How could the project team go about identifying the possible solutions?
2. What business applications would lend themselves to the use of OCR scanners?
3. Assume that a manager of a shoe manufacturing plant wants to practice management by exception. What are some types of reports that would be helpful?
4. The chapter identifies the three main types of outputs as reports, outputs from simulations, and communications. Where do they appear in the general systems model of the firm?
5. Of the eight system elements that can form the basis for system control design, which one do you believe to be the most important?

Case Problem: Cowpoke Creations

You are the new manager of information technology for Cowpoke Creations, a large manufacturer of Western clothing located in Calgary, Alberta. You previously worked as a senior developer for a large accounting firm where you specialized in auditing client's computer-based systems. Cowpoke was one of your clients and Rae Summerfield, the CIO, liked your work so well that she offered you the management job when it opened up.

Cowpoke is a good example of how information resources should be positioned in an enterprise. The information services organization is one of the major business areas of the company and Rae is a member of the executive committee. Rae works with the other executives in developing the strategic plan for Cowpoke, as well as the plans for each of the business areas. Rae is also chair of the MIS steering committee.

In your first meeting with Rae, she explains that the systems analysis section is in good shape, the previous manager having done a good job of building a staff of developers who have systems analysis experience. As a way for you to get your feet on the ground, Rae wants you to handle a complaint by the sales manager, Harold Hall, that the marketing information system is not functioning as intended. The system consists of a mathematical model but because it was implemented within marketing, Rae doesn't know the details. She wants you to call on Harold, find out what is going on, and report back to her.

You: Since I'm new to the organization, I would appreciate it, Mr. Hall, if you could give me a little background on your marketing information system.

Hall: Certainly. It all started about two years ago. I had a meeting with my regional managers and we decided that we didn't have enough information for setting the annual sales quotas for the sales representatives. We needed historical data about what each rep had sold in past years, plus their projections for the coming year. Only some of the historical data, and none of the projection data, was in the computer. I checked with Rae and she told me that we would have to wait about fifteen months before IS could get around to it. She always has a backlog. I kicked it around with my managers and we decided just to do it ourselves.

You: Do you have your own staff of information specialists?

Hall: We do. We have about a half dozen systems analysts and an equal number of programmers. We rely on IS for database and data communications expertise.

You: Well, could you please tell me about the problem with the marketing information system?

Hall: Our analysts did a poor job of not only designing the system but teaching us how to use it. It is very complicated-user unfriendly I would say. It's a mathematical model. Neither myself nor my regional managers are computer experts. So, every time we need to run the model, we have to ask our computer specialists to do it for us. It is very inconvenient, and not the way things were intended.

You: Did you or the other managers receive any formal training?

Hall: None to speak of. Our lead analyst gave us a demo but there are no written instructions.

You: You mention that the system is a model. I assume that it computes the quotas.

Hall: That's right, and the output is displayed on the screen in the form of a report. That's another thing. We would really rather get a hardcopy. And, it would be nice if we could also produce some graphs. But, nobody asked us. Our specialists used the old reports that we had been preparing manually and simply put them on the computer. Before we knew it, the system had been implemented. It would be too expensive to modify the system to give us what we need. At least, that is what our specialists say.

You: That's amazing. You didn't have any opportunity to approve the design as it unfolded or to exercise any kind of control over the development? For example, did the specialists sit down with you and ask you about your information needs? Or, did they ask you how well the system must perform in order to satisfy your needs?

Hall: None of those things. We had a brief meeting and then they went off to do the work. The next thing we knew, the system had been designed and implemented on the IS server.

You: How would you summarize the situation right now?

Hall: In one word: grim. No, seriously, I would say that we have a system that we can't use because it is too complex and if we could use it the output would not be in the format that we would like.

You: Are you mainly unhappy about the format? Does the information itself appear to be accurate? Have you encountered any errors?

Hall: So far, everything looks accurate. We've spent a lot of time going over the reports, trying to understand them, and I'm convinced that the right numbers are there. It does appear that the specialists gave us a good database, and that was one of the main things we were after.

You: Well, that's good news. Maybe all is not lost. Exactly what do you want from me, and from IS?

Hall: First, I would like to know where we went wrong so that if we ever do this again we won't make the same mistake. Also, I would like your recommendation concerning what we should do. As I see it, there are three possible solutions. Should we try to live with the system as it is now, should we ask our specialists to reengineer it, or should we call on IS to bail us out?

You: Well, let me tell Rae about our conversation and I am sure that she will get back with you shortly.

Assignments

1. Write a memo to Mr. Hall, for Rae's signature. Evaluate the marketing information system in terms of each of these five types of design effort-user interface, procedure, data, other system

interface, and system control. For each that is applicable, identify what was done correctly and what was not.

2. Write a second memo to Mr. Hall, also for Rae's signature, identifying which of the three solutions identified by Mr. Hall that you recommend that marketing take. Assume that the IS backlog has been reduced to approximately three months. After stating your recommendation, list the advantages and the disadvantages of following such a program.

Selected Bibliography

Agarwal, R., G. Bruno, and M. Torchiano. "An Operational Approach to the Design of Workflow Systems." *Information & Software Technology* 42 (Number 8, May 15, 2000): 547-555.

Briand, Lionel C., Jurgen Wust, John W. Daly, and D. Victor Porter.. "Exploring the Relationship Between Design Measures and Software Quality in Object-Oriented Systems." *Journal of Systems & Software* 51 (Number 3, May 1, 2000): 245-273.

Detlor, Brian. "The Corporate Portal as Information Infrastructure: Towards a Framework for Portal Design." *International Journal of Information Management* 20 (Number 2, April 2000): 91-101.

Fan, Ming, Jan Stallert, and Andrew Whinston, "The Adoption and Design Methodologies for Component-based Systems Enterprise Systems." *European Journal of Information Systems* 9 (Number 1, 2000): 25-35.

Gallegos, Frederick. "Audit Contributions to Systems Development." *In EDP Auditing* (Boston, MA: Auerbach Publishers, 1991), section 72-01-40, pp. 1-14.

Hix, Deborah, and Robert S. Schulman. "Human-Computer Interface Development Tools: A Methodology for their Evaluation." *Communications of the ACM* 34 (March 1991): 74-87.

Karabin, Stephen J. "Application Systems Control Standards." *In EDP Auditing* (Boston, MA: Auerbach Publishers, 1991), section 74-04-40, pp. 1-20.

Klein, Gary, and Philip O. Beck. "A Decision Aid for Selecting Among Information System Alternatives." *MIS Quarterly* 11 (June 1987): 177-85.

Kramer, Joseph., Sunil Noronha,, and John Vergo. "A User-Centered Design Approach to Personalization." *Communications of the ACM* 43 (Number 8, August 2000): 44-48.

Neumann, Peter G. "The Human Element: Inside Risks." *Communications of the ACM* 34 (November 1991): 150.

Stevens, W. P.; G. J. Myers, and L. L. Constantine. "Structured Design." *IBM Systems Journal* 2 (Number 2, 1974): 115-39.

Warnier, Jean-Dominique. *Logical Construction of Systems.* New York: Van Nostrand Reinhold, 1981.

Wilkinson, Bryan. "Systems Development and Design Checklist." *In EDP Auditing* (Boston, MA: Auerbach Publishers, 1991), section 74-04-10, pp. 1-17.

Yoon, Youngohc, and Tor Guimaraes. "Developing Knowledge-Based Systems: An Object-Oriented Organizational Approach." *Information Resources Management Journal* 5 (Summer 1992): 15-32.

Notes

1. The Association for Computing Machinery, ACM, has a special interest group that specializes in the computer-human interaction. The group is named SIGCHI and they publish a newsletter and sponsor conferences that provide information that is potentially valuable to systems developers.
2. Taken from Sirkka Jarvenpaa and Gary W. Dickson, "Graphics and Managerial Decision Making: Research-Based Guidelines." *Communications of the ACM* 31 (June 1988): 764-774.

3. The idea for the risk and control matrices came from Dr. Jerry FitzGerald, a management consultant. For more information, see Jerry FitzGerald, *Business Data Communications,* 3rd ed. (New York, N.Y.: John Wiley & Sons, 1990): pp. 488-496.
4. The idea of viewing controls in this manner was derived from *Systems Auditability and Control: Control Practices* (Altamonte Springs, Fla.: The Institute of Internal Auditors, 1977), pp. 45-86.

TECHNICAL MODULE H

WEB AND GRAPHICAL USER INTERFACE DESIGN

A strong case could be built for the argument that the user interface is the most important part of a system. After all, it is the part that the user sees and uses, and has a big influence on the user's perception of the entire system.

Web-based systems present particular challenges for developers. Whether your users are dozens of employees of a single company within a secure intranet or thousands of potential customers worldwide, the chance of working with all users is unlikely or impossible. Developers must rely on representative users to determine whether their user interface is as intuitive as it must be in these situations. Following guidelines for easy-to-read, easy-to-follow, attractive interfaces is the best way to ensure success for Web-based systems as well as systems that have a smaller audience that participates on the development team.

THE USERS AND THEIR MAIN EVENTS

In designing user interfaces it is necessary that the developers know who the users are and their expectations of the information system. It is also necessary to know how they will interact with the system—their main events. This understanding is the foundation of any good interface.

Who Are the Users?

There are two main groups of users. **Internal users** are members of the firm who use the outputs of the firm's information systems in performing their tasks. **External users** are individuals or organizations in the environment of the firm who also use the firm's information system outputs in performing their tasks. Examples of external users are customers, suppliers, governmental agencies, and stockholders. External users use the information system outputs in carrying out their relationships with the firm. For example, customers use invoices and statements in paying for their purchases, suppliers use purchase orders in filling the firm's orders, governments use tax reports in collecting taxes, and stockholders use financial reports in evaluating their investments.

An important point to recognize is that both internal and external users can interface with Web-based systems. Both types can participate in an intranet, which uses the Internet for communication within the firm and with selected environmental elements. For example, a firm can include its suppliers in its intranet. When the firm engages in e-business, external users can interface with the firm using the Web.

In designing Web-based interfaces, an important distinction exists between the intranet users and e-business users. The firm has much more control over the intranet users, and the design of their interfaces can follow the approach that developers normally take in working with internal users. E-business customers, on the other hand, present greater challenges because of their potentially larger number and dispersed geographical locations.

What Are the Main Events?

The users' **main events** are those user-initiated transactions that are supported by the information system. As an example, factory workers use the information system to clock on and off work at the beginning and end of each day, and clock on and off jobs that are performed during the day.

When engaging in user interface design, you first identify the users and then identify their main events.

TYPES OF INTERFACES

There are basically three types of interfaces that enable the user to interact with the system—outputs, inputs, and a combination of inputs and outputs.

- *Output interfaces*—The system uses output interfaces to provide the user with information. Such outputs include reports for internal users and documents for external users. These outputs can be printed or displayed.
- *Input interfaces*—Users use the input interfaces to enter data or information into the system. This type of interface is used by salespersons and data entry operators in entering sales order data into an order entry system.
- *Input and output interfaces*—The user uses combined input and output interfaces to enter data, information, and instructions into the system, and then receive the system's output. The system uses the input in performing its tasks. For example, a marketing manager enters a sales price into a pricing model and the model uses the price to simulate the effect that the price can have on sales. The output of the simulation is displayed or printed by the output interface. The system can also use the users' instructions in determining which task or tasks to perform. An example is when an executive specifies that a report is to be displayed in a graphic form.

When designing an output interface, developers are only concerned with communicating *to* the user. When designing an input interface, the only concern is receiving inputs

FIGURE H.1

Internal Consistency: Screens for System Have Consistent Layout

Title 1
Text entry
Text
Text entry
Text
Text entry
Text
OK
Cancel

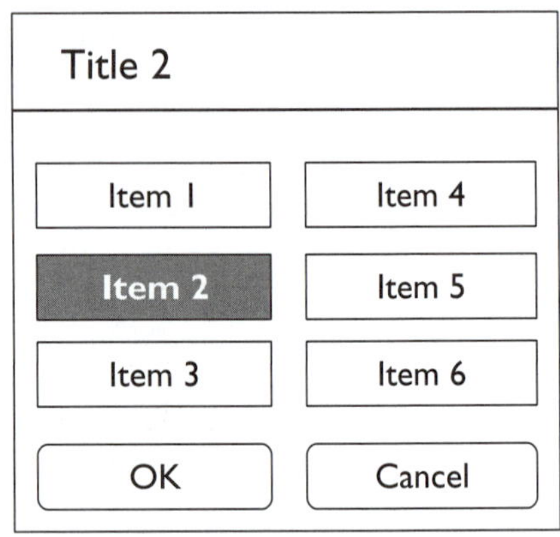

from the user. When designing combination input and output interfaces, developers must take into account the *two-way dialog* that exists between the user and the system.

THE GRAPHICAL USER INTERFACE

The direct interaction between the user and the information system is called the **human-computer interface** or the **user interface.** The first interfaces featured a dialog consisting of both alphabetic and numeric data in the form of commands, prompts and their responses, form filling, and menu selection. The ability of microcomputers and workstations to display data in a graphic form popularized what has become known as the graphical user interface.

A **graphical user interface (GUI),** is a means for the user to interact with the information system through the use of typography, symbols, color, and other static and dynamic graphics to convey facts, concepts, and emotions.[1] The underlying logic of the GUI is that graphics offer improvements over alphanumeric data by making it easier for the user to learn to use the system, improving system usability, and producing a more favorable user perception. This technical module addresses the special considerations that influence GUI design.

GUIs As a Means of Achieving Usability

Software developers incorporate GUI capabilities into their design to achieve usability. **Usability** is a concept that describes those product attributes that enable users to quickly, efficiently, and effectively use the product to accomplish *their* real work in a way that meets or exceeds *their* needs and expectations.[2]

The key to the GUI's contribution to usability is the favorable perception that the user forms of the software, based on the interface. This favorable perception enables the GUI to achieve an observable improvement in productivity. The ability of a GUI to achieve this productivity depends on its metaphor. A **metaphor** is an invisible web of terms and associations that underlies the way we speak and think about a concept.[3]

A good example of a metaphor is the electronic spreadsheet with its rows and columns. It has the same appearance to the user as a ledger sheet used by accountants; it is a natural way to array business data. When electronic spreadsheets were first introduced, business users were attracted to them because they provided a familiar metaphor. In a similar fashion, the use of icons to represent documents, folders, and diskettes offer an effective metaphor because they have the same appearance as objects typically found on one's desk. Achievement of such a **desktop metaphor** is a goal of systems designed for use by both business managers and non-managers; the metaphor provides a natural setting for information systems work.

When building a GUI, it is a good idea to focus on one or two metaphors and then add other functionality. You should study the users and understand what mental models they employ in their everyday work. Then, tap into those models by building in metaphors that both reflect and extend them.

GUI Requirements

A GUI design must satisfy several basic requirements.[4] The GUI must provide for:

- A comprehensible mental image, or metaphor
- An appropriate organization of data, functions, tasks, and roles
- A quality appearance, known as the *look*
- Effective interaction sequencing, known as the *feel*

A GUI design that satisfies all of these requirements will provide an effective means of communication for every kind of information system application. This is possible because graphic design relies on established design principles.

GUI Design Principles

The three main principles of GUI design are organization, economy, and communication.

FIGURE H.2

Grids Provide the Framework for GUI Organization

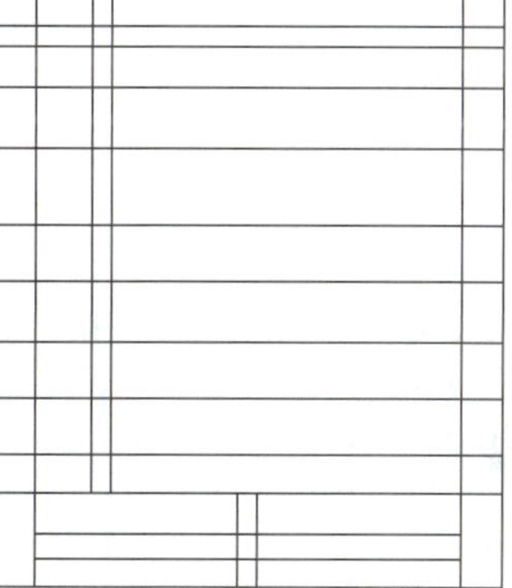

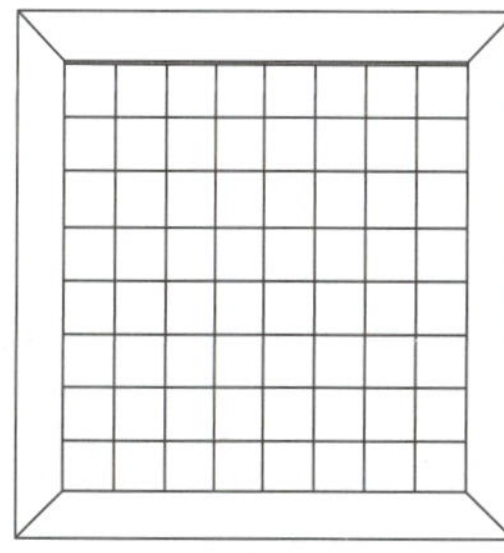

FIGURE H.3

Relationship Examples

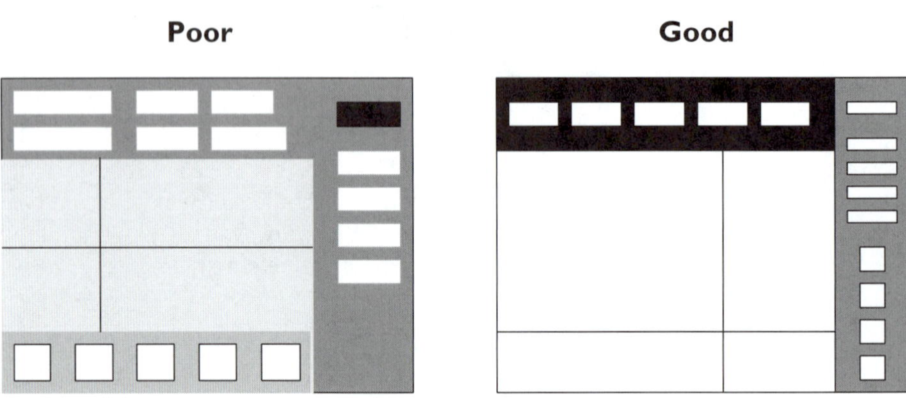

Organization

Designers achieve organization in their interfaces by means of several techniques—consistency, screen layout, relationships, and navigability.

Consistency is achieved by maximizing the regularity of the location and appearance of all components. There are two kinds of consistency—internal and external. **Internal consistency** deals with the regularity within a single system, and two examples appear in Figure H.1. In both examples, like items have the same general appearance. **External consistency,** on the other hand, deals with regularity across systems. One reason for the popularity of Microsoft Windows is the external consistency that it offers across the various software components.

Screen layout can contribute to organization by using horizontal and vertical grids to provide the framework, as illustrated in Figure H.2. The grid concept applies to entire screens, windows, buttons, and icons.

Relationships are established by grouping like items. This grouping can be enhanced by using such features as background color. Figure H.3 shows how the example on the right does a better job of defining relationships than does the one on the left. Relationships should be clear, consistent, appropriate, and strong.

Navigability deals with the ability of an interface to focus the user's attention on the appropriate material and to lead the user through the material in the proper manner. Figure H.4 illustrates an example of poor navigability on the left and of good navigability on the right. The good example uses title bars to identify major areas and bullets for subsidiary items within each area.

Economy

The second GUI design principle is economy. The main idea is to not use too many of the various graphical features that are available because overuse can actually diminish the ability of the user to communicate. Economy can be achieved by means of simplicity, clarity, distinctiveness, and emphasis.

Simplicity minimizes the work the user must expend to understand a display. Although both windows in Figure H.5 contain the same material, the one on the right has the simplest appearance. There are fewer shapes and arrangements. In this exam-

FIGURE H.4

Good Organization Assists Navigation

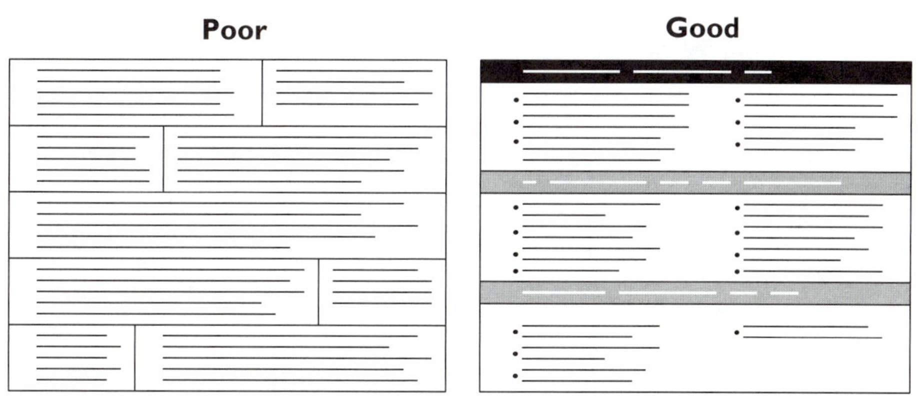

ple, simplicity is achieved by means of format. It can also be achieved by including only essential elements.

Clarity means minimizing the opportunity for ambiguity. For a novice user, the right-hand icon in Figure H.6 offers a higher probability of being perceived as a zoom operation than does the icon on the left. In viewing the icon with the flowers, the user would not be certain whether it represented a zoom out or a zoom in.

Distinctiveness enables the user to separate elements on the screen into logical groupings. In striving to achieve distinctiveness, as much harm can be done by too much as too little. Figure H.7 illustrates both extremes. On the left, there is not enough distinctiveness to help the user focus on the important elements. On the right, the use of too much distinctiveness, called the **Las Vegas approach,** is equally ineffective.

Emphasis is the final means of achieving economy. The designer should make it easy for the user to pick out important elements by keeping them to a minimum.

FIGURE H.5

Simple Displays Assist Understanding

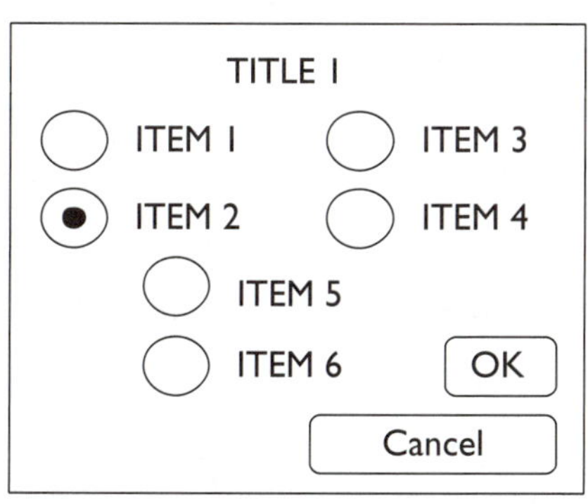

TABLE H.6

Choose Graphic Carefully

Techniques include minimizing clutter and adhering to vertical and horizontal grids. An example of good emphasis is the use of **stoplight colors** in displays of management information systems. Data printed in green represents things that are going as planned; data in yellow indicates items that might be getting out of control; data in red signals problems that demand the manager's attention.

Communication

The third design principle is communication, which is achieved through a balanced offering of legibility, readability, typography, symbolism, multiple views, and color. We discuss color in the next major section.

Legibility can be achieved by using a combination of characters and graphics that show up well. The emphasis is on communication rather than appearance. In applying this design principle, the designer should pay particular attention to the environment in which the GUI will be used. If the room is dark, a brightly lighted screen may produce too much glare. If the room is bright, dark backgrounds may introduce unwanted reflections.

Readability makes the display easy to interpret and understand. As a general rule, lines of alphabetic material should be left-justified, whereas numbers should be right-justified or aligned on the decimal point. Attempts to make the display more attractive, such as by centering lines of text, usually diminish readability.

Typography deals with the manner in which textual material is displayed. Some basic guidelines are listed below.

- Use no more than three type fonts.
- Use no more than three type sizes.
- Include no more than 60 characters on a line.
- Use combinations of uppercase and lowercase.

Two typography techniques to avoid are use of uppercase only, and the use of justified right-hand margins with fixed-width fonts. Either can slow reading speed as much as 12 percent.

Symbolism relates to the use of graphics that convey messages and information in the desired way. This is a complex principle to apply and can benefit from prototyping. A series of requirements prototypes can enable the designer and user to zero in on the graphics that are most effective in meeting the user's unique preferences.

Multiple views enable the user to see the information in various ways. Multiple forms can be used, such as tabular, graphic, and narrative. Information can also be displayed in multiple levels of abstraction. Such a capability can be achieved by using a technique called **drill down,** which enables the user to begin with a display of summary data and then guide the succeeding displays to present increasing detail. This is illustrated in Figure H.8a. A manager viewing the report sees that the western region is doing poorly in meeting its sales quota. The manager wants to know more, and brings up a report of the western region sales by product, as shown in Figure H.8b. The manager sees that VCR sales are not what they should be. If the manager wanted, he or she could bring up a third view, perhaps showing VCR sales in the western region by sales representative to identify those who are selling the product and those who are not. The GUI should enable the user to select the desired view.

These design principles provide guidelines to both systems developers and users as they engage in interface design. The information systems organization should incorporate these guidelines in standards manuals, style guides, templates, and clip art so that they can be more easily applied. Figure H.9 is an example of GUI design guidelines followed by a project team in developing a system for an automobile dealer.

The Use of Color in GUI Design

Color is an important means of achieving communication in a GUI design when it is used properly.

Objectives in Using Color

In designing graphical user interfaces that use color, two particular objectives should be kept in mind.[5] First, color can be used to impart information. Second, the interfaces should be designed so that the user can select the desired colors.

FIGURE H.7

Employ Proper Balance in Distinctiveness

Poor

Poor

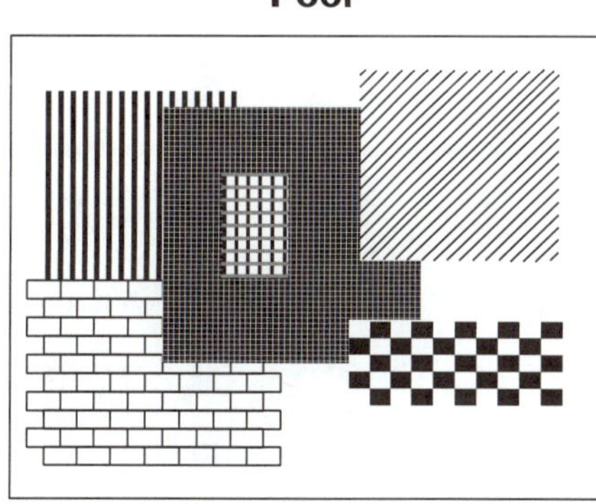

FIGURE H.8

The Drill Down Technique Illustrated

a. Company sales

COMPANY SALES (IN THOUSANDS OF DOLLARS) FOR PERIOD ENDING AUGUST 31, 2001			
REGION	YEAR-TO-DATE SALES	YEAR-TO-DATE QUOTA	YEAR-TO-DATE VARIANCE
EASTERN	425,000	410,000	15,000+
MIDWEST	378,500	360,000	18,500+
SOUTHWEST	163,250	160,000	3,250+
MOUNTAIN	150,000	155,000	5,000-
WESTERN	410,000	445,500	35,500-
TOTALS	1,526,750	1,530,500	3,750-

b. Western region

WESTERN REGION SALES BY PRODUCT LINE (IN THOUSANDS OF DOLLARS) FOR PERIOD ENDING AUGUST 31, 2001			
PRODUCT LINE	YEAR-TO-DATE SALES	YEAR-TO-DATE QUOTA	YEAR-TO-DATE VARIANCE
CAMCORDER	60,000	63,000	3,000-
CD PLAYER	92,300	95,000	2,700-
TAPE PLAYER	15,000	10,000	5,000+
TUNER, AM/FM	78,200	77,500	700+
TV	103,600	100,000	3,600+
VCR	60,900	100,000	39,100-
TOTALS	410,000	445,500	35,500-

Advantages of Using Color

Color can be used to:

- Call the user's attention to important material
- Improve visual search time
- Enable the user to organize material into hierarchies or structures
- Portray objects in a more natural manner
- Give graphics a dynamic dimension across both time and space
- Contribute to an accurate interpretation
- Provide an additional coding capability
- Make information more believable and appealing

These advantages serve to improve the user's perception of both the information that the system provides and the system itself.

Disadvantages of Using Color

In being alert to the potential disadvantages of using color, keep in mind that it can:

- Increase the cost of the hardware
- Fail to accomplish its objectives with color-deficient users, a condition that is inherited by approximately 8 percent of males and 0.4 percent of females
- Cause visual discomfort and afterimages when certain combinations are used improperly
- Achieve other than the desired effects when not used in accordance with users' particular cultures

These disadvantages can be minimized or avoided by adhering to color design principles.

Color Design Principles

The principles of organization, economy, and communication that we applied to GUI in general can be applied specifically to color.

Color Organization You can use color to organize material by assigning certain colors to particular groups and adhering to a consistent use of color from screen to screen and from system to system. The use of similar background colors is especially effective in achieving organization. By applying the same screen display color schemes to such hardcopy material as user manuals and system documentation, the advantages of organization can be expanded to include user training as well as systems maintenance, redevelopment, and business process redesign.

Color Economy A maximum of from three to seven colors should be used in those situations where the user is to remember the meaning of each color. A good design

FIGURE H.9

Project Specific GUI Guidelines

- The program has a graphical user interface in a multitasking environment.
- To simplify the interface to the task of data collection, all panels are full-screen with warning dialogs or help fields.
- Only a few actions are possible in each panel.
- Each action is initiated by clicking a button or by pressing a keystroke combination.
- There is only one entry and one exit to each panel.
- These entries and exits are consistent and uniquely symbolized.
- There is limited movement between panels to allow quick data entry.

FIGURE H.10

The Interface Design Process

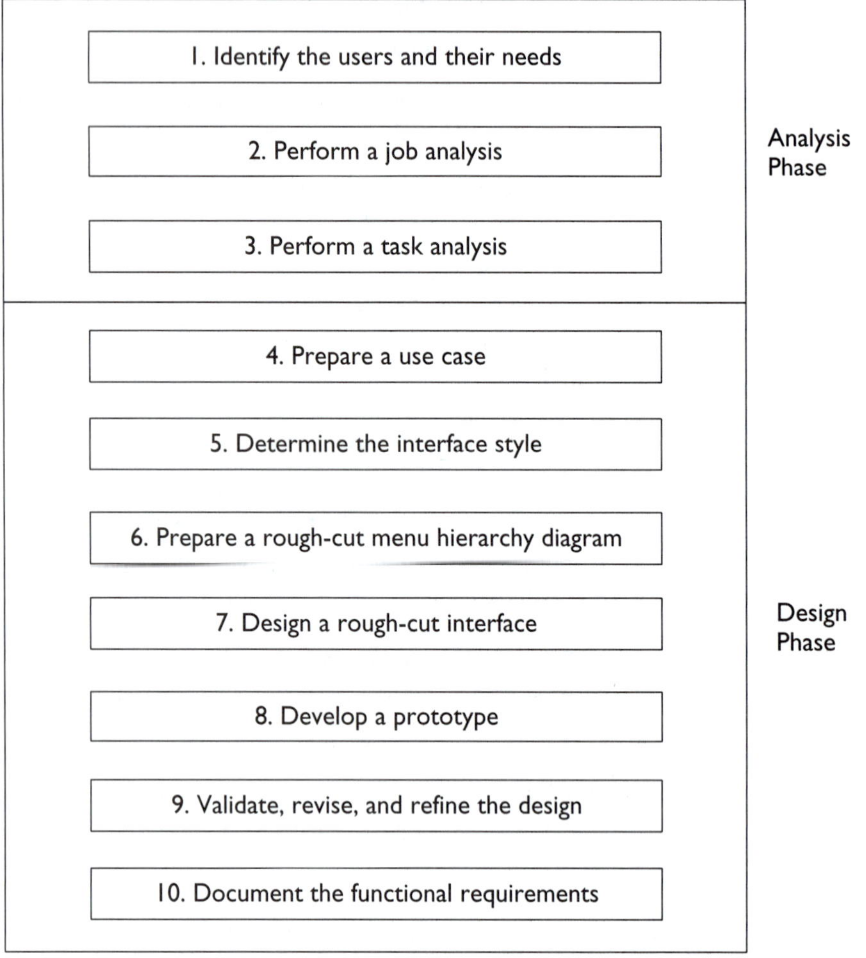

technique is to first design the screen for black and white, and then add color. Another technique is to use shape in conjunction with color as a means of accommodating all users, including those with deficient color vision.

Color Communication Viewers do not have the same sensitivity to colors in all areas of their vision. Typically, viewers are more sensitive to colors in the center of their vision than on the periphery. Keeping this in mind, use bright colors such as red and green in the center of the screen display and colors such as blue, black, white, and yellow near the edges. When users are older, make an effort to use brighter colors and to minimize the use of blues, which are difficult to discern.

Also pay attention to the environment in which the color will be viewed. When the room is dark, use white, yellow, or red for text, lines, and shapes, and use blue, green, or dark gray for the background. In a bright environment, use blue or black text, lines, and shapes on light backgrounds of magenta, blue, white, or light yellow. Regardless of the environment, the screen background can be a problem when it is more attention-getting than the foreground of text and data.

Finally, be aware that certain color combinations can cause irritation and produce afterimages. Particularly avoid strong combinations of red and blue, red and green, blue and yellow, and green and blue.

Good color is difficult to achieve for several reasons. We have seen how the environment is a factor. The space in which the color is used also has an influence. The size, shape, and location of objects influence how their color is perceived. You should also take into account many physiological and cultural influences. In coping with these influences, designers should use prototyping to determine good color sets and then make small refinements to learn the effects that certain color changes produce.

THE USER INTERFACE DESIGN PROCESS

User interface designs of all types evolve by following the methodologies described in this text—prototyping, RAD, and the phased development methodology. However, particular attention has been paid to the user interface design process, and ten specific tasks should be kept in mind.[6] These tasks are illustrated in Figure H.10.

This process can be followed in designing interfaces for users who will communicate with the systems that either do not use the Web, or use the Web by means of an intranet. In designing interfaces for e-business users, a different set of guidelines is involved and is explained later in the technical module.

1. *Identify the users and their needs.* Learn about users by means of interviews and surveys. Learn who the users are in terms of age, gender, educational background, experience, physical handicaps, and so on. Also determine their expectations of the new system. Learn how frequently or infrequently the users will use the system. Occasional use calls for very simplistic interfaces, whereas frequent use is facilitated by more advanced and powerful interfaces.

2. *Perform a job analysis.* Understand the user's job by breaking it down into its component parts and producing a **task list.**

3. *Perform a task analysis.* A **task analysis** is a subdivision of each task into its elementary steps that recognize the knowledge and skills required for each step. It is a type of skeleton for interface design—the architectural base around which the interface will be designed. However, it is not sufficient to simply understand the steps of the task; you must know how important the task is to the user.

4. *Prepare a use case.* A **use case** is a sequence of transactions performed by an information system that enables users to perform their tasks. We described use cases in Chapter 5 and included an example of a narrative use case in Figure 5.14. We also included both narrative and graphic examples of use cases in the description of the ASTA project. See Figures CS 4.3 through 4.7. The task analysis provides the basis for identifying the user main events, which are addressed separately in the use cases.

5. *Determine the interface style.* With an understanding of the users and their events, attention can turn to the interface. You select from the use of such

FIGURE H.11

A Menu Hierarchy Diagram

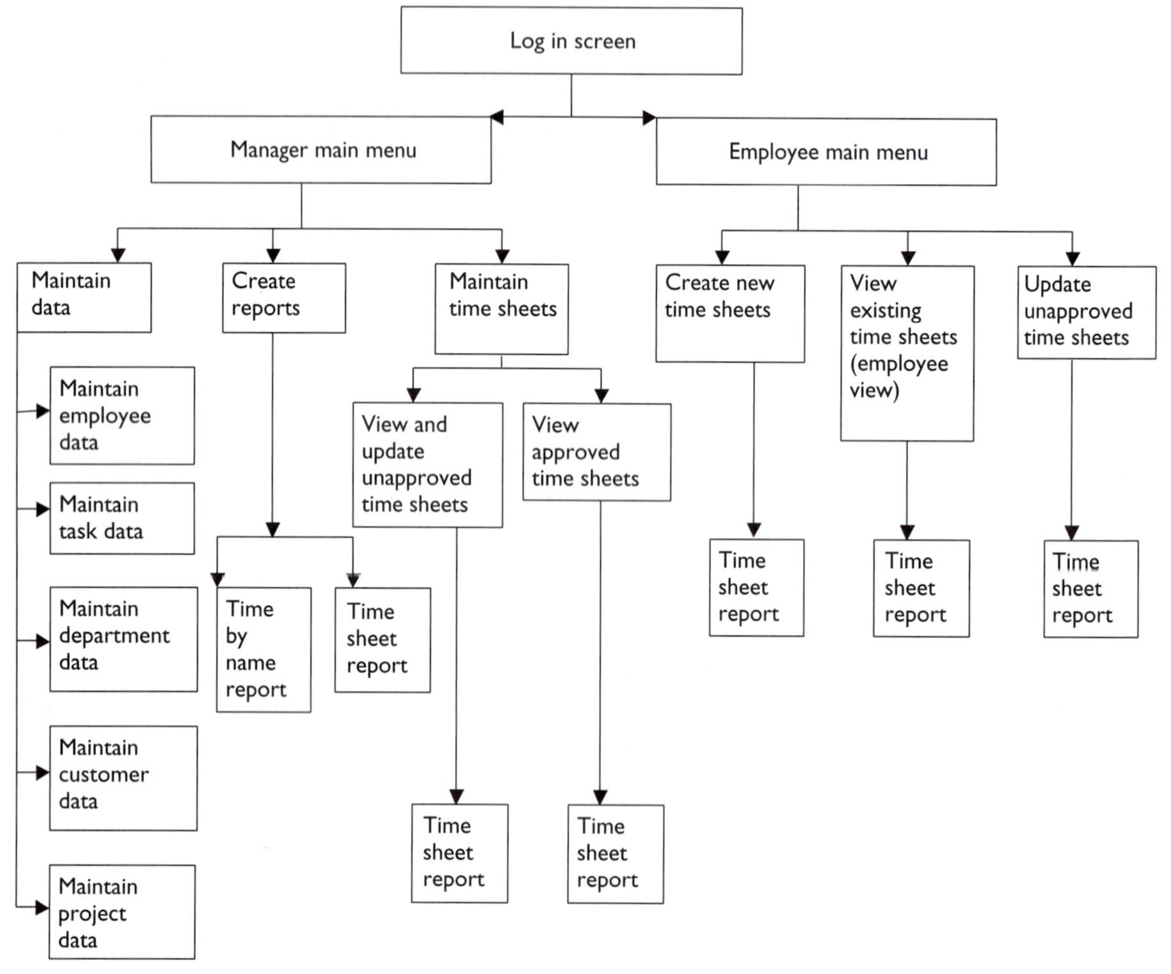

GUI features as windows, boxes, buttons, and so on by recognizing the objectives, advantages, and disadvantages of each. Although a wealth of suggestions apply here, we offer some general design advice below.

- Provide flexibility.
- Provide the user with the ability to undo errors.
- Provide user feedback.
- Allow users to be in control.
- Provide optional help.
- Use defaults for common or likely outcomes.

6. *Prepare a rough-cut menu hierarchy diagram.* A menu hierarchy diagram, also called a dialog flow diagram, uses rectangles to identify the menus or

screens and their arrangement. Figure H.11 is an example. The main menu is at the top and arrows indicate the direction of the navigation from one menu or screen to another.

7. *Design a rough-cut interface.* Position the major elements of the interface by paying attention to structure rather than appearance. Consider the use of a storyboard, or hardcopy, view of the interface as an alternative to one produced with software. Make certain that you adhere to the design principles and have the layout checked by a subject-matter expert.

8. *Develop a prototype.* Refine the rough-cut interface by putting it in a form so that it can be tried out by one or more users in a walk-through or simulation. Include all essential elements, but not necessarily in a polished form.

9. *Validate, revise, and refine the design.* Use walk-throughs, simulations, and tests with persons who either will use the interface or are representative of the users. Be alert to responses and incorporate improvements in new prototypes. Continue this process until objectives have been met or resources have been exhausted.

10. *Document functional requirements.* Write functional specifications that will serve as the blueprints for building the software. These specifications include an updated use case and menu hierarchy diagram that reflects the final design. The specifications should incorporate all screens and explain how they interact.

These recommended steps emphasize the importance of understanding user needs at the task level and of taking a deliberate approach to GUI design in the form of a rough-cut interface, prototypes, and attention to refinement and monitoring.

Web Interface Design for e-Business Users

E-business users who communicate with the firm by means of the Web often are not experienced in doing business with the firm, not experienced in using the firm's interface, and may not be experienced in using Web interfaces in general. For these reasons, the Web interface developers must be especially attentive to the users and their events. Many users may only visit the Web site a single time and the site must be designed to make that visit a successful one. The term **e-loyalty** has been coined to describe the type of repetitive visiting activity that a Web site should stimulate.[7]

Unique Layout of the Web Interface

The layout of the graphical user interface evolved over a period of thirty or so years, in response to innovations in hardware and software. The layout of the Web interface is the product of a much more recent evolution, being packed into just the past few years. Figure H.12 shows how a typical Web layout differs from the GUI. The convention that many Web home pages follow consists of a table of contents frame on the left-hand side of the screen and the material on the right-hand side. A packed screen is now expected on the Web page as viewers do not scroll. On the other hand, the convention that many GUIs follow enables users to scroll up and down the display to reveal additional material.

FIGURE H.12

Basic Layouts of Web and Graphic User Interfaces

Classic Web Page Grid

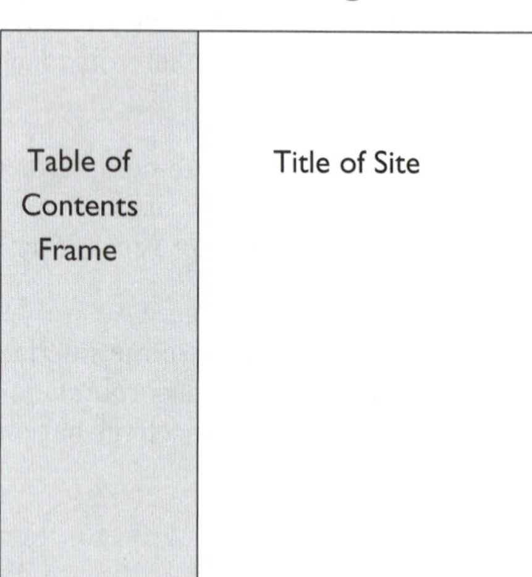

Simple Menu Grid

Title
Text entry
Text entry
Text entry
Text entry
Text entry
Text entry
OK
Cancel

Web Page Design Guidelines

Since the Web site might have a visitor's attention for only a brief time, the main design objective is to make the use as intuitive as possible. This goal is supported by Steve Krug in his book *Don't Make Me Think,* which provides the source of the following guidelines.[8]

Design the Home Page to Convey the Big Picture

Tell the user what the site is about by using a good short tag line and a welcome blurb. Only include essential elements, and rotate promotions frequently.

Design Each Page for Scanning, Not Reading

Users typically do not read the contents of a Web page, but scan them, looking for the first reasonable option. This activity is called **satisficing,** and can be achieved by omitting needless words. Prepare a rough-cut page and then delete half of the words. After doing that, you should try to delete half of the remainder.

Provide for Persistent Navigation

Studies have shown that the Back button accounts for some 30 to 40 percent of all Web clicks. To minimize this activity, each Web page should provide:

- An identification of the site and the page
- A clear delineation of the sections and options
- A clear indication of what is clickable
- A clear picture of where the user is in the overall scheme of things

- An ability to conduct a search
- A way to perform the necessary utilities
- A way to return home
- A sense of control (provide tabs to eliminate the need for continuous scrolling)

In meeting the navigation needs of the Web site, developers can prepare a site map, which provides a clear visual hierarchy of the relative importance of the Web site content. The site map is the equivalent of the menu hierarchy diagram used in GUI design. When more knowledgeable Web users arrive at the site, they tend to go to the site map first. It shows the advanced user where they can go without having to cope with unique home page styles, a text full of fluff, and unnecessary graphics. An example of a site map appears in Figure H.13. The home page is at the top. Arrows show the direction of the navigation.

FIGURE H.13

A Site Map

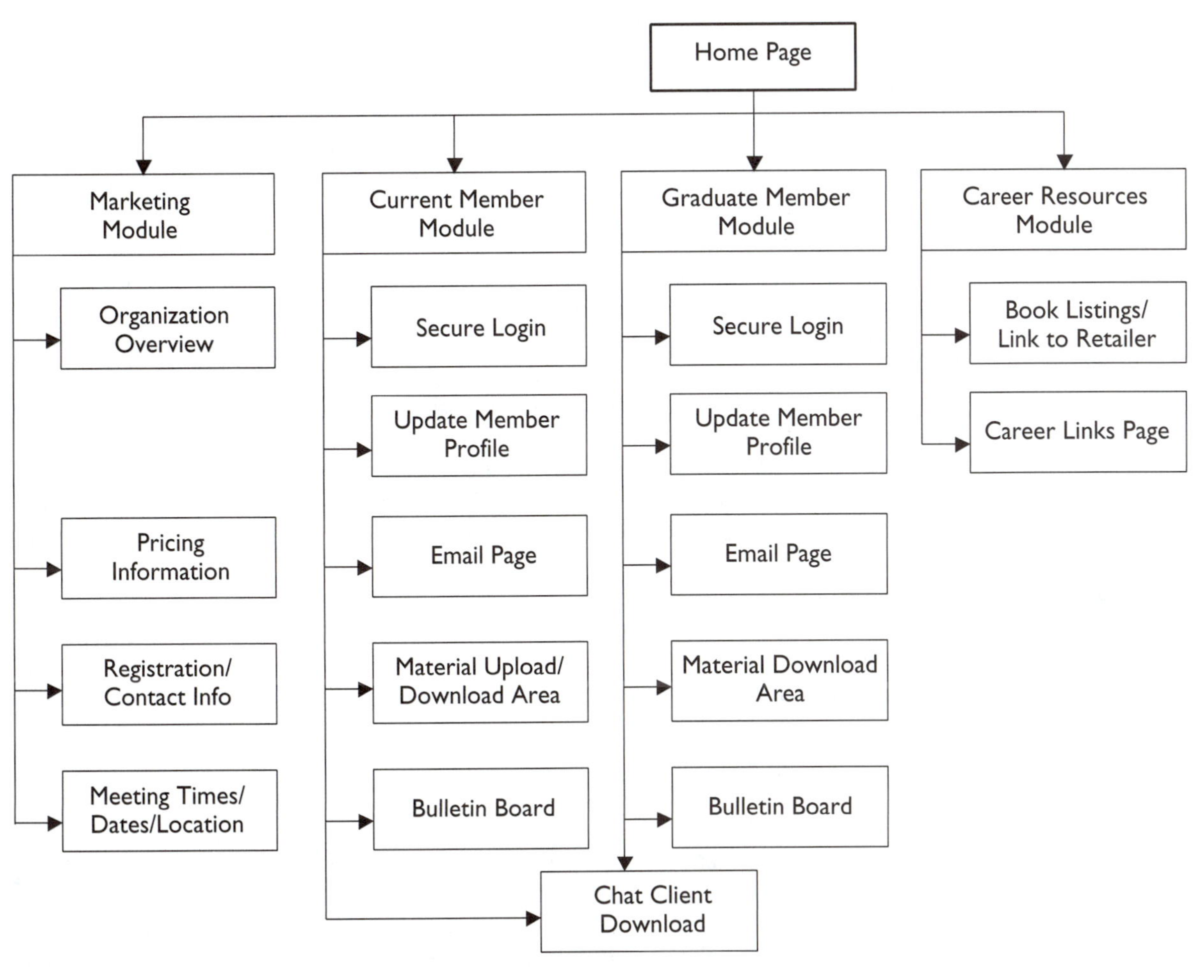

Web Page Color Guidelines

The issue of color use is just as important for Web pages as it is for GUI interfaces. Christine Rigden, of BTexaCT, offers the following suggestions as a way to minimize the problems of color discrimination by color-deficient users[9]:

- Never use color as the primary cue for information. Rather, use color as a means of adding emphasis.
- Make sure that text has good brightness contrast with its background.
- Make sure that the colors chosen for followed and un-followed links are far enough apart.

Choice of colors is important for all viewers, including those with normal vision. Forty of the possible 256 colors are slightly different on PCs and Macs, and the remaining 216 colors represent a **Web-safe color palate,** which has also been named the **Browser-Safe Color Palate.** Information on this palate, which gives better visual control over what the user sees, can be found at www.lynda.com/hex.html.

The Challenge of Web Design

Much less is known today about Web interface design than GUI design because of the newness of the Web as a means of linking users to systems. Another factor contributes to the challenge of Web design and that is the need for an artistic as well as technical talent. The layout of an attractive Web page is much like creating a good painting. The Web page designer must be an artist. Further, the judgment of the effectiveness of the Web layout is in the eye of the user. The Web page developer must identify the image that the user wants the Web page to convey and then incorporate that image into the site.

Since there is such variety in Web users, there can be no single process to follow in developing interfaces. The best approach is to design a site that meets a need, carefully think out the users and their events, execute the design well, and test it thoroughly before use.

Once the Web design is implemented, it must continuously be evaluated to assure that it is meeting its objectives. This assurance can be obtained by soliciting visitors' feedback through e-mail, online surveys, and forums or focus groups.

KEY TERMS

user interface, human-computer interface
graphical user interface (GUI)
usability
drill down

PROBLEMS

1. Design a GUI that will enable a manager to use the drill-down technique to prepare the two reports illustrated in Figure H.8. Use an opening screen that will enable the user to specify the operation to be performed. Then, use one or more screens to present the information. Use the storyboard approach. First, use pencil to sketch the layout for each screen on posterboard. Apply as many of the design principles as you can. When you are satisfied with the layouts, use a black marker to redraw the pencil lines.

2. Now add color to your storyboards, applying the color principles. Assume that the user is a fifty-year-old executive who has a dark office and does not have color-deficient vision.
3. Make an oral presentation to your class, explaining the screens and how they are used. In the process, explain how you applied the GUI design principles. Obtain feedback from the class concerning ways to improve the designs.
4. Take the class feedback into account and revise your screens. If you have design software available, use it. Otherwise, prepare a new set of storyboards.
5. Present your revised GUI to the class.

SELECTED BIBLIOGRAPHY

Bawden, David. "Online Retrieval: A Dialogue of Theory and Practice" (2nd Edition). I*nternational Journal of Information Management* 20 (Number 3, June 2000): 243-244.

Galitz, Wilbert O. *The Essential Guide to User Interface Design* (New York, NY: Wiley Computer Publications), 1997.

Hammond, Eric. "Hammock Swings Through Web Interfaces." Infoworld 22 (Number 29, July 17, 2000): 55.

Mandel, Theo. *The Elements of User Interface Design* (New York, NY: John Wiley & Sons), 1997.

Oard, Douglas W. "User Interface Design for Speech-Based Retrieval." *Bulletin of the American Society for Information Science* 26 (Number 5, June/July 2000): 20-22.

Rash, Wayne. "Rash's Judgment—Don't Overlook the Interface When Choosing Network Gear." *Internetweek* (March 13, 2000): 57.

Turk, Matthew, and George Robertson. "Perceptual User Interfaces." *Communications of the ACM* 43 (Number 3, March 2000): 32-34.

Wonnacott, Laura. "Web Site Design is a Combination of Both Science and Art that Satisfies Many Users." *Infoworld* 22 (Number 5, January 31, 2000): 60.

NOTES

1. This definition paraphrases one in Aaron Marcus, "Designing Graphical User Interfaces: Part I," *UnixWorld 7* (August 1990): 107.
2. John S. Hoffman, *Principles of Human-Computer Interface Design,* unpublished manuscript, 1992, 1-5.
3. Thomas D. Erickson, "Working with Interface Metaphors," in Brenda Laurel (ed), *The Art of Human-Computer Interface Design* (Reading, MS: Addison-Wesley), 1960, 66.
4. This material on GUI requirements and design principles in the next section draws heavily from the three-part series titled "Designing Graphical User Interfaces," by Aaron Marcus, which appeared in the August, September, and October 1990 issues of *UnixWorld.*
5. Gitta Salomon, "New Uses of Color," in Brenda Laurel (ed), *The Art of Human—Computer Interface Design* (Reading, MS: Addison-Wesley), 1960, 271.
6. Hoffman, pp. 4-5 through 4-28.
7. Ellen Reid Smith, e-loyalty: How to Keep Customers Coming Back to Your Website (New York, NY: Harper Business), 2000.
8. Steve Krug, Don't Make Me Think! (Indianapolis, IN: New Riders Publishing), 2000.
9. Christine Rigden, "'The Eye of the Beholder': Designing for Colour-Blind Users," British Telecommunications Engineering 17 (January 1999). 2-6.

CASE STUDY INSTALLMENT 5

ADVANCED SYSTEM TECHNOLOGY ASSOCIATES

CONSTRUCTING AND INSTALLING THE ASTA SYSTEM

It's the end of Week 10 of the client project and the Queen and the Programmers are putting the final touches on their effort. The team finally got out of the analysis, design, and preliminary construction loop with the system modules and began final construction last week. The team is now set for their regular Friday meeting in the snack bar. Rachel has alerted the Cowboys that they would be talking about testing, documentation, and training.

PLANNING THE FINAL CONSTRUCTION AND INSTALLATION

"The way we've got this laid out," Rachel said, looking at the Gantt, "testing is team effort. Everybody but Gary is going to be involved. I'm scheduled to develop the test specs and the rest of you will carry out the various tests. Gary, you need to get on the documentation of the users manual. It shouldn't be too difficult since we're keeping it short and sweet. As soon as that's wrapped up, maybe you can give Kim, Tracy, and Sean help on the developer manual. They are likely to be tied up on testing for a while. So, Gary, you might end up with most of the documentation by yourself."

Gary indicated a willingness to follow that plan but reminded Rachel, "You and I are supposed to do the training. I can't see how I can work on all these things at the same time."

"No argument there. Tell you what—I've probably got more free time now than anyone so let me handle the training. I know the system inside and out and know all of the users so I should be able to handle it. If I need help, I'll ask for it."

The rest of the team assured Rachel that if she would do the training they would take care of everything else.

"As usual," Rachel said, "we're trying to finish the project and also finish the next delivery report. Our final delivery is due a week from this Thursday. What do you want to talk about first, the project or the report?"

PLANNING THE FINAL DELIVERY REPORT

Most everyone said "report," so Rachel asked them to pull out their final delivery specs. The team had done very well on the first two deliveries and they felt it was because they finalized the contents a couple of days before the due date. Seeing no reason to change, the team followed the same strategy for this final report and established next Monday as the deadline for the sections.

"Compared to the tons of material we had to crank out for the other two reports, this one should be a piece of cake," Rachel said, calling the team's attention to the table of contents. We start off with a status memo. That tells the client exactly where we stand—the fact that we've met our schedule. Since I've been after everyone to follow the schedule, I should be able to do it in my sleep. Put me down for the status memo. Then we have the users and developer manuals. We've already assigned those. We also need a quick reference guide, which will probably be only a pocket-card-sized summary of the major user operations. Gary, since you're doing the users manual, can you take care of the reference guide?"

Gary, seeing the finish line and wanting to do any and everything to get there, said "Sure, why not? But, while I've got your attention—you remember that I've done all of that object-oriented documentation. I'd like to add that to the developer manual."

"That's an excellent idea," Rachel said. "And since it's new, you should be prepared to explain it at the presentation." Gary agreed and Rachel moved to the next item. "The report specs mention an installation guide. There's a sample in the specs. It deals with things like training and organizational culture. Sean, could you do that? Tracy and Kim will have the responsibility for the installation but I think it would be good for someone to help them out by doing the guide. Is that OK with you?"

Sean nodded "Yes."

Rachel continued, "Then we need a training guide. Since I'm going to do the training, I'll take care of it. Finally, we have the future recommendations section. It's

FIGURE CS 5.1

Test Specifications

Test Specification ASTA Skill Set System			Page 1 of 2		
Designed by: Rachel			Module or Screen: Search skill set		
Test Data Source: Sample manager search info			Objectives: Test and verify functionality of search skill set screen		
Test Case #	Description	Test Steps	Expected Results	Actual Results	Performed by/ Date
1	Test functionality of searching one skill category	Select a single category by placing a check and click search	System will generate a second screen with subcategories of the selected skill	Same as expected	Rachel 12/01/00
2	Test functionality of searching multiple categories	Select multiple categories by placing checks and click search	System will generate multiple screens with subcategories of the selected skills	Same as expected	Tracy 12/01/00
3	Test functionality of matching records	Select a category of skill and click search	The system will match skill category	Same as expected	Tracy 12/01/00
4	Test functionality of searching by an employee name	Enter an ASTA employee name and click search	System will match request	Same as expected	Tracy 12/01/00
5	Test functionality of searching by a department	Select an ASTA department from the list box and click search	System will match request	Same as expected	Tracy 12/01/00
6	Test functionality of searching by an employee title	Select an ASTA employee title from the list box and click search	System will match request	Same as expected	Tracy 12/01/00
7	Test for null values	Click the search button without entering anything	System will display a message box for null values	Same as expected	Tracy 12/01/00

really important because it is our way of communicating to the client a course of action to follow after we're gone. Who wants to do that? Tracy and Kim—why don't you get on that as soon as you have the developer manual complete?"

The two remaining Cowboy Programmers repeated Gary's "Why not," and Rachel put away her report specs and said, "OK, now let's talk about getting this project completed."

COMPLETING THE PROJECT

The two remaining phases in the Gantt chart were final construction and installation. The final construction activities consisted of testing, documentation, and training, and

FIGURE CS 5.2

Sample Users Manual Table of Contents

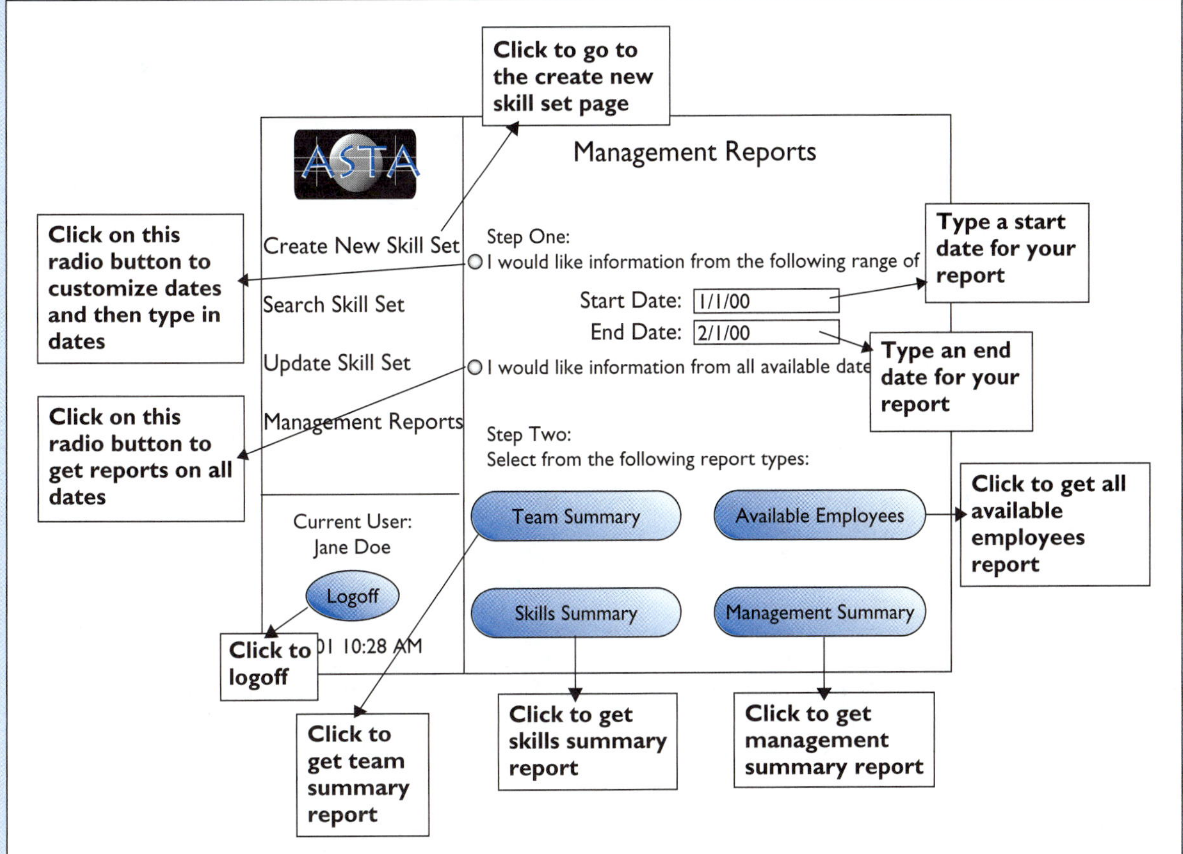

Management Reports

- The management reports page is restricted only to project managers. This page lets managers create customized reports.
- To view reports using selected dates, click on the first radio button, then type in start and end dates.
- To view reports from all available dates, click on the second radio button.
- Once the date option has been selected, choose from one of the four report types by clicking on the button.
- To get a report on team summary, click the **Team Summary** button.
- To get a report on skills summary, click the **Skills Summary** button.
- To get a report on management summary, click the **Management Summary** button.
- To get a report on available employees, click the **Available Employees** button.
- Choose from the other four options on the left anytime to navigate to a different page.
- To logoff, click the logoff button.

FIGURE CS 5.3

Sample Developer Manual Page

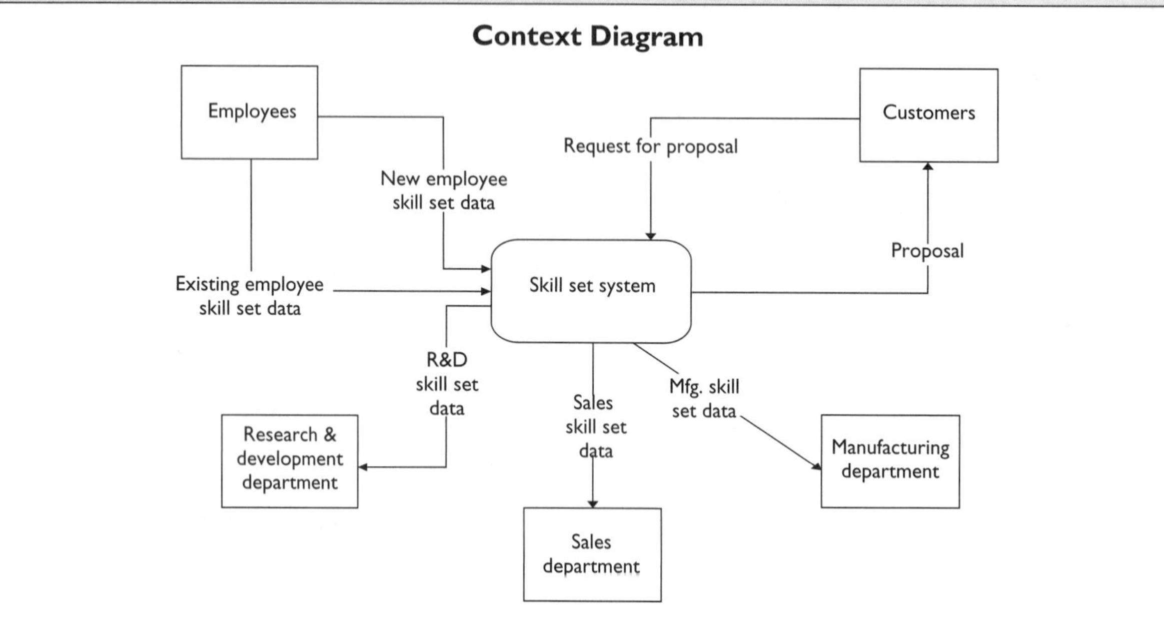

The context diagram describes ASTA's skill set system in the context of its environment. The skill set system is connected to its environment by data flows. The R&D, sales, and manufacturing departments receive skill set data from the system. Employees can enter new employee data to create their skill set profile or update their skill set by entering existing data. The customers can request and receive proposals from the skill set system.

had all been discussed when planning the final delivery. The team then talked about how the installation would proceed. ASTA was going to hire some temporary employees to accomplish the data entry. Kim and Tracy were to install and test the database. The team would do any necessary debugging. Then, the only thing left was to present the final delivery to Mel and Yolanda. With this strategy reviewed, the team meeting broke up and everybody set out to do their assigned tasks.

Testing

This is not the first time the team has been involved with testing. Each of the five system modules included module testing, or unit testing, in one form or another. The team had decided to test the project management reports module by using prototypes, and test the skills inventory database design module and the skills data entry module by providing the users with Beta versions. The team used unit tests for the employee update module and the security login module, and developed test specifications for each.

As the team prepared to do system testing, Rachel had put together the system test specifications. Figure CS 5.1 is an example of her work. Kim, Tracy, and Sean conducted the tests, and Rachel documented the results. This was all in accordance with the Gantt. The tests went well, with a minimum of debugging required.

Documentation

The documentation work consisted of the users and developer manuals. In putting together the users manual, Gary kept in mind that the two main groups of users would be the employees who enter the skill set data, and the project managers who retrieve the information output. He made liberal use of screen shots and tried to keep the narrative to a minimum. Since the team had designed the system for easy learning and easy use, this objective of simple communication was easy to achieve. Figure CS 5.2 is a sample users manual page.

Sean and Kim and Tracy also made liberal use of illustrations in the developer manual. The sample page in Figure CS 5.3 shows how they integrated the DFD context diagram into a narrative overview of the system. Rather than just including the diagrams separately, they tried to support each with a narrative. This would make it easier for the client and future developers to understand the diagrams.

Training

Once Rachel decided how to best perform the training, she documented it in the form of a training guide, shown in Figure CS 5.4. She decided to use Gary's users manual and quick reference guide as the student texts. A copy of the reference guide appears in Figure CS 5.5.

Several days before training began, copies of the users manual and quick reference guide were provided to the department managers for distribution to the attendees. Separate sessions were held in the conference room for HR, R&D, manufacturing, and sales. Rachel had worked up an exercise beforehand to illustrate an operation that each group would be performing on the operational system, and she selected someone from the audience to perform the exercise as she stepped them through the users manual. Then, the employees went back to their offices and tried the exercises themselves. Rachel dropped by the offices to make sure things had gone all right. She also followed the same approach in training the managers, only emphasizing information retrieval.

Installation

Kim and Tracy had primary responsibility for the installation and developed the installation guide in Figure CS 5.6 to make sure everything went smoothly, which it did. Now, all that remained was the final presentation.

Presenting the Final Delivery Report

As the team waited in the conference room for Mel, Yolanda, Elizabeth, Rick Gomez, Sue Kim, and the project managers to arrive, the students realized that they were back where the project got started. It seemed so long ago when Mel and Yolanda had briefed the team in this same room. Once all of the client representatives were seated, Rachel distributed report copies to Mel and Yolanda and the team addressed the sections using Microsoft PowerPoint slides for visual support.

FIGURE CS 5.4

Training Guide

Training Guide

The objective of the ASTA skill set system training is to prepare the employees to enter and update their skill sets using their workstations, to prepare project managers to retrieve skill set data, and to prepare all managers to produce summary reports.

Trainer
Rachel Sanders

Attendees
Attendees will include employees, project managers, and other managers. Separate employee sessions will be conducted for the following departments—HR and finance, R&D, manufacturing, and sales. Department managers will determine which employees will attend and notify them one week ahead of time (not later than November 28) of their responsibility to attend. The managers will again remind the employees the day before the sessions. It is expected that all employees who will be working with the skill set system will be trained. All managers will attend a single session.

Training Dates and Times
All training sessions will be conducted on December 5 at the following times:

HR and finance employees	8:30 AM
R&D employees	10:00 AM
Manufacturing employees	1:00 PM
Sales employees	2:30 PM
Managers	4:00 PM

Location
The training sessions will be conducted in the ASTA conference room.

Equipment
Notebook computer and wall display screen.

Supplies
Users manual and quick reference guide for each attendee. Rachel will deliver copies of the manual and guide to the department managers at least three days before the scheduled training for distribution to the trainees.

Topics
System components (all sessions)

- Review the purpose and major functions of the skill set database.
- Launch the system as a normal user. Display the main page of the database.
- Review various records, tables, forms, and their relationships.
- Discuss the inputs from the various sources.
- Review the output records.
- Discuss the security and login process

System functions for employees (employee sessions)

- Entering new records.
- Editing records.

System functions for managers (managers session)

- Searching records.
- Generating reports.
- Creating backup files and necessary products for archives.

FIGURE CS 5.5

Quick Reference Guide

Quick Reference Guide

	Login	Personal Skills	Search Employee	New Employee	Run Reports
Functionalities	Access to password protected data, skills, and search function	Access for updating the skill set matrix and adding new skills acquired	Access the locality of employees by selecting a city, product, or skill level	Allow data entry of personal and skill information	Allow generation of reports to be viewed and printed by project managers
Access Level	■ Human resources ■ Sales ■ R&D ■ Support staff	■ Human resources ■ R&D	■ Human resources ■ Sales ■ R&D ■ Support staff	■ New ASTA employees ■ Human resources	■ Human resources ■ Sales ■ R&D ■ Support staff
Simple Steps	1. Enter login 2. Enter password 3. Click "OK" 4. Click on desired command button	1. Select Update Skill Set 2. Select desired category for updating	1. Select Search Skill Set 2. Select desired search criteria	1. Select Create New Skill Set 2. Enter the requested information	1. Select Management Reports 2. Select desired reports for generation

Rachel summarized the status memorandum and Gary went through the object-oriented diagrams. The diagrams were well received. Several of the ASTA employees were more familiar with object-oriented tools than DFDs and were glad that the team had included the UML illustrations.

There was no additional discussion of the developer manual or the remaining documentation since it had all been used during the training and installation. The only section to be discussed was the future recommendations. Kim used a slide of the system overview that they had prepared for the first delivery to focus everyone's attention on the remaining Web project. A copy of Kim's slide appears in Figure CS 5.7. This was a fitting way to end the project—by laying the foundation for next semester's Systems Development team to add the Web capability.

As the team walked to their cars, Gary tapped Sean on the shoulder and said, "Check it off." Sean said, "What? The final delivery?" "No," said Gary. "The whole project." Everyone had a good laugh. The pressure was off.

FIGURE CS 5.6

Installation Guide

Installation Guide

Conversion Strategy

Direct cutover installation strategy will be used to convert from the old manual system to the new automated system on December 7. The staff will be trained to use a pilot version of the new system on December 5. Additionally, a user acceptance review will be evaluated before the cutover. In case of a possible system failure, ASTA will be able to perform daily operations until the new system is fully functional and operational.

Before the initial installation, one of the following is recommended:

Platform and operating system requirements	
Platform	Operating System
Microsoft Windows NT	Windows NT 4.0, Service Pack 4 or later
Microsoft Windows 2000	Windows 2000 Server v.5.0.2195
Sun Solaris (SPARC) system	Sun Solaris 2.7 or 2.8
HP 9000 (8xx)	HP-UX 11.0
IBM RISC System/6000	IBM AIX 4.3.2 or 4.3.3

Memory	Disk Space	Media Device
32MB RAM	60MB hard disk	CD-ROM drive

Database	Versions
IBM DB2 Universal Database	Enterprise Edition 6.1, 7.1
Informix Dynamic Server	7.2, 7.3 Dynamic Server 2000(9.2)
Oracle Server	7.3.4, 8.0x, 8.1.6
Microsoft SQL Server	6.5, 7.0; SQL Server 2000(8.0)
Microsoft Access	97 or higher

Initial Installation

Initial implementation and testing of the new system will occur on Yolanda's computer. The following steps will be followed until the new system is fully installed.

Step 1 Insert floppy disk into computer disk drive	**Step 2** Open the disk on drive a: to display the ASI.mdb file	**Step 3** Open directory for installation
Step 4 Copy and paste ASTA.mdb file into directory	**Step 5** To complete the installation, click the Add button—and select the appropriate ASTA package. Follow through by clicking the "Open" and "OK" buttons	**Step 6** Test the newly installed module ■ Perform all skill input procedures ■ Perform all search precedures ■ Perform logon and logoff procedures ■ Perform basic troubleshooting

FIGURE CS 5.7

System Overview

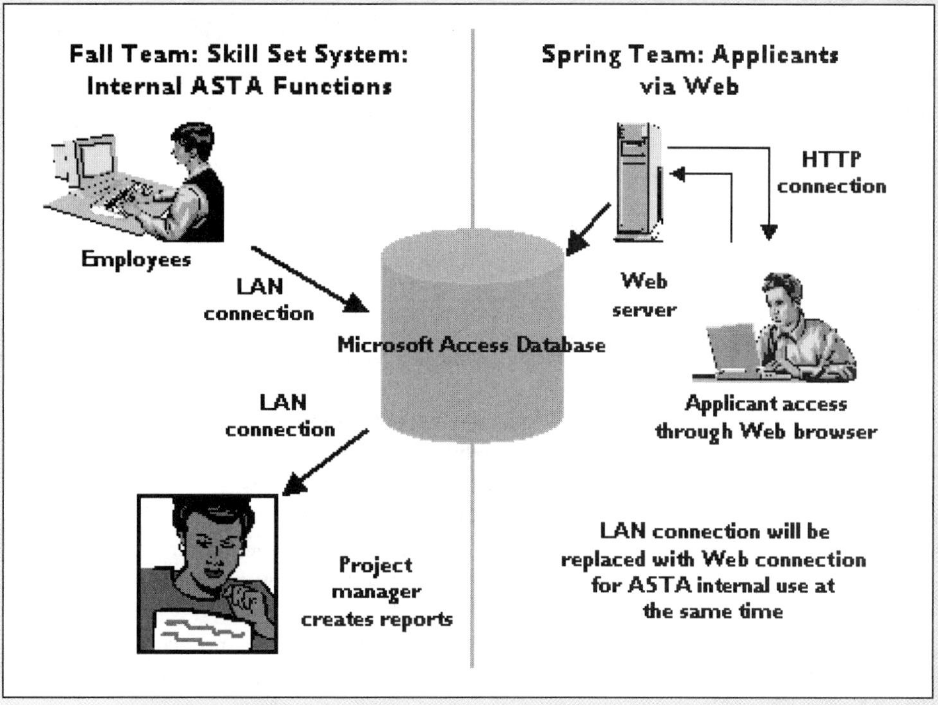
Fall Team: Skill Set System:
Internal ASTA Functions
Spring Team: Applicants
via Web
HTTP
connection
Employees
LAN
connection
Web
server
Microsoft Access Database
LAN
connection
Applicant access
through Web browser
Project
manager
creates reports
LAN connection will be
replaced with Web connection
for ASTA internal use at
the same time

CHAPTER 7

PRELIMINARY CONSTRUCTION

LEARNING OBJECTIVES

- Understand what is included in the implementation portion of the system development life cycle.
- Identify the preliminary construction activities and understand their timing.
- Understand what can be involved in preparing facilities for the new system-what work is performed and who performs it.
- Describe the implementation support that can be provided by hardware vendors.
- Explain what is included in the development environment.
- Identify the two questions that must be answered when the firm considers custom-written software.
- Appreciate why testing is necessary and how to execute a modular testing strategy.
- Use a decision logic table (DLT) to test all possible conditions that a program can encounter.
- Explain the importance of user training, and planning the training as early in the system development life cycle as possible.
- Understand what is included in a training environment and why it is valuable.
- Recognize the effectiveness of a JAD session to obtain user approval of the construction of each system module as it is completed.

INTRODUCTION

We are still in the iteration loop of the phased development methodology. We have completed the analysis and the design of a system module and are now ready to perform the preliminary construction. We will continue in this loop until the user approves the module deliverable. We will repeat this looping process for each system module.

Preliminary construction consists of two basic activities—constructing the new system software modules and test data, and demonstrating the new system to users and project sponsors. The construction of the software modules and test data involves the preparation of physical facilities, installation of hardware, coding or purchasing of application software, building of test files, and preparation of training materials and documentation. The demonstration of the system can take the form of a JAD session that has four possible outcomes—the users can accept the module with no change, they can request minimum change, they can request significant change, or they can cancel the project.

Implementing a system can account for half or more of the project effort and cost. The goal of project management is to minimize the percentage of resources absorbed during implementation by planning, analyzing, and designing as carefully and thoughtfully as feasible. Putting more time and effort in the earlier ideas-on-paper work during preliminary investigation and each iteration of analysis and design should pay off in an implementation effort that is efficient and orderly.

Solving the Transition Terminology Puzzle

During the time that the development project rolls along, a multitude of terms are used that relate to the transition of the old system to the new. The terms include *implementation, construction, conversion, installation, cutover,* and *changeover.* As the development team goes about its business, each member may use these terms to mean different things since (as with most of the vocabulary of computing) there are no universally agreed-upon definitions. In order to minimize the confusion in this text, we offer specific definitions below.

Implementation is the process of converting the design of the new system to a production system consisting of hardware, software, people, data, and information. This includes testing and a wide variety of activities we will cover in the last three chapters of this text. In phased development, planning for implementation activities can begin as the design evolves, with the performance of the activities spanning the three final stages—preliminary construction, final construction, and system test and installation. The implementation span is illustrated in Figure 7.1 with the large outer box containing three inner boxes, each representing one of the final SDLC stages.

The two **construction** stages include creating software, data sets for testing, and databases, and conducting training, creating user and developers manuals, and other implementation activities. We use the term **conversion** to describe the translation of data files from the existing system to the format and content required by the new system. That activity is not identified in Figure 7.1 but occurs during the two construction stages.

The large rectangle in the lower portion of the figure represents the system test and installation phase, and here is where the number of transition terms increases. A major process during this final phase is the transfer of the system to the users, and it consists of three steps. The first is **installation,** which is the transfer of production files (software and data) from the development environment to the production environment or a staging environment that mirrors the production environment. The second step is the acceptance test, and the third is cutover. **Cutover,** also called **changeover,** is the transition from the use of the old system to the new one. Cutover signals the end of development and the beginning of production.

Preliminary Construction Overview

At this point in the SDLC, we have reached the preliminary construction phase. We have analyzed and designed a single module of the new system and we are ready to start construction of that module. As shown in Figure 7.2, there are two primary steps to this phase of development:

1. Construct new system software modules and test data.

2. Demonstrate the new system modules to users and project sponsors.

FIGURE 7.1

A Structure of Implementation

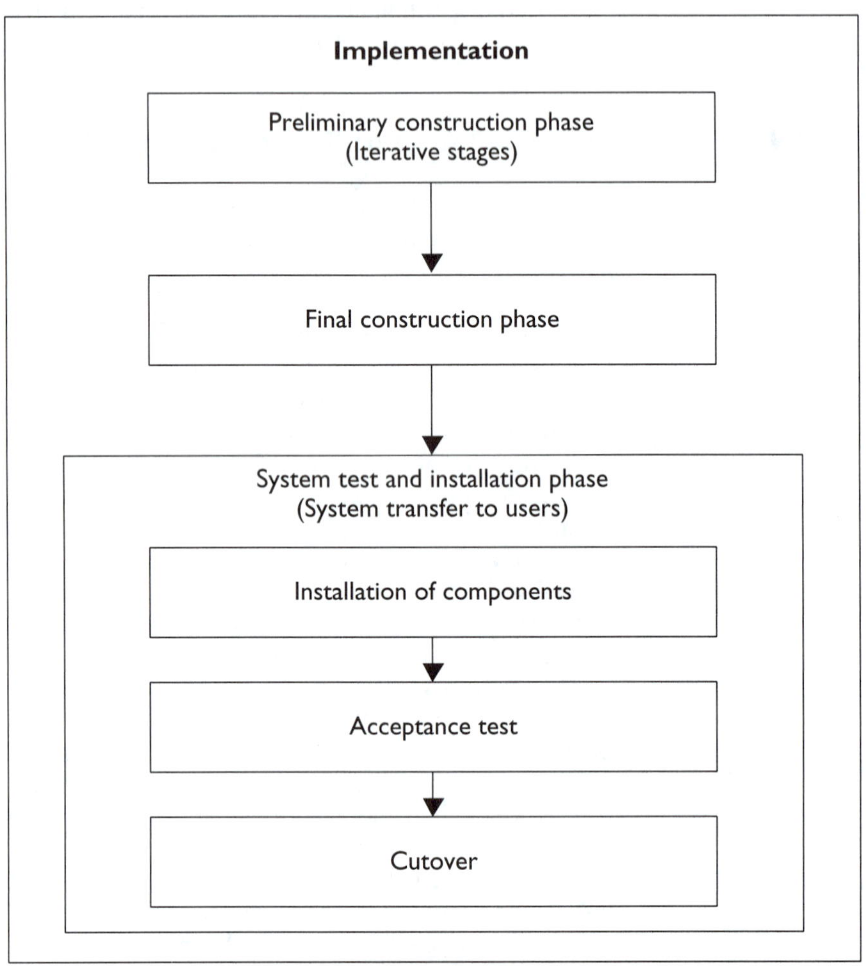

The project team members who have the major implementation responsibility base their construction work on the logical design, which is prepared during analysis and design. The logical design is contained in the project dictionary. Figure 7.3 on page 426 shows the contents of the project dictionary as the first iteration of preliminary construction begins. Preliminary versions of a users manual and a developers manual are included. The users manual will include instructions for system use, and the developers manual will include selected portions of the project dictionary to be used in maintaining the system.

The project team's role in system construction is similar to that of a builder in constructing a house. Just as a builder works from an architect's blueprints, the project team works from the system design specifications to turn plans on paper into a tangible product. For example, through the efforts of the programmer, program specifications will become working software and data files. A member of the project team may help the user purchase hardware and prepare the installation site.

Using the knowledge gained from observing procedures and interviewing users, the team will write user manuals and create training materials. The team member with administrative responsibilities may write a job description for a database specialist and then be involved in the process of hiring someone to fill that role. Preliminary construction consists of a wide variety of activities, but they can be summarized into the two main steps listed above. In the sections below, we first describe the construction activities and then those related to demonstration.

Construct New System Software Modules and Test Data

Construction can involve numerous and varied activities and often requires the combined skills and knowledge of a large development team. Managing these efforts is vital to the success of the project. How closely the constructed system conforms to the designed system depends largely on how well the five system components of people, data, information, software and hardware are integrated into a single, smoothly functioning system. The success of this integration is determined by the coordination of the members of the project team.

The Timing of Construction Activities

A list of activities commonly performed during construction appears in Figure 7.4 on page 427. As we follow a phased development approach, we do not perform the activities in a strict sequence. Rather, the construction and test activities alternate. You

FIGURE 7.2

Preliminary Construction Phase Overview

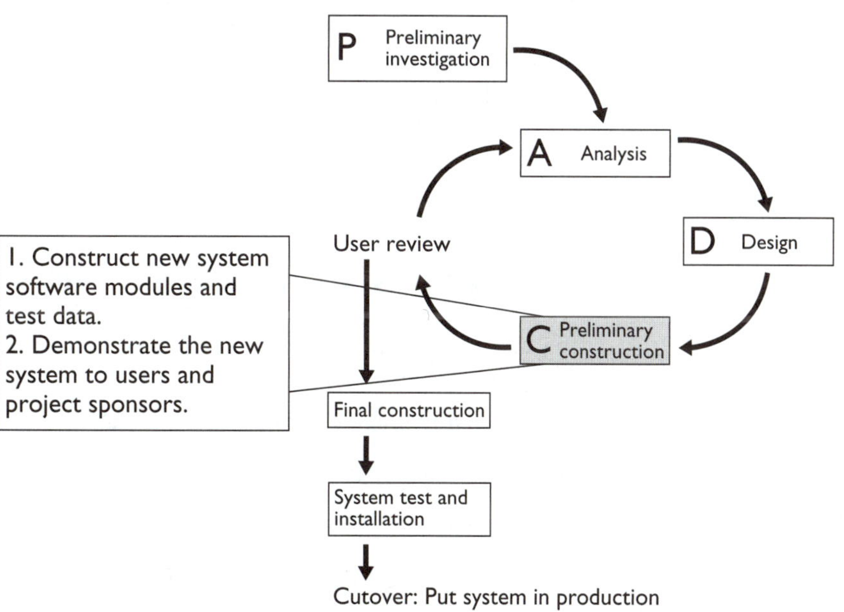

FIGURE 7.3

The Project Dictionary at the Beginning of the First Preliminary Construction Phase

Enterprise Analysis
- Organization Background
- Organization Chart

Problem Definition

The Project
- Project Overview
- Project Risk Evaluation Form
- Risk Reduction Strategies

Project Planning
- Planning Summary
- Milestone Summary
- Network Diagram(s)
- Gantt Chart(s)

The Existing System
- Existing and New System Component Summary
- Process Models
- Data Models
- Object Models

The New System—will become more complete with each iteration
- System Objectives
- System Goals
- Goal Analysis Form
- System Constraints
- System Boundaries
- System Performance Criteria
- Functions/Components Matrices
- Process Models
- Data Models
- Object Models

Users Manual—Table of Contents and sample excerpts

Developers Manual—Table of Contents and sample excerpts

Appendices
- Interview Notes and Tapes
- Input/Output and Programming Standards
- Sample Input/Output Documents
- Client Meeting Agendas
- Team Meeting Agendas

should never build an entire system without repeatedly testing the hardware, software, information, data, and people components as they are assembled. By building small, well-designed test files, and then using these files to verify that each component works correctly, you can identify problems early and correct them before they mushroom into colossal headaches during production use.

In following a phased approach, the preliminary construction and testing activities (steps 1 and 2 in Figure 7.4) will be interspersed with analysis and design activities. Then, the final construction and testing activities will follow the standard pattern in steps 3 and 4 of the figure, and will be succeeded in order by installation, approval, and cutover. Therefore, steps 1 and 2 may vary depending on the development approach that you adopt, but the final steps (3 through 7) will be basically the same no matter what approach you follow.

The Preliminary Construction Activities

Using the first action steps in Figure 7.4 as a guide, the five main activities of preliminary construction include:

- Plan and prepare the physical facilities
- Plan, obtain, and install the development environment hardware
- Obtain software tools and code or obtain application software
- Build the test files and production database
- Plan and prepare training materials and documentation

These activities will most likely *not be completed* during preliminary construction. And, planning for these activities will likely begin *before* preliminary construction. The work is spread over multiple stages of the SDLC as illustrated in Figure 7.5.

Plan and Prepare the Physical Facilities

The construction of a house and the construction of an information system both begin with the foundation. In system construction, the physical computing facility is the foundation, whether it is a large, specially constructed area with expensive mainframe equipment or only a revamped user area with a personal computer. The construction of a large computer facility is a complex undertaking beyond the scope of this book. Usually, projects will involve modifying an existing facility rather than constructing a new one.

Figure 7.4

Checklist of Implementation Activities

1. Perform **preliminary construction**
   - Plan and prepare the physical facilities
   - Plan, obtain, and install the development environment hardware
   - Obtain software tools and code or obtain application software
   - Plan and prepare training materials and documentation
2. Perform **preliminary testing**
   - Create a test environment: build test files and prepare development and staging environments
   - Test components
   - Test system
3. Perform **final construction**
   - Revise software in development and staging environments
   - Build the test files and production database
   - Document procedures
   - Hire and train personnel
4. Perform **final testing**
   - Test subsystems
   - Test system
5. Perform **system installation**
   - Transfer tested software to production environment
   - Transfer production files to production environment
6. Obtain management approval of completion
7. Cutover to new system

FIGURE 7.5

Preliminary Construction Activities Span Multiple Phases

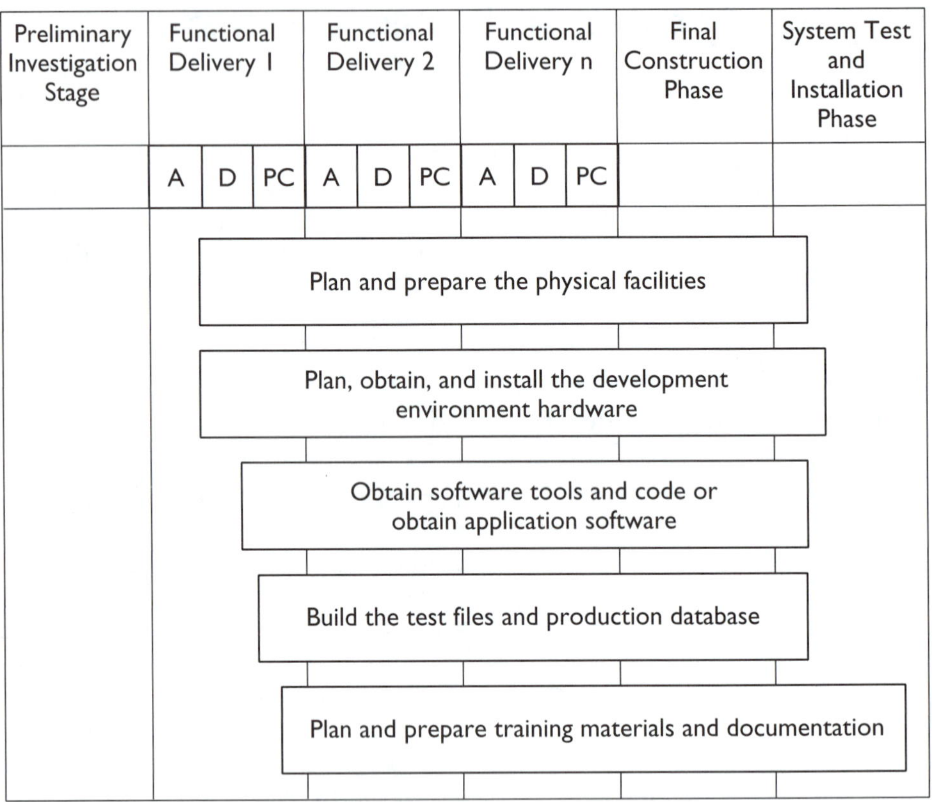

Modification of an existing facility includes such activities as redesigning the physical layout to accommodate new equipment, installing a new environmental control system with such features as air conditioning, fire protection, power surge protection, and power backup, and altering the lighting and noise reduction features of the users' work areas.

As an example, consider modification of a facility to accommodate a new automated order processing system for a telemarketing firm. Previously, customers phoned in their orders to operators who manually completed an order form for each customer. The new system provides each operator with a workstation connected to a server housed in another room. Preparing the facility for this new system involves running electrical and communication lines to each operator's workstation. One of the main concerns in preparing this facility is simply keeping all of the wires out of the operators' way.

Responsibility for facility preparation commonly rests with the manager of computer operations. This person works closely with the project team and the IS steering committee during the facility preparation. Timing is critical. In some instances, the new system cannot be finally tested until the facility is completed.

Since the construction of a large computing facility can span months, the work performed during one of the early iterations of preliminary construction activities might be limited to working with an architect on the design of the facility, and perhaps obtaining bids from contractors. Such activity is usually controlled and coordinated by the firm's purchasing department. The project team contributes by providing information concerning the projected physical design of the new system.

To avoid all the work of creating or expanding facilities, some companies arrange for a wide variety of computer services from an outsourcing firm or application service provider. An **application service provider** helps customers define their goals, provide software tailored to the customer's specific business objectives, and host the solution by providing server space and technical support on the provider's site. Key advantages of using an application service provider for a company entering a new area of computer applications, such as Internet order processing, include:

- An off-site facility with the necessary environmental control features
- Vendor expertise in hardware and software, including communications
- Experienced 24/7 (24 hours, 7 days a week) technical support
- Capacity for server expansion that can evolve with increases in system activity

With the physical facilities in place, the hardware can be installed.

Plan, Obtain, and Install the Development Environment Hardware

The required hardware configuration is determined during the design phase. Installing and configuring servers for a large Web-based system requires specialized expertise. Usually, the hardware vendor or vendors will work with the operations staff to install computers, servers, disk drives, communications equipment, and high-speed printers. If a vendor does not provide installation support, computer consultants are available to assist with the installation. The development team works with the operations staff to install and configure most PCs for client/server systems or Web-based systems.

As with the facility preparation, hardware installation activity during this phase might be limited to identification of vendors that can provide the needed units. For large companies, leasing hardware is a frequent choice since the process of upgrading both hardware and operating systems can be left to a firm that specializes in the particular platforms chosen by the company. Once the scope of services is identified, requests for proposals (RFPs) can be prepared and made available to several vendors. A structured approach to the evaluation of software proposals is described in Technical Module G. The same approach may be taken to evaluate vendor proposals for leasing, selling, outsourcing, and renting hardware.

Obtain Software Tools and Code or Obtain Application Software

The Development Environment

As soon as possible after the platform for the production system is chosen, the developers should create a development environment, often called the develop-

FIGURE 7.6

Coding and Unit Testing Occur in the First of Four Software Staging Environment

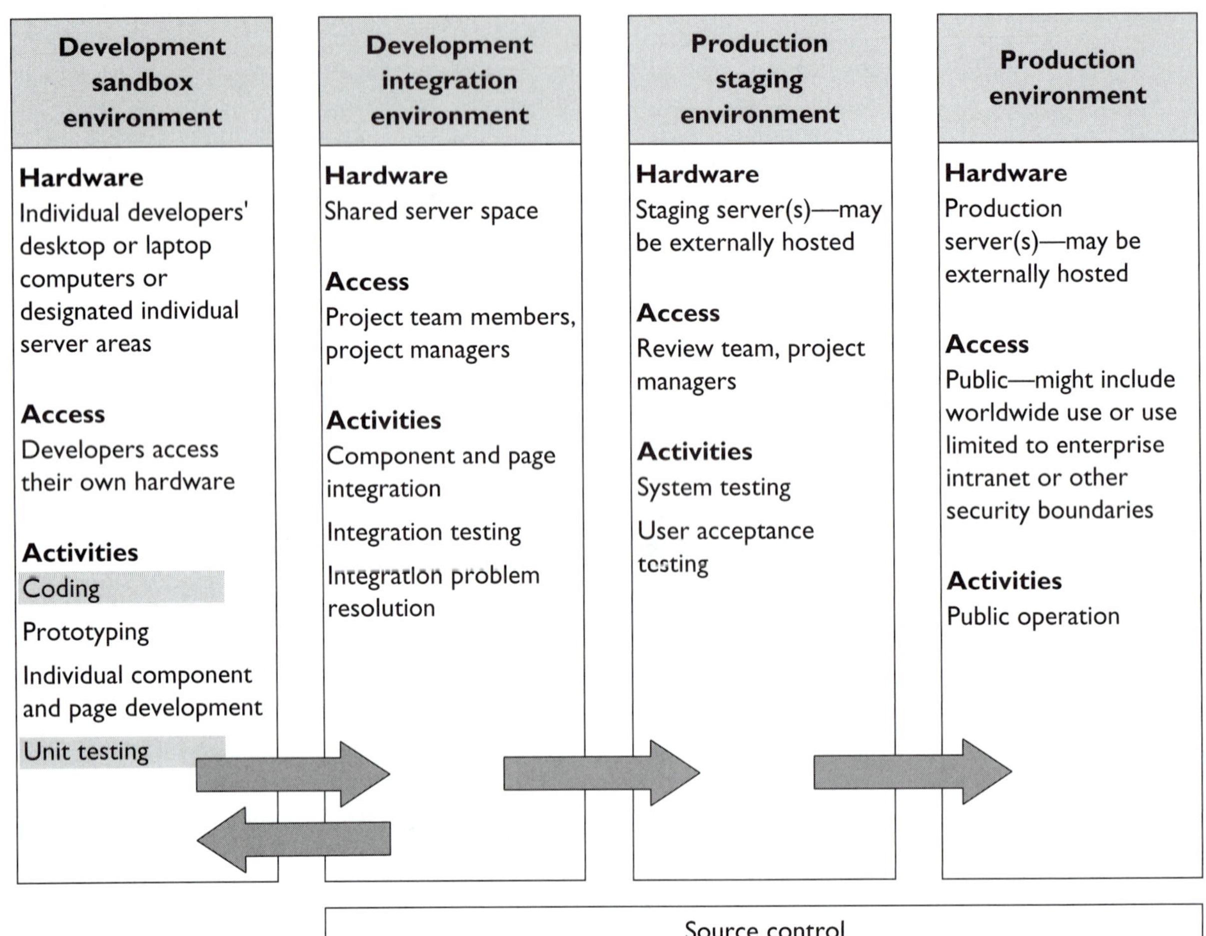

ment sandbox. A **development sandbox** includes the necessary software development tools and preliminary test data that are required to construct the new system. It is an environment that duplicates project files locally, giving team members the ability to develop prototypes and explore new development paths independently.

The term *sandbox* emerged from the idea that developers require an area where they can build "sand castles." Nothing is permanent in the sandbox, allowing developers to exercise their creativity and rapid development skills while not interfering with the clients' stable production environment. Ideas, proofs of concept, and prototypes can be built in the sandbox with little constraint on the resources normally required to install, configure, and execute software in production. Once a software module or series of modules has been completed and approved, the module(s) can be taken out of the sandbox and promoted into an integrated test environment for further testing with all system components before installing the software in the production environment. See Figure 7.6.

Developers using sandboxes should have regular communication, ensuring that each team member is kept up to date with the master project. Locally duplicated sandboxes, called **variant sandboxes,** allow team members to simultaneously work on different releases of the same project. This speeds and simplifies post-release maintenance. Version control software, such as Microsoft's Visual Source Safe, may be purchased to help manage this process.

The recommended approach is to assign one team member to create the initial variant sandbox so that other team members can be working on other parts of the project. The lead programmer creates a quick sample module and tests it in the production environment to be certain that the sandbox has the same or a compatible version of the development software. The advantages of creating a development environment separate from the production environment are listed below.

- Reduce the risk of introducing errors into the production environment.
- Reduce the risk of not completing all functions by including test data for all possible errors and time periods, such as quarterly and year-end reports.
- Save time and money by working with short test data files and working with less expensive hardware with easier access (such as a desk top development environment that simulates a Web-based production environment that includes dozens of servers).
- Eliminate any potential interference with production activity for completed systems and earlier versions of application software.

To gain these advantages while minimizing confusion for multiple versions of a system, a development environment should include:

- Short data files
- Copies of the latest software files developed by the team
- Copies of job control language for any batch processes
- Systems documentation to aid revisions
- A change log that identifies the version, author, and date for each revised software module

Each individual developer creates new code in his or her individual variant sandbox. This is shown as process bubble 1 in the data flow diagram in Figure 7.7. In this diagram, the lower portion of each process symbol identifies the actor or actors who will perform the process. All of the software files are stored in a development integration environment; this is shown as the second environment in Figure 7.6 and illustrated as a data store in Figure 7.7. Developers copy team software into their own sandbox (process step 2) and test whether their code works with the team code. They revise their code as needed (process step 3) and update the team storage of files in the development integration environment. Once the team has completed all of the functions for the current development phase, a user review (process step 4) will determine whether the developers should proceed to the next development phase.

Installing Purchased Software

When a system is based on purchased software, the development team's responsibilities are reduced. The purchase agreement usually specifies that the vendor will help

FIGURE 7.7

Software Integration Process: Testing and Revising

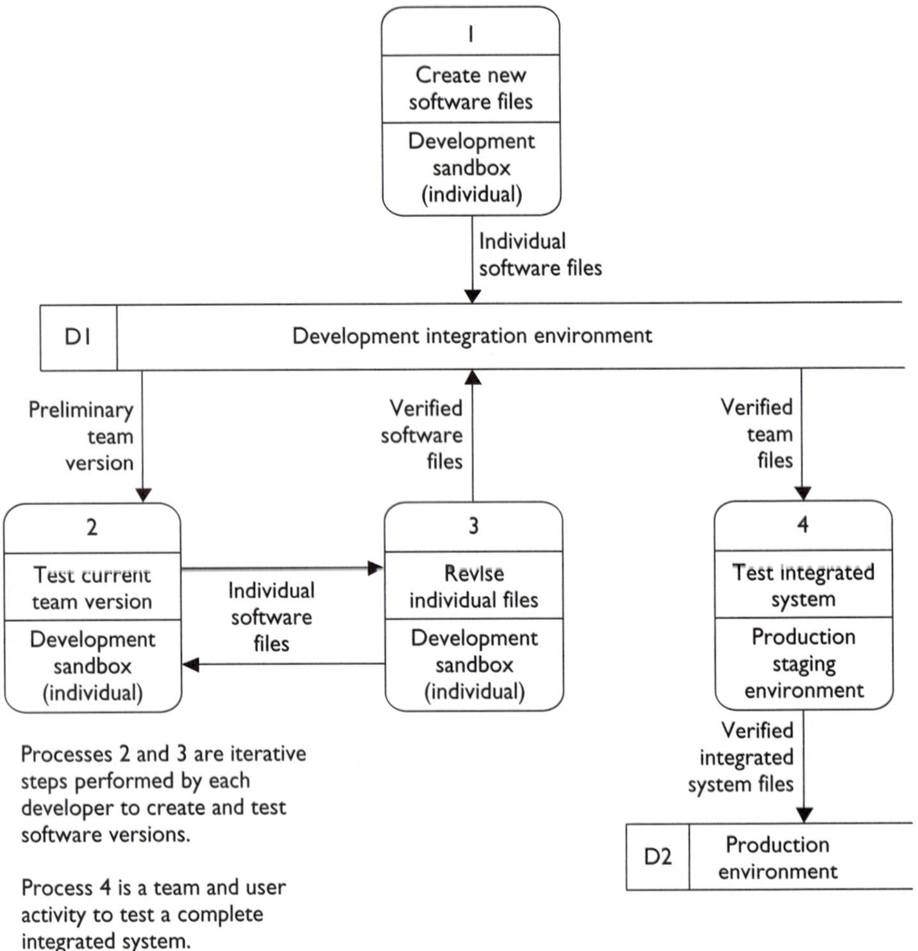

install software for large scale systems. This is the case with such large, enterprise resource planning systems as SAP. The installation should be a part of the phased construction activities. It should be installed in modules and tested and reviewed with users at each step. This is the same process that is followed with custom software. The main advantage of this approach is that any problems in meeting the user's requirements are quickly identified.

The task of configuring such parameters as server locations and the communication port settings, and correcting bugs are the vendor's job. In these situations, it is also generally the vendor's responsibility to test the software to ensure that it satisfies the functional requirements.

The development team or a technical support team will usually install software that is purchased for PCs, following instructions provided in the software documentation. Exceptions are software that is custom-prepared by third parties such as an outsourcing firm or application service provider, and also expensive integrated or networking software. Both of these items will often be installed and tested by the outsourcing firm or application service provider.

Selecting Purchased Software

When more than a single software vendor have products that can meet some or all of the functional requirements of the new system, the systems approach can be followed in making the selection. First, the possible products are identified; then they are evaluated; and finally the best is selected. This selection process is explained in Technical Module G on the evaluation of possible system solutions.

Coding Custom-Written Software

Although building the software component from scratch requires more time and effort than installing purchased software, the development team often has no choice. When prewritten software is not available to meet the requirements, software must be coded from the specifications developed during the design phase.

Who Should Write the Software?

A major decision involves identifying who should prepare the custom-written software. Should it be the developers or the users? Although users often do not have the knowledge and skills for such responsibility, a key ingredient in phased development is a high level of user involvement in development. Therefore, efforts should be made to involve the users as much as possible.

In deciding who should be responsible for the custom programming, four factors should be considered.

- The availability of end-user development tools and CASE tools
- The complexity of the hardware component
- The relative importance of functionality versus efficiency
- The frequency of changes and the volume of exception reports that are anticipated

For a large, complex system project, the specific requirements for all of the criteria except the first one are likely to change during detailed design activities. Before construction begins, it is worthwhile to review the requirements and determine whether the earlier decisions about who will code the software still apply.

Professional programmers should write software for large complex systems. Similarly, if efficiency and transportability are vital requirements, software should be coded in a language that has the best runtime efficiency, such as C, C++ or Java. But, if the software will run on a PC and users have developed similar applications themselves, having them write the software should reduce the total system development cost. Depending on the nature of the system, some portions may be written by programmers and other portions by users when a mix of development tools is chosen.

What Development Tools Should be Used?

When the development team codes the software, another question arises: What development tools should be used? Should the team use a programming language as C, C++, or Java to maximize run time efficiency? Or should the team use a tool with

TABLE 7.1

Evaluation of Development Languages: JAVA AND C++

Evaluation Criteria	C++	Java
Ease of use	C++ is more difficult to use than Java. It also has more unnecessary complexity.	Java has a more consistent semantic structure that minimizes the number of underlying concepts. It has uniform syntactic conventions.
Ease of learning	C++ has a longer learning curve than end-user development tools; available integrated development environments speed learning.	Java is easier to learn for programmers who already know C or C++; without that prior knowledge Java will be slightly easier to learn for a beginner than C++ due to less complexity.
Run-time efficiency	Though C++ pointer arithmetic and aliasing prohibit some optimizations, run time is faster overall than Java.	Java's garbage collection raises questions about efficiency and guaranteed timing, especially in real-time systems.
Reliability/error checking	C++ has many well-known coding traps (e.g., = vs. ==, & vs. &&, premature semicolon in control structures). There is little checking at run-time, thus few errors are detected early.	Java has fewer coding traps. There are multiple run-time checks (e.g. bounds checking and checks for null values.)
Realtime ability	C++ provides some functions for handling local and calendar time; real-time calls are operating system dependent.	Java supports delays in centiseconds and clock access in milliseconds.
Maintainability	C++, mainly due to the fact that it isn't as easy to use, is also not as easy to maintain. However, C++'s object-oriented features, IF USED, improve maintainability because they force interfaces to be defined and used.	Though not completely, Java does promote ease of maintenance by using document comments (//*) and standard documentation conventions, which aid in readability.
Portability	C++, like most other languages, compiles into the machine code of the particular platform, making it less portable than Java.	Java is specifically designed to compile into what is called byte code, which a program called a Java Virtual Machine (JVM) then interprets on the desired

Source: Wheeler, David (1996). Ada, C, C++, and Java vs. The Steelman [Article posted on Web site]. Retrieved August 1, 2000 from the World Wide Web: http://www.adahome.com/History/Steelman/steeltab.htm.

more built-in features to speed development time? Generally, the factors in this choice will be the same ones affecting the choice between user and programmer coding. The programmer's familiarity with the language, the degree of low-level machine control required (for light sensors and other special peripheral devices), portability, and efficiency are all factors to consider. In addition, the nature and frequency of changes in user requirements may make using an end-user development tool the only feasible choice. Table 7.1 identifies the relative advantages and disadvantages of using Java and C++. The developers will consider such features when making the language decision.

For large systems, it is wise to design the system so that portions that require run-time efficiency will be written in the most efficient language and portions that will change frequently are written in easy-to-learn, easy-to-use, but slower processing tools, such as Microsoft Access. This mix takes advantage of each language's strengths for specific functions. A data warehouse is an example of an approach that combines development by IT specialists and users working with different tools. IT specialists write the main data entry and processing programs in a language with superior run-time efficiency for high-volume work. Users are trained to generate their own exception reports, which were described in Chapter 6, in order to reduce the development time devoted to satisfying frequent small requests. Ideally, the user can query the database and obtain the needed information without having to specify the requirements for a programmer.

To take advantage of a mixture of software sources, however, you must have a database management system that allows access with user-friendly tools, or the development team must construct interfaces to allow this flexibility.

Another consideration enters into the choice of the language, and it is maintainability. User-friendly tools and CASE tools reduce the time required both to understand and to modify the code. When execution efficiency is important, however, the development team cannot take advantage of the reduced development time. Instead, they need to select tools that will take longer to program and will not be as easy to maintain.

Whatever development technology is chosen, programmers must write code that is very flexible. That is, the code should be portable and adaptable. To achieve this goal, programmers need to follow standards.

Programming Standards

Firms establish **programming standards** to serve as the guidelines for the programming staff so as to produce maintainable and flexible systems. These standards specify conventions for naming data elements and documenting program code, as well as structured programming practices for formatting and organizing code. These programming standards are extensions of documenting standards that guided the project team through the preliminary investigation, analysis, and design phases by prescribing formats to be followed for process and data models.

Below is a list of some guidelines for minimizing errors in spreadsheet development by users as well as IT specialists.

- *Know your problem.* Determine and summarize requirements before starting to build your spreadsheet.
- *Design modules top down.* Decompose the spreadsheet into smaller, less complex modules; for example, an overall construction bid spreadsheet would be linked to spreadsheets determining labor, material, and overhead costs.

- *Keep modules small.* Each spreadsheet should solve a single function (for example, overhead costs).
- *Document your work.* Label formula cells and rows with totals on the spreadsheet itself as well as in all user documentation.
- *Organize your spreadsheet.* Separate your spreadsheet into four sections, using blank lines for clarity: the introduction, the input section, the calculation section, and the report.

Spreadsheets often include errors that are hard to detect.[1] Their "What if" modeling capability makes comparing figures under different scenarios easy, but sometimes the figures being compared are nonsensical. For example, when adding a row for overhead costs to an existing spreadsheet, a programmer could easily make the mistake of inserting the row outside the range of rows totaled to compute the final costs. Overhead costs would be in the spreadsheet, but they would not be included in the computation of total costs. Such mistakes can be prevented if developers follow such simple standards as those described above.

Why would a firm adopt programming standards? Studies have shown that adopting and enforcing programming standards makes code easier to read and easier to maintain. In many cases, debugging time has been reduced by as much as 50 percent when structured programming practices were followed.[2] As illustrated in guidelines above, structuring the process and setting standards can be valuable for end user development. Setting standards is even more important for a more complex development environment. An example of more complex standards is provided in Figure CS 3.6 for the ASTA team's work with Microsoft Visual Basic and Access.

Build the Test Files and Production Database

As the system is constructed, you will test the individual components. For the *people* component, you will test to ensure that the users understand the procedures and can interface with the system as intended. For the *data* and *information* components, you will conduct tests of the database to ensure that its contents are complete and compatible with the system being developed. For the *software* and *hardware* components, you will conduct tests to ensure that the programs are working properly and that the equipment configuration performs as it should. **Testing** is the process of ensuring that the system quality goals are met when the system is installed.

Testing the People and Information Components

One of the big challenges in developing a Web-based system for widespread use is the inability to know all possible interpretations of your interface instructions by users you will never meet. In Chapter 5 we recommended arranging test audience reviews of the initial Web interface requirements. These user representative tests should be made several times in the development process so that changes in the navigation of a complex Web-based system do not become confusing for the potential customers or contributors to a site. For public users the system should require no training and a minimum of instructions on each screen.

The information component exists most often in the form of reports—printed or displayed. When developers provide users with reports generated by the system, it not only tests the outputs but the processes as well. The assumption is that if the reports are acceptable to the users then the processes that produce the reports are doing what they are supposed. Testing the information component is a classic example of black box testing—using the outputs as a check of the internal processes.

Testing the Data Component

In the excitement of developing a new system it is easy to pay so much attention to the people component and the software and hardware components that you overlook the importance of the database. This is especially true of small systems.

As the scale of the system increases, the attention that must be paid to the database increases almost exponentially. As much, or more, time should be invested in planning the creation of the database as the other components.

When the system being developed is replacing an existing computer-based system, the conversion from the existing database to the new one will be relatively straightforward when there are only minor changes in the data model. Substantial changes in the data model make the conversion much more difficult. The conversion can be so difficult that larger firms will often outsource this activity so that their developers can concentrate on the other system components.

When the system being developed is replacing a non-computer system, the data conversion must allow for the fact that the existing data resource most likely contains innumerable errors, omissions, and inconsistencies that are unacceptable to a computer-based system. When converting from manual data files to electronic ones, someone must reformat the data so that it can be entered onto electronic media by a data entry clerk. One of the authors worked with a small insurance company who divided up all of the data coding among all of the employees, including the president. Every day during his lunch period, the president would go down to the file department and fill out the coding sheets for his files. With the president doing his share, the other employees didn't dare complain about the extra workload.

The ASTA team recognized the importance of the database to the skill set system and allocated one of the eight project phases to database design. Major milestones were established for the database work, as shown in Figure CS 3.4, to such activities as reviewing the ER diagram with the client, installing a beta version of the database on the client's PC, and refining and debugging the database. To build the database, ASTA hired a data entry clerk from a contract employment firm to enter all the skill set data from Yolanda's paper files. The data entry clerk was not only faster than Yolanda, but this approach allowed Yolanda more time to help with testing the system reports and the completed database while keeping up with all her other tasks.

Testing the Software and Hardware Components

Unit testing is the process of testing each new software module in the development sandbox. You will build test data files to evaluate the reliability of the system. You will observe users and system operators to be sure that the procedures you have constructed are clear and that you have accurately represented the tasks to be performed.

Every system is eventually tested. You can test the system now, while its errors and inefficiencies can be corrected relatively easily and inexpensively. Or, you can let the users test the system after it is installed and risk frustrated users and expensive revisions. Testing after installation is analogous to leaving it to the homebuyer to discover

FIGURE 7.8

The Format of a Decision Logic Table

Condition stub	Condition entry
Action stub	Action entry

that there are no electrical outlets in the kitchen. The builder should check such details as the house is built, so system omissions and errors are discovered *before* the wallboard goes up and the drywall is applied. Testing during the iterative preliminary construction stages in phased development will occur first in each development sandbox. The users will then review verified code in the development integration environment (Figure 7.6).

Your success as a systems developer depends on your attention to detail and your awareness that, no matter how many times you have done something correctly in the past, there is always a chance that this time you have done it wrong. Avoid living dangerously; always test before you install. Better yet, follow the guideline for phased development to frequently review your work with users.

Testing all Possible Transaction Combinations

One of the big challenges in planning a testing process is to make certain you have tested all possible transaction combinations that the system can encounter. A decision logic table can be used to meet this challenge. A **decision logic table (DLT)** is a process modeling tool that is used for documenting situations where multiple conditions influence actions to be taken.

A DLT has the format illustrated in Figure 7.8. In the *condition stub* area, all of the conditions that can influence one or more actions are listed. In the *condition entry* area, the letters Y or N are used to identify whether the conditions exist. In the *action stub* area, all of the actions that can be taken are listed. In the *action entry* area, the letter X is used to specify the actions to take.

Figure 7.9 is a simple example, showing how two conditions influence the choice of a strategy for preparing custom software. The strategy is carried out by taking one of four actions, depending on the conditions.

- When the firm has the development software that has been selected for use in preparing custom application software, and the IS staff is trained in that development software, then the staff is assigned development responsibility.

- When the firm has the development software but the IS staff is not trained in its use, a training program is launched.
- When the firm does not have the development software but the IS staff is trained in its use, the firm obtains the software.
- When the firm does not have the software and the IS staff is not trained in its use, the code preparation using the development software is outsourced.

This DLT example shows how the tool can be used to guide a high-level decision. An example of how a DLT can capture the logic of software is shown in Figure 7.10. This is the type of logic that could be incorporated in an order entry program. The programmer can use such a diagram to guide the testing process to ensure that all possible logical paths are tested. The two action columns with dashes (-) indicate condition combinations that should not occur-new customers with past-due receivables. The programmer would include an error routine to detect such a situation.

The value of the DLT to testing is that it forces you to consider all condition possibilities. In the credit approval example, there are three conditions, but there are eight possible combinations (Y/N columns). The formula for determining the number of combinations is:

$N = 2^C$

Where N = number of combinations

c = number of conditions

In the Figure 7.9 example, the formula would be

$N = 2^3 = 8.$

The programmers would ensure that tests for all eight conditions are conducted.

Plan and Prepare Training Materials and Documentation

During each iteration of analysis stages, when the characteristics of the new system begin to emerge, attention should be devoted to user training. Web-based sys-

Figure 7.9

A Decision Logic Table of Key Custom Software Decisions

The firm has the selected development software?	Y	Y	N	N
The IS staff is trained in using the selected software?	Y	N	Y	N
Assign code preparation to the IS staff	X	X	X	
Obtain the selected development software			X	
Train the IS staff in the use of the selected software		X		
Outsource the code preparation				X

FIGURE 7.10

A Decision Logic Table of Credit Approval

Present customer?	Y	Y	Y	Y	N	N	N	N
Good credit rating?	Y	Y	N	N	Y	Y	N	N
Past-due receivables?	Y	N	Y	N	Y	N	Y	N
Grant unlimited credit		X			-		-	
Grant credit up to $5,000	X				-	X	-	
Grant no credit			X		-		-	X
Forward to credit manager				X	-		-	

tems are likely to have a subset of users who will never be trained, such as customers for an airline reservation system. But there will always be a subset of users who will take over ownership of the system and there may be several subsets of users who will be trained in processes that the public will never see. Examples are travel agents, airline boarding control clerks, airline financial analysts, and flight schedulers. Before the system can be turned over to user-owners, appropriate user groups must be trained. First, training planning is conducted, addressing such issues as who should be trained, what material should be communicated, where and when the sessions will be held, and who will conduct the sessions. Large firms have special teams that are dedicated to planning the training program for each project, and then administering it. In smaller firms, persons from the human resources unit or members of the project team can perform all of the planning activities. A user on the development team is ideal for conducting the training sessions since she or he thoroughly understands the system and understands user terminology, concerns and issues. If no user is available for preparing or conducting training, a developer who has worked closely with users is the next best choice since the users will have confidence in the developer's capabilities.

Training can be conducted in one-on-one sessions or classroom settings, depending on the number of users. Attention can be given to the details of system operation, correcting errors, receiving help, and other subjects that the user needs to understand. When a user manual is prepared to support the system, it can be used as a textbook for training.

For systems with a large user group, complex processes, and turnover in the user group, developers should create a training environment. This will be worthwhile whenever repeated training is likely. For example, large airlines hire dozens of airline clerks for airports worldwide. Training on airline reservation systems is a key part of their job training. The advantages of creating a training environment separate from the production environment are as follows.

- Reduce the risk of introducing errors into the production environment, such as adding a fictitious passenger to a real flight and forgetting to delete the passenger.
- Reduce the risk of not training for all functions by including training data relevant for situations that do not occur every day in the production environment, such as handling passenger transfers for a canceled flight.
- Save time and money by working with short training data files and working with less expensive hardware with easier access. An example is a desktop training environment that simulates the server connection of the production environment but is in fact completely based on the PC.

FIGURE 7.11

JAD Review and Confirmation Workshop

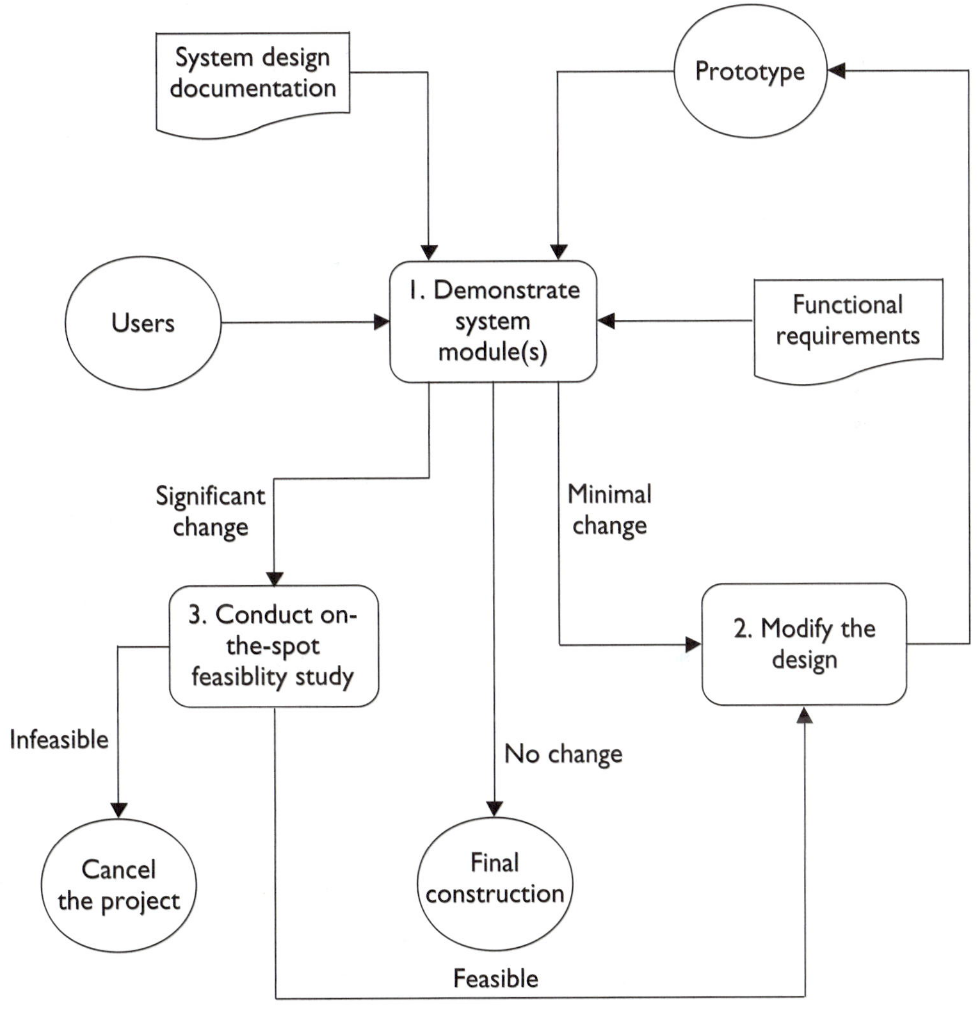

PROJECT MANAGEMENT TOOLBOX

Management of Preliminary Construction

In describing the analysis stage, we referred to it as "where the rubber meets the road," recognizing the importance of identifying the user's requirements accurately. That is the systems analysis view. Developers who rightfully recognize the importance of constructing and installing the software that performs the necessary processing use the same phrase when referring to implementation. This is the implementation view. As with an automobile, there is more than one place where the rubber meets the road and all are important.

If user-driven development has meant saying, "yes" to every request up to the first iterations of preliminary construction, the development team is probably feeling some stress. A very serious question to ask after the first iteration of preliminary construction and user review is:

- *Are we on schedule?* If so, earlier estimates about the schedule for future phases will probably continue to meet team targets. If not, should we adjust the scope, schedule, or resources? This juggling of schedule, scope, and resources can be illustrated by a triangle, as shown in Figure 7.12 Or you can regard the schedule, scope and resources as the three legs of a stool that must be kept in balance or the project will fail.

If the team is behind schedule there are additional questions.

- *Is the schedule realistic?* If not, should the schedule be expanded or the scope reduced or resources expanded? A typical optimistic developer will decide that the problems faced up to this point are due to some unique problem. For example, "Our key user has been very busy, but now she has seen our prototype, she says she will spend more time reviewing our work and give us more feedback and be faster responding. " Or "We waited a long time to find out what the development tools would be, but now that these are chosen and resources are committed, we should be able to move forward quickly." Optimism is a key virtue of a "can-do developer" but it can lead to serious problems for the developer as the project

- Eliminate any potential interference with production activity for completed systems and earlier versions of application software.

To gain these advantages, a training environment should include:

- Short data files that cover all conditions and match training instructions
- Training instructions as part of a tutorial or notebook
- Results for training actions so students know if they have been successful

Training is usually timed to occur just before the user must begin use of the system. Some firms adhere to policies that restrict training to the two-week period prior to turning the system over to the users.

Once the developers have tested all of the system modules and prepared the training materials, they are ready to proceed to final construction where the modules are integrated into a single, functioning system. Before that happens, however, user approval must be obtained. This is the decision point in phased development where users decide whether to repeat the analysis, design, and preliminary construction activities for additional functional deliveries or revisions or go on to final construction. The project team must demonstrate the system to users and project sponsors.

FIGURE 7.12

Balancing Scope, Schedule, and Resources

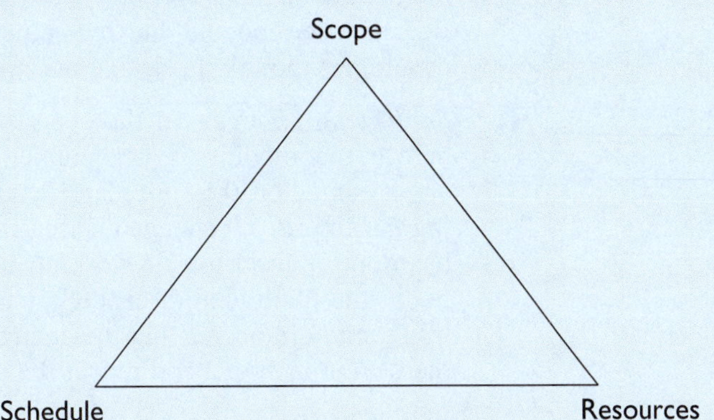

nears the final completion date. One way to increase resources is to ask developers to put in 50-, 60-, or 70-hour weeks for the last weeks or months of a project. It is better to be realistic early and cut the scope or add resources (additional team members, consultants, training for developers, purchased object libraries with completed code for some functions, and so on).

- *Is the scope realistic?* If not, should phases be created that are more in line with business objectives and an enterprise analysis of what is possible within a reasonable time frame? The solution may be to review some of the assumptions made in preliminary investigation. Is this the right project to pursue at this time? Is this the right scope for our organization at this time? It is best to view the lessons learned at each user review point from the broadest perspective, not a programmer's perspective of creating code to meet a specification.

DEMONSTRATE THE NEW SYSTEM MODULES TO USERS AND PROJECT SPONSORS

Frequent user reviews are an integral part of phased development. Whether you use a requirements prototype or an evolutionary prototype, user approval is solicited after each iteration of preliminary construction. The project team demonstrates to users and project sponsors the work that has been done for one or more modules. The project sponsors can include the IS steering committee or management on any organizational level. The demonstration can be accomplished in a small group meeting informally in an office or computer lab, or it can take the form of a JAD session. Figure 7.11 on page 441 is a flowchart of a JAD session devoted exclusively to the decision of whether to accept the system module as demonstrated. This session is called a **JAD review and confirmation workshop.**[3]

In step 1, the module is demonstrated in the presence of users. The users and developers use the functional requirements from the preliminary investigation phase and the system design documentation from iterative design activities as the basis for evaluating the demonstration.

There are three possible outcomes.

- *No change*—The users and project sponsors may determine that no changes are necessary. In this case, the module is completed and is ready for integration with other modules in the final construction phase.
- *Minimal change*—When the users and project sponsors are generally satisfied with the module, but recommend some relatively minor changes, the developers modify the design in step 2 and revise the prototype.
- *Significant change*—In the event that significant changes must be made before the module is acceptable, the developers, users, and sponsors engage in an on-the-spot feasibility study in step 3. If it appears that making the significant change is infeasible, the project is cancelled. If the team has done a good job of working with the users and sponsors up to this point, the likelihood of cancellation is extremely remote. When the feasibility study indicates that the changes are feasible, the developers modify the design in step 2 and repeat the prototyping.

Although we include this JAD session at the end of each preliminary construction stage, it could be conducted at any point during the system development life cycle. In fact, the more frequently the JAD sessions are conducted, the more likely that the project team will remain on target in developing a system that meets the users' needs.

We have now completed the analysis-design-preliminary construction iteration. If other modules remain, the iteration is repeated. If not, the development moves to the final construction phase where the modules are integrated.

SUMMARY

In phased development, planning for implementation of the new system can begin as early as analysis and design, with the actual work being performed during preliminary construction, final construction, and system test and installation. Preliminary construction and preliminary testing are interspersed with analysis and design. Then, the remaining tasks of the system development life cycle can be taken in order-final construction, final testing, system installation, management approval, and cutover. The two steps of the preliminary construction phase are (1) construct new system software modules and test data, and (2) demonstrate the new system modules to users and project sponsors.

Preliminary construction includes some portion of the preparation of the physical facilities, installation of hardware, purchase of prewritten software or the coding of custom software for each system module, building of test files, and preparation of training materials and documentation.

Facility preparation for Web-based systems is much more complex than that for stand-alone PC systems and must be timed so that unavailable facilities do not hold up such other efforts as hardware acquisition and testing. Hardware acquisition can begin during preliminary construction but will not likely be completed until final construction. As with the facilities, hardware acquisition is timed so that the units are in place when needed.

The new system software can be purchased from software vendors or custom coded by the firm's programmers or outsourcers. A combination of both approaches is another possibility. Regardless of which approach is selected, the availability of a development sandbox can facilitate independent coding by team members. The sandbox includes software development tools and test data.

When pursuing a strategy of custom coding, two key questions must be answered: Who should write the software, and what development tools should be used? The answers to these questions are complex and depend on the capabilities of the users and developers, the system being developed, and the development tools that are available. When acquiring purchased software, vendor selection is very important. When the purchased software is acquired and the custom code is prepared, the programs are tested to ensure that they perform correctly. Successful unit testing during preliminary construction stages will lead to easier system testing in the final construction stage.

Training materials should be planned and begun during preliminary construction as soon as the basic characteristics of the system have been defined. Early reviews of training by users will ensure that training conducted during the final construction stages will meet the users' needs.

The output of preliminary construction could be a prototype that is demonstrated to users and project sponsors. This demonstration can be conducted for only a few persons when the system is small and modest. For larger and more complex systems, a JAD review and confirmation workshop can provide an effective setting.

Key Terms

implementation
construction
conversion
application service provider
development sandbox
variant sandbox
programming standards
testing
unit testing
decision logic table (DLT)

Key Concepts

- Planning for the implementation activities begins as soon as the new system design begins to emerge
- The development environment
- Staging environment
- The importance of the selection of the programmer and the development technology
- The importance of testing
- Training environment
- A JAD session can provide an effective setting for achieving user approval of any portion of development activity

Questions

1. What distinguishes phased development from the traditional system development life cycle?
2. When does implementation begin?
3. What are the two steps of each iterative preliminary construction stage?
4. What are the five main preliminary construction activities?
5. Who is usually responsible for preparation of the physical facility of large-scale computer systems?
6. Why is the collection of software development tools and preliminary test data called a development sandbox?
7. What are the contents of a development environment?

8. In what way is the installation of large purchased software systems, such as SAP, similar to the installation of custom software?
9. What factors influence the choice of person or persons who should write custom software?
10. Why would you want to mix end-user development tools and more complex development tools to create a system?
11. What sort of guidelines are spelled out in programming standards?
12. Why should testing be performed as the software is produced and not afterwards?
13. What contribution can decision logic tables make to planning a testing program?
14. What are the contents of a training environment and why would you create one?
15. Who can administer a training program?
16. When a JAD review and confirmation workshop are used for the demonstration of the preliminary construction for the users and project sponsors, what are the three possible outcomes?
17. What can the project team do to minimize the chance of the project being scrapped during preliminary construction?

Topics for Discussion

1. The general rule is that "if purchased software is available to do the job, buy it." Are there any instances when a firm would pass up such software and decide to prepare custom code? If so, what are they?
2. If the JAD review and confirmation workshop concludes that significant changes are necessary, and an on-the-spot feasibility study be conducted, should the developers try to convince the users and project sponsors that the changes are feasible when they would be extremely difficult to achieve?

Case Problem: "It Was a Nightmare!"

You went to college with Ryan Valdez, and have kept in contact with him ever since, as you developed your information system consulting business and he became the president of PowerCo, the local electric utility. So, when he called on the phone and asked you to have lunch with him, you eagerly accepted. It turned out to be a business lunch, as Ryan unloaded on you his bad experiences in implementing a new fixed assets system. You recall from your accounting courses that fixed assets are buildings, furniture, vehicles, and other things that are not easily converted into cash. Ryan explains that the current PowerCo fixed assets system is very old, having been coded in COBOL, and many of the processes have to be done by hand.

It seems that PowerCo had purchased a prewritten software package to do the fixed asset work and had attempted to implement it. As it turned out, the implementation was one bad experience after another. And, to make matters worse, the college student who ended up with a lot of the implementation responsibility turned in her resignation last Friday.

You: How did you come to purchase the software package?

Ryan: Our fixed assets expert Bob Popp was playing tennis with a friend who had heard we were looking for one, and he recommended one named Redbud. Bob is a member of our accounting department. He liked what he heard and reported it to our vice president of finance, Amy Wilson, who passed it on to the IS steering committee.

You: Are you a member of the committee?

Ryan: No. It just consists of the vice presidents.

You: Sorry for the interruption. Please go on.

Ryan: Although the system sounded good, Amy thought that we should do a system study before purchasing something, so the committee directed Bob to obtain as much information on the package as possible. He spoke with the programmer who had developed it but, after hearing what the package would do, he had mixed feelings. He felt that we needed something simpler. He shared his sentiments with Amy and she agreed.

She called a meeting of the IS steering committee and we probably would have killed the Redbud issue at that point, but our CIO, Judy Jones, liked the idea of using a package. You know, our IS shop has been overloaded and can't implement new systems fast enough. Judy saw this as a chance to get some relief. Judy has a big influence on the steering committee and when she came out for the package, everybody else except Amy went along with the idea. So, we decided to make the purchase.

You: You haven't mentioned a strategic plan for information resources that might spell out the process to follow when developing a system. Do you have one?

Ryan: No.

You: Then what happened?

Ryan: We put together a project team. Since we didn't have to worry about doing any programming, the team consisted of only Bob and three accounting clerks who were to do the data entry-entering the fixed asset data into the new format and adding any additional data that Redbud would require. Amy convinced Judy that the team should include someone from accounting who is experienced in software development, so Pat Jackson, senior developer in accounting, was given that responsibility.

You: Did you have a development plan, like a Gantt chart or something?

Ryan: No Gantt chart, since it seemed like it would be so simple. The only plan was to let Pat handle any questions dealing with software and Bob any questions dealing with fixed assets. The accounting clerks were to do most of the work but Pat convinced us to hire part-time clerks instead, which we did. But it didn't work out at all since they were put under the supervision of accounting department supervisors who had not been trained on the system and could not answer the clerks' questions.

You: Just a minute. The accounting supervisors weren't trained? Was anyone trained?

Ryan: No. When we asked the Redbud vendor if they could give us some training, they said they didn't have anyone to spare. And this cost us dearly. When the clerks asked the supervisors questions they couldn't answer, they referred the clerks to Bob. This worked OK but Bob was sent out of town for a month to work on another project, and with him gone, there was nobody to answer the questions. As a result, much of the entered data was full of errors.

You: When did you find out about the data errors?

Ryan: Not until shortly before the planned cutover date of October 31 a year ago. The team tried to run the package with the new data and it was a nightmare. The data was full of errors. Bob took a look at it and decided that it would be a mammoth task to clean it up. When the steering committee found this out, they postponed the cutover for a whole year. All of the data had to be reentered but the committee didn't want to incur any more costs than were absolutely necessary. We decided to let the part-time clerks go and hire a part-time college student to do the reentry. We brought in Helen Bennett, a real sharp accounting major at the university.

You: So, you didn't really do any software testing until you were ready to install the entire package. Right?

Ryan: We assumed that since the software was prewritten, the vendor had tested it.

You: You've mentioned data problems. Are you aware of any problems with the software?

Ryan: As soon as Helen got underway on cleaning up the data, she ran the first batch through Redbud to see what would happen, and encountered some things we hadn't anticipated. The interface between Redbud and the general ledger system wouldn't work. There was no procedure for the offices to follow in transferring an asset to another location. We wanted to prepare management reports identifying which assets had been transferred from one location to another but since we only assign asset numbers to cars and trucks, there was no way to determine which assets were involved. There were several other disappointments as well.

You: Do you know whether Redbud consists of modules?

Ryan: That I do know. It's got a depreciation module, a database module, a reporting module, and some more that I can't recall.

You: Have you been able to get any help from the Redbud vendor?

Ryan: Hardly anything. The system is not documented and I've mentioned the lack of training.

You: Well, from what you tell me, I don't imagine that the team demonstrated any parts of the system to people in accounting to get their feedback-to make sure that it was doing what it was supposed to do.

Ryan: To my knowledge, there was never any such demo.

You: So when Helen found out about the software glitches, what did this do to the cutover schedule?

Ryan: Well, it didn't have any affect at all at first. Helen went on full-time for last summer and was able to clean up the data and complete the data entry. But she believed that the cutover date coming up this fall was unrealistic because there are still unanswered questions about the software. She wanted another postponement but the steering committee decided to stick with October 31. By the end of the summer, Helen was responsible for all fixed asset systems, supervision of all fixed asset payments, and the implementation of Redbud. Before leaving work last Friday, she told Judy that she had accepted a job offer to work in New Orleans and would be leaving September 1. That's only ten days off. What should we do? We've got all this money and time invested in a system that looks like it doesn't even fit the way we do business. I know you have a lot of experience in software development. Can you tell me where we went wrong and what we can do to get things back on track? We're willing to completely start over if that is the thing to do. Most importantly, we don't want this to happen again.

After thinking it over for a moment, you decide to break down your response into three areas-weaknesses in the PowerCo infrastructure, errors made prior to preliminary construction, and errors during preliminary construction.

Assignments

1. What are the weaknesses in the PowerCo infrastructure that make system development difficult?
2. What errors were made prior to preliminary construction?
3. What errors were made during preliminary construction? Hint: Use Figure 7.5 as a checklist.
4. What can PowerCo do to prevent such a fiasco in the future?

SELECTED BIBLIOGRAPHY

Apte, Uday, and MaryAnne Winniford. "Global Outsourcing of Information Systems Functions: Opportunities and Challenges." In Khosrowpour, Mehdi (Ed). *Managing Information Technology in a Global Society* (Harrisburg, PA: Idea Group Publishing, 1991): 58-67.

Borck, James R. "Cobol-to-Java Conversion: Application Transformation." *INFO WORLD* 22 (Number 33, August 14, 2000): 53-56.

Li, Eldon Y. "Software Testing in a System Development Process: A Life Cycle Perspective." *Journal of Systems Management* 41 (August 1990): 23-31.

Linthicum, David. "Standards Smooth Software Development." *Network World* 15 (Number 32, August 10, 1998): 31.

Nelson, R. Ryan, Ellen M. Whitener, and Henry H. Philcox. "The Assessment of End-User Training Needs." *Communications of the ACM* 38 (Number 7, July 1995): 27-39.

NOTES

1. Dan N. Stone and Robert L. Black, "Building Structured Spreadsheets," *The Journal of Accountancy* 68 (October 1989): 131-142.
2. Edward Yourdon, *Managing the Structured Techniques,* 2nd ed. (Englewood Cliffs, NJ: Prentice-Hall, 1979), 4.
3. The term JAD review and confirmation workshop and the concepts presented in Figure 7.11 were taken from Sandra Donaldson Dewitz, *Systems Analysis and Design and the Transition to Objects,* (New York: McGraw-Hill, 1996).

CHAPTER 8

FINAL CONSTRUCTION

LEARNING OBJECTIVES

- Identify the tasks involved in final construction.
- Appreciate the importance of software testing and know some techniques to ensure that it meets its objectives.
- Recognize the features of database preparation that can produce a huge drain on development resources.
- Identify potential hardware vendors and evaluate their products.
- Explain what is involved in preparing facilities to house large-scale hardware.
- Describe the types of documentation that are necessary to meet the needs of users, participants, and technical personnel.
- Understand the role of the developer in the education of users and participants.

INTRODUCTION

We are finally out of the loop! We accomplished analysis, design, and preliminary construction for each system module and are now ready to put all of the pieces together. The integration of the modules into a system comes during the final construction stage. During this stage, construction of the software and databases is completed. The software and databases are then tested, hardware is obtained, facilities are made available to house the information resources, the documentation is completed, and training programs are conducted. Preparation of the database can be made difficult when the data is in a format that must be converted to fit the new system, when the new system requires data that has not previously been maintained, and when the firm is large and is the type that must maintain large historical files.

The goal of software testing is the identification of problems before installation. Testing problems can arise due to lack of proper attention by the developers, but these can be minimized or eliminated through good planning.

Additional hardware is acquired following basically the same procedure that was used during an early preliminary construction phase for purchasing software tools or application software. RFPs are provided to hardware vendors who then prepare proposals. Evaluation of the proposals can consider both quantitative and subjective factors. Once hardware is selected, it can be obtained through such payment plans as rental, lease, lease-purchase, and purchase. Before the hardware can be installed, work may be required to prepare the facility. This work can be sizeable for large-scale systems.

All of the final construction work is summarized in documentation, which includes such user materials as manuals, tutorials, and quick reference cards. More technical documentation takes the form of technical operations manuals, installation manuals, developer manuals, and system documentation.

Prior to cutover, users and participants must be trained. This training can be conducted by one of the users who is a member of the development team, by one of the developers, by the firm's human resources unit, or by consultants.

THE FINAL CONSTRUCTION TASKS

We have reached the fifth stage of phased development as illustrated in Figure 8.1. Each module of the new system was analyzed, designed, constructed, and tested during the earlier phases. The new system now exists in the form of separate, tested modules if an evolutionary prototyping approach has been taken. If a requirements prototyping approach has been taken, a complete model of the system exists, but the software must now be rewritten partially or entirely in the chosen production environment development tools.

During the final construction stage, the tasks are continued that were performed in preliminary construction. The tasks of the final construction stage include:

1. Construct and test production-ready programs
2. Construct and test a production-ready database
3. Obtain additional hardware
4. Prepare the facility
5. Test the hardware components
6. Complete the documentation
7. Train participants and users

Planning is important throughout the system development life cycle, but its importance increases as the new system cutover approaches. The large number of final construction tasks and the manner in which they are intertwined demands that close attention be paid to planning. We describe how planning can be approached for all seven tasks.

CONSTRUCT AND TEST PRODUCTION-READY PROGRAMS

If the new system is to use purchased software, the vendor or vendors should have delivered that software during preliminary construction. The project team members familiarized themselves with the software and tested its modules. If the new system is to use custom-written software, the coding and testing of the modules has been accomplished. Whether you use custom-written or purchased software, whether you install new hardware or use the old hardware for a new purpose, you need to thoroughly test the software components as a system.

Some basic guidelines to follow during the testing process are listed below.

- Test each function in the system separately.
- Check the flow of control through the entire system to insure that the desired paths exist and modules communicate correctly with one another.

FIGURE 8.1

Final Construction Phase Overview

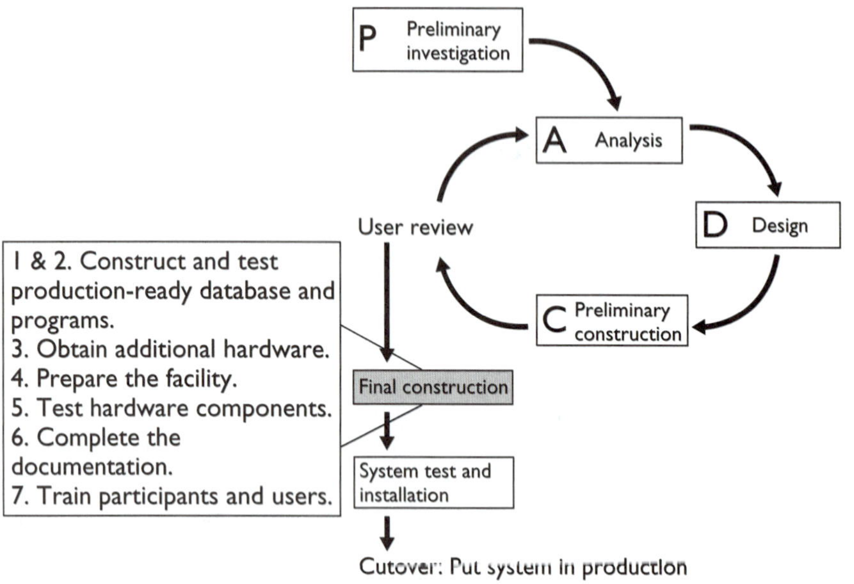
P Preliminary investigation
A Analysis
D Design
C Preliminary construction
User review
1 & 2. Construct and test production-ready database and programs.
3. Obtain additional hardware.
4. Prepare the facility.
5. Test hardware components.
6. Complete the documentation.
7. Train participants and users.
Final construction
System test and installation
Cutover: Put system in production

- Test valid, invalid, and boundary values.
- Test data that is not supposed to change for consistency.
- Verify error-detection routines.
- Have users test interactive systems.
- Test user interfaces.
- Test system backup and disaster recovery procedures.

Some questions to ask during the testing process are listed below.

- Does each requirement that applies to the module have its own test case?
- Does each design element that applies to the module have its own test case?
- Has a "list of common errors" been used to write test cases to detect errors that have occurred frequently in the past?
- Have all simple boundaries been tested—maximum, minimum, and off-by-one boundaries?
- Have compound boundaries been tested, that is, combinations of input data that might result in a computed variable that's too small or too large?
- Do test cases check for the wrong kind of data, for example, a negative number of employees in a payroll program?
- Are representative, middle-of-the-road values tested?

- Has compatibility with old data been tested? Have old hardware, versions of the operating system, and interfaces with legacy applications been tested?

Choosing an Approach to Testing

There are two approaches to testing system accuracy: black box and white box testing. Although both are designed to create accurate systems, one focuses on error-free functions and the other on error-free code.

Black box testing concentrates on the system's functions—whether the system creates accurate output. It is based on the assumption that if what goes in and what comes out are correct, the system must be correct. Users are ideal black box testers, as they have the best knowledge of the system's intended function.

In **white box testing,** also called **glass box testing, code review,** and **code walkthrough,** each program module's code is checked by reviewing each line or by creating data to verify each line. The best white box testing is a code walkthrough by the programmer and the analyst. Research indicates that more than twice as many errors are found when someone besides the author participates in the walkthrough.[1]

The Goal of System Testing

The goal of testing is to locate system errors before installation. These system errors can take several forms. They may be software coding errors that produce incorrect output or hardware design errors that reduce system efficiency. They may be in the form of faulty procedures documentation that causes the user to enter invalid data. Errors may also appear in the master files, whose accuracy is vital to successful production runs. And errors may take the form of omissions in design specifications that unacceptably limit system performance. The point is that you need to test for more than simple errors in coding—the bugs that plague programmers.

Potential Problem Areas in Testing

As one of the last activities in the system development life cycle, testing is the development activity most likely to get pushed beyond the scheduled completion date. As a way to meet the completion date, developers may omit or do a haphazard job of testing the system. A remedy for this tendency is the phased development approach. Early demonstrations to users are a good test of requirements determination, design, and system construction. We explained the process of unit testing in Chapter 7 when we addressed preliminary construction activities. If unit testing was completed during each iteration of analysis, design, and construction for each functional delivery, then many of the errors will have been found before system testing in the final construction stage.

Even if adequate time has been allowed for unit testing, problems may surface due to **developer fixation.** Developers design test procedures for *expected* problems; they may not understand the production operations well enough to anticipate all the things that could go wrong. One solution to this problem is to have a user design the test data files for unit testing and system testing. Another is to follow **systematic testing procedures** that cover *all functions,* even those that you feel certain will work. We explained the use of decision logic tables (DLTs) in Chapter 7 as a way to ensure that all possible transaction conditions are tested. DLTs are a systematic testing approach.

FIGURE 8.2

Final Testing Occurs in the Last Software Staging Environment

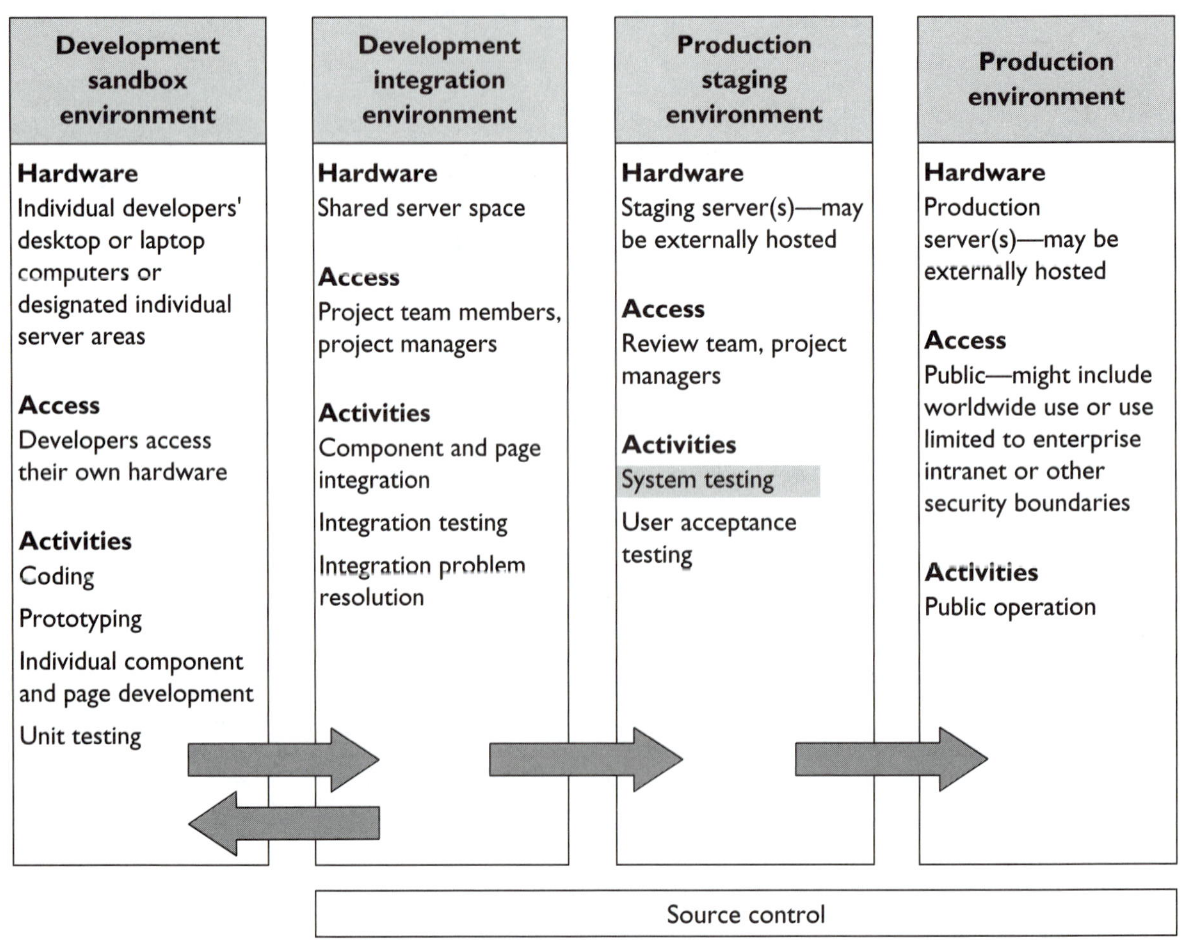

Any systematic test data files built during earlier development should be saved and made a permanent part of the testing environment. This environment can be used for system testing in a hardware environment that mirrors the production environment. This production staging environment is illustrated as the third environment in Figure 8.2. Systematic testing and user testing are particularly helpful if the development team members become weary of the project and are not as reliable as they were during earlier phases.

Developer fixation is an even greater problem in maintenance—"such a small fix couldn't have created any errors"—so the existence of an easy-to-use, documented testing environment is especially important for the ongoing maintenance part of the life cycle. When software is revised, the system may be tested quickly with the systematic test data files built and documented during earlier development. During maintenance, a quick fix may introduce errors in unexpected ways, and these are likely to be discovered through systematic testing. Testing for all possible errors, not just the ones likely to be directly affected by a new change, is called **regression**

testing—testing goes back (regresses) to cover earlier tests to be certain that the changes did not impact other features of the system.

The particular system features that most need to be addressed in system testing are:

- The system's compliance with user specifications, as well as the completeness and accuracy of the specifications
- Programming assumptions
- The coordination of the five system components (people, data, information, software, and hardware)
- The coordination of coded modules
- All input, process, and output conditions

Ensuring that the system performs in an *effective* way by meeting user specifications is only one dimension of testing. Testing must also ensure that the system performs in an *efficient* way.

Documentation of Testing

Since testing is a planned process that is critical to the success of the system, it requires extensive documentation. The documentation should detail the entire test plan, including the specific tests to be conducted, the sequence in which they will be conducted, and the tentative test schedule. The test documentation should contain listings of the test data and the broad performance standards expected of the system. Results of test runs are also filed with the test documentation.

One standard documentation form used by many organizations is the test specification, shown in Figure 8.3. Notice that this form provides headings for the major details that need to be documented, including what will be tested, how it will be tested, what results will verify that the system passed the test, who will perform the test, and when. Figure CS 5.1 is one page of 20 test specification pages completed by the ASTA development team.

Planning the Construction and Testing of Production-Ready Programs

As project manager, you need to specify testing procedures as carefully as you planned the previous phases of the project. Your test plan should cover the following:

- Personnel and supplies
- Preliminary tests of each component
- Final tests
- Documentation of test plans, data, and results

Personnel and Supplies

To ensure that testing is carried out in an organized manner, it is necessary to form a **test group** responsible for developing the test data and for carrying out tests at each stage. The test group also evaluates adherence to standards and inspects system documentation. An independent **quality assurance group** with permanent, experienced

FIGURE 8.3

A Test Specification Form

Test Specification					Page __ of __
Designed by:			Module or Screen:		
Test Data Source:			Objectives:		
Test Case #	Description	Test Steps	Expected Results	Actual Results	Performed by/ Date

members often evaluates large projects. Smaller projects cannot afford this luxury; their test group is a changing team of people drawn from programming teams that have completed their modules.

Whenever possible, users should participate in tests. The participation of users increases their commitment to the system and gives developers insight into how well the user requirements are being met. All of the time, effort, and resources consumed by development may be wasted if you fail to gain and maintain user confidence. When you encourage users to participate, warn them that errors and omissions *will emerge*. Explain that their role is to help identify the errors that must be eliminated before the system is put into production. Involving users in the testing process also educates them about the costs and benefits of system features and serves as training in the use of the system.

Planning test activities requires that you identify all the supplies needed for the tests. If the project involves installing new hardware, you need to be sure that you have the various types of storage disks, printer paper, and so forth—not only the right kind but also a sufficient quantity. Keep in mind that supplies will be needed for the many backup files maintained during testing. If you are installing purchased software, be sure that you have enough copies of system and user documentation so that access to reference materials is not a problem. Planning for supply needs may seem a trivial concern, but you should remember, "For want of a nail the shoe was lost…for want of a nail the kingdom was lost." Don't let the little things foul up your project; plan for even these mundane needs.

Preliminary and Final Tests

Black box and white box testing can be performed in two basic ways—preliminary and final. In preliminary tests, the components are tested individually to determine their ability to meet the acceptance criteria—the functional requirements that have been identified as the basis for accepting the system. Preliminary tests, called unit tests, were performed during preliminary construction. Final tests are performed during this phase and can be continued into the system test and installation stage.

To plan for both preliminary and final testing, you need to specify the tests to be performed, the people responsible for performing them, and the paperwork required to document them. Preparing a Gantt chart of these activities will help you manage the process more effectively. The Gantt chart in Figure 8.4 delineates the test activities for testing purchased software for a restaurant. You will notice that the work breakdown structure used in this chart varies from the A-D-C-R used elsewhere in the text. Since there are no official standard codes, the firm can specify the set or sets as the standards that it wants its systems developers to use.

Creating a production staging environment as similar to the final production environment as possible is an important part of final testing. The unit testing environments in the development sandboxes are purposely constructed for programmer efficiency. Work will typically be done on a PC with small test files so that the testing and revising iterations go quickly. Final testing needs to stress the system the same way it will be stressed in production. Final tests are called **stress tests** or **volume tests** because they use the production database and have the same amount of activity that is expected during peak loads for the production system. The stress tests will test the network and hardware as well as software and database performance.

Documentation of Test Plans, Data, and Results

Documentation of testing takes time, so this activity needs to be included in the plan for testing. An administrative assistant, user, or business analyst might be assigned the task of writing and organizing the documentation of testing as well as carrying out many of the testing activities.

Construct and Test a Production-Ready Database

Factors Influencing Database Preparation

The success of a new system depends to a great degree on the integrity of its data. Four factors influence the difficulty of preparing a production-ready database. They are size of the firm, type of firm, data availability, and data format.

Size of the Firm

All else being equal, the preparation of a database for a large firm is more difficult than for a small one strictly because of data volume. A small firm might be able to schedule its database preparation to begin one month prior to the planned cutover, but an industry giant might have to provide a lead time of six months, a year, or even longer.

Type of Firm

Certain industries require large databases of historical data. The insurance and banking industries are examples. When firms in these industries convert to new information systems, the databases must reflect what has happened in the past. For example, the

FIGURE 8.4

Gantt Chart of Preliminary Test Activities

Project Planning Documentation		Page 1 of 1
System: Fast Run Software—Warranty Period Testing		Date
Symbols: Scheduled activity; Completed activity	Analyst: Tracy Bell	Signature

Activity	Individual Assigned	M	Tu	W	Th	F	M	Tu	W	Th	F	M	Tu	W
		August 13-29												
Preliminary tests														
PT1 Build test data files	Fred													
PT2 Test with vendor data	Tito													
Verify results with our data														
V1 Verify labels	Fred													
V2 Verify log entries	"													
V3 Verify end-of-day log	"													
V4 Verify summary report	"													
Test process with our data														
T1 Start-up	Tito													
T2 Data entry	"													
T3 Label generation	"													
T4 Termination	"													
T5 Check Generation	"													
T6 Backup	"													
T7 Error recovery	"													
T8 Database maintenance	"													
T9 Management review	Fred, Tito													
System tests														
S1 Build production files	Fred													
S2 Test production files	Tito													
S3 Repeat V1-V4	Fred													
S4 Repeat T1-T8	Tito													
S5 Management review	Fred, Tito													

record for a hospitalization policy that was issued in 1988 should reflect all of the activity since that date—changes in coverage, addition of dependents, claims history, and so on. Similarly, the record for a bank customer who is paying off a five-year automobile loan taken out three years ago should reflect all of the payments that have been made. Firms such as insurance companies and banks cannot simply create their databases as transactions occur; they must capture historical data that can exist in large volumes and various formats. In the previous chapter we told the story of the insurance company that divided up the work of coding their policyholder files to fit the new system format, and assigned each portion to a home office employee, including the president. In such a situation, the workload can be so massive that it can easily develop into a morale problem where grassroots support for the project becomes eroded. The insurance company was able to turn a potentially bad morale situation into one that had just the opposite effect because of the enthusiasm of the president to do his part.

Data Availability

A potentially difficult situation is when data required by the database does not currently exist in the firm. Perhaps certain data has not been maintained on such environmental elements as customers or suppliers and a data gathering effort must be launched. Surveys and questionnaires must be designed, the data gathered, follow-up action taken for non-respondents, and the data stored in the database and verified. When efforts such as these are required, the developers should not attempt to do all of the work themselves; the scope is far beyond the time and resources that they can devote. Instead, the developers should enlist the help of others in the firm, such as marketing researchers in the marketing unit and purchasing agents in the purchasing unit, as well as data gathering specialists outside the firm such as consultants.

However, it is not always necessary that the firm embark on data gathering when the data does not currently exist. There are thousands of commercial databases on the market. Some are available for sale, and some, such as DIALOG and BRS (Bibliographic Retrieval Service), can be accessed in an online manner by paying a subscription fee.

Data Format

When the new system requires that the existing data be converted to a different format or to a different storage medium, the process is called **file conversion.** The most difficult file conversion is from a manual system to an information system. Converting even a small manual database of 5,000 or fewer records may consume as much as three to four person-weeks, depending on how complicated the data entry process is. For example, keying a customer file will be much easier if all the data for each record is available from a one-page customer order form than if the data must be extracted from five different documents. If the old system was automated, some data conversion may still be required—especially if incompatible hardware or software is being installed or if requirements demand that data be organized in a new format.

Conversion Procedures and Controls

Procedures must be followed to ensure the validity of the files prior to conversion. The developers or users make a preliminary review of each manual or computer file, purging unnecessary records and verifying that the file is accurate and current. Then a **freeze date** is set; after this date, no further updates are made to the files awaiting conversion. Instead, updates are tracked separately so that files can be brought up to date after conversion is complete.

Measures must also be taken to ensure the integrity of data during conversion. One simple control technique involves grouping records in batches of 50 or 100 each and assigning each batch a unique number. A total is then calculated for one selected field by manually summing the values on the various records in the batch. This total is compared to the total accumulated as the records are converted. A discrepancy indicates a conversion error. For financial records, a batch total of a field such as account balance or total cost of order is used. For non-financial records, a total of a numeric field such as patient number or part number can be used. The term **hash total** is used for a total of numeric data that has no purpose other than to establish a control.

As you can see, constructing and testing a production-ready database is one of the more rigorous implementation activities. It requires both careful planning and attention to detail. Given its complexity, database creation should be treated as a subproject, and a team of users and developers should be assigned to plan, monitor, and perform its many tasks.

Responsibility for the Database

The manager of database administration, assisted by a staff of DBAs, has the responsibility for making the database available. DBAs are members of the project teams during the system development life cycle and monitor system performance during production.

Planning the Construction and Testing of a Production-Ready Database

Early in the SDLC, perhaps in one of the first iterations of analysis activities, the project team should anticipate any possible difficulty in preparing the new system database. The team should pay attention to the factors listed above that cause the effort to be sizeable. The team should then list the steps of the preparation, decide who will do the work, and schedule the time.

DFDs, ERDs, class diagrams, and the data dictionary can provide a good starting point for identifying the files that will be involved. All data stores in the DFDs are likely candidates for master files that must be converted. With the files identified, the ERDs, class diagrams, and data dictionary can identify the data elements that are involved.

When the level of database activity appears to exceed the capabilities of the development team and the firm's employees, consideration should be given to outsourcing either part or all of the work.

Obtain Additional Hardware

During an early iteration of design activities, the project team determined the hardware requirements of the new system. This determination came about as the byproduct of the data and process modeling activity. During an early iteration of preliminary construction activities, the process of obtaining the hardware was begun. When the hardware needs of the new system are modest, perhaps consisting of a few PCs, the needs can easily be met during preliminary construction. When the needs are more robust, the activity of obtaining the hardware can continue to final construction.

Regardless of the scale of the hardware acquisition, the process must be an informed one, with a good understanding of the products and their vendors.

Sources of Hardware Information

Four sources are especially effective in providing information about available hardware. They are the hardware vendors, computer magazines, reference books, and the Internet.

Hardware Vendors

All hardware vendors, large and small, promote their products by means of advertising and personal selling. You have seen computer ads on TV and in magazines. Other promotions, such as direct mailings and sales calls, are aimed at persons who are in a position to make or influence hardware decisions. If you become an information specialist and become a manager in a large organization, the hardware suppliers' sales representatives will most certainly call on you in person. The reps will make certain that you remain current on their products by providing you with manuals, perhaps conducting onsite seminars, and offering invitations to attend courses on topics of special interest at the vendor's headquarters or education center. If you have a big budget, the reps are likely to bombard you with freebies (t-shirts and trinkets, such as pens and paperweights displaying their company logos), free demo units, and factory tours. They will want to know what you are paying for your equipment, and in many cases, they will undercut their competitor's prices by such a large factor that your CFO would have a hard time not choosing them. Often, they will offer to run the break-even analysis and cost justification planning for you to give to your management as a way to justify selecting their hardware and services.

When it is important for you to attend courses offered by vendors, the vendor or your employer will pick up the registration, travel, and other expenses. One of the advantages of working for a large computer user is the opportunity to remain on the cutting edge of new technology through vendor contacts.

Computer Magazines

The popular computer magazines that you find on newsstands and in libraries contain articles that describe the latest hardware and software. Most of the magazines are focused on the PC market. PC Magazine has a reputation for testing hardware in real life situations that push the equipment to the limits. *Information Week* and *E-Week* are two weekly periodicals that contain reviews of computer products of all types and sizes. Numerous magazines are available that focus on specific development tools and specific areas, such as networking. By reading current magazines, you can take a giant step toward staying current in computer technology.

Reference Books

Your company, city, and college library most likely has one or more sets of reference books that are devoted to descriptions of computing hardware. An example is the Data Pro series on various types of hardware, from DataPro Information Services. Such sets provide descriptions of the units, accompanied by performance statistics and prices. The books are kept current with revisions. For platform considerations and a wide variety of development and system support topics, Microsoft Press provides a series of reference books. These resources are used for certification. Many IS personnel keep them after earning certification and consult them often. A list is available at www.microsoft.com/mspress. For example, *Microsoft SQL Server Reference Library* and *Inside Microsoft SQL Server* specify how to create high-performance data warehousing, transaction processing, and decision support applications. Networking Essentials is a reference for troubleshooting and diagnosing networking problems.

The Internet

There are many sources of hardware information on the Internet. Each of the hardware vendors has its own Web site, providing information about the company and its products. In addition, there are sites that offer information about multiple vendors' products. For example, there is a *PC Technology Guide* sponsored by Direct Connection at www.webopedia.com. There is also *TechWeb* at www.techweb.com and cmpnet.com, sponsored by CMP Media. Gartner, Inc., a research and advisory firm, has a Web site at www3.gartner.com that displays Dataquest research and a wide variety of technology related resources. Ziff Davis, the publisher of *PC Magazine,* mentioned above, provides articles and supplementary information on their sites at www.zdnet.com and www.cnet.com.

One feature of the information systems field that makes it so interesting is the constant change. It seems that every day something new is announced. This constant change imposes a big responsibility on users but an even bigger one on information specialists. Regardless of your career path you must make an effort to stay current on computer technology. One of the advantages of a college education is the preparation that it provides for conducting literary research. By applying that skill after graduation you will be able to keep up with the ever-moving information systems field.

The Hardware Selection Process

Once the project team identifies the vendors that can possibly fill the hardware needs of the new system, the team can prepare a **request for proposal,** or **RFP,** that invites vendors to submit proposals recommending the use of their products. In all likelihood, the firm has a policy for RFP preparation and the team will coordinate this effort with the purchasing department. Figure 8.5 is a common outline of an RFP.

The contents of the RFP are the secret to the successful acquisition of hardware. The RFP includes such details of the system design as: (1) performance criteria, (2) equipment configuration, (3) transaction volumes, and (4) file sizes. In addition, the RFP specifies the installation schedule that the vendor must meet in making the hardware available when it is needed. It is necessary to provide such details if each vendor is to propose a configuration that satisfies the physical design of the new system. The firm wants to be in a position to make an *apples-to-apples* comparison of the vendors' proposals and that is possible only by specifying the design in a detailed way. Otherwise, each vendor will recommend those units that they perceive to give them a competitive advantage and the firm will be forced to make an *apples-to-oranges* comparison.

When vendors wish to submit a bid, they prepare written proposals and often supplement them with oral presentations to the project team and perhaps the IS steering committee. Figure 8.6 is an outline of a typical proposal.

Evaluation Criteria

The selection of a hardware vendor is a semi-structured problem. Some of the elements, such as the performance ratings of the equipment units, are highly structured and easily measured. Other elements, however, must be evaluated in a subjective way.

The selection can consider the following evaluation criteria:

- *Equipment Performance*—How will the hardware perform in terms of its speeds, error rates, mean times to failure, and so on? Can it handle the expected number of simultaneous users? Is memory capacity adequate for the target applications?
- *Equipment Maintenance*—What service will the vendor provide to keep the hardware in running order? Is the server operating system supported in the infrastructure specified in the current strategic plan for information resources (SPIR)? Are performance utilities and other products available to increase server performance as needed?
- *Education*—What does the vendor offer in terms of educational programs for users and the technical support staff?
- *Industry Knowledge*—How knowledgeable is the vendor in meeting the needs of the firm's particular industry? Most industries have unique data processing requirements and a vendor who is aware of these needs can provide valuable consultation in how to best apply the hardware.

The project team can consider these evaluation criteria in a structured way by weighting the criteria and rating each on a quantitative scale. In Technical Module G on the evaluation of system alternatives we describe such an approach in evaluating different software possibilities. The same approach can be used to evaluate hardware and also software vendors.

Verification of Hardware Vendor Claims

It is always a good idea to verify the hardware vendors' claims and there are several ways to go about doing this. The simplest approach is to read the hardware reviews in the computer magazines. Two potentially more productive approaches are to seek out other users of the same equipment, and require the vendors to solve benchmark problems.

FIGURE 8.5

An Outline of a Request for Proposal

1. Cover letter
2. Introduction
3. System objectives and constraints
4. System design
   - 4.1 Summary description
   - 4.2 Performance criteria
   - 4.3 Equipment configuration
   - 4.4 Transaction volumes
   - 4.5 File sizes
5. Installation schedule

FIGURE 8.6

An Outline of a Vendor Proposal

1. Cover letter
2. Summary of recommendations
3. Introduction
4. Advantages of the proposed equipment
5. Equipment configuration
6. Equipment specifications
   6.1 Performance data
   6.2 Prices
7. Satisfaction of the performance criteria
8. Delivery schedule

User Contacts Persons connected with the project can contact a sampling of the vendors' customers for the purpose of gauging the performance level of the hardware products. Members of information systems, the IS steering committee, or the firm's purchasing department can make the contacts.

Benchmark Problems When the firm's hardware order is extremely important to the vendors, such as a multi-system order to be placed by a national chain, the firm can impose what is called a benchmark problem. A **benchmark problem** is a process that must be performed by each vendor using its own hardware, which provides a major basis for evaluating that hardware. For example, all vendors must use their equipment to update a master file with transaction data. The vendors use data provided by the firm, and the processing is monitored in terms of such performance factors as throughput time, error rate, and storage utilization. In some cases, the firm supplies the software and in others the vendor is expected to do the programming.

Different Ways to Pay for Hardware Resources

The low prices of PCs have made outright purchase a popular form of payment for hardware resources. Every day hundreds or thousands of individuals pay for their PCs by writing checks or using credit cards. Business organizations often purchase the low-priced units the same way. However, the steady improvement in the price/performance ratio of computer technology and the continuous introduction of new software tools influences most organizations to consider four additional payment alternatives—rental, lease, lease-purchase, and outsourcing. Each payment method offers advantages and disadvantages. Rental is only available for PCs; the other three options are popular choices for servers and communication equipment as well as PCs.

Rental Plans

Some hardware vendors offer rental plans that enable their customers to make monthly payments for their hardware and to cancel the agreement with short notice—only thirty or ninety days. This is the most flexible payment method because it provides the firm with the ability to easily and quickly return equipment that is no longer wanted.

By paying the rental amount, the firm does not have to worry about paying equipment maintenance, which is provided by the vendor at no extra cost. Large computer systems require both scheduled and unscheduled maintenance. **Scheduled maintenance** is work that is performed to prevent equipment failure. It is like changing the oil in your car every 12,000 miles. The term **preventive maintenance (PM)** is also used. **Unscheduled maintenance,** on the other hand, is work that is performed to repair a failure that has already occurred. It is like fixing a flat tire. Hardware maintenance must be performed by trained technicians, called **field engineers,** or **FEs.** The hardware vendors provide FE services to their rental customers. The rental approach offers some real advantages. However, it is the most expensive of the payment methods in terms of the monthly cost.

Lease Plans

Lease plans are very similar to rental plans but bind the firm to a longer period of time, usually a minimum of one year. Lease therefore lacks the flexibility of rental but the monthly payments are lower. The same contractual stipulations concerning maintenance apply.

Lease-Purchase Plans

Some leases include a clause that provides the firm with the option to purchase the leased equipment. A certain percentage of the lease payments that have already been made can be applied to the purchase.

Purchase Plans

When the firm uses the hardware for a long period, such as three to five years or more, it is most economical to purchase it outright. The title passes from the hardware vendor to the firm, which assumes responsibility for maintenance, insurance, and taxes. Some of the larger firms have their own FEs, and other firms acquire FE services from the hardware vendor or from maintenance firms by means of a separate maintenance agreement. Equipment maintenance is one of the most popular services provided by outsourcers.

A big deterrent to purchase is the large investment that the firm must make at the outset. Another is the risk of investing in technology that could quickly become obsolete.

Outsourcing

The Application Service Provider is a new business model for arranging hardware, software and technical support services from a vendor. Some of the large hardware vendors combine sales, leasing, and maintenance services for firms in one contract. Third-party outsourcers are also common. Contract negotiations include specific details about a full range of computer equipment, operating systems, utilities, testing, and maintenance plans. These plans can provide for 24/7 on-site service or a contract for Monday through Friday service with 48-hour response and penalties for exceeding specific downtime minimums.

For large system configurations, the selection of the hardware payment option is an important decision for the firm. Sometimes, the decision makers specify that such special studies as payback analysis and net present value calculations be performed to determine which option is best. These techniques are described in Technical Module F.

Putting the Hardware Decisions in Perspective

The two main decisions relating to hardware selection concern the choice of the vendors and the payment method. The vendor decision is essentially a semi-structured one, which can be influenced by both company politics and the emotions of the decision makers. Some firms are dedicated to particular vendors, having built a strong relationship over the years. These firms will not consider other vendors, even though the others may offer superior hardware or lower prices. The decision concerning the payment method is more structured, and is less susceptible to non-economic influences.

The amount of attention that is given to these decisions varies with their importance to both the firm and the vendors, and with the amount of money involved. These decisions typically are not made by the project team. Rather, they are made on a higher organizational level—by the IS steering committee or the executive committee. The CIO plays a key role.

Planning the Obtaining of Additional Hardware

When it is necessary to obtain new system hardware, the timing is critical to completion of the project. The hardware delivery should be scheduled to occur right after the facility is ready and other such preparatory work as software and database creation have been completed. In those cases when software testing or database conversion cannot be performed until the hardware is in place, timing is even more critical. In some instances, when the new system hardware cannot be obtained in time for use in testing the software, the firm can make arrangements with another user of the same hardware to use it on a temporary basis. Also, hardware vendors often have such facilities as test centers and service bureaus where hardware can be used for testing.

In planning for the obtaining of additional hardware, the developers should schedule all of the other final construction work and then identify the ideal hardware delivery date. Then, the developers should estimate the time that will be required to prepare the RFP, receive the proposals, evaluate the proposals, select the vendor or vendors, and provide the vendors with enough time to make the equipment available. With these estimates, each step can be scheduled. Vendors should be contacted as soon as possible to determine the lead time that each will require in filling an order.

This is one portion of the final construction activity that is not entirely under the control of the firm. The ability of the vendors to meet the needs of the firm must be considered. Of all the final construction activities, this is the one that is the most difficult from a scheduling standpoint.

Prepare the Facility

The size of the physical installation task is in direct proportion to the size of the equipment to be installed.

Installing Small-Scale Systems

The installation of such small-scale systems as PCs and workstations presents no real problems. The minimum facility that is needed is desk space, an electrical outlet, and some type of network connection. In addition, attention can be given to room lighting, which can influence how users view screen displays. We discuss the influence of room lighting on perception in Technical Module H.

Installing Large-Scale Systems

The installation of racked servers and networking equipment can require a large, complex construction project. Facilities must be made available with the following features:

Security

The firm protects its centrally located information resources from unauthorized use, damage, or destruction by keeping the computer room locked. Access is gained by opening the door with a key, inserting a magnetically encoded identification card into a reader, entering numbers into a combination lock, or satisfying more exotic screens, such as those employing fingerprints, palm prints, or even lip prints.

Raised Floors

Servers are connected by cables the size of garden hoses and larger. Rather than lay the cables on top of the floor, where they would pose a hazard and be susceptible to damage, the cables are located under the floor. When the computer room is built, the floor is raised a distance of two feet or so above the regular floor. In addition to providing space for the cables, the raised floor also provides a plenum for directing a cooling air flow through the various units.

Temperature and Humidity Controls

The computer units operate best within certain temperature and humidity ranges. Computer rooms often have their own air processing and chilling units to ensure that these environmental conditions are met. Cool air is pumped from below the raised flow into the server racks that are designed to allow optimal airflow around the racked servers. Most servers now have thermal sensors that will automatically shut the hardware down if the server gets too hot. The sensors may be set to trigger the operating system to first shut down cleanly.

Pollutant Controls

The air conditioning and heating units also remove such pollutants as dust and paper fibers from the air. When the computer facility consists of several rooms, each with its own type of equipment, separate air pressures can exist in each room to control the flow of pollutants. For example, the room housing the central processing unit (CPU) can have a high pressure and the room housing the printers can have a low pressure. When doors are opened between the rooms, any pollutants in the printer room will not flow to the CPU room.

Fire Controls

Smoke and fire detectors are located both on the ceiling of the computer room and under the raised floor. Fire suppression systems utilizing chemicals or gas rather than water are installed to put out fires.

Uninterrupted Power

Power distribution units owned by the firm enable it to separate the computer units from the source of municipal power. These distribution units prevent hardware from being damaged by sudden fluctuations in voltage, such as when lightning strikes a transformer. In addition, many firms install auxiliary power generators to produce their own electricity when the municipal power goes out.

Installation Requirements of Networked Systems

When systems require networked configurations, the installation consists of providing the necessary data communications circuits. Transmissions that span relatively short distances, such as those in a department, building, or several adjacent buildings, can be handled by a **local area network,** or **LAN.** Transmissions over slightly longer distances, such as within a city, can be handled by a **metropolitan area network,** or **MAN.** LAN circuitry can consist of twisted pairs, coaxial cables, or fiber-optical cables. MAN circuitry is usually comprised of fiber-optical cables. Both LAN and MAN circuitry is provided by the using firm. The twisted pairs consist of four wires and are the type of circuitry that is used in your telephone. Twisted pairs are the least expensive circuitry but do not offer the high quality transmission of the other choices. Coaxial cables are the type of circuitry that is provided by cable TV services and can transmit the widest variety of signals, including television signals used in video conferencing. Fiber-optical cables offer the greatest security against unauthorized tampering because of the requirement for special equipment to tap into the circuit.

Transmissions that span distances across a state or nation or around the world can be handled by a **wide area network,** or **WAN.** WAN circuitry choices include fiber-optical cable or microwave transmission. The WAN circuitry is provided by such a common carrier as AT&T or Sprint.

Planning the Preparation of the Facility

Because physical facility construction is similar to any type of building construction, the construction firms are skilled at developing schedules, which can become a part of the contractual agreement. As with the hardware planning, the facility preparation is not a responsibility of the developers. That responsibility ordinarily falls to the manager of computer operations, who works with the general construction contractor as well as the vendors that are to supply the security systems and environmental controls. Because of lengthy lead times, the physical installation must be planned far in advance and coordinated with the delivery of the computer hardware.

TEST THE HARDWARE COMPONENTS

Often systems are developed using an organization's existing hardware resources. In such situations, you will need to test the hardware to make sure that it can handle the added load your application will place on it. Sometimes hardware that performed adequately before a new application was added does not perform adequately afterward. The increased processing load, the expanded number of accesses to files, or the greater number of terminals that can be active simultaneously may so degrade the hardware's performance that response time and turnaround time become unacceptable.

If you are installing new hardware, you will need to test it to make sure that it meets specifications. When you solicited bids from vendors, you stated the **technical specifications,** or the capabilities the hardware would have to possess. These technical specifications include processing speed, communication ports supported, disk access speed, printer speed, and memory capacity. Before you purchased the hardware, you probably ran several benchmark tests at the vendor's site to determine the hardware's ability to meet these specifications. Now you need to test the hardware at your site with your data. These tests will assure you not only that the hardware runs properly but also that you have prepared an appropriate facility to house it. For example, you have the cabling, electrical supply, and temperature and humidity environment that are adequate. Tests commonly performed on hardware are listed in Figure 8.7.

Planning the Testing of Hardware Components

When planning the cutover to the new system, time should be allocated to testing the hardware components. The hardware should be tested using new system software and data. The data volume should be adequate to test the ability of the hardware to meet the peak load requirements.

FIGURE 8.7

Common Hardware Tests

Test the access speed.	Is there enough capacity to ensure an acceptable response time when multiple users log onto the system? Can the user retrieve data from the system without an unacceptable delay?
Test the processing speed.	Does the hardware meet the response time requirements of the user's production schedule? Does the system process transactions at an acceptable rate?
Test the server capacity.	Is the storage capacity adequate for the volume of data required?
Test the peak load.	What happens when simultaneous server hits increase? How many users can access the server without a decrease to an unacceptable level? Can the printer withstand the peak volume of printing activity expected?

FIGURE 8.8

Common Sections of a Users Manual

1. System overview
   Purpose of the system
   Narrative and graphical overview of system inputs, processing, and outputs

2. General procedures and information
   Sign-on and sign-off procedures (mainframe system or microcomputer network)
   Operating instructions (definition of function keys)
   Procedures for loading and running programs
   Explanation of standard error messages

3. Procedure documentation (repeat for each major procedure)
   a. Procedure overview
      Summary description of procedure
      Data flow diagram(s)
   b. Detailed procedure description
      Detailed procedure narrative or data flow diagram of work flow
      Screen formats, including sample formats and detailed explanations of screen options (add, insert, delete)
      Description of source documents and instructions for data entry, including all codes and uses of codes
      Output descriptions
      Sample output forms with detailed explanations and instructions for receiving and distributing output
   c. Data definitions
      Description of data used in procedure
      Data ownership and responsibility
      Data access security considerations
   d. Interface areas
      Data received from other procedures/user groups
      Information provided to other procedures/user groups

4. Glossary terms

The amount of time required for testing depends on the scale of hardware involved. The technical operations staff is the best candidate for performing the testing. Planning of the testing should be a joint effort by the project team and the manager of technical operations.

COMPLETE THE DOCUMENTATION

The project team assembles new system documentation for two groups. One group consists of users. Before too long, the team will turn the system over to its users and they must be able to use it independently of support from information specialists. This independence can be achieved by means of a well-written users manual. The other group that will use the documentation consists of information specialists who will implement and maintain the system. This documentation takes the form of one or more technical manuals.

Users Manuals

Users manuals provide information that nontechnical users need to use the system. Determining just what that information should include requires knowledge of the procedures that the users will perform. For example, the user of a system running on a single PC or a small local area network often performs the tasks of both a business area user and an operator. If the user is expected to install software, load and run programs, and format diskettes, instructions for performing these technical procedures must be provided in the users manuals. In a large system built around a series of networked servers, a technical operator will usually perform these procedures; therefore they need not be addressed in the user documentation.

Users manuals focus on the data entry procedures that users commonly perform. They explain such tasks as transferring data from a source document to the computer via a data entry screen. They also describe the reports the system will generate and the steps the user must follow to produce the desired output. Figure 8.8 lists the topics most frequently included in a users manual. Figure CS 4.2 is a users manual table of contents and Figure CS 5.2 is a sample page created by the student team for the ASTA skill set system.

Users manuals are often supplemented with quick reference guides and tutorials. A **quick reference guide** is a page or pocket-sized card of frequently used commands and procedures such as system log-on, data entry, report capabilities, and logoff. (Figure CS 5.5 is a quick reference for the ASTA system.) **Tutorials** are software-based lessons that introduce the user to the capabilities of the system. The users manual for a general ledger accounting system might include a tutorial with lessons on creating a ledger, processing transactions, and posting daily updates to the ledger—all with dummy data. The experience of using the system correctly to create and process dummy accounts builds the user's confidence and reduces the likelihood of errors later on.

Developing useful, usable manuals requires a good dose of common sense and consideration for the readers. Following the documentation standards that the firm imposes on its developers will help you to prepare user-friendly manuals. In addition, every users manual must be edited and proofread thoroughly. The development team and users should check its contents to ensure that all information is clear and correct. After the project manager verifies that the manual conforms to the organization's documentation standards, the manager of the user area or the project sponsor approves the final version of the manual so that it can be copied for distribution to users.

Technical Manuals

Since users manuals usually take precedence, **technical manuals** are often forgotten in the rush to install a new system. Both are extremely important, however. There are three types of technical manuals.

- *Technical operations manuals* describe start-up, run control, and end-of-day procedures for the system hardware and software that are to be performed by members of the firm's technical operations unit. These manuals also give instructions for running supervisory programs, performing hardware maintenance, logging errors, ensuring security, and recovering from a general system failure. Figure 8.9 lists the typical contents of a technical operations manual for a large information system.

FIGURE 8.9

Contents of a Technical Operations Manual

1. Introduction
   - Purpose of the manual
   - Hardware configuration
   - Computer room layout
   - Emergency service numbers

2. Hardware operations
   - Step-by-step powering up instructions
   - Hardware checks and restarts
   - Log-in and log-out procedures
   - Instructions for operating peripheral hardware
   - Hardware switching (processor to processor, disk to disk, or printer to printer)
   - Equipment failure recovery procedures
   - Preventative maintenance cycle

3. Supervisory programs
   - Start-of-day procedures, including on-line system start-up, operating system and communications network start-up, database start-up, file space allocation, and transaction log initialization
   - Run control and error recovery procedures, including input control, authorization and special requests, output control, quality and distribution, and system utilities
   - End-of-day procedures, including batch processing, security backup procedures, and shut-down procedures

4. Error logging and recovery
   - Logging errors for hardware and software
   - Hardware engineering liaison
   - Software engineering liaison
   - Recovery procedures

5. System security
   - Computer room security
   - Restricted access zones
   - System security, access, and passwords
   - Network security
   - File security and backups
   - Fire prevention procedures

6. Software library maintenance
   - Cataloging procedures
   - Version control, including simultaneous, current, and previous versions
   - Update procedures
   - Software backup procedures

7. Glossary of terms

- *Installation manuals* describe how to install hardware and software and how to configure the system for the current operating system and peripherals. These manuals also describe the main memory and peripherals required to use the hardware or software being installed. Software installation manuals also list and describe all program and data files. Often a separate installation manual is not prepared, in which case information about installation is given in the technical operations manual (for large systems) or the users manual (for PC-based systems, if the user is expected to install the system). The installation guide for ASTA is part of the developer manual table of contents in Figure CS 4.1 and the guide itself is Figure CS 5.6.

- *Developer manuals* serve as a reference for maintaining the system and for future systems enhancement or reengineering. The developer manual gives an overview of any custom-written software and describes how each program module fits into the system. It provides the process, data, and object models that were prepared during analysis and design, such as use cases, DFDs, ERDs, class diagrams, the data dictionary, program listings, and input-output format samples. The developer manual also describes and documents the procedures for requesting and implementing changes to the system after changeover. For an example of topics to be included, see Figure CS 4.1; Figure CS 5.3 is a sample page.

Planning the Completion of the Documentation

Different information specialists prepare the users and technical manuals. Planning the completion of these documents should be based on the outlines of the contents. For that reason, a decision should be made on the content as soon in the construction process as possible.

Using the users manual outline in Figure 8.8 as an example, users and developers on the project team can prepare the system overview, describe the general procedures, and explain the portions of the procedure documentation with which they are familiar, such as DFDs and source documents. Programmers can assemble the section dealing with screen formats and sample output forms, and database administrators can prepare the section on data definitions.

The technical manuals are primarily the responsibility of the programmers and the manager of technical operations. In the technical operations manual in Figure 8.9, the programmers describe the supervisory programs, and error logging and recovery. The programmers work with technical operations personnel, under the guidance of the operations manger, to prepare the hardware operations section. The system security and software library maintenance sections are prepared by operations personnel.

Train Participants and Users

Shortly before cutover, the participants and users must receive education and training concerning their roles in the new system. The users will use the new system and must learn how to interface with the information system and interpret the output. The participants will not use the output but will work within the system, performing such tasks as data entry. The training prepares the participants to perform their duties. A real key to realizing operational feasibility is preparing the participants and users to support the system.

When small numbers of participants and users are involved, the education can be accomplished informally, in one-on-one sessions. Larger projects can require that the material be communicated in classroom settings. The responsibility for conducting the sessions can be assigned to special educational groups that exist in information systems or human resources units of large firms. For smaller scale operations, members of the project team can conduct the sessions. The users manual frequently serves as the textbook for the sessions. In Chapter 7 we explained the value of creating a training environment and what that environment should include for systems with many users and significant turnover in the user population.

Consultants and representatives of hardware and software firms can also help. There are also many other organizations that offer various forms of computer training and education. For example, the Association for Computing Machinery (ACM) frequently holds workshops and seminars on such topics as CASE, artificial intelligence, and computer graphics.

It is best to schedule the sessions to occur immediately prior to cutover so that the material will be fresh on the participants' and users' minds. It is also best to schedule training when there are no more than a few remaining errors in the system; otherwise the early trainees will be frustrated by system failures and will spread discouraging news about the impending system changes. For these reasons, the actual training sessions will not occur until the final stage—system testing and installation. However, planning should begin earlier—during construction, design, analysis, or even preliminary investigation. The manager of user education for a large corporation maintains that training planning should begin as soon as you know you are going to develop a system.

Planning Participant and User Training

Planning training activities can be a complex task. Reserving rooms and equipment, preparing materials, and determining a feasible, convenient training schedule require a lot of effort and coordination. The development team's workload is reduced somewhat if the hardware and or the software vendors conduct some of the training sessions and provide some of the training materials. Hiring a consultant or a training specialist to handle these tasks may be a good idea if the organization lacks the resources to plan, prepare, and conduct its own training. Most of the time, however, the development team is extensively involved in training users and technical staff.

The steps in planning a training schedule are outlined below.

1. Schedule training to occur during the two-week period before cutover.

2. Reserve classroom facilities, instructors, equipment, and training materials at least one month in advance of the training date.

3. Notify all trainees three times: one month, two weeks, and two days prior to their training session. Require that trainees confirm their ability to attend their scheduled sessions. Coordinate with user management to prepare a list of participants for each training session.

4. The day before training, check the classroom facility to make sure that the necessary hardware and software are available and functioning properly. Also ensure that adequate copies of any additional training materials are available.

5. Train the technical support and maintenance staff first.
6. Next train user-managers so that they can help train their operational staff.
7. Train users with similar functions or from similar business areas together.
8. Schedule one or more make-up training sessions as needed.
9. Conduct a survey or informal review session to evaluate the effectiveness of the training provided.

Figure 8.10 is a form that developers can use to plan and solicit approval for training activities. Two major concerns are determining effective training methods and

FIGURE 8.10

A Training Plan Approval Form

Training Plan Approval Form				Page
System				Date
User Department	Project Manager	Signature		
Describe Type of Training, Topics, and Instructor(s) for Each Topic:				
Tentative Schedule:				
Date	Time	Topic	# Hours	# Participants
Participants:				
Requirements: Room: Equipment: Training Materials:				
Title	Quantity	Buy/Develop	Cost	
Approved by:				
Systems Group	Date	User-Sponsor	Date	

PROJECT MANAGEMENT TOOLBOX

Project Management Tips for Final Construction

Although the completion of the analysis-design-preliminary construction looping activity means that the focus of the project is on a single phase—final construction—that phase is anything but simple. There is so much activity going on—software, database, hardware, facilities, documentation, and training—that to an observer it would have all of the appearances of a three-ring circus. The analogy does not end there; like the well-planned and coordinated circus acts, the final construction acts must be managed.

This is a mammoth task—too much for one person and one management tool. The person or persons responsible for the overall development project (IS steering committee, CIO, or project manager) should assign responsibility for each of the final construction major tasks to appropriate individuals and insist on management mechanisms for each. A table, such as the final construction management grid in Figure 8.11 illustrates this philosophy.

In this chapter, we identified the seven tasks that occupy the developers' attention during final construction and they are listed down the left-hand column. For each, the sequence of analysis, design, construction, and review can be followed. As illustrated in the *analysis* column, objectives should be established for each task, responsibility for each should be assigned to an individual, and each should be planned in accordance with its own Gantt chart. In the *design* column, examples are included of tools that can be used to design the manner in which the tasks are to be carried out. Many of these tools are illustrated in the chapter, but several are not. For example, the chapter illustrates a program test specification form (Figure 8.3). No such form is included for database testing but a similar form could be designed. The *construction* column recognizes that the tasks are performed, and the *review* column recognizes that for each a formal appraisal is made to ensure that it met its objectives.

identifying the room, equipment, and training materials required. An example of a short guideline for the training steps for the ASTA skill set system is provided in Figure CS 5.4.

SUMMARY

The final construction stage includes seven tasks—constructing and testing production-ready programs, constructing and testing a production-ready database, obtaining additional hardware, preparing the facility, testing the hardware components, completing the documentation, and training participants and users.

There are two basic approaches to testing—black box, which focuses on system output, and white box, which addresses lines of code. The goal of testing is to locate errors before installation, but problems arise due to the fact that it comes late in the SDLC and developer fixation causes attention to be aimed at expected problems. Testing should be aimed at ensuring compliance with user specifications; compliance with programming assumptions; coordination of the system components; coordination of coded modules; and validation of all input, process, and output conditions. Planning for testing considers such factors as personnel and supplies, preliminary tests for each component, final tests, and documentation.

FIGURE 8.11

Final Construction Management Grid

Task	Analysis	Design	Construction	Review
Program testing	Objectives, responsibility, Gantt chart	Test specifications	Program tests	Review of program testing
Database testing	Objectives, responsibility, Gantt chart	Test specifications	Database tests	Review of database testing
Hardware acquisition	Objectives, responsibility, Gantt chart	RFPs, proposals, contracts for vendor rental, lease, and purchase	Hardware installation	Review of hardware installation
Facility preparation	Objectives, responsibility, Gantt chart	Construction contracts, security plan, selection of environmental control vendors	Facility construction	Review of construction
Hardware testing	Objectives, responsibility, Gantt chart	Test specifications	Hardware tests	Review of hardware testing
Documentation	Objectives, responsibility, Gantt chart	Outlines of manuals	Preparation of manuals	Review of manuals
Training	Objectives, responsibility, Gantt chart	Training approval form	User and participant training	Review of training

The preparation of the database can be a challenging task. When file conversion is required to put old data into a new format, the process can require as much time and effort as development of new system software. The factors that influence database preparation effort are the format and availability of the data, and the type and size of firm.

One of the most difficult parts of obtaining needed hardware is the identification of potential vendors. This task has been simplified considerably by use of the Internet. Additional information can be obtained from vendor marketing activities and such publications as computer magazines and reference books. Once the vendors are identified, they can be provided with RFPs and they respond with proposals. The proposals can be evaluated quantitatively, in addition to verifying claims by contacting other users of the same equipment and requiring the vendors to solve benchmark problems. Hardware can be rented, leased, purchased, or acquired through lease-purchase.

The work of preparing the physical facility is minimal when small-scale hardware is involved. However, for large-scale systems, the work can take the form of a full-scale construction project that must address such requirements as security, raised flooring, temperature and humidity controls, pollutant controls, fire controls, and uninterrupted power. Networked systems impose additional requirements in terms of communications circuitry.

The hardware should be tested after it is obtained, with tests of access speed, processing speed, storage capacity, and performance under peak load conditions.

The documentation of the construction effort takes the form of a users manual and technical manuals. The users manual can be supplemented with a tutorial and quick reference guide. Technical manuals can exist in the form of a technical operations manual, an installation manual, and a developer manual.

The concluding task of the final construction stage is training of participants and users. The systems developers can have the primary responsibility for the education, conducting classes or training sessions. Other sources, both inside and outside the firm, can also contribute when the task falls outside the capabilities of the project team.

KEY TERMS

developer fixation
systematic testing procedures
test group
quality assurance group
file conversion
request for proposal (RFP)
benchmark problem
scheduled maintenance, preventive maintenance (PM)
unscheduled maintenance
field engineer (FE)
users manual
technical manual
technical operations manual
installation manual
developer manual

KEY CONCEPTS

- Black box testing
- White box testing, glass box testing
- Regression testing
- Stress testing, volume testing
- Factors influencing the difficulty of database creation
- RFP specifications require vendors to propose products to meet the specific needs of the new system
- The preparation and testing of software, and the installation of hardware can depend on availability of physical facilities
- Versions of technical manuals are prepared for different technical users

QUESTIONS

1. Which of the final construction tasks must be tested?
2. What is the difference between black box and white box testing?
3. Who is ideal for engaging in black box testing? Why?
4. Who is ideal for engaging in white box testing? Why?
5. What is the goal of system testing?
6. What is developer fixation? How can it be overcome as a testing problem?
7. What is regression testing? Why is it important?
8. What kind of testing would a test group perform?
9. What is the difference between preliminary and final tests?

10. What is stress testing? Why is it important?
11. What is meant by file conversion? Does it only apply to manual, noncomputer files?
12. Identify four factors that influence the difficulty of database preparation.
13. What documentation provides a good starting point for planning database construction?
14. Since the hardware vendors are expert on their own products, why not let them propose the configuration that they feel is best suited to the firm's needs?
15. How can you verify the claims of hardware vendors?
16. Why would a firm go to the trouble of setting up a benchmark problem? Why would a vendor participate in it?
17. Which hardware payment plan should the firm choose when it is uncertain whether the system will succeed?
18. Which payment plans include equipment maintenance?
19. Identify two uses of a raised floor.
20. Which LAN circuitry is least expensive? Which offers the greatest security against tampering by a computer criminal?
21. Who should perform hardware testing?
22. Who should prepare the users manual? The technical manuals?
23. Who can perform participant and user training? Why wait so long to perform it?

Topics for Discussion

1. The chapter identifies banks and insurance companies as types of firms that maintain data for long periods of time. What are some other types?
2. Is it easier to prepare a database from computer files maintained on magnetic tape and disks, or from such manual files as paper documents? Explain why.
3. What do you think about the view of the manager of user education for the large corporation that planning for that education and training should begin as soon as you embark on a development project—even before the design of the system is known?

Problems

1. Go to your library and look over the selection of computer magazines. Select one that has an article on some piece of hardware that interests you and write a short summary.
2. Repeat problem 1, only select a software article.
3. Go to your library and find a hardware reference book. Select a piece of peripheral equipment that is reviewed and write a one-page paper that evaluates two vendors' products. Identify the vendor that you would recommend and give your reasons.
4. Access the Web site of a hardware vendor and write a short summary of their products.
5. Access the Web sites of the *PC Technology Guide* and *TechWeb*. Write a short paper comparing their contents.

Case Problem: Splashdown (C)

In only a short time on the job you have made a name for yourself as a good forms designer. Your boss, Mildred Wiggins, who is the manager of systems analysis, first asked you to design a form for use in determining whether to prototype. Now, she wants a repeat performance in terms of a form that can be used to estimate the expected difficulty of database creation. The scene is Mildred's office.

Mildred: I was reading this IS book and it said that there are four factors that influence the difficulty of database creation. Two of them relate to the firm and don't concern us. However, the other two relate to the data and are a concern.

You: What are the two data factors?

Mildred: Data format and availability. If the format is one that is similar to that of the new system, and it the data exists in an electronic form, the database work won't be too bad. Also, if the data is something we've been gathering in the past, it should be no problem.

You: And, when those conditions don't exist, it can be a real hassle, right?

Mildred: Right.

You: Well, that makes a lot of sense. Sounds pretty simple to me. Why do we need a form?

Mildred: Well, there are bound to be other considerations. That is why I called on you. You'rc an information specialist. Can you think of anything else that might apply?

You: I would have thought that the big factor is the size of the file or files. If we have a lot of data, we expect difficulty. Right?

Mildred: That's part of it but we have to consider other factors as well. Any other ideas?

You: Accounting applications are notorious for their large data files. So, if it is an accounting system we can anticipate more database difficulty than for, say, MIS or DSS. Isn't that right?

Mildred: That's correct. If an application is data oriented, we should give a lot of attention to database creation and get started as soon in the development as possible. On the other hand, if it is information oriented, such as MIS, DSS, or an expert system, there might not be much database work at all and we can postpone the work until later. Many MISs and DSSs use data from the accounting databases.

You: That's a good idea. Another thing we might want to include is the expertise that we have within IS. If we have experience with the database in question—maybe we have staff members who developed it—the time required to become familiar with the format would not be as long. If we don't have expertise, we might want to plug in some extra time for orientation.

Mildred: You're right on target. Any other good ideas?

You: Well, I'm afraid I've about run out of gas. Let's see (thinking), the time frame might be a factor. If the user needs the system right away, we might not have time to develop the database in the normal manner.

Mildred: That's a good point. Any more gas in your tank?

You: No, only fumes. Have we covered everything?

Mildred: The only thing I can think of is the age of the data. If it's really old, we can anticipate problems in file conversion. The data might have been created by different generations of systems and not conform to a uniform format. That could pose some real difficulties. Let's include that and come up with a prototype form. I'd like the form to use quantitative weights and rates for each of the criteria. We can vary both based on the situation. A high score would signal potential database creation problems. I'd like for you to work up a form. If you think of anything else that we haven't discussed, go ahead and include it.

Assignments

1. Design the form that Mildred has requested. Use your word processor or similar software. It should consist of a series of scales such as the following:

The data is:

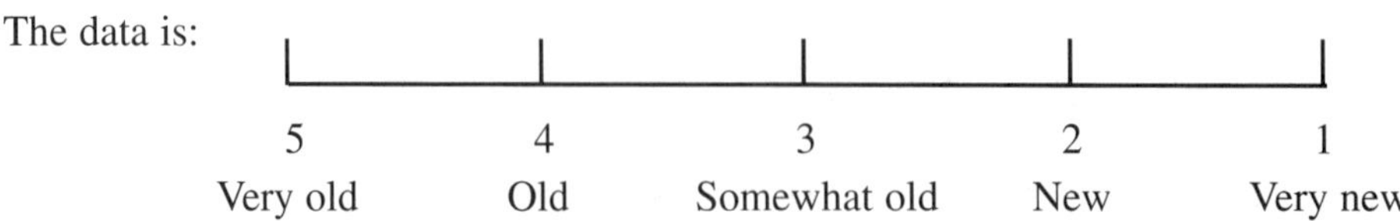

Each scale will have a weight. The weights should add to 1.00. For each scale, multiply the weight times the points to obtain the weighted points. Add the weighted points for an overall score. Make the form as user friendly and self-explanatory as possible.

2. Review Case Study Part 1 and use your form to project the degree of difficulty that can be expected in developing the skill set database. Attach the completed form to a memo to Yolanda, advising her of the potential difficulty and recommending appropriate actions to minimize the difficulty. She is deciding on the preferred sequence of project phases as illustrated in Figure CS 2.1 and your data might be helpful.

Selected Bibliography

Ameen, David A. "Evaluating Alternative Computer Acquisition Strategies." *Journal of Systems Management* 41 (September 1990): 15-20.

Connolly, P. J. "Building Better Apps for Your Business Via Thorough Testing." *Infoworld* 22 (Number 38, September 18, 2000): 58.

Dash, Julekha. "Compuware Introduces Remotely Hosted Software for Internet Testing Service." *Computerworld* 34 (Number 39, September 25, 2000): 88.

Kit, Edward, *Software Testing in the Real World* (Reading, MA: Addison-Wesley), 1995.

Gelperin, David, and Bill Hetzel. "The Growth of Software Testing." *Communications of the ACM* 31 (June 1988): 687-695.

Li, Eldon Y. "Software Testing in a System Development Process: A Life Cycle Perspective." *Journal of Systems Management* 41 (August 1990): 23-31.

Shea, Billie. "Software Testing Gets New Respect." *Informationweek* 793 (July 3, 2000): 97-106.

Roper, M. "Software Testing—Searching for the Missing Link." *Information & Software Technology* 41 (Number 14, November 15, 1999): 991-994.

Note

1. Gerald M. Weinberg, *The Psychology of Computer Programming* (New York: Van Nostrand Reinhold, 1971), p. 57.

CHAPTER 9

SYSTEM TEST AND INSTALLATION

LEARNING OBJECTIVES

- List the three basic steps of installing the new system.
- Identify the goals of installation.
- Explain the importance of the user acceptance test.
- Understand the importance of cutover and the different options that are available.
- Describe a post-implementation evaluation, identify who conducts it, and explain how it is conducted.
- Identify the different types of system maintenance and strategies that may be followed to reduce it.

INTRODUCTION

As indicated in the previous chapters, a system takes form gradually. During preliminary construction, each system module was constructed and tested. This testing involved primarily software and data. During final construction, the system modules were integrated and the system was subjected to further testing. This testing involved the software, data, and hardware. In the last stage of the phased development methodology, system test and installation, further testing is done. During this stage, all of the system components are subjected to testing—not only the software, data, and hardware, but also the people, procedures, and facilities. This final test of the complete system package is called the user acceptance test since it is used as the basis for verifying that the system is acceptable to the user.

The main goals of installation are to meet the system specifications within the constraints of time and cost and to turn over control of the system to the production staff. The three basic installation steps are to (1) design and perform the system test, (2) install the system components, and (3) conduct a user acceptance test. When the user accepts the new system as it is constructed, the developers turn the system over to the user and the system goes into production. This process is called cutover. There are several approaches that can be taken to cutover—pilot system, immediate, parallel, and phased. Some time after cutover, a post-implementation evaluation is conducted to ensure that the system is performing as intended.

As the system is used, it becomes necessary to maintain it. There are different types of maintenance, but all can be minimized by following reduction strategies as the system is being developed.

This chapter concludes the description of the system development effort. The user now begins to enjoy the benefits of the project.

INSTALLATION: THE END OF DEVELOPMENT

Inexperienced developers and users may think that the newly created system can simply be handed over to the users for production use, but several important activities remain. Just as we cannot simply ask the users what they need during requirements determination, we cannot just give the system to the users at installation. The activities of this final stage are designed to smooth the transition from old system to new, from the development environment to the production environment. The three main steps of the system test and installation stage, as shown in Figure 9.1, are:

1. Design and perform the system test
2. Install the components
3. Conduct a user acceptance test

The system test concludes a planned testing program that began with preliminary construction. When the system passes this test, all of the components can be installed. The components are those that have provided the basis for the system development—people, data, information, software, and hardware. The user acceptance test confirms that the system is performing correctly and that the users' needs have been met. Installation and cutover are exciting and demanding activities for both users and developers. At cutover, the users assume full ownership of the system, and the developers have the pleasure of seeing the system in production use.

THE GOALS OF INSTALLATION

We have finally reached the final stage of systems development and have arrived at the system test and installation phase. The system has been constructed; only the transfer to the users remains to be completed. Installing a system is a time-consuming process, whether you are developing a new system or revising an existing one. This investment of time, money, and people must be managed so as to realize the goals of installation, which are:

- Install the system, meeting all specifications for all five system components (people, data, information, software, and hardware) in a reasonable amount of time and at a reasonable cost.
- Turn over control of the system to a well-trained, committed production staff.

To achieve these goals, you need to think in terms of the larger goals of organizational relevance, project management, and system quality emphasized throughout this text. The system should support the firm as it works toward meeting its strategic objectives, the development project should be carried out efficiently and effectively, and the delivered system should be one that meets or exceeds the quality standards that users expect.

Install the System

The first goal of installation stated above may seem obvious and trivial. Of course you will install the system—that is what installation is! Yet, if you consider the full text

FIGURE 9.1

System Test and Installation Overview

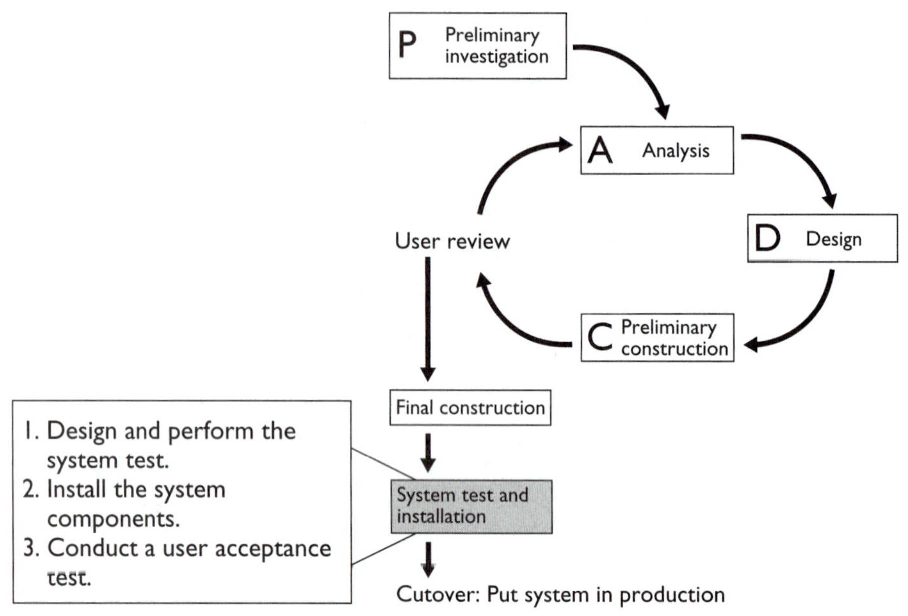

of that goal statement, you will see that it places three stipulations on installing the design. The system installation should:

- Meet all *specifications* for all components
- Be completed in a reasonable amount of *time*
- Be completed at a reasonable *cost*

The first stipulation relates to the system quality goals in terms of functionality, maintainability, and portability. These goals become the criteria for evaluating the system that you develop. As you test each system component, you need to keep these criteria in mind. Is the user interface transparent? Are the hardware and software reliable and efficient? Are the procedures clear and consistent? Are they well documented?

The second and third stipulations relate to project management goals. Because estimating the effort required to develop a system is extremely difficult, a project manager's development plan often fails during installation and a project that seemed to be on schedule falls seriously behind. One way to avoid this problem is to prepare a detailed implementation schedule with lots of milestones to help you measure progress. *These milestones should be product deliveries for each activity on the implementation checklist.* Scheduling tangible product deliveries will allow you to obtain the feedback you need to keep track of the team's progress.

Also very important to meeting the project management goals is the coordination of the divergent activities performed during implementation. You need to plan for contingencies in your schedule; finishing task A on time may be critical to starting and finishing task B as scheduled. As project manager of a large team, you will need to manage the team's communications and resources to maximize team productivity. Because schedule overruns inevitably lead to cost overruns, your success as a project manager depends on your ability to manage the process as you produce a quality product.

Turn Over Control of the System

The second goal of installation relates largely to the people component of the system. You want to be certain that cutover is a positive, orderly transition and that the production staff feels confident and positive about assuming responsibility for the system. To achieve a successful cutover, you must manage the installation activities so that users do not become frustrated by delays, confusing procedures, or malfunctioning hardware or software. To maintain the users' commitment to the system, you need to involve them in the testing process—especially the testing of procedures. The people who will use the documentation are the best judges of how clear and complete your instructions for using the system are. Many elegantly designed systems have failed because the systems developers failed to secure user commitment. You can avoid the wasteful expenditure of time, effort, and money that such a failed system represents by continuing to involve the users as you test and install the system and by remembering that people are the component for which the data, information, software, and hardware are designed.

The three steps of the system test and installation stage, described in detail below, provide a systematic way to ensure that these goals are met.

Design and Perform the System Test

The system test brings together all of the components of the new system that were assembled during the three final SDLC stages—preliminary construction, final construction, and system test and installation. We graphed this multi-stage assembly process in Figure 7.5. The system test includes the physical facilities, the hardware, the software, the production database, the trained users, and the documentation. The purpose of the system test is to determine how the components perform as a single functioning unit.

System tests are often performed after hours—in the evening or over one or more weekends. Ideally, a production staging environment is created so that the difference between its system testing and the final system test in the production environment, as shown in Figure 9.2, will be trivial. The same test data files that were built to test the software and hardware during the construction stages should now be used to test the system.

The system is put through several test runs. One test run may require the users to enter a small set of standard production data to verify that the data entry screens are easy to read, that the procedures for recovering from data entry errors are clear and correct, and that the system produces the expected output. Another more extensive test run might test the system's capacity—will it handle the expected peak production volume? One or more of these tests should be a walkthrough with several users. How well does the system meet specifications for response time? Can it process the expected data volumes as quickly as required? What are its storage, throughput, and output limits? When pressed past its limits, does the system degrade gracefully?

Yet another test run might introduce intentional hardware failures to test the backup and recovery procedures. Is the audit trail accurate? Have transactions been logged correctly? Do the users understand how to perform the necessary manual backup procedures? Can they restart the system without losing data or duplicating transactions?

FIGURE 9.2

System Testing and User Acceptance Testing Occur in the Last Software Staging Environment

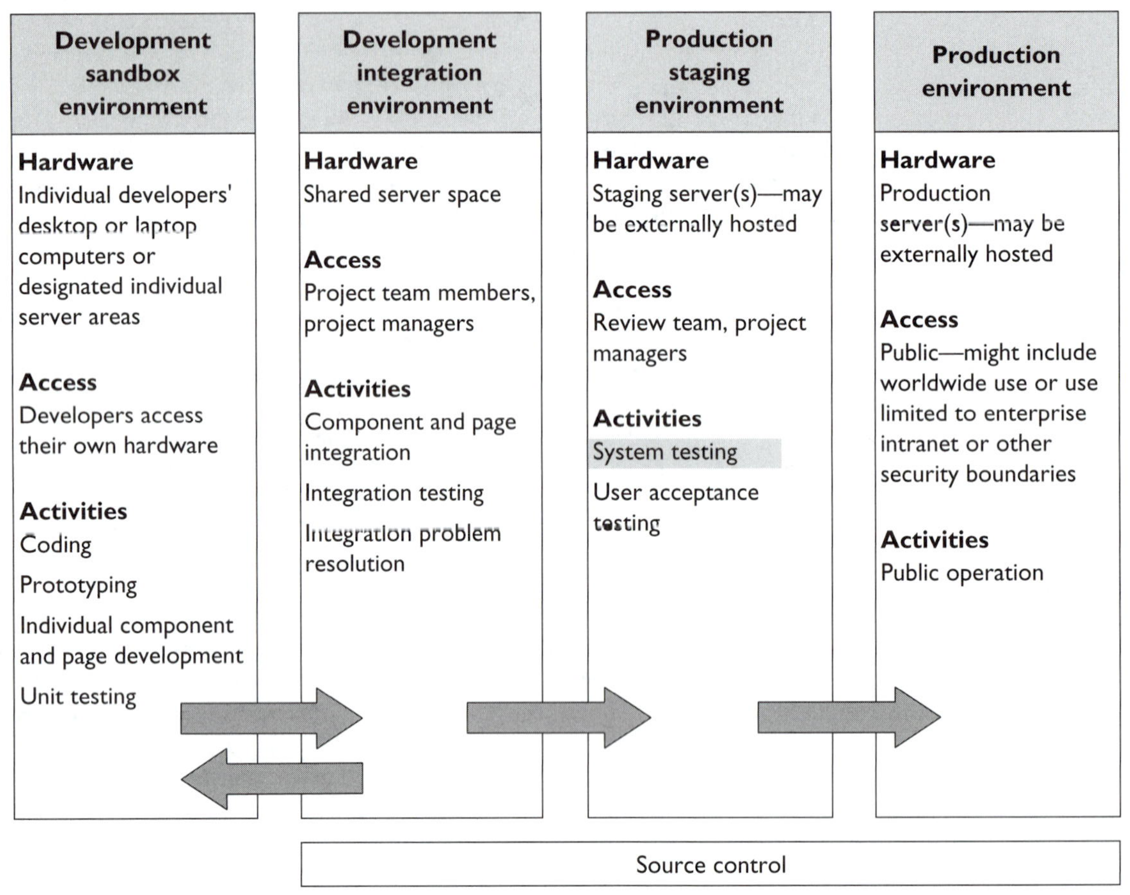

Once these controlled tests have been completed and the results meet user acceptance criteria, the system is ready for installation.

Even after the system has been accepted by the users, testing is not usually complete until the system has been used for day-to-day production operations. Systems that have passed all the tests mentioned above have been known to collapse during their initial production runs. Such a breakdown is particularly disastrous in a real-time environment such as airline reservations or consumer banking.

The Economics of Testing

Testing is a time-consuming, labor-intensive activity that can rapidly become very expensive. We have emphasized the importance of testing; now we need to give you some indication of how much testing is enough.

A guideline that some firms have followed is that "Every piece of code should be proved correct." In some situations, this guideline is appropriate; in others, it is not.

For example, if the system being built is extremely important to the firm, if system failure would incapacitate the company or threaten human life, or if even a small failure or minor error would greatly diminish the system's integrity or security, then, by all means, test everything. Because prototyping and intensive testing are high-cost activities, however, this expense is justified only for high-risk systems.

Other types of systems that warrant thorough testing are those that account for money, such as the accounts receivable, purchasing, accounts payable, and payroll subsystems of the AIS. Testing should be performed to a level that the users and the internal auditors are satisfied that the data is an accurate representation of the funds that are represented.

Thoroughly prototyping a routine system, such as one that prepares a management report or performs a statistical analysis, or rigorously testing a purchased software package is wasteful. Managers do not need 100 percent accuracy when using information for decision making; they are wise enough to supplement the information with their own judgment and experience. Likewise, it is not necessary to subject purchased software to complete testing when there is evidence, such as verification by other using firms, that the software functions as intended.

The value of the information provided by excessive testing (in the form of absolutely error-free runs, user satisfaction that the system operates correctly, and so forth) may be much lower than the cost of obtaining it.

Install Components

Installation is the period during which production files and operations are transferred from the old system to the new one. Installation requires that the affected components of the old system be replaced or modified by the components of the new system. For example, additional personnel may join the user group or operations staff to oversee functions of the new system. At a minimum, the current users will begin to perform different procedures as they use new hardware or software to accomplish their job objectives. As we recognized during the iterative preliminary construction phases, building data files for the new system is a major task in installation.

Managing the installation process requires careful planning, attention to detail, and concern for security and control. The development team's installation plan will include the following:

- The installation schedule, which identifies the tasks, who will do them, and when they will be done, as described in a Gantt chart
- Installation procedures and controls to maintain data integrity and to cross-check the old and new systems
- A contingency plan in case any aspect of the old or new system fails during conversion
- A timetable for the systematic dismantling of the old system, including removing old hardware, software, and documentation, and archiving final copies of reports, programs, and files from the old system

Figure 9.3 is a checklist of common installation activities categorized by system component. This form will help you to plan these tasks, to document their completion, and to secure approval as tasks are completed. Figure CS 5.6 is the installation guide written by the development team for the ASTA skill set system.

FIGURE 9.3

Installation Plan Checklist

Installation Plan Checklist	Date		Page	
System	Analyst			
Activity (check all that apply)	Person Responsible	Start Date	Finish Date	Approved By
I. People _____A. Hiring of new personnel _____B. Training _____C. Formation of installation team II. Procedures _____A. User manuals _____B. Technical manuals _____C. Printing/distribution of paper forms _____D. User acceptance test _____E. Removal of out-of-date documentation III. Data _____A. Control procedures for file conversion _____B. Review of current file _____C. Freeze date and file conversion _____D. Update of converted files _____E. User acceptance test _____F. Archiving of old files IV. Software _____A. Application program library _____B. System program library _____C. Backup program library _____D. User acceptance test _____E. Removal/archiving of old software V. Hardware _____A. Electrical outlets, cables, etc. _____B. Supplies _____C. Device installation _____CPU _____Communication _____Printer(s) _____Terminals _____Other____________________ _____D. System security _____Power backup _____Off-site storage _____Access restriction _____E. User acceptance test _____F. Removal of old hardware				

Note: This form should be revised to reflect the system components—people, data, information, software, and hardware.

Many project managers feel that the number and complexity of these tasks warrant the formation of a special installation team. An **installation team** is composed of users and developers—perhaps some from the original development team—who begin planning for installation early in the project. Although a special installation team may not be necessary for small system projects, it might be justified when the project requires extensive file conversion.

Conduct a User Acceptance Test

Once all components have been installed, the system is subjected to a final user review—the acceptance test. During the **acceptance test,** users test the system under routine and exceptional conditions to determine whether it satisfies the acceptance criteria that were established during requirements determination. Users scrutinize documentation; measure system response times; study input screens and reports; evaluate backup, recovery, and security procedures; and rate the system's usability and reliability. Any components or functions that fail to satisfy the acceptance criteria must be modified. In other words, the development team is not off the hook until the users signal their acceptance of the new system by signing off on each criterion. Figure 9.4 is an example of a user acceptance test form.

When the user accepts the new system, it is time to put it into production. This activity is called cutover. Cutover marks the transition from system development to production. Development is ended and a period of productive use begins.

Cutover to the New System

When the users have thoroughly checked the system and are satisfied that it meets their needs, a formal meeting is conducted with the development team, users, and information systems management. At this meeting, the installation and new system are officially assessed, and the users sign off on the acceptance criteria, thus accepting responsibility for the new system.

The task of changing from the existing system to the new one is called **cutover.** There are three basic cutover strategies:

- Immediate cutover
- Parallel cutover
- Phased cutover

In addition, there is a fourth strategy that is used in conjunction with the other three:

- Pilot system

Figure 9.5 shows how the old system is terminated and replaced by the new one. The different strategies provide options for making this transition. Each of the three main strategies incurs different installation costs and a different degree of risk. Immediate cutover offers low cost yet high risk. Parallel cutover is a high-cost strategy but features low risk. Phased cutover offers a compromise in terms of medium cost and risk. Each can be an effective strategy, depending on the nature of the system being installed.

FIGURE 9.4

User Acceptance Test Form

User Acceptance Test Form	Date	
System	Review Date	
Review Prepared by		
Acceptance Criteria	Approved by	Date
1.		
2.		
3.		
4.		
5.		
6.		
7.		
8.		
9.		
10.		

Acceptance Acknowledgement

The undersigned representatives agree that this project, identified above, has been completed in a satisfactory manner.

Information Systems Management		User Management	
Authorized Signature	Date	Authorized Signature	Date
Title		Title	

Pilot System

A **pilot system** is one that is installed in only one part of the firm's operations as a way to measure its impact. Once the pilot performs satisfactorily, the system is installed in the remainder of the firm in an immediate, phased, or parallel manner. A pilot system is like a test marketing activity that a firm can follow to evaluate the reception that consumers will give a new product. As an example, a soft drink firm can use such a city as Phoenix to test the appeal of a new drink.

Immediate Cutover

When **immediate cutover** is followed, the old system is dismantled and the new system is put into operation simultaneously. In other words, the old system is shut down and immediately replaced by the new system, with no transition period during which parts of both systems are live.

Because of its high risk, the immediate cutover strategy requires careful consideration and planning. Installing a system with the immediate cutover strategy is somewhat like performing a high-wire act without a safety net. If problems arise or errors are encountered, there is no net to fall into or old system to fall back on. Another factor making immediate cutover a risky strategy is that it does not allow you to verify the operations of the new system by comparing its output to the old system's output. This difficulty in comparing outputs of the old and new systems very often cannot be avoided. In many cases, the new system is such an improvement over the old one that the outputs are completely different.

Even so, the immediate cutover strategy is sometimes a good—even *only*—choice. For example, installing a new communications network usually requires the disconnection of the old communications system. Since the new system can be tested thoroughly before cutover and since operating the two systems concurrently is not feasible, immediate cutover is an appropriate strategy. When installation is simple and

FIGURE 9.5

The Four Approaches to Cutover

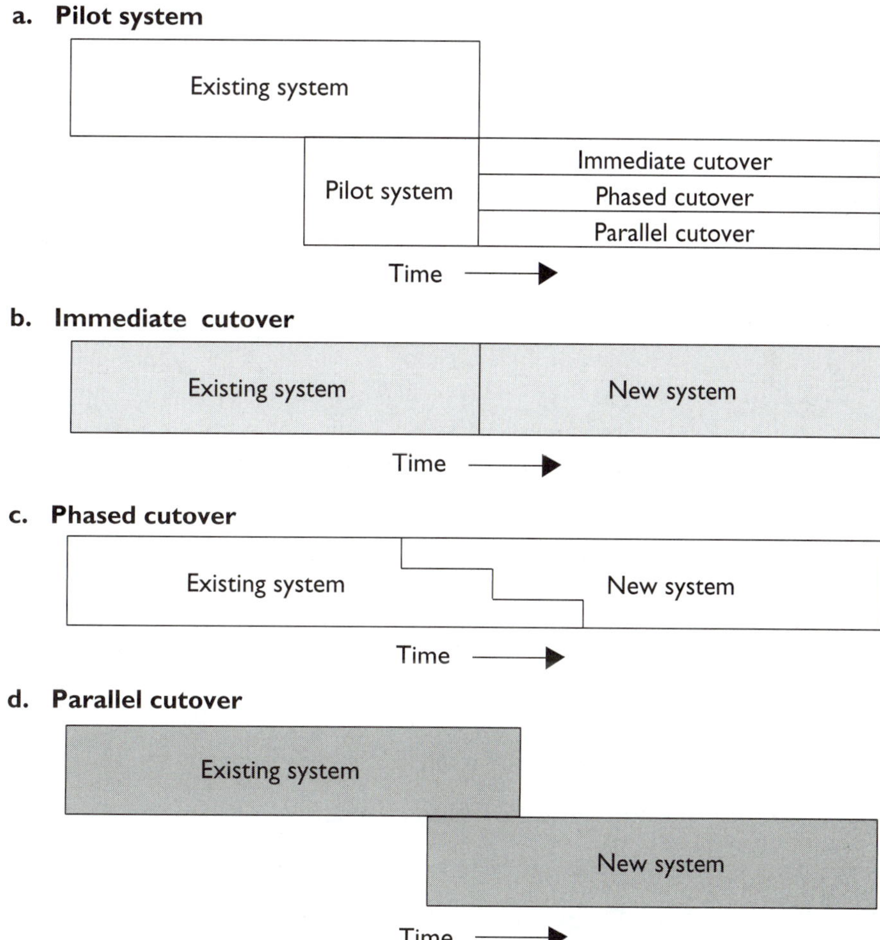

straightforward or when any other installation strategy would be too costly or too complicated, immediate cutover may be the only feasible choice.

The risk of immediate cutover can be reduced by conducting a final test of the installed system during a slow period or after working hours. In the case of the communication system mentioned above, the network would probably be closed for several hours to all but a few users involved in the final test. This test would be conducted at night or on a weekend so that very few users would be inconvenienced. After the low-volume test, the network would be opened to all users. Similarly, a department store might make a final check of its installed point-of-sale system by conducting a rehearsal run while the store is closed to customers.

Parallel Cutover

With the **parallel cutover** strategy, the new system is run simultaneously with the old until the accuracy and reliability of the new system can be verified. The greatest advantage of this strategy is that it is very low risk; its greatest disadvantage is that it is very high cost and often requires complicated procedures.

Parallel cutover reduces risk in several ways.

- It allows you to verify the new system's outputs by comparing them to the old system's outputs.
- It builds user confidence in the new system by allowing users to verify it in a production environment.
- It builds user comfort with the new system by enabling the users to become accustomed to its operations.
- It provides a safety net—the still functioning old system—in case the new system fails. This feature is often called **fallback** because it allows you to fall back to the old system if necessary.

The high costs and complicated logistics associated with parallel cutover may make it infeasible. Running both systems simultaneously strains the organization's resources; the same number of people who ran only the old system before must now oversee the operation of both systems. When a manual system is being replaced by an automated one, users must continue to perform all of the old manual procedures while also performing all of the new procedures of the automated system. The increased workload and mental strain of parallel cutover can quickly take its toll. If both the old and the new system are automated, computer resources may be pushed beyond their limits, resulting in increased downtime and turnaround time. These complications can actually increase the likelihood of system failure while attempting to reduce the difficulty of coping with that failure.

In summary, several factors can make parallel cutover prohibitively difficult.

- Too many resources may be required.
- Comparing the new system to the old may be too difficult.
- The required procedures or logistics may be too complicated.
- There may be no equivalent operation in the old system (for example, when a manual ticket reservation system is computerized).

The overall risk reduction achieved through the parallel cutover strategy, however, may justify living with these complications and planning for them. Several techniques for managing parallel cutover are listed below.

- Phase in the parallel operations whenever possible. That is, instead of running all aspects of the new system in parallel with the old, bring the new system online function by function or file by file.
- Bring in temporary staff or reduce the workload of users during parallel operation.
- Plan for additional computer resources. For example, order more supplies and ask other users to reduce their requirements or to reschedule their computer activities to avoid conflicts.
- Prepare interim quick-reference procedure sheets by placing procedure summaries on placards and encasing them in plastic. These sheets should contain both old and new procedures—for example, the procedure sheet for creating a balance sheet would give the steps for the old manual system and then the steps for the new computerized system. These quick-reference sheets will guide users through complicated procedures and alleviate some of their stress.
- Maintain user morale by recognizing their increased workload and showing your appreciation of their contribution. Schedule frequent morale-boosting activities.

Another way of dealing with these problems is to perform a **modified parallel cutover** strategy. With this approach, the new system can be tested using old data to simulate a historical parallel run. That is, a new computerized accounting system might go live over a weekend, running old but genuine data from the old manual system. The output from the new system could be compared to that generated by the old system to verify the new system's operations. Furthermore, the users could operate the new system in a no-risk environment, thus avoiding not only the stress of running both systems simultaneously but also the anxiety of using the new system to produce output that affects the organization. Although this alternative is feasible only for small systems with few users, it deserves consideration when circumstances permit.

One question that must be addressed when the parallel cutover strategy is adopted is how long to continue the parallel operation before dismantling the old system. The length of the parallel cutover period will vary depending on the complexity of the new system and the consequences of its failure. A short period of parallel operation, perhaps only a few days, is appropriate when the new system is fairly straightforward and errors in its functions are neither critical nor life-threatening. In contrast, when a large organization installs a new accounting system, it may continue parallel cutover through several accounting cycles because the validity of the system's data and reports is crucial to the organization's survival. The adage about ends justifying means comes to mind—the cost and complexity incurred by a more extended parallel cutover period are justified by the peace of mind and risk reduction achieved.

Phased Cutover

An installation strategy that achieves a happy medium on the cost and risk scales is **phased cutover,** in which the system is installed in phases. This is similar to the phased development approach that we have been following for system development. Phased cutover differs from phased development in that the first is an installation strategy whereas the second is a development approach. A system being installed with a phased cutover strategy may have been developed by following any development methodology—traditional life cycle approach, prototyping, RAD, and so forth.

The phases of the installation can be:

- *Subsystems of the system*—Each subsystem is cut over separately. For example, when a manufacturer cuts over to a new accounting system, order entry is cut over first, inventory is cut over next, followed by billing, and so on.
- *Organizational units*—The system is put into use in only one part of the firm at a time. The parts can be organizational levels, business areas, geographic sites, and so on. A good example is when the Air Force cuts over to a new aircraft maintenance system. The system is installed airbase by airbase.

The order of functions for phased cutover by subsystem is usually determined either by the needs of the users or by the logical progression of functions. In the first case, system functions are installed one by one on the basis of user priorities. For example, when a new marketing information system is being installed, users may determine that the salesperson territory assignment subsystem should be installed first.

Putting Cutover in Perspective

Cutover is an exciting time both for the users, who gain full control of the system, and for the developers, who see months of labor finally brought to fruition. Cutover signals the end of the project, but it would not be complete without recognition of the outstanding contributions of the key developers, users, and managers. Everyone will be refreshed by a celebration that alleviates the psychological letdown associated with the end of an intense activity. Although post-project recognition ceremonies or celebrations may seem frivolous, they are valuable motivational tools that formally mark the end of a project, revitalize users and developers, and restore some of the stamina needed to take on tomorrow's projects.

CONDUCT THE POST-IMPLEMENTATION EVALUATION

After cutover has been achieved and the users have adjusted to the system, an evaluation should be conducted of the project and the delivered system. A **post-implementation evaluation** investigates the results of the project and alerts developers to ways in which future projects can be improved. It also provides feedback on how well the development team met the system objectives, stayed within the project constraints, and estimated the project schedule and budget. This feedback serves as a measure of team performance and helps developers become better estimators.

Focus of the Evaluation

The post-implementation evaluation report, generally prepared two to three months after cutover, addresses the three goals of system development:

- *System quality*—Does the system do what it is supposed to do? Does it function reliably and efficiently? Is it well documented to facilitate maintenance? Can the system adapt to changes in the organization? Is it compatible with other systems?

- *Project management*—What project management approaches were used? Were they successful? Why or why not? Were management and users kept abreast of the status of the project schedule through reviews at major milestones? Was the system completed on time and within budget? What lessons were learned about managing a project such as this one? Should the firm adopt any new policies to take advantage of these lessons? Are the users satisfied with the system? Are they pleased with the way the project was conducted?
- *Organizational relevance*—Does the system improve an operational task critical to the organization's objectives? Does it support management control or provide strategic value? Is it producing the benefits that were expected? Do the system benefits justify its ongoing production costs?

As these questions indicate, the post-implementation evaluation relies on information gathered from the development team, the users, and management. This information, along with technical data about the system's functionality, will be used to evaluate the project outcomes.

The Evaluators

Two groups can perform the majority of the post-implementation evaluation. They are the developers and internal auditors. The developers are primarily concerned with whether the system is meeting the users' objectives, as perceived by the users. The developers therefore gather feedback information from the users by means of personal interviews, mail surveys, telephone surveys, or any other appropriate means, such as JAD sessions.

The internal auditors, on the other hand, are primarily concerned with whether the new system is processing the data properly. Does the conceptual system accurately reflect the physical system? This conclusion can be reached by studying the system storage contents and outputs.

Other participants in the evaluation can include anyone who is a stakeholder in the system, such as members of the executive committee and the IS steering committee, users, and perhaps representatives of other firms, such as suppliers and customers, that are linked to the system in some way. In an effort to ensure an unbiased audit, the firm often contracts with consultants or other external specialists. There have been instances where students in local undergraduate and graduate information systems courses and programs conduct the audits as term projects.

With potentially so many people involved in the evaluation, a wise strategy is to assign one person the responsibility to lead the post-implementation effort. This person would not necessarily have to be the same one who led the development project team. In fact, it would be better to select a different person as a means of ensuring unbiased reporting.

The Evaluation Process

The post-implementation evaluation consists of a five-step process.

Step 1. Review Project Documents

The first step in the evaluation process is to compare the old system, the promised system, and the delivered system. Reviewing earlier project documents, especially the

FIGURE 9.6

Post-Implementation Project Summary

Post-Implementation Project Summary	Page
System	Date
Prepared by	

Schedule

Date Implemented (Mo/Yr) ________

Duration of the project, in months (from authorization to implementation):

- Earliest estimate ________
- Authorized estimate ________
- Actual duration ________

Size

Size of the system:

- K lines of code ________
- K bytes of object code ________
- Number of programs ________
- Other ________

Was this an enhancement project?

☐ Yes ☐ No

If yes: How much bigger is the new system than the old system? ________ %

What portion of the old system was replaced?

________ %

How many people and departments receive data from the system?

- People ________
- Departments ________

Cost

Cost of the project, in $ thousands (from authorization to implementation):

- Earliest estimate ________
- Authorized estimate ________
- Actual cost ________

Costs include (check all that apply)

- ☐ Internal systems personnel
- ☐ External systems personnel
- ☐ User personnel
- ☐ Computer research charges
- ☐ Purchased software
- ☐ Purchased hardware
- ☐ Other ________________

Was the project cost justified? ________

Using ROI? ________ %

Using Payback? ________ %

Using Present Value? $ ________ (thou)

Other? ________________

If the project was not cost justified, what was the basis for proceeding? ________________

____

Technology

Hardware technology (check all that apply):

- ☐ Mainframe or mini
- ☐ On-line terminals
- ☐ Personal computers

Principal language(s) ________________

____

(ignore operating systems or small amounts of code)

requirements document and the cost-benefit analysis, will refresh your memory and help you identify the objectives and expected benefits of the development project. The documentation review will also provide the technical information needed for a summary of the delivered system, such as the one shown in Figure 9.6.

Step 2. Plan the Post-Implementation Review

The next step is to prepare a plan for the evaluation, which involves identifying individuals to be interviewed and assigning evaluators to the various tasks involved in gathering the data and reporting the findings. The team leader for the post-implementation evaluation decides which users, team members, and managers are to be interviewed. The criteria for evaluation are those established through the review of the project documents.

Step 3. Conduct Interviews

Except for the information gained from studying error logs and other documentation of the system in operation, most of the information on the success of the project will come from interviewing users, developers, and managers. The guidelines for conducting interviews, covered in Chapter 5 when we described systems analysis, apply here.

Of critical importance in post-implementation interviews is gathering the interviewee's true feelings. Many users will hesitate to express negative comments about the project management or system quality, especially if the person conducting the interview is one of the developers. You can overcome this hesitance by using a questionnaire such as the one shown in Figure 9.7 to elicit user responses. As we recognized in Chapter 5, a mail questionnaire often is capable of obtaining sensitive information that cannot be obtained by face-to-face interviews or telephone surveys. After the user has completed the form, an evaluator should follow up by asking the user about his or her expectations of the system and lessons learned.

The development project team and management should also be interviewed. Interviewing several team members and managers should provide a representative sample of assessments of the project and its outcomes. Figure 9.8 shows an interview form or questionnaire that can be used to gather team members' comments on a project. Figure 9.9 lists some questions that delve into the development project manager's assessment of the system and whether it satisfied organizational relevance goals.

Step 4. Prepare the Evaluation Report

The emphasis in the post-implementation evaluation report is on (1) evaluating the project's satisfaction of the systems development goals, and (2) recommending policies and strategies to facilitate future development projects. A model for such a report appears in Figure 9.10.

The report is a reference for future systems development projects. It serves as a *guidebook* for estimating and managing projects, as a *sourcebook* for technical problem solutions, and as a *handbook* on user-developer relations. Therefore, the time required to compile and document its information is time well spent.

Step 5. Submit the Report to Management

The team leader for the post-implementation evaluation should present a summary of the highlights of the report to appropriate representatives of upper management.

FIGURE 9.7

Post-Implementation User Evaluation Form

Post-Implementation User Evaluation	Evaluation Date	Page 1 of 2
System	Evaluator	

Please evaluate the project on the criteria listed by circling the response that best describes your viewpoint.

	Very Unsatisfactory						Very Satisfactory
Functionality							
Reliability							
1. Comprehensiveness of options on screens and menus (all necessary choices provided)	1	2	3	4	5	6	7
2. Sufficiency of help options	1	2	3	4	5	6	7
3. Integration of functions	1	2	3	4	5	6	7
4. Accuracy of data	1	2	3	4	5	6	7
5. Reliability of system	1	2	3	4	5	6	7
6. Security	1	2	3	4	5	6	7
Clarity							
7. Consistency and predicitibilty of system.	1	2	3	4	5	6	7
8. Ease of learning and use	1	2	3	4	5	6	7
9. Clarity of instructions, prompts, error messages, and help messages	1	2	3	4	5	6	7
10. Clarity of choices on screens and menus	1	2	3	4	5	6	7
11. Clarity of report formats and labeling	1	2	3	4	5	6	7
Efficiency							
12. Response time	1	2	3	4	5	6	7
13. Number of keystrokes	1	2	3	4	5	6	7
14. Ease of movement between functions	1	2	3	4	5	6	7
Ease of Maintenance							
Understandability							
15. Clarity and completeness of user documentation.	1	2	3	4	5	6	7
16. Clarity and adequacy of training materials.	1	2	3	4	5	6	7
Modifiability							
17. Ability of screens and menus to continue to be used, even when changes are implemented.	1	2	3	4	5	6	7
18. Frequency of requests for modificaiton.	1	2	3	4	5	6	7
Testability							
19. Completeness and helpfulness of test plan.	1	2	3	4	5	6	7

Post-Implementation User Evaluation	Page 2 of 2

	Very Unsatisfactory						Very Satisfactory
Portability/Scability							
Portability							
20. System can be used at other offices.	1	2	3	4	5	6	7
21. System can be used on other hardware.	1	2	3	4	5	6	7
Adaptability							
22. System similar to other systems already in use.	1	2	3	4	5	6	7
23. System not dependent on other systems to be functional.	1	2	3	4	5	6	7
Team's Performance							
24. Met agreed milestones.	1	2	3	4	5	6	7
25. Interested in future needs.	1	2	3	4	5	6	7
26. Cooperative attitude	1	2	3	4	5	6	7
27. Used non-technical terms.	1	2	3	4	5	6	7
28. Kept user informed on progress.	1	2	3	4	5	6	7
29. Thorough training.	1	2	3	4	5	6	7
Overall Project							
30. Level of user involvement	1	2	3	4	5	6	7
31. Management committment	1	2	3	4	5	6	7
32. Overall satisfaction	1	2	3	4	5	6	7

Comments ____________________

Members of the post-implementation team, the original project manager, appropriate users, and information systems managers should attend the presentation to answer questions, provide supplementary information, and express dissenting opinions.

The presentation of the report marks the official end of the system development project.

Putting System Use in Perspective

We have described the activities that are performed to put a new system into use. These activities required a considerable investment of time and money by the firm. The expectation is that the system will have a long and productive life. During this life, users will use the system and there may be periodic post-implementation evaluations, perhaps every two or three years, to ensure that the system is still meeting its objectives. During this period the system is maintained, perhaps by a maintenance team that is part of the information systems unit.

Systems Maintenance

Systems maintenance is work performed on an operational information system for the purposes of enabling the system to continue to accomplish its objectives in terms of efficiency and effectiveness. There are four basic types of maintenance:

- *System compatibility maintenance* is necessary any time the system is revised to interface with a new system.
- *System efficiency and reliability maintenance* is geared toward improving the overall performance of production systems that are running correctly but inefficiently.
- *Emergency needs and errors maintenance* is repair work that is necessitated by normal deterioration. This type of maintenance is required by the hardware component; hardware will deteriorate if you do not maintain it. Software, on the other hand, deteriorates with maintenance. As revisions alter the original structure of the programs in a piecemeal fashion, the integrity of the software deteriorates.
- *User enhancements maintenance* consists of revisions to improve or augment the user outputs being generated or to conform to new output requirements. New reports and revisions to current reports account for most user enhancements. Acting on requests for changes and learning about new requirements consume a tremendous amount of developers' time over the system development life cycle.

Since so much time and so many information systems resources are spent on maintenance, improving productivity depends not only on reducing initial development effort but also on avoiding frequent revisions. Several strategies can be followed to reduce system maintenance.

Strategies for Reducing Systems Maintenance

Systems maintenance can be reduced by following two basic strategies, plus addressing efforts at specific kinds of maintenance.

FIGURE 9.8

Team Member Project Evaluation Form

Team Member Project Evaluation	Date
System	Evaluator

Please evaluate the project on the criteria listed by circling the response that best describes your viewpoint.

	Very Unsatisfactory						Very Satisfactory
System Quality							
Functionality							
1. Error rate	1	2	3	4	5	6	7
2. Timeliness of report delivered	1	2	3	4	5	6	7
3. Completeness of reports delivered	1	2	3	4	5	6	7
Maintainability							
4. Quality of documentation (user and technical)	1	2	3	4	5	6	7
5. Quality of testing procedures documentation	1	2	3	4	5	6	7
6. Quality of programming standards	1	2	3	4	5	6	7
7. Clarity and functionality of modules	1	2	3	4	5	6	7
Portability/Scalability							
8. Ability of system to be used at other sites	1	2	3	4	5	6	7
9. Ability of system to be used on other hardware	1	2	3	4	5	6	7
10. Procedural flexibility	1	2	3	4	5	6	7
Project Management							
Timeliness							
11. Meeting of agreed-upon milestones	1	2	3	4	5	6	7
Cost							
12. System cost	1	2	3	4	5	6	7
User Commitment							
13. Involvement during development	1	2	3	4	5	6	7
14. Enthusiasm about completed system	1	2	3	4	5	6	7
Overall Project							
15. Background of development team	1	2	3	4	5	6	7
16. Performance of development team	1	2	3	4	5	6	7
17. Priority assigned by management	1	2	3	4	5	6	7
18. Upper-management commitment	1	2	3	4	5	6	7
19. Overall benefits from the system	1	2	3	4	5	6	7
20. Overall rating	1	2	3	4	5	6	7

Comments:

Basic Strategies

The system can be developed to eliminate the need for unnecessary changes, and to reduce the effort of changes when they must be made.

- *Eliminate unnecessary changes*—During the preliminary investigation and iterative analysis phases, you define the functional requirements right the first time, and during construction you make use of thorough testing.

- *Reduce effort of changes*—During the iterative design phases, you design the system so that changes can easily be made, and during the preliminary and final construction phases you incorporate the ease-of-change features into the system. Thorough documentation and use of CASE tools also reduce the effort of changes.

FIGURE 9.9

Project Management Evaluation Form

Project Management Evaluation	Date						
System	Evaluator						
Please evaluate the project on the criteria listed by circling the response that best describes your viewpoint.							
System Quality	Very Unsatisfactory						Very Satisfactory
1. Satisfaction of users							
a. Were user requirements met?	1	2	3	4	5	6	7
b. Is the data valid, integrated, and secure?	1	2	3	4	5	6	7
c. Is the system easy to use, responsive, and stable?	1	2	3	4	5	6	7
d. Were schedule and budget requirements met?.	1	2	3	4	5	6	7
2. Satisfaction of the IS group							
a. Does the system conform to IS data and architecture goals?	1	2	3	4	5	6	7
b. Is it easy to operate, audit, and maintain?	1	2	3	4	5	6	7
c. Does it operate within cost and schedule requirements?	1	2	3	4	5	6	7
Project Management							
3. Control of progress (Throughout the project, were the status of the project schedule, budget, and features to be delivered communicated clearly to all user managers?)	1	2	3	4	5	6	7
4. Tradeoff among cost, schedule, and features (particularly with respect to technical issues of development)	1	2	3	4	5	6	7
5. Team leadership (Did team leadership enhance team productivity and provide members with the opportunity to develop and enhance their skills?)	1	2	3	4	5	6	7
Organizational Relevance							
6. Value added to the enterprise (Does the system improve efficiency or effectiveness, in tangible or intangible ways, in the short or long run?).	1	2	3	4	5	6	7
7. Total cost and delivery dates for the system.	1	2	3	4	5	6	7
8. Overall rating	1	2	3	4	5	6	7
Comments:							

FIGURE 9.10

A Model for the Post-Implementation Evaluation Report

1. Executive summary
2. Table of contents
3. Conclusions and recommendation
   3.1 Major successes and failures
   3.2 Recommendations for future projects
4. Overview of the project
   4.1 Project objectives
   4.2 Project participants
      4.2.1 Development team
      4.2.2 User organization
      4.2.3 Vendors, consultants, etc.
5. Project summary
   5.1 Project characteristics
      5.1.1 Size and complexity
      5.1.2 Project management strategies
      5.1.3 Development tools used
6. Assessment of outcomes
   6.1 System quality
      6.1.1 Functionality
      6.1.2 Ease of maintenance
      6.1.3 Portability/scalability
   6.2 Project management
   6.3 Organizational relevance

In addition to these basic strategies, specific strategies can be pursued to reduce certain types of maintenance.

- *Reduce system compatibility maintenance*—System compatibility maintenance can be reduced by developing portable systems. A portable system functions well in various environments and with various devices. Its hardware architecture allows it to interface with a number of printers and storage media and to operate under a standard operating system. A portable system is built in such a way as to ensure program-data independence, so that later changes in data requirements involve only minor alterations to the software. A portable system also is easily adapted to changes in security and user procedures.

- *Reduce system efficiency and reliability maintenance*—System efficiency and reliability maintenance effort can be reduced by employing structured techniques and conducting frequent tests as you develop the system. Structured walkthroughs at each stage of the development process will help you ensure that the system meets user requirements and does what it is supposed to do. Thorough testing of all system components during initial construction phases will catch errors caused by both people and machines. It will identify inconsistencies or omissions in both user procedures (for example, data entry) and program instructions (for example, data retrieval, manipulation, and reporting). Often improving the efficiency of a system is a simple matter of training users to follow the procedures closely and to take advantage of all that the software and hardware can do.

- *Reduce emergency needs and errors maintenance*—Emergency needs and errors maintenance can be reduced through better analysis, design, and testing. No matter how well you follow the guidelines for creating an efficient, reliable system, there are likely to be a few unpleasant surprises in production—errors that occur due to unexpected actions by users, regulatory changes, unannounced changes in systems that interface with your system, and other types of difficult-to-predict changes. The better analysis is, the fewer surprises there will be. Similarly, good design and structured or object-oriented development methods that adhere to standards make it easier to find the code that needs changing and make the necessary changes without causing new errors. If a testing environment was created and documented in the initial development effort, then the revised system can be tested thoroughly with little additional effort. This reduces the risk of introducing new errors into the system and causing another iteration of emergency fixes and error maintenance.

- *Reduce user enhancements maintenance*—User enhancements maintenance can be reduced by ensuring that the original development of the system is user driven. By involving users in every phase—from preliminary investigation through all the iterations of analysis, design, and construction—you increase the likelihood that the system will meet user expectations. Some of the strategies we have stressed throughout this text to promote user involvement include having users develop all or part of the system (for example, procedures) and using prototypes in a phased development process to acquaint users with system features before the system is fully ready to install. You can also reduce the number of user enhancements if, early in the development process, you encourage users not only to identify their current needs but also to project their future needs. Although it is certainly not necessary to include every conceivable feature that users think they might need, you should design the current system so that it can be easily enhanced to fulfill future needs.

Of course, any system will be easier to enhance and to maintain if it has been designed and built with ease-of-maintenance in mind. Clear and complete documentation, structured modules, and a consistent format will reduce the effort required to ensure compatibility, to improve efficiency, and to enhance the capability of the system.

The End of Maintenance

At some point, management may decide that it is time to make major changes in the system. A decision might be made to redevelop the system by repeating the system development life cycle. Or a decision might be made to drastically reengineer the system by means of business process redesign (BPR), in which case a reverse engineering effort is followed by forward engineering.

We described redevelopment and BPR earlier when we covered preliminary investigation activities in Chapter 4 and will not elaborate on that material here. The point to understand is that system installation does not signal the end of attention to the system by top management, users, and information systems personnel. As long as the system remains in production, it is monitored on a virtually day-to-day basis as a vital element in the firm's operations.

PROJECT MANAGEMENT TOOLBOX

Management of System Test and Installation

We presented the functions/components matrix in Chapter 1 as an effective way to capture the major features of a system. It seems only appropriate that we use that same format to manage the achievement of the system and its objectives.

Figure 9.11 is a functions/components matrix that can serve as a checklist of topics to be reviewed when managing the final development stage of system test and installation. The cells identify only the topics, and project management can call upon considerable detail in verifying that the objectives identified by the topics have, in fact, been achieved. For example, all of the Data, Information, Software, and Hardware cells contain the same entries of (1) meets functional requirements, and (2) technical manual documentation. In using this information, it is necessary to know what the functional requirements and the types of documentation are. Take, for example the Data/Input cell. The functional requirements might specify that for a data entry of sales order data, the data elements to be entered include customer number, customer order number, item number, and quantity. The technical manual documentation that is needed might consist of an object class diagram and a data dictionary that contains the data attributes. Project management verifies that these requirements have been met.

The same detail is required to use the entries in the People cells. Using the People/Input cell as an example, perhaps the functional requirements state that data entry operators will only have to input the data that uniquely identifies an order. Consideration of the facilities might consist of evaluating the room lighting to ensure that the data entry operators can easily view the screens and checking to ensure that all of the necessary equipment, fixtures, and supplies are present. In a similar fashion, an evaluation is required to determine whether the users manual and the technical manuals contain adequate descriptions of the data entry process, and that user training covered all of the input routines.

Because of the summary nature of the cell entries in the figure, it is easy to overlook the value of using a functions/components matrix format for the final evaluation of project achievement. What the matrix contributes is a framework that ensures that project management pays attention to all of the major factors that bear on meeting the project objectives.

PUTTING SYSTEMS DEVELOPMENT IN PERSPECTIVE

We have described systems development in considerable detail. The phased development approach that we selected as the basis of our description consists of six stages and each stage consists of multiple steps. It is easy to see how this many steps would be required to develop a complex system on such a large computer platform as a mainframe or a server in a client/server network. It is not so easy to see the steps being required to develop a simple system on a small computer, such as a PC or a workstation, but they are. Of course, there would be some differences, since no two development projects are exactly the same, but the basic development methodology applies to all types of projects.

Take, for example, a project where a financial manager develops an electronic spreadsheet-based system on her microcomputer for use in tracking cash flow. The manager (user) will define the functional requirements of the systems and probably develop it a part, or module, at a time. As each module is completed, the manager subjects it to tests to ensure that it is performing as intended. When the entire spreadsheet is assembled, the manager uses more testing before putting it into production.

FIGURE 9.11

System Test and Installation Matrix

	Input	Processing	Output	Storage	Control
People	Meets functional requirements Facilities, including equipment, fixtures, and supplies Users manual procedures User training Technical manual procedures	Meets functional requirements Facilities, including equipment, fixtures, and supplies Users manual procedures User training Technical manual procedures	Meets functional requirements Facilities, including equipment, fixtures, and supplies Users manual procedures User training Technical manual procedures	Meets functional requirements Facilities, including equipment, fixtures, and supplies Users manual procedures User training Technical manual procedures	Meets functional requirements Facilities, including equipment, fixtures, and supplies Users manual procedures User training Technical manual procedures
Data	Meets functional requirements Technical manual documentation	Meets functional requirements Technical manual documentation	Meets functional requirements Technical manual documentation	Meets functional requirements Technical manual documentation	Meets functional requirements Technical manual documentation
Information	Meets functional requirements Technical manual documentation	Meets functional requirements Technical manual documentation	Meets functional requirements Technical manual documentation	Meets functional requirements Technical manual documentation	Meets functional requirements Technical manual documentation
Software	Meets functional requirements Technical manual documentation	Meets functional requirements Technical manual documentation	Meets functional requirements Technical manual documentation	Meets functional requirements Technical manual documentation	Meets functional requirements Technical manual documentation
Hardware	Meets functional requirements Technical manual documentation	Meets functional requirements Technical manual documentation	Meets functional requirements Technical manual documentation	Meets functional requirements Technical manual documentation	Meets functional requirements Technical manual documentation

Granted, the manager most likely will not complete all of the documentation that a project team would produce on a large project, and would not engage in formal planning supported by such documents as a Gantt chart or network diagram. The manager would take shortcuts made possible by the fact that the user and the developer are the same person. However, the manager would not deviate from the main path.

The real value of phased development is that it can be applied to projects of all kinds. It is a framework. We have supplemented this framework with tools that contribute to successful project completion—planning tools like Gantt charts and network diagrams, data and process modeling tools like class diagrams, analysis tools like the functions/components matrix, design tools like risk and control matrices, construction tools like the test specification form, and installation tools like the installation plan checklist. The methodologies and the tools provide developers with a proven, systematic way to develop information systems. By using the tools that you have learned, you can apply them to any system development project that comes your way, as a user or as an information specialist.

SUMMARY

Installation has two main goals—to install the system design as specified, within time and cost budgets, and to turn control of the system over to the user.

The basic steps of installation are design and perform the system test, install components, and conduct a user acceptance test. The system test requires that all of the components be brought together—the people, data, information, software, and hardware. Although testing is always necessary, the amount depends on the type of the system. Systems that have a direct influence on company performance demand that everything be tested. Installation consists of the transfer of production files and operations to the new system. The acceptance test is a thorough test of the system by the user. Cutover signals the end of the development effort.

Cutover to the new system can be accomplished four basic ways. A pilot system can precede an immediate, parallel, or phased cutover. Immediate cutover is the most straightforward but is the riskiest. Parallel cutover offers the least risk but may not be practical because of the strain that it puts on the information resources. Phased cutover offers a balance between cost and risk, and can be accomplished with phases representing subsystems or organizational units.

Shortly after cutover, the system is subjected to a post-implementation evaluation by all of the stakeholders—users, developers, internal auditors, perhaps consultants, and (for very large or important projects) upper-level managers. The review evaluates the system in terms of the three goals of system development—system quality, project management, and organizational relevance. The evaluation is conducted by interviewing users, developers, and managers and a report is prepared and presented to management.

After the system goes into production, it is necessary to perform maintenance so that it can continue to satisfy the functional requirements. The four types of maintenance are system compatibility, system efficiency and reliability, emergency needs and errors, and user enhancements. The first two types improve the performance of a system that is running correctly. The user enhancements increase the usability of the system for the user. The two basic strategies for reducing maintenance are to eliminate the need for unnecessary changes, and to reduce the effort to make the changes when they are required.

When maintenance is no longer effective and the system is still necessary, management can authorize a redevelopment effort or business process redesign. The system life cycle therefore continues for as long as the system performs a useful function.

KEY TERMS

installation
installation team
acceptance test
cutover
pilot system
immediate cutover
parallel cutover
fallback
modified parallel cutover
phased cutover
post-implementation evaluation

KEY CONCEPTS

- The installation requirements to satisfy system specifications within time and cost budgets
- Use of product deliveries as major milestones
- The system test integrates all of the system components—people, data, information, software, and hardware

- Testing is always required but the degree depends on the characteristics of the system
- The inverse relationship that exists between cutover risk and cost
- Cutover phases can be based on subsystems or organizational units
- The large numbers and varieties of people who can participate in the post-implementation evaluation
- Use of system development goals as measures for the post-implementation evaluation
- System maintenance is triggered by causes in addition to error correction
- System life is extended through maintenance, redevelopment, and business process redesign

QUESTIONS

1. What are the three steps of the system test and installation stage?
2. One of the three goals of installation applies to the system. Which is it? To what do the other two apply?
3. What items on the installation checklist can serve as project milestones?
4. What distinguishes the system testing in this phase from that performed during preliminary and final construction?
5. Should every piece of code in the new system be proved correct? Explain.
6. Name four components of an installation plan.
7. What name is given to the final test before cutover?
8. What is cutover? What are the three main strategies?
9. What is the difference between a pilot system and a phased cutover?
10. Of the cutover strategies, which is least risky? Most risky?
11. How does parallel cutover reduce risks?
12. Which cutover strategy offers a fallback benefit?
13. Why would a firm not elect to use parallel cutover?
14. What is a modified parallel cutover?
15. Identify two ways to install a new system in phases.
16. As described in the chapter, a post-implementation evaluation is made of the system, the development process, and a third area of concern. What is the third area?
17. Who conducts a post-implementation evaluation?
18. The first step of the post-implementation evaluation is to review project documents. What is the purpose of this review?
19. Why would personal interviews of users be a better way to gather information in the post-implementation evaluation than use of a JAD session?
20. The post-implementation report serves as three kinds of books. What are they?
21. Identify four types of systems maintenance. Which one often includes redesign of reports to increase their value?
22. What are the two basic strategies for reducing maintenance?
23. What options are open to management when it is clear that maintenance is no longer effective in keeping a valuable system alive?

TOPICS FOR DISCUSSION

1. Are there any types of systems that would require no testing? Very little testing?
2. Should a firm agree to have students in an information systems course conduct the post-implementation evaluation?

3. If the development team included an internal auditor, is that person a good candidate for conducting the evaluation?
4. Do all four types of systems maintenance indicate a poor systems development job?

Case Problem: Katie's Gifts

You are fresh out of college, having earned an information systems degree. Rather than follow the traditional path of working for an established firm, you decided that the best way to learn how to apply information technology to solve real-world problems would be to open your own consulting firm. You return to your hometown, a fairly large city, where you have a lot of contacts.

Things haven't gone as well as you expected. You thought the phone would ring off the wall—calls from your friends who are in business and need computing help. One day, your expectations are met when you receive a call from an old high school friend who owns a gift shop. The shop specializes in wedding gifts and carries lines of china and silver. It seems your friend, Katie, has bought a PC and wants to be able to use it in her business. Although she didn't go into any details, it sounds like it should be a pretty simple task. So, you head on over.

You exchange greetings, Katie gives you a tour, and then she leads you into her office where her PC occupies a prominent spot.

Katie: It's good to see you. I'm so impressed that you have become a computer expert. That is just the kind of help I need.

You: I would love to help. I probably shouldn't tell you this, but you are my first client. I can't wait to get started. What is it exactly that you need?

Katie: Pretty simple, I imagine. My father talked me into getting this PC. It's a good one but I never studied computers in school and don't know the first thing about setting it up. I have word processing, a database package, and a spreadsheet package—all from Microsoft. In looking through some of the manuals, I noticed an example of how you can use the database to build a customer file. I would like to be able to put our bridal registry on the PC. It's in a three-ring binder now.

You: What kind of information do you keep in the binder?

Katie: Of course names and addresses, and the date of the wedding. Then we include details on the china and silver patterns that have been selected. I would also like to be able to tell customers what has already been purchased so that they can make an informed choice and select items that will really be appreciated.

You: That sounds simple. What would you like for me to do?

Katie: Just tell me how to go about it. I don't know where to start.

You: We went through something like this in a systems development course that I took at school. We studied a phased development approach. I think we ought to use it. I could list out the steps to be taken and then we could work together to take them. How does that sound?

Katie: Great. Can we get started now?

Assignment

1. Make a list of the stages and steps of the phased development process model. Refer to the discussion in Chapter 3 and use it as a basis for your list. For each step, place a checkmark if it should be taken, even in a modified form, and place an X if it should not be taken at all.
2. Of the checked steps, are there any steps that you should take by yourself? If so, add your name as the responsible party. Are there any steps that Katie can take by herself? If so, list her as the responsible party. For those steps where you and Katie should work jointly, add both your names.

3. Can you think of any steps that should be taken that are not in the phased development methodology? If so, list them.

SELECTED BIBLIOGRAPHY

Berger, David. "How to Avoid the Many Pitfalls of Software Installation." *PEM: Plant Engineering & Maintenance* 23 (Number 1, February 1999): 10.

Cloud, Avery C. "An EDP Control Audit With Teeth." *Journal of Systems Management* 41 (January 1990): 13ff.

Gallegos, Frederick. "Audit Contributions to Systems Development." *EDP Auditing* (Boston, MA: Auerbach Publishers, 1991): section 72-01-40, 1-14.

LaMonica, Martin., and Michael Parsons. "SAP Makes Moves to Ease R/3 Implementation." *Infoworld* 19 (Number 35, September 1, 1997): 37.

Williamson, Miryam. "From SAP to 'nuts!" *Computerworld* 31 (Number 45, November 10, 1997): 68-69.

GLOSSARY

A

acceptance test The final user test for a new system, during which users test the system under routine and exceptional conditions to determine whether it satisfies the performance criteria that were established during requirements determination

activity diagram A dynamic model that is a version of the statechart diagram, but emphasizes the activities or processes of an object

actor An external entity with which a system interfaces

application service provider A service organization that helps firms define their goals, provides software tailored to the firms' needs, and hosts solutions by providing server space and technical support

association A linkage between an actor and a use case or a use case and a use case

attributes The distinguishing characteristics of an entity, expressed as data elements

B

balanced DFDs Leveled data flow diagrams that are developed in a top-down manner and are consistent in how they represent processes and data structures

batch processing Accumulating transaction data into a batch and processing the entire batch at once through each step of the procedure

benchmark problem A process that must be performed by each vendor using its own hardware, which provides a major basis for evaluating that hardware

break-even analysis An economic justification method that compares the monthly costs of both the existing and new systems and identifies the month when the costs are equal

break-even point The point in time when the cost of a new system is equal to that of the old system

business process redesign (BPR), business process reengineering This redevelopment of existing physical and conceptual systems, without being constrained by their current form

C

cardinality The number of times a type of relationship occurs between entity types

class diagram An illustration of the object classes that exist within a use case, and their associations

client/server computing The use of a network that includes a central computer (a server) and individual workstations (clients) for all computing needs of a firm

closed system A system that is not connected to its environment; these systems are usually theoretical

closed-loop system A system that controls itself and adjusts its performance to the desired level by using a control mechanism and a feedback loop

collaboration diagram Illustrates how selected object classes of the class diagram collaborate in processing a transaction

compliance The state of a system when it falls within the constraints set by the firm's management and the elements in the firm's environment

component diagram Provides a physical view of the system by illustrating the software components that comprise the system

composite key An identifier that consists of multiple attributes

conceptual system A system that represents a physical system, but does not exist in a physical sense

connector symbol In a data flow diagram, a circle that contains the number of the process to which a data flow is directed or the process from which a data flow comes

consistency checking A process supported in CASE tools that ensures that the diagrams and data repository entries are complete, do not violate any methodological rules, and are consistent within and among diagrams

construction The process of creating software, data sets for testing, and databases; conducting training; creating users and developers manuals; and other implementation activities that are performed during the two SDLC phases of preliminary construction and final construction

context diagram A data flow diagram of the highest level, which describes the system in the context of the environment

conversion The translation of data files from the existing system to the format and content required by the new system

cost-benefit analysis A study of the costs and benefits that will result from developing and using a new information system

critical path method (CPM) diagram A type of network diagram that uses a single time estimate (the best that can be made given the available information) for each activity

cutover The process of changing operations from the existing system to the new system

D

data Detailed facts and figures that by themselves are relatively meaningless to the user

data dictionary A detailed description of the data in a firm's database, primarily consisting of a narrative description of the characteristics of each attribute of each entity type

data flow One or more data elements that travel together

data flow diagram (DFD) An object-oriented documentation of the processes, data repositories, data flows, and elements of the environment of a system

data store A place where data is kept

decision logic table (DLT) A process modeling tool that is used for documenting situations where multiple conditions influence actions to be taken

decomposition diagram A type of diagram that subdivides a system into its lower systems, or subsystems

definition effort The process of systems analysis that determines what the problem or opportunity is, where it is located, and what caused it

deployment diagram Illustrates the nodes of a system, composed of software components

descriptor attribute An attribute of an entity type that provides descriptive information but not identification

developer fixation A condition that results when developers focus their attention when testing a system on the problems they expect rather than on the entire system or the problems that may occur when a user is actually using the system

developers manual Technical documentation of the developed system, to be used by information specialists and developers in the future in maintaining, revising, or reengineering the system.

development sandbox A set of files including the software development tools, program code under construction, and preliminary test data required to construct each module of the new system.

drill down A graphical user interface design technique in which information is displayed in multiple levels of abstraction, which enables the user to begin with a display of summary data and then guide the succeeding displays to present increasing detail

E

encapsulation The practice of listing operations for an object class that only show what functions are performed, not how they are performed

enterprise analysis The study of the firm in its environment for the purpose of understanding the firm's mission and objectives, its responsibilities to its environmental elements, and the level of its resources

entity An occurrence of an entity type

entity type An environmental element, resource, or information flow of such importance to a firm that it is described with data

entity-relationship diagram (ERD) A diagram that identifies the entities within the system that are described with data and the relationships between the entities

evaluation criteria The judgment standards used to determine which solution best meets the needs of the users

evaluation table A table of columns for two to four possible solutions with rows identifying key features, advantages, disadvantages, issues, and questions that will lead to the selection of the best solution

evaluation worksheet A table for comparison of two to dozens of possible solutions by comparing weighted ratings for each solution based on selected criteria

evolutionary prototype A prototype of an information system that eventually becomes the final system after a series of iterative changes based on user feedback

exception report A special report that can be used to practice management by exception

executive committee The top-level managers of a firm who make decisions regarding the long-term strategy of the firm

executive sponsor A top-level manager from the user area who establishes management support of a JAD session by being present for the beginning and conclusion

F

facilitator The person in a JAD session who provides direction to the discussion and creates a climate that enables the group to reach a consensus

fallback A feature of parallel cutover that allows developers to return to the old system if the new system fails

feasibility study An abbreviated form of systems analysis that is intended to determine whether a system project should be pursued

feedback loop The flow of information and signals between a system's output, control mechanism, and input

field engineer (FE) A trained technician who can perform maintenance on equipment

figure 0 diagram A second level data flow diagram, which shows the major processes contained in the context diagram

file conversion The process of converting the existing data to a different format or to a different storage medium

forward engineering The process of developing a new system to replace an existing system that has been analyzed using reverse engineering; the new system can be developed by following the SDLC methodology in the normal fashion

functionality The users' view of how they would like a new system to function, which is influenced by what the existing system does and does not do

Gantt chart A project management tool that lists all of the project activities and uses bars to indicate the timing of each activity

graphical user interface (GUI) A means for the user to interact with the information system through the use of typography, symbols, color, and other static and dynamic graphics to convey facts, concepts, and emotions

group collaborative session A meeting of persons for the purpose of achieving agreement on a discussion topic for which diverse opinions may exist

I

identifier attribute, key An attribute of an entity type that can be used for identification

immediate cutover An installation strategy that involves dismantling the old system and putting the new system into operation simultaneously

implementation The process of converting the design of the new system to a production system consisting of hardware, software, people, data, and information

in-depth personal interview A face-to-face session involving a person who asks questions and another person who answers them, usually a developer and user, respectively

information A result of data that has been processed by an information processor; meaningful to the user

information engineering (IE) A top-down methodology for developing systems that begins with enterprise planning and strategic planning for information resources

information integrity The condition that exists when the firm's data accurately represents its physical systems

information processor A device, computer or noncomputer, that transforms data into information and makes information available to its users

information systems steering committee The management committee that makes strategic decisions concerning the firm's information systems, and provides top-level control of ongoing systems projects

inheritance The concept that attributes and operations of a superclass apply to all of its subclasses; the only attributes and operations listed for a subclass are those not encapsulated by the superclass

installation The period during which production files and operations are transferred from the old system to the new system

installation manual Instructions that the firm's information specialists should follow in installing software on the firm's hardware.

installation team A group of users and developers, possibly from the original development team, who begin planning for the installation early in the project

integrated CASE tool A computer-aided software engineering tool that supports the firm's strategic planning and all system development life cycle stages

J

joint application design (JAD) session A formal approach to systems design using a group-decision support setting; the purpose is to obtain agreement and understanding among users and members of the project team concerning the important elements of a system project

L

leveled DFDs Data flow diagrams that are used in a hierarchy to document a system

lower CASE tool A computer-aided software engineering tool that is used during the construction and installation stages to help the programmer develop, test, and maintain program code

M

magnetic ink character recognition (MICR) A hardware component that is capable of reading a very specific type of ink (magnetic ink)

mainframe computing The use of a large central computer for all data processing and storage

maintainability The ability to keep the system on target in meeting users' needs

management by exception A management technique that requires management to become involved in the physical system of the firm only when performance is not meeting the established performance standards

mandatory relationship A relationship in which the entities must always exist; the entities cannot exist on their own

message A communication of information from one object to another in anticipation that the receiving object will perform some kind of activity

middle CASE tool A computer-aided software engineering tool that is used during the analysis and design stages to document the existing and new systems

milestone An activity that, when completed, can represent measurable progress in the development process

modified parallel cutover A type of parallel cutover that involves testing the new system using old data to simulate a historical parallel run

multiplicity The number of times that an object class can participate in an association

N

net present value An economic justification method that determines the benefits of a system and discounts those benefits to reflect the fact that they are measured in future money, which has less value than existing money

network diagram A project management tool that uses a pattern of interconnected arrows to represent work to be done

nominal group technique (NGT) A group interview technique developed to facilitate meeting procedures and to maximize individual contributions by minimizing inhibitions caused by pressure from peers or superiors

normalization The process of converting data to a series of normal forms for the purpose of eliminating redundant elements and creating a structure as flexible and efficient as possible

O

object A valuable resource of the firm that is described with data

object class A grouping of similar objects in a system, used to create class diagrams

object class diagram A diagram that identifies the object classes and shows their communications linkages

object diagram A snapshot of the status of an object at a point in time

objective A condition or situation to be attained that is of major importance to a firm and is usually integral to its strategic plan

objective question A question that can be answered only in certain, predefined ways, such as true/false or multiple choice

observation Viewing an activity or process as it is being performed or as it occurs

online processing Processing each transaction individually as it occurs so that the master file is updated with each transaction

open system A system that interacts with its environment; one that is connected to its environment by resource flows

open-loop system A system that cannot control itself because it does not have a control mechanism and/or a feedback loop

operations The processes performed by the objects of an object class

optical character recognition (OCR) The ability of a hardware component to read data that is printed in ordinary ink

optional relationship A relationship in which an entity type can exist on its own or in a relationship with another element

P

parallel cutover An installation strategy that involves putting the new system into operation while temporarily keeping the old system in operation

payback analysis An economic justification method that determines how long it will take for the cumulative benefits of the new system to equal its cumulative costs

payback point The point in time when the new system benefits and costs are equal

performance criteria The specific operating standards that the new system must satisfy in order to meet its objectives, which are jointly agreed upon by the user and the developers

periodic report, repetitive report, scheduled report A report that is produced on a regular basis (i.e., weekly or monthly)

PERT (program evaluation and review technique) chart A type of network diagram that takes three time estimates for each activity (optimistic, most likely, and pessimistic), averages them, and uses the result as the actual estimate for the activity

phased cutover An installation strategy that involves moving operations to the new system in stages or phases

physical system A system consisting of tangible elements that can be seen and touched

pilot system A system that is installed in only one part of the firm's operations as a way to measure its impact

portability, scalability The ability of the system to adapt to a changing environment; called scalability when the issue is adapting to growing data storage or increased transaction processing

post-implementation evaluation Investigation of the results of the project, ways in which future projects can be improved, and how well the development team met the system objectives, stayed within project constraints, and estimated the schedule and budget

preparation effort The process of taking a systems view of a firm to analyze its information system needs

problem Either a positive or negative situation that exists for which a solution must be found

process A transformation of data

program flowchart A diagram that uses interconnected symbols to show the detailed processes performed by a single information system program

programming standards Conventions that the programmers of an organization are expected to follow in coding their programs.

project dictionary A collection of system documentation that the project team members create throughout the SDLC

project management All of the actions that are taken to ensure that a project is carried out as planned, and uses a project management mechanism consisting of the project plan, project managers, and information flows

project management mechanism The components of the control mechanism of a project, namely project managers, the project plan, a system of scheduled meetings and reports for monitoring project progress, and a project budget

project plan A list of all of the activities or tasks that must be performed during the process of developing the system

project request form A form that users or their representatives fill out to describe their computer support needs and is usually a part of a formal procedure for evaluating users' needs

proposal A document submitted by vendors describing its products and services and why it should be selected to provide those products or services to the firm

prototype A model that contains the essential elements of an object to be produced in the future

pseudocode A narrative documentation of a system that looks like information system code, but is not; there are no guidelines for pseudocode

Q

quality assurance group An independent group with permanent, experienced members who evaluate large projects

R

realtime system An online system that controls one or more processes as they occur

relational structure A database structure that consists of multiple data tables that can be integrated using their attributes

relationship The association that exists between and among entity types

repository, central encyclopedia An electronic storage of all of the system documentation, including data elements, data structures, data flows, process logic, and object classes

request for proposal (RFP) An invitation to vendors to submit proposals recommending the use of their products in a system; the RFP must contain design details so that the responses from the vendors will be specific and comparable

requirements prototype A throwaway model that serves only as the blueprint for the final system

reverse engineering The process of analyzing a system to identify the elements and their interrelationships, and to create documentation on a higher level of abstraction than currently exist

S

scheduled maintenance, preventive maintenance (PM) Work that is performed on a regular basis to prevent equipment failure

scope The definition of the area within which a system is to be applied and a development project is to be focused

scope creep A problem in system development created by users continually increasing the demands on the new system as it is being developed

scribe The person in a JAD session who maintains a record of all of the input from participants and creates a written report

sequence diagram A dynamic model that show how the object classes of a use case communicate with each other by means of messages

solution effort The process of developing a new or improved system to solve the problem identified; also called systems design and implementation

special report A report that is produced only when triggered by a request or a specific event

statechart diagram, state chart A dynamic model that shows the different states that an object assumes as the use case evolves

strategic business plan A long-term plan developed by the executive committee of a firm that will guide the firm's actions

strategic plan for information resources (SPIR) The guidelines for future development and use of the firm's information resources so that they support the strategic objectives of the firm

structured English A narrative that describes the system on a very detailed level, following specific guidelines for structure and syntax established by the firm; similar to pseudocode, but with guidelines

structured interview An interview in which a developer prepares a list of questions ahead of time and makes an effort to stick to that list and sequence

subjective question, open-ended question A question that puts no specific constraints on how the respondent must answer, such as an essay question

subsystem A system that resides within a larger system

supersystem, suprasystem The highest level system, one that is composed of other systems

supplier, vendor A firm that provides products and services to other firms for use in producing their products and services

survey A form of questioning, either in person, through mail, or by phone, that relies on a single set of questions asked of a large number of people

SWAT (skilled with advanced tools) team A team of systems developers who are especially skilled in carrying out some particular aspect of system development

symptom A condition that results from the existence of a problem

system A group of elements that work together to accomplish an objective

system flowchart A diagram that uses symbols to show how the major processes and data of a system are interconnected

system study A thorough analysis of the existing system at the planning stage intended to determine the objectives and requirements of the new system

systematic testing procedures Testing of all functions of a system, even those that are certain to work

systems developer A person who actively participates in the development of an information system, contributing specialized knowledge and skills

systems maintenance Modifications to a system to ensure that it continues to meet the users needs

systems view A way of analyzing the firm system for the purposes of defining problems and achieving solutions

T

technical manual Documentation of the system for technical users who will be responsible for performing advanced functions, maintaining the system on a daily basis, and updating it

technical operations manual Instructions that the firm's technical operations staff should follow in running the system on the firm's hardware

test group People responsible for developing the test data and for carrying out tests at each stage; also responsible for evaluating adherence to standards and inspecting system documentation

testing The process of ensuring that the system quality goals are met when the system is installed.

U

unit testing The process of testing each new software module in the development sandbox

unscheduled maintenance Work that is performed to repair a failure that has already occurred

unstructured interview An interview that begins with no formal plan and follows a path that is determined largely by the user's answers

upper CASE tool A computer-aided software engineering tool that is used either prior to the SDLC or during the preliminary investigation stage for strategic planning for information resources and enterprise modeling

usability A concept that describes those product attributes that enable users to quickly, efficiently, and effectively use the product to accomplish their real work in a way that meets or exceeds their needs or expectations

use case A step-by-step narrative description of all of the processes that are performed by a system

use case diagram A graphic representation of the key features of the narrative use case report

user interface, human-computer interface The direct interaction between the user and the information system

users manual Documentation of the system that provides information that nontechnical users need in order to use the system correctly

V

variant sandbox A copy of the necessary software development tools and preliminary test data that are required to construct the new system that allows team members to simultaneously work on different releases of the same project

W

Warnier-Orr diagram, action diagram A process modeling tool that is capable of documenting a system at all levels by describing processes with verb-object statements arranged in groups within brackets

Web-based computing The use of the Internet (or World Wide Web) to allow computing on the client or user level

work breakdown structure A method of uniquely identifying each activity or task in a project, particularly used in Gantt charts

workflow diagram A high level data flow diagram that specifies the organizational units in a firm and the processes they perform

INDEX